Psychological Medicine

Psychological Medicine

AN INTRODUCTION TO PSYCHIATRY

Peter Storey MD FRCP FRCPsych DPM
Consultant Psychiatrist to St George's Hospital
and Springfield Hospital, London

TENTH EDITION

Previous editions by
Curran, Partridge and Storey

CHURCHILL LIVINGSTONE
EDINBURGH LONDON MELBOURNE AND NEW YORK 1986

CHURCHILL LIVINGSTONE
Medical Division of Longman Group Limited

Distributed in the United Stated of America by
Churchill Livingstone Inc., 1560 Broadway, New York,
N.Y. 10036, and by associated companies, branches
and representatives throughout the world.

First edition 1943
Second edition 1945
Third edition 1949
Fourth edition 1955
Fifth edition 1963
Sixth edition 1969
Seventh edition 1972
Eighth edition 1976
Ninth edition 1980
Tenth edition 1986

Previous editions by Curran and Guttman, Curran and
Partridge and Curran, Partridge and Storey
ISBN 0-443-03065-0

British Library Cataloguing in Publication Data
Storey, Peter
    Psychological medicine : an introduction to
    psychiatry.—10th ed.
    1. Mental illness
    I. Title   II. Curren, Desmond
    616.89   RC454

Library of Congress Cataloging in Publication Data
Storey, Peter.
    Psychological medicine.

    Rev. ed. of: Psychological medicine/Desmond
Curran,
Maurice Partridge, Peter Storey. 9th ed. 1980.
    Bibliography: p.
    Includes index.
    1. Psychiatry.   2. Mental illness.   I. Curran,
Desmond.   Psychological medicine.   II. Title.
[DNLM: 1. Mental Disorders.   WM 100 S884p]
RC454.S785   1986   616.89   85-15131

Printed in Great Britain by
Butler & Tanner Ltd, Frome and London

Preface

It is sad to record the death of Dr. Maurice Partridge, who died in 1984 after a long illness. He was a wise doctor, a fine teacher and a good friend. He was part author with Desmond Curran after the death of Eric Guttman, so that 'Curran and Guttman' became 'Curran and Partridge' and continued to grow in reputation.

As I have been, in effect, the sole revising author of the last few editions, the title of the book has been changed, with the strong recommendation of Professor Curran, who still takes a keen interest in each edition, forty three years after the first.

The chapter on the Legal Aspects of Mental Illness has been written because of the new Mental Health Act of 1983 (England and Wales) and 1984 (Scotland), and I am grateful to Dr. D. Chiswick, Senior Lecturer in Forensic Psychiatry in the Edinburgh University department of psychiatry for help with the latter.

A new chapter on Psychosomatic Medicine has been written, as many friendly critics have suggested. Much new material has been added, especially in Chapter 11 where the sections on Anxiety States and Hysterical Conditions have been largely rewritten, as has Chapter 13 on Mental Handicap. Other new material has been added in other chapters and much pruning also carried out. At the request of several medical students, to whom I am most grateful, I have included summaries of some chapters which I hope will help in revision for examinations.

London 1986   P.S.

Contents

1. Introductory   1
2. The aetiology of mental illness   17
3. Symptoms encountered in mental illness   44
4. Classification of mental disorders   59
5. Psychiatric case-taking   66
6. Organic mental states   77
7. Psychiatry in the aged   114
8. Schizophrenia   124
9. Affective disorders   160
10. Disorders of personality and of sexual development   209
11. Personality reactions and neurotic states   236
12. Obsessional states   297
13. Mental handicap   309
14. Alcoholism and drug addiction   323
15. Psychosomatic medicine   351
16. Treatment   375
17. The legal aspects of mental illness   441
    Bibliography   470
    Index   474

1

Introductory

Psychiatry is a word derived from two Greek words meaning respectively 'mind' and 'medical treatment'. It has thus an exact meaning: it is that branch of medicine that aims at the treatment of mental ill-health. Its aims are therapeutic and it is an integral part of medicine. In this it differs from psychology, with which it is often confused.

Psychology means 'study of the mind'. Since no experience can come to us without participation of the mind, it is clear that such a study must be vast. Psychology has studied the processes involved in such mental functions as perception, memory and learning. It has studied the nature of intelligence and of personality. It has studied behaviour, both of individuals and of groups. It has applied such studies to different aspects of life with the consequent development of specialities, such as educational psychology, vocational psychology, industrial psychology. Apart from normal processes, it has studied abnormal ones, as in abnormal psychology. But it differs from psychiatry in that it is not an integral part of medicine, though in some way related to it, and its aims are not therapeutic, although it has made many contributions to therapy, and more and more clinical psychologists are involved in treatment.

This book provides no synopsis or outline of normal psychology, because we feel the subject cannot usefully be compressed into a small enough space. Several books on the subject are recommended in the bibliography.

Psychiatry may be defined as that branch of medicine the special province of which is the study, prevention and treatment of mental ill-health, however produced.

The scope of psychiatry

Put in the most general terms, mental ill-health is experienced subjectively as a substantial impairment of comfort and happiness, and

1

is shown objectively as a substantial impairment of efficiency or of the capacity for satisfactory social relationships. The range of clinical material is thus very wide, extending from those whose conditions are sufficiently severe to call for institutional treatment, through those whose conditions, though less severely disabling, may none the less be potent sources of personal misery and social inefficiency, to the 'social problem group' of maladjusted misfits, delinquents and drunkards.

It may be said with truth that many of these are social rather than medical problems. In practice, however, many of them become the subjects of psychiatric care. Whether they do so or not is determined by practical considerations. It is not a theoretical question of where the boundaries of psychiatry begin and end, but a practical one of who is best equipped to deal with the particular problem that is presented. It is not that psychiatry wishes to make territorial demands, but because delinquency and alcoholism are often bound up with problems of personality and psychiatric illness that such cases are often referred for psychiatric opinion and advice.

Mental health should be seen as a spectrum rather than as a category. At one end we have a rarely realised ideal of health, with emotional stability, an absence of distorting neurotic feelings, personal happiness, and good relations with family, work and society. Few people are in that ideal state the whole time, and most would be represented somewhere along our hypothetical spectrum. At the other end it shades off through varying degrees of unhappiness and difficulties in coping into mental illness. This concept is a gross oversimplification of course: many people function well in certain respects and poorly in others, and some major mental illnesses affect people who otherwise cope quite happily with life.

It is worth noting that in some respects each culture and subculture will have its own views of what constitutes an 'ideal' relationship with, for example, society. This is shown very clearly in the clash of opinion between the USSR and the Western world about psychiatric illness as an explanation of political dissidence. Another example currently causing problems in Britain, especially in immigrant families, is the incompatibility of traditional Indian and modern British views about the ideal relationships between children and parents.

The mentally healthy person copes with life and its problems, including those of growing up, without undue subjective distress, and without causing undue distress to others, unless subjected to extraordinary pressures. Even when under great pressure, he or she remains able to recognise what the problem is, and to tolerate much distress, without losing self control or the ability to respond in an adaptive and coping way.

The size of the problem

Mental disturbances are common, and many of them are seriously disabling. Statistics produced in different parts of the world and in different historical periods are very difficult to interpret, because of varying diagnostic practices and different methods of case identification and recording. Even between the USA and the UK there are some big diagnostic differences. For example, in some parts of the USA quite different criteria for the diagnosis of schizophrenia are in use from those in this country, differences which may not be apparent in, for example, an article about treatment or prognosis. Different diagnostic practices should always be allowed for when reading foreign articles or books.

Many people believe that there has been a rapid increase in rates of psychiatric illness in the West, but there is no good evidence for this idea. Rather, we have increasingly elaborate psychiatric services, a decreasing willingness to tolerate distress, and an increasing demand for help — from professionals — with problems and symptoms which in the past were accepted as part of a burdensome life which could not be changed and so must be borne. At present the demand seems limitless.

Nor is there solid evidence that modern urban life is more 'stressful' than rural life, or than life in less developed countries. Although we invoke 'stress' so frequently, in fact it remains a poorly defined concept. We all tend to identify our own problems more than those of others, but when rural communities in under-developed countries, for example, are studied adequately, a high incidence of both major and minor mental disturbance is always found; even if to the nostalgic Westerner the life seems peaceful compared to his own.

We have made progress in quantifying some of the factors which lead to schizophrenic relapse and depressive illness, by the use of life events schedules and by studies of the emotional interactions in the families (p. 128), and this field is developing rapidly. It remains difficult to be precise about the relationship of mental or psychosomatic illness to factors such as long working hours, excessive responsibility, frustration, continually suppressed anger pressure to 'beat the clock', and very many other matters which clinical observation and common sense tell us are frequently relevant. A central problem here is that what to one person is a pleasure is to another a pain.

Frequency of mental illness

There are several different methods of identifying and describing the frequency of mental illness, the details of which would be inappropriate here (see Bibliography) but some of the main findings are worth mentioning.

In an extremely thorough study of a Swedish rural community, in which a psychiatrist examined every individual within a brief period of time, the prevalence figures were: psychoses 1.7%; neuroses (excluding minor disturbances) 13%; mental deficiency 1.2%. The estimated cumulative risk in this population, was that by the age of 60 years, 43.4% of men and 73.0% of the women would have had some significant mental disorder; and that 'severe impairment' would have been suffered by 7.9% and 15.4% respectively of men and women. These are very high rates, but many studies around the world have come up with similar, and often with higher rates. For example, surveying a population in Manhattan, but using a questionnaire method, with very different definitions, 815 out of 1000 people were found to have some psychiatric symptoms, and 234:1000 were considered significantly impaired, and to be 'psychiatric cases'. When the Swedish and American researchers concerned in these two reports did a kind of cross-check study, they found that if the American criteria were applied to the Swedish population, the neurosis rate rose from 13.1 to almost 40%; the mental deficiency rate from 1.2 to 10%; but that the psychosis rate did not change. These details are given as a reminder of the difficulties of making comparisons in this field, and of maintaining a critical attitude when presented with mental health statistics.

In Britain many surveys have also been done. One important general practice study showed that individual doctors varied in their estimates of psychiatric morbidity in their own practices between 37.8 and 323 per 1000. This almost tenfold difference is determined by doctors attitudes, interests, and skills, more than by population characteristics; although emotionally disturbed patients do tend to join the lists of doctors likely to give them a sympathetic hearing. Socially unstable poor populations also have much higher psychiatric morbidity rates than more settled and prosperous areas.

Mental illness among medical patients

Many studies have concentrated on medical and surgical wards and outpatient clinics, and all find high incidences of psychiatric problems.

Again there are major differences depending on the method of study, the criteria used, nationality, and so on. Some examples are: a 51% incidence of psychiatric symptoms in newly referred medical outpatients in a London hospital; a 34% incidence in patients with small intestine disease at another; significant depression in 43 of 150 medical inpatients; and of a series of patients with abdominal pain presenting to a surgical clinic, almost 50% had an alcohol problem.

Very often the psychiatric symptoms of these medical and surgical patients are unrecognised until the special study is made. It is as important for the doctor to take a brief psychiatric history and examine the mental state in *every* patient admitted, as it is to ask about dyspnoea and measure the blood pressure. Not only is suicide a common cause of death, but psychiatric symptoms cause much personal suffering.

In many of the patients picked up in these surveys outlined above, there might be no useful treatment, or the disturbance may be only a transient reaction; but in some, serious mental illness might be usefully treated.

Hospital admission statistics

Hospital admission rates are much higher now than they were 20 years ago, although, as has been pointed out earlier, this does not mean that mental illness is commoner, but rather reflects altered attitudes and improved facilities.

In England and Wales first admissions to psychiatric units of all kinds rose from 98 to 137 per 100 000 of population between 1954 and 1970, an increase of 40%. Total admissions rose from 162 to 374 per 100 000, a 125% increase; which is due at least in part to the high number of readmissions inseparable from our present system of encouraging early return to the community.

Between 1970 and 1975 however, there was a 10% fall in first admissions, the first fall since figures were first collected in 1898. This fall continued until 1981, after which date the official figures are not available at the time of writing (1984). The overall fall in first admissions was from 137 per 100 000, as already mentioned, to 106 per 100 000. Readmissions however, continued to rise, and first admissions for alcohol related conditions have doubled over the 10 years. The total number of psychiatric in-patients in England and Wales has fallen from 165 000 in 1961 to 96 400 in 1981, whereas outpatient attendances have increased a great deal.

The chances of an individual being admitted to a psychiatric unit of some type during his or her lifetime therefore fell slightly in 1975 to approximately 1 in 8 women and 1 in 12 men, from the earlier high point of 1 in 6 women and 1 in 9 men. The commonest age for first admission is between 20 and 30 years of age. The rates fall to a minimum at about 60 years old, and rise steeply after 65, as dementia becomes increasingly common.

The normal and abnormal in psychiatry

The word 'normal' is used in different senses. When we say that a person is of normal height, we refer to someone who is neither very small nor very tall, but whose height approximates to the statistically average. But when a dentist says that someone has normal teeth, he means something different; he means that the teeth are without blemish, which is far from statistically average. In general medicine, 'normal' is often used to indicate an absence of physical pathology. In psychiatry, we use the word 'normal' in the first sense, to denote something that is more or less average rather than something that is perfect or ideal. That is to say, the normal can only be judged against its background and normality and abnormality are essentially statistical concepts.

In considering single characteristics, such as height or colour of the hair, it is clear that we must allow for a wide range of variation; in such a far more complicated matter as behaviour, the range is bound to be even wider. Behaviour that passes as normal in Brixton might not be considered so in Cheltenham. When society is viewed as a whole, therefore, we must allow a very wide range as coming within normal limits. We must not stigmatise as pathological something that merely happens to conflict with our own standards. Whereas in general medicine the criteria of normal liver function tests may be fairly strictly defined, the criteria of psychiatric abnormality are less exact, although it is true that in both the normal shades into the abnormal by gradual degrees. Extraordinary behaviour in itself is not evidence necessarily of mental illness. The diagnosis of mental illness requires the additional presence of other symptoms so that the whole condition can reasonably be regarded as constituting a psychiatric syndrome. In brief, normal people can behave in extraordinary ways. The statistically abnormal, or merely eccentric person is not necessarily a psychiatric problem. Abnormality leads to psychiatric problems when there is failure to adapt to society and when such failure of adaptation causes either social nuisance to others, or distress to the individual concerned. Such distress usually arises either from inefficiency at work or from inability to make or maintain satisfactory social relationships.

Development of psychiatry

The first flowering in Europe was during the great period of the Greek and Roman Empires, when disciples of Aesculapius and later Hippocrates first claimed to treat the mind, until then the province of mysticism rather than of science. Clinical observation led to the development of therapeutic programmes; the patients were studied as individuals, treated with sedatives, and soothed or stimulated by special baths or music. It is of historical interest that balneo-therapy was revived within our own time and that music again had a therapeutic vogue in the 1950s. But after the decay of the Roman Empire psychiatry, as a clinical study or field of scientific enquiry, virtually ceased to exist until the effects of the Renaissance came very slowly to reach the problem of mental illness more than a thousand years later. It was not until the end of the eighteenth century that psychiatry began to flower again.

In Britain a special fillip was given to this process by a chance but important event: the development of recurrent attacks of sustained and uncontrollable excitement by King George III. The picture, as described by Fanny Burney, the authoress, in her diary of 1789, when governess at the Court, is that of mania: the severe insomnia, the intense over-activity of the King, the persistent overtalkativeness until the royal larynx became quite hoarse, the continual pottering and ill-directed bustle, and indeed the erotic pursuit by the Monarch of Miss Burney herself through the shrubberies at Kew. (Recent historical research has suggested porphyria as the cause.) The agitated medical consultations and the difficulty of the treatment aroused public interest so that the progress of the august patient did much to focus attention on the welfare of less eminent sufferers. By the beginning of the 19th century scientific enquiry and humanitarianism had again begun to exert effect.

Attention was paid at first mainly to the major mental illnesses, the insanities. The workers occupied themselves first with introducing a more humanitarian approach. The abolition of restraint was advocated by Pinel in France, and by Conolly in Britain. The provision of suitable forms of occupation was encouraged by Tuke. By about 1850 the custodial care of the patients had been improved altogether beyond recognition. These advances have been continued and extended, even during our own time. the huge barrack-like hospitals of the 19th century, though themselves an advance at the time, came to hold many more patients than they were designed for; and by our standards, are much too institutional, with enormous wards and long corridors. They cannot easily be made warm and homelike, with a comforting atmosphere, which is what is needed.

Following this, the trend has been to have psychiatric units in general hospitals serving a certain district, in the hope that ultimately large mental hospitals would become unnecessary, because chronic patients could be maintained mainly in the community. In 1985 at the time of writing, we can still see a need for long term hospital care of a fair number of chronically ill patients in the future; and there is still a need for much greater resources both in hospitals and the community.

Factors other than that of better organisation have helped towards improvements in treatment. Pharmaceutical advances with the provision of better drugs have contributed enormously, especially over recent years; and so has public enlightenment. There have been developments in clinical psychology, psychotherapy, nursing practices, occupational therapy, social work, and in diagnosis and the selection of treatment. The remoteness of the mental hospital from ordinary life has been much reduced, as has the stigma that attached to it. More and more patients stay only briefly in hospital, returning soon to live at home, or if appropriate, in hostels, sheltered lodgings and so on.

At the same time that the reforms were beginning in the 19th century, clinical studies were also afoot, directed at first mainly to observation and thence to the descriptive classification of illness. Here the difficulties were peculiar owing to the wide variations from case to case, the absence of objective signs, and the fluctuations shown by the illnesses in their often very long duration. None the less by the end of the century, and largely owing to the work of German psychiatrists, culminating in that of Kraepelin, the confusion previously surrounding psychiatric illnesses had been largely resolved. The organic states such as those due to neuro-syphilis had been clearly demarcated from the major 'functional' mental illnesses, and a workable Classification had been mapped out (see p. 59). This was an enormous advance; in view of the difficulties a remarkable one, and far greater than may be generally realised.

The extent of the advance can be gauged by comparing events at the beginning and end of the century. In 1815, Dr Thomas Monro, physician to the Royal Bethlehem Hospital, gave evidence to a Board of Enquiry. Many of his patients had been kept in chains for years, and he described his practice in the following words: 'The patients are ordered to be bled about the latter end of May or the beginning of May according to the weather. And after they have been bled they take vomits daily or every other day for a certain number of weeks. After that we purge the patients. That has been the practice invariably for years, long before my time, and it was handed down to me by my father, and I don't know any better practice'. These routine hit-or-miss methods, indiscriminately applied to fettered patients, may be contrasted with the brilliant lecture-demonstrations, teaching the symptomatology of different illnesses with lucid exposition of the differential diagnostic points, that were given in his humane and enlightened hospital by Kraepelin only 75 years later.

The value of these methods of descriptive classification was great. To take a specific example, it would have been impossible without them to have linked general paralysis of the insane to its prodromal condition, primary syphilis, a connection which also needed advances in histo-pathology of course. In this way, they have paved the way for the subsequent development of treatments for a variety of conditions. More generally, they brought order almost for the first time to an otherwise chaotic subject; by emphasising the features held in common, they correctly brought together into a related group the apparently heterogeneous illnesses that we now know under the collective term 'schizophrenia', and by long-term study they showed that the apparently contrasting conditions of mania and melancholia were essentially related to each other as the contrasting phases of the same illness, manic-depressive psychosis. These, and other observations, produced clarity from chaos, and by aiding prognosis made for the more effective management of the various conditions.

However, there were drawbacks. First, there were many points at which the classification broke down, owing to the tendency for mixed states to occur, and for illnesses to change their forms as they progressed. Second, and more formidably, these methods yielded no positive indications either as to aetiology or to specific treatment. Kraepelin's approach to psychiatric illness was that which is traditional in general medicine. He viewed psychiatric conditions as disease entities, with an aetiology, pathology, symptomatology, course and prognosis of their own. On this basis he achieved much, but the aetiology and pathology persistently eluded him — except in general paralysis of the insane. He sought for a pathology in terms of structural lesions of the brain, or of biochemical disturbances affecting cerebral function. He did not find it. He was therefore led to infer that the aetiology and pathology depended on hereditary and constitutional factors of an unknown kind. The inference was probably fundamentally correct, although the rôle of psychological and social factors in the precipitation and modification of the illnesses was largely ignored at first, and the approach did not directly contribute to the problem of treatment. To that extent, the Kraepelinian approach was sterile. Once the classification, whatever its imperfections, had been more or less generally accepted, it was on that sterility that attention came to be focused, although its enduring value is shown now by the fact that different treatments have specific benefits in diagnostic groups based on those Kraepelin originally described.

Around the turn of the century, therefore, other methods were explored. At this time Sigmund Freud, a Viennese neurologist, came upon a number of cases whose symptoms seemed to date from particular incidents that they were at first unable to remember, but whose occurrence was later elicited under hypnosis. With recovery of the memory and adjustment of the patients' attitudes towards the incidents concerned, some cases improved. From this sprang the concept of the 'unconscious mind'. This was in itself nothing new, for it had been written and spoken of by various 19th century thinkers, such as Samuel Butler, the author of *Erewhon*. But its application to psychiatry initiated a trend away from the formal and traditional concepts of mental illness as a disease process, as in other medical conditions, in favour of viewing such illness in a more dynamic way in terms of reaction to events past or present, conscious or unconscious. This was a new conception, and to some extent a sound one. Further, it was attractive in that it offered therapeutic possibilities. Freud's ideas gave rise to *psycho-analysis* (see p. 389), in which mental disorders were seen as arising from a failure of normal emotional development in childhood.

At about the same time, Adolf Meyer in the United States also began to conceive of mental illness in terms of reaction, and developed what he called the *psycho-biological* approach. This was conceived on a wider basis that the psycho-analytic theory, was realistic, and took cognisance of physical factors in mental illness. Its essence was that each patient should be considered as an individual, and his illness interpreted in terms of the effect upon him of the life-situation through which he had passed.

Both psycho-biology and psycho-analysis have made contributions to knowledge, and it is difficult to assess which has had the greater influence. It is possible that Meyer, with his practical approach, had the greater influence within the profession; it is a mark of this that most standard psychiatric textbooks have for many years taught in terms of 'schizophrenic reaction-types' and 'manic-depressive reaction-types' instead of treating schizophrenia and manic-depressive psychosis as illnesses in their own right, as had Kraepelin. Psycho-analysis, on the other hand, has had a greater vogue amongst people of a less scientific and practical kind. Its concepts have dominated psychiatry in the United States since the Second World War, but are rapidly losing ground there. Curiously, there is an increased interest in psycho-analytic views among psychiatrists in Germany, where earlier psycho-analysis was largely ignored; and a much greater interest in the biological and medical aspects has developed in the United States.

In everyone, patient or non-patient, there is an interaction of psychological, social, physical, and constitutional factors. A proper balance of these is the ideal way of understanding.

Some popular fallacies of the last sixty years

Ideas, derived from psycho-analytic theory, that if all be laid bare, then various unconscious factors may be revealed hitherto impeding the development and progress of the patient, encourage belief in limitless possibilities of 'cure'. Such belief takes no account of the potentialities, which may be limited, with which the individual started life.

Once ideas of the limitless are current, limitless hopes may be raised. In this connection, mention may be made of the alleged applicability of psychiatry to politics and international relations, as though wars could be prevented and revolutions outmoded by sexual hygiene or breast feeding. The currency of these ideas has done nothing to enhance the reputation of psychiatry.

Conversely, the fact that the Kraepelinian school was therapeutically unproductive within its time has led to the fallacy, rarely expressed but often implied, that to say a condition is primarily constitutional is also to say that it is untreatable. This is not the case. Phenylketonuria is a genetically determined disease (as is diabetes mellitus to a large extent), and therefore 'constitutional', but it can be treated by avoiding phenylalanine in the diet (see p. 317). Many similar examples could be produced.

Another common fallacy is that all mental illness is a flight from reality in a conscious or unconscious attempt to find a pleasanter milieu. This may or may not be the case in an individual instance, but as a general proposition it is nonsense.

Again, there tends to be a popular idea that the psychiatrist encourages free expression, frowns upon discipline and recommends the utmost licence. This is also nonsense, and seems to have arisen from misinterpretation of the term 'repression' which Freud's translators used in a special sense.

PSYCHIATRY AND THE REST OF MEDICAL PRACTICE

In addition to the psychoses, neuroses, and the various syndromes and reactions described in this book, emotional factors are important throughout the practice of clinical medicine in all its branches. They must be considered in situations ranging from reactions of patients to their doctors, and vice versa; through such problems as the attitude of a patient to his renal dialysis, of a spouse to a colostomy, of a mother to breast feeding; and reactions like those of a child to a grandparent's death or the arrival of a new baby in the family. There are no situations in clinical medicine in which people's feelings are not relevant, and in which emotional reactions of unexpected intensity may not suddenly disturb something outwardly straightforward. We outline in this section some of the more important types of problem which can arise. Chapter 15 deals with Psychosomatic medicine and Liaison psychiatry, and therefore also considers the relationship between psychiatry and the rest of medicine.

The doctor–patient relationship

Doctors are in an unusual position in society, carrying so much personal responsibility, and belonging to a closed professional group with long traditions and a powerful mystique. Few people feel neutral about them or approach them for help as they would a plumber. It might be easier if they did. Accompanying the rational appraisal the patient makes of the doctor, and beneath the surface of the professional interview, many patients have a childlike dependence on, and an idealised image of, their doctor. The more ill the person, or the child or spouse who is the focus of treatment, the more complete is the 'handing over' of responsibility to the doctor and to the profession. It is true that with an increasingly sophisticated population a more critical view is being taken of doctors, but most people still react when ill as their parents did. This trusting dependence is on the whole welcomed by doctors, and by nurses, as it makes it easier to organise and carry out treatments which often involve discomfort, pain and even danger, as in major surgery; it is also welcomed because it makes people feel valued and respected — something everyone likes.

Doctors are supported in the responsibility they carry by the structure of the medical profession. To the outsider it often seems like a union 'closed shop', and is often criticised and resented, but the profession enables individuals to carry responsibilities and problems under which an unsupported individual would collapse.

Occasionally, perhaps because of some mishap, but more commonly arising from the personalities of the patient and doctor concerned, the relationship is strained or even breaks down. The patient's bitterness and anger are often based not only on the outward reality of what has happened, but often on a sense of betrayal or rejection, more appropriate to the feelings of a child for a parent than of one adult to another. We are then dealing with co-called 'transference' problems.

The term 'transference' is one introduced by Freud. It refers to the way in which emotions are 'transferred' from important childhood figures to people in adult life, where they can seriously distort relationships by bringing in an inappropriate intensity of feeling, often accompanied by an expectation of some strong emotional response — usually of a parental kind. All this happens without the individual concerned clearly recognising the existence of these feelings, never mind their source in earlier life (see p. 392).

Doctors, and most especially psychiatrists, who should know better, are more prone than any other group of people to find themselves in difficult transference situations, which can get completely out of hand unless recognised. For example, if a woman regularly attending her doctor has, in addition to the objective reality of her symptoms or problems, powerful but unconscious feelings for him derived from her feelings for her own father; and if that father had been dearly loved but had abandoned the family for another woman when she was 7 years old, then trouble is quite likely. Any steps the doctor takes to end the series of consultations may be experienced as further abandonment, and the violence of the emotions generated can be surprising and disturbing. These situations can be avoided best by recognising that they can and do occur, and openly discussing the possibility with the patient in a calm way, as described in the section on psychotherapy (p. 386).

Doctors being human they too have their own emotional preferences and sympathies, dictated by their own development and experiences; and transference distortions (called 'counter-transference' in psychoanalysis when they refer to the doctor's unconscious feelings for the patient) can also occur. At a day-to-day level this is often no more than that an individual doctor may be happier dealing with, for example, middle-aged women than with men of his own age, or vice versa.

The special position of doctors, especially male, leads them often to become the object of amorous feelings often inextricably mingled with the kind of transference feeling mentioned above. Their position also facilitates sexual advances by either doctor or patient, and the very strict rules laid down for professional conduct by, for example, the General Medical Council in this country, are a recognition of these dangers. The Hippocratic Oath contains ' ... refraining from all wrongdoing or corruption, and especially from any act of seduction, of male or female, bond or free ... ' which perhaps reflects the same problems in a very different culture.

Difficulties of the student in psychiatry

The difficulties in establishing the aeriology of the major mental illnesses have been, and are, so great that psychiatry lacks much of the precision found elsewhere in medicine. This, together with the difficulty of measuring mental characteristics and the frequent absence of physical signs, tends to discourage the student who has been rightly imbued with the importance of exact observation, and who expects symptoms to be correlated with signs. The insistence of the curriculum on pathology, in a strictly organic and physical sense, makes the student less at ease when dealing with conditions whose physical pathology cannot be directly demonstrated. Moreover, the sin of 'missing' the organic lesion encourages concentration on the organic aspects with neglect of the psychological ones, rather than viewing the patient as a whole.

The student is also often discouraged by the personality of some patients who may arouse antagonism by being demanding, critical, ungrateful, aggressive, anti-social in various ways, or otherwise difficult to form a comfortable relationship with. It is very important to be aware of one's own reactions in such circumstances, and try to ensure that they do not alter the way the patient is treated. We must often lay aside our value-judgments.

As we all have problems, and they may be the same as those of the patient, a student or a doctor may have difficulty in taking an objective view of the patient and his life, and may tend to avoid an issue or become too entangled with it. Detachment comes from awareness of one own feelings and with practice.

Mental illness still has a stigma, and this can even lead to a reluctance to diagnose it, especially in someone whom the doctor likes, or can identify with. Again, an awareness of one's own feelings is needed.

Aims of psychiatric teaching

The first essential is that the student should feel at ease with people and their feelings, especially those who are mentally ill or emotionally disturbed, and be able to cope effectively with them. Too often the student — and the qualified doctor — feels ill at ease, and cannot cope himself with emotionally tense situations. He tends to withdraw, either physically or by changing the subject to something like physical symptoms, with which he feels more comfortable. In the consulting room, the doctor may respond by the too rapid prescription of a tranquilliser or by too rapid and therefore empty reassurance.

To be at ease and able to cope effectively needs practice. The student should talk to, and formally interview, as many patients as possible during his psychiatric training. While clerking surgical or medical patients at other times he should always make some enquiry about their emotional and social life, and avoid the tendency to put patients in rigidly defined compartments which depend on the presenting complaint, so that hernia sufferers are asked only about hernias, and phobic patients asked only about their fears.

In addition to being at ease with the patient, the student also needs a working knowledge of psychiatry, how to take a history, and how to examine the mental state.

As in general medicine and surgery, he has to learn how to approach the problem, how to gather information, and how to think constructively about it. This is more basic than learning the clinical features and treatment of the main psychiatric syndromes, important though that is. One of the greatest difficulties comes in the gathering of the information, because it needs an openness of mind and alertness to subtle clues to detect the presence of some emotional disturbance during a brief consultation about headache or dyspepsia.

The necessary basic knowledge can be obtained without too much difficulty, and it can be applied to individuals, if, when the history is taken, a reasonable estimate of the mental and emotional characteristics of the patient is made at the same time as the physical assessment. This need cause no great trouble, as will be shown. It will repay by increasing the accuracy of the diagnosis and prognosis as well as helping in general management, whatever the nature of the condition that is being dealt with. Such an assessment may not be very exact, but it is a great deal better than none at all. After all, medicine is not an exact science; it is an art which uses scientific methods when it can. The essence of being a good clinician is not to use a calculating machine or ready-reckoner, but to exercise a judgment trained in assessing a large number of variables, amongst which psychological factors are not the least important. Apart from problems that are specifically psychiatric, there is inevitably some psychiatric aspect to every case, and it should never be neglected.

2

The aetiology of mental illness

In psychiatry mind and body are considered inseparable, but this has not always been so. The nature and causes of consciousness have never been fully understood. It seems certain, however, that mental activity does depend on the integrated functioning of the nervous system, and therefore on the physical conditions necessary to sustain that function. For mental activity to be possible, there must be an adequate supply of blood to the brain, the blood must be within certain limits of acidity and alkalinity, and must contain certain quantities of oxygen and sugar. Thus, mental activity depends on physical conditions. For our present purposes, therefore, mind and body should not be considered as separate entities, as in the so-called psycho-physical dualism of the earlier philosophers, but should be considered as together forming a whole.

This concept is necessary for the understanding of mental illness. In every case both physical and mental factors have to be considered. The mental and physical makeup of a person are usually referred to together as the 'constitution'. The constitution is the whole person as he is at any one time, whatever the causes may be. One very important aspect of someone's constitution is the personality, considered specifically in Chapter 10. The constitution is not a fixed or immutable thing, but develops and changes as life goes on. It includes not only the hereditary endowments both physical and mental with their innate tendencies, and the intrauterine environment, but also the effects of development and experience as shown by the patterns of behaviour that the person has acquired. In fact, the constitution predisposes the individual to react, both physically and mentally, in certain ways.

In order to understand any mental illness, one has to consider first the patient's physical and mental make-up, i.e. his constitution, second, the psychological and physical stresses imposed by his environment, and third, the effect of those stresses upon that constitution. That is, we have to consider in every case, the interaction of psychological and physical factors with those of the constitution —

17

that is on the total make-up of the individual. These three groups of factors are invariably present and operative in every case, though their practical importance may vary much from one case to another. The terms psychological, physical and constitutional, denote only different aspects of the whole individual; they overlap, and their separation under these headings is artificial, but it is convenient for description and understanding.

Causation of mental illness as a process

Just as there is never a single and simple cause for normal behaviour, so there is never a single and simple cause for mental illness, which arises always from a variety of factors that combine to produce their effect. In fact, causation is a process involving physical and mental factors, both past and present.

For example, a person may develop a severe attack of rheumatic fever in childhood and as a result may develop mitral stenosis. His physical constitution has then been altered. If many limitations then have to be placed on his activities at home and at school, these will alter the direction of his interests and his adjustment towards his fellow-children, i.e. they will alter the mental aspects of his constitution also. If the attitude of his family has also been over-solicitous and over-protective, he may tend to take excessive care of himself and thus show unnecessary invalid tendencies. Such a person is then more likely to be disturbed by minor symptoms than the average person would be. Such a person developing palpitations in later life may then become excessively disturbed by them, fearing that they herald further heart disease, even though they may be only the normal products of anxiety in some particular situation. His fears may then lead him to be further anxious, with continuance of the palpitation as a result. Such a case can only be understood by considering the psychological, physical and constitutional factors that are involved, through study of the personal history of the patient.

Again, and apart from mental and physical factors that have occurred in the past, the patient may be affected in many ways by immediate environmental influences that exert both psychological and physical effects. Thus, unemployment may lead, through reducing income, to the physical effect of undernourishment as well as to the mental effect of reducing self-confidence. These two may then combine to lower the resistance to mental stress, leading to a rundown condition that may interfere with the appetite and general metabolism.

Here again the case can only be understood by considering all three groups of factors, psychological, physical and constitutional, and it will be realised that such consideration calls for a medical training and a sound knowledge of general medicine, with which psychiatry must always be linked.

Relative importance of psychological, physical and constitutional factors

It has already been said that, though these three groups of factors are present in every case, their relative importance will vary from one case to another. In the first example given above, that of the man who experienced abnormal anxiety over palpitations in relation to his previous experience of heart disease, the principal factors were his fears, i.e. psychological factors, for it was those that caused the palpitations, and therefore the anxiety, to continue; but the physical factor of the mitral stenosis and his constitutional tendency to invalid reactions also contributed. In general, the cases in which psychological factors are aetiologically predominant should be intelligible in the following way. (1) The patients should be in clear consciousness and full touch with their surroundings; (2) their normal intellectual powers should be intact; and (3) they should be free from hallucinations, delusions, and misinterpretations (see chapter 3 for symptom definition); and they should be free from physical lesions that could satisfactorily explain the symptoms. The symptoms should be comprehensible, in the light of the previous history and personality as a reaction to recent or immediate situations. But at this point it may be laid down as a general rule that where the patient shows (1) a physical abnormality that reasonably accounts for the symptoms, or (2) disturbance of consciousness, or (3) hallucinations, delusions or misinterpretations or (4) intellectual deterioration, the psychological factors are unlikely to be of predominant importance, and the principal causes should usually be sought elsewhere.

Now, suppose that we have two patients with typhoid fever, and one develops a delirium in course of it. He becomes confused, does not know the date or where he is, sees the pigs that he has bred running over the end of the bed, and hears the imaginary voices of his relatives calling, while he mistakes the identities of those around him. It would be difficult indeed to explain such a state as a mere psychological reaction. On the contrary, we know from previous experience of such cases that the delirium will pass as the physical condition improves. We recognise it as an accompaniment and ascribe it to the toxic effects of the illness; that is, the physical factors are of predominant importance. But the psychological factors also contribute, for the voices that he hears are the voices of his relatives, the animals that he sees are those with which he is familiar; that is, the individual symptoms are the products of his own personal experiences. These last have not caused the state, however, but have merely lent it individual and personal colouring. They have contributed, but in a way of secondary importance. What of the constitutional factors? These also have contributed, for we had two patients, and though the illnesses were equally severe with equal toxic effect, only one developed the delirium. The inference is that there is some difference in their make-up, which causes one to be more susceptible than the other. Thus, the physical factors are indispensable for the development of the delirium, the constitutional factor allows it to develop given the physical conditions, and the psychological factors supply the individual colouring that will make one person's delirium different from another's.

Again, suppose that an elderly person is brought for advice on account of failure of memory and intellectual grasp. She has left the electric fires on all night, through forgetting to turn them off; she has gone to the shops but on arrival cannot remember what she wants to buy; she has failed to keep appointments because she cannot remember which day is which or where she should go. She herself complains that her memory is bad. On examination, we find that she does not know the date even approximately, that she remembers wrongly the ages of her children, that she cannot recall the dates of many important events in her life, especially the more recent ones. Physically, she shows no signs except peripheral and retinal arteriosclerosis of a gross kind, perhaps with some muscular rigidity such as often occurs in old age. There are no immediate environmental or psychological stresses; the previous personality has not been abnormal. There is no reason why she should wish to be as she is; indeed, it causes her hardship and much inconvenience. We correlate the mental and physical findings, and deduce that the failure of memory is secondary to the arteriosclerosis which has led, through inadequate circulation, to deterioration of the brain. Here, the physical factors are again predominant. We infer that the genetic constitutional factors are of some consequence, because there is a marked family history of the same sort of condition. The psychological factors are represented by her being able to remember some things that are of special significance to her in preference to others that she has forgotten; they partly determine what use she makes of her decayed powers, but they have not caused the decay and, as factors, are relatively unimportant.

Here again the assessment of the relative importance of these three groups of factors is made on a common-sense basis, on scrutiny of the case as a whole, and on comparing it with others in our clinical experience. Where physical factors are predominant, the clinical picture will be (1) one of intellectual deficits, or (2) along the range from clouding of consciousness, through confusion (in the simple sense of putting the left shoe on the right foot, getting into the wrong bed unwittingly as a drunk man might do, or mistaking the obvious use of commonplace objects), and sub-delirious states to full delirium. Such states cannot reasonably be explained in terms of psychological factors mainly; these will always be subsidiary, though lending a personal and individual colouring. Constitutional factors will certainly be present, and in the last analysis may be considered responsible for allowing the development of the condition, as when one patient with typhoid develops a delirium and another does not. But physical factors will be the aetiologically predominant ones.

Let us now consider a more complicated case. Suppose that a youth is referred for advice because, after a few weeks during which he has been moody and failing to get on with his work, apparently on account of pre-occupation with his own thoughts, he has announced that his health is being undermined by radioactive emanations from a hydrogen bomb, that he has a mission to save mankind but is prevented from carrying it out by Russian agents who interrupt his thoughts, disarrange his books and papers, and spy upon him in the street.

After taking a detailed history from the patient and his relatives, we find that he has been reasonably normal until a few weeks previously, though liable to religious doubts and slightly concerned as to the possibilities of war and its consequences, including those on his career. There have been no recent changes or stresses in his home environment or conditions of work.

On examination, we also find that he hears hallucinatory voices that criticise him and quote Biblical texts. But he is in clear consciousness, in touch with his surroundings though slower than usual, is not confused though somewhat bewildered by what he believes to be going on, and is without signs of physical disease.

How are we to construe such a case? Are we to say that this is a psychological reaction provoked by the cumulative load upon his mind of religious conflict and concern over future war? We reflect that many people have religious doubts, and many are afraid of a future war; but it is a long way from that to developing a mission to save mankind, to feeling already under the influence of the hydrogen bomb, hearing imaginary voices and being persecuted by Russian agents. We think that this youth has a severe mental illness, with disordered perception (hallucinations), false beliefs (delusions and misinterpretations), leading to a serious disturbance of function. The psychological factors of religious doubts and worry over war would seem inadequate as causes of a disorder of this severity and massiveness.

It is true that the more we study this youth, the more probably shall we discern some connection between the delusions and hallucinations on the one hand, and his own mental pre-occupations on the other. But that is not to say that the latter have *caused* the former. The mere understanding that there is some connection does not explain why he should have come to have these beliefs, to have accepted them as true, or why he should have hallucinations. We cannot consider this a mere psychological reaction without doing violence to the facts. It looks more as though we are dealing with some basic illness, to which the personal pre-occupations have lent an individual colouring as in the case of typhoid delirium that we have previously considered.

But this patient is not delirious and we can demonstrate no signs of physical disease. We are thus in the difficulty that the psychological factors seem inadequate to explain the whole, and that the physical factors, though we may suspect their existence since there is a disturbance of function, are not obvious. In this dilemma, rather than stretching the facts by attributing the state to psychological or physical causes, it seems most logical to invoke constitutional factors as the cause. This may be vague, non-committal and an admission of imperfect knowledge. But at least it is likely to prevent serious error, such as we might fall into if we adopted conclusions unwarranted by the available facts. In attributing the condition to constitutional causes, we are only saying that we believe there is something in the patient's make-up that has caused him to break down in this particular way, and that the environmental stresses do not seem to have been of prime importance. We shall be fortified in this conclusion if we find, as we often shall, a family history of the same sort of condition in the patient's own or preceding generation.

We may take much the same view in cases of long sustained and uncontrollable excitement, and in cases of long sustained and severe melancholia. there may have been precipitating factors in the first place, and initially the state may have appeared comprehensible as a reaction to them. But, as the reader may agree when he comes to read the description of these conditions in Chapter 9, there are few psychological factors that could justifiably be used to explain the long continuance of states of such severity, even though they may have acted as precipitating agents.

In general, we invoke constitutional factors when there is an absence of *adequate* and demonstrable physical or psychological factors, and when genetic factors can be demonstrated, as in schizophrenia and the major affective illnesses. It is true that the patient may react to these illnesses with anxiety or disturbance of mood; such might almost be considered a normal reaction to the abnormal experience of such illness. But such added reaction is secondary and is not causal.

It will be realised that in this aetiological exercise of assessing the relative importance of constitutional, physical and psychological factors, we are seeking a satisfactory quantitative relationship between the condition as we see it and the causes that we can find to account for it. Detailed knowledge of an individual patient may show us why the particular symptoms that he has take the form that they do (as when the delusions of an oft-convicted felon take the form of being persecuted by the police), but it does not necessarily explain why he has the symptoms in the first place, when he has not had them before. Further, the exercise becomes less difficult with increasing experience, because the more cases one sees the more does one realise that there are groups of cases that have symptoms in common. By attending to the clinical picture one may then recognise it as belonging to a particular group. One may then know from experience what weight should in general be attached to the constitutional, physical and psychological factors in that particular group of illnesses. That is one should attend to the symptomatology of the condition and try to classify it, rather than seek to explain the individual symptoms essentially in terms of reaction.

The questions are: 'is the patient ill, if so in what way, and why?' If a woman seriously believes that the plants in her garden are repeatedly dug up by a busy neighbour and replaced very exactly by weeds, it may be concluded that she is ill, and that her illness takes the form of at least one delusion; it is not enough to say that she thinks as she does because she is a keen gardener and dislikes the neighbour; to conclude that that is the explanation of the illness is to mistake the pathogenesis of one particular manifestation with the aetiology of the whole.

The need for a multiple aetiological approach, taking all three groups of factors into account, can sometimes be seen in almost diagrammatic form. Thus, a man lost his job and became profoundly depressed. Previous loss of job had not had this effect. But on this occasion the loss occurred during an attack of influenza. Even with the cooperation of these physical and mental factors, the occurrence of severe depression is unusual. But here there was evidence of constitutional predisposition in that the patient's mother had committed suicide while in a mental hospital for melancholia. Few cases show their mixed aetiology quite so clearly, but all possess it, and in every case both the symptomatology and the relative importance of the various causes and their interaction have to be assessed.

Aetiological fallacies

Neglect of this basic principle of multiple causation by psychological, physical and constitutional factors, is responsible for two main aetiological fallacies and over-simplifications. First, the view is sometimes held, though less often than in the past, that mental illness must always have an essentially physical cause. The train of thought seems to be that if normal mental activity depends upon physical conditions, then any mental abnormality must be physically determined. In practice, this is sometimes but by no means always the case. The mental symptoms in intellectual deterioration or delirium may properly be attributed to the underlying physical disorder, as we have seen. But of course this is not necessarily so in other conditions. Psychological factors may be predominant, as in many cases of excessive anxiety, and there is no scientific basis for supposing that mental symptoms cannot arise as their more or less direct consequence. Constitutional factors may also be predominant, as in the cases of schizophrenia, mania and melancholia that we have considered. In fact, any of the three groups may be of prime aetiological importance, and to insist on the essentially physical as a cause is mistaken.

Even where the physical factors are aetiologically predominant, the psychological factors must necessarily make some contribution to the picture; as we have seen, the individual differences between one case and another depend upon them. That one patient sees snakes and another sees archbishops depends upon their personal preoccupations and experiences. That one patient's suspicions are directed towards the Catholics, or Jews, and another's towards cyclists or Freemasons, depends on the prejudices and attitudes that the individual has developed.

More than this, although the physical factors may be aetiologically predominant, the whole pattern of the illness may be constitutionally determined, as in the case quoted above where a severe depressive illness was precipitated by influenza. Again we see that insistence on the purely physical as 'the cause' is fallacious.

The second main fallacy is the converse one that mental symptoms are entirely dependent on mental causes. This is equally erroneous. We have already considered some of the schizophrenic, manic and melancholic states in which no satisfactory physical pathology can be demonstrated, and how it may then seem logical and natural to turn to the psychological factors for the aetiological explanation. As we saw in the introductory chapter such attempts have often been made. Psycho-analysis in particular has sought explanations of these illnesses in purely psychological terms; Meyer's psycho-biology has sought to explain Schizophrenia, in particular, as a gradual retreat from reality under the cumulative effects of a persistent failure of adaptation. More recently theories of schizophrenia have been put forward based entirely on abnormal relationships within the family, or on other social pressures; and some have even suggested that a schizophrenic breakdown can be seen as a useful adaptation to unbearable stress — a difficult view to hold for those who actually deal with these patients. The interplay of genetic and environmental factors in the development of schizophrenia and affective illnesses is considered in more detail in the relevant chapters (p. 126 and p. 163).

Very striking examples of the misunderstandings which can arise are found when a person with melancholia experiences feelings of guilt, which may happen as a symptom of that illness, and efforts are then made to explain both the guilt and the melancholia as arising from some trivial misdemeanour, perhaps committed years before and having been no source of concern meanwhile. As an extreme form of this illogicality, the case may be quoted of a severely depressed patient who brooded persistently on the fact that she had once taken, uninvited, an extra piece of cake at a wedding 20 years before. She sought to explain her illness — as did the relatives — as arising from this amoral act and the worry that it had occasioned. But of course the illness was constitutionally determined; the brooding was a symptom, not a cause; the fact of having taken the cake merely lent direction to the sense of guilt which was part of the illness itself.

Again, a patient with general paralysis of the insane may have delusions of grandeur. It is reasonable to suppose that these represent his wishes, but it is not reasonable to suppose that his wishes caused the illness. On the contrary, they merely account for some of the symptoms he shows in it. In fact, although intimate knowledge of the patient may explain the particular form of some of the symptoms, it is not necessarily enough to explain the illness itself. Although psychological factors will always be present and will lend some individual colouring, their existence must not lead to the fallacy that a mental illness must have purely mental causes.

We will now consider these three groups of factors, constitutional, physical and psychological, in turn. We will consider them in that order, on the principle of dealing with the more constant and basic ones first. It will soon be further apparent how artificial is their separation, and how much they are interrelated and overlap.

Constitutional factors

It is generally recognised that the make-up of an individual at any given time is due both to nature and to nurture, to the hereditary equipment with which he started and to the influences upon him of what has happened subsequently.

Some genes, like those for eye colour and Huntington's chorea (p. 108) exert their effect independent of any known environmental influences; but usually genes can be seen as setting limits to an individual's potentialities. This is seen very clearly with height, in which nutrition also plays an important rôle, although a food intake larger than optimal does not lead to increased height, but to obesity.

The importance of the genetic equipment in (a) setting a limit to potentialities, and (b) leading to very diverse manifestations mostly falling within the bounds of normal variation, has not, however, been so widely recognised for psychological as it has been for physical phenomena. This is partly because the greater complexity of the problem has hindered the development of precise knowledge, but no doubt partly also because of a natural reluctance to accept such a frustrating doctrine of personal limitations. None the less, there is evidence in its favour, and this is illustrated by the work of Kretschmer who has described different physical types which are associated to some extent with corresponding personality types. The chief of these are:

(1) The 'asthenic' (lepto-somatic) type — This is characterised by narrow build, an angular profile, and a lean, dyspeptic, hungry look. Asthenics appear taller than they really are. The musculature is poor and gives a tendency to droop. The chest is long, narrow and flat, with a subcostal angle of less than 90°. The skin is pale and the hands and feet tend to be cyanotic. There is some association between this build and an introverted personality whose emotions tend to be cold leading to aloofness, whose interests tend to be intellectual and abstract, with an inclination towards contemplative rather than active pursuits, in

line with the fact that the reserves of energy are usually small. There is some affinity between this build and schizoid personality (see Chapter 10) and a liability to schizophrenic breakdown.

(2) *The 'pyknic' (pyknosomatic) type* — Here the physique more resembles Humpty-Dumpty, Falstaff or John Bull. It is characterised by large body cavities, a short neck, and small but graceful extremities. Pyknics are liable to look shorter than they really are. The thorax and abdomen are wide and deep. The subcostal angle is greater than 90°. The musculature is good unless, as is not uncommon, the person has run to fat. The skin is ruddy and the peripheral circulation good. There is some association between this build and a personality characterised by emotional warmth and sympathetic responsiveness, a tendency to extroverted activities and to maintaining the common touch, towards activity rather than contemplation, and a high endowment of energy. There is some affinity between this personality and cyclothymia (p. 164) and a liability to manic-depressive developments.

(3) *The 'athletic' (athleto-somatic) type* comes between the other two. It is characterised by broad shoulders, narrow hips, good proportions of trunk and limbs, large bones and a well-developed musculature, especially in the proximal muscle groups. Any associated personality type is less well-defined than with the asthenic and pyknic physique, but this physique is disproportionately common in young criminal delinquents.

Kretschmer's work has been carried further by Sheldon and his associates who have concluded, as a result of physical measurement, photography and psychological study of normals, that in physique there are three basic dimensions, endomorphy, ectomorphy and mesomorphy, each of which makes an approximately equal contribution to the statistically average individual, while those other than average are variants along one of these three dimensions. The endomorphs (with large body cavities and massive digestive viscera) are akin to Kretschmer's pyknic type with temperamental characteristics to match; the mesomorphs, with predominance of bone, muscle and connective tissue, are the analogue of the athletic type; the ectomorphs, in whom delicacy and angularity of appearance are striking, with temperamental accompaniments of restraint and inhibition, correspond to the asthenic type.

The associations between physique, personality and liability to breakdown are of interest and sometimes have practical value in the assessment of certain mixed psychiatric syndromes. But they are by no means invariable and there are many exceptions; they exist, therefore, only as general trends in a broad sense. The fact that these associations

Fig. 2.1 Asthenic type

Fig. 2.2 Pyknic type

Fig. 2.3 Athletic type

between body build and temperament exist, is a striking illustration of the importance of 'constitution' as described earlier.

More powerful evidence, perhaps, comes from the study of intelligence. This, as measured by intelligence tests, appears quite comparable to height in being largely determined by the hereditary endowment [i.e. the genes] and in exhibiting a normal curve of distribution in the population. That is to say, just as there are large numbers of people of medium height, while the numbers become smaller towards the extremes of tallness or dwarfism, so there are large numbers with medium intelligence and the numbers become smaller towards the extremes of intelligence, high or low. However, the full genetically determined potentialities may not be realised if the environment is markedly unfavourable at any stage of development. Among the factors identified as harmful or limiting have been intrauterine ones such as heavy maternal smoking, toxins such as lead, and infections; perinatal factors such as anoxia; early severe malnutrition; and an upbringing with little intellectual, perceptual or emotional stimulation and richness.

Although such personal characteristics as character and temperament are not as easily susceptible of measurement, there is no reason to suppose that all mankind starts life with equal potentialities in these respects. On the contrary, minor variations in every aspect of attribute of character can readily be observed, with extreme variations less common. That is, a normal curve of distribution exists, just as in intelligence and height.

Studies of identical twins brought up together and apart have shown that such fundamental attributes as degree of outgoingness, proneness to anxiety, and basic levels of drive (energy) seem to be largely determined genetically.

Constitutional factors, therefore, may contribute to mental breakdown through the limitations that they impose upon the individual as regards his physique, personality, intelligence and temperament. But they may do more than this by providing a predisposition to the development of mental disorder on a genetic basis.

Genetic influences

Broadly speaking, genes can be considered under two headings, those of minor and those of major effect. Variations in intelligence and character and in liability to minor 'nervous' symptoms are now attributed to the influence of many genes of small but additive effect.

Whilst it is true that any individual may show nervous symptoms under sufficient provocation, there is evidence that all people are not *equally* liable to such developments. The liability to such a response varies from person to person, in contrast to the universal tendency to respond to infection with fever. The differences between individuals in this respect cannot be accounted for solely, or even mainly, on the ground of the environmental stresses that they have met, but are considered attributable, in part at least, to the influence of these genes of minor effect.

Such a genetic endowment does not necessarily result in breakdown, but it renders its possessors more susceptible to the effects of stress, as is shown particularly by studies of identical twins. It will be realised that, however little is known of the mechanisms of genetic influences, the tendencies that they confer make their appearance at different times of life. Thus, although the tendency to brown eyes and dark hair is innate, the appearance of some characteristics may be delayed, just as an innate tendency to baldness may not be manifest until later life. In the same way, the liability to breakdown may appear early if it is marked, or if it is mild may be delayed until the individual comes under considerable stress.

The extent to which this occurs is complicated by the fact that a man may be normal or average in many respects, but an extreme variant or abnormal in one or in only a few. He may be abnormal, for example, only in extreme sensitiveness, conscientiousness or aggressiveness. That is, his liability to breakdown may be of a very specialised kind, which may be brought out only by particular environmental stresses, or by internal stresses arising from incompatibility of contrasting character traits provoked by special situations.

It is in the production of these minor abnormalities that the genes of minor effect have influence. The genes of major effect, by contrast and as their names implies, are responsible for the constitutional loading that contributes to the development of major abnormalities, of a more marked, more clearly cut and more specific kind. There are certain rare conditions in which this is plainly demonstrable, such as Huntington's chorea and phenylketonuria. The latter can be shown to arise from a single recessive gene. The former can be shown to arise from a single dominant gene; its onset in the potential victim is inevitable and certain, so that the only way that he can avoid the disease is to die of something else before he reaches the time of life at which it develops. In recent years phenylketonuria has become preventable by giving a diet free of phenylalanine, thus demonstrating that to identify a genetic cause for a disease does not mean the outlook is hopeless, although that is the attitude of most people. It is possible that similar results will be possible in other genetically determined diseases.

Conditions in which the genetic relationships are so clear cut are few, but that they occur at all is of great significance as regards genetic influence in general. Such genetic influence can be discerned, though in a less obvious and plain form, in such other major psychiatric disorders as schizophrenia and manic-depressive psychosis. Just as the ordinary man is most unlikely to fall below an adult height of 4 feet, and it needs pathological dwarfism to produce that effect, so is he unlikely to sink into a really profound depression of psychotic or melancholic type (see Chapter 9).

There is, of course, no reason why specific genes of large effect, resulting for example in a classical manic-depressive psychosis, should not be combined in the same individual with several genes of small but additive effect. In fact, this does appear to happen. If the genes of minor effect make for stability, the resultant is the occurrence of manic-depressive psychosis in an otherwise stable person; if they are unfavourable ones, the resultant is manic-depressive psychosis in someone already predisposed to minor abnormalities and neurotic reactions. In practice, manic-depressive psychosis can afflict both types of individual.

The above outline represents a convenient working hypothesis, which may help in the understanding both of individual cases and of the difficulty in obtaining more exact data concerning the heredity of mental illness in general.

Environmental influences

Apart from these hereditary factors, a person may acquire patterns of reaction, either through being encouraged or through not being checked in their development, which, through repetition and long continuance, become characteristic and all but automatic. Those who have been encouraged to run for help in any difficulty may so continue until their dotage. Those, obstinate and of sterner stuff, who, though hopelessly lost, refuse either to ask the way or return to the starting point, may show a like intransigence as part of their normal approach to life. Such persistent and characteristic behaviour may be so integral a part of the personality as to justify its being called constitutional. In this sense there are thus both psychological as well as physical constitutional factors, as is only to be expected since 'physical' and 'mental' are but different aspects of the constitutional whole.

The upbringing is obviously of great importance in encouraging the development of behaviour patterns that are of a helpful kind. Life makes many demands on our powers of adaptation, and successful adaptation calls for flexibility. What is required is that a person should not be unduly rigid on the one hand, nor liable to panicky impulsive action on the other. To maintain the mean between these two requires steadiness of mind, and the best way of acquiring it is to be reared in a steady atmosphere.

Children are imitative by nature, and they should have steady people to emulate if they are to become steady themselves. Tradition and cultural influences are of great formative value. Repeated changes of background, living with different relatives or in different places with repeated changes of school, may make demands on the child which he is unable to meet and therefore have an unsettling effect. The child also needs affection and this should be of a steady kind on which he knows that he can rely. Where the parents are loving and over-protective at one moment but angry and threatening the next, in accord with their own caprices, the effect is to discourage steady attitudes. Likewise, the child requires discipline but this should be of a consistent kind that he is able to understand. If he is to learn to respect the rights of others, his own rights should be respected also; if the discipline is unduly repressive the naturally spirited child will rebel and the timid child will become cowed. The same may happen if there is invidious discrimination so that one child is deprived in favour of another. All children need moral support, but this should stop short of over-protection. Financial security is obviously helpful.

In summary, the home background should be emotionally and financially steady, with affection that can be relied upon and is properly distributed, with reasonable liberty but with reasonable and consistent discipline. Within this framework the normally constituted child should grow up normally enough, although there are many sad exceptions as when people with apparently normal backgrounds become drug or alcohol dependent.

Where there are marked departures from these requirements, the growing child may adopt attitudes unhelpful to his adaptation, and these may well persist not only into but throughout adult life. Poor management of the home situation in the early years may result in such persistent traits as jealousy, resentment, intolerance of frustration and authority, incapacity to show affection, undue dependence, inferiority feelings and inability to meet people on even terms. These may be a considerable handicap and hindrance, and may be so ingrained in the personality as to be habitual and therefore, as has been said, a part of the constitution.

However, while no one doubts that it is a good thing to have come from a happy home, it is perfectly possible to emerge from an unhappy one and yet have a good personality. The converse is also true. This illustrates how difficult it can be to evaluate genetic and environmental influences in any given case. The latter can probably be of paramount importance. If it should seem that undue emphasis has been laid on the genetic rather than the environmental influences in the foregoing discussion, this does not arise from any intention of minimising the importance of the environment, but from the necessity to draw the attention of the student to the possible importance in any given case of more recondite factors, of whose existence he should be aware.

Summary

In summary, hereditary factors are of prime importance in setting limitations to the development of physique and intelligence: they also make a substantial contribution to the personality and temperament. There are certain broad trends in the association between certain types of physique and personality. It is probable that many genes of minor but additive effect provide a predisposition to the development of minor mental abnormalities, and that specific genes of major effect are associated with the development of more marked mental abnormalities in the form of specific and major illnesses. In all these ways the constitutional factors will always have contributed to the patient's development, and their influence must not be ignored, whatever other apparent causes there may be of the condition that the patient presents. Nor does the apparent absence of hereditary predisposition mean that constitutional factors are absent. The importance of environmental as opposed to hereditary factors having influenced the development of the constitution is less likely to be overlooked, as everyone knows of the importance of early environment. The genetic and environmental influences should be weighed in every case, or at least some attempt in this direction should be made. Where acquired attitudes of mind and habits of reaction have become so habitual as to be an integral part of the personality, they also may be considered constitutional. The more precise genetic data concerning particular psychiatric syndromes will be found in the appropriate chapters.

Physical factors

By physical factors are here meant the states of physical disorder or disease that are studied in general medicine, such as infections, intoxications, disorders of nutrition and circulation, metabolic, endocrine and degenerative disturbances. Now, the origin of these may be exogenous, as in infections, or constitutional, as in the degenerative disturbances, or both, as in the intoxications. We have already noted that one patient with typhoid fever may develop a delirium, whereas another equally ill may not. Likewise, a chronic alcoholic may develop delirium tremens, but another who drinks more under the same conditions may remain free from delirium. The inference is that their make-up is different, and that there must be constitutional factors involved, as well as the physical ones. This again emphasises the artificiality of the separation. Reminding ourselves, therefore, that the terms 'physical' and 'constitutional' are not mutually exclusive, we may consider the physical factors in mental illness under three headings:

   1. Those that produce their effects through permanent changes in the physical structure

   2. Those that are associated with mental symptoms though in the absence of permanent changes in the physical structure; in these some transient but reversible structural change is to be inferred

   3. Those about which we may speculate but know nothing certain.

Factors producing permanent structural changes

In this first group are such degenerative conditions as the senile and presenile dementias; the late results of cerebrovascular disease including major strokes and diffuse arteriosclerotic dementia; the late results of head injury and sometimes of cerebral tumour; chronic alcoholism; occasional cases of poisoning with carbon monoxide or heavy metals; general paralysis of the insane due to tertiary syphilis; and numerous other rarer causes. The clinical pictures arising from these causes have enough in common to be recognisable as showing an 'organic type of mental reaction'. The cardinal features of these organically determined states are impairment of intellect and personality, often with emotional changes, and they are described in Chapter 6.

Factors producing transient physical changes

The second group, those associated with mental symptoms though in the absence of permanent changes in the physical structure, comprise a considerable variety. First, we may mention the variable and reversible physical changes that accompany emotion, and are an integral part of emotion as experienced in the mind. These are mediated by the autonomic system, and the commonest are palpitation, sweating, tremors, various symptoms arising from the alimentary tract, and frequency of micturition. More dramatic and widespread in their effects than these physical accompaniments of emotion are toxic states of exogenous origin, i.e. the febrile and toxic deliria, which present the above symptoms of the 'organic mental reaction' with additional features of disorientation, clouding of consciousness, with misinterpretations of what goes on around them (amounting to fleeting delusions), and often with hallucinations. Such states can occur in any severely toxic condition, in uraemia, carbon monoxide and metallic poisonings, and in the course of chronic alcoholism. Cases that die show degenerative changes in the nervous system to an extent that varies with the severity and chronicity of the poisoning. It is a reasonable inference that in those who survive there have been changes of such lesser degree as to be reversible.

Uncertain physical factors

It remains to consider the third group of physical factors, those about which we may speculate, but of which we have no certain knowledge. First, as to structure, although much work has been done, histological studies have not succeeded in establishing any definite connection between mental symptoms and cellular pathology except in such degenerative conditions as the dementias, in states where irreversible damage has been done by toxicity, and where there has been localised damage with resultant mental symptoms of organic type as may occur with cerebral tumour or after head injury, or following vascular accidents. That is to say, histology has been of help where there has been permanent and irreversible damage, but has otherwise told us little.

Many studies have claimed to demonstrate that patients with chronic schizophrenia have evidence of cerebral atrophy, dilatation of the third ventricle on lumbar air encephalography; and others have tried to demonstrate histopathological changes either at post mortem or by brain biopsy. None of these studies has been really convincing, however, although one must realise that the techniques are relatively crude. Computer assisted tomography is now being used in this field, and recent studies have shown cerebral atrophic changes in chronic schizophrenia, which strongly suggests some organic brain disease. Much research is being done in this field currently.

Electroencephalography has not yet lived up to earlier hopes in studies on schizophrenia and other mental illnesses, although it is so useful in neurological investigation and has helped to elucidate the nature of sleep. Patients with schizophrenia often do show abnormalities on their e.e.g., but there is no general agreement on the meaning of these, and it may be that the abnormalities are the result of the abnormal mental state rather than indicators of underlying causal disturbance.

Endocrine studies have in recent years been more productive, especially in manic-depressive illnesses and other affective disorders, and biochemical research and theorising has had an enormous impact, on treatment especially, with the development of drugs. More detail is given on these subjects on page 170.

Summary

In summary, then, physical factors are of predominant importance in the production of degenerative, confusional and delirious states. They are also accompaniments of emotion and an integral part of emotional experience. In this respect they contribute to those emotional reactions precipitated mainly by psychological factors; but they usually play small part in their causation. It is probable that physical factors, in the form of endocrine, biochemical and metabolic disturbances, play a considerable rôle in the development of major mental illnesses such as schizophrenia and affective disorders. Our knowledge, however, is at present so incomplete that the attribution of major mental illnesses, other than degenerative conditions and deliria, to physical factors is at present no more than speculative.

Psychological factors

Psychological factors will colour an organically caused illness, will precipitate and modify a functional psychosis such as schizophrenia or mania, and will be the main factor in leading to a neurotic disorder in most cases (see Chapter 11).

Individual emotional reactions

Emotional reactions may occur as a result of changes either in the individual or in his environment, and they may happen suddenly or gradually, according to the nature of such changes. Such sudden changes are bereavements, injuries or illness, unexpected financial reverses, or the loss of a job. Gradual changes may occur as the result of ageing, with inability to accept the limitations imposed by increasing ill-health and frailty, or when it slowly becomes apparent that a long struggle towards some desired end is resulting in failure from which there seems no escape, or when a situation of early promise has ended in disappointment. Sexual difficulties and frustrations may also be important factors.

In general, the failure of adjustment that such emotional reactions represent results from a discrepancy between the demands made upon an individual and his ability to cope with them. It will be noted that such demands may be made upon the patient not only by the external situation but also by himself, through his ambitions and his social and ethical standards. Such reactions are, therefore, the product of the interplay between a particular situation and a particular personality, and their pattern depends on the nature of the emotional currents that the situation evokes. In conditions where the psychological factors are predominant, attention should therefore be focused upon these emotional currents. For example, overwork is often cited as a cause of nervous breakdown. But where the patient has in fact worked to an abnormal extent, what is important is not the overwork itself but the emotional strain under which it has been done or the reasons which drove the patient to undertake it. Indeed, it can almost be taken as an axiom that overwork is a euphemism for overworry. The key to understanding breakdowns in which psychological factors predominate lies, therefore, in the emotional response that results from the interplay between the provocative situation and the patient's personality.

More complex emotional reactions

Sometimes these may be easily intelligible, as when the stress is one which would shake anybody, such as a bereavement or being bombed. More often, however, the intensity of emotional responses and their time-relationship to stresses become intelligible only with knowledge of the patient's personality.

Where the time relationships are unexpected, this is usually because (1) worries and stresses tend to be cumulative in their effects, and the 'last straw' effect is often seen in precipitating depressive illnesses, (2) the initial symptoms may, through causing worry or through other reasons, have led to other symptoms, with the later development of further and secondary reactions, (3) people come to need the stimulations to which they are accustomed, and in the absence of such may feel disorganised and at a loss; and decrease of tension may be as emotionally upsetting as increase of tension, (4) there is an unexplained but common tendency for symptoms in both depressive and schizophrenic patients to follow about 3 weeks after some emotional turmoil or upheaval.

The intensity of the emotional response also may seem anomalous, if the situation has had some special significance for the patient that is not at first clear to the observer. This is especially liable to happen if the patient is subject to inner conflicts, which involve the higher emotions attached to values, standards, ideals and ambitions.

Mental mechanisms in neurotic states

The patient may prefer not to look at these difficulties mentioned above, or he may see only their less unpleasant aspects. But this does not do away with the emotional currents themselves; all that happens is that the patient finds himself in the grip of something that he does not understand. He finds his situation the more difficult to manage as a result. These points may be illustrated by simple examples. A soldier in the front line may fully realise that he is homesick and terrified; but with goodwill he may fully do his duty. On the other hand, although the stress was far less overtly severe, the conscientious secretary of a business man found herself unable to carry on owing to a functional dyspepsia. This was attributed to overwork, for which there was some evidence, and to dental sepsis, for which there was not. After dental extractions and a holiday had not resulted in improvement, in that she relapsed as soon as she returned to work, it emerged that the real cause of her trouble was that she had fallen in love with her employer. She had not admitted this to herself since she was a girl of strict standards and he was a married man. Her feelings had actually induced her to work long hours for him, and she had persuaded herself that her emotion was one of admiration only. After she had realised the true nature of her difficulties, she changed her job and did well.

It may be thought that the foregoing is an extreme example, but failure to understand the factors that induce our feelings and dictate our actions is to some extent present in everyone; and even if it is not always obvious in ourselves, it is plain enough in those around us. The average man is surprisingly deficient in introspective desire or capacity; his self-knowledge is often limited to a vague awareness that he finds difficult to put into words. This absence of clear formulation has an important bearing on the therapeutic results that can follow a diagnostic interview which obliges a patient to formulate for the first time and to express his feelings in words. Few psychiatrists have not had the experience of receiving thanks for 'putting things so clearly' after an interview during which they have scarcely opened their mouths. Nor is lack of self-knowledge confined to the simple or to the tongue-tied and inarticulate; the self-esteem of those with intelligence, introspective gifts and verbal facility, is often subtly self-satisfying rather than accurate. In fact, it is very difficult to make a just self-estimate.

The difficulty is much increased by the normal tendency to attend to those aspects of ourselves which give us satisfaction, with a relative disregard of our own less satisfactory aspects. The emphasis is naturally upon the former. It is easy to make mistakes in describing what is in and on our minds as it is to make mistakes in describing some outside event, especially one in which we have been unpleasantly involved. In each case, desires, prejudices and expectations will distort observation and falsify recollection, so that the real constituents of the scene will be ignored, wrongly described or emphasised, or a wrong attribution of their origin made. This is especially likely to be so if the results of more accurate introspection are disconcerting or damaging to the self-esteem, and thus calculated to arouse emotions of an unpleasant character. That is why, while many people do not mind complaining of their poor memory, so few complain of their poor intelligence and judgment, although the latter can scarcely be less frequent or serious in their effects. Again, a man will pride himself on his capacity for compromise where others will see only weakness; or upon his high standards and strict discipline, where others see only the reflection of an irritable and aggressive personality.

Memory, and therefore our conception of our past, is apt to be affected in the same way. Unpleasant facts tend to receive preferential treatment in the normal process of forgetting. Murderers tend to develop an amnesia for the murders they have committed. Less dramatically, patients tend to forget, when giving their work record, the jobs that they disliked or did badly. the authors themselves have been reminded by their friends of discreditable past episodes, though they have again forgotten them. More vividly, a sergeant of sensitive disposition was the only survivor of a group of men who all came from his own village; he forgot all details of the actual engagement, an amnesia facilitated by his having to break the news to his fellow-villagers. Again, another patient could recall a quarrel with his wife, but not that he had threatened suicide if she did not behave better. He was ashamed of it.

Thus lack of self-knowledge, both past and present, tends to keep us in ignorance of our true selves, largely through a shift of emphasis from what is unpalatable to what gives us satisfaction. This, as will be mentioned, is to some extent a merciful provision. But where a person has inner conflicts, this mental mechanism tends to operate more strongly, and by obscuring the issue makes the conflicts more difficult to resolve. As such conflicts give rise to unpleasant emotional responses, the patient is left under a greater or lesser handicap according to their severity.

It will thus be realised that in these conditions in which psychological factors are of prime aetiological importance, what happens is that particular circumstances lead to emotional repercussions in a particular personality; the causes may have to be sought more in that personality than in the circumstances; consequently, they may lie more in the past than in the present. The true nature of the emotional disturbance may be obscured from the patient by that lack of self-knowledge which is common to all of us, and by psychological mechanisms, shared to some extent by all of us, which prevent us from accurate assessment of ourselves and of our reactions to situations.

Psychoanalysts have made the major contribution to studying 'mental mechanisms', and one does not have to accept the whole of psychoanalytic theory in order to use their findings. In particular, they have described various types of *ego defence mechanism*. These may be described as 'habitual, unconscious mental processes, which may be healthy and helpful or pathological and harmful, which have the effect of resolving conflict between inner drives and external reality'. Examples might be clearer than further explanation, and further details should be sought in the psychoanalytic literature. Only a few will be mentioned here.

Some ego defence mechanisms

Repression This is one of the best known, by name at least. Unacceptable memories are kept out of consciousness, although emotions associated with them may not. For example, a man who wept after his mother's death but could not say for whom, or denied feeling sad, might be showing repression. If he denied that he had been weeping, or refused to accept that his mother was dead, he would be showing denial.   *Denial*, as illustrated above. In a crude form is more likely in schizophrenics, in less extreme and unrealistic forms is a 'neurotic' defence.   *Intellectualisation.* Thinking about strong impulses and wishes in a detached sort of way, and not putting them into action.   *Displacement.* Directing powerful feelings towards some person or thing which is intrinsically less important, and therefore safer. Lavishing love on a pet, or making jokes in very difficult situations, can be examples.

The preceding ego defences, and others not named, are commonly used in daily life, more often by people with neurotic character problems (see Chapter 11). Some are more commonly used by people with more severe personality problems, for example: *Projection* which is attributing your own bad feelings to others, and in extreme forms is clearly psychotic, as when someone who has had fears that he might be homosexual comes to believe that strangers are joking about the fact that he is indeed so.

Some ego defences are regarded as characteristic of more mature and stable personalities, such as *sublimation,* in which emotional drives which cannot be openly expressed are put into some creative or useful activity, perhaps into art (a classical psychoanalytic concept), or as when aggression is channelled into sport.

There is an interesting article on the subject by Vaillant referred to in the bibliography, in which 18 ego defences are considered in relation to overall mental health and success in various fields of life.

Advantageous use of the same mental mechanisms

These psychological mechanisms can be useful in promoting the adjustment of the individual, in that they may buffer him comfortably from the unpalatabilities of reality. They become handicaps only when the emotional repercussions aroused by conflict are too powerful for adjustment by such methods; they then become harmful to those whom they prevent from realising the true nature of their difficulties. In ordinary life these mechanisms can be of value in adapting the picture of reality so that it becomes emotionally acceptable. Repressed facts do not disappear completely; they remain potentially available, but are not recalled owing to emotional interference. The less tolerable they are to the conscious mind, the less easily are they recovered. Although it is often said that such facts are 'repressed into the unconscious', it will often be found that patients are in fact capable of remembering them, but prefer to keep them in some separate mental compartment, and so manage to disconnect them from the stream of consciousness rather than remove them altogether.

The extent to which such mechanisms are successful in maintaining adjustment over a long period of time is variable, and depends much on chance. Sublimation tends to be the most satisfactory mechanism, and many who adopt it live happily and successfully, without indication that their mode of life has any but its prima facie value. It was pure ill-luck that moved an admirable schoolmaster of advanced years to reflect one day while playing bridge with his headmaster's wife: 'What a fine thing a boy's bottom is'. That he did so was the first sign of the cerebral tumour from which he soon afterwards died, and which disintegrated the psychological mechanisms by which he had held his feeling and actions in check so that they accorded with personal and social propriety.

The development of physical symptoms from emotional causes

The foregoing is an example of how physical factors may influence psychological ones. But it must never be forgotten that psychological factors can also set physical ones in train. Emotional upset, however caused, may produce symptoms of mental or bodily distress, or both combined. The rôle of the autonomic nervous system in causing palpitations, sweating, abdominal discomfort and other physical symptoms is considered in more detail in the section on Anxiety states (Chapter 11) and that on Psychosomatic medicine (Chapter 15).

Summary

In summary, we may say that psychological factors are always present in mental illness. Where they are not aetiologically predominant they will at least account to some extent for the differences between one individual clinical picture and another, as, for example, in the pattern of delirious states or the form taken by delusions. Where they are aetiologically predominant, the states to which they give rise are characterised by emotional disturbance rather than by distortions of the mental content, and in the sense that they do not lead to psychosis are relatively minor conditions, though they may be markedly disabling. Such emotional disturbances arise from the effect of particular situations on the personality, and represent some degree of failure of that personality to adjust under stress: although often the stress may have been imposed by the personality itself rather than by the situation. For this reason, as well as because the same situation may evoke different emotional responses in different people, the key to states where the psychological factors are predominant usually lies more in the personality than in the situation. To understand the personality, it is necessary to know the past history and development as well as the present circumstances, for it may be the former that determine the faulty adaptation: and very often it is, though not always. Emotional disturbances of more or less subtle kinds arising from inner conflicts are usually more potent causes of breakdown than are the more gross emotional disturbances arising from severe external stress. The comparative subtlety of the former makes the emotional difficulty harder for the patient to cope with, as do lack of self-knowledge, the normal tendency to obscure one's deficiencies from oneself, to rationalise one's actions and to fail to see what one does not wish to see. These tendencies, though present in all people and often useful in promoting adjustment, become handicaps when they prevent the clear formulation and understanding of emotional disturbances that have already led to breakdown. Such understanding may be the more difficult to gain because emotional disturbances often lead to physical symptoms, either indirectly through auto- and hetero-suggestion or directly through their effect on the autonomic system, with the result that they may dominate the clinical picture and obscure the real causes. The patient may fail to see the connection between the physical symptoms and the psychological state, either through ignorance or from choice. That psychological factors can lead to physical ones, and especially so in people of a particular constitution, serves to emphasise that all three groups of factors must always be taken into consideration.

3

Symptoms encountered in mental illness

It is essential that the student should know the more important symptoms encountered in mental disorder, and that he should be clear as to the meaning of the technical terms used to describe them. Contrary to popular belief, fewer technical terms are used in psychiatry than in other specialities. This has disadvantages, since it often leads to well-known terms being used in a special and technical sense that differs from their ordinary meaning. For example, 'hysteria' means something quite different to the psychiatrist from what it means to the layman.

Unconsciousness

An unconscious patient is neither aware of his environment nor capable of responding to stimuli in any well-directed way (*inaccessibility*). He is subsequently incapable of recalling any mental activity during the period in question. This is called anterograde as opposed to retrograde amnesia. States of unconsciousness are best observed after severe concussion, in deep anaesthesia and as a final stage of many intoxications. The duration of anterograde amnesia is good evidence of the severity of concussion, and a probable indication of the length of time that the patient will be off work (p. 89). Between unconsciousness and consciousness there are various types and degrees of disturbed consciousness.

Disturbances of consciousness

These are mainly due to physical causes, and the general characteristics are as follows:
1. Deficient grasp, that is of the meaning of what he observes.
2. Disturbances of attention and concentration.
3. Slowness of thinking.

4. Disturbances of memory (*retention*).

5. Lack of direction in thought and action.

Consequently the patient shows: Disorientation (i.e. he has lost his bearings as regards place, time and other people).

Confusion (by which is meant something simpler than may be normally experienced on being confronted with an income tax form or legal enactment. The patient is confused when he mistakes the use of a knife and fork, puts the right shoe on the left foot or cannot find his own bed).

Disconnected and often incomprehensible behaviour.

Subsequent amnesia.

Three intermediate states between consciousness and unconsciousness are often recognised:

1. *Dimming or clouding of consciousness.* Less than normal rather than anything abnormal is experienced. All mental processes are slow. Association of ideas is scanty. Thinking is difficult or impossible. These patients are apathetic and bemused, show no initiative, are easily fatigued, and it is hard to attract or to hold their attention. They tend to pass into a dreamless sleep, stupor or coma. In mild cases the patients may answer and behave rationally under examination, but readily relapse when left to themselves. In cases of moderate severity, although out of tough with their surroundings, they may be roused to answer simple questions correctly. And in severe cases it may just be possible to get an occasional appropriate response by forcible questioning or commands.

2. *Delirious states.* The consciousness is clouded, and the continuity of mental processes is interrupted or shattered by abnormal experiences such as hallucinations. Restlessness is a most common feature.

3. *Twilight states.* There is rarely a peculiar alteration of consciousness and personality for certain periods of limited duration, with subsequent amnesia. Such are mainly encountered in epilepsy (p. 96) and also, uncommonly, in some hysterical states (p. 276).

Attention

This is the term used for describing the experience that certain objects are in the centre of consciousness, whilst others lie more towards the periphery. This distribution may be achieved either voluntarily or involuntarily. Attention may be disturbed in various ways:

1. It may be difficult or impossible to *arouse* the attention of the patient. This generally occurs in organic states resulting in disturbed

consciousness; but it may also occur in states of 'retardation', perplexity, or self-absorption due to depression or schizophrenia.

2. It may be difficult or impossible to *keep* the attention of the patient, (*a*) because the patient returns to predominant preoccupations (depression and schizophrenia); (*b*) because the attention of the patient is readily distracted by stimuli from the outside, this distractibility preventing concentration on any given subject for any length of time (manic and certain organic pictures); (*c*) because of variation in the level of consciousness where this is dimmed or clouded. Such variation should always arouse suspicion of organic intra-cranial cause.

Disturbances of volition, general activity, motor behaviour

Lack of initiative may be a life-long characteristic, especially in dullards and inadequate people. When it appears as a new symptom this is usually in states of debility after physical illness, neurasthenic states, and in depression and schizophrenic psychoses, but it is not uncommon with cerebral lesions, especially those involving the frontal lobes. *Retardation* denotes a condition, not natural to the person but associated with illness, characterised objectively by slowness of speech and action, but in fact due to difficulty in execution. (It is rare for retarded patients to experience slow thoughts and empty minds.) It is most often seen in depressions and some schizophrenic states, and when of rare severity may result in stupor. Patients with organic mental conditions can also be slow in the uptake.   *Stupor* means complete suppression of speech, movement and action not accounted for by profound disturbances of consciousness. Though less common than formerly, it is produced by schizophrenic disturbances of will, but it may result from extreme retardation in melancholic patients. *Flexibilitas cerea* (a peculiar type of 'wax-like' rigidity of the muscles), *catalepsy* (the tendency to keep up postures which have been imposed), and *negativism* (automatic resistance to all outside stimuli) are symptoms sometimes found in schizophrenia and also in some conditions of organic cerebral disease.   *Psychomotor overactivity,* together with an increased speed of action, can be seen in all states of excitement, most commonly in manic conditions, in which it is sustained, and sometimes in organic confusional states in which it is less sustained and more variable. Impulses may follow one another so rapidly that none is carried out or completed. Psychomotor overactivity can also occur in certain abnormal personalities under the influence of alcohol.

In *Catatonic excitement,* which occurs in schizophrenia, the motor behaviour is generally more disintegrated, and features like *stereotypy* (monotonous repetition in speech and movements), mannerisms and grimacing are often observed and are highly characteristic.

Perseveration denotes a repetition of a phrase or movement, apparently due to inability to change to a new one, as when the patient asked to answer a question continues to give an answer previously given. It may be most marked in the field of speech and may be regarded as part of a dysphasia. It is common in all organic psychiatric conditions.

Suggestion means influence by processes other than reason; *suggestibility* is the capacity — varying in each individual — of yielding to such influences. This normal attribute is increased in states of disturbed consciousness. It is strikingly present in the hypnotic state. In schizophrenics it may reach the extreme degree of *automatic obedience. Echopraxia* and *echolalia,* i.e. the automatic repetition of actions which are seen, or of words which are heard, are particular examples of this.

Abnormal impulses, Such as *kleptomania* (the impulse to steal) and *pyromania* (the impulse to set things on fire) do sometimes occur in obsessive-compulsive states, i.e. as impulses experienced against the will and under a subjective feeling of compulsion. Where thefts and arson have been committed, however, there is usually some much simpler explanation despite the pleas often put forward by those who are brought to justice. When there is a subjective experience of compulsion, there must be an internal struggle against the compulsion for it to be considered 'obsessive-compulsive' (p. 50).

Disturbances of thought

There is frequently confusion in the student's mind when considering thought disorder, of which '*schizophrenic thought disorder*' is one particular type, but which is so frequently mentioned that the existence of other forms is ignored.

By the term '*schizophrenic thought disorder*' we mean a complex disturbance of the grammatical use of language, both with the spoken and written word. There is a basic disturbance of the associations of sound or meaning, or both, which leads to a rambling vagueness, or to more severe disturbances. It is described in the chapter on schizophrenia (p. 134) in more detail. The term 'formal thought disorder' is now commonly used to emphasise that the disturbance is of the form and structure of speech. A delusion is *not* part of thought disorder.

Thought blocking and *neologisms*, both mentioned below, are also very characteristic of schizophrenia, but are not necessarily present even in the presence of severe thought disorder.

Retardation, encountered mainly in depressive states, is characterised by slowness or difficulty in thinking, often accompanied by a poverty of ideas of which the patients are clearly aware. When both speech and movement are slowed, the usual term is *psychomotor retardation*. Many depressive patients who are retarded do not, however, so much complain of slow thoughts or empty minds as of thoughts that go round and round but do not get on. An extreme poverty of association may lead to a form of perseveration very like that seen in organic conditions.

Circumstantiality means slow progression of thought because of a continual tendency to digress into detailed accounts of trivial matters — such as the exact date and time of some event many years ago. It is very characteristic of those with obsessional personalities; but also occurs in unintelligent or very self-centred people. As a new development it suggests schizophrenia or organic brain disease.

Flight of ideas is typical of mania. Manic patients think quickly and have a great wealth of association which prevents them from pursuing a purposive line of thought. Flight of ideas is an exaggeration of what Schopenhauer attributed to certain authors. 'They write as if they were playing dominoes. The incidental number of the last piece determines the next, and the following piece has no relation to the last but one.' An example of 'flight of ideas' is provided by a manic patient who said 'maternal, paternal, infernal, Dante'.

The term *Incoherence* is self-explanatory. It may occur in normal people who are emotionally upset. When persistent it should suggest either organic confusion or schizophrenia.

Blocking, or sudden interruption in the stream of thought, occurs in schizophrenia.

Neologisms are frequently invented by schizophrenics. A patient, for instance, described a drawing: 'Cordron. A theme of curved and fancy lines, stcollic st, from steeple word from the point on the top of the post collic (unexplainable) word matching the point; caller from the cordron and cross piece. Squirrel, wirrel from wearl; the curls in the lines which look like a wearl pool.'

Predominant ideas are convictions not based on reason but on an emotional foundation. They are not necessarily pathological, and every normal person tends to develop them in the fields of politics, religion, and love. They must be distinguished from from obsessional ideas (p. 50).

A *delusion* is a false belief which cannot be corrected by an appeal to reason or logic, making due allowance for the individual's cultural and religious background. *Secondary delusions* are those which arise as explanations of, or understandably from, some other disturbance. For example, a depressed patient who feels very ill, has severe constipation and is losing weight, may believe with delusional intensity that he has cancer of the bowel. Another, plagued by guilt, may feel that the police are watching him.

A *primary* (or *autochthonous*) delusion has a different quality. This is a delusion which springs suddenly into the mind of the patient, often after a period of puzzled unease, in which the world seems full of some hidden meaning, threatening and vague (*delusional mood*). Suddenly, he sees, or less often hears, something — in itself ordinary — but perceives it in an extra-ordinary way. This is the '*delusional perception*', which introduces the primary delusion. For example, a young man, a student of German history, spent all night wandering around the City of London, in a world full of mystery and fear. At dawn he saw a traffic light change from red to yellow to green — and he 'knew' that this was a signal to him, and that it was now his task to complete Bismarck's work and re-unite Germany.

Delusional mood, delusional perception and primary delusions, are three of the so-called 'first rank' symptoms of schizophrenia discussed in Chapter 8.

Many delusions are secondary to hallucinations, but they can occasionally develop from a real event or experience as the result of systematic although emotionally biased reasoning.

Delusions are also classified as those of grandeur, of selfreproach, of poverty, of reference*, of persecution, or as hypochondriacal delusions, according to their content.

Quite often the content of delusions can be understood rather simply, as can some auditory hallucinations. For example, someone usually troubled by marked feelings of inadequacy and failure may develop delusions of grandeur when psychotic; and someone troubled by fears that he is unattractive to women and has homosexual doubts or urges, is likely to hear voices commenting, unfavourably, on his sexuality if he develops schizophrenia.

The fact that the content can be understood in this way does *not* provide an adequate explanation for a delusion developing. This is the

---

*i.e. erroneous ideas that things happening have special reference to the patient.

old problem of 'content and form'. In psychiatry the 'form' of a psychotic illness is usually more basic than the 'content'. This is demonstrated by the fact that in the nineteenth century patients had religious delusions and hallucinations, whereas now they are more likely to be about hypnosis and X-rays, although the underlying schizophrenic illness is the same.

The term *Paranoid* as used in psychiatry ranges from ideas of being done down and put upon, to a more fully developed resentful sense of hostile environment coupled with a tendency towards the formation of delusions of a systematised character to explain it. In this way its use may range from an attitude of mind not in itself at variance with reality, to definite delusions of persecution. It may, therefore, reasonably include a man who thinks his boss is doing him down, which may be more or less true, and a man who is patently mistaken in thinking himself persecuted. In deciding the truth of the matter, what is important is the evidence rather than the patient's belief; a man's wife may be unfaithful, but more evidence is required than a belief arising from a torn scrap found in the waste-paper basket.

Obsessional ideas (compulsive thoughts) must be distinguished from delusions and from predominant ideas. Compulsive thoughts are recognised as being abnormal and foreign to the personality, and yet still as belonging to the individual, and as the product of his own mind. They are resented and resisted. The patient struggles against the obsessional idea, but may fight for his delusions. Predominant preoccupations are not obsessional in that they are fully accepted and should be distinguished from compulsive thoughts on that account; i.e. for a student to be preoccupied with examinations is not abnormal. In content, obsessional thoughts are often banal and pointless, but they are sometimes indecent, blasphemous or aggressive.

Passivity and related experiences

Passivity experiences are those in which the patient feels that some other power — human or non-human — is influencing, controlling or making his thoughts, feelings, utterances or movements. He may feel like a robot, or he may feel that the influence is only partial or that it is an attempt to control him which has not yet succeeded. He does not recognise the thought or impulse as the product of his own mind, unlike an obsessional thought.

The related experiences of the title are in a way the opposite of passivity, in that instead of some force coming into the mind, there is the experience of thoughts or feelings leaving. Thus there is *thought broadcasting*, when the patient feels that what he is thinking or feeling is coming out into the open, as it were, so that others can pick it up, and perhaps record it. *Thought withdrawal* is rather more selective, so that only certain thoughts or ideas are being extracted; *thought insertion* is the exact opposite of thought withdrawal.

All of these are *experiences*, and not perceptual distortions or ideas, and they have in common a loss or disruption of the boundaries or limits of the self. They are disturbances of the ego-boundary, to use another term. They are absolutely characteristic of schizophrenia, and each of them counts as a first rank symptom in diagnostic importance. As with other such symptoms, they lose that importance if there is any organically determined clouding of consciousness or if psychoto-mimetic drugs, such as LSD have been taken.

Disturbances of affect

Affect means emotion or mood. Disturbances of affect may consist of variations in intensity or duration, or the emotional response may be abnormal because inappropriate to the particular situation. The term 'Affective Disorders' (p. 160) refers to sustained disorders of mood rather than to transient emotional reactions.

Intensity. Increased intensity of emotion is often complained of by hysterical and histrionic 'sensitive' patients. Of more significance as regards seriousness of illness is the converse, i.e. poverty and loss of emotion (*affective loss*). This is common in depression as a complaint (feeling 'numb' or 'frozen') and as an objective finding in schizophrenia.

Shallowness of affect. This may be a life-long feature of some people — (certain hysterical psychopaths and dullards). Where it appears as a new feature it is suggestive of schizophrenia or organic deterioration. Again, certain quite normal individuals are acutely aware of complete emotional detachment after a psychic shock, such as seeing an accident. This is usually a transient experience of no significance.

Incapacity to control the emotions and their expression is characteristic of organic syndromes (*emotional incontinence and lability*). Normal emotional experiences, such as elation, depression, irritability, anxiety, may become morbid by reason of their intensity and duration, but the extreme degrees of melancholy are never experienced by the normal individual. Extreme anxiety, amounting to panic, may be felt by normal people in terrifying situations, such as torture or in burning buildings.

Irritability is increased in normal people by fatigue, overwork and hunger. It is liable to be marked after head injuries, in epileptics, and in patients whose emotional control has been reduced through organic changes.

Ecstasy may be described as a feeling of overwhelming bliss combined with an all-pervading sense of clearness of perception. It is often associated with a feeling of suspicion and fear, and not infrequently accompanied or followed by the appearance of autochthonous delusions. True ecstasy is probably beyond the experience or imagination of normal persons. States of ecstasy are chiefly seen in schizophrenia.

Incongruity of affect. This exists when the patient's emotional reaction is markedly different from that expected in the given situation. It is mainly used to describe schizophrenic patients, who often laugh or smile in an empty and fatuous way at inappropriate times. (This may not reflect their inner feelings, the normal expression of which is disturbed.)

In an unemotional psychopath incongruity of affect may be striking, e.g. when he acts without embarrassment or distress when caught in a major delinquency.

Ambivalence denotes the simultaneous existence of contradictory emotions. It is a part of normal experience, but in very exaggerated form is commonly seen in schizophrenia.

Anxiety may occur in any psychiatric syndrome. It is often 'free floating', that is, not clearly about anything in particular, but a pervasive feeling. In other people or conditions it may be clearly related to some obvious and understandable stress, or may be in the special form of a *phobia* in which the patient recognises that the anxiety is related specifically to some object or situation in an irrational way.

Anxiety includes an unpleasant sense of fear, concerned with what might happen in the future, associated with symptoms due to autonomic over activity or adrenaline output in the 'flight or fight' response. These include palpitations, sweating, dry mouth, tremor, nausea, giddyness, weakness, and others. The subject is considered in more detail on page 240 in the section on *anxiety states*.

Tension is a very common complaint indeed, and one made by many people in whom there is no evidence of psychiatric disturbance. It is the opposite of relaxation, and is closely related to anxiety but without the autonomic disturbances. It is less related to the future, but more to a sense of difficulty of coping with the present and immediate past; but there is also a general sense of the awareness that things might go wrong, and that one must remain 'keyed up', alert, and controlled, in order to cope with the situation. Tension in muscles, often experienced as a painful ache, is almost invariable in those who complain of tension. (see p. 256)

Disturbances of memory

The function of remembering is generally divided into (1) Registration, (2) Retention, (3) Recall.

1. *Registration.* Registration of the material to be remembered may be disturbed by lack of concentration. Thus in manic states the distractibility prevents the patient from perceiving properly what is happening. The manic patient will therefore tend only to remember subsequently those things that by chance, or because of their special impressiveness, did not escape his attention. By contrast, registration may be prevented by intense pre-occupation with something else, as in the absent-minded professor. In states of unconsciousness nothing can be recorded, hence the subsequent amnesia. When consciousness is dimmed or clouded, only a partial or patchy recollection of what has taken place remains. This may even extend to a complete amnesia if registration was grossly deficient. Serious defects of registration usually arise from organic cause.

2. *Retention.* Disturbances of retention should only be assumed if it is certain that registration and recall are unaffected. Retention for short or longer periods of time (the latter being essential for learning) may be disturbed to a different degree. The capacity for retaining visual and auditory material may also differ markedly. In general, the capacity to retain material is better if associations are present with which it can easily be connected. Poverty and slowness of association may stimulate a memory disturbance. Again, serious defects of retention usually arise from an organic cause.

3. *Recall.* Recall may be either automatic or voluntary. In morbid mental conditions automatic recall is often preserved whilst the capacity for voluntary recall (i.e. involving conscious effort) is frequently impaired. These phenomena can often be observed in normal individuals who are fatigued, or in the aged, and the disturbance is most marked in trying to recall names. It is generally possible for a person to recognise something immediately which he could not recall on voluntary effort, or only to be able to recall facts when something associated with them is recollected. Voluntary effort quite often seems to interfere with recollection.

The ability to recall is facilitated by richness and rapidity of association: consequently poverty or slowness of association may make memory disturbances appear more severe than they really are. All disturbances of recall cannot, however, be explained as being due to loss of initiative or poverty of association. Nor should all memory disturbances be attributed to 'repression', although this may play an important part in determining which material is not recollected. Thus, although failure to recall may have an organic basis, emotional factors may play a larger part than is usual in failures of registration and retention.

When memory impairment is due to organic brain disease this is usually for recent events rather than for remote ones. The gaps of memory, or amnesia, consequent upon sudden damage to the brain (head injuries, epileptic fits, apoplexies) are often for a longer period than that of the actual unconsciousness. This is frequently seen in *retrograde amnesia* after injury to the brain, as when a person cannot remember the accident or the events for a variable length of time preceding it. The amnesia for the period of unconsciousness, or of disturbed consciousness, is due to lack of registration. *Anterograde amnesia* (that is, loss of memory for a period after consciousness has apparently been regained) is due to a state of altered consciousness during the period which the patients do not remember afterwards.

Total loss of memory over a long period, or over the whole of life, is generally a hysterical symptom, and inconsistencies between the knowledge which the patient shows and what he claims to have forgotten may show that this material is very near the surface of consciousness: in other words, if not deliberate deceit, self-deception plays an active part. The material is available if the patient cares to look, but he succeeds in keeping it out of sight and apart from the rest of his mental content (*dissociation*, p. 266). Such hysterical amnesias are also related to *fugues* (see p. 275). In these the patient wanders off in a dissociated state. The motive is usually to avoid some difficulty or situation which he feels incapable of facing.

A normal quality of remembering is that it tends to mould the past according to desire and to fill in defects in memory with facts which may have been in the past rather than with facts which are genuinely recollected; and the conviction that such false recollection carries is often very striking. When there is a pathological loss of memory the gap is often filled in with elaborate fabrications. Broadly speaking, the less critical the patient, and the more active his initiative, the more capable he becomes of producing such fabrications, and of changing them under cross-examination. This, called *confabulation*, is often striking in the Korsakoff psychosis (p. 105) and organic dementias.

The feeling of familiarity which is experienced on recognition may also, in certain abnormal conditions, be attached to facts or things that have not previously been known to the individual. This experience of déjà vu is known to many normal persons when fatigued or sleepy, and it may be a prominent feature in certain neurotic syndromes, and sometimes in disturbances of temporal lobe function.

In the Korsakoff psychosis patients not infrequently get the order of past events wrong, so that the disturbance does not so much involve correct fact as correct sequence.

Disturbances of intelligence

Variations in the amount and type of intelligence are very great. A poor native endowment is the main feature of *mental* handicap (p. 309), sometimes called *amentia*. An acquired impairment of intelligence that is irreversible is known as *dementia*. The mentally handicapped have never been intelligent; the demented may have been but have lost the faculty. The onset of dementia is gradual, except where it has followed some severe head injury or acute illness with destructive effect on the brain, such as meningitis or certain poisonings. In the progress of dementia, memory and creative thinking suffer first, abstract reasoning next, until finally primitive tasks such as the definition of words or the findings of opposites or common qualities, become impossible. A moderate degree of dementia may show itself only in an ability to cope with new problems and situations, though ordinary activities and familiar tasks can still be managed. Severe degrees of dementia interfere with even the simplest activities, such as dressing, eating and care of toilet.

Apart from amentia and dementia, it will be realised that various factors of a more or less transient kind may interfere with a person's intellectual application, so that there may be a relative failure in performance without actual deterioration in the intelligence itself. In such cases, if there is uncertainty whether the condition is recoverable or not, it is preferable to use the general term *intellectual impairment* rather than dementia, since this last implies irreversibility.

In trying to assess intellectual impairment of whatever kind, it is always necessary to compare the patient's present performance with his past performance, as shown by the school career, occupational training and work record. In addition, special tests may be used. These mainly depend on the facts that the patient's vocabulary and general knowledge give a fair idea of his educational and intellectual level, and are relatively resistant to mental deterioration, so that if preservation of these faculties contrasts sharply with performance on other tests, the presumption is that deterioration has occurred. It will be realised that the lower the original intellectual level, the more difficult it is to estimate impairment. (See p. 86.)

Disturbances of sensation

Hallucinations. These may be defined as sensory perceptions (mental impressions of sensory vividness) without objective stimulus, e.g. seeing a pink elephant when no pink elephant was present. *Illusions* are real perception falsified, e.g. mistaking a dark stain on a pillow for a bed bug. These definitions may be accepted for practical purposes, but it should be borne in mind that normal sensory perception is far from being an objective picture of reality but is conditioned and modified by many personal factors, both sensory and extra-sensory. In other words there is always a personal contribution to a perceptual situation, but the amount of this personal contribution varies enormously. This holds true for illusions and hallucinations as well as for normal perceptions.

Some anomalies of sensation may be mentioned that should be separated from hallucinations and illusions in the stricter sense. Thus, distortions of visual impressions, owing to detachment of the retina, noises in the ear or labyrinthine sensations due to vascular disturbance, numbness or tingling in the extremities due to pressure on the peripheral nerves, all being disturbances of the apparatus of sensation, are better kept apart. The same applies to flashes of light, if produced by stimulation of the optic nerve, or the more complex subjective experiences produced by stimulation of the sensory areas of the cortex or cerebral pathways.

Visual hallucinations are most commonly found in states of impaired consciousness (delirium and twilight states), and should always suggest the predominance of some organic disease affecting the brain. Some normal individuals, however, experience visual hallucinations just before they go off to sleep (*hypnagogic hallucinations*). Temporal lobe epilepsy may lead to very elaborate and complex visual hallucinations. Visual hallucinations in toxic and delirious reactions may range from kaleidoscopic patterns appearing when the eyes are shut, to the most complex visions of varying scenes, persons, animals and objects, either still or moving at various speeds. The impression may be vague, or very clear and detailed. The hallucinated objects may be projected in a real setting, i.e. a man may be seen sitting in a real chair, but may be transparent and uninfluenced by any physical happenings around him. Schizophrenics may experience symbolic visions, often possessing a quality of intense significance; but visual hallucinations in schizophrenic conditions are more usually in the nature of vivid mental pictures rather than experiences which are thought to be part and parcel of the external world, and, except in acute phases or episodes, are rare in our culture. There is evidence that they occur more often in schizophrenics from very different societies and have been described as common in schizophrenics in Saudi Arabia.

Auditory hallucinations. These are most common in schizophrenic states but also occur in toxic confusional conditions, and sometimes in involutional melancholia and senile dementias. They are usually localised in the head, but may appear to come from outside. Less frequently they are located in some part of the body; this is very typical of schizophrenia. They usually occur in the form of voices of varying distinctness, and even when the exact words are not clearly heard the general import is often felt to be plain. They may speak to him, or they may speak about him, commenting on his actions perhaps. This distinction of second person and third person is important. Voices speaking about the patient are characteristic of schizophrenia; as are the voices which echo, anticipate, or immediately follow his thinking — the '*echo de la pensée*' or *echoing thoughts*. Noises, such as creaking, shooting, ringing and so on, may also be heard. Auditory hallucinations often have an illusional foundation.

Tactile hallucinations. Tactile hallucinations are described by schizophrenic and delirious patients. The patient may feel he is being touched or blown upon, or may experience a drizzling sensation of sand or dust. The genital organs are often the seat of tactile hallucinations, which may be elaborated into a belief that the patient has been the victim of rape. Some schizophrenic patients feel that their body, or some part of it, has changed in size or weight. Statements about a change in the internal organs, such that the heart has become a stone, or that the bowels are blocked, may be metaphorical expressions, but are sometimes accepted later as statements of facts, and, in so far as this is the case, become delusions.

Olfactory hallucinations. Olfactory hallucinations, which always seem to have an unpleasant character, are frequently complained of in schizophrenia, occasionally in temporal lobe epilepsy and severe depression, and rarely in delirium.

Hallucinations have many points in common with sensory perceptions, but they also possess certain distinguishing qualities, quite apart from the absence of appropriate stimulus. Their perceptual character, or the conviction that they represent something of external origin, varies from case to case. Hallucinations appear to be more obtrusive in character than perceptions, and tend to occupy the foreground of the patient's mind and to absorb his attention: otherwise the fact that patients are unable to disregard voices and other sensations that are practically meaningless could not be explained.

The content of the hallucinations is determined to a varying extent by the past history of the patient concerned. Elementary hallucinations are more easily explained on a neurological level, but more complex hallucinations of visions and voices can often be traced, as regards content, to the previous experiences, attitudes, views and fantasies of the particular patient. It is sometimes possible to distinguish the physiological from the psychological element in their production. Thus, patients with delirium tremens usually see small and moving dots, as do patients with small scotomata. Elaboration of these into rats, mice, etc., depends upon extrasensory factors. Similarly the more complex hallucinations of cocaine addicts (cocaine bugs under the skin) are built around the nucleus of their tactile sensations. In other instances it is not easy to discover a sensory element in the development of hallucinatory experiences, nor any illusional basis.

Depersonalisation. This is 'a state in which the individual feels himself changed throughout in comparison with his former state. This change extends to both the patient and the outer world and leads to the individual not acknowledging himself as a personality. His actions seem to him automatic; he observes his own actions like a spectator. The outer world seems strange to him, and has lost its character and reality' (Paul Schilder).

The sense of the outer world being changed is sometimes known as *derealisation*, as opposed to the feeling that the patient is himself changed, which constitutes depersonalisation in the more strict sense. Depersonalised patients complain of loss of feeling, whereas observation of their behaviour shows natural emotional responses. There are, however, cases when the subjective poverty of emotions is followed by objective 'affective loss' (p. 51).

Depersonalisation and derealisation may be experienced in a variety of psychiatric conditions: anxiety and obsessional states, depression, schizophrenia, disturbances of temporal lobe function, temperamental adolescent states and after electrical treatment. They are not necessarily of ominous significance.

The problem of *time perception* and its disturbances is still obscure. They may be observed chiefly in affective disorders, after head injuries and some cerebral operations, and in delirious or subdelirious states. The patients may complain that time moves too fast or too slowly, or in extreme cases that it seems to stand still or rushes on so fast that they cannot follow.

4

Classification of mental disorders

We have already mentioned (p. 8) that one of the main contributions of the nineteenth century to psychiatry was the establishment of a workable classification of mental illness. This followed the lines traditional in general medicine, and consisted of a series of more or less rigidly defined 'disease entities', each with an aetiology and pathology (presumed but in only a few instances demonstrable), symptomatology and course of its own. Later it came to be realised that many psychiatric conditions were not so much actual diseases in that sense as the individual reactions of particular personalities to situations that they found difficult or stressful. The old classification then had to be adjusted to include this concept, and mental illness thus came to be divided into two great groups: (1) *the psychoses*, and (2) *the neuroses*. The *psychoses* were the disease-entities, major illnesses, which in their full form involved insanity (e.g. schizophrenia, manic depressive psychosis); the psychotic patient experienced life in a distorted way, owing to delusions, hallucinations or misinterpretations, which were symptoms of an illness arising mainly from constitutional causes and probably of an obscure physical sort. The *neuroses* were minor illnesses in the sense that the patients experience only such mental symptoms as anxiety or tension not in themselves outside the real of normal experience, which were unrelated to insanity and did not lead to it, but arose as a response to difficulty or stress, though experienced to an exaggerated degree.

The validity of the distinction between psychosis and neurosis has been disputed from time to time on the following grounds. First, it is sometimes objected that there is no sharp borderline between sanity and insanity, or therefore between neurosis and psychosis, so that certain cases cannot be assigned definitely to either group, and the difference between neurosis and psychosis then becomes one of degree rather than of kind. Second, it is sometimes objected that the supposed aetiological differences (as arising from attitudes of mind, on the one hand, and from presumed obscure physical causes, on the other) are an invalid distinction in that physical causes for the psychoses have not been satisfactorily established. Third, it is sometimes objected that neuroses cannot be distinguished from psychoses on grounds of severity of the illness, because a person who has, for example, a mild state of hypomania may be far less handicapped than an entirely sane person with a heavy load of neurotic symptoms.

We hold to the usefulness of the distinction, particularly for schizophrenia and bipolar manic-depressive illnesses. In these the rôle of genetic and constitutional factors is most clear; physical treatment is most useful and purely psychological treatment least effective; and the departure of the patient from normal modes of thought and experience is most striking. In unipolar depression (without manic upswings) the distinction is more blurred, but remains important.

The purposes of diagnosis should always be remembered: they are to be able to offer the best treatment, assess most accurately the prognosis, and to facilitate research. In so far as groups of patients genuinely have features in common by which they can usefully be distinguished from others, diagnosis is a worthwhile task. In psychiatry, there is at times too much enthusiasm for finding the exact pigeon-hole, yet losing sight of the purpose.

We submit the following classification of the psychoses:

1. *Organic psychoses.* The main features are disturbances of consciousness and of the intellectual functions of memory and grasp. They range from clouding of consciousness through delirium and, where the condition is more than transient, Korsakoff's syndrome, to dementia. Physical factors are predominantly important in their causation. The conditions will be discussed later.

2. *Functional psychoses.* These receive this non-committal name because their aetiology is not yet proved. They are two in number:

a. *Schizophrenia.* This is not so much a specific illness as a group of heterogeneous conditions which have features in common. The main features are progressive introversion with disintegration of thought, of emotional responses and of the personality. Constitutional factors are largely responsible.

b. *Affective disorders.* It is now recognised that this group includes:
   (i) *Bipolar manic-depressive illness,* in which there are sustained phases both of depressed and elevated mood; and
   (ii) *Unipolar depressive illnesses* in which abnormally elevated mood does not occur.
   Schizophrenic illnesses can be defined fairly clearly and do

not merge with neurotic conditions, but depressive illnesses cover a very wide range, varying from minor and purely reactive states of depressive mood, to true psychoses with agitation, delusions and hallucinations.

All the foregoing conditions are liable to be major illnesses in the sense that they may lead to the patient viewing life in a distorted way owing to the occurrence of delusions or misinterpretations. For example, in the organic psychoses the failure of grasp leads to suspiciousness with delusional beliefs that sinister goings-on are afoot; the failure of memory leads to beliefs that things mislaid have been stolen, that people who are dead are alive, that people and things are other than what they are, and so forth. In schizophrenia there are invariably distortions of content (delusions, hallucinations, misinterpretations) at some stage and in some form. In manic-depressive psychosis the manic (i.e. excited) phase may lead to grandiose but false ideas, such as an engagement to Royalty or the possession of riches, in line with a mood of exaltation; and the depressive phases may lead to false beliefs of actual or impending ruin, death and destruction or delusions of cancer, in line with the pessimistic mood. This is not to say that every single psychotic case necessarily has distortions of content, but that the type of illness is one in which distortions of content *can* occur, as shown by clinical experience. Many patients with recurrent depressions of manic-depressive type may escape the development of delusions in fact, as may those with mild recurrent excitements; but the patterns of these illnesses are such that they belong to the manic-depressive group, in which it is known that distortions can occur, though they may happen not to do so in a particular individual case. After all, it is possible to have mild or severe attacks of bronchitis, without the severity affecting the diagnostic category to which it belongs. In the bipolar affective illnesses typical delusions might well develop in any subsequent breakdown, despite their absence before.

On the other hand, distortions of content do not occur in the neuroses, whether mild or severe, and, although they may be very disabling, these are benign illnesses in the sense that they are not associated with such grave developments. Traditionally, the neuroses are listed as follows:

1. *Anxiety and phobic anxiety neuroses,* characterised by the prominence of anxiety, which is undue, unduly easily provoked, and unduly persistent. Psychological and constitutional factors are both important in their causation.

2. *Neurotic (or reactive) depression,* characterised by a variably depressive mood (of different symptom-pattern from that of manic-

depressive depression) occurring as a personal reaction to conflicts or situations of stress.

3. *Hysteria,* characterised by the patient developing and making use of some symptoms to serve some particular personal purpose, but without awareness or without full awareness of the motives for doing so.

4. *Obsessional neurosis,* characterised by the repeated and involuntary intrusion into the patient's mind of thoughts or impulses, of which he cannot rid himself by an act of will.

Traditionally, these are described as separate entities, as in early editions of this book. We have come to the conclusion, however, that it is more logical to consider them under the general heading of 'Personality Reactions' — except for obsessional neurosis which does have such special features of its own as to warrant its being considered separately. The manifestations of anxiety, reactive depression and hysteria are, after all, not so much those of illness in the formal sense, as of the patient reacting to the life situation with anxiety, with depression or hysterically; moreover, the patient may react in all three such ways at the same time, or with any of them at different times, i.e. with anxious, depressive or hysterical symptoms occurring in different degrees and combinations. Rather than trying to view such cases as suffering from *either* an anxiety neurosis, *or* neurotic depression, *or* hysteria, we have come long since to prefer a more elastic approach, thinking in terms of 'How much anxiety, how much depression, how much is hysterical?'

Our classification has therefore become, so far:

1. *The psychoses*
   a. *Organic psychoses*
   b. *Functional psychoses*
      (i) Schizophrenia
      (ii) Affective disorders
2. *Personality reactions* with anxiety and depressive symptoms, and hysterical features.
3. *Obsessional states.*

There remains a heterogeneous group of cases whose common feature is a failure of normal development, whether in the field of personality, sex, or intelligence. Thus, the psychopathic personality, as described on pages 219 shows failure to develop emotional maturity as a main feature; cases of sexual deviation represent a failure of normal development in a different sphere, as do those with anomalies of intelligence. These are essentially 'Disorders of development'; we group them under two headings: 'Disorders of Personality and of Sexual Development', and 'Mental Handicap'. We consider 'Personality Reactions and Neurotic States' and obsessional states also in two separate chapters.

The classification thus becomes:

1. *The psychoses*
   a. *Organic psychoses*
   b. *Functional psychoses*
      (i) Schizophrenia
      (ii) Affective illnesses.
2. *Personality reactions* with special reference to anxiety and depressive symptoms and hysterical features. Sexual difficulties, psychopathic and other developmental disorders are often relevant.
3. *Obsessional states.*
4. *Disorders of personality and of intelligence (disorders of development).*

This classification is not exhaustive, and there is considerable overlap in practice, but it provides a scheme into which most patients can be conveniently fitted. The student may be helped by the following diagrams. Suppose that the organic conditions are represented by a circle (A), the schizophrenic conditions by another circle (B), and personality reactions by a third circle (C). These circles should not be considered as quite separate from one another as in Diagram 1, but rather as overlapping as in Diagram 2.

Individual cases can then be represented as at any point within the system of circles. For example, the area A1 would represent an organic condition in almost pure culture, A2 would be an organic condition with personality problem as well, and C2 would be a mixed picture with a schizophrenic and personality problem combined; and so on in various combinations and proportions. The same principle holds good for the various subdivisions within the main groups. Thus it is not uncommon to meet with cases that can most conveniently be described as obsessional states with depressive features and so on.

Multi-dimensional diagnosis

Psychiatric diagnosis (or classification) is not, however, exhausted by describing a clinical picture in terms of its diagnostic category. The

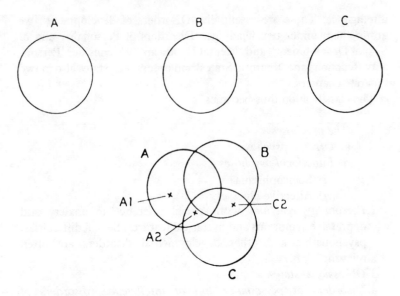

Fig. 4.1 Relationship of various syndromes.

reader will have observed that in the foregoing discussion of classification, reference to aetiology was not entirely omitted. There is in fact a certain affinity between the nature of the cause and the type of condition that ensues. This relation is closest between organic causes and organic states; but hysterical states have a close relation to specific psychological factors and psychopathic reactions to a particular type of constitution.

When attempting to make a more complete psychiatric diagnosis, (1) the *aetiological* should be distinguished from (2) the *descriptive* aspect. The latter consists of the syndrome that is observed. The aetiological aspect comprises the assessment of the physical, psychological and constitutional factors and their relative importance in bringing about the condition in question. (3) No condition can be fully understood without taking into account personality reactions as seen in the light of the past history and environment. Therefore, a complete psychiatric diagnosis should include the essential characteristics of the patient's *previous personality*. (4) The practical value of any diagnosis lies in its therapeutic and prognostic implications. The symptoms as such may have little significance in assessing these. Therefore, in making the diagnosis, the expected course of the condition, assessed by clinical experience in the light of the clinical picture, aetiology and personality of the patient, should also be indicated.

An example of a diagnostic formulation that would satisfy all these criteria might be:

'Acute recoverable anxiety state, reactive to a terrifying accident, in an immature, ill-adjusted personality of low intelligence', or

'Acute delirium, due to chronic alcoholism and malnutrition, in a hypomanic personality with pre-existent organic deterioration.

It is, of course, possible and may be desirable to go into more detail, in particular by weighing the various aetiological factors and assessing their importance in either bringing about the condition or in colouring it. For example, a case might be diagnosed as follows:

'A transient depressive reaction with anxiety and obsessional features in a dependent, sensitive, over-conscientious foreign youth following interrogation by the police over suspected customs irregularities', or

'Progressive pre-senile dementia coloured by alcoholism in a retired general with highly aggressive pre-morbid personality.'

Diagnoses of the above kind are sometimes called multi-dimensional'.

Classifications are inventions and not discoveries; and the student can save himself a good deal of puzzlement about individual cases if he realises that a psychiatric diagnosis is essentially a short-hand description.

5

Psychiatric case-taking

It is just as important in psychiatry as in general medicine to have a scheme of examination, for unless the examination is systematic, important aspects may be missed. The examination of the psychiatric patient differs from that of the general medical case mainly in (1) the attempt to cover a wider range, (2) the need for more informality, and (3) the greater need for corroborative information. These three main points may be briefly explained.

(1) *The wider range* is necessary because in psychiatry it is particularly important to assess, as will later be seen, how far the patient's present state differs from, or how much it is merely an extension of, what has gone before; this demands some knowledge of his previous personality and habits of reaction.

(2) *The greater informality* is desirable for much the same reason, namely that one aims to see the patient as he really is, and therefore unhampered by artificial constraints. Although there must be a scheme of examination, this should be reasonably elastic in application, since it is desirable that the patient should express himself freely, and he will be prevented from doing so if the examination is conducted in a rigid and formal fashion. What is required, therefore, is for the doctor to carry the necessary framework in his head so that he can mentally tick off the items as the patient produces the necessary information, which will be done both spontaneously and in answer to questions. As the scheme of examination is rather extensive, the student may find that he cannot carry it in his head all at once. He need not be dismayed if he has to keep the written scheme before him and follow it in detail with his first few cases. Indeed, he will be wise to do so. Although the scheme may seem rather formidable at first sight, it is logical enough to be memorised with no great difficulty, and with a little practice can then be quite easily applied from memory. Once it is held in mind, it will be found unnecessary (and is often undesirable) to pursue each item in the set order. Even so, the student will be wise to indulge in

short cuts only when he has had some experience and practice; otherwise his short cut may be to the wrong shop.

(3) *The corroborative information* is necessary not so much from any lack of co-operation and unreliability among psychiatric patients (though these are sometimes found), as from the difficulty of seeing ourselves as we really are and therefore of giving an unbiased account of ourselves, so that an objective description of the patient and his condition from relatives or friends is likely to be helpful and may be indispensable. Thus, to take two extreme and perhaps cynical examples, patients on a criminal charge and pleading their abnormal mental condition as a defence, tend to remember numerous neurotic traits in their past lives as well as a large number of mentally afflicted relatives; whereas applicants for pensions of the grounds of neurotic disability, tend to forget previous breakdowns and any family history of similar problems. The critical sifting of evidence obtained from outside sources as well as from the patient will not only make for greater accuracy but may also save much time in the end. The relatives or friends should often be seen separately, and it is better to see them after the patient, to lessen the feeling that he is 'being talked about behind his back'. Sometimes it is better to see the other informant with the patient if it seems likely that the patient may feel resentful.

It can be very helpful to have information from a social worker or community psychiatric nurse who has seen the family at home. The general practitioner often has a store of information about the patient and the family.

EXAMINATION OF THE PATIENT

This consists of two parts, the *interview* and the *physical examination*. It is always desirable to perform a thorough physical examination, with special attention to the central nervous system; but unfortunately the pressures of hospital life often lead to this being omitted in out-patient departments. In fact a sizeable percentage of psychiatric patients have a significant physical illness, particularly those admitted to acute psychiatric wards.

The purpose of the psychiatric *interview* is threefold: to gain a picture of the patient's state of mind: to understand the setting, the personality and the development of the patient in which the state of mind has occurred: and to create or maintain a helpful relationship between the doctor and the patient.

The establishment of the right atmosphere must be kept in mind throughout. The first essential is to listen, and the second is to give enough time — at least an hour for a first interview and preferably more. The rapport between patient and doctor is based on the latter's interest in the patient's complaints. The patient should be encouraged to talk and should be diverted as little as possible. It always pays to spend time on the patient's description of his symptoms, in which he will incidentally reveal a good deal about himself. Throughout the diagnostic interview the doctor should play a secondary rôle. He should never seek to impress the patient, but should allow the latter to be himself. It is inevitable that the doctor will have to ask some questions, but these should be as few as possible. If questions have to be asked on intimate topics, they should be asked frankly and without diffidence, since diffidence is easily imparted. In fact, the interview should be conducted on level terms as between equals, but unnecessary trespass on the patient's feelings and private affairs should be avoided. Where the patient shows marked hesitation or defensiveness over some sensitive point, the issue should not be forced. Note of his attitude should be made and the matter may be reopened later as may be necessary.

It is very important to avoid leading questions, that is, phrased in such a way that they tend to lead to a certain answer, and stop the flow of conversation. Most of us use these all the time, and it is a difficult habit to break. For example — 'Your father died when you were on holiday, you must have been upset,' is much less useful than 'How did you feel about your father's death?', or perhaps better still 'Tell me about that.' And 'What about boyfriends?' is better than 'Have you a boyfriend?'

The student will find practice of the greatest help. As well as carefully avoiding leading questions, moralising must also be eschewed. The interviewer may think the patient has behaved badly, is incompetent, or of dull intelligence, but critical remarks, critical tones of voice or dismissive gestures and so on must not appear. Only when a good relationship has been established can such elements be brought in, and then they should be introduced deliberately, with therapeutic purpose. The patient must be accepted for what he is. It is however very important for the doctor to recognise his own feelings about the patient, even though he does not express them, and this applies to positive as well as negative emotions. He may find this difficult at first. It is almost irresistible to put questions in such a way as to suggest the answer (e.g. 'you didn't?' 'it wasn't?') and this fault is often combined with an inflection or facial expression which leaves little doubt in the patient's mind not only as to what answer is expected, but as to what reception a different answer might receive. The reticent or allegedly uncooperative patient is usually the product of a poor examination technique, for most people like to talk about themselves; most patients are surprisingly willing to discuss even their intimate problems with small encouragement, and many are grateful for the opportunity. But any rapport that may have been established tends naturally to be broken by such a remark as: 'You don't mean to say that a great big chap like you is afraid of the dark?' Moreover, a poor technique of examination can easily result in inaccurate as well as inadequate information, and this is especially likely to be so if the questions asked are not geared to the patient's intelligence. Finally, it is permissible to laugh with a patient but never at him.

Scheme of examination

The following items are suggested as a frame of reference:

Particulars

Name. Age. Sex. Single, married, separated, divorced. Occupation. Religion. Address and telephone number. Addresses and telephone numbers of next-of-kin and private doctor.

Complaints

These should be noted in detail, if possible verbatim.

History of the present illness

Begin by establishing 'when did you last feel quite well?', and then take a careful chronological account of the development of symptoms both mental and physical, so that they can be related to important life events before and during the development of the illness. It is common to find that the more carefully this account is taken the further back the history extends, and the more clearly the relationship to life events appears.

Personal history

The importance of different epochs of life and development will, of course, vary considerably with the age of the patient; neurotic traits in childhood will obviously have less significance in a senile case than in an adolescent.

(1) *Early development.* Birth injuries. Whether brought up by parents or not. Dates of weaning, walking, talking. Home atmosphere: relationship to parents and others in the family; sleeping arrangements. Neurotic traits, e.g. morbid fears (of dark, etc.), thumb-sucking, stuttering, temper-tantrums, enuresis and other difficulties in toilet-training, sleep-walking, night-terrors, food fads.

(2) *School record.* Scholastic attainments; social adaptation as regards friendliness, participation in games and recreations, home-sickness, discipline and discipline difficulties.

(3) *Work record.* Jobs held, why taken on, how long held, reasons for leaving, financial returns.

(4) *Social record.* Attitudes towards relatives and friends, towards authority (including anti-social trends, lying, stealing, rebellion), towards religion and politics. Steady, or variable and moody? How spare time is spent. Hobbies, interests. Successes and disappointments. Ambitions. What makes life worth living?

(5) *Sex.* Development. Information, how acquired. Masturbation and attitudes towards it. Sex experiences and attitudes towards them. Menstruation. Marriage. Pregnancies, miscarriages, abortions. Contra-ceptive measures. Menopause. Difficulties in sex life. Happiness or otherwise of marital relations. Details of the sexual history may well not be forthcoming, particularly at a first interview with a reserved person. It is usually unwise to push the patient for more information than he is willing to give, but you should let him know that it might be important.

Medical history

(1) Physical illnesses, and how readily recovered from. (2) 'Nervous' or 'mental' illnesses, and whether or not in circumscribed attacks, whether treated, and if so, where. (3) Attitudes towards health, bodily disturbance, and treatment; use and abuse of drugs.

Family history

Enquiry is often best delayed until the patient's confidence has been gained. Obtain the occupation of the father and, if possible, of other relatives as well, and where they lived. This is often a good indication of the social and cultural background, and of how far the patient has travelled, geographically and culturally. Determine the place of the patient in the family and the numbers of sibs (i.e. brothers and sisters). Do not begin by asking whether there is insanity or suicide in the family, but ask first after physical health, then after 'nervous' and 'highly strung' relatives with special reference to interference by these conditions with happiness and efficiency. Then ask about major mental illnesses (noting if admission to hospital was required), including epilepsy, alcoholism, drug addiction, criminality, suicide. Take care in each case to distinguish between the two sides of the family. Try to determine more of the home atmosphere, whether happy or not, and the 'healthconsciousness', as regards how seriously minor ailments were taken and how far robust attitudes were encouraged. Apart from the possible genetic implications, the family history and background are of importance as indicators of the early environment. Note the ages at which the parents died, as depression in later life is associated with bereavement in childhood and around puberty.

Personality traits

Indications of these will already have been yielded by the facts elicited, and the life history will probably have brought the patient's outstanding personality traits to the examiner's attention. They will afford some guidance as to how far the patient is a positive and effective person, how far he is negative and inadequate, and how far his present state contrasts with his previous personality. The main indications will be afforded by whether the patient has tended to show *fight* by trying to overcome difficulty, or *flight* in trying to dodge or run away from it; *self-confidence* in social relations, as opposed to shyness or timidity; *initiative,* or lack of it; *self-reliance* in forming judgments and making plans, or dependence on others; *rigidity* so that he is hard to influence, or undue suggestibility; *adventurousness* or a tendency to caution and counting the cost; *enterprise* or preference for the old and familiar; *dominance,* leadership, or self-subordination; *candour,* or suspiciousness; *warm-heartedness,* or emotional coolness; *equability,* or moodiness; *conscientiousness,* or irresponsibility; and so on. The list might be extended indefinitely, but these are the sort of trends to be looked for. People are relatively seldom all of a piece and consistent; contradictory attributes may often be observed and should cause no surprise. When they occur, however, they may be valuable indications that the patient has problems within his own personality, as when a person shows obvious see-sawing between aggressiveness and submissiveness, and can achieve no harmonious integration of such contrasting traits. The more the personality traits are discrepant in relation to each other, the less stable is the personality likely to be.

This may be both diagnostically and prognostically important. The assessment of the patient's stability is considered later (p. 75).

Having thus established the nature and development of the complaints, the setting in which they have occurred, the type of personality and its development, as judged by the heredity and facts of the life-history, it remains to complete the formal examination of the mental and physical state.

Mental status

(1) *Appearance and behaviour.* Tidy or unkempt? Easy or difficult to make contact with? Calm or agitated? Cheerful or depressed? Any noticeable oddities, such as mannerisms or grimaces? Behaviour appropriate or inappropriate?

(2) *Talk.* The form rather than the content is considered here. Does he talk readily or reluctantly? Abnormally fast or slowly? To the point or discursively? Are there any incoherences, strange words, puns? Any sudden stops or changes of topic? Does the form of talk vary much with the subject?

(3) *Orientation.* Does the patient know where he is, the time of day and the date, and recognise he is being examined by a doctor?

(4) *Mood.* Is this disturbed? In what way? Note the appearance, for this may give some indication. Non-committal questions should be asked: How do you feel in yourself? What is your mood? How are your spirits? Many varieties of mood may be present — not merely degrees of happiness or sadness, but irritability, fear, worry, restlessness, bewilderment, indifference, and others conveniently included under this heading. It should be noted particularly (a) how much the mood is constant; (b) how much it varies with circumstances — can the patient 'snap out of it' to normality? (c) what are the influences that change it; (d) whether it is appropriate to the circumstances. Are suicidal ideas present (see p. 201)?

(5) *Thought content.* Are there any special worries or preoccupations.

(6) *Distortions of content.* (a) Are there any delusions or misinterpretations? Does the patient show abnormal attitudes towards people or things in his environment? Do people treat him all right, or in some special way? Ask the patient if he has self-conscious feelings that people are talking about him or looking at him. If yes, does he believe it or imagine it? In what way do they do so? Does he feel he is under some outside influence or control? Have things happened that have perplexed or puzzled him? Did they seem to have some special meaning? Does he read things in newspapers, see things in

advertisements, hear things on the radio that refer specially to him, and, if so, kindly or unkindly? Does he depreciate himself, e.g. in morals, possessions, health, or does he appear to regard himself grandiosely?

(b) Are there hallucinations or other disorders of perception? Auditory hallucinations are far the most common. Do the patient's thoughts turn to words in his head? Does he hear them spoken? Does he hear his name called when alone, hear himself talked about when alone? Does he experience peculiar body sensations, feelings of deadness or electricity? The frequency, vividness, and timing of such occurrences should be noted, and the patient's reactions to them and beliefs as to their origin.

(7) *Obsessive-compulsive phenomena.* Does the patient experience thoughts or impulses that repeatedly intrude against his will? Does he have to repeat actions unnecessarily, e.g. go back to make sure doors are locked or taps turned off? Does he have unreasonable fears? What is the relation of these symptoms to his emotional state, especially as regards anxiety and depression? Does he have insight into their illogicality?

(8) *Cognitive (intellectual abilities).* Much the most sensitive indicator of minor organic brain disease is impairment of recent memory for *unimportant* information, which is why trying to learn a name and address is useful. Emotionally important material may be learnt readily by someone with definite impairment. (a) *Memory.* Good or bad? Better for recent or remote events? Evidence of deterioration? Test by comparing the life-history as given by himself and others, or by examining history for gaps and inconsistencies. Ask about recent events such as admission to hospital (or journey to consulting room) and subsequent happenings, what eaten at last two meals, what knowledge of current events. Does he know his way around the ward, the names of some staff members, and the name of the ward? Note any selective impairment of memory for recent or special incidents. Test further by giving series of digits to repeat, first forwards and then backwards (a normal person should be able to repeat at least seven forward and five backward); and by giving a name, address and three words, which he must repeat immediately, two minutes later and five minutes later.

It is also useful to test visuo spatial ability by getting the patient to draw a 5 pointed star, draw a clock face with the hands at a certain time, and draw some complex design from memory.

(b) *Concentration.* Ask the patient to subtract 7 serially from 100 (93, 86, 79, etc.) and note time taken and number of mistakes.

Impairment on this test can indicate poor concentration and attention from any cause, but also dyscalculia.

(c) *General information.* Tests must be geared to his educational level and interests. Suitable questions are: name of the Monarch and her immediate predecessors, Prime Minister, Chancellor of the Exchequer, six large cities in Britain, capitals of European countries, dates of beginning and end of last war.

(9) *Intelligence.* Standardised tests are discussed on page 311. The assessment of intellectual deterioration will be found on page 86. A fair estimate can be gained by going over the school and work record and discussion of the patient's jobs and hobbies. Simple rough tests are the definition of abstract words, e.g. 'envy' and 'surprise'; the explanation of proverbs, e.g. 'the early bird catches the worm', and differences, e.g. between a dwarf and a child, or idleness and laziness.

(10) *Insight.* Does the patient regard himself as ill? Does he understand the extent and nature of his abnormality? Does he think he can get well?

(11) In every patient details should be recorded of any disturbance of appetitite and weight; and also of sleep, noting whether there is delay in getting to sleep, early morning wakening, or whether sleep is fitful and broken. Physical examination follows, with emphasis on the central nervous system.

ASSESSMENT OF THE CASE

When the complaint, its development, the setting and personality in which it has occurred, are considered in the light of the full history and results of mental and physical examination, it should be possible to arrive not only at a diagnosis but also at a prognosis and a provisional plan of treatment. The diagnosis and prognosis will depend also to some extent on the stability of the patient's previous personality. The assessment should be made on the *facts* as revealed by the life-history and examination. Reliance should not be placed on mere subjective impressions. The following are the main pointers.

The work record is important. Personality difficulties are indicated by frequent unemployment, frequent changes of job, and failure to increase earning capacity with age. This does not necessarily apply to adolescents, who often vary their jobs until they settle down. Suspicion should also be aroused where jobs are often changed on alleged health-grounds, through becoming easily fatigued or intolerant of noise, because of difficulties with colleagues or superiors, or in favour of open-air or lighter work. Where such changes are attributed to medical advice, it will often be found that the doctor was merely prevailed upon to endorse the patient's or relatives' own views.

Apart from work, the most valuable evidence of difficulties, such as vulnerability is the failure to *sustain* interests and personal relationships. There will be instability where there is no pertinancity in hobbies, and where there is no constancy in friendship or the love-life. Most vulnerable or inadequate people show small output of physical energy and distaste for games or activities where they can hurt themselves. Many lead sheltered and restricted lives because they regard themselves as highly strung or requiring protection from undue effort. Many also lack humour, and though capable of laughing at others, are prevented from laughing at themselves by their egocentricity.

Finally, the family example and tradition are often most important in setting the ethical and social standards as well as the 'health-consciousness' of the patient; knowledge of these is therefore desirable for understanding his reaction to life.

The main questions are as follows:

Is the present state foreign to the patient's previous personality? The answer depends on (a) how long it has been present; (b) how far the personality was previously stable; (c) whether, if anything similar was previously experienced, that was in circumscribed attacks; and (d) how far the personality was stable between such attacks. If the present state appears foreign to the previous personality and has not been experienced before (or experienced only in circumscribed attacks with normality between), we start to think in terms of (i) organic syndromes, especially when impairment of memory and grasp is prominent, or (ii) conditions belonging to the schizophrenic or affective groups. That is, we think in terms of specific illnesses. This is especially so where the state is not easily construed as a reaction to circumstances. Such a decision may be easy, but it may require judgment. For instance, profound gloom with hopelessness of recovery, guilt, and unworthiness occurring in an ordinarily stable person, even after a bereavement, would be taken as something more than a mere reaction to the event, viz. a true depressive illness.

Is the present state explicable as a reaction of the patient's personality to circumstances? The answer depends on: (a) the nature of the symptoms. We should expect anxiety, emotionalism, poor control, a variable degree of depression, and difficulty in getting to sleep. We should *not* expect intellectual impairment, distortions of content or perception (delusions, misinterpretations and hallucinations), or severe guilt; (b) whether the present symptoms are in line with previous instability; Or (c) are such as the previous personality (as judged by the life-history) might reasonably be expected to show in the circumstances. If the symptoms are not foreign to the previous personality, but seem to arise from it, and to be reasonably construed as provoked by the circumstances, we start to think not in terms of specific illness but of an essentially reactive neurotic state.

Are we dealing with an unstable personality who, apart from symptoms arising from the instability, is also developing a specific illness? This question is more difficult to answer. It depends on (a) the extent and constancy of new symptoms; (b) their nature; (c) how far they conform to those found in the more specific illnesses. Such assessment may be far from easy. These are cases that may require some observation before a firm opinion can be given.

As regards treatment, the more the illness appears a specific one, whether organic, schizophrenic, or manic-depressive, the greater is the likelihood of some physical treatment being required. The more the condition seems to arise from attitudes of mind as part of a personality difficulty, the more will psychological management and psychotherapy be required.

6

Organic mental states

Certain principles determine many of the manifestations of impaired brain function from brain lesions of any type: trauma, ischaemia, degenerative conditions, infections and others. It is for these reasons that throughout this chapter the term 'brain damage' refers not only to the results of trauma, but also to any other cause of brain cell disease or death. In the first part of this chapter we consider the basic principles, and describe some of the aspects common to all patients with damaged brain, whatever the pathology. There are then a few paragraphs on the assessment of impairment, and then the second section of the chapter dealing separately with some of the major syndromes and the organic psychoses.

General principles

Rate of onset. The more acute the injury or damage the more likely is consciousness to be disturbed. Slowly progressive tumours or atrophy do not disturb consciousness until very late, whereas quite minor head injuries do so early.

Severity and extent of damage. Naturally the more severe and extensive the damage the greater the effects, although there is much individual variation, and site of damage is also very important in this. Overall, the larger the quantity of brain tissue damaged or dead the more severe the long term effects will be.

Site of damage. This is important because of the localisation of brain function, as with the differing effects of right and left hemisphere lesions, or frontal as opposed to parietal lesions.

The actual pathology is irrelevant, except in so far as it determines the rate of onset, site, and extent of damage. There is no final difference between the effects of a stroke and the surgical removal of a tumour, if similar areas of the brain are involved.

Mental changes

Although undoubted brain damage may occur with no detectable mental changes, most patients with neurological signs of cerebral hemisphere damage will have some psychological deficit; and mental changes may persist when the physical signs have cleared up. This chapter is therefore also concerned with those many thousands of patients with strokes and head injuries, not very often seen by psychiatrists, in whom mental changes may be more important than their physical disability. Not only is an understanding of their psychological deficits and difficulties helpful in management, but these patients are quite often significantly depressed; and many of them can be helped by antidepressants or electrical treatment (q.v.). Too often however, depression is ignored, or is considered as an inevitable result of the stroke, so that no treatment is offered.

In non-progressive brain damage, spontaneous improvement after a single insult — such as a stroke or head injury — continues for some time. Young children may go on improving for a decade or more; young adults for 3 or 4 years; the elderly for only 6 to 12 months. In all cases however, the rate of change is greatest in the early stages, and the position at 12 months is a fair guide to the future. In older people a fairly accurate prognosis is possible at 6 months.

Interview with the patient alone may be misleading, as another informant may clearly describe personality changes not detected at interview. In fact, if organic personality deterioration is obvious at interview it must be fairly severe.

It is important to realise that dementia is not an 'all or nothing' affair, but that there is a continuum ranging from mild forgetfulness to gross dementia; and that in many patients with progressive brain disease, specific defects — for example, receptive dysphasia, visuo-spatial agnosia, or personality change — may dominate the clinical picture for some time before more generalised changes appear. The level of function may also vary from day to day.

Brain damage *alters the capacity to respond adaptively.* Patients are less able to cope with tasks of various types; less able to tolerate emotional stress; and are subject to new stresses arising from their disabilities. When stressed beyond their capacity they become increasingly anxious, and this sometimes becomes so severe that the patient ends up trembling, mute, unable to respond adaptively to the situation, at times even becoming incontinent; and is afterwards confused and exhausted. This is called *catastrophic anxiety*. A typical situation in which it develops is that of the partly paralysed stroke patient trying to cross the road before the lights change, who stops in the middle of the road trembling, unable to move either way. Lesser degrees of anxiety accompany many activities, depending on the patient's particular physical or mental disabilities and his previous personality. In many cases the result is a progressive reduction of activity, particularly after a bout of catastrophic anxiety, so that the patient withdraws from danger as it were, and his life becomes more and more limited.

The long term effects of any brain damage, including the ability of the patient to cope with life and the way he feels about it, can be seen as the result of the interaction of two main sets of factors — organic and personal: the organic factors depending on the extent and site of damage as mentioned earlier. The subdivisions used here are of course to some extent arbitrary and overlapping.

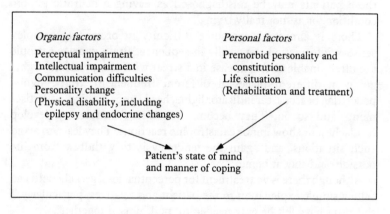

Fig. 6.1 Factors affecting the long-term effects of brain damage.

ORGANIC FACTORS

Perceptual impairment

The importance of this is often missed, because the disabilities do not arise from straightforward impairment or blunting of the sense of light touch and pinprick, to which neurological examination is too often confined by the non-specialist. The most striking disabilities arise in patients in whom parietal damage has led to visual inattention in one half field ('sensory extinction') who cannot perceive stimuli arising simultaneously in both half fields, although they can see them adequately if presented separately. This is not just an academic neurological curiosity, because every time the patient stands on the kerb with traffic moving in both directions he may be *functionally* blind in the affected half field. The anxiety generated by his mistakes in assessing traffic etc. may lead him to stay at home; and he cannot easily explain his problem to others, nor comprehend it himself, because he can see adequately most of the time, as for example when talking to the doctor.

Other important sensory disabilities, associated again with parietal damage, arise from severe impairment of visuo-spatial perception and memory. The patient may no longer be able to assess the size or shape of a room or a space to cross, he cannot remember right from left, he gets lost, bewildered, and frightened. Again, mounting anxiety in the face of the inexplicable leads to a progressive reduction of activity, and at times to withdrawal to the safety of one or two rooms only. Some of these patients may be misdiagnosed as having a neurotic phobic condition, or as 'not really trying'.

There is almost always some difficulty in processing complex sensory information, especially in sequence. Brain damaged people are often unable to feel at ease in a street with many flashing lights going in different places at different frequencies: traffic lights, pedestrian beacons, car indicator lights, head lamps dipping, advertisements and so on. They become bewildered and tense, develop headaches, or show minor catastrophic reactions. They learn to avoid such situations, and again the tendency is to withdraw from life outside, and stay at home.

Although there is no treatment for perceptual loss, great benefit can follow simple explanation to the patient and relatives, particularly if the latter have felt he only needed to 'pull himself together'.

Intellectual impairment

This is itself a vast subject, and a great deal of work has been done, mainly by psychologists, in studying the effect of cerebral lesions on intellectual performance. Only a few of the main clinical aspects are mentioned here.

Rigidity. A common early sign of impairment is difficulty in 'switching set', that is in turning attention from one subject to another. For example, if watching television intently the patient may seem unable to hear a question asked by his wife, so that she may say he is going deaf. He may be unable to follow a conversation in which several people are taking part, because he cannot switch from one aspect to another easily, although he can discuss matters intelligently with one other person.

There is a narrowing of interest, and even without any memory difficulties in the usual sense of the word there is a lessened ability to take in new ideas. These changes are very familiar with increasing age.

Concentration. When there is clouding of consciousness this is always disturbed, but it is also impaired in many alert patients with chronic brain lesions. An early manifestation is of a paradoxical change from very intense concentration (as mentioned under 'rigidity') to a state in which the attention wanders and flickers from one subject to another. The 'set' of concentration having been broken, it may take some time before it can be re-established. Later in the course of progressive brain disease it is permanently impaired.

Concrete thinking. As impairment progresses there is a lessened ability to grasp abstract concepts, and thinking becomes more elementary and 'concrete', as shown in the well-known proverb tests. For example, people of average intelligence and education when asked a proverb such as 'People who live in glass houses should not throw stones', will explain it in terms of human relationships. The brain injured, even if of previously high intelligence, may respond with 'the stones would break the glass'.

Memory. This is a complex activity, including the registration of new information, the immediate recall, capacity for retention of new information for short and longer periods of time, the ability to recollect, and the ability to recognise. All of these may be disturbed to varying degrees. Memory for words and for visual material is often impaired selectively; the former more by dominant and the latter by non-dominant hemisphere lesions.

Clinically the most common early manifestation is *forgetfulness*, in which everyday recent information and recent activities are not remembered. Even with quite severe brain damage, memory for the distant past may be well preserved, and family informants have been known to say that the patient's memory is improving because he dwells on his childhood with such loving detail. As the lesion progresses, all memory functions break down.

The *Korsakoff state* is a particular type of memory loss, first described by Korsakoff in alcoholics. It is dealt with on page 105.

Comprehension. The ability to understand the meaning of words and of events etc., is disturbed when consciousness is clouded, as are all intellectual functions, and it deteriorates with generalised brain damage. In patients with receptive dysphasia, verbal comprehension is specifically disturbed, and the patient may be severely disabled by quite small localised lesions in the dominant temperoparietal regions. At interview this disability may be mistakenly diagnosed as a global dementia, although the patient may be able to function quite well in some situations — as in caring for himself, or even reading. An opposite situation is seen when a patient has relative sparing of the dominant hemisphere, and his well preserved verbal abilities give a false impression of his intelligence and ability to cope. This may lead to difficulty if he therefore takes on tasks beyond his competence.

Communication difficulties

Severe dysarthria is common after strokes, and even more after head injuries, especially when there has been brain stem damage and the muscles of the tongue, pharynx, and face are all spastic. Speech may become incomprehensible to others, and, especially when intelligence is well preserved behind the speech disorder, the frustration and sense of isolation which results is most painful and depression and despair are very common.

Dysphasia is of two main types, expressive (or motor) and receptive. Mixed forms are common with more extensive lesions. Expressive dysphasias are easy to recognise, except when very mild, when there may be no more than a slight difficulty in finding the names of things or people. When severe the frustration of the patient is obvious, and easy to empathise with.

Receptive dysphasia is much easier to miss, unless it is specifically tested for. It is easy to be misled by a bright manner, appropriate social behaviour and normal polite phrases — 'What lovely weather we are having' — into thinking that someone understands fully what is being said, and has a good grasp of, for example, their financial situation. If more care is taken to get the patient to express their own ideas the true picture might appear. In someone with a mixed dysphasia, in which both expressive (motor) and receptive elements are present, you may have to test understanding by giving the patient increasingly complex instructions to carry out. For example, put a number of objects on the desk, and ask the patient to group them by weight, to wrap a coin in paper and put it in an ash tray, and so on. Severe receptive problems disturb comprehension and communication so much that the patient may seen effectively demented. If the other hemisphere is undamaged there will be good preservation of visuo-spatial and other abilities, and the individual may function alone quite well, although without useful verbal skills.

Personality changes

These fall into three main groups, which may overlap clinically, especially if the brain damage is diffuse or multifocal.

Apathy, irritability, anxiety. These are perhaps the commonest early changes. Characteristically the patient tends to withdraw, to be apathetic and uninterested compared to his previous self; and to respond to any form of outside stimulus or interference — such as being asked to do some chore — by a little explosion of anger, or by becoming tremulous and anxious. This can be seen as a protective mechanism in a way, as it has the effect of lessening the demands made on the patient by others, and lessens the chance of him being stressed beyond his capacity, when real catastrophic anxiety might ensue.

Exaggeration of premorbid personality traits. This is common. For example: the introverted suspicious character may become more difficult and paranoid; the friendly extrovert excessively jolly and tactlessly interfering; the obsessional, careful with his money, becomes frankly miserly; and so on.

Frontal lobe syndrome. This occurs in patients with frontal lobe damage, in whom intellectual functions are relatively little disturbed, but who show disinhibition and alterations in drive and activity. Sexual and aggressive impulses, normally controlled, are expressed openly and without shame. In eating habits, manners, dress, cleanliness, and other conventionally determined things, the patient becomes slipshod and careless. He may be casually incontinent. Conscience loses its force, worries and anxieties are no longer troublesome, and some patients with only mild changes may feel a good deal happier and more carefree. Most patients become relatively apathetic and less active, but a few become restlessly over-active, and, when this is combined with disinhibition of sexual and aggressive impulses, great social problems may develop.

It is in the family circle that the main impact of these personality changes is felt. When a man becomes aggressive, irritable, and sexually disinhibited after a head injury, the lives of his wife and children may become absolutely intolerable; although he may return to work, and seem to his work mates merely a bit odd and unpredictable. Drugs such as benperidol and cyproterone acetate, which lessen libido without feminisation can be helpful when sexual disinhibition is a problem.

With more severe damage patients often become fatuous seeming, and emotionally dependent and labile. Marked emotional incontinence, with sudden changes from empty laughter to tears and an expression of agonised grief, occurs mainly in those with bilateral damage to the pyramidal tracts at any level. Such patients may be unresponsive to a verbal approach, but tricyclic antidepressants (q.v.) often seem to make them calmer and happier seeming. In the late states of progressive brain disease there is an obliteration of all personality characteristics, as the patient ceases to communicate and respond in the final stages of dementia.

PERSONAL FACTORS

Premorbid personality and genetic factors, and the patient's environment and life situation, largely determine his reaction to the organically based deficits. Anxious vulnerable people, who have found life difficult to cope with at the best of times, may be overwhelmed, and regress into complete invalidism and despair. Even someone of previously stable temperament, who struggles hard against a disability, may be unable to cope if he is hard up and confined to a fifth floor flat in a wheelchair; or if his wife is suddenly taken ill or leaves him. An accountant suffers much more from dyscalculia than does a manual worker, whose earning power may be unaffected. The manual worker may become unemployable if left with a limp and a weak arm, whereas the accountant could continue in his own work; and so on. In every case these personal factors must be considered.

There are some particularly difficult situations which crop up again and again. One of these is common in all branches of medicine; that which develops when a person of hysterical and manipulative personality develops a disability which leads to the family rallying around, perhaps even ending a period of estrangement. The secondary gain of increased attention often outweighs the gain from physical improvement, and the illness becomes hysterically prolonged. Driving and perfectionistic people, who cannot tolerate anything less than the best, are often overwhelmed by the effects of a stroke. They start off working very hard at their exercises, but suddenly despair at their lack of progress, and may become quite deeply depressed and even suicidal.

In families in which there has been a struggle for dominance between husband and wife, or in which one spouse has resented a dependent and submissive rôle, an illness like a stroke can profoundly disturb the relationship between them, sometimes with tragic effect. For men especially, to find that they are no longer turned to as head of the family by the children, can be humiliating and distressing. For nearly all a loss of self-respect, a loss of purpose and meaning in life, results from these illnesses which not only lead to physical impairment, but to a real loss of intellect and personality.

A very common problem after head injury in adolescents and young adults arises from conflicts about independence and dependence. Typically some young person, who may or may not have had problems in asserting his independence from his parents has a severe head injury in a road accident. (Similar situations can arise whatever the source of the brain damage, but road accidents are over-whelmingly the most common.) To the parents it seems clear that their forgetful, clumsy, disinhibited son or daughter, is incapable of much responsibility, and needs care and protection; and an unbiased observer would often agree with them. The injured person, who may be strikingly insightless, disagrees and there are continual clashes, in which the patient is abusive and may be physically violent and which he justifies as a natural reaction to excessive parental control. The parents can usually only cope emotionally by reverting themselves to attitudes and behaviour which were appropriate for a young child. A 20-year-old having a tantrum like a 4-year-old can be a terrifying sight, and the lives of families with brain damaged offspring can be extremely turbulent and difficult. As the damaged individual slowly improves, the parents may fail to change their attitudes appropriately — they find it difficult to 'let go' and the clashes continue.

It is a general finding in people with significant organic personality change who are not in institutions, that the only people able to cope with looking after them in the long term are their parents, unless they have established a happy marriage of some duration. A young wife with young children can very rarely cope with a brain damaged husband, and he usually returns to his parents, who cope themselves, as mentioned earlier, by reacting to him as to a child. An older wife may be able to stick by her husband, even if he has severe personality change, if there have been long years of love and mutual esteem. She may be motivated more by pity and duty, and by the memory of affection, than by anything else, because it must be realised that the brain damaged person often seems like a completely different personality inside the same body. A wife in such a situation (and the converse is true in the rarer cases where a wife is brain damaged) also usually copes emotionally by treating her husband as a child. That almost always means that she stops all sexual intercourse, even if she does not exactly recognise why, as one cannot have sex with one's child. The husband as a consequence feels rejected and frustrated, and this in turn can lead to great conflict.

PSYCHIATRIC SYMPTOMS

The increased tendency to anxiety has been mentioned earlier; but many brain damaged patients also become depressed — at times very severely — more commonly in those with a family or personal history of depression. It is worth remenbering that brain damage is no contraindication to antidepressant drugs or even e.c.t.; and if patients have symptoms of depressive illness, with sleep disturbance, anorexia, diurnal variation, feelings of unworthiness etc., they should certainly be offered treatment. In others the depressive mood is fluctuating and shallow seeming, part of the personality change. In these patients treatment is rarely successful, but in doubtful cases it should be tried. Side effects from tricyclic drugs are more common in the brain damaged, who easily become ataxic; so that the dosage should be small at first and cautiously increased. The tetracyclic antidepressant mianserin is relatively free from atropine-like side effects, and is well tolerated by the brain damaged. It does lead to postural hypotension at times, so the dose should be built up gradually from 10 mg to a maximum of 60 mg daily.

A few brain damaged patients develop obsessional symptoms, and, particularly if the temporal lobes are involved, may develop schizophrenia-like symptoms, which are described in the section on temporal lobe epilepsy.

Organic syndromes may show much variation in their course, as the intensity and severity of the interference with cerebral function fluctuates, and as the patient's reactions change. The principal syndromes to be described, which may thus overlap considerably at times, are (1) *Organic neurasthenia*, characterised by emotionalism, oversensitiveness and debility, in relation to any physical illness, not necessarily involving the brain; (2) psychiatric aspects of *head injury*; and (3) psychiatric aspects of *epilepsy*; (4) *post-encephalitic states*; (5) *organic psychoses*: with delirious and subdelirious states characterised by clouding of consciousness; dysmnesic syndromes (characterised by difficulty in remembering and confabulation); and (6) *dementias*.

Assessment of intellectual impairment

This can be done clinically and by using standard psychological tests.

Clinical assessment

The account given by the patient and his relatives may be sufficient, if definite change in the ability to do his previous work, marked forgetfulness, inability to follow a previously enjoyed T.V. show etc. has developed. Simple tests may also be helpful: Repeating a name and address immediately and 2 minutes later, repeating three simple words after 3 minutes, subtracting 7 serially from 100, doing mental arithmetic, explaining well known proverbs, giving an account of recent world news, the names of members of the Royal family, etc. These time-honoured methods, although unstandardised, do give some indication, so long as the doctor has used the tests often enough to know how people may be expected to react. With inpatients in hospital their knowledge of the name of the ward and ward sister, the geography of the ward, the times of meals etc. can all be asked about; and at interview the patient's recollection of previous interviews can be informative.

Psychological tests

If after clinical examination there is still doubt about the presence of organic impairment, psychological tests, usually given by a clinical psychologist, can be used. Unfortunately it is in those borderline cases where the clinician is uncertain that the test results are also ambiguous. Naturally the patient should not be sedated at the time of testing, and the tests are unreliable in those who are markedly depressed or otherwise disturbed.

Intelligence tests

On the standard tests used for IQ assessment, such as the Wechsler Adult Intelligence Scale, brain damaged patients tend to perform relatively better on the verbal scales, which measure vocabulary, than they do on the performance scales, which measure the ability to solve problems and do mental arithmetic etc. There is therefore a discrepancy between the two scales, so that for example, the verbal IQ may be 126, but the performance IQ only 84. A gap as wide as this almost certainly indicates organic brain damage. However, if the discrepancy is between say, verbal IQ 110 and performance IQ 90, the difference of 20 points is found at times in the general population, with a certain known frequency, and the position remains uncertain. These equivocal tests are still extremely useful however, if later testing is done, because in progressive brain disease the scores will worsen; and if the patient is recovering they will improve.

Learning tests

These are, in our opinion, more generally useful than the intelligence tests, in that they are more sensitive to minor impairment.

Verbal learning. These test the ability of the patient to learn new words and their meaning, that is to extend their vocabulary; or they test the ability to learn pairs of words which have no logical connection in meaning. Examples are the Walton Black and the Inglis paired associate test.

Visuo-spatial tests. These test the ability to retain and reproduce diagrams which are shown to the patient for a standard time. The Benton Visual Retention Test and the Graham-Kendall Test are perhaps the best known in this country.

These two groups of tests can be said, to a limited extent, to test the two cerebral hemispheres separately, in that there is a tendency for visuo-spatial impairment to be commoner with nondominant, and verbal impairment to be commoner with dominant hemisphere lesions.

As with any test equivocal results are common, and again it can be most useful to do the tests serially to assess change. For details of these tests and the many others available, psychological texts should be consulted.

ORGANIC SYNDROMES AND PSYCHOSES

Organic neurasthenia

This can occur as a complication of debilitating physical illnesses, usually in their later stages or during convalescence, but it can occur also in the early stages of, or in convalescence from, the more severe organic mental syndromes about to be described. It is characterised by over-sensitiveness, emotionalism with lability and fatigue, often coupled with querulous irritability, headache, hypochondriacal attitudes, insomnia and subjective complaints of memory disturbance and difficulty in concentration. The course is variable but is apt to be prolonged in those with vulnerable or inadequate personalities who become readily demoralised. Treatment consists in improving the physical condition, protecting the patient from stress, allaying his anxieties as far as possible, and judicious rehabilitation.

PSYCHIATRIC ASPECTS OF HEAD INJURY

Mental symptoms are often produced by injury to the head. In the majority of cases, however, these mental symptoms are of secondary importance, the surgical aspect of the case needing and receiving primary attention. Moreover, such mental symptoms as are shown usually disappear as the patient recovers from his injuries, so that most cases of head injury are scarcely regarded as psychiatric problems at all. However, modern care is leading to an ever increasing number of survivors of severe head injuries, who in the past would have died. Most of those who have been unconscious for several weeks are left with permanent mental changes, often very severe; and less severe injuries may also leave permanent damage.

Concussion

Concussion is a transient loss of consciousness after head injury, more common if the head is free to move at impact, presumably because of the swirling motion of the brain within the cranium. It is very rarely, if ever, followed by long-term organic brain damage unless it occurs repeatedly as in 'punch drunk' boxers, but it may be followed by a 'post-concussional state' (p. 92).

Pathology

The brain has a porridge-like consistency, and sudden deceleration leads to a fluid-like swirling of the contents of the skull, with shearing stresses in the brain tissue which lead to damage to both neurones and to small blood vessels. Swelling of the brain follows, and consequent compression of the brain stem at the tentorial gap, leading often to permanent generalised spasticity even if the hemispheres are not much damaged.

Severe head injuries

The severity of a head injury in terms of long term mental change is closely correlated with the duration of post-traumatic amnesia (P.T.A.) This is defined as the time from the moment of injury to the resumption of normal continuous memory. A patient with a P.T.A. of less than an hour will probably be back at work within a month, but a P.T.A. of much more than a week is likely to be followed by some permanent mental deficit, and a return to work delayed by a year, with intermediate durations of P.T.A. and recovery along a continuum Retrograde amnesia, that is amnesia for a period of time before the injury, is almost invariable if the P.T.A. is prolonged, but its duration is a much less accurate guide to the future.

Head injury has frightening connotations to almost everyone. The family who await recovery are almost always dreading severe and permanent damage, and the longer they wait the more likely that becomes. The injured person when he wakes up is also likely to be very fearful as awareness returns, and personality factors must be considered from this stage on, as mentioned earlier (p. 84). The manner in which the patients complaints and anxieties are handled can have a marked influence on the degree of anxiety and invalidism afterwards, and a robust attitude towards activity is necessary in those with no organic damage, especially if they are of anxious or hypochondriacal temperament.

Post-traumatic confusion and delirium

Some degree of confusion, that is, disorientation and impaired grasp of the surroundings, often occurs after even minor head injury, as with concussion ('Where am I?' asks the rugby player as he sits on the ground holding his head.) If confusion is prolonged into hours and days, as follows more severe injuries, particularly during the slow recovery phase after coma or semi-coma, delirium (p. 100) may develop; that is, features such as hallucinations, and states of excitement or fear, may be added to the confusion and disorientation. The patient will be unable to lay down new memories, as is easily shown on testing (p. 86) and there will, in the future, be no memory for this period, which is of course that later recognised as post traumatic amnesia. As people recover, the degree of confusion and of memory formation fluctuates, often leading to the development of 'islands of memory' towards the end of the period of post traumatic amnesia.

It cannot be emphasized too much that there are no clinical features in the mental state of the confused person which indicate the cause of the confusion. If a man has had a very minor head injury, because he bumped his head while suffering from hypoglycaemia, the mental state examination gives no clue to the fact that his confusion is actually caused by hypoglycaemia.

The clinical findings and differential diagnosis of confusional and delirious states are described later in this chapter (p. 100), and will not be repeated here; but it is worth noting that alcoholics and elderly people who already have some degree of senile or athero-sclerotic dementia (p. 118) are more likely to develop confusion after quite minor head injury.

Post-traumatic twilight states are rare. It occasionally happens that a patient after a minor head injury with concussion (p. 89) finds himself at some strange place, with no recollection of the accident or of the intervening period, although he may have behaved quite normally to outward appearances.

Long term effects of severe head injury

The principal features have been described under the headings of perceptual and intellectual impairment, communication difficulties, and personality change, on pages 79, 80, 82, and the interplay of these organically determined features with various personal factors also outlined (p. 84). These general principles apply to the results of brain damage arising from any cause, of which closed head injury from road accidents is much the commonest.

Outwardly the patients tend to resemble each other greatly, with generalised spasticity of all four limbs and of the face and tongue, and also affecting the muscles of the larynx and pharynx, leading to a monotonous and scanning sort of speech. Brain damage is usually diffuse, but depending on which parts are most damaged, and on personality factors, we commonly see one of three clinical pictures, often overlapping; a euphoric, talkative, disinhibited type; a sullen, morose, irritable-explosive type; and an apathetic, slow, inactive type. All may occur with or without marked intellectual change, but the more severe the personality change the more likely is intellectual change to be present.

These personality changes make many patients extremely difficult to live with, and great emotional stress often develops in the families. Sadly, the greatest incidence of head injury is in the impulsive and poorly controlled young men who contribute so much to the road accident statistics, especially with motor cycle accidents. People of somewhat psychopathic temperament are more likely to have accidents, and less likely to wear seat belts in cars, and show even more disturbances of behaviour after their head injuries than do people of previously more stable temperament.

Prognosis

The long term outlook depends very largely on the amount of brain damaged, and also on personality and environmental factors. The younger the patient the longer recovery will continue, so that a child of under 5 years might continue to improve for up to 8 or 9 years, a young adult about 4 years, and a 70 year old for about 1 year. It is wise to wait at least 6 months before offering a prognosis. When there is much anxiety, or litigation is outstanding, forecasting the outcome is often more difficult.

Treatment

Rehabilitation, with physiotherapy, remedial gymnastics, graded occupational therapy, and job retraining, in an enthusiastic atmosphere, is the most effective way of preventing invalidism and rebuilding confidence. Job placement, using the D.R.O. (Disabled Resettlement Officer) and Labour Exchange facilities if necessary, helping the patient to find work with which he can cope without strain, is the next step. If he cannot settle in his old home, because of personality changes, a hostel or other sheltered accommodation may be needed. Discussion of his difficulties, practical help from social workers, encouragement and emotional support, explanations to the relatives, antidepressants or other appropriate drugs as necessary, and one or two years of anticonvulsants as prophylaxis against post-traumatic epilepsy, are all part of the treatment. Patients should be pushed towards such facilities as are available, but the number of special centres designed to cope is all too few.

Post-concussional (post-traumatic) syndrome

This syndrome is quite common after minor head injuries in which there has been only transient loss of consciousness, that is, concussion. It does not occur after the more serious illnesses in which there is unequivocal evidence of brain damage.

The symptoms are monotonous. There is almost always headache, dizziness and poor concentration, irritability, easy fatigue, undue sensitivity to noise and light. Frequent brief spells of shallow depression are also very often present.

It rarely lasts for more than a few days after a sporting injury and is much more likely to be disabling and prolonged after injuries in which there is the possibility of industrial or insurance compensation. People of previously anxious or vulnerable personality are also much more commonly affected. There is, however, a sizeable number of affected people in whom none of these factors can be identified with confidence. There is also some published evidence of minor brain damage in this syndrome.

Very many people with the syndrome seek compensation and those doctors who do a lot of medico-legal work naturally see them. Undoubtedly there is often conscious exaggeration of symptoms (that is, malingering) and perhaps more often unconscious (or hysterical) elaboration (see p. 273) in these compensation cases. Many patients exist however, in whom the syndrome develops without a compensation case, although one can quite often identify some other 'secondary gain' (p. 282) even in these. A typical example would be that of someone who becomes unable to take any share of responsibility for the control of turbulent children because of his incapacity, and leaves it all to his wife.

In identifying possible financial or other gain, it is too easy to dismiss the patient's complaints as unreal, or as an expression of personal weakness or greed. One should not, however, forget the fear which any injury to the head generates in people, with the apprehensions of being permanently crippled or demented and so on, and accidents often occur in terrifying circumstances, in which death may have seemed very close. A 'traumatic neurosis' as a response to such a threat is perhaps understandable.

In some patients, especially in those who have also suffered a whip lash injury, there may be a disturbance of vestibular function, which can be demonstrated by the presence of positional nystagmus for instance, and which by causing vertigo adds to the unpleasant experiences.

It is important that doctors and nurses do not encourage the development of undue anxiety after head injury, and a generally robust attitude is best, emphasizing the benefits of early activity and of occupation.

Overall the syndrome is probably best seen as one in which the symptoms are at first directly due to some transient organic damage, perhaps combined with anxiety. It soon clears up in most people however, and its prolongation is probably always due to more purely psychological factors, of the sort outlined above.

Prognosis is difficult to assess. Most of those who are seen by doctors are interested in compensation, and this acts as a powerful deterrent to getting better. The old idea that the patients all improved after settlement is certainly false, and in fact many of these patients remain unhappily disabled. Early settlement of litigation is, however, likely to be helpful, but many claims drag on for 4 or 5 years, while the affected individual goes from doctor to doctor for further opinions, a system well designed for the perpetuation and elaboration of neurotic or hysterical symptoms.

Treatment is uncertain and difficult. The best course is almost certainly rehabilitation in a centre which can offer both physical activities and psychological help to the patient and the family. Rapid settlement of claims would probably lessen the degree of neurotic or hysterical elaboration, but is difficult with the British legal system.

Compensation problems

The hope of financial gain, in the form of pension or compensation, is often over-emphasised as an aetiological factor in the production of post-traumatic disabilities. When such an intention is fully conscious, the case is one of malingering, but this is probably rare. When the intention is not fully conscious its psychological significance varies considerably; but assessing the inner motives and degree of insight in such cases is extremely difficult.

In some cases the intention seems to be to punish the guilty or to receive just consolation for an innocently suffered wrong. In other cases the money enables the patient to succumb to or keep up a neurosis which has its real origin in conflicts not necessarily connected with the accident at all. In yet another group of cases the accident acts as a psychological trauma; the experience of a serious threat to life or limb releases anxieties with which the patient is unable to cope, and leads to a neurotic reaction. Each case must be considered individually in the light of the patient's personality and life-history, and these do not reveal clear evidence of neurosis or psychopathy in every instance. All that can be expected and is usually found are character traits which render the individual liable to break down under particular stress, but which may not previously have given rise to serious maladjustment or to the formation of symptoms. Even so, there is a higher incidence of post-traumatic disability after industrial than after sporting accidents, in the insured as opposed to the uninsured, and in soldiers as opposed to civilians. Compensation factors are often very important, and when the head injury has been trivial many cases seem to recover when the compensation case is settled.

Mental symptoms in encephalitis lethargica

Though now rare, sporadic cases seem to occur. In the acute phase the mental symptoms show nothing specially characteristic. In recovery, there is inertia and sloth with restlessness, irritability, moodiness and hypochondriasis. Subsequently, Parkinsonism may develop, with ptyalism, oculogyric crises, 'coordinated tics' (compulsions to make purposive but unnecessary movements, such as straightening or smoothing) and other obsessive-compulsive symptoms. Later developments may be depressive, schizophrenic or paranoid. The Parkinsonian slowing may give an erroneous impression of dementia, whereas the reduction in intellectual function is really only slight, arising from slowness and lack of initiative.

Encephalitis lethargica in childhood may produce gross personality change with hyperkinesis, aggression and loss of all moral sense leading to stealing, lying, cruelty, sexual aberrations and indiscipline. Follow up studies have shown, however, that about one third of cases regain social adaptation and that another third develop Parkinsonism.

Psychiatric aspects of epilepsy

Epilepsy is a very common condition, and although few epileptic patients present psychiatric syndromes, there are important psychological problems for almost every epileptic. In childhood and adolescence, the fits are especially frightening, not only to the child but also to his parents and siblings, his schoolfellows and even the teachers. He becomes the focus of attention, must be specially treated, may be forbidden to ride a bicycle, to go swimming and many other things, and has his future career choice restricted. Everyone treats him as 'different', and parents can very easily become seriously overprotective.

If the child is lucky enough to have the fits fully controlled these features tend to fade away, but for the others life is certainly made more difficult. Within the limits of the fit type and frequency, children should be encouraged to live as actively and normally as possible, and a lot can be done by careful and repeated counselling of all those involved.

In addition to the natural anxiety and despondency caused in many patients, some epileptics are prone to spells of surliness and irritability, often accompanied by spontaneous mood changes. These spells may be ended by a fit. Phenobarbitone also causes depression, sometimes quite serious, in a certain number of epileptics.

Epilepsy itself does not lead to intellectual or personality deterioration, but a progressive lesion causing the epilepsy may do so, of course. High levels of medication, repeated head injuries and cerebral anoxia in the unfortunate few who are poorly controlled are other factors. Persistent focal discharges in the dominant hemisphere, even without fits, lead to difficulties in learning and impair verbal skills generally.

In a few patients a picture amounting to 'dementia' can be produced by continuous abnormal electrical discharge without actual fits.

In adults emotional disturbances and the major epileptic syndromes are commoner in patients with a focus in the temporal lobe than in others.

'Epileptic personality'. A few epileptics of longstanding, poorly controlled and usually institutionalised, become slow, narrow, bigoted, religiose, pedantic, suspicious and irritable. They can be extremely difficult to contend with in a ward, and become very unpopular with others. Most mental hospitals have a few such patients. The factors mentioned earlier which lead to personality deterioration are usually present, combined with the effects of chronic institutionalisation.

In a number of epileptics, it seems that temporal lobe disturbances at certain critical periods of life prevent normal personality development, which cannot be recouped, even if the fits are later stopped. The development of transvestism (q.v.), for example, has been linked to this in some people.

Aggressiveness. This is undoubtedly a characteristic of some epileptics, especially those with temporal lobe lesions acting as the focus.

Epileptic psychoses

Confusional states and twilight states. These are uncommon, and are clinically indistinguishable from other confusional states, although the history gives a clue. They may follow a fit, or seem to occur instead of a fit, as an ictal phenomenon, especially in temporal lobe epilepsy. Rarely patients in these states are seriously violent, but mainly they present as 'blank', perplexed, tense, failing to grasp their environment or what is said. They may wander about in the street, urinate in public, or do other things of which society disapproves. The term 'twilight state' is often used. There is complete amnesia afterwards for all these states. They can be stopped by intravenous diazepam, if it can be given; intramuscular diazepam must be used if intravenous injection is impracticable.

Temporal lobe epilepsy is sometimes encountered in psychiatric departments, usually because the peculiar subjective experiences involved have led to an erroneous diagnosis of anxiety, hysteria or psychosis. It can be understood as focal epilepsy, with the focus in the temporal lobe, the complex functions of which are intermittently disturbed. It is characterised by periodic disturbances of consciousness with entry into a transient dream-like state, with or without loss of touch with reality and with more or less confusion.

In the milder forms, the patient remains correctly orientated but may feel in a dream or as if something is happening that has happened before. Simultaneously he may experience altered affect often in the form of intense panic, sometimes with feelings or loathing or revulsion. At the same time his perceptions may be distorted so that familiar things, though recognisable, assume an altered appearance often tinged with unpleasantness or horror, and he may experience inexplicable tastes or smells. His thoughts may become disordered or inappropriate, so that he may find himself struggling to remember something without knowing what it is he has to remember, or may find nonsensical phrases recurring to his mind in a way he cannot control. There may be accompanying autonomic disturbances, such as sinking feelings in the abdomen, dryness of the mouth or palpitation. In the motor sphere, the patient may perform stereotyped but inappropriate automatic acts, such as chewing, spitting or aimlessly moving things from one place to another. In fact, there may be a disturbance at all levels of nervous function, autonomic, sensorimotor and psychic, of varying complexity in each.

The attack may be ushered in by an aura, of a simple epigastric kind as in more ordinary forms of epilepsy, or of a complicated and highly organised kind such as suddenly seeing the appearance of some figure or pattern; a sense of there being some body or object, uncertainly glimpsed and only partially apprehended, behind one or other shoulder is specially characteristic. Usually the attack lasts but a few seconds or a minute or so. On recovery, the patient may have an almost complete or only a vague and partial recollection of the incident, but is usually left anxious or frightened by such an unexpected trip into the unknown.

More severe attacks can last for longer periods of time, during which all contact with reality is lost so that the patient can only remember the very beginning of the attack. He may then 'come to', and find himself somewhere unexpected, or inexplicably wet, or without some possession he should have had.

The main diagnostic points are as follows. The longer attacks are rare and must be distinguished from states of hysterical dissociation (p. 266). In this, the main guides will be the personality of the patient, the essentially episodic nature of the condition, the genuineness of the disturbance of consciousness, the purposelessness of the behaviour, and the ready resumption of normal conduct on recovery. The shorter attacks are commoner than may be realised, and their essence is their suddenness and transience, coupled with an eerie, nightmare quality which the patient will emphasise but may find difficult to describe. Where anxiety is a component, this is usually of a supernatural intensity, different from anything the patient has normally experienced and different from the anxiety he feels lest the experience should recur. A sober account of a sudden, transient, queer disturbance, with astonishment that it should have happened and uneasiness lest it should happen again, will suggest the diagnosis, especially if the patient is of previously stable personality and there is no evidence of motive or secondary gain.

The treatment of temporal lobe epilepsy is principally by anticonvulsants, which are better described in a neurological text. Phenothiazines may also be useful in the control of psychotic symptoms so long as the patient is already on anticonvulsants. As for any other type of epilepsy, onset after adolescence should lead to investigations to exclude a cerebral tumour or other lesion. If the attacks cannot be controlled by drugs, or there is behavioural deterioration between attacks, temporal lobectomy may be necessary. This can only be done if the contralateral temporal lobe is perfectly intact, as very severe memory disturbances of Korsakoff type (q.v.) may develop with bilateral damage to or removal of the medial temporal lobe structures.

Transient psychoses. In addition to the chronic schizophrenic-like psychoses of epilepsy described later temporal lobe focus epileptics occasionally suffer from brief, acute psychotic illnesses, resembling both schizophrenia and affective illnesses, or mixed schizo-affective illnesses. They usually last only a few days, although sometimes many weeks, and may be suggestive of a functional psychosis or have a more or less marked admixture of confusional symptoms.

The schizophrenia-like psychoses of epilepsy

A certain proportion of patients with long standing epilepsy, mainly of temporal lobe origin, develop an illness closely resembling chronic paranoid schizophrenia with delusions and hallucinations, but with relatively well preserved affect. The development of schizophrenia-like symptoms is commoner when the lesion is tumour or hamartoma, rather than when it is mesial temporal sclerosis, and is particularly common in left handed females.

In our experience of such patients organic impairment of memory and other intellectual function is also marked. Both anticonvulsants and phenothiazines are useful in treatment, but the symptoms are difficult to control completely.

The occurrence of epilepsy must not necessarily be regarded as a bar to higher education or to academic training, as the follow-up of epileptics has demonstrated. Another encouraging point is that, contrary to previous medical belief, a normally intelligent person who develops idiopathic epilepsy is much less likely to deteriorate mentally than one who develops symptomatic epilepsy. Just as there are societies for sufferers from conditions such as diabetes and polio-myelitis, the British Epilepsy Association (at present at 3 Alfred Place, London, W.C.1) sets out to help epileptics, and may offer guidance over problems of employment and social contacts. Finally, the greater efficacy of the various anticonvulsant drugs that have been developed over the last twenty years renders control of the seizures less difficult than it used to be, and in only a few cases does serious deterioration develop.

Encephalitic and post-encephalitic states

The major epidemic of encephalitis lethargica 'sleepy sickness') which swept the world after the first Great War left in its trail some severe disabilities. Many developed parkinsonism, some developed intractable obsessive-compulsive states, and many young people who were affected developed personality disorders of psychopathic type. Various forms of encephalitis, for example, that due to herpes virus, now occur quite frequently. In the acute stages they can present with mental illnesses closely resembling schizophrenia, except that some clouding of consciousness will be apparent at some time (most often they present with obvious clouding, usually severe enough to cause stupor or coma). Residual effects of diffuse brain damage are not uncommon, with intellectual and personality deterioration.

ORGANIC PSYCHOSES

These can be divided into three main groups:

1. Acute states of clouded consciousness, including delirium and sub-delirium; usually known as acute confusional or toxic confusional states, or 'acute brain syndromes'.

2. the dysmnesic syndromes (Korsakoff states) in which recent memory is mainly affected; and

3. the dementias, which are characterised by irreversible impairment of intellect and personality; also called 'chronic brain syndromes'.

In common usage in medicine the term 'organic psychosis' is often restricted to the first group, but really all belong conveniently under the same heading.

Delirium and sub-delirium (confusional states)

These terms are used to describe states of clouded consciousness in which there are symptoms such as hallucinations, delusions, depression, excitement and fear, as well as clouding with its attendant confusion and disorientation. Sub-delirium is used to describe the less florid cases, but is not exactly defined.

The characteristic acute organic mental symptoms, the presence of which must *always* arouse suspicion of organic disease, are:

1. Disturbances of consciousness;
2. Disorientation for time and place;
3. Failure of grasp of the environment and of what is occurring; and
4. Objective impairment of memory.

These are the features of confusional states in general, which are extremely common in medical and surgical wards, especially in the elderly, while florid delirium is quite rare. Most confused patients are old and frail, suffering from heart failure or chest infections, and with some degree of pre-existing senile or arteriopathic cerebral disease. They often call out in a confused and frightened way, and may be noisy and disturbing to others, especially at night — when they cannot see clearly enough to keep their flickering sense of orientation. They are not often more disturbed than that, but when they are they cause great management problems, and the mental distress and excitement can worsen the physical state.

Aetiology of delirium

In addition to the age associated factors mentioned above, constitutional factors are important in that some people become clouded and delirious more easily than others, for unknown reasons. Children are also particularly prone to delirium, which may accompany high fever with common childhood fevers, especially those viral illnesses such as measles and mumps, in which some degree of encephalitis is common.

Psychological factors are only secondary, in that they determine the content of the fears, hallucinations, and so on. Genetic factors also influence the content, as someone with a family history of schizophrenia is more likely to develop schizophrenia-like symptoms in a delirium than someone else. If an individual has successive delirious illnesses, even from different physical causes, the mental symptoms will be almost identical in each.

As was emphasised at the beginning of this chapter, the disturbances due to organic factors do not tell us anything specific about the underlying pathology. They tell us only that organic disease is present and interfering with the function of the brain. We must then make a *medical* diagnosis. As an example, the mental disturbances due to hypo- and hyper-glycaemia in the same patient in successive weeks, might be identical. The history and physical findings, supplemented by blood sugar estimations, distinguish one from the other.

The physical factors which can cause clouding of consciousness, and thus lead on to sub-delirious and delirious states, are very numerous. Anoxia, as with congestive heart failure or extensive lung disease, is a common cause, as are various infections, including meningitis, encephalitis, pneumonia and typhoid. Some severe infections, however, rarely lead to clouded consciousness: for example, cholera and bacillary dysentery.

Any drug which can lead to unconsciousness in overdosage will cause clouding in an intermediate dose: alcohol and barbituarates are perhaps the commonest, but tricyclic antidepressants, bromides, amphetamines and many others can be responsible. Alcohol and barbiturates can lead to states of clouded consciousness either directly or by sudden withdrawal in the physiologically dependent. Metals such as lead and manganese, and very many complex industrial poisons may be responsible also.

Electrolyte and metabolic disturbances are quite common precipitants, particularly potassium depletion following diuretics. Prolonged vomiting as in hyperemesis gravidarum and pyloric stenosis; and self induced vomiting in anorexia nervosa or bulimia (p. 368), can disturb electrolyte balances enough to affect the mental state, as can severe diarrhoea. Hypo- and hyper-glycaemia can both cause states of clouded consciousness.

Prolonged malnutrition, with vitamin deficiences, predisposes to clouded consciousness, as in Pellagra (Riboflavine and Nicotinic acid especially), and vitamin B_{12} deficiency can do the same. Prolonged shortage of these vitamins leads to dementia.

Finally, head injuries, cerebrovascular accidents, and many other acute cerebral disorders, are quite commonly responsible.

The EEG is almost always disturbed in confusional states, which may occasionally be helpful in diagnosis. Characteristically, there are slow waves of very high voltage.

Symptoms and signs

Specific illnesses do not give rise to specific kinds of delirium. The clinical picture tends to be much the same whatever physical agents are involved. The only exception to this is that the more prostrating the underlying physical condition, the more torpid is the patient likely to be.

(a) *Physical.* Where the condition is of any severity, it is common to find a sluggish reaction of the pupils, nystagmus, diplopia and slurred speech, together with other evidence of incoordination that may be brought out by attempted movements. Control of the bladder and even rectum may be defective, leading to incontinence.

(b) *Mental.* The essential features are (i) clouding of consciousness, leading to (ii) disorientation, (iii) severe impairment of immediate recall and of recent as well as of more distant memory, and therefore (iv) difficulty in grasp. With these are associated (v) restlessness and (vi) increased suggestibility and responsiveness leading to confabulation. The difficulty in grasp and the increased suggestibility are coupled with (vii) an anxious or fearful affective state. The patient is perplexed. The combination of these leads to (viii) misinterpretations which, owing to the emotional condition, are usually of a paranoid sort. Apart from the foregoing there are commonly (ix) hallucinations, especially visual ones; these are often of a frightening kind and enhance the paranoid condition. Finally, unless the patient is so toxic as to be stuporose, the delirious state is characterised by (x) a remarkable variability in all the symptoms from one time to another.

Thus, the extent to which consciousness is clouded will vary from moment to moment, but the attention is at all times poorly sustained, so that the patient's concentration is very bad and his thinking laboured and even disconnected. The patient tries readily, and though he may be transiently roused from his confusion will soon sink back into it, so that, though momentarily accessible, he will soon become inaccessible again. This may prevent him from grasping the simplest thing, even his whereabouts, and he may not even be able to give his name, so that he is disorientated for time, place, and person.

The restlessness depends largely on the degree of physical debility; a spry alcoholic in delirium tremens may show highly purposive and coordinated movements, whereas the patient who is physically prostrated will merely toss, turn and flop. In the more active patients investigatory and occupational activities are highly characteristic; for example, they may drive imaginary cars, enact telephone conversations or tell imaginary rosaries.

Visual hallucinations are very common in the more acute intoxications, and when so real as to be accepted by the patient as part of the external world they are almost pathognomonic. Auditory hallucinations, though less pathognomonic, are about as common; they may persist for some time after evidence of gross confusion has disappeared.

The marked variability of the state is shown also in the paranoid attitudes and delusional ideas, which are typically transient, shifting and ill-systematised. Where there is a variable difficulty in grasp coupled with anxiety and fearfulness, it is inevitable that doubt and suspicion should arise; again, the heightened suggestibility and disturbed perception encourage the development of misinterpretations. These are the starting point for the formation of delusions, but the latter are not sustained owing to the poor memory, confusion and impaired grasp, although in the course of any delirium the patient will feel himself at some time and to some extent the subject of persecution and annoyance. Such feelings will lead to various degrees of disturbed behaviour, ranging from querulousness with the expression of ideas of reference, to more crystallised notions of plots, of being poisoned, kidnapped or tortured, or being involved in gang warfare or revolutions.

In mild cases the patient may behave normally enough in the day, later to become restless and confused as night falls.

In summary, delirium is a clouded, confused, restless but essentially variable state, with a striking frequency of visual hallucinations and paranoid features, accompanied by a labile (variable) mood that is predominantly anxious, fearful, depressed and irritable. Its vividness is increased by the heightened suggestibility and responsiveness, but will be decreased pari passu with the extent to which the patient is physically prostrated. The whole picture is strikingly coloured by the personality and previous experiences of the individual sufferer — this being shown in its simplest form when aggressive people become even more aggressive when drunk.

The essential *organic mental symptoms* are the clouding of consciousness, the confusion, the impaired grasp and memory, and the variation in the level of consciousness from one time to another.

Differential diagnosis

This depends on the occurrence of organic mental symptoms in association with some physical condition that may adequately explain their development. These symptoms are readily missed if certain others, such as anxiety or depression, are particularly marked. Special attention must therefore be paid to the examination of the patient's sensorium, in order to elicit evidence of clouding, and of impairment of grasp and memory. The difficulty of differentiation from manic or schizophrenic excitement may sometimes be very great — even for a time impossible. In the doubtful case, the characteristic variability of delirious symptoms may be a crucial diagnostic point. Visual hallucinations make it almost certain that the diagnosis is of an organic state, except in patients from much less developed societies in which visual hallucinations occur in schizophrenia sometimes.

Course and prognosis

This depends on the severity of the underlying physical illness and on the physical condition of the patient, and in most cases complete mental recovery occurs when the underlying illness resolves. However, the development of acute confusion in the elderly, and even in the young when debilitated by a long physical illness, is quite often a prelude to death. In the elderly a delirium may settle only to reveal some degree of dementia persisting. In other cases, restlessness and excitement may lead, through the physical prostration that they cause, to a fatal outcome that would not otherwise have been expected. Wild and impulsive deliria of that sort are prone to occur in unstable and psychopathic people, in the young and in the severely mentally subnormal; their prognosis is accordingly less good. Another risk, which may be quite real in depressed patients, is that of suicide; a history of a previous suicidal attempt should be an indication for special precautions.

Treatment

The first essential is to make a medical diagnosis of the underlying cause. Extensive investigation may be necessary, although an accurate history from an informed person, and a thorough physical examination will usually provide the answer.

It is also essential to ensure adequate nourishment and fluid intake, if necessary intravenously. Since avitaminosis can be a factor, vitamin medication should be given. This can be done by the intramuscular or intravenous route, as well as by mouth. A suitable preparation for the former is Parentrovite as described later.

If possible the patient must be helped to rest, without excessive sedation. Barbiturates should be avoided, because as the effect wears off they can increase the confusion. The phenothiazines, in a dosage which produces tranquillisation without deep sedation, are probably best. Chlorpromazine can be given by intramuscular injection, in doses of 25–100 mg every three to six hours, as required. Paraldehyde should not be used.

Skilled nursing remains extremely important. It is best in a quiet room, preferably with a very limited number of nurses, so that the patient can more easily become familiar with them. Everyone in contact with a delirious patient should remember how easily misinterpretations and excitement develop, and should repeatedly tell him that he is in hospital and who the speaker is. The room should be well lit to avoid frightening shadows, and whispering about him in earshot should be avoided.

There remain a very few obscure and intractable cases who remain delirious even after the causative illness has apparently been effectively treated. In these cases, electrical treatment (p. 429) can be rapidly successful, two or three treatments quietening the patient, relieving confusion and stabilising the emotional state.

In *alcoholic delirium tremens,* all the foregoing principles of treatment apply. The treatment of this important, and increasingly common condition, is given in the chapter on Alcoholism (p. 323).

DYSMNESIC SYNDROME

Korsakoff's psychosis

In this condition the memory disturbance is the most striking feature, not the difficulty in grasp or clouding of consciousness. In the full blown state the patient is unable to hold new verbal memories for more than about 90 seconds, so that he is unable to remember what he was talking about before then, and he tends to confabulate, that is to fill the gap by making something up.

Aetiology

The Korsakoff state develops whenever the tracts which run from the hippocampus through the fornix to the mammillary bodies are interrupted bilaterally. In alcoholics thiamin deficiency may lead to degenerative changes in the mammillary bodies, and a Korsakoff state may follow Wernickes' encephalopathy in which there are other mid brain disturbances, or delirium. In alcoholics peripheral neuritis is usually present as well. The term Korsakoff's 'psychosis' should properly be reserved for this picture in alcoholics. A Korsakoff 'state', in non-alcoholic patients, may follow head injury, destruction of the relevant areas by tumour or surgery, or cerebrovascular accidents. It is not uncommon in an incomplete form, in arteriosclerotic dementia.

Symptoms and signs

At first sight the patients may present no overt abnormality. They may even appear to be abnormally quick on the uptake, and they often speak with great fluency and plausibility. But examination reveals gross defects in memory. These are most obvious in the appreciation of time relationships, especially for recent events, and may be so marked as to cause gross disorientation in time. As if to compensate for these defects of memory, the patients are specially liable to *confabulate* in course of which they often show a striking suggestibility. At first their confabulations may seem plausible, but on longer acquaintance it will be realised that their tales are quite untrue, even though they are embroidered with extraordinary detail, and that with a little suggestion and encouragement they will tell of adventures that are preposterous, fantastic and beyond any hope of credulity.

Visuo-spatial memory is not affected, and a patient may know his way round a ward, which he cannot remember being in even after many months, in a paradoxical seeming way.

Apart from the disturbance of memory and confabulation, the patients are usually markedly cheerful, almost euphoric, but in a silly and fatuous way. This cheerfulness is usually punctuated, however, by marked irritability. In addition, they are usually indolent, with abnormally little initiative, and there is some impairment of intellectual grasp.

Course and prognosis

In alcoholics great improvement may result from massive thiamin dosage, given intravenously at first, and then for months by mouth. Improvement can continue slowly for up to eighteen months or more once it has started. If there is no improvement after one month the outlook is bad.

It is a matter of urgency to begin treatment with thiamin in large doses if Wernicke's encephalopathy or Korsakoff's psychosis is suspected. Blood can be taken to assess serum pyruvate for reference later, but treatment should not be delayed. We have seen permanent memory loss follow delays while elaborate tests were performed.

For the non-alcoholic Korsakoff states no treatment is usually possible, although, as with all forms of brain damage, there may be spontaneous improvement.

THE DEMENTIAS (SEE ALSO CHAPTER 7)

Dementia is an irreversible impairment of intellect and personality, due to organic damage or disease affecting the brain. The term is mainly used for the progressive dementias, several of which are described in this book, but it also applies to non-progressive damage such as that due to head injury, encephalitis, anoxia, or any one of many other insults to the brain. The term 'chronic brain syndrome' has the same meaning.

The two most important dementing illnesses are *senile* and *arteriopathic (arteriosclerotic) dementia.* They are not described in this section, where they might be expected, but in the chapter on Psychiatry in the Aged, because of the many practical problems which they cause in old people and their families. The main clinical features of progressive dementia will therefore be found on page 118, which should be read in conjunction with this section. Apart from the ages, and those aspects of life which largely depend on age, such as increasing frailty, the clinical descriptions apply overall to the pre-senile dementias as well.

There are a few illnesses, such as hypothyroidism and vitamin B_{12} deficiency, which lead to permanent dementia if untreated but which remain reversible for quite a long time after onset. Their detection is essential, and is considered later in this section on page 110.

PRE-SENILE DEMENTIAS

A pre-senile dementia is one which comes on before the age of 65, by arbitrary definition. They are very much less common than dementia in later life. Alzheimers disease is about ten times as common as Pick's disease.

Alzheimer's disease

The essential feature is the early onset, usually between 40 and 60 years of age. It is commoner in women. This condition can often be distinguished from the other pre-senile dementias by the relative preservation of the patient's social behaviour and emotional responses by comparison with the severity of the dementia that such preservation covers. In this respect Alzheimer's disease resembles arteriosclerotic dementia. Symptoms of aphasia, agnosia, etc. are frequent, but less well defined than when they result from focal lesions of vascular origin. As the condition progresses, stereotyped movements and speech are usual, and the latter finally deteriorates into repetitive utterances that are intelligible but meaningless. The histopathology is indistinguishable from senile dementia, (p. 118) so that some neurologists refer to 'Alzheimers disease of senile onset' depending on the patient's age. Death usually occurs within 2 to 5 years of onset.

Pick's disease

This is similar in that it gives rise to a profound dementia, but the deterioration is more general so that social preservation is lacking. Gross restlessness is a rather frequent finding. The underlying pathology differs from Alzheimer's disease in that the latter condition is found to be diffuse at post-mortem, whereas cases of Pick's disease show only circumscribed areas of cerebral atrophy, in the frontal or temporal lobes or both. It is because the frontal lobes are especially affected that personality is relatively more damaged. Microscopically the degenerating neurones form 'balloon cells', and there are also neurofibrillary tangles and plaques as in Alzheimer's disease. Death usually occurs after 6–10 years from the onset.

Huntington's chorea

This condition is of special interest in that it is hereditary and transmitted by a single autosomal dominant gene. It affects therefore half the offspring of any sufferer on average. It usually occurs at middle-life or soon after, but there is often a pre-morbid history of eccentricity. The symptoms and signs do not develop in any set order. The choreic movements may be the first developments, and, if they are, curious smacking of the lips may be the earliest one, later to be followed by spasmodic sudden jerkings which may be of a generalised kind. In other cases, the choreic movements may be preceded by changes in character, of which irritability is specially common, and may later lead to ungovernable rage, while lack of prudence and impaired judgement are usual. These changes in character may or may not precede the dementia, which, in its turn, may or may not precede the chorea. The dementia itself has no special features. The course is essentially downhill, the prognosis is hopeless, and there is no treatment, except that thiopropazate (Dartalan) often lessens the severity of the movements. The family history will be of special aid in the early diagnosis of this melancholy condition, and may also be some prognostic guide. The average survival from onset to death is about 12 years.

Genetic counselling is essential if the disease is to be contained, and it is a painful task to warn family members of the risk to their offspring, and of course to themselves, but it *must* be done.

Creutzfeldt-Jakob disease

This extremely rare disease is included because of the interesting developments in understanding its cause. There is rapidly progressive dementia with marked motor and sensory impairment leading to multiple neurological signs, because of widespread cortical atrophy. The cause is apparently a slow virus, and passage through animals has been demonstrated. It is probably identical with the illness 'Kuru' affecting certain Pacific peoples who eat the brains of enemies.

Other pre-senile dementias

Many pre-senile dementias do not fit pathologically into any of the named illnesses above, and are often called 'simple' or 'non-specific' dementias. They lead to cerebral atrophy as do the others, and the clinical picture is no different.

General Paralysis of the Insane (GPI)

General Paralysis (or Paresis) is an inflammatory disease of the brain due to syphilis, coming on 10–20 years after the primary infection usually, and leading, if untreated, to spastic paralysis with profound dementia and death. It is commoner in men than in women, and only affects a small percentage of syphilitic patients.

In most patients mental changes precede physical disabilities, although Argyll-Robertson, or other abnormal pupil signs, are found quite early.

It is now a rare disease in the Western world, presumably because of the more efficient treatment of early syphilis. Nevertheless, a serological test for syphilis is essential in every patient being investigated for dementia. There are no particular mental symptoms which distinguish it from other dementias.

The cerebrospinal fluid shows characteristic changes in the Lange (colloidal gold) curve, and in the follow up after treatment the CSF should be studied at six months and one year, to confirm that the disease is inactive. Details of diagnosis and treatment should be sought in a neurological text.

The prognosis for mental recovery depends on the stage at which treatment is begun, as penicillin, or other appropriate antibiotics, will arrest the disease, and a fair amount of functional recovery will occur.

'Treatable dementia'

This somewhat paradoxical heading is to remind the reader that there are some conditions which lead to progressive dementia if untreated, but can be effectively treated if diagnosed early enough. If untreated the damage is permanent. It is therefore very important indeed to bear them in mind whenever confronted by a dementing patient, and to exclude them by careful investigation.

The conditions concerned include the following:

1. *Deficiency and metabolic disorders.* Hypothyroidism, deficiency of vitamin B_{12} and folic acid (and very rarely of other vitamins of the B complex), hyperparathyroidism and spontaneous hypoglycaemia if repeated. Uraemia may present as apparent dementia, as well as leading to confusional states.

2. *Space occupying lesions.* Primary and secondary tumours, subdural haematomata, and very rare conditions such as cysts or giant aneurysms.

3. *Others.* Syphilis and rare inflammations; normal pressure hydrocephalus. Unrecognised alcoholism is an important possible cause which should always be kept in mind, as alcohol can cause diffuse brain damage, irreversible after a certain stage. Very rarely chronic poisoning, for example, by lead or manganese might be responsible.

Remember that drug abuse, especially with benzodiazepines and barbiturates, can cause apparent dementia; and in the elderly severe retarded depression can produce a pseudodementia, as described in the chapter on Psychiatry in the Aged.

Differential diagnosis of dementia

It was emphasised at the beginning of this chapter that the mental effects of damage to brain tissue depend on the site and extent of the damage, and the rate of onset, and not on the pathology, except for the ways in which the pathology determines those factors. Clinically then, one can only diagnose 'dementia', and after that medical and neurological investigation is necessary to exclude a treatable cause. This is exactly parallel to the acute confusional states.

In an old and frail person, with a considerable degree of impairment, especially if there is a history of repeated small strokes, elaborate investigation is inappropriate. In younger people the opposite is true, and every effort must be made to see if one of the treatable conditions listed above is present. The difficulty comes with the patients in between 65–75 years of age, in deciding whether or not to investigate fully. The investigations are expensive, but not dangerous, now that Computer Assisted Tomography has replaced air encephalography and angiography for screening purposes. Thyroid function and a full blood count to exclude megaloblastic anaemia are worth doing even in the very old, along with routine studies of the urine and a chest X-ray. Occult infection makes many mildly demented patients much worse.

Brian biopsy is very rarely justified on clinical grounds, as there is a considerable morbidity.

Special investigations

It has been emphasised that the features of the mental state in organic brain damage are of little help in establishing the cause of the deterioration. 'Dementia' may be confidently diagnosed on clinical grounds, but in many cases further investigation is needed. Formal psychometric testing (p. 86) is commonly needed if the presence of dementia remains uncertain. Serial testing may be decisive. In the old, or when a history of cerebrovascular accident or head injury is obtained, it may be considered unnecessary to subject the patient to extensive investigation, but even in these cases a subdural haematoma may be suspected, and investigation may become desirable.

The physical investigations are those used in neurology and neurosurgery; and they are capable of demonstrating the presence of tumours or other space occupying lesions, vascular malformations, cerebral infarcts, and cerebral atrophy. They are always preceded by a full neurological examination, blood serology, skull X-rays, and often by a lumbar puncture.

Electroencephalography

Patterns of electrical activity in terms of frequency and amplitude vary with age, level of awareness and metabolic state, as well as with local cerebral disease. (Medication of the types used in psychiatry can alter records considerably.) In general the electroencephalograph (EEG) has little diagnostic specificity and early hopes for its especial application to psychiatry have not been fulfilled. No clinically useful correlations with emotion or thought processes have been discovered, though interesting research trends are appearing with more subtle recording techniques.

A single normal record does not exclude organic cerebral disease. On the other hand the finding of a grossly abnormal record in a psychiatric patient should make one hesitate to accept a condition as purely functional. Records taken from psychiatric patients show a higher overall incidence of mild and nonspecific abnormalities than are found in the population at large. More marked abnormalities are often seen in the records of psychopathic patients; these resemble the under-developed records of children and it has been postulated that these patients suffer from a failure of maturation of the brain. Severe and often unilateral abnormalities in the records of aggressive patients reflect possible structural disease of the temporal lobe and are sometimes associated with temporal lobe epilepsy. Some phasic mental disturbances may also have a basis in temporal lobe epilepsy. A special technique using sphenoidal electrodes for recording activity from the underside of the temporal lobe may be useful in these cases to provide evidence of pathology in a surgically accessible area.

The EEG now has an established place in the investigation of those cases in whom intellectual loss or clouding of consciousness suggest an organic pathology. It may provide valuable help in distinguishing primary from secondary dementia and in excluding the pseudo-dementia of the retarded depressive. In confusional states with paranoid ideas, a diffusely slowed EEG weighs the diagnosis in favour of an organic condition rather than schizophrenia.

In barbiturate takers and barbiturate coma the EEG shows a characteristic fast rhythm induced by these drugs. During the withdrawal phase from barbiturates, the increased tendency to develop fits is indicated by a lowered threshold for the appearance of epileptic activity during photic stimulation.

Finally occasional hysterical conversion states may be recognised with the EEG. A dominant rhythm responsive to light excludes blindness, and the appearance in the record of a cortical evoked response following auditory stimulation excludes deafness. A patient in a catatonic stupor or hysterical coma has a normal waking record.

EEG recording is simple and painless. With its limitations borne in mind it can be a valuable diagnostic aid in psychiatry.

Radioactive isotope scan

This method is also painless, but the patient must lie still for up to one hour, and it is therefore unsuitable for restless patients.

Radioactive tagged elements (e.g. technetium) are injected into the blood stream and the pattern of take-up in the brain recorded by means of a scintillation counter. Characteristic patterns or 'maps' of take-up are shown by different types of tumour, etc., and very clear demarcations of normal and abnormal tissue may be obtained.

Cerebral angiography

Radio-opaque materials are injected into the internal carotid, or other appropriate arteries. Serial X-rays taken with careful timing can then demonstrate various arterial and venous phases of the cerebral circulation. In addition to its value in the identification and localisation of tumours and vascular malformations, atheromatous and stenotic disease of the arteries may be demonstrated.

Brain biopsy

Needle biopsy of the brain may be performed through burrholes, and the material obtained examined microscopically. Tumour cells or the changes characteristic of various dementias may be identified.

Computer assisted X-ray tomography (CAT scanning)

This method has proved of very great value. The head is scanned by a beam of X-rays in a series of slices a few mm apart, and the relative density of tissue measured. A computer is used to print the data as a picture which is inspected by the radiologist. There is no discomfort or morbidity, but the patient must be able to lie still for about one hour. Recent results of CAT scanning in alcoholism and schizophrenia are referred to on page 331 and 131. CAT scanning has more or less replaced air encephalography in which air was injected into the cerebral ventricular system via a lumbar puncture or cranial burrholes.

7

Psychiatry in the aged

A separate chapter on this subject is justified by the special problems posed by the elderly, and by the vast numbers of patients concerned.

Old age begins officially at 65 years, for purposes of retirement for example, but at that age many people are still bright and lively, with active minds and bodies. Enforced retirement may have harmful effects, especially in those with few interests outside work. It leads to depression, and often to an apparent increased rate of ageing.

The earliest mental features of ageing are increasing forgetfulness for recent events, and especially for recently spoken words, with easy fatigue, lessened ability to sustain concentration, and an increasing 'rigidity' of mental processes. This is not just a rigidity of opinion and attitudes, but an inability to switch attention easily from one aspect to another and back again. Comprehension of complex matters and sound judgement may be preserved for a long time, but these also, along with other intellectual abilities, do decline as death of neurones proceeds. Ageing merges imperceptibly into senile dementia in those people in whom neuronal death progresses more rapidly.

Other psychological developments, as age increases, are intertwined with physical and social events. Bodily strength declines, degenerative arthritis, poor eyesight, deafness, shortness of breath, and other disabilities advance; the ageing person finds life increasingly difficult, and is increasingly confronted by mortality as friends and neighbours die. Most serious is the death of a spouse, and it is now firmly established that there is a major rise in morbidity and mortality, especially from heart disease, in the first six months after a spouse dies. Social isolation increases as time passes, intensified by the limits imposed by frailty, and often by relative poverty. In many the diet also becomes more limited and vitamin deficiences become quite common, especially in elderly widowers living alone.

Social isolation is not only due to the factors outlined above. Much depends on personality. The eccentric woman hater, always relatively isolated, becomes more so; and as senile changes progress he is more likely than others to become paranoid and disturbed, and thus to come early to the attention of the social or medical services. Those of warm and outgoing personality, and especially those who have kept on good terms with their now grown up children, are more likely to be visited, or taken to live with the family when appropriate. The awkward, demanding and over-critical are more likely to be isolated.

Others who become isolated easily are the shy and reserved, the unmarried for any reason — for example those who stayed at home to look after mother years ago. Those who have such close relationships with their spouse that the rest of the world has been excluded, in a kind of childlike dependence, also do badly after bereavement.

When people live alone, without any social 'feedback', abnormalities of personality become more and more marked, a development intensified by senile cerebral changes. There is often increasing egocentricity and hypochondriacal self-concern. Functional psychiatric illness is more common in those with abnormal personalities of all kinds, and is increased by social isolation and physical disease. Suicide, for example, is common in lonely old people with chronic painful diseases. Organic brain disease is equally common in people of all types, but in those with abnormal personality it is much more likely to lead to florid behavioural disturbances.

The social structure in which the person lives is also relevant to all this. Small cohesive groups offer more support to the bereaved and ill than do disparate individuals recently rehoused in tower blocks of flats. Small cohesive groups can, however, be very rejecting of the eccentric individual who has never fitted in.

Psychiatric morbidity in the elderly

There is a large and increasing proportion of old people in Britain and the other countries of the Western world. The 1971 census of England and Wales showed almost 6 400 000 over 65 years, of which almost 2 250 000 were over 75 years. The number over 65 years is increasing by about 15% per decade, which means an increase of almost one third between 1971 and 2000. There will, with recent birth rate trends, be relatively few younger people to support the elderly, services for which are already grossly inadequate. No adequate plans to cope with this problem have yet been put forward within the National Health Service.

The best estimates we have of morbidity suggest the following: In those over 65 years about 10% have some significant dementia, in half of them quite serious; 30% have significant anxiety or depressive symptoms — in some of long standing, but in many of recent onset — of whom few are receiving any treatment other than benzodiazepines (q.v.). Many of these elderly people have multiple pathology, with psychiatric disorders co-existing with cardiovascular, gastrointestinal, and other diseases. Those over 75 years have still higher morbidity, and are less likely to have a living spouse.

Depression in the elderly

This section should be read in conjunction with the chapter on Affective Disorders, in which the aetiology, clinical features, and treatment are described in detail.

Depression is very common in the elderly, but is often unrecognised and untreated, as for example, in those who have had strokes, many of whom are seriously depressed. Doctors tend to feel 'I would be depressed too, if I were like that', and therefore do nothing about it, although such patients can often be helped by antidepressants.

Too many elderly depressives are given benzodiazepines or other minor tranquillisers (p. 418) which help associated tension and anxiety, but may make the depression worse, and often cause confusion and unsteadiness.

Serious depressive illnesses, with retardation or agitation, produce a picture easily mistaken for dementia (so called depressive pseudo-dementia). The distinction is extremely important as spontaneous remission in serious depression in the elderly is rather uncommon, whereas treatment is often very successful. Dementing illnesses usually develop over months and years, whereas depression deepens over weeks and months. It is only in the final stages of depression that psychomotor agitation or retardation and withdrawal are so marked that they interfere with communication and cause mis-diagnosis. A history from a family member or close friend can be very helpful here.

In the demented, depressive mood is less sustained; and incontinence, deterioration of personal habits, and behavioural disturbances of all kinds are much more common. More serious and sustained depression can occur at times in early dementia, and well being can be improved with antidepressant treatment.

Treatment

The forgetfulness of the elderly is a big problem with drug treatment, and makes the use of monoamine oxidase inhibitors unwise in someone who lives alone and has memory difficulties. Electrical treatment

(ECT) tends to cause more memory disturbance in the elderly than in others, but may still be very useful, and so may tricyclic antidepressants. The elderly are prone to many disabling side effects with tricyclic drugs generally, including confusion, glaucoma, constipation (which can even develop into paralytic ileus), retention of urine, cardiac arrhythmias, and postural hypotension. If they are prescribed, small doses, such as amitriptyline 10 mg three times daily, should be used to begin, and the dose increased as side effects allow.

The tetracyclic drug, mianserin, is free of these side effects, is equally effective, and is in our opinion preferable. Dosage should start with 10 mg, and build up slowly to 40 or 60 mg daily. Other more modern drugs such as trazodone may also be tried.

Paranoid psychosis in the elderly

This section should be read in conjunction with the chapter on schizophrenia, especially pages 140–145. Paranoid psychoses in the elderly are common, particularly in those of suspicious and reserved temperament, and social isolation, especially that related to deafness, is often a factor. In some, there are classical 'first rank' symptoms of schizophrenia, but in others there are only persecutory delusions. Personality is usually well preserved, and the term 'paraphrenia' is often used for these states. There is no general agreement on terminology, unfortunately, but we suggest 'schizophrenia of late onset' when truly schizophrenic symptoms are present, and 'paranoid psychosis' when they are not. Treatment is as for schizophrenia, but the delusions are sometimes very resistant to treatment.

In some patients persecutory delusions are the first sign of a dementing illness; and paranoid features are common in confusional states and depressive illnesses.

Confusional states in the elderly

The most important diagnostic point here is to distinguish transient confusion from dementia, remembering that confusion is an integral part of advanced dementia (Ch. 6 on 'Organic States' should be consulted for the account of confusional states). The problem presents in those for whom no history is available, perhaps because they live alone, so the doctor cannot easily tell how long the patient has been disorientated and confused.

Confusion arises in those with and without some degree of pre-existent dementia, more easily in the latter. It can be due to any infection, especially urinary, to electrolyte imbalance from diuretics, head injury (elderly people are prone to fall), and numerous other causes; and very commonly to chest infections and heart failure. Careful physical examination and investigation is necessary.

A common cause of confusion in the elderly is drug intoxication. Normal doses of tricyclic antidepressants or benzodiazepines can lead to it; and too many patients have a large variety of drugs prescribed, often at different outpatient clinics. The very commonly prescribed hypnotic nitrazepam is often responsible. The bathroom cupboard may easily contain psychotropic drugs, diuretics, anti-inflammatory drugs for rheumatism, and painkillers. If the patient is already forgetful, mis-dosage is common, and confusion with added falls may develop.

Another cause of transient confusion, especially in those already slightly demented, is a major emotional upheaval — such as bereavement or a sudden enforced change of house, or admission to hospital. The death of a spouse may 'uncover' dementia, as mentioned later, but quite often upheavals and turmoil lead to confusion which settles down in a few days.

DEMENTIA

This section should be read in conjunction with the chapter on organic states (Ch. 6). The possibility of depressive pseudo-dementia, and of deterioration due to treatable causes, must always be remembered.

Senile dementia

Senile dementia is the commonest of all dementias, affecting about 5% of those over 65 and considerably more of those over 75 years. There is a marked hereditary element. Pathologically, senile dementia and Alzheimer's disease are indistinguishable, and they should be regarded as the same illness: the age 65 years being an entirely arbitrary division. Most cases start after 70 years. Microscopically neurones disappear, senile plaques and neurofibrillary tangles appear, and cerebral atrophy develops, with dilation of the ventricles and broadening of the sulci. The frontal lobes are affected early in many cases, with consequent early personality deterioration. There is much evidence to suggest that a defect of cholinergic transmission, associated with lessened choline acetyltransferase activity, is fundamental to the condition. This has led to attempts at treatment with choline and other appropriate substances, but so far without benefit.

Major emotional upheavals, such as the death of a spouse, often seem to precipitate the illness, but this is probably more a matter of 'exposing weakness' in that the patient is less able to cope with the stress, and therefore suddenly deteriorates.

The clinical picture is one of progressive deterioration of intellect and personality, in which memory disturbances are very prominent, but which affects all aspects of mental life sooner or later. These clinical features also apply to the pre-senile dementias.

The onset is typically gradual. Memory fails for recent events, the patient becomes slower, vitality diminishes, interests narrow, comprehension begins to lessen, emotional blunting occurs with increased egocentricity. There may also be emotional lability with unexpectedly easy tears or empty laughter. Irritability is common in short lived bursts, and any mental or physical task — even a call to join in a conversation — may lead to anxiety with tremor and restlessness, if the patient is unable to cope with it; and catastrophic anxiety (p. 78) may also develop in similar but more demanding situations. As the deterioration progresses it becomes less and less possible for the patient to get involved in any task, and therefore these distress signals of failure to cope diminish.

Sleep becomes disturbed, and the normal rhythm reversed, often leading to restless pottering all night. Very frequently, confusion increases at night to such a degree that the patient loses touch completely with time and place, and goes out for some imaginary appointment or to visit a long dead mother miles away. Such nocturnal wandering is dangerous, especially on cold winter nights, and is very worrying to relatives and neighbours. It is perhaps the single most common reason for referral for psychiatric care.

Personal standards and habits deteriorate. Early on there may be an unexpected and out of character sexual offence, such as exhibitionism or sexual interference with a child, as social inhibitions decline; and clumsy shoplifting or other theft might occur. Incontinence always develops at some stage, at first seemingly because the demented patient ceases to care where she empties her bladder, later because she cannot anyway find the way to the W.C., and later still, because all sphincter control is impaired. Habits of eating, personal hygiene, standards of dress, all deteriorate.

Memory loss leads to mislaid articles and misunderstandings, and persecutory delusions of a transient and poorly organised type are very common, more so in those of previously suspicious temperament.

There are usually focal disturbances at some stages, such as dysphasias and dyspraxias, but not so markedly as with arteriopathic dementia, and focal neurological signs do not occur. Visual, and less commonly, auditory hallucinations, and misinterpretations are common.

In some the illness advances very rapidly, so that within a few months there has been a total change of personality, and great physical weakness, and death follows soon. Others may endure for several years, especially if well cared for, although towards the end the patient may seem devoid of any mental life at all; hunched up, incontinent and inaccessible.

Arteriopathic dementia (Arteriosclerotic dementia, multi-infarct dementia)

This is the other type of common dementia in the old, although it can develop in younger people, especially if hypertensive. Clinically it may be indistinguishable from senile dementia, and in many there is microscopic evidence of both pathologies. Certainly in the later states the clinical description given for senile dementia applies here too, except that neurological signs are common.

In the classical form the most marked feature is that the illness has a sudden onset, with a 'little stroke' causing transient dysphasia, confusion, or weakness and unsteadiness, depending on the site of the lesion. The patient then improves quite quickly, although rarely returning completely to normal. Recurrent attacks, with lesions in different parts of the brain, lead to the step-wise deterioration classically described. There is a tendency for personality to be preserved more than in senile dementia, for any given degree of intellectual impairment. Focal neurological signs and specific psychological deficits due to local brain damage are almost invariable at some stage.

The pathology is not now regarded as primarily due to thrombosis in sclerotic arterioles in the brain. One cause increasingly recognised is micro-embolism due to clumps of platelets formed on the surface of atheromatous plaques in the major vessels of the neck or aortic arch. Aspirin lessens platelet 'stickiness', and is under trial as a long term treatment. A neurologist's advice should be sought before starting this regime. Peptic ulceration is a contra-indication.

Another cause of patchy infarcts in the brain, causing dementia, is failure of perfusion through seriously narrowed major arteries. Any episode of hypotension, as from a myocardial infarct, haemorrhage during an operation, a prolonged anaesthetic while sitting up in the dentist's chair, and so on, can lead to permanent brain damage and dementia. Great care must be taken in anaesthesia for the elderly for this reason.

Hypertensive encephalopathy, commoner in middle-aged people, can also lead to some degree of non-progressive dementia if prolonged.

Treatment of dementia

There is no drug treatment known to arrest the progress of these dementing illnesses, although aspirin may help in some cases of micro-embolism, as mentioned. Cyclandelate 400 mg three or four times daily is claimed to improve cerebral blood flow, and improve mental functions. Although there is no convincing evidence, in such grim conditions it is perhaps worth trying these drugs, so long as side effects are not troublesome.

Antidepressants (q.v.) can be very useful in relieving depressive states even in the demented who cannot describe their feelings verbally. A changed demeanour, improved sleep and appetite, and the disappearance of weeping, indicate that treatment has been helpful.

Paranoid disturbances can be helped by phenothiazines and thioxanthines as used in schizophrenia, but in smaller doses. Depot injections prevent accidental overdosage by the forgetful. Thus, 10 mg of flupenthixol or 12.5 mg of fluphenazine decanoate intramuscularly every two or three weeks may lessen suspicion and paranoid outbursts, and make the patient calmer and happier-seeming. Sometimes a paranoid old lady at home can in this way at least accept a home help or meals on wheels which she has been refusing.

Extrapyramidal disturbances develop easily in the elderly with brain damage, and the drugs should be stopped if they occur. Anti-parkinsonian drugs tend to cause their own side effects, and the correct amount is unlikely to be taken by a forgetful person, and so their use is not recommended except for occasional small intramuscular injections.

Care and management

Except in the more severely demented, who pass beyond response before they die, every attempt should be made to keep the demented person active, physically and mentally. Company, trips out, occupational therapy, music and simple games, are all helpful when pitched at the correct level. Those who can be cared for in the family are obviously most fortunate, and whatever chores they can cope with should be given to them.

A well balanced diet may need careful supervision. Bowel function is most important, as constipation is a frequent cause of mental disturbance and nocturnal restlessness in the demented, as well as leading to faecal incontinence from overflow. Both bowel and urinary incontinence can be helped by regular 'habit training' in hospital. Chiropody is another helpful adjunct, as feet become painfully neglected often.

Doctors must realise that one of the most useful functions they have in caring for these patients is in maintaining the morale of the family or staff who do most of the necessary work. If doctors do not show interest the level of care deteriorates, especially in large hospitals with heavy case loads.

For the patient at home, attendance at a day centre or day hospital, or 'holiday' admission for a few weeks as an inpatient, relieves the burden on the family, and can help a family to keep their demented relative at home. These services are considered in the next section.

In the terminal stages of dementing illness life can be preserved by vigorous treatment of infections and so on, but in our opinion this should not be done. In hospital the situation should be discussed with the nurses and the family, and an agreement reached that the patient should be allowed to die peacefully. (Pain and discomfort should always be relieved if possible). The feelings of the nursing staff must be considered seriously here. Those who spend their working life in psychogeriatric wards caring for the old people cannot just 'switch off' their attentions, and it may seem to them that this is what a decision to abandon certain forms of treatment implies. In Britain many nurses have entirely different cultural backgrounds to those of the medical staff, and they should not be expected to share attitudes which may seem to others self evident.

Services for the elderly mentally ill

Two parallel sets of services exist, those of the health and the social services, which should be harmoniously integrated.

The medical services start with the general practitioner, who can call on services from health visitors and district nurses, and can refer to, or ask for, a domiciliary visit by a psychiatrist, geriatrician, or other appropriate specialist. The patient can attend a day hospital, or become an inpatient. Community psychiatric nurses have an important role; they may be attached to the family doctor or to the psychiatric team.

The local authority Department of Social Services provides social workers and assistants, home helps, domiciliary occupational therapy, meals on wheels, attendance at social or luncheon clubs or at occupational day centres. Finally, they provide residential old people's homes (so-called Part III accommodation), some of which may also have a day centre function. Local authority homes vary a great deal in the amount of confusion and disturbance with which they can cope, whereas hospitals of course have to cope with the most disordered.

All the services mentioned above, which are aimed largely at keeping the old person more happily at home, are very seriously overstretched at present in the UK. There are many demented old people still at home who would be better off in hospital or a home, and whose families would also be much relieved.

8

Schizophrenia

The word schizophrenia, literally 'split mind', describes a range of mental disorders, and many students find the concept a baffling one, as such varying clinical pictures are given the same name. It does *not* mean the split personalities of Jekyll and Hyde type, who are usually psychopathic or hysterical, and a better analogy is of a widespread splintering or fragmentation of the mind.

The concept is perhaps best understood historically. Until German psychiatrists began their careful clinical studies with long term follow up in the 19th century, most of the mentally ill were lumped together as 'insane'. Many died of such illnesses as syphilitic General Paresis or because of lack of care or from concurrent infection; a great many deteriorated; and some recovered. By the end of the 19th century, building on the work of many others, Kraepelin had firmly established two major groups among those who did not die of organic brain disease — Manic Depressive illnesses and Dementia Praecox. They were distinguished essentially by the finding that the manic-depressives recovered, although they often relapsed; while those with Dementia Praecox did not, ending up in a characteristic end-state (the 'precocious dementia') despite rather widely varying patterns of early illness. The essential difference was therefore prognostic. Later Bleuler suggested the name 'the schizophrenias', and broadened the concept, leading the way to include patients who did not necessarily end up 'demented', but who share some of the characteristic signs and symptoms at the onset. We no longer use the plural, not all psychiatrists are in favour of the broader concept, and some have broadened it beyond useful limits.

It is important to realize that many psychiatrists abroad, particularly in the USA and USSR, would not share the views put forward here, and this should be remembered when reading foreign articles or books. That does not mean that our view is necessarily more correct — although we may think it so — but that conclusions about aetiology and treatment, for example, cannot be applied if the diagnostic criteria are different. In the USA, for example, patients are diagnosed as schizophrenic in some centres, especially those with a psycho-analytic orientation, who in Britain and continental Europe would be regarded as suffering from depression in a setting of personality disorder.

Schizophrenia should not be thought of as a single 'disease' with varying manifestations, but as a group of related syndromes which have important things in common. It may well be that varying causes for the syndromes will one day be clear, or that they represent different reactions, determined by constitution, to some common causative factors.

These syndromes are grouped together because they show similar disorders of thinking, emotional reaction, will power, motility, and similar types of hallucination and delusion. They are characterised by a marked tendency to drift out of contact with reality into an inner subjective world dominated by fantasy and delusion. Thinking becomes unrealistic and distorted and emotional reactions shallow and inappropriate. During the early stages the clinical picture may vary considerably from patient to patient. Frequently a gradual change of personality in the direction of increasing ineffectiveness, oddness or eccentricity is observed, often accompanied by non-specific symptoms that are apparently neurotic; but the onset may be sudden and the symptoms florid.

In those patients who do badly, a relentless progression sometimes occurs, and individual differences become less marked. In very severe cases, the end result is a characteristic form of profound mental deterioration, the patients living in a world of their own, unoccupied, inaccessible, and apathetic, but without that clouding of consciousness of true intellectual impairment which are seen in organic psychoses (p. 99).

In other patients, presenting similarly perhaps, the illness can remit entirely, leaving no apparent ill effects. In most there are various intermediate patterns, so that prognosis can be extremely varied. This is dealt with in more detail later in the chapter (p. 150).

Epidemiology

Schizophrenia is a very common illness, affecting about 0.8% of the population between the ages of 15 and 45 at some time in their lives. In 75% of cases the onset is between 17 and 25 years of age, but there is a smaller wave of increased incidence between 40 and 50. There are about 150 000 people with some disabling form of schizophrenia in the

United Kingdom now. It is rather more common in men than in women.

Until fairly recently approximately one quarter of all hospital beds in Britain were for schizophrenics, but modern treatment and changes in discharge policy have reduced this considerably. It is most often found in areas of social disintegration, poverty, and rootlessness, such as characterise urban centres, and particularly areas with many lodging houses such as are found near large railway stations. It is commoner in people working in semiskilled or unskilled occupations (social classes IV and V on the Registrar General's classification). However, these findings are due to the downward social drift of those who are developing schizophrenia, or who are already ill: the social class of the families of origin is distributed normally, and they have usually moved into the decayed urban area shortly before being admitted to hospital — the way they enter the official statistics. The illness affects people of all grades of intelligence. It occurs throughout the world, and has been found in all types of society which have been adequately studied.

Aetiology and pathology

Genetic aspects

Ideas about the relative importance of genetic and environmental influences in the development of schizophrenia have been changing recently. Older studies suggested concordance rates in identical twins as high as 90% if they had been brought up together, falling to 78% if they had been separated for 5 years. These figures were probably artificially raised because they were based on hospital statistics only, and overall it seems that the concordance rate in identical twins is about 45%. In non-identical twins it is about 10%, and is higher if they are of the same sex. The identical twin who develops schizophrenia seems often to have been smaller, weaker and less dominant from birth than his mentally healthier co-twin. Where one parent is schizophrenic, the chances of the illness developing in the children are 10 to 14%, rising to about 40% if both parents are schizophrenic. If a grandparent was schizophrenic, but the parent healthy, the risk to a child is only about 3% compared to the general population risk of about 1%. The risk for full siblings is 14%, and for half siblings about 7%.

These figures show the very great importance of hereditary factors, but leave much room for environmental influences, including, of course, the intrauterine environment.

Environmental stresses alone do not seem to lead to schizophrenia unless the basic genetic predisposition exists. This has been shown in long term follow-up studies of babies separated at birth from their mothers, who were mental hospital inpatients, and brought up in foster homes and orphanages. Only the children of schizophrenic mothers developed schizophrenia themselves, with a frequency of about 12%, a rate similar to that for children brought up in the home with a schizophrenic parent. Similar results have come from studying children who have been fostered from early infancy by other families. The fostered children of schizophrenic parents develop schizophrenia in about 10% of cases, whereas other fostered children do not, and nor do the biological children of the foster parents.

A schizophrenic hereditary loading is associated not only with an increased risk of schizophrenia, but also of character disorders and neurotic states, and there is some evidence of an increased incidence of people with artistic interests and talents among the relatives. The term 'schizophrenic spectrum' has been used to cover the wide range of presumed manifestation of the genes. The facts of schizophrenia heredity do not fit any simple genetic pattern of dominant or recessive genes, and there are probably several genes involved. In some people, the hereditary loading is so marked that they are almost certain to develop schizophrenia, however favourable the environment might be, but in most cases they inherit a character or personality vulnerability, which predisposes to schizophrenia in an unfavourable environment.

Environmental aspects

Genetic factors, although necessary, are insufficient to explain the development of the illness, as appears from the 45% concordance in identical twins. There is still uncertainty about the environmental stresses involved, although a good deal is known about the stresses which can lead to relapse in known schizophrenic patients. It seems reasonable to assume that similar factors affect the patient in his first illness, as in subsequent breakdowns, and clinical impressions support this idea.

Factors leading to relapse

Life events

Relapse in known schizophrenics often follows a few weeks after a build up of 'life events', as described on page 165 for affective illnesses.

Life events are defined in various ways in different research schedules, but essentially they include such matters as births or deaths in a family, loss of jobs, car accidents, a brother's marriage, jilting by a girl friend, move of house, and very many more. Known schizophrenic patients tend to be very vulnerable to such events, in which emotional experiences presumably lead on to neurochemical and psychophysiological changes — which then develop their own momentum, and lead on to a breakdown and the development of psychotic symptoms. In assessing the importance of precipitating life events, one must be careful to identify those which are the consequence of early schizophrenic deterioration, rather than a causal factor. For example, a young man might lose a job and a girl friend over to space of a few weeks *because* he is becoming ill, rather than become ill as a reaction to those stresses.

High 'Expressed Emotion' Another important factor known to lead to relapse, and almost certainly involved in the precipitation of first illnesses as well, is the nature of the family interaction. In families where much open criticism and hostility is expressed about the patient, relapse rates are higher. This is particularly true where the patient spends many hours of each week in close contact with family members. These factors explain, at least in part, why patients often do better in a hostel, or somewhere else less emotionally intense, and also show that the marked withdrawal from family life, and in fact from all emotional involvement, which is so characteristic of schizophrenia, may be serving a useful purpose. Medication, such as phenothiazines, lessens the relapse rate in these 'high expressed emotion' homes.

It is worth pointing out that the same relationship between high expressed emotion and breakdown often exists in the families of those who present with anxiety and depressive symptoms. In considering these findings one should remember that the target of the criticism has probably been behaving oddly, uncooperatively or notably unsuccessfully for a long time. The parents may have started without particularly critical attitudes, and may treat the more normal siblings quite differently. In other words, what looks like being 'the fault' of the parents may be understandable as the reaction of ordinary people to an extra-ordinary situation. Unfortunately, there is a clear vicious circle of worsening with more criticism, followed by even more criticism and so on.

Schizophrenic people on the whole do not cope well with emotional intensity of any type, and seem to live most contentedly within a rather narrow range of emotional and other environmental stimulation. What to many are the very things which make life worth living — love, responsibility, variety, a challenge — are to the schizophrenic an intolerable stress. They also tend to cope badly with too little stimulation, and the apathy and lack of willpower which so many chronic schizophrenics show, (the schizophrenic 'defect'), and which is such a problem in rehabilitation, is part of this. They tend to lack self-generated drive, and unless stimulated do very little.

There have been many claims that specific patterns of family relationship or mother-child interactions are related to the development of schizophrenia, but it is more likely that the effects are non-specific, in that any intense family conflict or disturbance is experienced as stressful, and those with a constitutional predisposition to schizophrenia become more liable to breakdown. Other children or family members might react differently, depending on temperament: some developing neurotic or depressive symptoms perhaps, but others coping more actively, for example by leaving home. Clinically, it is often apparent that the family life of a schizophrenic is difficult and full of resentment and tension, and the patient may do much better when he leaves home and enters the relatively neutral atmosphere of a hostel. The parents' reaction to an eccentric and later mentally ill child often leads to deterioration in the family relationships, and one or both of the parents may have personality abnormalities related to the schizophrenic heredity, if they are not themselves actually psychotic. In other cases one sees families where the parental reaction is excessively tolerant and protective, and the patient may regress and become more dependent and childlike than he might otherwise. Attitudes within the family can however be modified, as outlined on page 155.

It is our clinical experience that first attacks of schizophrenia, in those with a clear cut onset, often follow life events which, in others, would lead to feelings of depression: for instance, the loss of a girl friend or of a job, as mentioned earlier. In a good many of these patients, treatment with phenothiazines alone leads to the emergence of depressive mood after thought disorder and delusional ideas have settled down.

Although there is evidence that first attacks of schizophrenia are precipitated by such stresses as leaving home to join the army or go to college, it is important to note that there is no increase in schizophrenia among combatant troops, nor in prisoner of war camps. The environmental stress should be seen as precipitants of illness in vulnerable people, rather than the cause. By the time soldiers have gone through their initial training period, most of those predisposed to major mental illness will in fact have been weeded out. The guiding principles generally adopted in connecting the development of schizophrenia with traumatic events, e.g. in awarding war pensions, are (1) that the stress should have been demonstrably severe, and (2) that the symptoms should have followed shortly after the stress without a long latent interval.

Schizophrenia is commoner in the long term prison population, but this is due to the repeated offences of some schizophrenics, rather than to the psychic trauma of prison.

Psychophysiological aspects

There is a good deal of evidence that in schizophrenia there are raised levels of activity in some central and autonomic nervous system activities, especially in the ascending reticular activating system, producing quantitative or qualitative changes in 'arousal'. It is not just that arousal is generally raised, thus affecting all functions, but that some systems and functions are differentially affected, and the delicate balance of activating and inhibitory feed back systems disturbed. Skin conductance, heart rate, electromyography, finger pulse volume, and other measures have been used, and all show changes in schizophrenia.

Psychophysiological and psychological studies of the different ways in which the dominant and non-dominant hemispheres behave show quite marked differences between schizophrenics and others. There seem to be asymmetrical dysfunctions of various subtle types shown, for example, by tests which compare the ability of the right and left hemispheres to distinguish certain sensory stimuli or time intervals between stimuli.

Skin conductance can be shown to rise in the presence of a relative who is critical or hostile, and to fall with one who is more neutral emotionally. It is not only in acutely disturbed patients, where one would expect it, that high arousal is found, but also in chronically ill and withdrawn patients. Abnormalities of the galvanic skin responses have been shown to be present years before psychiatric breakdown in studies of the children of schizophrenics, who have been followed up after the testing. Children who did not break down later, but were otherwise well matched, did not show the same abnormalities. In this last study it was demonstrated that various perinatal complications seemed to be related to later schizophrenic breakdown, in these children with a schizophrenic heredity. This is a reminder that environmental influences begin very early in life, immediately after conception.

Studies of the *electroencephalogram* (EEG) in schizophrenia have so far been disappointing. Although there is general agreement that abnormalities of various types are present these might be reflections of the abnormal mental state rather than directly related to underlying causes of the illness. There has been a revival of interest in the subject recently with studies of cortical evoked potentials, the use of computerised techniques, and more careful clinical correlation with EEG findings. A recent study suggests that different schizophrenic subgroups have different EEG abnormalities.

Neuropathological studies in schizophrenia used to be very popular, but for several decades little work has been done in this field. Of the many claims made of histopathological changes in schizophrenia, none has been substantiated. However, cerebral tumours, especially those involving the limbic lobe, can produce illnesses indistinguishable from schizophrenia.

Computed Tomography in Schizophrenia Now that computed tomography (CAT scanning) has enabled us to demonstrate intracranial abnormalities painlessly and without complications, there has been a revival of interest in the old idea that schizophrenic patients have cerebral atrophy, with dilation of the cerebral ventricles. Many, but not all, recent studies have indeed demonstrated ventricular enlargement, but the subject is still not clarified. Some studies suggest that atrophic changes are commoner in those without a clear family history, suggesting that some cerebral disease or damage has precipitated the illness in those patients.

Biochemical studies in schizophrenia have waxed as neuropathological studies have waned. The findings that substances like mescaline and LSD (lysergic acid di-ethylamide) could produce states somewhat resembling acute schizophrenia without clouding of consciousness (unlike any other drugs known before), and that these substances had molecules related to those of adrenaline, was a powerful stimulus to research.

Currently much research centres on dopamine and dopaminergic pathways, largely because all neuroleptic drugs useful in schizophrenia have dopaminergic-blocking effects which are proportional to their potency against schizophrenic symptoms. It is thought that the meso-limbic dopaminergic pathway is that relevant to schizophrenia, and that effects on the nigro-striatal pathway, also dopaminergic, are responsible for the extra-pyramidal side effects of these drugs. Supporting evidence comes from the fact that dopamine releasing and dopamine-mimicking substances and amphetamines can cause a schizophrenic-like paranoid psychosis.

Against the theory are the lack of schizophrenic symptoms after laevodopa, the fact that Parkinson's disease, with low dopamine levels, can co-exist with schizophrenia, and various other inconsistent findings. There are at least two different types of dopamine receptors known at present, and there may well be more, which complicates matters.

Premorbid personality. Children who later develop schizophrenia are not only characterised by abnormal psychophysiological test findings. They tend to be nervous, conforming, quiet children, who work hard at school but achieve less than might be expected from their diligence. They also tend to be friendless and withdrawn, and they often gradually develop the so-called 'schizoid' personality which almost 50% of schizophrenics show before breakdown. (The schizoid personality is described on p. 214). In those patients in whom the schizophrenic illness develops gradually from a schizoid type of personality, so that one can hardly say when deterioration began, the prognosis is bad.

In other people the premorbid personality is not schizoid, but wayward and impulsive, unpredictable in reactions, easily anxious and upset, and generally vulnerable seeming. Yet others have normal seeming personalities, and in them the illness is usually of later onset and the prognosis is better. It is a general rule in psychiatry, certainly applicable in schizophrenia, that the more abnormal the premorbid personality the worse the prognosis.

In older people, especially those who develop paranoid schizophrenia or other paranoid states, the personality is often paranoid. By this is meant over-sensitivity, looking for slights, tending to blame others when things go wrong, and generally seeing the world as a hostile place, full of individuals and institutions who are out to do one down.

Although, as indicated above, environmental factors play a part in causation, no means of preventing the illness are known. In particular, there is no evidence that the development of child psychiatry in Child Guidance Clinics or individual psychoanalysis have any prophylactic value, although such evidence would be very hard to collect.

Parents should not be given the impression that they are to blame for the illnesses of their children, although it is helpful to try and lessen the family tensions and hostile criticism by discussion in many cases as mentioned later in this chapter (p. 155). On the other hand, as regards eugenics, many relatives of schizophrenics are haunted by fears for themselves and their children to an extent that is quite unjustified actuarially.

Schizophrenia seems sometimes to be precipitated by febrile

illnesses, childbirth, and occasionally by head injury. It is difficult to know how far these events may be causal or coincidental. For example, although schizophrenia seems to occur far more often after childbirth than during pregnancy, the actual incidence of puerperal schizo-phrenia* is much less than the incidence of schizophrenia unrelated to childbirth in women of child-bearing age. Further, an attack of puerperal schizophrenia may have been preceded and may be followed by confinements without psychiatric incident. In women with already existing schizophrenic illnesses, pregnancy and labour may be uneventful, but they may cope poorly with the child, owing to a general lack of drive, and may not be able to give emotional warmth or love because of the affective changes.

As far as head injury is concerned large scale studies show no more schizophrenia in the brain injured than in the normal population, except in those in whom there is temporal lobe damage. Temporal lobe epilepsy may produce illnesses very like schizophrenia, (see p. 98) and there is an overlap of the two illnesses in some way.

As the result of a careful study of the biography and background of individual cases, some understanding can be reached of the meaning of the symptoms to the patient, and this understanding can be a great help in establishing rapport, and thus in treatment and management. This is true, of course, of all disease. In our view psychological theories fail to account for the actual origin of schizophrenic symptoms, whatever light they may throw on the form that these may take.

Symptoms and signs

It has already been said that the schizophrenic disorders are a group of illnesses that have certain signs and symptoms in common, although not all of these are present at any one time in each patient, and some of them may never appear. The different forms are liable to have different modes of onset and to run different courses, as will later be described. We may consider the disturbances under the headings of signs and symptoms, as in general medicine, distinguishing those features which we observe, and of which the patient may be unaware, from those features of which he complains or which he describes.

---

*The student will sometimes come across references to 'puerperal schizophrenia', 'puerperal mania' and 'puerperal depression'. Sometimes these are referred to collectively as 'puerperal psychoses'. Puerperal psychoses are not special entities of their own. All that is meant is that the patient has had an attack of schizophrenia, or of mania, or of depression that happens to have been related to childbirth. See also page 169.

Signs in schizophrenia

The principal objective signs come under the headings of thought disorder; emotional disturbance; disturbances of will and volition; disturbances of motility; and withdrawal.

Thought disorder

A poverty of ideas and associations may be all that is noticeable at first, but a sense of sudden interruption or blocking in the stream of thought is more typical. Some patients experience countless non-identifiable thoughts rushing through their mind.

By 'thought disorder' we mean the manner in which thought is expressed, rather than any disturbed *content* of thought. Delusions, for example, do not count as 'formal thought disorder', and many deluded patients can think clearly and normally, and express themselves perfectly. Thought disorder is more a matter of disturbances of associations and a breakdown in the structure of sentences and even of words, as well as more subtle disturbances such as concrete thinking, described in this section. We tend to consider speech and writing almost exclusively as the ways in which thought is expressed, but of course, a person's actions can be, and often are, dictated by thoughts, and when a patient performs some bizarre or unexpected action, if asked to explain he might well produce a thought disordered reason.

Thought disorder can also affect mathematical and scientific logic, although only another mathematician is usually able to assess it properly.

The most important characteristic of schizophrenic thought disorder is a disturbance of associations, which can show in various ways. The term 'knight's move', taken from chess, indicates the way in which the schizophrenic can jump from one subject to another, apparently unrelated, because the intermediate thought or association has been suppressed. The opposite is even more common: associations which are largely irrelevant or tangential to the subject of conversation are not excluded, but are woven into speech, often deviating the patient from what he wants to talk about. For example, a young man talking about his boyhood in Cardiff, said 'I lived near Cardiff Arms Park, and we all used to go to the rugby internationals there, with a leek*. But that seemed to make it difficult to go on holiday because I

*Footnote for foreign readers: a symbol of Welsh national pride.

thought there was a leak in the boat when I went to Spain with my parents, and wanted to jump overboard.'

There are many varieties of schizophrenic thought disorder. Many patients show a vague and stilted wooliness in expression, so that the meaning is never exactly clear. Thus an early schizophrenic wrote: 'Poor people are entitled not only to the benefit of 'Education', because some of them don't need it, but also to compensation. I don't mean money they have lost, or not made the best of, but moral compensation as well — to reimburse them for what they have failed to obtain.'

The development of a gnawing anxiety that something may have gone wrong with one's mind because of an inability to understand what the patient is getting at, possesses some diagnostic value in schizophrenic thought disorder, particularly when it is coupled with a history of impairment in social efficiency or in social relationships and evidence that the method of expression exhibited has not been a lifelong characteristic. Conversation with schizophrenics is apt to continue without any progress being made and without the elicitation of definite facts, owing both to the patient's obscurity of expression and tendency to reply in vague, evasive generalities of the 'sometime', 'may be', 'yes and no', 'perhaps' variety. Schizophrenics tend not only to be woolly and vague, but woolly in an odd way, whilst occasional remarks demonstrate they are very much in touch.

Again, in certain instances the utterances of schizophrenics may appear not only bizarre but comic as well, yet what may sound like a joke was not meant to be one. This arises from an inability on the part of the patient to separate the abstract from the concrete and to distinguish clearly between metaphors and facts. For example, a schizophrenic girl, when asked why she was turning round in a circle, replied that she felt she was in a knot and was trying to unravel herself: and a schizophrenic sailor seriously maintained that in his opinion, or rather experience, the brain was divided into three parts, second sight for'ard, understanding amidships and memory aft, adding that the top of the mind should be kept empty in order to have a place to air one's views.

The 'concrete' thinking of the schizophrenic can be tested by asking the patient to explain the meaning of a proverb, such as 'people who live in glass houses should not throw stones'. All proverbs are about human life, but a thought disordered schizophrenic might well explain this one by saying 'of course they shouldn't, they'll break the glass'. Similar concrete answers can be given by brain damaged people, and the test is inappropriate for people of below average intelligence, or those for whom English is not their first language.

From the subjective point of view, schizophrenic patients may, in the early stages, complain of difficulty in concentration. Many such patients turn their attention to subjects that lend themselves to vague speculations, such as mysticism and spiritualism, and so-called philosophy and psychology; and this if often interpreted as an over-compensation for their vaguely felt incapacity. But when the thought disorder becomes worse, the patients usually lose insight gradually. The thought disorder colours the various delusional systems, and contributes to the misleading appearance of intellectual impairment.

The elements of language may be well preserved, but various mutilations of individual words may occur, so that the verbal production of these patients may resemble that of an aphasic. In the most severe stages, language is disintegrated into a sequence of incomprehensible syllables and neologisms ('word salad').

In the early stages there is often an inclination for highbrow, odd or artificial expressions (mannerisms of speech), and the newly coined words or neologisms that appear later usually result from the patient's urge to describe his experiences, for which purpose an ordinary vocabulary is inadequate. The neologisms invented can be ingenious, e.g. 'teleognosis'.

It is quite common for patients to be able to converse sensibly on some neutral topic, and yet to become thought disordered as soon as important personal matters are touched on. It is not as though the patient deliberately screens himself from distress, but more as though a rise in inner tension (or 'arousal') alters cerebral function so that thought disorder appears. When drug treatment controls thought disorder in acute schizophrenia, depression and anxiety are often revealed.

It should be clear that it may be impossible to distinguish mild thought disorder with certainty from the woolly vagueness, for example, which many mentally well people demonstrate. Similarly, anxiety will often make people think less clearly, or even cause temporary thought block, as in interviews or examinations. Severe thought disorder is unmistakeable, but when mild it cannot be relied on as a diagnostic aid. (see p. 148)

Emotional disturbance

The most characteristic change in emotion ('affect') in schizophrenia is a loss of normal responsiveness, leading to what is called *flat* affect; less commonly there is an inappropriate response, the so-called *incongruous* affect, as for example, when someone smiles when you would expect him to be sad. Both represent a loss of normal emotion, and they tend to be later developments.

In the early stages of schizophrenic illnesses marked anxiety and depression are frequent, although they may not be clearly expressed, but hidden behind an expressionless or even incongruous mask. If the patient is asked to describe his feelings in writing, or to fill in a questionnaire, for example, it may become apparent how bad he feels behind his blank facade. Sudden suicide attempts may also be made by people who seem detached and uncaring. Later in the course of the illness, and less often early in it, the real loss of affect and true 'flatness' or 'incongruity' develop. The inability to express emotion clearly is associated with rather immobile features, lack of gesture, monotony of voice, withdrawal from others and often an inability to hold eye to eye contact. It is important to realise when dealing with a schizophrenic patient that you may not know 'how he feels' in the ordinary sense of that phrase, which is an important part of the difficulty there often is in establishing rapport. It is worth pointing out that in Parkinsons disease it is easy to miss even severe depression, because of the immobile face, paucity of gestures, monotonous voice, and so on. In a schizophrenic patient in whom drug induced Parkinsonism has developed, there is a further difficulty in assessing the emotional state, but the difficulties described occur in those who have never had medication.

A schizophrenic illness often starts with unspecific, vague, emotional disturbances. The patient becomes irritable, over-sensitive or depressed, sometimes in reaction to an upsetting experience, sometimes without any demonstrable external cause. Relatives often say that he has become 'more difficult'. He becomes casual, sometimes flippant, often unpredictable in his responses. He may become rude, aggressive, suspicious. He may show a callous brutality and even commit brutal crimes, showing no emotional concern when caught. A mixture of hyper-sensitivity and detachment may be a very striking feature. The loss of emotional rapport may often be felt by friends and relations before it becomes clearly manifest in the patient's behaviour, and even good observers may find it extremely difficult to describe it in terms of specific illustrations or actual happenings. Even after a psychiatric interview nothing more tangible may be left than the feeling of a glass wall between the patient and the interviewer.

In other instances the patient may be able and willing to give an introspective account of his change and may be pathetically aware of the gradual loss of his emotions. In some cases the change is experienced as a loss of feeling in the perception of the outside world:

the sunshine has become less bright, the flowers less colourful, people's faces less lively; in psychiatric terms, the syndrome of depersonalisation and derealisation may occur at that stage. In other early cases, and more often in advanced cases, the loss of normal emotional response is disguised by a silly, cheerful indifference, and an empty giggling is one of the most often seen affective disturbances. This indifference or fatuousness is often the main feature of the typical incongruity and inadequacy of affect of the fully developed case. This emotional disturbance may be shown by the behaviour, e.g. if a patient laughs when talking about serious topics, gets violent on trivial provocation, gets dirty, neglects his clothing and fails to be ashamed when his attention is drawn to it; or if he exposes himself, or masturbates in public, as deteriorated cases do.

But in other cases the disturbance is much more subtle, and, in assessing it, one is up against the patient's (and his relatives') tendency to rationalise it, and one has to consider very carefully what emotional reaction would be appropriate in the light of the patient's normal (i.e. pre-morbid) personality. As with many other symptoms, it is the change of his reaction, as seen against his past, that is of real significance.

In those patients who do badly, emotional shallowness, progressive apathy, and loss of interest are associated with the patient's increasing withdrawal from contact with the outer world, so that he becomes more and more solitary, self-absorbed and frequently hypo-chrondriacal, until finally he appears to live entirely in a world of his own. Even in those who do well otherwise, there may be some lasting flattening of affect, with a detachment from others and their feelings.

Disturbances of will and volition

'Lack of energy' is a frequent complaint in the early stages of the illness. Friends and relatives may describe the patient's poverty of initiative, loss of drive, lack of decision and determination. More often such disturbances must be inferred from the description of the patient's behaviour and mode of life. His work history is often the best indicator. A psychopath may frequently change his job because he quarrels with his superiors or workmates, but an early schizophrenic can give no adequate reason for such changes or, if he does, his reasons are illogical or coloured by his abnormal emotional condition.

More characteristic still is a gradual downward trend in the type of work the patient is given by his employers. There is often no gross negligence or misconduct, just a very slow falling off of that initiative and spontaneity required in independent and responsible work. This deterioration may be so gradual that nobody can date its onset; it may go on for years until such a patient, without ever having shown more dramatic symptoms, is found sitting about the house doing nothing or ends up as a tramp, drifting about the world without aim or purpose.

When the loss of initiative and spontaneity becomes more profound, and when it affects more primitive biological functions, it leads to those chronic conditions once a feature of mental hospitals — immobile figures sitting or standing about the wards. These states are now much less often seen, because patients are not left without occupation or stimulation as they used to be.

Disturbances of motility (catatonic disturbance)

There are several different types of motor disturbance, but they can be put under the two main headings of acute and chronic. They are all generally much less frequent and severe than they used to be because of earlier and more appropriate and effective treatment, although older patients with chronic catatonic disturbances are still common in mental hospitals, having had less effective treatment on admission decades before.

The common forms of acute catatonic disturbance are either extremes of overactivity (catatonic excitement) or of underactivity (stupor). Both are associated with very high levels of autonomic arousal, and can be precipitated by some form of rough handling, such as can happen when a patient is taken compulsorily by the police to hospital. The patient is in fact usually terrified, often by the strange mental experiences he is undergoing, such as hallucinations or passivity feelings (see below), in combination with the situation in which he finds himself. A state of stupor can switch to one of excitement suddenly and patients may become destructive, noisy, or aggressive without apparent motive. These sudden outbursts of activity are sometimes carried out in obedience to hallucinatory voices, but in other instances patients who are able and willing to provide information can give no reason for them. As one girl said: 'It's just as much of a surprise to me as it is to you', and she adhered to this even after recovery.

The patients may adopt strange attitudes, or peculiar positions, apparently expressive of such states as terror or ecstasy, or they perform wild and apparently purposeless, incomprehensible, movements. The movements themselves are often not performed with the normal degree of precision and coordination.

The chronic catatonic states do not have the same emotional disturbances behind them. They are mainly stereotyped repetitions of curious movements, such as knocking, rubbing or rocking, but may be more complex, and sometimes seem to hold in themselves the distorted reflection of some old purposive activity.

There are often disturbances of muscular tone, and a stiffness or awkwardness or lack of normal gracefulness is present; and with tic-like additions and distortions bizarre mannerisms develop. There is often also facial grimacing, commonly including a marked pursing and pushing forward of the lips. Some awkwardness and mannerisms may persist even after otherwise good recovery.

In other instances there may be a sustained increase of tone so that fixed postures are maintained for long periods, and, if these are deliberately altered by someone else, the patient will retain a new position. This state is known as *flexibilitas cerea*. If flexibilitas cerea is combined with stupor the result is *catalepsy*.

As with the disturbances of volition, these disturbances of motility are sometimes projected and rationalised, in that they may be attributed to the effect of outside influences and sometimes to that of hallucinatory voices.

Withdrawal and introversion

These go together almost always, and are an important aspect of schizophrenia, present in nearly all patients at some stage. They are especially prominent in slowly developing illnesses of poor prognosis, and, combined with the characteristic apathy, lead to patients just sitting on their own, often lost in a dream world of fantasy. The degree of withdrawal shown is often extreme, as with two patients who had been in the same ward, with adjoining beds, for over ten years, but did not know each other's names.

Symptoms in schizophrenia

The symptoms of schizophrenia can be put under the main headings of *delusions; hallucinations* and other perceptual disturbances; and *passivity experiences* and related phenomena.

(1) *Delusions* do occur in other psychotic conditions, although much less often than in schizophrenia. They have little diagnostic value in schizophrenia unless they are *primary or 'autochthonous'*.

The essence of primary delusions is that they appear suddenly, fully developed with an unshakable quality of conviction, without any logical connection with the immediate environment or circumstances at the time. They are often preceded by a strange feeling that the world is full of some hidden secret or mystery, or that things are charged with hidden meaning (delusional atmosphere). A chance observation or remark is immediately realised to have an intense personal significance or meaning. The traffic lights turn green in succession — this can only mean he is a Royal Personage; a piece of paper torn up — this means the unsuccessful destruction of a letter from the husband's mistress, and so on. The term 'delusional perception' is used for that moment in which some apparently natural event is misinterpreted or perceived strangely by the schizophrenic. (See also p. 148 for Schneider's 'first rank' symptoms).

So called *secondary delusions* are also common. They are delusional misinterpretations of something experienced, and they explain the experience. For instance a nasty taste in the tea means that it has been poisoned; abdominal pain and constipation indicate that the bowels have been blocked by a piece of plastic inserted by the doctor overnight. Secondary delusions can also occur in severe depression, or with organic states.

The degree of systematisation and elaboration of the schizophrenic delusions depends to a large extent on the severity of the co-existing thought disorder. Delusions of persecution, often by political or religious bodies, are the commonest, followed by hypochondriacal delusions, typically with a bizarre quality, and delusions of jealousy, grandeur or self accusation. Favourite themes are the erotic, the philosophical, the religious, the mystical, the political and the hypochondriacal, frequently strangely combined often with a paranoid or grandiose colouring and backed up by misinterpretations of the most varied kinds, involving pictures or advertisements in the newspapers or what is heard on the radio.

Delusions of reference are extremely common, in which the patient is convinced that, for example, the television news contains secret messages about him, newspaper headlines are giving him hints as to what he should do, and so on. Very similar delusions can occur in depressive states, and so these do not have great diagnostic value.

The patient's attitude to his delusions is typical in that he does not usually react appropriately and thus will go to his doctor when it would have been more logical to have gone to the police.

(2) *Hallucinations* of any of the senses may be found; but auditory hallucinations are the most frequent and characteristic (p. 57). Their clarity varies. Some patients are able to describe the character of the voices in great detail and the impression may be so vivid that the patient answers hallucinatory questions and discusses the statements

of his supposed interlocutors. Other patients, although they are immediately aware of what the voices say, cannot repeat the exact words or otherwise describe the sensory character of their experience. The voices are generally disagreeable, threatening, aggressive, and abusive, and frequently make allusions to sexual matters. Sometimes the voices give orders that are often carried out to the letter, and hence it is always important to determine what hallucinatory commands are received.

The most characteristic voices are those which talk about him, argue about him, or comment on his actions in the third person. These are only found in schizophrenia, whereas voices talking *to* the patient may occur in severe depression and in some organic states.

Another characteristic type of schizophrenic hallucination occurs when the patient hears his own thoughts, either immediately before he has conceived them (they are 'dictated to him'), or simultaneously with the process of thinking, or immediately afterwards ('echo of thoughts'). In later stages the voices become more incoherent and incomprehensible, and neologisms often appear. Voices sometimes develop from obsessional thoughts; these increase in vividness, as if they were heard, and finally they are being heard 'inside the head' (pseudo-hallucinations) until they are finally experienced as coming from outside.

Visual hallucinations in the strict sense of the word are rare, at least in Western cultures. Disturbances of visual sensation and perception are not so uncommon in the early stages of the illness. The vividness of visual perception increases or decreases; faces or objects change shape, appear distorted. True visual hallucinations in acute stages of the illness are sometimes described as small images or pictures, often distorted or bizarre, flashing through the visual field. In rare cases of religious-ecstatic excitement the beginning is sometimes marked by one overwhelming vision of Christ or God in His Glory, or of something else appropriate to that particular person's culture and beliefs.

Complex and organised visual hallucinations, such as of living figures or identifiable objects, strongly suggest an organic state, like delirium tremens, and not schizophrenia. The diagnosis of schizophrenia should not be accepted in such a patient until thorough investigation has excluded organic causes.

'Pareidolic' illusions are not uncommon in the last stages of the illness when the patient, withdrawn and autistic, allows his phantasy freer play, and sees faces, people, and monsters in the clouds, wall-surfaces, etc.

Hallucinations of taste, smell and touch are often woven into the delusional systems or are quoted to confirm it. Bodily sensations such as tinglings and 'shooting' feelings are quite common, and genital hallucinations occur, which the patient may interpret as meaning that sexual intercourse has taken place. Hypochondriacal delusions of a bizarre nature are often combined with hallucinatory and passivity experiences. For example, one middle aged patient has almost continual complaints of suprapubic pain which he insists is due to being stabbed inwardly by a scythe, wielded by a tiny woman inside his bladder, who does it to prevent him marrying.

(3) *Passivity experiences and related phenomena.*These are very common in early schizophrenia, and are found only in that illness, so they have great diagnostic value. In chronically ill patients they may not be described.

True passivity experiences are those in which the patient is aware of some outside power or force, human or non-human, influencing his own thoughts, feelings, reactions or bodily activities. It is a direct experience, not an 'as if' feeling. There are no words which can easily describe these experiences, so analogies are used: 'it's like telepathy' or 'hypnosis', or 'cosmic rays affecting the brain' or 'it's like being a robot'. It is not surprising that secondary delusions grow up around these strange and frightening feelings.

Related experiences are those in which the patient's own thoughts and feelings seem to leave his mind so that they can be 'picked up' or 'read' by others (thought broadcasting); or taken away from his mind (thought withdrawal); and the experience of having some other thought or idea slipped into the mind from outside (thought insertion). Very often nowadays schizophrenic patients believe that their thoughts are being electronically recorded somewhere, an idea which, like many others, clearly shows the influence of a changing culture on the content of delusions.

Clinical forms of schizophrenia

The well known classification into Simple, Hebephrenic, Catatonic, and Paranoid schizophrenia has been largely abandoned, because of the marked overlap between the sub-types, and because at different stages the same patient might fall into different sub-types. A brief outline of them is, however, given here because they have some historical interest, and because the term paranoid schizophrenia and the related terms paraphrenic and paranoia are still used, sometimes loosely.

(1) *Simple schizophrenia (schizophrenia simplex).* This term was used to describe those patients in whom there was a very gradual onset of personal deterioration, eccentricity, loss of affect and of drive. They do not have the characteristic symptoms, only some of the signs, of schizophrenia. Bleuler, who popularised the concept (and introduced the word schizophrenia), included in it the eccentric and 'schizoid' relatives of schizophrenics; and many vagrants and 'drop-outs' were thought of as belonging to this group. It is rarely diagnosed nowadays, because of the impossibility of distinguishing it confidently from personality disorder, the effects of alcohol, a life of vagrancy, and so on. It is a term better not used in our view.

(2) *Hebephrenic schizophrenia.* This is characterised by onset at about puberty, with affective flattening and incongruity, with marked thought disorder, and a poor prognosis. Some cases begin suddenly, with marked depression or anxiety, but hebephrenic deterioration sets in later.

(3) *Catatonic schizophrenia.* In this group catatonic disturbances are prominent, onset is later than in hebephrenia, usually with an acute onset of stupor or excitement, or of perplexity; and impulsive acts, often violent, are common. As mentioned earlier, catatonic motor disturbances are usually associated with great fear or terror, and frightening hallucinations and delusions are common. There may be difficulty in distinguishing catatonic excitement from mania at times. Prognosis is uncertain, some patients doing very well.

(4) *Paranoid group* These psychoses are the latest in onset, the majority of them starting in the fourth or even fifth decade. They begin with paranoid ideas, and the development of hallucinations completes the picture. The delusions are not generally systematised, and various delusions often co-exist without being related or combined. The discrepancy between the grotesque delusions, the terrifying hallucinations and the poor emotional response which they evoke, is often very striking, and this may enable the patient to have some insight into his condition. Thus, he may complain: 'I am suffering from ideas of persecution'; and a German paranoid schizophrenic wrote to his physician during the war: 'I have been given the Iron Cross. The schizophrenic indifference is appreciated in the front line.'

The name *paraphrenic* has been given to those sufferers from paranoid psychoses who, in spite of more or less systematised delusional ideas and in spite of hallucinations, yet retain their personality in a relatively intact state. Thus, the patient may show few symptoms of withdrawal or thought disorder, and the emotional rapport may remain strikingly good. Paraphrenic psychoses begin later in life than the other paranoid psychoses, often at the time of the climacteric or the beginning of the involutional period. The preservation of the personality may be due either to the fact that the pre-psychotic personality was resistant to the development of the illness, or to the late onset, or due to both reasons. Apart from actual paraphrenia with its tendency to systematised delusions, more loosely organised paranoid states of a more variable kind appear quite commonly in the old age groups and may yield to treatment.

The term *paranoia* was used by Kraepelin to denote those cases whose personalities were essentially preserved, and whose delusional systems developed insidiously and by logical steps in an essentially systematised way, such development being unaccompanied by hallucinations. Paranoia, in this sense, is no longer regarded as a special clinical entity, but rather as an incompletely developed form of paraphrenia. The delusions of these patients are commonly grandiose as well as persecutory, so that they may believe themselves descended from royalty or other exalted personages, or believe that they are prevented from holding titles or high office through the machinations of eminent persecutors. Thus, though the term *paranoid* essentially implies hostility and resentment, the term *paranoiac* connotes megalomania and grandiosity with which hostility and resentment are usually combined.

Some paranoiacs live at liberty as queer inventors, founders of eccentric sects, or as apostles of peculiar social reforms; many are ultimately admitted to mental hospitals because of some friction with society. Owing to the preservation of the personality, the firm belief in their own delusions, and the logic of their well-systematised reasoning, paranoiacs are often capable of persuading others of the righteousness of their cause. This is specially likely to arise when the paranoiac lives alone in secluded circumstances with a submissive partner; the latter may then come to share the delusions, a condition known as *folie á deux*. The number of people who share the delusions is, of course, not necessarily restricted to two, but depends upon the circumstances. When such a state of affairs comes to light, with resultant separation of the parties concerned, the secondary sufferers from the condition readily recover through the corrective effect of mingling with more normal people, although the real sufferer from the disease does not.

Pseudo-neurotic schizophrenia. This is a term mainly used in the United States, to describe patients with severe personality problems, difficulties with and anxieties about nearly all aspects of life, with rigid and insightless views, and not responding appropriately to psychotherapy. As described it does not really fit into European ideas about schizophrenia.

Schizo-affective psychosis. This is considered on page 151.

The definition and diagnosis of schizophrenia

Definition

As mentioned near the beginning of this chapter, there are marked differences of attitude towards schizophrenia and what the term means, in different countries and different centres. It must be accepted that these are no hard and fast rules, no exact boundaries, and of course, we have no solid basis in known organic pathology or aetiology. It is most important therefore that we do have a clear understanding of our limitations, and that when we are setting up a drug trial or comparing prognosis in different cultures, for example, we make clear the diagnostic criteria used.

There are two main diagnostic attitudes and corresponding criteria at present used in the Western world, with various local elaborations. One takes into account the longer term disturbances of emotion, loss of will power and so on, but for diagnosis of the newly presenting case, emphasises the characteristic acute symptoms as represented, for example, by *Schneiders first rank symptoms* (see p. 148). These have the great benefit of being easy to identify as absent or present, and, it is worth noting, respond extremely well to the types of medication which are currently used. Schneiders criteria therefore offer a very practical diagnostic approach in terms of immediate treatment, are simple to use, and have high reliability in the sense that several observers will independently agree closely on the absence or presence of the first rank symptoms.

The principal disadvantage of an approach based on acute symptomatology is that many patients with acute and florid psychoses may have Schneider's first rank symptoms, and yet may in other ways be regarded as suffering from hypomania or mania, with elation, overactivity and so on, and may have major mood swings of bipolar type (see p. 189). Treatment with phenothiazines and lithium together is likely to be helpful in those most closely resembling hypomania. The prognosis in these acute 'affect laden' illnesses is very much better than in schizophrenia of insidious onset with early loss of normal affect.

The other major approach is in essence a return to Kraepelin's original view of Dementia Praecox: that is of a condition which always led to deterioration of some degree. In the United States, where in many centres there has been a powerful movement away from a psycho-analytic view of psychoses to an older 'European' view, this has led to criteria (such as those of Feighner and certain research criteria) in which evidence of chronicity and of some permanent defect is required before a diagnosis of schizophrenia can be accepted. The use of these criteria does mean that in a study of treatment or of any other aspect of schizophrenia, no patients with basically affective illnesses, will be included. There is, however, an element of circular argument in it: because advances in treatment of acute schizophrenic illnesses will not be recognised as such, since by definition a schizophrenic must be chronically ill and have a defect. There is no simple way out of this maze. The present author believes that it is most practical to use the acute criteria of Schneider, with a proper awareness that there is a border zone with the affective illnesses, indicated by the use of the term schizo-affective (see p. 151), 'affect laden', or 'schizophreniform', terms which are more or less synonymous.

Diagnosis

A distinction must be made between schizophrenic *symptoms,* which may occur in numerous psychiatric conditions, and schizophrenic *illnesses.* The mere presence of symptoms, often rather loosely called schizophrenic, such as paranoid delusional misinterpretations and catatonic phenomena, does not necessarily mean that the patient is suffering from schizophrenia; the former can occur in depressions and the latter in organic disease. Again, there are many paranoid personalities, suspicious, touchy, ready to take offence, who feel unwanted and that the world is against them, who are not suffering from schizophrenia.

One serious difficulty is that several of the most important features of schizophrenia are often difficult to identify with confidence in the early stages, particularly thought disorder and affective and volitional loss. For example, a girl who giggles as she gives a muddled account of some physical disorder to her doctor may be showing incongruous affect and thought disorder; or she may be a nervous and shy girl, too embarrassed to speak about the problems she intended to discuss with him. An adolescent boy who moons about the house all day, who avoids his old friends, plays records for hours at a time, and keeps promising to get a job but never makes the effort, may be developing the withdrawal and volitional loss of schizophrenia. He may instead be suffering from depression, or may be taking drugs, or there may be serious problems in the family to which he is reacting.

First rank symptoms

There are however a number of very clear cut 'first rank' symptoms on which a diagnosis of schizophrenia can be made with fair confidence in the early stages, so long as there is no clouding of consciousness of organic type, and so long as no psychotomimetic drugs such as LSD have been taken. These first rank symptoms (a term introduced by Kurt Schneider) are not indicators of outcome, nor are they important in the life of the patient and his family in the way in which, for example, loss of affect is important. The term 'first rank' refers only to their usefulness in diagnosis.

They are diverse in quality, but some of them are naturally related to each other. *Primary delusions,* which have been described on page 140, are frequently preceded by a period, lasting days or weeks, in which everything seems strange and perhaps threatening, in which the world seems full of mystery and hidden meaning. This is the so-called *delusional atmosphere.* Suddenly, the patient perceives something which makes everything clear — he sees a blackbird hop across the garden and knows that therefore the earth and sun will collide in a hundred days; or sees the milkman wave at the neighbour across the street, and knows that this means that he has passed the test to be relayed into outer space. That is *delusional perception* — the object or event witnessed is not an hallucination, but it is given a special delusional significance. The characteristic schizophrenic hallucination is of *voices in the third person,* talking about him, commenting on his actions, and often conversing about him.

Another group of first rank symptoms can be regarded as evidence of disturbance of the 'ego-boundary', that awareness of the boundary between ourselves and the outside world and people. The schizophrenic has experiences which transgress that boundary: he feels that other thoughts or powers get into him, and make him do things, think things, feel things, which are alien to him. These are *passivity feelings,* and are extremely common in early schizophrenia. Various terms such as *made feelings* and *made thoughts* refer to these. In addition to alien intrusions he may feel his own thoughts and emotions leaving him in various ways. Thus there may be *thought broadcasting* and *thought withdrawal,* while *thought insertion* is the opposite, and has the quality of a passivity experience. An uncommon and unrelated symptom is *echoing thoughts,* in which the patients own thoughts seem to be spoken, in his head or outside it, just before or after he actually thinks them. These are not usually experienced fully as hallucinations, that is as a real voice coming from outside, but more as a half spoken thought.

Other useful diagnostic features

Another important diagnostic point is the lack of insight many patients show into the abnormality of their behaviour, which is neither explained nor excused by the schizophrenic as similar behaviour would be by others.

In taking the history, careful enquiries should be made as regards increasing introversion and emotional indifference or shallowness. Has the patient done less and less? Has he seemed increasingly vague and dreamy? Has it seemed difficult to get at what he is driving at? In order to establish the diagnosis of a progressive schizophrenia, it is necessary to discover whether the personality of the patient has changed in a schizophrenic way that cannot be accounted for by environmental or developmental factors. The more extroverted the previous personality, the more noticeable will be a change towards introversion, seclusion and emotional shallowness and detachment. The greatest difficulties arise in sensitive, shy, shut-in personalities, and in such the nature of the disease is seldom recognised except in retrospect, unless the unrealistic or bizarre quality in the complaints or behaviour betrays their schizophrenic origin at the time of their occurrence. Here again the lack of insight, as shown by lack of explanation, of excuse, or of realisation of the need for these, possesses diagnostic value.

The early presenting symptoms may be of a non-specific kind and resemble those of a state of anxiety or depression; and the true diagnosis may be only permitted or suggested through the development of additional symptoms, especially passivity feelings, hallucinations or primary delusions. Sudden inexplicable behaviour, anti-social or not, that seems senseless or startling should always suggest schizophrenia, so long as it is not obviously gainful.

Amphetamines may produce illnesses very like paranoid schizophrenia, and so may psychomimetic drugs like LSD (see p. 349). Rarely, schizophrenia-like pictures may develop in physical illnesses with some confusion (in the organic sense), or clouding of consciousness, for example in encephalitis. The only clue in the history may be from the nursing staff who report that the patient becomes muddled and confused at night. Also rare are schizophrenia-like illnesses with tumours in the limbic system or elsewhere. Diagnosis is of really vital importance, because these very rare conditions are usually potentially fatal.

Real clouding of consciousness only occurs rarely and transiently in the most acute forms of schizophrenia. The differential diagnosis from other acute psychoses is of less immediate importance since most psychotic patients need hospital care. In the differential diagnosis from hysteria, a fair rule is that where there is reasonable ground for doubt, the case is one of schizophrenia.

Course and prognosis

Having read the section on 'Definition and Diagnosis', it will be clear that overall prognosis must depend on the criteria used to define schizophrenia. Even for those who base the diagnosis largely on the acute symptomatology, as we do here, and thus include patients of better prognosis, it is a grave illness in many cases. It used to be said that its course could be crudely compared with that of a switchback downhill, but that the gradient was difficult to predict since the downhill course might stop or spontaneous remissions occur. About one third of the cases recovered or showed considerable improvement after the first attack, while the other two thirds failed to do so, and if followed up after ten years were either in mental hospitals or had died. The chances of a spontaneous remission were greatest within 2 years and were negligible after 5 years from the onset. It had been worked out that if a patient had remitted for 3 years, he was probably safe for another 7 years, but recovery from a third attack was improbable. But this state of affairs has been considerably altered by the introduction of the phenothiazines and later drugs, and other improvements in care. It is still advisable to start treatment early but more can be expected than formerly, even for the more chronic type of case.

One major difficuly in discussing prognosis will be a surprise to the medical student, used to assessing degree of recovery by the patient's symptoms, signs and level of function. Most patients on adequate doses of neuroleptic drugs have no symptoms, anyway, although there may be marked signs in the sense of lack of drive or emotional flattening. (Excessive drug dosage increases apathy and flattening, and must be carefully monitored). Discharge from hospital and gainful employment are unfortunately unreliable indicators.

A simple closure of hospital beds, as an economy or as an expression of attitudes to mental illness, will cause many to be discharged from hospital. A shortage of hostel places or sheltered lodgings will prevent discharge of others. In other words, public and medical attitudes can be more important in this than clinical and personal well-being. Gainful employment also depends more on the state of the economy and the national unemployment rate than on clinical factors in many cases.

These factors make it very difficult to compare recovery rates now with those of some years ago, and with those of other countries and varying rehabilitation methods. Although very many chronic schizophrenic patients have been discharged from hospital in the past thirty years, it is difficult to know how much they have gained as a result of this, or how much their relatives have suffered. The idea that discharge from hospital is necessarily a good thing is too naive a view. Discharge should be to a better life than hospital can provide, but unfortunately it has not always been so.

Despite the disclaimers above there is no doubt that prognosis has greatly improved for patients admitted to hospital in the past 25 years and treated from the beginning with phenothiazines or other neuroleptics, and offered active social and work rehabilitation; and without doubt the most important single cause of relapse and re-admission to hospital is stopping drug treatment. This applies to many who are symptom free, working and living successfully and happily in the community, as well as to those in a more precarious balance.

The *prognosis* in any individual case remains difficult to assess in the early stages. There is no doubt that the more the illness resembles an acute affective illness the better, something which lies at the heart of the uncertainties of diagnosis and definition already considered.

Schizo-affective psychosis was a term introduced about 50 years ago for a psychosis of acute onset, with florid schizophrenic symptoms, in someone of good previous personality in which there was an understandable precipitant, marked emotional disturbance, either depressive or manic in quality, and in which complete recovery occurred in that not only did all symptoms remit but there was no schizophrenic defect left. Other workers in other countries used terms such as *schizophreniform psychosis, marginal psychosis,* and *affect laden schizophrenia,* all of which are essentially different terms for the same clinical picture. One can add to these features a family history of affective illness, good intelligence, and an endomorphic or pyknic build (see p. 27) and you have a complete list of the good prognostic features in schizophrenic illnesses. If many or all of these are present together then some will regard the illness as essentially affective and the schizophrenic symptoms as unimportant. Others will take the view, as the author does, that the schizophrenic symptoms indicate the use of phenothiazines (or other dopamine blocking drugs) as well as lithium, and make it more likely that later there may be a recurrence of more seriously schizophrenic type. It is essentially a matter of definition, as explained earlier.

There is also no doubt that overall the prognosis is worse in those illnesses with the opposite features. An insidious onset, a schizoid or otherwise poorly integrated personality, no obvious precipitant, early emotional loss with flattening or incongruity, low intelligence and loss of drive and interest are ominous. Asthenic physique is probably more common in those who do badly. Many schizophrenics with a very poor outcome seem to be unusually clumsy as children, with marked asymmetries of the face or body, and in these perinatal or other brain damage may play a part. Certainly, acquired brain damage, as from head injury, or co-existing epilepsy, naturally enough makes it more difficult for the unfortunate sufferer to cope with life and worsens the prognosis.

By *schizophrenic defect* we mean the characteristic picture, compounded of emotional blunting and lack of drive, often with some degree of vagueness or woolliness of thinking, which tends to follow symptomatic recovery from a schizophrenic illness — both the first breakdown and subsequent relapses. In many patients each relapse leads to further step-wise deterioration, so that even patients who seemed at first to have a good prognosis, judged from the criteria just given, can end up doing badly. It is schizophrenic defect rather than the active symptoms which make schizophrneia such a serious illness, as it leads to permanent social and personal decline in so many of the sufferers.

Treatment

There are three principal methods of treatment, all applicable to nearly every patient: the use of phenothiazines and other anti-psychotic drugs; environmental changes; and rehabilitation. In many patients there are also other aspects to be considered, which are mentioned later. In all psychiatric illnesses, as in all other illnesses, a relationship of trust and confidence between the patient and those treating him is of the greatest importance.

Drug treatment

The phenothiazines remain the mainstay of drug treatment in schizophrenia, although other groups such as butyrophenones and thioxanthenes also have a place, and are prefereed by many psychiatrists. It is striking that all the drugs useful in the control of schizophrenic symptoms are liable to produce extra-pyramidal disturbances, although their efficacy is not proportional to those side-effects as was once suggested. Drugs used for the relief of depression and anxiety do not cause similar side effects. This clinical fact supports the current theories that abnormalities in dopaminergic neuro-transmission are important in schizophrenia.

In clinical use the drugs available can be considered under three simple headings: more sedative; less sedative; and depot injections. Details of the use of the drugs are given in the chapter on treatment, which should be read in conjunction with this section.

The more sedative drugs such as chlorpromazine and thioridazine are most useful when the patient is very tense or disturbed, frightened perhaps by hallucinatory voices and other symptoms, or potentially violent. After the florid disturbances have settled many patients are too sedated by these drugs, and they benefit from a change to something less sedative, such as trifluperazine. If a patient is not markedly disturbed he can be started on one of the less sedative drugs. Thought disorder, and perplexity with passivity feelings, often seem to respond best to trifluperazine.

The great benefit of the depot injections is that patients cannot so easily stop taking their medication, which is the commonest single cause for relapse and readmission to hospital. Some just forget to continue because they feel well; many others stop because they feel so much better that the drugs seem no longer necessary; some object to side effects; and others very naturally object to the idea of having to remain on drugs indefinitely. It is obviously important to explain to the patient and his family the reason for the prolonged drug therapy and also to concentrate on minimising side effects. A lower dose may be necessary, and antiparkinsonian agents are often very helpful. A change of drug, for example from fluphenazine (a phenothiazine) to flupenthixol (a thioxanthene), may be the best course of action. The depot injections are on the whole less sedative, but overdosage with resultant apathy and slowness can develop insidiously, and the patients often benefit from missing one of the monthly or fortnightly injections and re-starting on a smaller dose.

All schizophrenic patients should be given phenothiazines or one of the antipsychotic drugs in the early stages of the illness, and the majority should continue to take them either continuously or intermittently. There are many chronic schizophrenic people in long stay hospital wards who receive bigger doses than they need, almost as a matter of therapeutic habit. In fact, while living in the sheltered atmosphere of a hospital they may seem to need no drugs at all. It is different outside hospital however. Many schizophrenics are liable to relapse in the face of quite minor stress, or even when confronted by changes of routine. The antipsychotic drugs lessen this overreaction. Even in well run and harmonious long-stay wards patients are not certain to avoid all relevant stresses; for example, relapse can follow the departure of a nurse to whom the patient is attached, or an upheaval such as redecoration of the ward.

The side effects of these drugs, and ways to combat them, are described in more detail on page 412. Some other drugs, such as pimozide, which have more limited uses, are also discussed.

Environmental change

In the early stages of a schizophrenic illness the patient is nearly always better treated in hospital. A day hospital can be as good as an inpatient stay, if the home situation is suitable and the patient not too disturbed. Hospital care allows drug treatment to be supervised more closely, many patients feel much safer and the family situation, which is ofen extremely disturbed and tense by the time the patient first presents, can then simmer down. In hospital the patient can be observed in much more detail. The way in which he relates to other people and the degree of withdrawal, suspicion, anxiety and depression can all be assessed; and as he improves, his concentration, interests and abilities at work, and his level of drive or apathy can also be studied. The reports of nursing staff and occupational therapists on these matters can be almost as important at times as the actual care which they give the patient.

During the patient's stay in hospital, contact should be made with the family, both by direct interview and if possible by a social worker who can visit the home. (At the time of writing unfortunately the social services are very hard pressed, and social worker services are hard to obtain.) Through these contacts with the family a better idea of any relevant stresses within the family can be obtained. The family can often be helped to come to terms with the problems generated by the patient and his illness, and there may well be problems which have contributed to the breakdown for which help can be offered. When the family atmosphere is full of emotional tension and conflict many patients do better not to return home, but to go and live in a hostel or some other more neutral environment. In some homes there is too little tension, and the patient is allowed to sink back into an overprotected invalid's life, with almost no demands being made upon him.

Environmental change through family therapy

The role of 'high expressed emotion' in precipitating relapse in known schizophrenics (and presumably in precipitating first breakdowns too) was described on page 128, along with a warning to avoid regarding the parents as somehow deliberately and maliciously driving their unfortunate child mad. That view has been put forward, and has been fashionable in some circles. It is both untrue and unfair, and by introducing a note of hostility and condemnation of the parents only serves to increase the guilt and sense of failure which they naturally feel, as well as making it more difficult for them to help in treatment. When tensions in the home are marked, and much hostile criticism is being voiced, a decision must be made whether to advise the patient to move out into the more neutral atmosphere of a hostel or some other accommodation, or to try and improve the family atmosphere.

In the last few years various studies have shown that by careful explanation to the family of the part played by expressed emotions, of the nature of the illness, and using a kind of educational family therapy, the atmosphere can be much improved and the relapse rate lessened. In those families which are poorly organised and chaotic, an extension of the method to include advice on how to solve various day to day problems, with some support and encouragement along these lines, has also been shown to be helpful.

Rehabilitation

In those patients who were generally well integrated personally and socially, and who have made a good recovery from a brief illness, no rehabilitation may be needed. In very many cases however, the patient was poorly integrated before, and has had a long illness. He may need to learn to work steadily, to keep regular hours, to look after himself in terms of personal hygiene, money, clothing, and even diet; and he needs to be motivated to do all these things. Forces acting against him will include the apathy and loss of will power so characteristic of schizophrenia, unhappy experiences of failure, illness, and rejection in previous work and living situations, and the social isolation experienced by nearly all chronic schizophrenics.

Rehabilitation is usually centred around work, but many other factors need to be tackled. A regular programme of industrial type work, with regular pay and productivity agreements (all very small in hospital settings) is the mainstay of rehabilitation in most mental hospitals, which is obviously most suited to those who previously did similar jobs. It is much more difficult to devise rehabilitation programmes for other types of work, although clerical skills such as filing, shorthand and typing can be taught easily in hospitals. Many men can be interested in woodwork, which has a creative quality and domestic work, shopping and cooking is valuable for many, including men who are leaving hospital to live on their own. Some patients need practice in such matters as making telephone calls and how to deal with interviews for jobs. Others might become too inhibited and withdrawn to go into a café, restaurant, or big store, and all of these problems can be tackled. Occupational therapists can also provide help in general socialisation, for example by conducting quizzes, encouraging patients to take part in running a hospital magazine, and to take responsibility for some activity or for some other patient.

It can be very helpful to transfer the patient to a special rehabilitation ward after he has settled down in the admission ward, when his symptoms have responded to drug therapy and the change of environment. The emphasis then should switch to self help, as opposed to nursing care, to a regular day of work in occupational therapy, and to social rehabilitation. Social workers can help with family problems, work prospects and with accommodation, and psychologists can offer training in social skills and other personal help.

The atmosphere of the ward is extremely important. Nurses must be continually aware of the need to encourage self reliance, social interaction with other patients and the staff, regular hours and regular attendance at the occupational therapy department, and good personal hygiene in those who have deteriorated in that way. The more unnecessary restrictions, arbitrary authority, and lack of individual care and concern, the more likely are patients to slip into withdrawal and apathy. It must be clearly understood, however, that it is in the very nature of schizophrenia for such changes to occur, and the most perfect environment, although it can mitigate the tendencies, cannot prevent them.

Towards the end of the stay in hospital the problems of overriding importance are of work and accommodation. Many can go back to doing the job they were doing before, but most patients with schizophrenia find it difficult to function at their previous level, and need some help from social agencies such as the Disabled Resettlement

Officer (DRO) who is based at the local labour exchange; and from various industrial training schemes run by government agencies. Some can be employed in sheltered workshops such as those run by Remploy. Obviously, the level of employment and the state of the national economy can make a huge difference to the prospects for a discharged patient.

Discharge of the chronic schizophrenic patient

Suitable accommodation is often a bigger problem than finding a suitable job. Many patients have no home at all if they have spent long in mental hospitals, or may have been rejected by their families. A great deal has been said about the necessity to provide suitable accommodation, and many promises have been made, but over the country as a whole little has been done. As more active treatment and rehabilitation methods have developed, and the staff of psychiatric hospitals have aimed at the rehabilitation and discharge of long-stay patients to 'community care', more and more patients with chronic schizophrenic illnesses have left hospital but found themselves no better off outside. Many fail to cope with the rigours of life and are repeatedly readmitted to hospital, only to be discharged again. Others end in prison because of petty offences; some live in common lodging houses or doss houses; and others live rough. As the policy of vigorous treatment and early discharge from hospital developed, it became apparent almost 20 years ago that many fewer mental hospital beds would be necessary, and plans to phase out many mental hospitals were made and to provide suitable facilities in the community. Unfortunately the new facilities have not been adequately developed, and if more hostels are not provided, there may be even a majority who would be happier and healthier in hospital, than fending incompetently for themselves in the community.

Subsidiary treatment

We have said that the three main pillars of treatment are antipsychotic drugs, environmental change and rehabilitation. In a good many patients other specific treatment is needed.

Depression and anxiety. These are often present, especially in the acute stages, although they may be overshadowed by the symptoms and signs of schizophrenia and they might not be easy to detect, as described earlier, on p. 137. As mentioned before, the control by drug therapy of delusional ideas or of hallucinations may uncover quite marked depression, which may benefit from antidepressant drugs or electrical treatment. When using antidepressants in schizophrenia, especially those of the MAOI group, it is important that adequate doses of a phenothiazine or other antipsychotic drug are given. Otherwise the schizophrenic symptoms may be made worse.

It is unwise to offer any formal psychotherapy for depression or anxiety in an acute schizophrenic, even if the depression seems related to conflicts and problems in an understandable way. Discussion of the problems and emotional support are always indicated, and sometimes practical or social help is needed. Explanatory or insight-directed psychotherapy, particularly of psychoanalytic type, unfortunately tends to make schizophrenic patients worse, as they often cannot deal with the emotional problems and conflicts brought to the surface in the course of psychotherapy, and become more disturbed in consequence. In North America psychotherapy is often used in acute schizophrenia, but nearly always in conjunction with phenothiazines. There is, however, no evidence that those who get the psychotherapy do better than those who get drug treatment without psychotherapy.

Electrical treatment is not only helpful in the treatment of depressive symptoms, but it is dramatically and rapidly successful in catatonic stupor; in the states of acute perplexity and bewilderment which some patients develop; and in states of turmoil and tension which in some patients renders them almost inaccessible. Although electrical treatment is often helpful symptomatically, and can make the patient feel much better, it seems to have no effect on the long term results of treatment, in terms of remission and relapse rates.

Psychosurgery This was extensively used, in the form of pre-frontal leucotomy, before the phenothiazines were introduced. It may have some place in the treatment of severe and intractable tension where all other methods have failed to produce relief, but if so it must be very rare.

Insulin coma therapy (deep insulin treatment). This is no longer used, but a brief account is given in the chapter on treatment (Chapter 16). It remains of historical interest because it was the first treatment to produce good results in schizophrenia, and it sparked off new hope and interest in therapeutic possibilities.

Helpful organisations. Both patients and their families, and other interested people might find helpful some of the leaflets and information put out by the National Association for Mental Health, 39 Queen Anne Street, London, W.1. and by the National Schizophrenia Fellowship, 29 Victoria Road, Surbiton, Surrey KT6 4JT.

SUMMARY

(1.) Concept originally of Dementia Praecox, with bad prognosis; broadened later to 'the schizophrenias'. Disagreement persists about the definition and diagnosis of the syndromes. (p. 146)

(2.) Common illness, affecting 0.8% of population. Genetic factors important, and probably necessary. Concordance in identical twins reared apart about 45%. Environmental stresses include perinatal damage, marked conflict, 'high expressed emotion', and life events.

Premorbid personality often schizoid; or anxious, vulnerable, achieving little despite effort.

(3.) *Principal signs* (p. 134)

(a) Thought disorder

(b) Disturbances of affect — flattened or incongruous.

(c) Loss of drive and will power.

(d) Withdrawal and introversion.

(e) Catatonic (motor) disturbances.

(4) *Principal symptoms* (p. 140)

a) Delusions (especially *primary*) and *delusional atmosphere, delusional perception.*

(b) Hallucinations, (especially *voices in the third person*).

c) *Passivity feelings* and other ego-boundary disturbances (*thought broadcasting, thought withdrawal, thought insertion*).

(5.) *Echoing thoughts*

See page 143 for notes on simple, hebephrenic, paranoid and catatonic pictures and paranoia, paraphrenia, and page 151 for schizo-affective psychosis.

(6.) See page 146 for definition and diagnosis.

(7.) *Prognosis* —

Good features:

sudden onset of florid symptoms, good personality, understandable precipitant, well marked affect, good intelligence, family history of affective illness, pyknic build.

Bad features:

insidious onset, schizoid or otherwise poorly integrated personality, early loss of affect and drive, no obvious precipitant, low intelligence, asthenic build, brain damage.

(8.) Treatment (p. 152) — Phenothiazine and other dopamine blocking drugs.

Environmental change (including educative family therapy)

Rehabilitation.

Subsidiary treatment for associated depression and anxiety.

9

Affective disorders

INTRODUCTION AND CLASSIFICATION

The affective disorders are the commonest of all seen by psychiatrists, the term including those abnormal states in which disturbances of mood and emotion are the prime features. (The Latin word 'affectus' means emotion or mood.) They include various types of depression and the manic-depressive illnesses, and range in severity from mild and transient reactions to severe psychoses.

In one thorough survey in London, the life time risk of suffering a depressive illness for which in-patient or out-patient treatment is offered, has been estimated at 12% for men and 20% for women. Similar figures have been produced elsewhere. This gives some idea of the importance of depressive disorders, as they are among the most common presenting in general practice.

Later in this chapter the clinical pictures of *endogenous* and *reactive* patterns of depression are described in their classical forms, but in fact there are major disagreements among psychiatrists about this classification. Many regard the two forms as qualitatively distinct conditions, which at times overlap to produce mixed clinical pictures (often called the bimodal hypothesis); yet others see them as shading one into the other, as part of a continuum of depressive disorders with mixtures of endogenous and reactive features in most patients, and with the classical forms representing the extremes of the continuum the unimodal hypothesis, as illustrated). The writer favours the latter. It is not necessary to take sides in the argument, but it is worth stressing that the more the clinical picture resembles the classical endogenous pattern, the more likely is physical treatment with antidepressants or electrical treatment to be helpful.

Bipolar manic-depressive illnesses do clearly form a group on their own, and have a fairly clear cut tendency to breed true. Nevertheless they overlap with the others, in that the clinical picture in the depressed phase of a manic depressive illness is identical with that of classical endogenous depression. In fact, until fairly recently, the terms 'manic-depressive' and 'endogenous' were often used inter-changeably to describe a depressive illness, and only modern genetic studies have separated the two, and it is now useful to use the term 'bipolar' manic-depressive in order to make the distinction clear, and indicate that mood swings up and down have both occurred.

Another important introductory point is that in deciding which pattern of depression a patient shows, in order to determine treatment, it is the pattern of symptoms which is important. It does not matter very much whether or not the depression has been precipitated by emotional trauma or not, as many depressions of endogenous pattern, and also many bipolar manic depressive illnesses, are triggered off by emotional factors, despite the fact that the word 'endogenous' means 'arising from within'.

In this book we do not use the terms 'psychotic' and 'neurotic' depression, but a brief note might be useful, as the terms are widely used, more or less as the equivalents of 'endogenous' and 'reactive' respectively. 'Psychotic' depression means that the patient has such a severe illness that he has lost contact with reality, and developed delusions or hallucinations; or (rather confusingly) that he has the type of depression in which those psychotic symptoms might develop if the illness became more severe. 'Psychotic' depression does correspond with 'endogenous' depression. 'Neurotic' depression implies that the symptoms are neurotic in quality, that the patients are neurotic in personality, and that their depressive state is a neurotic syndrome, which is naturally classified with the other neuroses. In fact reactive depression is classed as a neurosis by those who regard it as qualitatively distinct from others.

The term 'neurotic' depression is unsatisfactory, in our view, because there are patients who develop depression as an understand-able reaction to very severe emotional stress, who are not at all neurotic in personality. The term 'reactive' includes these people comfortably.

It is clear that the classification is less than perfect, but this is inherent in the subject. The purpose of classification is to aid in treatment and prognosis, and until some other criteria, perhaps biochemical or neurophysiological, are discovered, that put forward here seems as efficient as any other. It has the benefit that it does not require each patient to be put into a single category of endogenous or reactive depression. It also includes without difficulty those patients in whom the clinical picture changes with time.

The classification of the affective disorders offered here is therefore:

(a) *Depressive illnesses,* the range of which can be illustrated as in Figure 9.1, (although no mathematical relationships should be read into the diagram), and which are described on page 172.

(b) *Bipolar manic-depressive illnesses,* which are described on page 189.

When a patient is said to suffer from swings of mood, people sometimes say 'Don't we all?' Of course we do, and they may be normal, but they may also be pathological. Thus, *elation* which is the opposite of depression, may follow some successful achievement; it is transient, natural, and normal enough; unless it is associated with other psychiatric symptoms there is nothing pathological about it. So seldom, if ever, does it call for medical care that elation, unlike depression and excitement, may be said never to constitute an affective disorder on its own.

Excitement also may transiently follow some sequence of events that has caused a person to become 'strung up'. It may be observed, for example, after motor accidents or committee meetings that have caused frustration or annoyance. If it is transient, it is normal enough. But if excitement occurs as a main feature in a person's behaviour, in the absence of outside cause, and is sustained over a considerable period of time, it may be considered pathological. This occurs in manic-depressive psychosis.

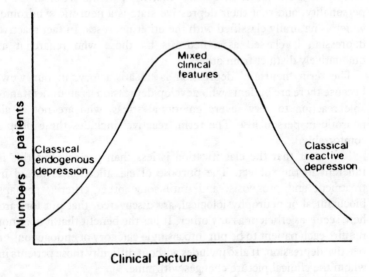

Fig. 9.1 The range of depressive disorders

Depression likewise may follow such reverses as failure in examinations or in securing a coveted job, of which it may be regarded as a normal and natural consequence, and is usually transient. More severe and less brief episodes may follow bereavements, major financial reverses or being jilted. These may not be abnormal in view of the precipitating causes. But, as with excitement, depression can occur as a main feature in a person's behaviour and be in duration and severity out of proportion to any apparent outside cause. It may then be considered pathological, although the normal shades into the abnormal by insensible degrees.

The excited and depressive phases of manic-depressive psychosis show a mood disturbance that is undue and unduly prolonged. The excited phases are known as *hypomania or mania,* according to their severity, and are less common than the depressive ones.

AETIOLOGY OF AFFECTIVE DISORDERS

Many factors are known to be involved in the development of both bipolar manic-depressive and purely depressive illnesses.

Genetics

Several studies have shown that bipolar manic depression is genetically independent of other (unipolar) depression, while the rare recurrent manic illnesses without depression resemble bipolar illnesses genetically. In other studies no clear cut genetic differences emerge between depression of endogenous, involutional, and reactive patterns, which is one of the reasons why they are not considered as qualitatively different in this book. It can be taken that the genes involved are not recessive, as in that case affected siblings would be more common than affected parents or children, whereas the risk is, in fact, much the same in all first degree relatives; nor are the genes sex linked. It seems that the method of transmission is polygenic and complex, and that what is inherited is an increased tendency to develop depression, which may never show unless the right environmental factors are present at the right time. In some people, as with schizophrenia, the genetic loading seems so pronounced that they become repeatedly depressed without much environmental stress. Recently it has been claimed that a good deal of alcoholism is genetically related to depression, and one certainly sees many alcoholics who drink, or who begin drinking, to relieve depressive feelings. Genetic factors also show in the response to treatment, as relatives tend to respond well to the same drugs.

Personality and constitution

Remarkably little is known about the personalities of those most likely to develop depression, perhaps because people of nearly all types of personality can be affected.

Bipolar manic depression is distinctly more common in those of *cyclothymic* personality, that is to say people in whom there are sustained mood swings above and below average, not amounting to illness. Relatives of manic depressives also often show this personality characteristic. Many of these people seem to be set at a higher level of drive and activity than are ordinary mortals, may be extremely productive and successful people, sociable and extroverted, and 'the very last person you would expect to be depressed', as is so often said.

There are several common personality traits in those prone to recurrent depression. A good many are anxious, emotionally labile, chronically pessimistic people, easily upset and worried. Others are outwardly calm for most of their lives, but always troubled by feelings of inadequacy and inferiority. Yet others are chronically melancholic and brooding, never seeming happy in any circumstances; and there is a large group with very varied neurotic problems and conflicts. There are no personality traits which distinguish reliably between those who do and those who do not develop affective illnesses.

Physical make-up shows some correlations with affective disorders, in that bipolar manic depressives, and those of cyclothymic personality, are rather more likely to have a pyknic (endomorphic) body build (p. 27).

The effect on personality of early life experiences has been the particular study of psychoanalysts (p. 389) and naturally there have been many attempts to relate character development and later depressive illness to infantile experiences. There is no single and generally accepted psychoanalytic theory of depression at present, but there is a general consensus that the child gains secure self esteem by developing good relationships with the parents or their substitutes; and that in later life depression, with loss of self esteem, is associated with disturbances in this area. This view is quite compatible with what we observe in many patients, but by no means all.

There is also evidence that the death of a parent in childhood, especially in early puberty, predisposes to depression, and that this is more marked when the parent of opposite sex is the one to die. It is as if the child is sensitised to grief and mourning at this stage, feelings which are rekindled in later life, especially by 'loss' as described later.

Emotional and psycho-social precipitants of affective disorders

As mentioned earlier, the bipolar manic depressive illnesses are the most likely to develop without any obvious precipitant, but in many of them some factors can be discerned. A prolonged period of angry frustration in which the patient feels he is making great effort but getting nowhere, is quite a common background to a manic upswing. Both upward and downward swings can be precipitated by events which would in most people cause anxiety or sorrow. A good example was that of the doctor who unexpectedly received a haematological report on his son which indicated leukaemia, and within a few hours was hypomanic.

In all other depressives, there are many types of situations which can call forth depression. Perhaps the commonest is the 'last straw' sequence, in which there has been a long period of cumulative stress, including perhaps money worries, marital disharmony, problems at work or with the children, and during which the patient has felt progressively more troubled and strained, until there is some further episode or problem, not intrinsically very important, and the patient becomes truly depressed. Other depressive illnesses, however, follow some single major blow, of which the commonest is some important loss or threatened loss. The loss of a spouse is perhaps the commonest single major event of this type, but of course much depends on the importance to the individual of such situations. The death of a child or parent; the loss of a child through marriage or emigration; loss of work, of prestige, of self respect, of health, of a limb, or even of a much loved home or pet; all these at times can precipitate depression.

In recent years the importance of both loss and of 'last straw' sequences has been demonstrated statistically by the use of 'life-events schedules', in which a systematic enquiry is made about all kinds of events which disturb the pattern of life. These range from the apparently trivial to the obviously important, cover both joyful and distressing events, and include such things as change of job, marriage of a sibling, move of house, death of a relative, and many more. Patients with depression show more life events, as defined in these schedules, particularly of the type in which some important person leaves the circle of the patient, by death or in some other way. Life events schedules of this type also show similar patterns in schizophrenic relapses, and in some physical illnesses. All these precipitating events have a rather extraordinary tendency to be followed by illness in about three weeks, as though in some way a chain of events is triggered off in the individual which takes three weeks to come to fruition.

The interaction of social and psychological factors in the causation of depression has been clearly shown in a number of studies. For example, women have been shown to be more vulnerable to depression if they had lost their own mothers before the age of 11, had three or more children under 14 at home, had no paid employment outside the home and had no intimate or confiding relationship with their partner. These factors were not by themselves sufficient to cause depression, but seemed to make the women more vulnerable to the effects of life events. Other surveys have produced similar, if not identical, results.

Bereavement depression. One of the most important items on any 'life event' schedule is the loss by death of some loved or otherwise important person, and it deserves some separate consideration.

Normal grieving is said to go through several stages. Commonly at first there is a feeling of 'numbness' or even an absence of any response, especially while the individual is continuing to cope with related practical matters, such as arranging the funeral or coping with elderly relatives. By the end of a week or two this has usually ended, and the second stage, of 'the pangs of grief' develops. There is weeping, a deep sense of loss and distress, anxiety, and often a restless 'searching' type of behaviour — analagous probably to the searching behaviour of so many other animals when separated from their offspring, for example. These pangs of grief are usually triggered off by some reminder of the dead person, such as photographs, letters, or familiar favourite possessions. The frequency and intensity of these pangs slowly diminishes.

At the same time there is a persistent sadness, and a state very like that of a depressive illness, with anorexia, sleeplessness, loss of interest and impaired concentration, and loss of sexual drives. A lost, bewildered feeling, in which life seems pointless is very common. As mentioned in chapter 15 on psychosomatic medicine, there are immunological changes, and the death rate rises in the bereaved in some groups.

Usually people go through these stages, with sadness and loss, but emerge after some months, and take up life again. In some the stage of chronic sadness drags on and on, and after 6 months it is usual to regard such a state as a form of depressive illness — a pathologically protracted bereavement. This is more likely to happen when there have been conflicts in the relationship between survivor and the dead person. An example is that of a woman who has never left the parental home, but has ended by caring for an elderly parent for years. There may have been deep affection, but also childlike dependence emotionally, and strong resentment against the mother for all the years during which the daughter might have been enjoying a different sort of life, with marriage, travel, friendship and so on all 'sacrificed' to the care of the parent. In such cases, which are indeed common, natural grieving is complicated by the guilt which the survivor feels for all the bad thoughts she may have had, for any cruel things she may have said or done to the mother, and for wishes that she would 'hurry up and die'. Another situation which leads to very prolonged grief is that of the marriage in which the couple, often childless, have spent almost all their time together, without other interests of any kind. They have done the shopping and housework together since his retirement, they have no outside friends, and no resources. They may have been blissfully happy together in life, but in death the survivor is lost, like an orphaned child, and severe depression and emotional collapse is common.

The importance of bereavement in causing mental and physical ill health is increasingly recognised. Organisations such as CRUSE, for the widowed, and numerous bereavement counselling groups set up by voluntary organisations or local authorities are useful to refer bereaved people to. Special types of psychotherapy aimed at guiding people through normal grieving, have been developed. They aim at helping people to go through the normal processes of grieving which may have been distorted by the sort of ambivalence mentioned before, or may have been suppressed by misguided attempts 'to carry on normally'. If the clinical picture of depression which arises from a prolonged grief reaction is essentially biological or endogenous in form, then antidepressants can be the most appropriate first treatment.

The interaction of psychosocial and physical or physiological factors, and the difficulty of separating them out, is illustrated clearly by post-natal (puerperal) depression. In this book we consider it in the next section, concerning physical factors in depression, but it could equally well be in this section, as in some women the psychosocial elements may seem predominant, and in others the hormonal. This point is elaborated later, as it is in the case of hormonal and psychosocial factors in the menopause.

Physical factors in the development of depression

Severe depressive illnesses can be triggered off by physical illness, influenza being the most frequently responsible. Glandular fever (infectious mononucleosis) is also quite often followed by depression, much more commonly in females. Quite minor head injuries, which lead to no significant organic cerebral damage, are another well known trigger.

Prolonged states of depression occur in any illness in which there is organic cerebral impairment, as after strokes, serious head injuries, cerebral tumours, and the dementias due to degenerative changes. In all these conditions the patient is usually very aware of his impairment, as described in Chapter 6 and depression is a very natural seeming reaction. It is very important not to view the depression as inevitable and untreatable because the circumstances are so grim for the sufferer. Relief from the worst of the depression, even if not cure, can often be achieved by treatment.

The role of the *menopause* in depressive illnesses is well known but obscure. There is no doubt that for a period of several years around the menopause, women are more likely to become depressed, and the symptoms often include 'hot flushes' and sudden drenching sweats which are known to be due to oestrogen deficiencies. Some people regard all menopausal mood disturbances as due to hormonal imbalance, and suggest that oestrogens are needed rather than antidepressants. Of the patients whose depression is severe enough to lead to psychiatric referral this is certainly not true, and the use of oestrogens, including the nonsynthetic ones, often has little effect on the depression, even if it relieves the flushes and sweats.

Hormonal factors are of course not the only important ones in the menopause. Even though a woman may be glad to be relieved of the nuisance of menstruation, the menopause means the end of an era. Options which were previously open are now closed; she may well feel inherently less attractive sexually because the biological purpose of sex has gone; and her husband may react to her differently for the same reason, even if he is not fully conscious of it. At more or less the same time her children are becoming grown up, and she is that much less needed, while probably having fewer interests outside the family than her husband. He is at his prime, probably, as far as his work is concerned, unless his job is strictly manual; and in the professional and managerial occupations work is often increasingly demanding at this time.

The menopause is therefore a period of great change, personally and socially, and in the depression which is so common at this time these factors often play a part. Similar problems of personal and social readjustment are at their greatest for men when they retire from work, at which time they become more prone to depression. By then their wives have made the necessary adjustments, but the retiring man is 20 years older and that much less flexible, and does not even have the organization of the home to fall back on as a useful daily task. The loss of prestige, interest, occupation, and companionship which follows retirement, are often more serious blows than the loss of income.

Post-natal depression

The puerperium is another time of major upheaval in both hormonal and psychological terms, during which depression is more common than at other times. To some people any depression occurring within twelve months of childbirth is 'puerperal', but this seems too extended a period to us, and three months seems to be more suitable. In the typical puerperal psychotic depression the mother is well for a period of about three to seven days after the birth, and the depression comes on very suddenly and at times with great severity; so that unexpected suicide is sometimes the first manifestation. Very many women go through a period of 'the blues' after childbirth; in most it does not need specific treatment, but it may develop into a true depressive illness.

The incidence of depression depends of course on how it is defined and on the population studied. Using standardised interview methods, about 10% of women seem to have depression marked enough to call for treatment, but the problem is often missed and much avoidable suffering experienced. In others, the illnesses are psychotic in quality and are always recognised. There are depressive delusions or mixed manic and depressive pictures, pure hypomania or even mania, and psychoses with affective and schizophrenic symptoms intermingled are often seen. The incidence of serious affective psychoses was about 16 times as high in the puerperium as in the preceding 2 years in one survey. Those most likely to develop them were unmarried women, especially primipara and those after Caesarian section. These illnesses tend to come on in the first week after delivery, as mentioned above.

In many others depressive mood develops slowly, after the woman has returned home, perhaps to the exhausting demands of other young children, themselves upset by the arrival of another rival, and to poor living conditions, and a husband who still expects the sort of pampering he has always been used to. In these cases the depression has more of a reactive and understandable quality. Obviously, treatment must take all these factors into account.

In addition to the major hormonal changes and other physical changes as the body reverts to its non-pregnant state, the physical fatigue often caused by the care of a new baby, such factors as blood loss and infection (much less common now in the Western world), there may be very important psychological difficulties. Not every baby is whole-heartedly wanted, and there is quite often underlying hostility and jealousy, about which the mother feels deeply guilty.

Among the serious consequences of persistent post natal depression we must include rejection of the baby or inability to cope with it, which can have long term effects on the child's development if the depression lasts for many months, and harmful effects on the other children, and the marital relationship. Many agoraphobic states seem to date back to post natal depression, even years later.

Although these personal and social factors as just outlined can be very important, there are many puerperal depressions in which hormonal changes, or perhaps some biochemical changes at present not appreciated, seem to be of overriding importance, which alter the mother's state of mind in some profound way. The term 'puerperal psychosis' is often used to cover both depressive and schizophrenic illnesses in the puerperium, as there is an increase in the latter at this time as well. In less developed countries, as in Britain a few decades ago, toxic confusional states are common in the puerperium, largely because of infection and blood loss. In a fair number of puerperal mental illnesses it is difficult to make a diagnosis, as affective and schizophrenic features may be very mixed.

Biochemistry and depression

The very 'physiological' or 'biological' disturbances of the endogenous depressive pattern, (described clinically on p. 172) the hereditary background of much depression, the part played by endocrine and other physical factors in causation, and the response of patients to physical treatment, had long suggested that some biochemical disturbances underlay depression. This attitude was strengthened by the introduction of antidepressants and of lithium in treatment, and an enormous amount of research has been done in this field, which we will not attempt to review in this book, where we comment on only what seems to be of most importance.

The amine hypothesis.

This hypothesis states that certain monoamines (e.g. serotonin, nor-adrenaline) have an important rôle as cerebral transmitters in those brain structures which are important in the control of mood. (The structures concerned are thought to be mainly if not entirely in the limbic lobe and especially in the hypothalamus.) When the concentration of these monoamines at important sites falls, depression results; and when the concentration increases the depression is relieved. Alternatively, decreased sensitivity of the post-synaptic receptors may be present. Similarly, manic disturbances are thought to be associated with increased concentrations of monoamines. It is known that reserpine, for example, decreases cell concentrations of serotonin, and also causes depression. The two main groups of antidepressants, monoamine oxidase inhibitors and tricyclic drugs, increase the concentration of monamines. It is thought that the former do this by inhibiting the breakdown of the monoamines centrally; the latter by inhibiting uptake peripherally. Whether or not his hypothesis will attain the dignity of accepted theory is uncertain, but it has been the centre of much very useful and interesting research.

Many other neuro-transmitters have been speculatively involved, but very little of a convincing nature has been produced despite a great deal of research activity.

Electrolytes. Alterations in electrolyte metabolism occur in severe depression, with an increase in intracellular sodium possibly related to changes in cell membranes. The finding that lithium is useful in the treatment and prevention of affective illnesses is presumably related to the fact that lithium is chemically related to both sodium and potassium, and consequently may interfere with their functions. Very rarely depression is caused by abnormalities of calcium metabolism, as in hyperparathyroidism.

Hormones. Changes in steroid hormones are known to be related to affective illnesses, although the relationships are uncertain. Examples are in the development of depression in Cushing's syndrome and in a number of people treated with steroids for physical illnesses, the very striking mood changes of the premenstrual period and the effect on mood of oral contraceptives, which in some people lead to depression and in others relieve it (depending not only on the person but on the constituents of the contraceptive). Cortisol production is increased in patients with agitated depression but not in those who are retarded and apathetic, and the increase is probably due to the overactivity and arousal rather than the depression.

Dexamethasone suppression test (D.S.T.) It has been claimed that in depressive illnesses, especially of endogenous pattern, a standard 1 mg dose of oral dexamethasone fails to suppress cortisol production as it does in normal subjects. There are too many conflicting reports for this to be used clinically as a diagnostic test at present.

Deficiencies of thyroid hormone can lead to depression, and overt myxoedema is often preceded and accompanied by depressive mood, sometimes to the extent of a true depressive illness, and hypothyroidism should be considered in patients who fail to respond to treatment. Hypothyroidism also causes intellectual impairment, which can be permanent if treatment is begun too late.

Vitamin deficiencies. Lack of vitamin B_{12} can lead to prolonged depressive states which respond poorly to treatment, and also causes intellectual impairment amounting to dementia at times. It is important to realise that these mental changes can long precede any anaemia or neurological signs. Similar states occasionally occur with folic acid deficiency. Estimation of the blood level of these two vitamins is a standard part of the investigation of presenile dementia, and is worth considering in depression when the patient fails to respond to treatment.

DEPRESSIVE ILLNESSES (unipolar depression)

We have already said, at the beginning of this chapter, that we preferred to view the range of depressive disorders as a continuum with the endogenous and reactive patterns at the ends of the spectrum, and many mixed pictures in between. We now give descriptions of those two classical patterns, and the reader must understand that they are given as illustrations, and not from inconsistency of purpose.

Symptoms and signs of the endogenous pattern

The essential symptoms are so simple that they may be easily overlooked; indeed, failure to diagnose depression used to be the commonest psychiatric mistake. Nowadays, for various possible reasons, such as the introduction of the anti-depressants with attendant publicity, the feeling that it is more 'respectable' for a patient to have a true depressive illness rather than a complicated neurotic personality problem, coupled with the fact that the former is easier to treat than the latter, depression is more often diagnosed, and perhaps over diagnosed. Another interesting change is that less severe forms of the illness are now seen, with less florid symptoms, presumably because of more efficient and earlier treatment. The symptoms and signs can be considered for convenience under two headings (1) physical and (2) mental.

The biological symptoms are, firstly, a persistent lowering of energy with consequently lowered drive and increased fatiguability. There is thus a reduction of activity. This is almost always accompanied by loss of sexual appetite, and by a characteristic sleep disturbance which consists in frequent and early waking. The patients can often get to sleep well enough, but this is interrupted after an hour or two, and they finally wake at three, four or five in the morning, after which they cannot get to sleep again, though some may doze fitfully and restlessly. Usually, but less invariably, there is constipation, loss of weight, and loss of appetite not only for food but for life in general (there is some evidence that early waking is secondary to a lowered food intake.) Amenorrhoea is not uncommon.

The mental symptoms run parallel. The reduction of activity is accompanied in the mental sphere by a feeling of being unable to cope as well as usual, coupled with a disinclination to do as much as usual. These almost necessarily involve a loss of interest, concentration, confidence and decisiveness, and lead to procrastination. The patient feels less than what he was, may feel inferior on that account, may thus become withdrawn, and anxious to avoid the company of others, except for those whom he knows well and from whose presence he may draw comfort and support. With the loss of interest the patient can neither experience enjoyment in the usual way nor 'get away from himself', and so remains to a greater or lesser extent selfabsorbed and preoccupied with his own symptoms. He then tends to think repetitively 'Why am I like this?' 'What has happened to me?' 'How am I going to get out of it?' 'Why has this happened *to me?*' In fact, the picture resembles that of general debility with the keynotes of generally reduced vitality and animation, with worry. As an indication of this reduced vitality, it may be mentioned that, according to Kraepelin, there is a reduction of the rate of growth of the hair and finger-nails. Many patients feel just generally 'ill', and do not emphasise the lowering of their spirits and mood particularly, until asked about them.

The condition is persistent and steady, showing little variation from one day to another, though most patients feel worse when unoccupied, and show a spontaneous rhythm, independent of outside events, of feeling lowest in the morning and a little less low towards evening — in a fashion somewhat reminiscent of the normal temperature chart. This so-called 'diurnal' or morning-evening variation is not invariably present though it is usual; very occasionally it is reversed. It will be noted that the picture is one of depression in a general sense, like a 'depressed area', the depression is not confined nor specifically related to the mood, but affects the interest, activity and total function of the patient, the so called 'vital depression'.

The diagnosis is reached by (1) exclusion of recognisable organic disease which might account for the loss of vitality, (2) careful comparison of the patient's state when he is seen, with his state when he is well. For a proper evaluation of this, of course, it is desirable (and may be essential) to interview the relatives or friends. It will then be found that, though the patient may show some degree of response to congenial company and other pleasant diversions, this is temporary and incomplete, and that in general he never reaches his normal level of animation or enjoyment. This comparison between the patient's state when well and when ill is often rendered easier by the fact that many of these patients are of normal personality. The change from a state characterised by energy, interest, extraversion, enjoyment, confidence, decisiveness and gregariousness, to one characterised by relative anergia, disinterest, self-absorption, joylessness, with lack of confidence, indecisiveness and withdrawal from company, may then be very striking, *provided that the comparison is sought.* The keynote is *reduction,* as opposed to the expansiveness of the contrasting manic or hypomanic phase in the bipolar manic-depressive.

The more severe cases are easier to diagnose. The reduction in activity may become very marked, leading to that generalised slowness called *retardation,* of which the indecisiveness already referred to is the first subjective experience. The indecisiveness may amount to gross vacillation, and may cause the depressed patient to raise hydra-headed objections to any course of action that may be suggested. The indecisiveness coupled with the retardation may result in *perplexity.* Depression of mood may now be the presenting symptom, and the patient may show a diffuse pessimism with hopelessness of recovery and suicidal preoccupation. By this stage the loss of interest may have increased so that the patient cannot experience normal emotion, is untouched by events of emotional significance (except perhaps by those that are sad and distressing), is unable to respond to a joke though intellectually he sees the point, cannot feel normal affection for others, gets no joy where he got it before, whether from music, from sights or from good company. In fact, there is an *affective loss,* which may be described in striking ways. 'I feel that I'm different from other people, and I usedn't to feel it, that they've got something that I haven't; I'm different from what I used to be, and I've lost something that I once had.' Another said, 'My heart feels as if it had been eclipsed'. A depressed Chinese scientist remarked, 'I have lost the function of my centre of happiness and my fighting spirit'. Another said, 'I feel that I have died inwardly'.

Self-absorption may become extreme, and the productivity of these patients, even in simple speech or letter-writing, may be negligible or non-existent, for they have little initiative or spontaneity. But this does not mean that their minds are empty. On the contrary, their thoughts tend to chase each other round, 'like', as one patient said, 'a squirrel in a cage'. The thinking continues, but in a restricted way and to no end, as though the mind were continually revolving in neutral without ever getting into gear.

Even the mildly depressed patient may be self-depreciatory; the markedly depressed patient almost always is. The self-absorption then encourages a brooding self-criticism with self-blame and preoccupation with past failures, real or imaginary, leading to the familiar 'If only I had acted differently', and 'If only I hadn't done that'. The remarks are given a self-reproachful twist; 'My heart feels as if it had been eclipsed' becomes 'I feel hard-hearted', and 'If only I had acted differently' becomes 'If only I'd had more will-power'. The patient supposes others to share his depreciatory feelings about himself, and may then feel unwanted and shunned. In this setting *ideas of reference* easily develop and lead to feelings of being critically spoken of, and of being able to discern disapproval or contempt in the innocent actions of others.

These feelings of self-reproach may be exaggerated into actual *delusions* of guilt or unworthiness, as the patients look into their past and find there causes for regret and self-blame. The line of thought generally follows the popular idea of moral and medical causation, so that the illness becomes attributed to masturbation by older patients, or to lack of consideration or failure to show affection or some other sin, real or imaginary. Whenever feelings of guilt are experienced in the absence of powerful justification, depression should be suspected. Delusions of punishment, present or impending, are a not unnatural consequence of the guilt-feelings. Other common ones, always in line with the melancholic mood, are those of impoverishment or ruin. Patients may thus refuse to eat, not only from anorexia, but because they feel they are unworthy or that they cannot afford the food. In many other patients there is increasing preoccupation with bodily health, with fear of cancer, and not infrequently delusional beliefs about this and other illnesses. These hypochondriacal delusions are most common in the elderly, but can occur at any age.

Hallucinations do not often occur in depressive states in Europeans, but are commoner in less sophisticated immigrants from less developed cultures. When they do occur in Europeans it is mainly in older people and they are almost always of voices talking to the patient, saying critical or hopeless things, or advising suicide. Their occurrence in younger depressives should suggest a toxic cause, or a schizophrenic element.

These states will be coloured by the previous personality. Touchy and over-sensitive patients will show paranoid trends, believing others to be against them in a way they may feel wholly or only partly justifiable, but such paranoid ideas will be consistent with the mood, and comprehensible in the light of it. Easily agitable patients will become agitated and importunate, and this may mask the real reduction of physical and mental activity. Obsessional personalities are likely to show exaggeration of their obsessional traits. These extraneous developments make it the more necessary to attend to the basic symptoms of the depressive state itself, if an accurate diagnosis is to be made.

As regards *signs,* these are few but variable. The patient can usually be observed to be less active and more easily fatigued than is normal. Retardation both of thought and movement (psychomotor retardation) may be obvious in the more severe case. Rarely, it may be great enough to lead to stupor, though in young people this should raise suspicion of schizophrenic admixture. The severely depressed patient will look sad, with what has been described as a 'frozen mask of misery'. Agitation may be obvious, with wringing of the hands. Sighing is frequent. The complexion is usually sallow, the pores of the skin may be more prominent, and the hair may lose its lustre. The patient may appear to have aged and loss of weight may be evident. There are no other physical signs except that the blood pressure is often raised above normal in those who are agitated and tense. In the milder or even moderately depressed case, the patient may be able to retain an appearance which can be most misleading.

Some patients start to drink heavily or to use other drugs, in order to relieve their distress, so that they present a very misleading picture. It is essential to recognise and treat the underlying depression in such cases, and not just concentrate on the drink or drug problem.

Finally, this whole state is steady and persistent, varying little from one day to another except in the stages of recovery, and little from one time of day to another except for the morning-evening variation. This syndrome is experienced in attacks, with periods of normality between, so that there may be a history of a previous attack often with a family history of the same thing. The clinical picture will vary with the severity of the attack, with the personality of the patient, and with the addition of anxiety, hysterical, obsessional or other modifying features. The milder attacks will show no distortions of content. But, underlying them all, the basic syndrome as described is virtually constant, and will be found so on enquiry.

The clinical picture of depression just described is that of the fully developed *endogenous pattern*. The most important features of it can be summed up as follows: a general and pervasive depressive mood and lowering of spirits (rather than being depressed 'about something'); disturbances of a biological type including sleep, appetite, weight, bowel function and diurnal variation; psychomotor retardation or agitation; and self reproachful ideas, at time amounting to delusions. Psychomotor retardation and agitation, and severe self reproach are relatively infrequent, but the others are all very common. The more of these features are present, the more likely is the patient to respond to treatment with antidepressants or electrical treatment, and in fact if depressive delusions are present it is best to use electrical treatment immediately. Patients with this type of depression will not benefit from psychotherapy, but need effective physical treatment soon, not only to relieve their distress, but because of the risk of suicide. Most serious of all are those rare cases with such intense self reproach that the patient feels that he has ruined the lives of his whole family, and that they too would be better off dead. Such feelings lead occasionally to the murder of the children and attempted suicide.

An uncommon pattern of depression now, but more common in the past, is a minor variant of the endogenous pattern, known as *involutional melancholia*. This term indicates a severe depression coming on for the first time in later life, in which marked agitation and the development of delusions and of a bizarre hypochondriasis are prominent. It affects principally, but not solely, people of rather rigid, narrow and obsessional character. The precipitants are those common to depression, especially those like retirement and death of a parent, which are likely to occur in an older person.

The onset is often gradual, and the earliest symptoms are of some physical complaint — most often of constipation — without apparent depression. Gradually depression develops, with the full range of endogenous depressive symptoms described earlier; and hypo-chondriasis and increasingly severe agitation become more and more prominent. The most characteristic picture then is of a deeply depressed man or woman, pacing or shuffling restlessly up and down, wringing the hands, and complaining of blockage of the bowels, or brains decaying, of cancer spreading through the body, or some other similar complaint. Delusions of poverty or of the imminent collapse of the family home, or of the family business, and similar concerns, are also common. Delusions of guilt, and even nihilistic delusions such as of being already dead may be present; and auditory and occasionally other hallucinations occur.

This florid type of depressive psychosis is much less often seen now, but before electrical treatment was introduced such illnesses often lasted many years, ending in death from self neglect or suicide; or in misery unrelieved by sedatives. The success of electrical treatment in these illnesses, which had previously been totally resistant to therapy, explains the impact on psychiatry which electrical treatment made after its introduction in the 1930s.

A strange and largely unexplained manifestation of depression in middle-aged women is *shoplifting*. It is not that most middle-aged shoplifters are depressed, but that a certain number are. They often steal goods for which they have no conceivable use, and may do it very obviously, as though hoping to be caught. In some cases it is clear that there are marked guilt feelings, and that they hope to be punished, but in others this is not obvious. Most magistrates are aware of this syndrome, and it is not uncommon for them to make the patient seek psychiatric help as part of the sentence, usually in the form of a probation order.

The reactive pattern of depression

At the other end of the depressive spectrum lies the pure *reactive depression*. Anyone may of course react to adversity with depressive mood, and everyone has a breaking point somewhere, but some people are much more vulnerable than others, and develop depression rapidly and repeatedly in reaction to life stresses which others might shrug off, or to which they might react in some other way. The most transient of these, lasting only hours or days, and in response to minor life stresses are not considered in this chapter, and are characteristic of those with vulnerable and inadequate personalities as described elsewhere (p. 218).

It is a mistake to think of depressive illnesses of endogenous pattern as being somehow more genuine and severe, and of reactive depressions as necessary milder; or to view reactive depression as always indicating a vulnerable or feeble personality. Some purely reactive states are very severe, cause great suffering, and lead to suicide; they may follow such prolonged and severe emotional stress that on hearing the patient's account one recognises that almost anyone would have been similarly affected. In many depressions of any length and severity, as has already been stressed, symptoms of the endogenous pattern slowly develop, and the clinical picture shifts towards the middle of the spectrum, but the pure reactive picture is described here.

Reactive depressions are common in adolescence, when the marked temperamental variations that so readily occur in children first begin to assume a greater length, especially among those who are prone to be passionate or love-lorn. In adolescents, however, such reactions do not usually last long, though their duration tends to increase with age.

The psychological factors are any that may be traumatic to the personality of the particular patient. Often they are sudden, such as an unexpected failure with serious consequences, an unexpected bereavement, or any other loss that cannot be compensated for. Being jilted, or reaching an impasse in a love affair that cannot have a successful ending, are not uncommon causes. Perhaps commonest of all are those difficulties in relationships with other people which arise from neurotic personality problems. Marital conflicts, sexual problems, unresolved problems with parents or children, recurring clashes and temperamental difficulties with friends or colleagues, are all commonly found in the background.

Sometimes the psychological factors may be prolonged and of cumulative effect, as, for example, in people who lead unstimulating lives in uncongenial climates, cut off from home associations and from the sort of company that they would ordinarily choose. Such people may conscientiously struggle on though increasingly bogged in a slough of despond from which, in the end, they have not enough spirit to raise themselves. Those who are obliged to toil at demanding work for which they do not care, under exacting superiors who offer no hope of promotion, and have to devote meagre earnings to the support of ungrateful relatives for whom they feel responsible, may likewise slide into a depressive state in reaction to their circumstances.

On the other hand, the development of depression may depend more on the individual qualities of the patient; an unintelligent housewife with few resources of her own and small capacity for satisfactory relationships may become worn down into depression through her anxieties over bringing up what for her become too many children, and through her inability to do things to her own or her husband's satisfaction through muddle-headedness which, through imprudent expenditure, prevents her from ever having anything to spare for such amusements as might otherwise be beguiling.

Physical factors may also contribute, not only in such dramatic form as mutilating accidents, but through the lowering effects of chronic pain or weakness, the restrictive effect of conditions such as arthritis, especially when combined with failing mental powers into the development of which the patient has insight.

In general, the psychological stress may have been severe; if it has not been, the patient will have a marked constitutional liability to depressive reactions, or one that has been exacerbated by physical causes. Where the stress has been prolonged and cumulative, the patient will often be found to have a good personality, without which he would have given up the struggle before the depression had become established.

Symptoms and signs of the reactive pattern

The main symptoms of the reactive depressive pattern is of depressive mood, recognised and described as such by the patient, and usually attributed to something in a straightforward way. Irritability, anxiety and tiredness are often present as well, but the loss of drive and of various mental functions, so characteristic of the endogenous pattern, are not prominent.

The degree of depression may be severe, with suicidal thoughts and even suicidal attempts. The patient will be pre-occupied with his state, and more so with the precipitating factors that have led to it. He will relate the two to each other, and in a way that carries conviction to the examiner. He will repeatedly mill over his affairs in his mind, and the more so if his circumstances are such as to call for some decision, over reaching which he may have some conflict leading to further anxiety. It is likely, however, that he will see the correct decision, quite clearly, though he may have difficulty in implementing it. His pre-occupations will interfere with his concentration to some extent, and may impair his work. But it is usually possible to distract the patient from his preoccupations, even if not for very long periods of time, and it will then be found that his mood improves and that he is responsive to other stimuli: that he is bogged down in his depression only to the extent to which he is pre-occupied with it, and it lightens with the provision of other distractions.

Physically, although there may be complaints of tiredness, this may not be much apparent; there may be some reduction of appetite; sleep is usually disturbed and the difficulty is usually in getting off; sexual activity tends not to be much interfered with, unless there is real tiredness or unless the precipitating factors are closely involved with the sex life. As regards signs, there may be none, beyond an appearance of gloom and some loss of weight, and those of anxiety where it is additionally present.

Elaborations of the basic condition may occur, either in the form of neurotic concern over the physical state, or of hysterical developments designed to exact sympathy and attention or to enforce some revision of the circumstances that have led to the depression.

Other presentations of depression

(1) Physical Symptoms. Many patients present with physical symptoms of various kinds, especially pain. These may be headache, pain in the chest, in the back, abdomen, or elsewhere. Others may have prominent somatic anxiety symptoms, with palpitations, dyspnoea and so on, as described in the section on Anxiety states (p. 240). Anxiety is a prominent feature of many depressive illnesses, and in some people somatic symptoms are so marked that they swamp the depressive symptoms themselves. Fears of cancer or of heart disease are very common, and these fears may reach delusional intensity. Constipation with cancerphobia is one of the most frequent of these presentations; and a fear of throat cancer, occurring mainly when anxiety has led to swallowing difficulties, is another. Many of these patients have extensive and repeated investigations before the depression is recognised.

It is a good practice for every doctor to ask all patients about their mood and spirits, unless the diagnosis is quite straightforward. The questions 'How are your spirits?' or 'How do you feel in yourself — in your mood?' do not take long to ask, and could save much suffering.

On the whole this 'somatisation' of depression is commoner in older people, in the less sophisticated and less verbal, and especially in those from underdeveloped countries and cultures. Where a sophisticated Londoner will complain of 'depression', and relate his malaise to difficulties in his marriage or at work (not always correctly), an Indian immigrant is more likely to complain of pain, weakness, premature ejaculation, or some other bodily symptom.

In most of these patients there will be some of the biological disturbances that are typical of depression, especially anorexia and weight loss, sleep disturbance, and diurnal variation in mood. It can be difficult to persuade the patient to view his illness as a manifestation of depression, and many are angry at the idea. It is often best just to use antidepressants, as described later, for a trial period, explaining your reasoning but not trying too hard to persuade the patient to share your views.

(2) Anxiety states. We have just described how one or more of the somatic symptoms of anxiety can be so prominent that they come to form the presenting symptom, and may then mask the underlying depression. The same is true of mental symptoms of subjective anxiety and tension, accompanied by the usual somatic symptoms, which can be very marked, and lead to a depressive illness being misdiagnosed as an anxiety state. This is a common and rather serious error, because only too often the doctor responds to an anxiety state by the automatic prescription of a benzodiazepine, or of a small dose of a neuroleptic such as haloperidol. Drugs of this kind do relieve anxiety, but often make depression worse.

It is a sound rule not to diagnose an anxiety state, in a previously non-anxious middle-aged person especially, until you have excluded both a depressive illness and the possibility of organic cerebral impairment, as pre-senile dementias often cause anxiety in the early stages. Unrecognised alcoholism is another hazard in diagnosis here. If a patient has a low anxiety threshold, and has had previous anxiety states as a response to external stress or internal conflict, one of which is seen to be present on this occasion, the diagnosis of anxiety state is on safer ground.

(3) Hysterical disturbances. These are less common as presentations of depression than are anxiety states, but in people of hysterical personality they are not uncommon, as depression seems to lower their 'hysterical threshold', as it were. There may be multiple complaints made in a very histrionic manner, obvious manipulation of the family and apparent secondary gain, but underneath there may be distinct depressive mood. Effective treatment can lead to what seems like a change in personality as the hysterical elements fade away. As with anxiety states, one must be careful to exclude underlying depression and organic deterioration when a patient first presents hysterical symptoms in middle life or later.

(4) Obsessive-compulsive symptoms. As with anxiety and hysterical states, obsessive-compulsive symptoms may appear in a setting of depression, and be so prominent that a diagnosis of 'obsessive compulsive neurosis' may be made. Depressive symptoms must be carefully sought, as these illnesses will only respond to antidepressant treatment, not to the behaviour therapy which can be so helpful in the chronic obsessive compulsive states in which depression plays no major part.

(5) Alcoholism. This deserves a separate heading as a serious problem, although it has been mentioned already. A significant number of people seem to be unable to tolerate depression without alcohol, even though they may be able to cope with other problems in a more stoical and mature way. In these patients no progress can be made unless the depression is treated at the same time that alcohol is withdrawn.

Course and prognosis of depression

Apart from those cases that end in suicide, depressive illnesses are usually benign in that most recover. In the more reactive patterns of depression a major change of circumstances can be curative, if for example an apparently dying child were to recover, or an alcoholic husband stop drinking. On the whole, however, although depression is often precipitated by such events, once the illness has developed it tends to run its course independent of external factors of that type. Really chronic depression, as a form of serious unhappiness, and with little or no endogenous element, occurs at times in people locked in very unhappy marriages, or other intense family situations, from which they are unable to free themselves, perhaps because of loyalty, religious beliefs, or for the sake of children. At times nothing can be done to help in such situations, other than to offer sympathy. In only a few patients without obvious major conflicts or external problems does serious depression persist despite treatment, and it is for this small group that psychosurgery may be necessary (see Ch. 16).

Untreated severe depression is rarely seen now, but before any modern treatments were instituted the average in-patient stay in a mental hospital for depression was over 12 months, and some stayed much longer. As they did not enter hospital easily in those days, the whole course was very long. At present depression severe enough to need in-patient treatment is usually relieved within 3 or 4 weeks, and the patient discharged within 6 weeks. Patients treated effectively with antidepressants as out-patients are usually very much better within 4–6 weeks, but those who do not respond to the first antidepressant given may be depressed for many months (The details of antidepressant drugs and of electrical treatment for depression are given in Chapter 16.)

In patients in whom reactive factors are predominant, and the endogenous features slight, antidepressants may not be indicated. If the depression has arisen from serious neurotic conflicts then some form of psychotherapy may be advisable. This can be given to the individual alone, or in a group; and if family conflicts are the centre of the problem, in so-called joint marital or family therapy. In our experience psychotherapy is not helpful in those who are still seriously and continuously depressed, and it is better for them to have been relieved of the worst of their symptoms by antidepressant or electrical treatment before starting psychotherapy, otherwise they may be too depressed to cope with the problems appearing in the psycho-therapeutic discussions, and end up in a worse state.

In many depressive states, especially in middle life, and especially in women in the years surrounding the menopause, it seems that the patient is prone to relapse repeatedly for periods of up to several years. During that time he or she may respond well to treatment, but relapse each time it is stopped, and never be completely well. At the end of this phase of uncertain duration there is a spontaneous change to a higher level of well being, and antidepressants can then be stopped and the patient remains well. In menopausal women it may be that endocrine changes are responsible, but on the whole it seems that this period represents the natural period of the depression, and that during that time antidepressants have suppressed the symptoms with greater or lesser success. In some of these patients lithium therapy is helpful in preventinq relapses during the period of vulnerability.

Some patients show a tendency to relapse at fairly regular intervals throughout long periods of their lives and in some the relapses tend to be at the same season of the year.

It is common to see patients in whom there is a history of a fairly serious depression years ago, perhaps untreated in the days before antidepressants were introduced (1950s), in whom some neurotic symptoms have persisted. Chronic agoraphobia (p. 261) lingering after puerperal depression is perhaps the commonest; but other anxiety, phobic, hysterical or obsessional symptoms may also follow this pattern. These patients can respond to antidepressants by losing their long standing neurotic symptoms, even if apparently there is no significant depression left, and a thorough trial of antidepressants is well worth while before beginning other therapy in long standing neurotic states with this type of background.

Excluding those with a predominantly reactive picture, only a few patients show no useful response at all to antidepressants and electrical treatment, although in a good many there are early relapses, often but not always due to adverse circumstances, and not always associated with obvious vulnerability and feebleness of temperament. These patients can be most difficult to help, and linger in everyone's minds as treatment failures. However, a good many of those who do repeatedly relapse can be helped by very careful drug control, the use of lithium salts, and personal and social support such as that provided by group therapy, and a day hospital or day centre. Some of these nonresponders are elderly people living alone, who are lonely but unwilling to give up their independence; or whose temperament is so seclusive or suspicious that they are unable to make use of the kind of social help offered by society.

It is important to consider three main possibilities when confronted by a depressed patient who fails to respond to treatment as expected.

Firstly, there is a sizeable group of people in whom there is a biochemical abnormality. In descending order of frequency these abnormalities are thyroid, vitamin B_{12} and folic acid deficiency; and much more rarely there may be disorders of calcium metabolism or other electrolytes. It is simple to exclude these, so long as the possibility is considered.

Secondly, there may be unsuspected organic brain disease or, much less often, some systemic disease such as carcinoma or tuberculosis. Slowly developing degenerative brain disease and cerebral tumours are particularly likely to be missed in younger people. In older people arteriosclerotic and senile changes are usually thought of, but may be missed.

Thirdly, there may be clinical features in the depression which have been missed or wrongly assessed, or which the patient has suppressed. In some patients in whom the symptoms are of endogenous type, drugs or electrical treatment may repeatedly fail to help because of some major conflict or problem which has not come to light. Conversely, patients in whom neurotic problems and conflicts are obvious may spend a very long time, often years, in psychotherapy of one type or another, because the importance of the endogenous depressive element is not recognised, so that they do not receive the drug therapy they need. Unfortunately there are many people who adhere rigidly to dogmatic theories of causation and treatment, and who persist indefinitely with inappropriate therapy despite the obvious failure of the method.

An illustration of the complexities which may exist was provided by a middle aged lady, living alone, who developed moderately severe rheumatoid arthritis and then depression with an endogenous pattern. She only responded slightly to antidepressants. The problem was reviewed and she was found to be hypothyroid, but although thyroxine helped her to feel better and to be more active, she remained depressed. Several months later she suddenly admitted that she did not live alone, but with another woman, to whom she was deeply attached, but who had become addicted to amphetamines and consequently was almost impossible to live with. Shame and loyalty had prevented her from telling the truth, but after the confession she improved and recovered completely when her companion went into hospital for treatment herself.

Depressive mood and the other symptoms of depression may be relieved fairly soon by treatment, but there are often consequences in the patient's family and social life which take longer to recover. Family tensions may be a factor in leading to depression, but they are also often much intensified by depression. Inability to work and consequent lack of money, irritability or emotional withdrawal, failure to cope with household tasks or as a mother, loss of sexual libido and the recriminations which follow, and many other accompaniments of depression can all seriously harm relationships in the family. The seriously depressed mother of a young child may be unable to respond to her young baby, and thus lead to both physical and emotional deprivation, with long term ill effects at times. The patient's withdrawal from normal social life during a long depressive illness may permanently damage friendships and lead to relative social isolation even after recovery. It can often help a great deal to discuss all these and similar problems with the family, and to try and get them to recognise the patient's unacceptable behaviour as part of an illness, and therefore something for which she should not be blamed, and which can therefore be better tolerated.

Treatment

As stated earlier, the more clearly the depressive illness shows the endogenous pattern, with the symptoms and signs just described, the more likely it is to respond to physical methods of treatment. These consist mainly of the various antidepressant drugs and electrical treatment (ECT).

The details of treatment are given in Chapter 16, but the basic principles are simple: antidepressant drugs should show some useful results within four weeks of full dosage being taken regularly, and should be stopped if no benefit appears. In serious depression with a suicide risk or self neglect, hospital admission is necessary as may be electrical treatment (ECT). Patients with depressive delusions nearly always need ECT. If the patient fails to respond to treatment, such as a tricyclic drug or ECT, the diagnosis should be reconsidered, and in particular there should be a search, as explained on page 185, for physical illness and for major life stresses that may have been overlooked, and which may be prolonging the illness. If no such factors are discovered, an alternative treatment should be given.

When a patient has responded to antidepressants, it is important not to stop them too soon. Many patients stop the drugs as soon as they feel better, only to relapse 3 or 4 weeks later. Very often the sequence is not seen as cause and effect, because it takes 3 or 4 weeks for the drugs to work, and a similar period to lose their effects. Drugs like tranylcypromine, which act within a week, lose their effect more quickly, too. It is wise to continue antidepressants for a minimum of 4 months after loss of symptoms, and the longer the depression has persisted before remission the longer the period of treatment necessary. 12 months or more on a tricyclic or tetracyclic antidepressant is often necessary. When the drug is withdrawn, it is best to do this very gradually, taking 3 or 4 weeks over each single minor dose reduction e.g., 25 mg at a time, using amitriptyline and similar tricyclics. This means that if the patient still needs the antidepressant there is no sudden and severe relapse, and the dose can be raised for 2 or 3 more months before reducing it gradually again.

Amphetamine-like drugs should be avoided because of the dangers of dependence, and benzodiazepines should not be regarded as antidepressants, although they can sometimes be given with antidepressants to relieve anxiety and tension. It is also best to avoid major tranquillisers such as haloperidol, which can make depression worse. Flupenthixol, however, is a useful antidepressant as well as being effective in schizophrenia.

Apart from the antidepressants, tranquillisers and hypnotics may be useful in the treatment of depressive illnesses. Sleep disturbance is a prominent symptom and is often helped by giving 100–150 mg of trimipramine or amitriptyline at night, or by nitrazepam 5–20 mg or dichloralphenazone 650–1300 mg. In agitated patients chlorpromazine 25–100 mg is often useful. In patients with marked early waking temazepam is most suitable to be taken in the early hours of the morning, as it has little hangover effect. In the relief of agitation and tension by day barbiturates are best avoided, because of the serious results of overdosage and the tendency for habituation to develop, although they are effective. Instead a sedative tricyclic drug such as amitriptyline may be helpful, and chlorpromazine or a benzodiazepine (see Ch. 16) can be added.

If the patient is able to work, it is better that he should continue to do so, although being kept under observation, and offered reassurance and encouragement meanwhile. Patients who do not normally work should be encouraged to pursue some routine, and should have definite activities prescribed for them where possible. In this the help of relatives may be necessary owing to the patient's indecisiveness and lack of initiative. At the same time the work or other activities prescribed should be well within the patient's limitations; he will not be able to cope with new things or strange people, and will be able to do less than his normal. It is a good rule that he should be encouraged to do what he normally finds pleasant, but should avoid what, however willingly undertaken, he would find irksome when well.

Where the depression is sufficiently severe to prevent the patient from working, and where there seems any serious likelihood of suicide, special measures are required. In mild depression a holiday may help, but in more serious states, especially with an endogenous pattern, the patient usually requires more support and protection, and holidays rarely help. Admission to hospital is preferable when patient or family feel they can no longer cope. If suicide seems a serious risk compulsory admission may be necessary.

Electrical treatment

This, also known as ECT for electroconvulsive therapy, revolutionised the treatment of severe depression. It is described in detail in Chapter 16, along with the indications for its use and the relatively trivial unwelcome side effects.

Psychological treatment

It must not be supposed that the treatment of depression is a routine matter of prescribing drugs and electrical treatment, even if the symptom pattern is purely endogenous. There is more to it than that. Account must, of course, be taken of the patient as a whole, and the various contributory factors, both external and within the personality of the patient, must be evaluated and dealt with as far as possible. Unsatisfactory conditions of work or of life at home, where contributory, will call for adjustments. Conflicts must be resolved as far as may be possible by psychotherapy. It is best not to undertake this, however, until a considerable measure of improvement has first been gained in any severely depressed case. Severely depressed patients are incapable of the intellectual effort involved, and much harm may in fact be done by obliging them to mill over their problems when they are in no condition to grapple with them. Confidence and trust in the doctor, other staff, and the treatment used are essential;

and the very act of 'handing over the problem' by seeking help is part of treatment.

When improvement is occurring, it is important not to yield to the temptations of (1) pushing the patient beyond his limitations, (2) discharging him or yielding to his requests to be discharged from hospital too soon. These amount to much the same thing. Stimulation of the improving patient should be gentle and gradual, for to encourage him to take on too much is to invite relapse.

Cognitive therapy.

In the last few years a new type of psychotherapy for depression has been introduced, derived more from behaviour therapy than from insight directed psychotherapy (see p. 394), although like the latter it concentrates on what the patient is feeling and thinking, as well as on what he does, like behaviour therapy.

The word cognition covers all the ways in which we 'know' something, including perceiving and remembering. There are three principle types of cognitive therapy: cognitive restructuring, cognitive behaviour therapy, and anxiety management. The former two are relevant to depression.

Details should be sought elsewhere (see bibliography), but in essence these approaches try and get the patient to use his reason, judgment, memory of the past and so on to recognise that, for example, he is not such a bad person as he feels he is, that other people are not ignoring him because they despise him, and so on. They also encourage people to do pleasant things, to divert and entertain themselves. In an informal and unstructured way, these methods have long been used to support and encourage depressed people, but in cognitive therapy they form the whole treatment. Several studies have demonstrated cognitive therapy can be as effective as tricyclic antidepressants, and of course, it can be given in addition to medication. It is much more time consuming than medication, and therefore more expensive, and its value in more severe depression has not yet been established. Perhaps its main benefit may turn out to be in lessening relapse rates.

BIPOLAR MANIC DEPRESSIVE ILLNESSES

These illnesses are much less common than unipolar depression, but are worth considering separately from the other affective disorders, because of their clinical features, genetic differences, and different treatment needs. The genetic aspect is considered in the section on aetiology, and treatment is considered both in this section and in Chapter 16.

CLINICAL

There is little to be said here about the depressive phase of manic depressive illness, because it is clincially identical with the classical endogenous pattern of depression described earlier. Agitation is rare but psychomotor retardation is common; the onset is often curiously abrupt; and both physical and emotional precipitants may be obvious, although often absent. Of all types of depression these are the most likely to come genuinely out of the blue, unrelated to circumstances or to inner conflicts, and not infrequently following some regular rhythm both in time and in relation to hypomanic upswings. It is in these illnesses that the importance of genetic and constitutional factors is most obvious; in which hormonal and biochemical changes are most clear cut; and in which psychotherapeutic treatment is relatively least important. In those patients in whom depressive or manic episodes are precipitated by neurotic or other personal conflicts, then psychotherapy can be very valuable when the patient has settled down to normal mood, and it can help to reduce the frequency of attacks.

The earlier in life a manic depressive illness appears, the more frequent is a family history of the same illness, and the more likely is the patient to have frequent recurrences. Although the personal sufferings of a patient with severe depression are very great, there is no doubt that it is the upswings which in the long run do the greatest damage, both to the patient's own life and to his family. To live with a manic depressive is for many to live in dread, because of the personal insults or violence which may suddenly develop; and because of the insecurity generated by unwise spending or investment, often enough leading to bankruptcy; or because of any one of a number of vitally important matters about which some unwise decision may suddenly be made, including, for example, suddenly giving up a good job, selling the house, or changing the children's school.

The manic phase

The onset is usually gradual, unless it follows a depressive phase, when the change can be very sudden. Many manic attacks seem more or less unrelated to outside events, but they are sometimes precipitated by external factors, of which the commonest are situations in which the patient has been subjected to considerable and continued frustration which he feels to be unwarranted and unjustifiable. In some cases an attack can be precipitated by an event which one would expect to lead to depression, and perhaps at some other time of the patient's life would have done so.

The term 'mania' is best reserved for illnesses so severe that the patient needs physical restraint, and 'hypomania' for all other degrees of severity.

Symptoms and signs

If there have been previous attacks, the development can often be recognised by the relatives before it is apparent to those who do not know the patient well. The patient may make gestures, stand in particular positions, or start to talk upon themes not in themselves remarkable, but which are peculiar to his manic phase. One of the commonest heralding signs is decorating the house, or doing other similar tasks, in the middle of the night. This may be happening for some days or even a week or so before there is any overt abnormality. This is usually followed by an increase in talkativeness, often with self-assertiveness, which is paralleled by an increase in activity. At first this may be well-directed, the patient still being able to do his work efficiently, though there is often some lack of restraint, so that he is less scrupulous about what he says and to whom he says it; he may confide family secrets and intimacies to people who are surprised to receive them, and he may be unduly familiar with acquaintances and strangers. At the same he may be extravagant, and if of a bonhomous disposition, may be overgenerous with gifts and in buying drinks for himself and others. In these ways he is almost always without insight into the fact that his behaviour is abnormal, and will insist that he has never felt better.

Just as the behaviour of the depressive is comprehensible in the light of his mood, so the behaviour of the hypomanic is also. And if called to account for his conduct, he will be able to produce plausible reasons for it which are hard indeed to refute except perhaps on economic grounds, which he will disregard. It may thus be very difficult to control the situation when, though not disturbed enough to admit to hospital compulsorily, he is spending beyond his means.

It will be noted that whereas the depressive phase is characterised by restriction and loss, the manic phase is characterised by expansion and self-assertiveness. The expansion, however, is more apparent than real. The themes upon which the manic or hypomanic patient talks are commonly the same themes, though they may preoccupy him only in the hypomanic phase, and they tend to be repetitive in conception and expression; the expansiveness lies more in a distractibility, and a tendency for the periphery of his mind to be caught by passing fancies.

If the patient passes beyond the hypomanic phase the total activity increases and becomes altogether out of hand. The patient gets up early, rouses the household with noisy bustle, goes out to gather spring flowers or to have a bathe, clears out lumber rooms, and may have performed before breakfast time innumerable activities to which he is normally quite unaccustomed. He then may plan unnecessary expeditions, may get in touch with people whom he has not seen for years, much to their surprise, make unnecessary telephone calls and send unnecessary telegrams. He may organise supper parties with boxes at the opera, to which he will take taxis but will arrive late owing to various things that have distracted him on the way, and there will be some confusion because the number of people he has asked will probably have increased since he made the arrangements which will probably have been in any event incomplete. These inconveniences will be brushed aside in flurry of further activity as he takes an inquisitive and extraverted, but superficial interest in all sorts of people and things, such as waiters, commissionaires, people encountered by chance at the bar, and so forth. Meanwhile, his plans for the evening may be undergoing many and rapid changes, as he may take up with people whom he meets, get fresh ideas from them, and may end up bringing strangers home for drinks in the small hours of the morning. The lack of restraint, the prodigal expenditure and the interest, though fleeting, in other people makes the patient a good target for parasites, hangers-on, and tellers of hard luck stories.

The patient may then retire for a few hours of uneasy sleep, after which the whole round of activity may begin again. His conversation similarly will be all but incessant, and one thought may so rapidly suggest another as to cause innumerable digressions without return to the main theme. The same distractibility characterises his actions, so that plans for effecting new improvements about the house will be broken off in favour of suddenly writing unnecessary letters, untidy with many afterthoughts and postscripts, which show the writer to be under characteristic pressure. One task after another is taken up but none completed.

At the same time, the patient usually feels possessed of marked clarity of thought, so that hesitations and doubts are cast aside, boldness is his policy and the decisions seem obvious, though his flurry of activity itself prevents him from implementing them. He may, however, offer advice freely, often in a way that carries conviction.

The pressure to which the patient is subject causes him to be intolerant of frustration, which, coupled with his over-confidence, makes him irritable and even markedly aggressive if unable to gain his ends. This is especially so if the customary lack of restraint has encouraged excessive drinking. Quarrels and even brawls are then quite liable to occur, and the more so when other people resent the inquisitive interference that such patients often show.

In such a state the patient's attention may be hard to hold, and their interest in what they are saying and seeing, coupled with their distractibility, may make it difficult to gain knowledge of their inner feelings. Such patients will often admit that their thoughts proceed at an unusual rate and follow each other with abnormal rapidity, but they will regard this as a satisfactory state of affairs and will not in the least concern themselves with its abnormality at the time. The mood is usually said to be 'elated' and the patient often described as showing an 'infectious gaiety'. Although this may occur, and the patient may laugh unduly often and loudly, it is by no means always the case. Many patients will say after the phase is over that, contrary to appearances, they experienced no real enjoyment, and an appreciable number will show a depressive content (occasionally even with suicidal ideas) even though their phase be a manic one. Excitement is thus a better term than elation, especially in view of the aggressive irritability that is so often seen.

As hypomania progresses further towards frank mania (and most cases do not progress as far) the tempo increases. The patient may shout, sing and dance, his conversation may become incoherent through pressure of talk which may be accompanied by gales of laughter, while the whole day is spent in a chaos of activity which seems purposeless owing to the rapidity with which one intention succeeds another. Violence often occurs. It is now that associations of ideas suggested by the sound of words will cause the patient to make rhymes and puns, and to show on the basis of such chance association, the so-called 'flight of ideas'. Lack of sexual restraint, which will previously have been noticeable in the ready introduction of risqué jokes, a tendency to philandering with erotic advances, may now amount to complete sexual shamelessness, with exhibitionism, overtly erotic behaviour and masturbation regardless of the circumstances.

In this state, the distractibility may cause the patient to be heedless of the passage of time, but he will otherwise be orientated. He may keep in remarkably good touch, and such patients often show a clear memory for everything that has happened, which is an indication for special care that nothing unsuitable should be said on the supposition that the patient is too distractible to notice it. Distortions of content (delusions and ideas of reference) may occur, but will be in line with the mood, so that the exalted patient may write cheques for a million, claim titles and confer them on others, boast of his physique and abilities and in general show grandiose behaviour; the patient who is excited and irritable may show marked paranoid trends, especially if previously he was a touchy person. Hallucinations, however, do not classically occur, and their presence should suggest the probability of intoxication or schizophrenic admixture. Judgement is impaired according to the extent of the grandiosity or paranoid trends, and the pressure under which the patient is acting.

Physically, the patient usually appears bright-eyed and with ruddy complexion. The voice is often hoarse through overuse. Loss of weight may become apparent as food is neglected in the general flurry of activity with which the patient increasingly exhausts himself. Sleep is disturbed both as regards getting off, and frequent and early waking, on which there is a tendency to resume activities immediately.

The contrast between the two phases of manic-depressive psychosis may be illustrated by the following table:

Depressive phase	Manic phase
Reduced animation	Excitement
Loss of confidence with feelings of inferiority and withdrawnness	Over-confidence with lack of diffidence, with gregariousness and tendency to interfere
Motor retardation up to stupor	Over-activity
Restriction and retardation of thought	Acceleration of thought; flight of ideas; often restriction of main themes of thought but peripheral expansion
Delusions of self-reproach, depersonalisation and hypochondriasis	Delusions of grandeur, mental and physical
Introversion	Extraversion
Suicidal ideas	Irritability and aggressiveness
Loss of sexual desire	Increase of sexual interest and diminished restraint
Sallow complexion	Ruddy complexion

Course and prognosis

In general, the manic phase, like the depressive one, may be regarded as benign since there is a tendency to spontaneous recovery. This is usually gradual. Often the first features of recovery are a diminution of irritability and aggressiveness, together with some return of restraint, as the pressure gradually subsides. The activity and talkativeness then become less. At this stage the patient may again be easily stimulated by having opportunity for excitement or for doing too much, but gradually he will return again to normal, if indeed he does not sink into a depressive phase. As with the latter there is great variation between one person and another in the length of attack; but manic attacks tend to be shorter than depressive ones. 3–6 weeks is a fairly usual duration. Where, however, such a phase occurs for the first time in a person over 40 years of age it is liable to be prolonged and the prognosis should be guarded accordingly. Since the introduction of lithium chronic mania very rarely occurs, although relapses cannot always be prevented.

Differential diagnosis

More attention may have to be paid to the evidence of relatives than to that of the patient. Although the latter may have little insight he may be astute enough so far to restrain himself as to put up a deceptively normal performance at interview. Allowance may have to be made for this in gauging the severity of the state, as well as for the fact that to live with an over-active and over-talkative hypomanic day in and day out is quite a different proposition from seeing him only for an hour in conversation. In some people with natural high spirits and a high endowment of energy, their normal state may be something approaching hypomania. The same is true of the cyclothymic when the swing of his mood is in an upward direction. But where a patient shows hypomanic behaviour for the first time, the diagnosis must be made by exclusion.

Many psychiatric conditions, like others in general medicine, are not clear cut, and there is an overlap with schizophrenia in the schizo-affective psychoses (see p. 151). For this reason, what is really a schizophrenic psychosis may be ushered in by behaviour of hypomanic or manic type. The previous personality and history of the patient may offer some guide; the less there have been schizoid features, the more normal the personality seems to have been, and the more there is a history of anything resembling cyclothymia, the more probable does the diagnosis of manic-depressive illness become in such a case. More important are the presence of such features as the first rank symptoms of Schneider, a bizarre emotional quality, and stuporose episodes, which all make a diagnosis of schizophrenia likely. In general the conduct of the manic or hypomanic patient should be congruous and in harmony with the mood. The family history is less helpful in the differential diagnosis owing to the tendency for mixed forms to occur.

Apart from the foregoing, there are only two main pitfalls. The first is when the patient is referred as a dipsomaniac, i.e. a periodic drinker to excess. The possibility must then be borne in mind that such drinking may be symptomatic of the increased bonhomie, lack of restraint and over-activity that commonly accompany the hypomanic state. This is much less common than excessive drinking as a response to depression.

The second main pitfall is when the patient is referred as a hypomanic, but may actually be suffering from some organic cerebral disease affecting particularly the frontal lobes. That now rare condition, syphilitic GPI in its expansive form, was particularly difficult to distinguish. Physical examination, intellectual deficits, and positive serology should be enough to make the diagnosis certain, but more detailed neurological investigation may be necessary.

Certain very rare lesions, such as tumours, in the neighbourhood of the third ventricle have been known to produce manic-like pictures, but where such uncommon conditions happen to be encountered, the condition is likely to be inconsistent, prolonged rather than episodic, with associated symptoms of headache, and with signs that, if not initially present, will develop as the lesion expands.

In summary, the difficulties in diagnosing hypomania or mania should not be great. Awareness of the existence of such a condition will put the student on his guard against dismissing as mere boorishness or foolish conduct, behaviour of a hypomanic or manic kind in a person not normally subject to it. The history of previous phases, or of depressive ones, will be a guide. The main differential diagnosis is from the excited forms of schizophrenia and from frontal lobe lesions of various types.

Treatment of the depressive phase

The treatment of the depressive phase is almost identical with that of other depression, using the antidepressant drugs and electrical treatment in the same way. The only important practical differences arise from the fact that as the mood starts to improve with treatment, there is a very real danger that the patient will become hypomanic. It is wise therefore to start lithium therapy (described in detail later) quite early in the course of treatment, to lessen the chances of this happening. It may also be wise to lessen the dose of antidepressants early, especially if MAOI drugs are being used; and to interrupt a course of electrical treatment before the patient has completely recovered, as a marked upward mood swing of the patient often seems to develop after only a few treatments, and to continue the treatment may encourage hypomania.

Treatment of the manic phase

The mildest cases will not seek advice at all. The less mild ones will be brought, more or less reluctantly, by relatives who are concerned about them, and more particularly about their extravagance. Where there is undue expenditure, any serious risk of social embarrassment or of losing a job through the behaviour, or where the relatives find him intolerably tiring to live with, the patient will best be treated in hospital. This is far more easily said than done. The patient is unlikely to agree. All the arts of persuasion and bargaining may be called for, and in persuasion use should be made of any physical symptoms or lesions that he may happen to have.

If the patient still refuses, as is likely, attempts may be made to reduce the over-activity by drug treatment, preferably doled out by the relatives and taken under supervision. It may be possible to arrange some holiday or change of scene, essentially of a quiet and unstimulating kind, on which the patient can take plenty of physical exercise, and indulge in some innocuous pleasure such as bathing, or pursue some innocuous hobby such as fishing. Instructions may have to be given to tradespeople, etc., with a view to preventing the running up of large credit accounts. Attempts should be made tactfully to control the intake of alcohol where this tends to be excessive.

The attack may then gradually subside, or the patient may become worse to the extent that compulsory detention is possible. Where there is extravagance leading to serious financial hardship, or where other social embarrassments are occurring, compulsory detention should not be too long delayed, but can only be undertaken as a rule where the behaviour is creating a real social nuisance.

Drug treatment

One very effective drug is haloperidol, but recent reports have suggested a high incidence of complications when used in conjunction with lithium. As lithium is so valuable in manic states, in treatment of the acute phase as well as in prevention the author has changed over largely to droperidol, which like haloperidol is a substituted butyrophenone. The dose of haloperidol varies widely, from 1.5 mg t.d.s. to 80 mg or more, in divided doses, and the dose range of droperidol is similar. They can also be given in large doses intravenously or intramuscularly. More sedative drugs such as chlorpromazine 300–600 mg daily can be added. These drugs control the patient's excitement and over activity partly because of the Parkinsonian side effects they produce. Antiparkinsonian agents, such as orphenadrine 50 mg t.d.s., are necessary in nearly all cases, but, curiously, side effects seem less common when very large doses are used. This is probably because of the anticholinergic effects of the drugs themselves which have an antiparkinsonian effect if in large doses. The same paradoxical loss of extrapyramidal symptoms with very high dosage occurs with phenothiazines. Haloperidol often causes rapid lowering of mood, and seems to lead to an earlier depressive down-swing than would otherwise occur. It is our practice to lessen the dose progressively as soon as the patient's excitement and elevated mood settle to near normal.

Lithium Carbonate. The actions and toxic side effects of this simple salt are described in Chapter 16. It is of most use in preventing recurrences of hypomanic upswings, but in many patients it helps to control the acute attack, and also contributes to more rapid recovery in the depressive phase. Side effects are more common if large doses are given at the start, and it seems better to give 400 mg of the delayed release preparation Priadel daily for a few days before increasing the dose to 800 mg or 1,200 mg, which in most people is enough to maintain the serum lithium between 0.8 and 1.4 mmol/l, the most suitable range. Many patients can be maintained adequately at lower blood levels, around 0.7 mmol. Regular estimations are essential as the drug is dangerously toxic if the level exceeds 2.0 mmol, and often ineffective if the level is below about 0.6 mmol.

Lithium has transformed life for most manic-depressives, as it is strikingly successful in preventing relapses in a very large number of patients. In those in whom it is ineffective or causes side effects, it is worth trying Carbamazepine, long used as an anticonvulsant, in a dose ranging up to 800 mg daily in divided doses, monitored by estimating the plasma level (therapeutic range 1.5–9.0 mg/l).

Treatment in hospital

In hospital, the aim should be to allow the patient just enough occupation and activity to enable him to work off something of the inner pressure that he feels, while at the same time preventing him from becoming further stimulated. This is not easy to achieve. The drugs mentioned above will be found useful, and if necessary can be combined with minor tranquillisers such as diazepam, up to 30 or 40 mg daily in divided doses. Attention must be paid to the intake of food and intake and output of fluids owing to the danger of intoxication. It is usually wise to cut down contacts with the outer world, such as visitors and the receipt of letters, at first and until the patient shows signs of settling down.

Electrical treatment

It may seem paradoxical that this should be applied to both the phases of manic-depressive psychosis, in view of their somewhat contrasting nature; but it is effective in each to some extent. It has, however, been largely replaced by the use of drugs in the treatment of hypomania.

General management

It is characteristic of the manic or hypomanic patient to dislike the restraints imposed upon him. He will constantly wish to be extending the range of his activities, and must be dissauded from this as far as possible. This almost always leads to bargaining, often of a more or less irritable kind. The best policy is to make concessions but only on the unimportant points. Often, the patient's humour may be exploited with advantage, and great use can be made of the distractibility by diverting the patient's attention from the main issues at hand. Occupational therapy and ward work can be useful as affording harmless channels for the output of hypomanic energy, but supervision will of course be required and care should be taken that the patient is stimulated as little as possible.

It is always a good rule to explain the state of affairs carefully to the relatives, not only with a view to recuring their co-operation, but because the lack of insight of manic and hypomanic patients leads them frequently to complain and sometimes to be litigious, as to which the family may be accordingly forewarned.

Psychological treatment

As with the depressive phase, it is necessary to evaluate the factors that may have contributed to the hypomanic or manic development (e.g. frustrations, conflicts, unsatisfactory conditions at home or at work), and adjustments should be attempted as far as possible. The patient will be far too distractible for such considerations in the early stages, and attempts to deal with them are likely only to stimulate him into further excitement. They should be delayed until reasonable tranquillity has been gained.

Despite the use of lithium, which is of tremendous benefit to many sufferers from manic depressive illness, in some patients recurrences cannot be prevented. It is then worth trying to achieve a higher level in the blood than usually considered safe, so long as it is done with careful supervision, as in some people this is successful.

Suicide

A few general facts may be given before considering the individual case. Although more women attempt suicide than men, effective suicide is rather more common in men than in women. The commonest time of year is the spring and early summer. As regards age, the commonest in most countries for men is in the seventies, and for women it is about 10 years earlier. There is a marked association with physical disease, and an even more marked one with alcoholism. Suicide is commoner in urban than in rural areas, among single people than among married, among the childless than among parents, among the socially isolated than among the gregarious, among those who have become impoverished than among those who have always been poor, among the unemployed than among the employed, among the rootless than among those who have attachments, and among Protestants or irreligious than among Roman Catholics. By these criteria, a single, childless, socially isolated, drifting, impoverished, unemployed, irreligious, seventy-year-old townsman with intractable organic disease may be a candidate, especially if liable to depressive illness or personality reaction, with a history of a previous attempt.

The frequency of suicide in the United Kingdom fell steadily after the second world war, but over the past decade has slowly risen. In 1975 it reached a low, with about 4000 deaths by suicide in England and Wales (a rate of approximately 8 per 100 000), but it was up to almost 5000 in 1983. Scottish figures followed a similar pattern. Death by suicide is almost as common as death in road accidents, something not widely appreciated. Rates in the United Kingdom are still much lower than for most developed countries.

Many patients go to their doctors in the days immediately before they commit suicide, but fail to reveal how they feel. In many of these cases their families have been at least partly aware of the severity of the depression, and may have encouraged them to make the visit. Unfortunately, because of diffidence and awkwardness, or because of the lack of time or the doctor's manner, they do not manage to communicate properly and get the help they need, but come away with a prescription — for indigestion mixture or an analgesic, as like as not. As has been mentioned elsewhere in this book, a question like 'How are your spirits?' should be a very common one.

Every patient with more than a mild depressive illness must be regarded as a possible suicidal risk.

At large, the most popular methods for suicide are by taking overdoses of drugs; but swallowing other poisons, hanging, cutting the throat or blood vessels, and jumping under trains are not uncommon. With the increasing spread of North Sea gas, in the United Kingdom, the use of the gas oven is less significant. Car exhaust gas is a not uncommon method. In hospital, suicidal attempts are most often made by jumping out of windows, hanging, self-strangulation, obtaining some sharp instrument with which to sever a blood-vessel, or hoarding drugs until a store has been obtained. Measures should be taken accordingly. Tricyclic antidepressants are very dangerous in overdose as are aspirin and paracetamol.

Suicidal talk should never be taken lightly, and this is especially so with depressive cases. A popular notion that 'those who talk about suicide don't do it' is entirely fallacious, though it is also true that the most determined patients of all may dissimulate their intentions.

The assessment of suicidal risk

This may be very difficult, but every doctor in clinical practice should understand how to do it, just as he should be able to examine the cardiovascular system. Students sometimes hesitate to explore the question, out of misplaced delicacy, or a fear that they might put the idea into the patient's mind, but in everyone who is suffering from depression some assessment of suicidal intent should be made, and recorded in the notes.

With the patient who has not made any suicidal act or threats, it takes only a few words to establish the facts. After an account of the patient's feelings, symptoms, social and personal problems has been taken, and a rapport established, suicidal ideas should be asked about openly and frankly. One can ask 'How is the depression at its worst? . . . ' 'Do you ever feel that you would rather be dead than put up with it indefinitely?' . . . and, depending on the answer to that question: 'Do you ever feel like ending your own life?' If the answer is 'Yes', then a more detailed assessment is needed. Very many depressives do feel that they could not tolerate such a state indefinitely, but they hope and expect relief from their suffering. Patients, with few exceptions, will tell the truth, and if they are evasive it should be taken as indicating strong suicidal thoughts.

A chapter on affective illnesses is the natural place to consider suicide, but not everyone who commits suicide is suffering from a depressive illness, and nor are all those who make more or less serious attempts. In assessing the likelihood of a suicide attempt, we may have to consider the following:

1. The seriousness of any attempt made recently
2. What the patient says about his feelings and intentions
3. The diagnosis
4. The method used or threatened
5. The immediate circumstances of the act
6. The social setting of the patient
7. Various sociological factors.

If someone has survived a suicidal act, then the likelihood of further attempts must be assessed, partly by how seriously ill he made himself, as well as by the factors given below. Remember, however, that people can make serious mistakes, both by under and over-estimating the potency of drugs, and the dangers of gas, electricity and so on. Quite a lot of those who survive serious attempts are quickly glad to be alive after all, but there are plenty who are not.

The patients' own statements of intent are the most important evidence of all, and an approach to the patient who is not known to be suicidal has already been outlined. After an attempt at, or threats of, suicide, the questioning must go further. For example:

'What did you hope would happen when you did this?' 'Can we feel confident that you will not try again?' and so on.

In addition to direct statements about suicidal intent, there must be an assessment of mood, of the degree of anger directed at others and himself (both very commonly found in suicidal patients), and of his determination. Any manipulative element in the suicidal threat or behaviour should also be assessed.

Diagnosis is sometimes very important. For example, suicide is very common in schizophrenia, especially in the early stages, when depression is a common symptom, and insight, with its attendant fear of future deterioration, is better preserved. Schizophrenics almost never make suicidal gestures, nor do they seek sympathy and attention by threatening suicide. They tend to violent and bloody acts, without warning. Because of the nature of their illness, it is more difficult to assess their mood and intentions, and great care must be taken.

Patients with psychotic depressive states, that is, with delusions or hallucinations, are also very much at risk, especially as they begin to improve from states of retardation which have inhibited any action. There is also a danger of murder, especially of children, by the deluded depressive who feels that she can bring only suffering to her family, and kills to spare them. If a patient expresses such delusional guilty ideas, full precautions must be taken.

Puerperal depression is another state in which very sudden suicidal attempts occur, usually within the first 10 days after the birth, as when some woman jumps out of a window, perhaps carrying her baby. Doctors and nurses become so accustomed to mild puerperal depression that it seems almost normal, which it is not. They may then ignore the danger signals of increasing restlessness, sleep disturbance, anorexia and developing fears and bizarre ideas about the baby and themselves. If a woman has had a previous severe puerperal depression (p. 169), of sudden onset especially, she should be carefully watched after delivery, and if necessary given prophylactic antidepressants.

Suicide is very much more common in alcoholics and drug abusers than in other people. Assessment can be very difficult because, unlike most other patients whom we are considering, they are less honest — both with themselves and others. Unfortunately, they tend to generate dislike and consequent rejection by both doctors and nurses, and staff must guard against this.

Many people who commit suicide have no true psychiatric illness, but are in chronic pain, lonely, see no hope of improvement and decide that on balance, they might as well be dead.

The method used is important, because some of them are nearly always associated with serious intent to die, and rarely with attention seeking or other non-serious attempts. These are: fire arms, hanging, drowning, jumping from heights, swallowing caustics or acids and, especially recently, the use of paraquat and similar weed killers.

The immediate circumstances are relevant in that they usually indicate the likelihood of discovery before death; and also how much the act was planned or impulsive, how much a reaction to immediate conflict, and so on. Careful preparations, such as making a will or sending the family away on holiday, are also important, as are some suicide letters, depending on their content.

By the social setting of the patient, we mean his family and the degree of happiness and support it may provide; and his work, friendships, interests, future prospects, and much that gives life meaning and depth. We can ask: 'What is there in life worth living for if he were well?' and seek for an answer along these lines. The more lonely, sad and empty the life before depression began, the worse the outlook.

Various sociological factors have been mentioned already, such as religion and marital state, and others are mentioned below in considering 'self-poisoning'. These factors are of great interest and importance statistically, but should not be relied on in assessing the individual patient.

Suicide precautions

If after careful assessment suicidal attempts seem likely, the patient should be admitted to hospital, if necessary under a compulsory section, as described in Chapter 17. Very occasionally, skilled home nursing, by professional psychiatric nurses, may be adequate. Few can afford this.

In hospital every nurse and other member of the staff should be aware of the risk, and, after careful and sympathetic explanation to the patient, there should be a search for tablets, razors, or other potentially lethal articles, and, when given tablets as treatment, care must be taken that they are truly swallowed. If there is any doubt, liquid medicines or injections should be given. It is wise to keep the patient in bed, or at least in pyjamas and dressing gown, and he should be accompanied to the bathroom, as one can drown in a bath with time and determination. The lavatories should not have projections from which people can hang themselves with pyjama cords, which should in any case be replaced by buttons. Sedation or tranquillisation is usually helpful.

Such stringent precautions are rarely necessary for long, as tranquillisation and antidepressant treatment usually have fairly rapid effects.

Self-poisoning

In the last few years there has been an enormous increase in the number of 'suicidal gestures' by taking overdoses of drugs, often trivial. In many cases there is no suicidal intent at all, and they are perhaps better called 'self poisonings'. The patient is usually a young woman or adolescent girl, of hysterical personality, and the overdose is an expression of despair, anger and frustration, or an attempt to change family attitudes or manipulate the situation. These patients have become a major problem in casualty departments and medical wards. There are so many of them in some urban hospitals that they seriously affect the work load, and if all were referred to psychiatrists — as is often recommended — the psychiatrists would have little time for their other patients. There is now little sense of shame or guilt attached to such self poisoning, and the massive increase is partly a matter of fashion in what is acceptable behaviour. Nevertheless a number of the patients are seriously distressed and some will go on to commit suicide effectively. The death rate from completed suicide is high among those who have taken apparently 'non-serious' overdoses in the past. It requires care and skill to distinguish those who need treatment from those who do not. The background of many of the 'self poisoners' is of social disorganisation, poverty, and personal inadequacy. They tend to come from unskilled working class families in which prison sentences, unemployment, children in care or on probation, are all much commoner than average, but they occur quite frequently at all social levels. There is rarely any evidence of psychiatric illness.

We know that careful assessment and appropriate treatment lower the chance of later death by suicide, and every case must be properly investigated. This initial assessment need not be done by a psychiatrist, as the skills can, and should, be learnt by every doctor who is dealing with these patients, who can then refer for psychiatric help the more disturbed and potentially suicidal. The essential factors in the assessment include interest, time and thoroughness.

Hypochondriasis

This word is used in various ways, but is best kept for clinical states in which the patient complains of various physical symptoms and disorders for which no physical cause can be found, over long periods of time, usually with great intensity of feeling, and in which the symptoms are not simply part of some other recognisable mental illness such as depression.

The most typical patient is more often a woman, over 55 years, of obsessional personality, being meticulous, rigid, tense, ruminative and usually over-concerned with bowel function throughout life; unhappily married or single, and poorly occupied. The patient's thoughts can seem almost totally dominated by concern about the symptoms. Bowel disturbances are perhaps the commonest problem, but any part of the body may provide the focus of concern. The main symptom may be pain, often described in extreme terms, although the patient does not look as though she is in agony, but may be less clear cut, and involve any system. The patient often goes to doctor after doctor, and hospital case records about her get thicker and thicker, while she collects an increasing number of reports and X-rays which she may take with her to consultations with new doctors. There may be some depressive mood, but these hypochondriacal states are distinct from depressive illnesses in which hypochondriasis is a symptom of a depressive illness, and is relieved by successful antidepressant treatment. Rather bizarre hypochondriacal states occur in schizophrenia also.

Patients with these chronic hypochondriacal states, often lasting many years, are very difficult to help. It may seem that their sufferings become their main interest in life, so that without them life would be more dull, and the interest of the whole family may indeed be focused on the patient's health. The symptoms, when not of pain, are commonly of 'throbbing' somewhere, or 'movement' in the abdomen, and it often seems that the patient is too aware of normal visceral or vascular activity which in most people does not reach consciousness. The patient is then 'listening in' with heightened awareness and a sense of distress to aortic pulsation, peristalsis, or some other normal body activity.

It is worth trying antidepressant drugs, as some of the states may be the residuum of incompletely resolved depression, but social distraction and useful occupation, giving the patient something else to take an interest in, is the most generally helpful treatment in an almost untreatable condition.

These states merge with those in which hysterical features are prominent, as described on p. 280 under Briquet's syndrome.

SUMMARY

'Endogenous and 'reactive' depression

Best seen as opposite ends of spectrum, most patients have features of both.

The more marked the endogenous pattern (largely biological symptoms), the more is physical treatment appropriate: (i.e. lowered drive, interest, concentration, appetite and weight loss, diurnal variation, loss of libido, retardation or agitation, constipation, self reproach, delusions.) Depression very commonly presents with physical symptoms or alcohol dependence.

(Transient minor depressive states in vulnerable people not included as 'Affective Disorder' but as 'neurotic reaction'.)

Bipolar manic-depressive disorders

Genetically distinct from 'unipolar' depressions above. (Recurrent mania like bipolar). Mania — requires physical restraint. Hypomania — anything less severe.

Symptoms

Over-activity, elation, irritability, excitement, grandiose delusions, loss of inhibitions, sleeplessness, flight of ideas.

Aetiology

Genetic factors important.

Depression — precipitated by 'loss', series of life events, puerperium, insoluble conflicts, pathological grief reactions, retirement, menopause. ('Loss' includes loss of people, work, health, self-respect). Alcoholism, viral infections, head injuries, steroids, drugs which deplete monoamines, Hypothyroidism, Vit. B_{12} and Folic Acid deficiency.

Monoamine hypothesis — that depression associated with low monoamine levels.

Treatment

Physical — ECT, especially if delusions or failure to respond to other treatment. Marked biological symptoms suggest good response.

Antidepressant medication Tricyclic drugs, MAOI, tetracyclic, tryptophan, lithium. Combinations (some suitable).

Psychological — Cognitive therapy, environmental change. (Insight psychotherapy best avoided in severe depression. Can be indicated on recovery).

Complications

Suicide major risk (about 5000 completed suicides annually in England and Wales). Impaired social life, work ability, lessened self confidence, alcoholism, all common sequels.

Prognosis

Most depressive illnesses recover with treatment, though may be recurrences over several years.

10

Disorders of personality and of sexual development

This chapter should be read in conjunction with that following. It considers those disorders of personality which can be regarded as constitutional; in other words, related to the basic nature of the person, and which we understand as the result of a life-long interaction of genetic and environmental factors. In clinical psychiatry it is mainly personality which is considered, although intelligence is often relevant, and even physical make-up may be important too. In the study of mental handicap intelligence is naturally more important. (See chapter 13).

We deliberately separate disorders of personality from 'personality reactions' and 'neurotic states', which are dealt with in the next chapter, in order to make clear the difference between enduring states and more transient and reactive conditions, in which of course personality is always important if not pre-eminent.

Personality is difficult to define, and no generally accepted theory of personality exists, nor is there any generally accepted way in which it may be described and assessed.

We use the word 'personality' here to sum up those enduring characteristics of a person which determine how he or she will react, in both behaviour and feeling, to the life situation and to changes in it. Many formal methods of describing personality have been put forward, but in practice there are three main approaches to the problem which are relevant here: (1) psychoanalytic, (2) quantitative and factorial and (3) clinical description of traits or types. An extensive literature exists about all of these and details of the first two in particular should be sought elsewhere, as only the merest sketch of them is given here. There are of course more ways of thinking about personality and its development, but these are the main ways in which it is described in practice.

(1) *Psychoanalytic descriptions of personality* arise naturally from psychoanalytic theories of personality development, in which people are viewed as passing through various stages in infancy and childhood,

and in which great importance is given to the role of unconscious processes. During the early stages of development libidinal drives are focussed on oral, anal and genital functions in sequence, and are gradually turned from concentration on the self outwards to other people. Thus descriptions such as 'an anal character', 'oral dependency needs', or 'narcissistic' are frequently used, and have fairly clear cut meanings in theoretical terms. To the non-psychoanalytic clinician they are often misleading, they are often used too loosely and sweepingly and they carry theoretical implications which may well not be justified in what should be a description rather than a speculative interpretation (see p. 389).

(2) *Quantitative and factorial methods* of personality description have mainly been developed by psychologists. They use questionnaires to obtain answers to questions relevant to personality, and by careful sifting and statistical analysis end by excluding all but the most useful and discriminating questions.

One of the best known is the Eysenck Personality Inventory (E.P.I.); the answers to which define an individual's place on two independent dimensions, firstly one of extraversion-intraversion and secondly one of neuroticism. The first is a measure of how reserved or outgoing the person is; the second measures emotional lability, largely in terms of symptoms which arise from overactivity of the autonomic nervous system. (It represents a constitutional predisposition, not, however, a neurotic 'illness'.) Eysenck's work is based theoretically on ideas derived from Pavlov: that is, that people who develop conditioned responses very easily are more likely to develop excessive and maladaptive responses, and thus to be neurotic. In our opinion this idea is indeed very relevant to many patients, including most of those with anxiety states and simple phobias, and also to those people who never consult a psychiatrist but who throughout their lives are 'anxiety prone' and habitually over-react to trivial stimuli. However, the Eysenckian concept of 'neuroticism' is much too narrow to include people with neurotic character disorders (p. 238); nor does it fit in convincingly with the nature of obsessional compulsive states (p. 297) or hysterical conversion (p. 264). At a theoretical level there are also serious doubts as to whether there is indeed a general factor of conditionability. The main use of the E.P.I. is in research studies involving large numbers of people. It is rarely of use in clinical situations.

The Cattell 16 P.F. (sixteen personality factor) Questionnaire provides a much more elaborate description of people than the two dimensional system of Eysenck, as it places people on sixteen different dimensions, and some of these can be combined to produce 'second order' factors. As with the E.P.I. the main use of the Cattell 16 P.F. test must be in research, as it has little clinical relevance.

A very different type of personality assessment is provided by the Kelly Repertory Grid, based on Kelly's theory of personal constructs. In essence the subject expresses his subjective feelings about people or things ('elements') in terms of 'constructs', which are chosen for their relevance to the person and problem being studied, but which may include for example 'kindness', 'aggressiveness' or 'motherliness'. After elaborate analysis, usually by computer, a picture of some of the subject's feelings and the way in which they are ordered and interrelated is obtained. In clinical work these so called 'grids' can be very illuminating, giving new insights into a patient's feelings and problems, and they are useful in assessing change, as for example in psychotherapy. They are, however, very time consuming to produce.

These are also questionnaires which are based more on clinical psychiatric concepts and ask about symptoms as well as putting questions related to underlying enduring personality characteristics. Two of these are the Minnesota Multiphasic Personality Inventory (M.M.P.I.) and the Middlesex Hospital Questionnaire (M.H.Q.). The M.M.P.I. is mainly used in North America, and contains about 550 questions, all originally chosen as usefully discriminating between patients already definitely diagnosed as psychiatrically ill. The M.H.Q. is much briefer and rates the patient on six scales, covering usefully the ordinary range of neurotic symptoms. Although the M.M.P.I. is used in clinical work in North America it is rarely used in Britain, and the M.H.Q. is used principally in research in this country.

In addition to the methods mentioned above there are also the so-called 'projective tests'. The best known of these is the Rorschach test, in which the subject is shown a standard series of ink blot designs and asked to describe what he sees. His answers are rated in a standardised way and his personality assessed accordingly. The rationale is very plausible — that he is expressing his fantasies and inner reactions — but the test has never been well validated (that is, objectively compared to other accepted measures and methods), and the results depend a great deal on the person doing the testing. The other well known projective test is Murray's Thematic Apperception Test (T.A.T.) in which a series of pictures capable of varying interpretations are shown to the subject, who has to tell a story about each one. Similar criticisms are levelled at this test, and neither of them is used extensively in Britain. Perhaps their greatest use is to identify particular conflicts or important emotional problems as a preliminary screening before psychotherapy, but they certainly do not give an overall view of the personality.

To the clinician, any system of personality description which is based purely on answers to a questionnaire must have serious shortcomings, for various reasons. For example, there is really no place in a questionnaire for objective assessments of such important matters as the person's capacity for effort or 'drive'; his ability to stick at things despite stress or difficulty; whether he becomes physically violent at times; his ability to form enduring relationships (as opposed to the ease or difficulty of meeting strangers which a questionnaire can well assess); or his 'likeableness'. All of these are of very great importance in the life of everyone, but several of them can only be well assessed from the reports of others or from the assessor's own responses. The benefits of questionnaires are obvious, in that they are not subjective, and they are reproducible; but in clinical psychiatry they are at best inadequate by themselves, and too often irrelevant.

(3) *Clinical assessment of personality.* Whatever theory of personality development is accepted, and whatever formal tests are used as adjuncts, in our view personality is best assessed by a combination of personal interview with the patient and with other people who know him well. Often certain features of the initial history which the patient gives will have more value in assessing his personality and predicting his future behaviour than anything else he says. For example, if a man has had twenty jobs in two years, and says he left each one because he was 'fed up' or 'didn't like being pushed around', then he is not likely to stick to any treatment régime and will very probably fail to keep his appointments. Conversely, a man who has spent thirty years in the same clerical job, and whose hobby is stamp collecting, is likely to be cautious, reliable, and a perfectionist. It is usually most natural and convenient to interview the patient's spouse, but other relatives or close friends, or even employers or work mates may at times be helpful. Naturally the patient's approval should always be sought for this. Another benefit of seeing the spouse or whoever lives with the patient, is that the home is often where conflicts and troubles are most intense, and light will probably be thrown on these as well as on the patient's personality and well being.

Although scientific exactitude is not possible when assessing personality by clinical interview, an attempt at rough 'measurement' of character traits should be made. In the same way that intelligence is distributed throughout the population on a more or less normal curve of distribution, so can we conceive of any personality characteristic. We should try to rate each patient roughly in this way for traits such as proneness to anxiety, outgoingness or reserve, obsessional features, capacity for sustained effort and interest, proneness to depressive mood and to irritability, sensitivity, suspiciousness and tendencies to blame others (paranoid traits), aggressiveness, attention-seeking, impulsiveness, and tendencies to avoid reality by denying problems or escaping from situations into day-dreaming or drink. All of these are often relevant clinically, and may be brought out during detailed history taking and interviews with others.

A good estimate of the patient's intelligence can also be made, by considering the educational background, work, interests, and of course by what is said and the way in which it is said. For each personality trait the patient is roughly rated as being average, above or below average, or perhaps very far from average in one direction or the other. There is a very wide range of normality, and it is important to remember that personality characteristics, although regarded as enduring features, are not independent of situation. For example, aggressiveness may be directed only at certain sorts of people in certain types of situations; perfectionism may be present in some activities and not in others; or irritability may be absent at work and severe at home. Nevertheless, on the whole these tendencies are mainly stable in given situations, and the way in which someone has behaved in certain circumstances in the past is usually a better guide to future behaviour than what he says he intends to do.

In keeping notes and when describing a patient's personality only the outstanding features will be mentioned, the unspoken implication being that any personality trait not mentioned is regarded as being near average in degree, or irrelevant. A patient might then be described simply as 'obsessional' or 'paranoid'; or as 'vulnerable' if throughout life he has reacted to stress by anxiety or depression, or by failure to cope in some way. In a more thorough description someone might be described as 'anxious, reserved and markedly obsessional' or as 'attention-seeking, lacking in drive and irritable'.

The reliable and valid assessment of personality is not only of interest to psychiatrists and other doctors. It is of the greatest importance to everyone who employs people, for example. Years ago the armed services decided that the best way to select people to be commissioned as officers was, after preliminary screening, to bring the candidates to live together for a time, under continuous observation. They could then be given various military tasks, of initiative for example, to see who showed ingenuity or powers of leadership. The way they got on with others while living together under those stressful conditions could also be assessed. Observing people in hospital can similarly help in personality assessment, although there is inevitable distortion because of the illness which has led to admission, and the unusual nature of life in hospital.

Accepting that there is a wide range of personality, and with the idea of a normal curve of distribution in mind, we can use the term 'abnormal personality' or 'personality disorder' when someone shows any extreme variation. The term is therefore essentially used statistically.

It should be clear that this method of personality description carries no theoretical implications, which is a benefit when the theoretical foundations of personality development are so uncertain. An elastic approach is required which recognises that certain instincts or drives provide the motive forces underlying human life and that, much modified and even distorted by genetic and environmental factors, these drives are always to be reckoned with. Psychological theories differ in the number of different drives they are prepared to recognise, but sexual drives, hunger, thirst and avoidance of pain are undoubted; to which many would add the drives to form personal and social bonds. Serious and persistent anomalies are common in the fields of sex and of personal and social bond formation; sexual anomalies are considered later in this chapter.

SOME TYPES OF PERSONALITY DISORDER

A number of types of disordered personality are commonly described, but no one should imagine that these 'types' are in any way entities; they can usefully be seen as examples. Personality is composed of numberless characteristics, present in an individual in varying intensity. In many these characteristics come together in certain ways, and we can then recognise the 'type'.

The schizoid personality

This description was originally applied because the combination of characteristics occurred in a large proportion of people who later broke down into schizophrenic illnesses, and also seemed commoner in the relatives of such patients. Recent studies of the relatives of schizophrenics shows a wider range of personality abnormalities and features, which are considered in the section on the aetiology of schizophrenia (p. 126). No clear cut relationship should be assumed with schizophrenia and the use of the word 'schizoid' to describe an illness or breakdown is incorrect, it must be used only to describe personality.

In general, the personality tends to be introverted, with emotions that are cold, leading to aloofness and seclusiveness, with interests of an intellectual and abstract sort, often nature-loving, and with an inclination towards contemplation rather than activity, in line with the fact that the reserves of energy are usually small. To that extent there tends to be fair uniformity, but in addition schizoid personalities may be ruthless, as part of their emotional coldness, or passive and withdrawing from competition when opposition is offered. To many also may be added qualities of queerness, eccentricity and oddness, and to others paranoid features of either aggressive or passive kind. Thus, the dreamy, bearded, sandalled utopian idealist is often a schizoid personality, just as much as is the wild-eyed, fanatical adherent of some political or religious sect. There is some correlation between the schizoid personality and an asthenic physique (see p. 26), and a tendency towards schizophrenic breakdown.

The cyclothymic (cycloid) personality

These frequently occur in the families of manic-depressives. They tend to be extraverted, good-natured, with emotional warmth and sympathetic responsiveness, sociable and adaptable, energetic and preferring activity to contemplation, practical and well in touch. This can alternate with periods of withdrawal, relative sadness, loss of drive and interest, like a minor depressive illness. The stages last for weeks or months, not hours or days. There is some correlation between the cycloid personality and the pyknic build ('the 16-inch neck in the 14-inch collar') and with a tendency to cyclothymia (see p. 27).

But as Nature is never tidy, not all who are liable to mood-swings have these engaging characteristics. Those whose moods veer mainly downwards are persistently gloomy for months at a time. Those whose moods veer mainly upwards are often unable to brook opposition and readily pass into irritable excitement. The behaviour of certain surgeons when vexed by difficulties in the operating theatre is often of this type.

The hysterical personality

This is the type that is liable to show hysterical symptoms par excellence, but it must be remembered that very many patients who show hysterical symptoms are not hysterical personalities (see p. 265).

A cardinal feature is the patient's desire to appear more than he (or more usually she) really is, with which is coupled a striking skill in self-deception. Hysterics are fond of picturing themselves in dramatic and romantic roles, and their emotions are vivid but shallow. They are easily influenced by people or ideas that appeal to them: they have a remarkable capacity for identifying themselves with, and imitating, others, and for dedicating themselves to various transient ideals. But these enthusiasms change readily. They are sentimental rather than realistic, often histrionic, and when confronted with difficulties tend to dodge them by taking flight into emotionalism rather than adopting effective action. They are immature in their thinking and emotional reactions, often sexually frigid and frequently incapable of long-term affection or sustained sexual relationships, though they are good short-term flirts and know how to dally with the other sex to satisfy their vanity. The instability of their emotions, vivid phantasy, and lack of solid qualities make hysterical personalities untruthful and unreliable, although they believe themselves to be candid. In fact, they deceive themselves more successfully than others. Hysterical conversion symptoms often provide the means by which they try to dominate their surroundings, with varying degrees of success.

Obsessional (anancastic) personality

This is traceable in about half of patients who develop obsessional compulsive neurosis. Minor obsessional features are generally recognised as quite desirable and are present in very many stable and well adjusted people. They include the characteristic qualities of orderliness, meticulousness, punctuality, caution, conscientiousness and a liking for routine, all of which if exaggerated can become disabilities. When orderliness becomes an end in itself, routines cannot be broken without anxiety and inability to cope, everything has to be checked, repeatedly, even though one knows it is ridiculous, and cautious appraisal is so prolonged that no decisions can be taken, then obsessional personality traits can become very burdensome.

Markedly obsessional people often find it difficult to 'let go' of things or of topics, and tend to hoard objects 'in case they will come in handy', and to continue some subject of conversation in boring detail and length. They find it difficult to do things swiftly, and if they come under pressure at work may be unable to cope, and may even break down into anxiety or depression in such circumstances.

It is worth distinguishing those obsessional features which the individual is glad he possesses, (sometimes called ego-syntonic) from those he would rather be without (ego-dystonic). The former group includes conscientiousness, punctuality, and neatness; the latter includes the well-known need (or compulsion even) to check gas taps, electric points, stamps on letters and so on, the inability to cope with unfamiliar things or routines, the inability to make decisions, the inability to speed up when necessary and the tendency to brood or ruminate unproductively and usually unhappily for hours on end.

There is often also what we can call emotional rigidity. Obsessional people take a long time to calm down after an upset, they find it difficult to end an argument with a spouse for example, but keep going over and over the same points. Marriage to someone of very different temperament, for example with hysterical features, can lead to much unhappiness for both. (See also Ch. 12 on obsessional states).

The paranoid personality

These are people who are persistently touchy, ready to feel aggrieved and put upon, prone to hold grievances and to be suspicious of the motives of those around them. On this account they often do not adjust well to society, and they are then liable to blame others for that maladjustment. Certain personality characteristics encourage the development of paranoid trends. Thus, rigid people have more difficulty in adjustment than do adaptable people, and are apt to be more put out by such difficulty. Aggressive people are more likely to feel aggrieved than are submissive people. Conceited people are more likely to feel slighted than are people characterised by humility. Over-sensitive people are more likely to be upset by, and see significance in, a casual attitude or unfriendliness shown to them by others. Dullards and the mentally handicapped are more likely to be put upon than the normally bright and their attitudes may be coloured by this or the fear of it. When these characteristics of rigidity, aggressiveness, conceit, over-sensitiveness and low intelligence are combined, even in varying proportions, in one personality, paranoid developments are far more likely to occur than in someone who is adaptable, modest and ready to take the rough with the smooth.

Circumstances may also encourage the development of the paranoid personality, such as restriction of freedom, continued frustration in whatever sphere, and prolonged failure.

Physical disturbances may aid paranoid developments through increasing the irritability and over-sensitiveness of the personality, as when a patient is subjected to prolonged and nagging discomfort from physical symptoms, or from a menopausal upset, or is prevented from normal activity or social intercourse by physical handicap. Deafness is of special consequence in this connection and so is chronic alcoholism. The former cuts the patient off severely from society, leaves him uncertain of what is happening or being said, and so provides a good soil for suspiciousness to flourish in. Chronic alcoholism encourages the failure from which paranoid developments often stem, and destroys those inhibitory faculties that make for reasonableness and well-balanced judgments, so that the latter became increasingly impaired as deterioration occurs.

Vulnerable personalities

These do not form a clear cut group. They are potentially unstable people and bad psychiatric risks. They are all liable to breakdown, but to break down in various ways, and in different ways at different times. Handicapped by constitutional loading, they have a small margin of reserve, and when pinched by circumstances are liable to develop various neurotic reactions as well as 'short-circuit' into uncontrolled or explosive outbursts. They may show one sort of reaction at one time, and another at a later one: or, if lucky, they may pass through life without overt symptoms. In general, they find life difficult to cope with and are 'inadequate'.

Scrutiny of such a case is liable to show a poor heredity, an unhappy early life in a home with incompetent parents, neurotic behaviour in childhood, poor work and health record, and more or less in the way of previous breakdown.

Salient personality characteristics are a low physical and mental resilience with tendencies to disapprove of more, to be afraid of more, and to enjoy less than is normal. They often have difficulty in mixing, inferiority feelings, and an egocentric tendency to protect themselves from potentially stressful situations. Their response to physical illness is likely to be of more prolonged invalidism than expected; and after minor head injury a post-concussional state (p. 92) is more likely to develop, and so on. They have low reserves of energy and find it difficult to keep going in adversity.

When breakdown occurs the commonest forms are states of anxiety or depression, or both combined, irritability and fatigue, poorly controlled emotionalism of non-specific sort, and explosive outbursts.

Finally, it may be well to point out that vulnerable personalities, though in varying degrees inadequate, may yet possess certain worthwhile qualities. Their poor capacity to cope with stress does not mean that they may not have talents and abilities, along with pleasant personal characteristics, which can flourish if life is easy. Doctors tend to see them at their worst.

Psychopathic (sociopathic) personality

This is an important and contentious subject, for several reasons. There are medico-legal implications because 'psychopathic disorder' comes within the scope of the 1983 Mental Health Act (dealt with in more detail in Ch. 17), as indeed it did in that of 1959. It is defined there as 'a persistent disorder or disability of mind (whether or not including a significant impairment of intellect) which results in abnormally aggressive or seriously irresponsible conduct on the part of the person concerned'. Such a person can be detained in hospital compulsorily only if 'medical treatment is likely to alleviate or prevent a deterioration of his condition'.

The term 'psychopath' has become a term of abuse, and one should avoid using it too freely, and especially avoid using it only because the person concerned inspires dislike and rejection, although psychopathic people do tend to inspire such feelings. In order to avoid this misuse of terms, psychiatrists began to use the more neutral-sounding term 'personality disorder' in an attempt to sound less critical and judgmental; but 'personality disorder' has unfortunately taken on a critical connotation for many people, and is therefore no longer so useful in its proper place — that is, as a term including all forms of disordered personality, as used in this chapter.

In Germany and other European countries the word 'psychopath' was used for someone with any abnormality of personality, in the sense of any major deviation from the norm which led to suffering either for that individual, or for society. 'Personality disorder' was meant to cover the same range. Using that system (developed by the same Schneider to whom we owe the concept of 'first rank' symptoms in schizophrenia), the term 'depressive psychopath' could be used to describe someone who was constitutionally gloomy and morose, and 'obsessive psychopath' someone whose checking habits, rigidity and indecision were personally disabling. In the Anglo-American usage the emphasis is on the sufferings caused to society by the 'aggressive or seriously irresponsible conduct' of the legal definition, which explains the alternative term 'Sociopath'.

The concept is linked historically with the 'moral insanity' described by Prichard in the early 19th century, who observed people who showed no moral feelings, compunction or ethical sense — although of normal intelligence — and regarded them as suffering from a mental disease.

There are many manifestations of psychopathic personality traits, but the main features can be summed up as follows: there is an *inability to tolerate frustration* and a need for *instant gratification*. The psychopath finds it *difficult to endure unpleasant emotions*, and feelings such as shame, anxiety or sadness cannot be borne, but lead to almost immediate action of some kind, known as *acting out*. This term includes running away from the situation, or being physically violent to people or things. The psychopath seems perpetually to be on a 'short fuse', exploding into some sudden activity, often anti social, and in the end usually maladaptive, because of an inability to tolerate unpleasant feelings or situations.

The psychopathic person *does not learn from experience* in a normal way, and makes the same mistakes again and again. For instance, a man who had just come out of prison for 'Taking and Driving Away' a car (for about the 10th time) had determined never to repeat the offence. On a lovely spring day, less than a week after release from prison, he did not even try to resist the impulse to take a car and have a run into the country. 'I didn't think of what might happen', he said to the psychiatrist later.

There is usually *difficulty in forming enduring relationships* and often an *emotionally cold and ruthless quality*. In some individuals this absence of normal feeling, and the lack of responsiveness to those who offer affection or care, is the most striking feature, and characterises some of the more violent criminal psychopaths, including, for example, mass murderers who seem to kill without personal motive.

Many psychopaths repeatedly break the law, and large numbers of long term prisoners, and especially those who are in prison because of repeated minor offences, have some psychopathic quality. In order to plan ahead some major crime, non-psychopathic characteristics are needed, but a major criminal might well use impulsive psychopaths to carry out the dirty work. Many of them are incapable of long term plans, and are as débris on the sea of life, floating from place to place and job to job and frequently submerged.

It is easy to see how psychopaths, following their characteristic pattern of irresponsible behaviour, may drift into criminality. Not all criminals, of course, are psychopaths, but an appreciable proportion are, and number among their ranks seducers, bigamists, confidence men, prostitutes, common adventurers and pathological liars who talk without the least regard for truth however certain their detection, for the sake of the immediate impression that they like to be able to make.

Emotional reactions of any sort may occur, such as sudden attacks of depression in response to some reverse, often ill-controlled and with much self-pity, sudden developments of anxiety when embroiled in some difficulty, uncontrolled rage which may result in throwing the china in a domestic tiff or in crimes of violence. Resort to alcohol (and other drugs) often occurs. Impulsive suicidal gestures, especially in association with alcohol, are frequent, though actual suicide is uncommon.

There are, of course, degrees in these things. The foregoing account presents a reasonably characteristic picture. But there are also modified forms of psychopathy. For example, a man may be irresponsible, changeable and unreliable in his domestic relationships but yet may stick at a job which satisfies him; or he may repeatedly and irresponsibly change jobs, show no social conscience, and yet sometimes stick to the woman of his choice in defiance of the usual rule that psychopaths show no constant or satisfactory personal relationships.

The foregoing are the general features which are more or less common to all psychopaths, but the latter can be further subdivided and classified to some extent. It is common to divide them into those that are predominantly inadequate, and those that are predominantly aggressive.

The *predominantly inadequate* have something in common with those of vulnerable personality, but show additional features of irresponsibility, lack of social conscience, and inability to learn from experience. These features, together with their lack of will-power and determination, are shown in their careers. Weak-willed and easily tired, they provide many of life's failures.

The *predominantly aggressive* type is actively antisocial rather than merely a burden on others. The aggressiveness may take the form of so-called 'short-circuit' (i.e. uncontrolled and explosive) reactions already mentioned. But that is not necessarily so. It may take more the form of the cold ruthlessness mentioned earlier, which enables its possessor to prosecute unscrupulous schemes, and to pursue with complete sangfroid courses of action which he knows to spell ruin to others.

The aetiology of psychopathic personality in a difficult and unsolved problem. The family background of many is turbulent and chaotic, often marked by violence and poverty, and with no steady loving parent. It seems that to have a promiscuous and psychopathic mother is even more likely to have severe ill effects on a child than to have an equally disturbed father. Genetic factors are also important, as has been confirmed recently by studies of twins brought up together and apart. Everyone with psychiatric experience has come across instances where a grossly psychopathic personality has emerged from circumstances which in themselves could in no way be incriminated for such a development. Other factors which seem to be relevant in some psychopaths include perinatal brain injury and encephalitis or other brain infections in childhood. In some large and muscular criminal psychopaths an abnormal chromosome pattern (XYY) seems more common than in the normal population, but large scale population studies shows XYY to be only weakly associated with any behaviour disturbance, and with rather low intelligence.

The chances of psychopathic personalities developing is enhanced by the frequency with which psychopathic persons marry each other, thus compounding environmental and any genetic factors.

The electroencephalogram is often abnormal in psychopathic individuals, and more than one abnormality may be shown in each EEG. About 30-50% show generalised slow wave activity, more marked in the more aggressive. About the same number, and again the more aggressive, show 'positive spikes', which are bursts of activity originating in the temporal lobes. Similar forms are found in less than 5% of the general population. These abnormalities may reflect an 'immaturity' in cerebral organisation, and certainly many psychopaths do settle down with age; but in some the EEG probably indicates minimal brain damage.

In summary, it will be seen that the answers are not known. There are various clues, but there are no satisfactory formulae. Aetiologically, each case must be judged on its merits. Many will be found to have no satisfactory explanation.

Course and prognosis

It is unwise to make a firm diagnosis of psychopathy in adolescents, because many people mature markedly from about 17-25 years of age. Even after that maturation can continue, and elderly psychopaths are relatively uncommon, except in prison. It has been claimed that those who show the 'immature' EEG pattern are most likely to develop favourably with time.

It is essential to remember that, like all disorders of personality, psychopathic personality is an enduring quality, and not something which comes and goes. A clear distinction must be made between people who have suffered damage to the frontal lobe, or those much rarer cases of mild chronic hypomania, in which behaviour can be identical with that of the psychopath. In the latter the disordered behaviour can be traced back to childhood or puberty, in the other two a distinct change has occurred at some time, although this may only be clear from the account of someone who has known the patient for a long time.

As regards treatment of the psychopathic personality, much justifiable pessimism is felt. The inadequate psychopath may show greater steadiness under firm guidance, especially if under the thumb of a suitable wife. Some may be helped by periodic and regular attendance in an out-patients department, where they can ventilate their difficulties, discharge their emotions, and be subject to a steadying influence much as though they were reporting to a sympathetic probation officer. Aggressive psychopaths will be more difficult to manage as their explosions are liable to have taken place, and their consequences to have been set in train, so rapidly and unpredictably as to have anticipated any steadying influence that might otherwise have been offered. In essence the psychopathic person can be helped to feel better if he is anxious or depressed, and it can have a steady influence if he becomes attached to a doctor or social worker who is prepared to give him some time. There is, however, no evidence that treatment affects the underlying personality disorder. In-patient treatment of psychopathic people should be kept as brief as possible, in for example the treatment of depression, as such patients often have a very disruptive effect on the ward. Certain special units have concentrated on providing help for psychopathic people, using intensive group therapy methods and trying to involve all the patients in the life and activities of the hospital community. Unfortunately little evidence has been produced which allows an assessment of the value of the method, although it has been very influential. In general, transformations through treatment do not occur in psychopathic personalities.

SEXUAL ANOMALIES

Anomalies in this sphere are certainly frequent, but the student should be aware of the very wide variations in practices, beliefs, attitudes, and feelings which exist within our own culture and in the world at large. They can properly be considered in the same chapter as disorders of personality because sexuality is an enduring aspect of personality, and the anomalies described are developmental in origin, with their roots in early life and in constitutional factors.

Homosexuality

Homosexuality means having a sexual propensity for members of one's own sex. Both the strength and the expression of this propensity vary in different individuals, and can also vary in the same individual during different epochs in life. For example, a homesexual phase is quite common in adolescence and should not cause undue alarm or concern.

Homosexuality is not an 'all or none' condition, and all gradations exist between apparently exclusive life-long 100% homosexuality without any conscious capacity for arousal by heterosexual stimuli, and apparently exclusive heterosexuality without any conscious capacity for arousal by homosexual stimuli.

Kinsey proposed a seven-point rating scale for the homosexual/heterosexual continuum with a maximum of 6 points for exclusively homosexual arousals and activity, 0 for exclusive heterosexuality, 3 for arousals and acts equally with either sex, and intermediate scores accordingly.

The prevalence of homosexuality is a matter of definition. Thus, according to the psychoanalytic school a homosexual component (sometimes conscious but often not), exists in everybody and, if this is correct, homosexuality in this sense is universal. But even if the criterion of homosexuality is confined to overt homosexual activities, the prevalence that is claimed comes to many as a surprise, and Kinsey's findings that 37% of the total male population have had at least some overt homosexual experiences to the point of orgasm between adolescence and old age provoked indignant scepticism. The lowest figure given in evidence to the Wolfenden Committee suggests that 1% of all males are exclusively homosexual and that another 4% have both homosexual and heterosexual impulses, and the Swedish authorities who provided these figures considered them too low.

Much more has been written about homosexuality in males than in females, and neither the law nor public opinion has been so concerned about the latter. According to Kinsey 4% of adult single women are exclusively homosexual (lesbian), but one informed British estimate is of less than 2%.

The main points to bear in mind is that a homosexual act or series of acts does not necessarily imply that the individual is the posessor of a predominantly homosexual make-up with a Kinsey rating of, say, 5 or 6.

Causation

No physical pathology has as yet been demonstrated, and nearly all biochemical and chromosomal investigations have been negative or inconclusive. Animal experiments show that the injection of male or female hormones into the pregnant female at certain critical periods of foetal development can produce homosexual behaviour in the offspring without any apparent physical deviation. On the whole individuals fit well into the 'gender role' in which they have been brought up, even when they have sexual ambiguities such as hermaphroditism. In some cases however, where the underlying constitutional and endocrine sexuality has been in opposition to the apparent sex, there has been a breakthrough of the opposing biological sexual features at puberty. Another factor indicating the importance of biological factors is the genetic evidence from identical and non-identical twins, although the concordance is not as high as earlier work suggested.

Environmental factors which seem to be of importance have been demonstrated in several independent studies, but they do not apply to all cases. An absent or weak and passive father, with the development of a very close and intimate relationship with the mother, is associated with an increased incidence of homosexuality in males, especially in youngest sons. There is less agreement about the family situation with lesbians.

It is probably best to view homosexuality as a kind of 'final common pathway' with several possible causes. Homosexual behaviour occurs in all human societies, and in nearly all mammalian species so the potential is probably present in everyone. Once homosexual patterns are established they may be kept going and reinforced more by social factors than by purely sexual ones, particularly in those many homosexual men in whom fear of women and a profound lack of confidence in their own masculinity leads to avoidance of heterosexual contact. Whatever the causes in the individual, the main features of psychosexual development have been laid down by puberty, and it is at this age that many individuals suddenly realise their sexual direction. The role of homosexual seduction is of little importance, and parents can be reassured on this point. Their own anxieties may well do more harm than the seduction itself.

Activities

The most frequent homosexual activity is masturbation with homosexual phantasies, and the proportion of homosexual, as opposed to heterosexual, phantasies in masturbation, both in the past and in the present, is a valuable indication of the Kinsey rating. Other common homosexual activities include mutual masturbation, bodily contact with ejaculation inter femora, oral-genital relations (fellatio) and anal intercourse (buggery). Individuals have their preferences or antipathies, but the majority of practising homosexuals indulge at some time or other in all types of homosexual activity both actively and passively.

Classification

What actually takes place physically or in phantasy is far less important than the preferred age of the sexual partner. Homosexuals can be divided rather sharply into those who are attracted by prepubertal boys (paedophiliacs, or child molesters as the Americans call them), and those who are not. The overlap between these two groups is small, in the order, perhaps, of 3%, and many of this overlap group are obviously unstable psychopathic individuals. Further, only a very small minority of the total homosexual population are paedophilics, and the popular concept of a sort of Rake's Progress, according to which those who indulge in homosexual activities with young men or youths are likely to end up by buggering little boys, has no foundation in fact. This main division between those homosexuals who are attracted by children and those who are not is a far more fundamental one than whether homosexuals are active or passive, which may vary according to circumstances.

Personality types

Homosexuals do not differ physically from heterosexuals, and only a small proportion are obviously 'camp', in an exhibitionistic way, although with the increasingly open attitudes of homosexuals, and increased tolerance of the rest of society, fewer homosexuals disguise themselves as heterosexual. All types of personality occur in homosexual people, as do all types of psychiatric illness. Whether there are more artistic people among homosexuals or not remains uncertain, because no proper survey has been done, but it often seems so. There are, however, plenty of homosexuals who are as boringly philistine as others.

It must be borne in mind, at least in the United Kingdom, that psychiatrists see highly selected homosexuals. Now that the law allows homosexual acts between consenting adults, and as public attitudes have become more tolerant, the homosexual is under less severe stress and almost no homosexuals are seeking medical help for homosexuality as such, although they are of course prone to all the usual psychiatric disorders. Anxiety and depression were very frequently seen in men, to whom a fear of exposure was often terrifying. Perhaps because of the more tolerant attitudes to female homosexuality, few lesbians ever presented to doctors.

Promiscuity is a striking characteristic of many homosexuals, and there is some evidence that the more promiscuous tend to be less stable. Currently, there is great anxiety among homosexuals, especially the more promiscuous, about fears of developing AIDS (Acquired Immune Deficiency Syndrome). Panic attacks, anxiety states, obsessive-compulsive states and depression, all focussed on AIDS, have become quite common, not surprisingly in view of the nature of the illness.

The assessment of homosexuality

Homosexual arousals and homosexual acts may have a totally different significance, both as regards prognosis and treatment, in different individuals. For example, the same homosexual act (and it must be remembered that so far as males are concerned all homosexual acts at a genital level committed with others, whether private or public, were until 1968 criminal offences), may be committed as a piece of adolescent experimentation, or it may be the result of temporary or permanent mental or physical disorder or disease, or it may be part of the individual's life style.

The following headings may be found convenient when confronted with a homosexual problem:

1. Transitional homosexuality. As already mentioned, homosexual arousals that may lead to homosexual acts are quite common in adolescence, and they are often best regarded as merely manifestations of sex without special significance.

2. What might be called the true homosexual with a Kinsey rating of 5 or 6, who only seeks other men as partners.

3. The bisexual individual who may have made some kind of heterosexual adjustment, perhaps a very satisfying one, but who still seeks or desires homosexual relations.

4. The facultative homosexual, who is predominantly heterosexual, but who takes part in some form of homosexual activity on rare occasions or in exceptional circumstances, e.g. on board ship or in the Services, and

5. The sort of person who may indulge in any kind of sexual activity as the opportunity arises, and who may well have psychopathic personality traits.

Treatment

When earlier editions of this book were written many homosexuals sought treatment to help them change their whole sexual orientation. In a few cases, almost entirely amongst those who had discernible heterosexual drives, such change occurred. They were driven to seek help mainly because of the great pressures exerted by society, but also because of religious scruples in some, and it was common to see married men whose marriage, often undertaken in order to 'cure' themselves, was threatened by their inability to control their homosexual feelings. Paedophiliacs still seek help, usually at the instigation of the courts, and there has been no increase in tolerance on the part of the general public to them. Most homosexuals however, now find that life is very much easier, especially in cities where with the growth of 'gay liberation' it is much easier to meet people of similar attitudes, and to join in the life of society, both homosexual and general. Those who are unable to profit from these changes are often those with neurotic or other personality difficulties who would find life difficult even if they were heterosexual. Treatment therefore is not often required.

The methods available can be listed as:
1. Endocrine or drug therapies
2. Aversion therapy
3. Intensive psychotherapy
4. Less intensive psychotherapy, counselling.

Endocrine treatments do not affect the direction of sexual drives, but can be used to control them. Female hormones or analogues such as ethinyl oestradiol 0.05 mg once daily or more can be given and will abolish all active drives, at the cost of feminisation. Benperidol, a butyrophenone, lessens or abolishes libido without feminisation in some people, as does cyproterone acetate. These are mainly used in paedophiliacs, in whom castration is used in some countries; and occasionally in people in whom frontal lobe brain damage has led to disinhibition of sexual control.

Aversion therapy was quite extensively used in attempts to alter sexual orientation, and some successes were achieved, especially if some heterosexual interest was there which could be encouraged and liberated. The methods were analogous to those used in alcoholism (p. 406) associating sexually arousing stimuli with unpleasant electric shocks. High motivation is needed to persevere with such treatment, as well as care in the selection of suitable photographs and other stimuli. It is unlikely that these treatments are being used anywhere in the Western world now.

Intensive psycho-analytic or other psychotherapies were very extensively used in an attempt to change sexual direction, and many individual successes were claimed, although overall the method must be regarded as a failure. Counselling, group therapies and other less intensive psychotherapies have a part to play in helping someone adjust to being homosexual, as they have in helping people to adjust to other major difficulties in life.

There remain homosexuals who, largely for religious reasons, do not accept their sexual drives as valid, and do not wish to live as practising homosexuals. They may seek help in controlling and coming to terms with their sexuality, and one or more of the methods mentioned might well be appropriate. There is no need to regard homosexuality as a disease in order to help people with what to them is a problem.

OTHER SEXUAL ANOMALIES (Sexual Deviations, Paraphilia)

It is not possible to describe all these. They are commoner than might be supposed, especially in minor forms, and whether or not they are considered as abnormal depends very much on the culture and attitudes of those judging. What to some people is sinful and disgusting is to others a minor sensual variation. Contemporary tolerance is much higher than a few decades ago and fewer people seek help, except for transexuals. If, the deviation becomes the sole sexual behaviour, always preferred to normal coitus, most people would regard it as abnormal, or as a 'perversion'. The individual is unlikely to seek help unless the spouse, or some legal agency, insists.

Sexual deviations are curiously rare in women and in psychotic patients. The commonest are exhibitionism, sadism and masochism. But there are also the trans-sexualists, i.e. men who wish to become women and, less commonly, women who wish to become men.

Exhibitionism. This is most often committed by a man of reserved nature, with marked inferiority feelings, who is usually either impotent or has no experience of even attempting intercourse. The act is usually one of suddenly opening a raincoat to expose the erect penis to some girl or woman in a quiet public place, but sometimes it may be done standing at a bedroom window. In some cases there is no erection. The man concerned seeks to shock and frighten, rather than to lead on to a sexual encounter. To be met with unconcern or even by laughter from some sophisticated person is felt as deeply wounding. The exhibitionistic act is a primitive and infantile way of reassuring the man about his manhood and potency although in some it seems more purely aggressive and hostile in quality. Treatment is essentially by psychotherapy, and aims at stopping the exhibitionism and helping the patient both to gain his self-esteem and to cope with his inferiority feelings in a different way. It is rarely very helpful.

In a few instances, exhibitionism only occurs when the individual is depressed, or under some particular stress, in which case, treatment has more to offer. Rarely it occurs because of cerebral disease with loss of sexual inhibitions.

In *sadism,* sexual pleasure is gained or enhanced by the exhibition of physical cruelty. This may occur during love play or intercourse, or apart from them. It may even occur without any basis in reality, as in sadistic phantasy (a main interest of the Marquis de Sade, after whom the condition is named). In masochism sexual pleasure is gained or enhanced by the subjective experience of pain, which may range from a mild infliction to severe flagellation. This, again, may or may not accompany other sexual activity, may occur only in phantasy, or may be self-inflicted by the subject when alone, then usually as a prelude to masturbation. Allied to masochism are such abnormalities as deriving sexual pleasure from being handcuffed or tied up. The condition is named after Sacher-Masoch who described his own state in his novels.

Combinations of sadism and masochism are particularly common, but as a rule several deviations will be observed in the same person, and the exhibition of only one is unusual. It is rare for sadists or masochists to seek psychiatric help for the sexual deviation, and when they do it is almost always at the instigation of the spouse, who threatens to leave. Many brothels provide sado-masochistic experiences (or sights thereof), and cater to individuals who in their marriages may repress those urges entirely.

In *Fetishism* sexual interest is diverted from normal intercourse onto objects which become sexually rewarding and satisfying in themselves when used in masturbation. The commonest articles are of women's underwear, but there is a curious and unexplained frequency of interest in shiny black leather and rubber clothing (testified to in the advertisement columns of newspapers). Other common fetish objects are shoes or slippers and silky objects. A considerable interest in all of these things, except black rubber or leather, is very common in normal sexual relationships, but it becomes a perversion when the fetish object becomes the main interest. There is commonly present a markedly obsessional element, and the impulses may be struggled against. However, the deviant sexual feelings are not seen as somehow silly or inappropriate as classical obsessional symptoms are.

Transvestism is also quite common and can be considered as of two almost distinct types, although in both men dress up in women's clothing. In the first type the women's clothing is clearly an elaborate fetish object, is associated with sexual excitement, and the man concerned either masturbates or has intercourse while so dressed. Such people may seek psychiatric help at the instigation of the spouse. It is important to note that this is not associated with homosexuality or transexualism (q.v.) or any desire to live as a woman. The second type does show some overlap with the first, but the essential difference is that the man does not seek excitement so much as a feeling of peace and contentment, and is often at his happiest sitting reading or watching television while dressed like this. These people however, are still heterosexual in their main drives, see themselves as men, and are not transexual, although obviously rather nearer to that position.

The *causes* of these abnormalities are complicated. In general, perversions can be regarded as gross exaggerations of sexual features that are not in themselves abnormal. Thus, a degree of self-display is not abnormal in sexual intimacy; in exhibitionism it is exaggerated until it becomes a substitute. Aggressiveness and submissiveness, and combinations of both, are involved in all personal relationships; where the relationship is close and emotional, they may become associated with and an integral part of love itself. Underlying a state of sexual excitement there may normally be an aggressive quality which is the accompaniment of a man wishing to wreak his will. The man who is 'a slave to his lover' may feel an erotic pleasure in submissiveness. These may be exaggerated into a sexual assaultiveness and an amorous self-abasement. Such developments are presumably facilitated by the close association, from whatever cause, between sexual excitement and pain. The assaultiveness and self-abasement, each with its painful association, may then become an integral part of the sexual excitement — in perversion, its most important part.

The predilections for special materials seem to arise partly from a visual and tactile appreciation which adds an aesthetic element to sexual feeling, and partly from association of ideas that may be peculiar to the person and may have its roots deep in his history. An example was of a man with a fetish of high heeled shoes. He had been brought up principally by servants and had longed for more contact with his mother. He recalled how he had spied on her as she dressed to go out in the evening, but through the keyhole his field of vision was restricted to her legs, feet and high heeled slippers.

The development of these tendencies into actual perversions seems to be in line with the constitutional trends. The sadist, although his sadistic qualities may be circumscribed, may have qualities of aggressiveness and waspishness with an emotional appreciation of situations that involve others in distress. The masochist, although his masochistic tendencies may be circumscribed, may tend to play a passive and submissive role in his general life, and to take pleasure in acts that come near to self-punishment. In many however, both features are present in the same person. The exhibitionist tends to be a showman in various ways. The lover of mackintosh, leather and silk tends to lead a rich sensory life, with attention to shapes, colours, scents, and the tactile and textural qualities of objects.

Circumstances themselves, as well as the constitutional trends, may aid these developments which are often assisted by lack of more normal sexual satisfaction, and so are more likely to arise where the circumstances impose frustration.

Prognostically, what is important is not the queerness of the abnormality itself, but the extent to which it interferes with the patient's actual performance. It may be a dominant feature to the extent that it worries the patient, but it is not prognostically ominous unless it shows signs of itself becoming a preferred substitute to more normal sexual activity, instead of an accompaniment. The more that it is confined to phantasy, and at the same time the less that it interferes with performance, the better is the prognosis.

Treatment is, for the most part, unsatisfactory. Exhibitionists are exceedingly difficult to treat on all counts except those few in whom it occurs only in a setting of depressive illness. Psychotherapy hardly ever, if ever, succeeds, and we have no evidence that the results of psychoanalysis are any better. Even repeated imprisonment seems to have little deterrent effect. Sadism and masochism, if tendencies rather than established perversions, may show improvement if the patient succeeds in checking his indulgence in these directions and then achieves a satisfactory marital relationship. In violent, dangerous sadists, anti-androgens such as cyproterone acetate may be used, or oestrogens. Aversion therapy (p. 406) can be very helpful in the fetishistic disorders, when the subject is highly motivated to change.

Trans-sexualists

These patients, though rare, come forward in increasing numbers and may present grave problems. They are usually men without chromosomal abnormality who wish to become women and often have been living as such; much less commonly, they are women who wish to become men. They complain that they are spiritually imprisoned in a body of the wrong sex, and of severe frustration as regards expressing and fulfilling themselves. For those who come for consultation, the mere adoption of the opposite sexual role is not enough, and they may not be satisfied by anything short of an actual physical change. If there is evidence of mental illness, such as schizophrenia, surgical intervention is inadvisable owing to the unpredictability of the outcome. Far more often, though they tend to be unstable and exhibitionistic, these patients are not psychotic at all. With increasing experience one realises that most of them are desperate and desperately sincere, often with a history of suicidal attempts, and the resolution with which they pursue their intention can be very striking. One of our patients, with some surgical knowledge, performed a bilateral orchidectomy on himself in two stages, and finally achieved a physical 'Sex change' through further plastic surgery after years of unremitting effort, for which it appears that 'she' is much the happier after an apparently successful marriage to another man. We could tell of others just as determined.

The earlier publications on the results of surgery and associated treatment were on the whole optimistic. More recently a number of gloomy reports have appeared, and in some centres treatment is no longer offered. Careful selection of appropriate patients is absolutely essential, and the work is very highly specialised.

Before surgery is performed the man should have oestrogens to increase breast size and diminish facial hair; and should live for at least a year as a woman in every possible way. Before and after surgery a great deal of counselling and other help will be needed. Those who are unable to cope with the delay are too impatient and impulsive to do well, and one should not give way to importunity.

SUMMARY

DISORDERS OF PERSONALITY

Definition

A disorder of personality exists if the personality differs so much from the mean that either the individual or society suffers from it.

Personality assessment and descrption

(1) *Psycho-analytic (best used only by psycho-analysts).*
(2) *Questionnaire methods, e.g. Eysenck Personality Inventory (most useful in research).*

(3) *Projective tests,* e.g. *Rorschach (dubious value).*
(4) *Clinical, including interview with relative. (The most useful in clinical practice).*

Some personality types (which are not entities, more examples):

(1) *Schizoid:* introverted, aloof, eccentric, emotionally cool. Occurs in many who later develop schizophrenia.
(2) *Cyclothymic:* a tendency to alternate between high spirited, energetic, outgoing phases and withdrawn, low spirited phases. Phases last for weeks or months. Occurs in relatives of bipolar manic depressives, as well as in sufferers from that illness.
(3) *Hysterical:* Immature, with rapidly changing shallow emotions, histrionic, manipulative, difficulty with enduring adult relationships. Often frigid. Prone to hysterical conversion disorders.
(4) *Obsessional (anancastic):* Cautious, meticulous, reliable, punctual, indecisive, can be mean. Prone to obsessive-compulsive disorders.
(5) *Vulnerable:* Low drive, little resilience or physical or mental stamina; break down easily with minor stress, mainly into anxiety and minor depressive symptoms.
(6) *Psychopathic (sociopathic):* Important medico-legal aspects because of Mental Health Act. (p. 442). Poor tolerance of frustration, 'act out' when under pressure, fail to learn from experience, difficulty forming enduring relationships, often emotionally cold and ruthless. Some predominantly aggressive, others inadequate. Personality changes little with treatment, but time may help maturity.
(7) *All types:* The more abnormal the personality the more likely is life to be stressful, with consequent neurotic and other reactions. (see Ch. 11).

SEXUAL ANOMALIES

(1) *Homosexuality:* a sexual propensity for own sex. A graded characteristic, e.g. Kinsey scale from 0 = exclusive heterosexuality to 6 = exclusive homosexuality. Prevalence uncertain, perhaps 1% of males Kinsey 6. Less known about homosexuality in women (Lesbianism).

   With increased tolerance and acceptance, a rare cause for seeking psychiatric help in our society (except for recent phobias, etc. about AIDS).

(2) *Exhibitionism*: Most commonly a reserved, sexually ineffective man exhibits erect penis to female, is gratified by shock or fear. If in setting of depression or unusual stress treatment can help, otherwise rarely useful.

(3) *Sadism/Masochism*: Gaining sexual excitement and pleasure from, respectively inflicting pain or having it inflicted. Can co-exist in same person, often mainly in fantasy. Psychiatric help usually only sought at request of partner. In minor degrees very common.

(4) Fetishism: Sexual excitement and satisfaction gained principally from objects (e.g., black rubber, high heeled shoes). Merges into normal interest in sexually associated objects.

(5) *Transvestism*: Cross-dressing, mainly heterosexual men in women's clothing. Can be
  (a) sexually exciting, e.g., preceding intercourse
      or
  (b) soothing, where cross dresser sits, for example, quietly knitting.
  Some of these merge into

(6) *Transexualism*: Mainly shown by men who wish to be, or 'believe' themselves to be, really women. Seek woman's rôle and often castration and other surgery after hormone treatment.

11

Personality reactions and neurotic states

In the previous chapter we have considered personality disorders, and have seen that personality is an enduring — or relatively enduring — feature of the constitution or make up of the individual. It is the result of the interaction of genetic and environmental factors, and is our starting point.

In this chapter we consider a broad range of abnormal personality reactions and neurotic states. We do not see neurotic disturbances as illnesses, but as the reactions of people with more or less abnormal personalities to stresses with which they cannot adequately cope. Some of these reactions are due to overwhelming stress in normally robust and stable people, in others the personality is too fragile to cope with even the most minor disturbance, and, of course, the majority are somewhere in between these extremes.

Obsessional-compulsive disorders, usually grouped with the other neurotic conditions, differ in that they cannot be conceived of so simply as reactions to stress, but have a more autonomous quality, and we therefore give them Chapter 12 to themselves. There is much overlap, however, and these classifications must be seen as matters of convenience, rather than as established entities.

As described in Chapter 9, we do not divide depressive states into two qualitatively distinct conditions — endogenous and reactive, or psychotic and neurotic. We think it more realistic to see all the major depressive states as a continuum but we exclude from that continuum the minor transient depressive reactions which therefore find a place in this chapter, along with anxiety, phobic and hysterical reactions.

Anxiety, transient depressive reactions, and hysterical reactions are described separately, but in practice are quite rarely found in pure culture. Usually it is a question of anxiety with hysterical features, or mixed anxiety and depression, and so on.

SOME DEFINITIONS OF THE TERMS USED

One of the main stumbling blocks to an understanding of the neurotic states and neurotic personality problems lies in the use of the words 'neurosis' and 'neurotic', which have unfortunately several overlapping meanings. It might be better not to use them at all if they were not so firmly established.

Originally the word 'neurosis', which was first used in 1776, indicated the belief that various symptoms arose from disorders of the nervous system; but a hundred years later it had shifted its meaning to indicate some functional disorder without any organic pathology.

There are four main ways in which the word or its derivatives are used now:

Firstly, the adjective 'neurotic' is widely used, in and out of the medical profession, to indicate that someone overreacts to relatively trivial life events, either with anxiety, tension, depression, or some other complaint, and usually also means that the person is difficult to get on with. This use of the term is non-technical, but broadly includes its other meanings, which are, however, worth dissecting out.

The second main use is medical and psychiatric, referring to the principal neurotic states or syndromes as outlined in an earlier paragraph, and we can say, depending on our classification, that there are three or four neuroses or neurotic states. (We prefer not to use the term neurotic *illness*, as in our view the word illness is better kept for the more serious psychiatric disorders, or for conditions in which there is some known structural or biochemical pathology.)

A third use, slightly modified, is the word 'neuroticism', introduced by psychologists in their attempts to measure how neurotic people are. A high neuroticism score means that someone has obtained a high score on a neuroticism questionnaire, and is analogous to a high score on an IQ test as a measure of intelligence. Most neuroticism questionnaires are heavily loaded with questions about palpitations, dry mouth, sweating hands, butterflies in the stomach, swimming sensations in the head, frequency of micturition, and others which are essentially related to autonomic overactivity. To this extent 'neuroticism' is a very limited concept, and is more or less the same as a tendency to become anxious with little provocation — what can also be called 'anxiety proneness'. It is important to realise that neuroticism as measured by questionnaires is not truly identical with any of the other concepts which the word neurotic covers, although closely related.

The fourth and last use of the word is in *'neurotic character disorder'*. So far the other three meanings outlined have all included the idea of some symptomatic disturbance, if only in the sense of autonomic overactivity leading to minor discomfort. In a neurotic character disorder, however, the disturbance lies in the way in which a person forms relationships with others, and there may never be any symptoms in the ordinary sense of the word. Perhaps the commonest example of such a neurotic problem is when a young man or young woman falls in love and marries, but does not see the spouse for what he or she really is — a fairly ordinary person. Instead, the young woman, for example, has reacted with feelings which more properly belong to her father, and she reads into her husband qualities of stability, protectiveness, reliability and so on which reflect her feelings for her father, and reflect also her emotional needs. This can be a complex and ambivalent situation and she may be reacting from a background of a very happy and loving relationship with her father, and unconsciously perpetuating it in marriage; or she may be seeking, and finding in an idealised way, qualities which were lacking in her own childhood. Similarly a young man may unconsciously seek a wife who provides him with a maternal kind of warmth and care.

Marriages based on emotional needs like these can be stable, satisfying and happy, particularly if they choose people who are appropriate, and who do indeed provide the kind of parental love and support which is demanded. We can say that those involved in these relationships have transferred into adult life feelings which orginally, and more properly, belonged to parents or to other important childhood figures such as siblings. As an example of this last we can take people who still behave in adult life as though they were competing with an older brother and react to people of approximately the same age with what is often called 'sibling rivalry'.

In everyone early childhood experiences mould personality, one aspect of which is the way in which we react to others and form relationships. In everyone some element remains of this 'transference' of emotion, and we should not be too quick to label it as neurotic but should reserve that term for people in whom there is such marked and inappropriate transfer of feelings that it causes difficulties in life. Obviously there is an important element of immaturity in those who have this kind of neurotic character problem, but they may be in other ways very stable and mature seeming, well able to handle the stresses and strains of life, and only having difficulties in certain specific relationships, usually in the home.

Serious trouble often develops in neurotic relationships of this kind at a stage when real life and the neurotic needs and demands are incompatible. A fairly common example is when a young man has enjoyed being mothered by his wife, but who feels relegated to a second place when a real baby comes along. Quite often such men become jealous and petulant, attention seeking in rather childish ways at times, become depressed, or start to drink to excess. A neurotic conflict exists when strong but basically infantile needs of an individual are in conflict either with reality, with other important needs of his own, or with the needs (neurotic or otherwise) of another person. Depending on the situation the individual copes in various ways, including of course the possibility of maturation of character, the development of insight, and resolution of the conflict. (This happy outcome does not necessarily need skilled professional help.) In many cases no satisfactory resolution is arrived at, and some uneasy truce or intermittent warfare continues, in any one of the many ways in which a marriage or family can be unhappy.

When such neurotic character disorders and conflict filled relationships exist in people who are constitutionally anxiety prone, or vulnerable to depression, or who have hysterical personality traits, then we find the kind of neurotic state with symptoms which we have already mentioned and which are described in detail elsewhere in this chapter and in others. In other words these neurotic character problems, and the conflicts which they generate, are among the most important causes and precipitants of the neuroses (i.e. the neurotic states or syndromes), the form of which depend mainly on constitutional factors. In addition to these internal psychological stresses, the neuroses may be precipitated by purely external factors, although of course many external problems in life, even including such matters as housing difficulties, are themselves partly or wholly caused by the personality of the sufferer.

In summary, the word neurotic has several meanings. First, it is used, often critically, about the generally over-reactive, difficult person who is unreasonably upset by day to day trivia, awkward and demanding in personal relationships. Second, it refers to one of the main neurotic syndromes, as a proper medical diagnostic term. Third, it is closely related to the idea of being abnormally prone to anxiety, but not necessarily with other personality difficulties. Fourth, and last, it refers to a type of character disorder in which feelings about childhood figures are transferred to people in adult life, so distorting relationships and making life difficult for both parties.

We obviously need a better terminology, but none has so far been developed. Confusion persists.

ANXIETY STATES

Before considering these, it must be clearly understood that, although anxiety is an extremely common symptom, anxiety states are relatively uncommon in pure form, and are seen much less often than are depressive states or phobias. In phobias (see p. 258) the main symptoms are indeed those of anxiety, but developing in certain defined circumstances; and in many patients with depression of various types (see Ch. 9), anxiety is a prominent symptom.

Anxiety has certain characteristics which help to distinguish it from other related emotional experiences, especially tension and depression into which it nevertheless merges. It is intimately bound up with an awareness of autonomic over-activity, so that the famous James-Lange theory was that anxiety as an emotion was indistinguishable from such feelings as palpitations, 'butterflies in the stomach' and other expressions of adrenaline output and sympathetic activity. It has been shown, however, in people with spinal cord lesions and loss of visceral autonomic awareness, that anxiety can be experienced without its usual physical accompaniments, although less intensely.

Anxiety is characterised as follows: it includes a sense of fear or something close to that, such as dread, terror, or panic. The feeling is unpleasant, and is concerned with what will or might happen in the future. There is a sense of threat, which in pathological anxiety is out of proportion to the actual threat as perceived by others, and usually as perceived by the patient, too. There are subjective bodily experiences, including palpitations, dyspnoea, constriction or pressure in the chest, tightness in the throat, weakness of the body (especially of the legs), dryness of the mouth, sweating, tremor, nausea, vomiting and giddiness (not rotatory vertigo, more a sense of unsteadiness). There is often an urge to micturate or defaecate and in extreme cases this can happen involuntarily, as can screaming, running or fainting.

Clearly, anxiety can be a normal and natural response, and its most extreme manifestations do indeed occur in, for example, people about to be executed or tortured. As a biological response it is part of the mobilisation of the organism for 'flight or fight', by means of the autonomic and endocrine systems. When very marked, it actually paralyses the will and leads to helplessness.

A mild degree of anxiety can improve both mental and physical performance, and those who do best in demanding and difficult activities, including sportsmen such as racing drivers, have the capacity to tolerate high levels of anxiety without deterioration in performance. In everyone, however, there is a certain level of anxiety beyond which performance progressively deteriorates. Some people actively enjoy danger, and find it stimulating, as the memoirs of mountain climbers make clear. They presumably experience unpleasant levels of anxiety at a later stage than would the rest of us. (It has been suggested that adrenaline is associated with unpleasant fear, and noradrenaline with the more pleasurable 'keyed up' states.)

Those of less robust personality experience disabling anxiety more easily than others, and are obviously more likely to seek help. In neurotic states the anxiety does not have a clear-cut relationship to a dangerous situation, such as the climbers stimulating fear of falling, but is either diffuse and 'free floating', or attached to a situation which the patient regards as ridiculous, as in a phobic fear of going out into the street. The diffuse and apparently meaningless anxiety is particularly hard to bear, and one of the functions of psychotherapy is to try and find the underlying sources of it, which can help to make it much more tolerable.

We should use the term 'Anxiety State' only when sure that the anxiety symptoms are not secondary to some other condition, such as depression or organic brain disease as described later.

It is worth making a distinction here between the kind of minor and often recurrent anxiety states seen mainly in general practice, and the more severe and less tractable ones treated by psychiatrists. The former are common in people who have a life long proneness to anxiety, mainly women, but who may have no other personality problem. They may cope well with life in every way, except that they easily become anxious. If something out of the ordinary happens, such as a daughter's impending marriage to an undesirable combined with serious illness in the husband, then the anxiety threshold is exceeded and the anxious mother goes to her doctor. With time, perhaps with some support and a tranquilliser, all this settles down, until the next time.

The more prolonged and difficult anxiety states arise when the precipitant is not some understandable and limited external stress, but where there is a complex problem of relationships due to an inner neurotic conflict, perhaps based on transference problems as outlined earlier in this section. It is unwise to give such patients tranquillisers freely, because with an enduring personality problem drug dependence is very likely. Psychotherapy is more likely to be the treatment of choice.

Aetiology

The general principle of multiple aetiology must be borne in mind; constitutional, physical and psychological factors will contribute to the condition.

Constitutional factors

There is a genetic predisposition to anxiety, and the genes involved are those of minor effect. It is due to their influence that many people have brisk autonomic responses which readily raise their tension. Upbringing presumably also plays a part, although this is more difficult to demonstrate by research than the genetic aspect.

There is a much greater tendency to anxiety in women than in men, as there is for depressive reactions also. Traditionally in our culture, men have been more prone to 'act out' when under pressure, by fighting, getting drunk, kicking the cat, and so on. Women have been more likely to suffer inwardly with anxiety and depression. Differential rates of admission to prison and mental hospital support this distinction. It will be interesting to see if the changing rôle and attitudes of women alters this balance.

Physical factors

There are some very important physical illnesses which can present with anxiety symptoms, more often if the patient has an anxious temperament or is subject to unusual stress at the time, but also in the absence of such factors. Organic brain disease, (including the pre-senile dementias, atherosclerotic and senile changes, cerebral tumours and early Parkinson's disease) is perhaps the commonest. Exhaustion, head injury, alcoholic abuse and endocrine disturbances are others.

Exhaustion, whether from long continued stress, from genuine overwork, or from the debilitating effects of illness, encourages the development of anxiety because, as has already been said, 'worries get a hold' more easily on those who are run down from whatever cause; because an exhausted man is less master of himself, more suggestible, and therefore an easier prey to such worries as he may already have or which may suggest themselves, than is the same man in good health. For these reasons anxiety is common after severe physical illnesses.

Head injury, especially when this is of a closed sort accompanied by concussion, is liable to give rise to an increased tendency to anxiety. This is commonly accompanied by irritability, and probably arises from a relative failure of autonomic control secondary to cerebral damage.

Anxiety is also often experienced by *alcoholics after drinking bouts,* and then appears to arise not so much from remorse as from actual toxic effect.

Prolonged heavy drinking, both before and after the development of true addiction, is often accompanied by a general increase in anxiety, usually responded to by taking another drink. These patients are often unwilling to reveal their alcohol intake, and may be misdiagnosed. If then treated with benzodiazepines or anti-depressants, the results can be disastrous. *Hypoglycaemia* and *thyrotoxicosis* can both lead to anxiety symptoms; the former in brief spells, the latter in a more sustained way. The former is much rarer as a psychiatric presentation, and is often missed. *Hypothyroidism* may also present with anxiety.

Anxiety is such a common complaint to general practitioners and other doctors, and in so few of the patients are physical factors important, that they are rarely considered, and therefore usually missed. It is a sound rule to consider physical illness factors (especially pre-senile dementia), and alcohol excess in any middle aged person presenting with anxiety symptoms for the first time. *Unrecognised depression* is another, and even more common, diagnostic trap.

Psychological factors

The commonest antecedent of anxiety is a sense of insecurity and very many of our patients have life long feelings of insecurity, often understandable in terms of disturbed early family life especially when there have been disruptive separations and no firm bond of love and esteem with a parent. In others, more recent events can lead to profound insecurity, such as the imminent break up of a marriage, threatened redundancy, the prolonged illness of a spouse or child, and many others.

In most patients who consult psychiatrists with anxiety states, there are both early background problems and more recent stresses and there are often also important conflicts of a neurotic type, as outlined on page 238. There is usually also a life long tendency to autonomic overarousal, so that they easily feel physical symptoms of anxiety in the face of quite minor day-to-day stress, and anxiety becomes disabling when they are in more severely testing circumstances.

In those who reach psychiatrists then there are often a number of important factors interacting which explain the severity and duration of the disturbance. Very many people develop mild acute anxiety states, in response to life's stresses, which settle rapidly with time and simple treatment. Those who reach psychiatric clinics have the more prolonged and serious disturbances, usually with complex multi-factorial origins.

Those who are always tense, who have few pleasures and relaxations in life, and who are over-conscientious and perfectionistic about their work and get increasingly 'wound up' over long periods, are more likely than others to develop anxiety states related to chronic work stress. The development may be slow, anxiety symptoms appearing after years of tension and cumulative strain.

Anxiety states can appear, paradoxically, when a long period of stress and difficulty suddenly ends. A typical example would be that of the mother of a sick child, ill for many months, who finally recovers. Within a few days the mother, who has kept herself going by exercising great self-control, and has been aware of very prolonged tension, suddenly develops an anxiety state. Such 'relaxation' reactions are quite common, and occur also with depressive states.

In relatively few patients in our kind of settled society do we see people reacting to really terrifying stress. A woman recently seen had been kept in a cellar during the Civil War in Lebanon, under continual threat of rape and murder for several weeks. On release she developed an overwhelming anxiety state, which several months later was still quite severe. Less dramatic 'traumatic neuroses' occur not in-frequently in people who have narrowly escaped in industrial, mining or road accidents, for example. In these also, secondary depression may develop as may hysterical developments related, for example, to unwillingness to go back to the scene of the danger, or to industrial compensation. The more isolated the individual is at the time of danger the greater the likelihood of a traumatic neurosis developing so that, for example, miners trapped in a group are psychologically better off than those trapped alone.

In all patients with anxiety states there is an interaction between personality factors (which are themselves the product of genetic endowment and life experiences), and environmental stress. In ordinary civilian life we largely see people with vulnerable and anxious personalities reacting to stresses of mild or moderate severity by the standards of others. At times we see the other end of the spectrum: people of normal personality reacting to extreme stress.

In summary, the psychological precipitants of anxiety are those which threaten security (including loss of life, pain and so on, as well as emotional security); which involve emotional conflict from which no escape can be seen; or they arise from prolonged tension, sometimes after its release.

Symptoms and signs

The characteristics of anxiety have been described at the beginning of this chapter, and those are the features found in anxiety states, in various degrees of severity and in varying combinations, in both acute and chronic forms. As anxiety is a psychobiological response, the patients have the characteristic physical signs as well as the subjective experience.

The mental symptoms vary from a mild uneasiness coupled with a feeling that something is going to happen, together with restlessness, to actual panic in which the patient is acutely afraid. In the typical case the fear is not clearly focused on any special object, but is general and permeates the whole mental state so that the patient experiences tension and disturbed concentration with inability to settle. Irritability is a common feature; the appetite is frequently impaired, so that loss of weight can be observed; and the patients find difficulty in getting off to sleep and wake unrefreshed after troubled dreams.

Headache is a common complaint, usually of the constricting 'tension' type, or of pressure on the vertex; but a muzzy unpleasant feeling in the head is very common, variably described as headache, 'woozyness', or 'giddiness', this sensation being more common with hyperventilation.

Hyperventilation is a common development in anxiety and phobic states. With the palpitations and other physical symptoms, and the sense of fear and dread, there is dyspnoea, with a sense of oppression in the chest, gasping for breath, or deep sighing respirations. In some people this leads on to a worsening of symptoms, because of the biochemical changes induced, and a vicious circle is easily established.

At times overbreathing becomes an established response to quite trivial stress, or even persists almost continuously to a minor degree. In those cases overbreathing can itself become a cause of panic attacks.

Hyperventilation lowers the arterial partial pressure of carbon dioxide ($P\text{CO}_2$), and increases the pH of the blood. These changes seem to precipitate anxiety and even panic in susceptible subjects, as do the accompanying changes in levels of ionised calcium. When hyperventilation is thought to be important in this way, a useful test is to ask the patient to overbreathe for 2 or 3 minutes, and to compare the results to that of his usual panic attacks.

The role of hyperventilation in producing lower levels of ionised calcium, and thus muscular spasms (carpo-pedal spasm, for example) is well known and more often recognised than the part played in producing panic.

Breathing into a paper bag can still be a useful manoeuvre in acute hyperventilation; and breathing exercises and education are a useful part of treatment for the more chronic over-breathers.

Acute anxiety states

Anxiety may occur in acute attacks, the first of which can often be traced back to some special experience. Subsequent attacks may then be provoked by any event that comes to be associated with the original trauma. More and more events come to be so associated, so that finally the 'conditioned reflex' may be set going by some stimulus with no obvious connection at all. This is specially liable to happen where the patient has interpreted the state as one of physical disease, and has become afraid of the symptoms themselves.

In some patients the clinical picture is one of recurring acute anxiety states, more or less identical with the panic attacks which occur in agoraphobia (p. 261), but without the obvious link to a phobic situation. In between attacks there will usually be a state of mild general apprehension and unease, with irritability, some impairment of concentration and lessened ability to cope with day-to-day life. Although no obvious precipitant may be described by the patient, it will usually be found that there is one, often quite simple to understand, which the patient may be unwilling at first to recognise. It will come to light only by exploring the patient's life and situation and by a very careful history of what was happening in the patient's life at the time. A striking example was of a man with random-seeming major anxiety attacks, sufficient to prevent him going to work. They turned out to be associated with visits to his wife by her cousin, with whom he suspected her of having had a homosexual affair in the past. The sense of insecurity and anguish, which he hardly allowed to enter his full awareness, and had certainly never talked about, triggered off the anxiety attack. A secondary gain of hysterical type (see p. 265) was also part of the picture, in that his symptoms kept him at home and thus thwarted any unwelcome affair.

As already mentioned, most simple acute anxiety states settle down with the passage of time and the lessening of stress and perhaps with treatment from the general practitioner, such as emotional support and a benzodiazepine. Those simple anxiety states mainly occur in anxiety-prone individuals as a reaction to an increase in life stress, and recur throughout life in similar situations. Such patients are rarely referred to psychiatrists unless the symptoms are unusually severe or puzzling, as was the case just described. It is reasonable to give a benzodiazepine to such patients, so long as it is for a brief period only. In patients with chronic anxiety states, or with chronic tension, the risks of dependence are high, and benzodiazepines should be used with caution. (see p. 418).

Chronic anxiety states

These develop either out of recurring acute attacks, or more gradually out of chronic states of tension, conflict and stress, as described earlier. There is no recognised length of time after which we call them 'chronic', but we imply a duration of a month or more. The patients are continually anxious and tense, with periodic exacerbations rising to panic levels at times. They are more likely to develop in those of less robust temperament and/or when the stresses are unrelenting, and also if an element of *secondary gain* develops (see p. 265). This is most commonly seen when someone, who has perhaps been struggling with an unpleasant work situation for years, breaks down into an anxiety state severe enough to keep him at home. Life is so much more pleasant at home that it is difficult to face work, and a change of job should obviously be part of the treatment. However, work may be hard to find or a pension might depend on staying with the same employers; factors like these are bound to make it more difficult to recover. Hysterical developments are not, of course, restricted to cases in which there is secondary gain centred on a work problem. Any disability or illness, not only an anxiety state, can become an excuse for an inability to meet some demand or cope with some responsibility, ranging from taking a share in coping with the children or with in-laws to being unable to be left alone by a husband keen on football or to have sexual intercourse because it sets off palpitations. Nor are all situations in which there is apparent secondary gain necessarily based on anxiety states. They may be straightforwardly simulated, or they may be purely hysterical (that is unconsciously motivated) without anxiety. In those in whom recovery does not occur there are four common clinical end states of chronic anxiety neuroses:

(1) *Hysterical elaboration* and exaggeration (p. 266) easily develops (as does deliberately simulated exaggeration), but most people

struggle on conscientiously, long after severe anxiety is firmly established, until they can no longer cope, and the pattern changes.

(2) *Exhaustion* often follows prolonged severe anxiety and tension, and merges imperceptibly into depression. The sufferer finds it more and more difficult to summon up the energy to cope, tension and misery are unrelenting, although the more marked physical symptoms of 'the adrenaline syndrome' often lessen. Retreat into chronic invalidism, with multiple vague physical complaints, is common at this stage, even in patients of quite robust personality who have tried hard to keep going.

(3) *Depression* becomes more and more marked in some, although the clinical picture usually remains reactive rather than showing the characteristic biological changes of sleep, appetite, weight and diurnal variation of mood of the endogenous pattern (see chapter 9 on Depressive States).

(4) *An 'organ neurosis'* is the fourth common end state. This occurs when the patient has been especially disturbed by symptoms from one particular system or organ, and focusses increasingly on that, remaining convinced that there must be organic disease causing the symptoms, and usually explaining the other anxiety symptoms as the natural consequence of being worried about an illness which no doctor has yet diagnosed. Considerable anger is often expressed at the incompetence or lack of investigative fervour that doctors have shown. Referral to a psychiatrist is frequently experienced as rejection by other doctors, which in some ways it often is. There may have been very long and intensive physical investigations, but the emotional state of life situation of the patient has not usually been enquired into at all, until the last test is negative. By then the investigations, and the ideas which the patient has picked up from doctors, nurses and procedures, have often powerfully reinforced the patient's own beliefs, rather than convinced him that he is physically healthy.

The commonest of these organ neuroses is of heart disease, which springs into the mind of many patients very naturally with their first panic attack with palpitations, gasping for breath, feeling faint and unsteady, looking pale and arousing a concern in onlookers which worsens the patient's anxieties and symptoms. It is perhaps remarkable that in so many patients it is easy to persuade them that the heart itself is not at fault.

In the World War of 1914–1918 an enormous number of soldiers developed 'cardiac neuroses' arising from the anxieties of the battlefield and intensified by the secondary gain of escaping from the battle and the likelihood of death in the trenches. The syndrome was widely known as 'da Costa's syndrome' or 'soldier's heart', and it was some years before its psychogenesis was understood. The presence of a functional systolic flow murmur (not understood then as now) made the diagnosis more likely.

Cardiac neuroses are the commonest, but similar concern can focus on *dyspepsia*, with a belief that there 'must be an ulcer'; on frequency of micturition and the search for cystitis; on nervous diarrhoea, with a diagnosis of 'colitis' (or now more frequently, 'irritable bowel syndrome'), or on headache and many other symptoms. In these organ neuroses, as with the other clinical pictures described, hysterical exaggeration and prolongation can occur if there is some benefit (secondary gain) accruing and a state of chronic hypochondria can also easily develop, in which the patient's life is dominated by the search for diagnosis and treatment.

In patients with organ neuroses there is often an understandable link with family or personal experiences. In those where the heart is the focus, very often there will be a history that a parent or sibling died at about this age of a heart attack or the patient might have had rheumatic fever as a child and had to spend some time in bed, with frequent auscultation for murmurs. The parents may have later reinforced the child's anxieties by forbidding him to play football and so on, so that a substrate of anxiety about the heart already exists. Analogous factors will often be found with other organs and symptoms.

In other patients the organ or system affected may have a different type of significance, as when a singer may be disturbed by the dyspnoea of an anxiety state and then develops anxieties about her lungs, coming to believe that some disease will ruin her singing career; or a surgeon can focus similarly on a tremor, and be worried about having multiple sclerosis. The more the worries about the symptoms the greater the anxiety, and the consequent vicious circle can be very hard to interrupt.

It is worth noting that the effect of emotion on autonomic function is clearly expressed in such phrases as 'He makes me sick', 'I can't stomach that', 'it gives me cold feet' and so on. Similarly, the effect of tension on skeletal muscle is shown by 'he's a real pain in the neck'.

Terminology in this area, as in others unfortunately, is confused. The term 'organ neurosis' is less commonly used now, and the symptom complexes just outlined are labelled by some as 'functional' or 'psychogenic' states (see p. 267) and others would call them 'psychosomatic' (see chapter 15).

Differential diagnosis

It has already been pointed out at the beginning of this section on Anxiety states that in pure form they are relatively uncommon, and on page 242, when considering aetiology, the importance was stressed of various organic illnesses, of depression and of alcohol. These points sum up the approach necessary for differential diagnosis: the term anxiety state should not be indiscriminately applied to everyone with anxiety symptoms, but it should only be accepted when confident that no other illness explains the presenting syndrome.

In addition, even when there is no underlying illness to explain it away, anxiety states are quite often modified by secondary gain, and depression creeps in so frequently at some stage that it is often very difficult to know whether to describe someone as having 'an anxiety state with secondary depression' or as suffering from 'depression with marked anxiety'. In practice one should not try too hard to identify pure syndromes, because what we are really dealing with are the multifarious ways in which human beings react to stress, determined by their whole personality, their life situation, and the nature of those stresses. The anxiety states are one broad category of types of reaction, merging into and modified by others. They are not rigidly constructed pigeon holes into which people must fit. It is entirely acceptable, therefore, in clinical practice if not for strict research purposes or for the designers of statistical manuals, to make a diagnosis such as 'a chronic anxiety state with secondary depression and a moderate degree of hysterical elaboration'. The purpose of diagnosis is to help in treatment and prognosis, and a more complex diagnosis can aid this.

Organic brain disease and depressive illnesses

These are the two most important underlying disturbances to identify. In the former anxiety reactions are 'released' as the individual finds it more difficult to cope with day-to-day life; and catastrophic anxiety reactions may also develop. These are described in Chapter 6. The role played by hypoglycaemia, thyrotoxicosis and alcohol is described on page 242 and is not repeated here.

Mixtures of anxiety and depression occur in three main ways. First, when the anxiety symptoms are sufficiently distressing to lead to a depressive reaction; and second, when the precipitating causes lead to anxiety and depression developing at the same time. In both of these the depressive symptoms are likely to be of the reactive pattern. Third, and most importantly, depressive illnesses of endogenous pattern, or of bipolar manic depressive type, can present — especially in people of anxious temperament — with severe anxiety symptoms. In fact, the depressive subgroup 'Agitated Depression' (p. 176) can be seen as the co-existence of severe depression and severe anxiety. If the depressive symptoms are not obvious they may be swamped by the anxiety and ignored by the doctor. It is essential for this possibility always to be borne in mind, and the correct questions must be asked. Patients with pure anxiety states do not commit suicide but depressives do. If the underlying condition is a depressive illness the only effective treatment will be that for depression, and treatment with benzodiazepines alone may lessen the anxiety but suddenly intensify the depression. Behavioural psychotherapy for anxiety symptoms can lead to a similar result, with the appearance of previously unrecognised depression.

It is a reasonable working rule that neurotic/ anxiety states do not develop in middle age for the first time in people of non-anxious temperament. Having established that no organic disease exists, the most likely cause for the symptoms is a depressive illness and antidepressant treatment is most likely to be helpful. This rule fails in those cases where overwhelming external stress occurs, as described earlier, in which case the stress will be apparent to both patient and doctor. Less often major stress occurs which is not described, perhaps because of shame. An example occurred when a middle aged army officer had kept secret the fact that he had been found by the police interfering sexually with a small boy, and developed a severe anxiety state in the days before his court appearance. This might be regarded as understandable and not a neurotic reaction.

In summary, the diagnosis of 'anxiety state' should be reserved for those conditions in which there are persistent characteristic signs and symptoms, in the absence of some other underlying illness, and in the absence of continuing adequate stress.

Course and prognosis

As has been described there are very many minor anxiety states, mainly occurring in anxious people when under some form of pressure, but in which there are no major emotional conflicts or other complications, and which settle down rapidly as the pressures lessen. These conditions rarely lead to psychiatric referral, but can form quite an important part of a general practitioner's work. The prognosis is excellent for each episode, but they may recur in the face of stress.

In the case of patients with more established anxiety states, who consult psychiatrists, the prognosis is less good. It depends on the balance between personal predisposition, stress, the clinical picture, and the efficacy of treatment. Overall, of any large series of patients with anxiety states referred to psychiatric outpatients, 60–70% will be found to be reasonably well on long term follow up after a few years.

In one large follow up study 68% had recovered or were only mildly impaired. The impairment included a more restricted social life, but there was no loss of earning power and the divorce rate was surprisingly perhaps, no greater than in controls. As a group they were noticeably unhappy and dissatisfied with life even after all symptoms had resolved, which presumably is a reflection of personality and life situation.

(1) *Predisposition.* By considering the patient's past life in terms of resistance or vulnerability to stress, capacity to cope with relationships, with work and with the practical difficulties of day to day life, a guide to the prognosis of any particular anxiety state can be obtained.

(2) *Stress.* What is stressful for one person is not necessarily so for another, and one's personal bias must be set aside in assessing this, in favour of what the individual patient says and what the past record indicates. If the stress lies in apparently insoluble conflict in the immediate family it is more difficult to modify than if it is at work. Almost always in chronic anxiety states the patient is experiencing emotional stress because his personality has led to a certain situation, conflict, or interactions with which he now cannot cope. He may see it as externally imposed, but usually he has contributed if only, as a simple example, by having got himself into a certain type of work situation which now proves chronically stressful. Psychotherapy which leads to an understanding of the nature of the stress, and the part the patient has played in its development, is crucial here.

(3) *The clinical picture.* The prognosis is worst in those cases in which there is some benefit to the patient in the prolongation of symptoms, either by unconscious 'hysterical' developments or deliberately. This is, of course, a matter of motivation.

In those who present mainly with exhaustion, as the result of a prolonged struggle to keep going against the symptoms and who are therefore more highly motivated, the outlook is better. Depression as a major development may improve prognosis, as depressive symptoms are often helped by anti-depressant medication, and the anxiety symptoms can improve with them.

In those with firmly fixed 'organ neuroses', treatment is made more difficult because the patient is often unwilling to see the problem as a psychiatric or psychological one.

(4) *The efficacy of treatment* will be considered in the next section, and also in Chapter 16.

Treatment

The essential preliminary is a good history, yielding a sound working knowledge of the patient's personality, habits of reaction, past performance and present difficulties, with an accurate chronological record of the onset of stress and the development of symptoms (see p. 243). As always the history should include information from the spouse or other relevant person. A careful physical examination, and if necessary some investigations, may be helpfully reassuring if the patient has not already been assessed in this way.

The first decision to be taken about treatment is often whether or not the patient should remain at work, and less often, to consider whether admission to hospital as an in-patient or day patient is needed. If the important stresses are at work, if performance there is impaired and especially if the patient feels worse at work, it would be wise to stop. In those in whom the major stresses are at home, the workplace can be a refuge. The doctor should be alert to the possibility that symptoms may be used to manipulate the situation, including that at work, especially in very chronic anxiety states.

Treatment in any given individual depends on the cause. As with all psychiatric treatment it can be considered under three headings: environmental change, physical treatment, and psychotherapy.

Environmental change

Admission as an in-patient is rarely necessary for patients with even the most severe anxiety states, except for a few very distressed and unable to cope, with homes in which it is impossible to rest, and in which domestic stresses are the principal cause of the disorder. Admission removes the individual from the stress, and allows for a period of drug treatment and some start with psychotherapy, or necessary counselling. Formal psychotherapy, aimed at insight, (see p. 394) is best carried out in out-patients or perhaps day patients, rather than with in-patients, in most psychiatric units. Day hospital admission (p. 381) can be a very appropriate setting for patients with anxiety states.

Change of work or changes in how work is carried out and similar matters, will almost always be considered in the history taking and counselling which must go on, even if there is no formal psycho-therapy. Perhaps the most profound changes of environment are those

254 PSYCHOLOGICAL MEDICINE

which can come about in the marital and other family relationships, including separation and divorce, which sometimes is the only way in which the stresses and conflicts can be controlled. Doctors and other professionals involved should be most careful not to take the responsibility of advising people to end their marriages, although very often discussion of the possibilities will be necessary.

Under 'change of environment' we can perhaps consider the value of proper planning of relaxation and pleasure. So many people with complaints of long standing anxiety, tension and depression have never had or have given up old hobbies, pleasures and interests and their only relaxation from the pressures of work is to drink or to watch television. People should be encouraged to examine the way in which they spend their leisure time, and to seek pleasant distractions.

Physical treatment

The most common physical treatment is with medication and there is absolutely no role for ECT. Before considering drug treatment it is worth mentioning that *regular physical exercise* can be helpful in relieving and preventing states of anxiety and tension. Swimming, jogging, brisk walking, and sports and games in which there is enough exercise to lead to some tiredness can be helpful. Clearly, this aspect is also closely linked to that of entertainment and pleasure mentioned in the previous section.

Various relaxation or quasi-relaxation techniques, such as meditation or yoga can also be helpful. Dancing, dance therapy, massage, methods emphasising control of bodily movement (for example, the Alexander technique) can all offer relaxation. They are much healthier and more effective in the long run when appropriately combined with discussion of conflicts and practical steps to be taken, and with psychotherapy if indicated, than a reliance on benzodiazepines alone.

Drug treatment

In some, if very acutely disturbed, a period of *modified narcosis* with benzodiazepines can be used to interrupt the panic and the vicious circle of increasing anxiety about the symptoms themselves. A short-acting drug such as lorazepam (2.5 mg every 4 hours) can be given until the patient is relaxed and sleeping for much of the day. The dose is then cut to one large enough to maintain that state for 3 or 4 days, followed by gradual withdrawal over a similar period, when it will often be found that there is a marked improvement, sufficient at least to approach the underlying problems more calmly and constructively.

This is most likely to help if there have been major external stresses. It should be avoided in recurring states of anxiety with marked domestic conflict and a vulnerable personality, where the treatment would soon become too easy a retreat into invalidism.

Antidepressants can often be helpful, especially the more sedative ones such as amitriptyline or trimipramine. 50 or 75 mg of trimipramine at night is a useful hypnotic and has some persisting anxiolytic effect during the day. Amitriptyline in doses such as 10 mg t.d.s., which are usually ineffective in depressive states, can be helpful for anxiety, and larger doses can be used as necessary. These tricyclics do not lead to dependence and tolerance does not develop.

Benzodiazepines are overwhelmingly the most often prescribed drugs for anxiety and tension, and they are described more fully in Chapter 16. They are very well tolerated and lead to rapid and pronounced lessening of anxiety without much sedation. They are grossly over-prescribed, handed out for minor disturbances and trivial complaints to a patient population which increasingly expects to have to suffer no unpleasant feelings, even in the face of real life problems. Doctors bear much of the responsibility for the development of these attitudes.

Benzodiazepines also have serious disadvantages, especially if, as so often happens, they are relied on as the sole treatment. In a brief self limiting anxiety state, which arises as a result of transient stress, it is reasonable to use them to lessen anxiety if the disturbance is severe enough to justify medication. When someone has an enduring personality problem, or the anxiety is in response to long standing marital conflicts for example, then to use drugs alone is insufficient. The tranquillisers will do nothing to solve the problems, tolerance will develop so that the dose will be increased, and side effects such as ataxia and mental slowing then develop. Benzodiazepines also have an alcohol-like effect and often lessen self-control, and lead to instability of mood, especially in higher doses. After a time the patient may well be psychologically dependent on them, and true addiction does develop at times.

Many serious problems in people's lives cannot be helped by medical intervention, although much can be done by psychotherapy, advice, emotional support, help with environmental changes such as housing problems, and other social or personal measures. It is often better to do nothing than simply to put someone onto tranquillisers if there is no likelihood of a change in the life situation. There is a temptation for the doctor to prescribe tranquillisers in order to satisfy the patient and cut short what seems to be an unproductive interview about an unchangeable life problem. *Barbiturates* should never be given to relieve anxiety in someone with long-term problems, as the dangers of addiction are considerable and the suicide potential high. They are best not used at all in psychiatric problems.

Another serious disadvantage of the routine use of tranquillisers for everyone with anxiety symptoms is that a sizeable proportion of the patients are likely to be suffering from unrecognised depression, and to be made worse by tranquillisers, or to have organic brain disease or some other physical illness presenting in the early stages with anxiety.

Counselling and psychotherapy

By counselling we mean here advice on daily living, such as on exercise, discussion of problems and of attitudes to difficult personal relationships at work and so on, which are an integral part of the management of any patient, and which are particularly important in people with chronic states of anxiety and tension, in whom the whole pattern of life so often seems unwise.

By psychotherapy we mean the formal methods of psychological treatment, with regular interviews as described on page 394 in Chapter 16. Such psychotherapy, both behavioural and insight directed, is often necessary, especially in those in whom conflict in the family is a central issue. The patient must be encouraged to look at the underlying problems and take necessary decisions. However, those decisions should be those of the patient and not the therapist.

Tension states

Tension is a very common complaint, and a common diagnosis, but it has been little studied and is usually thought of as a variant of anxiety in which the autonomic and 'adrenaline' symptoms do not develop. It is the opposite of 'relaxation'. It includes the feeling that one must remain controlled, keyed up and alert in order to cope with any difficulties that might arise. Moreover, there is a feeling that this stage of alertness and control has had to be unpleasantly prolonged already for some time and that the longer it lasts the more unpleasant it will become. A feeling of bottled up anger, which must not be allowed to blaze out, is often part of the picture.

Tension in muscles, almost always accompanied by feelings of mental tension, and painful aching, is often the principal symptom. A 'tight band' around the head, tension with stiffness and pain in the muscles of the back and shoulder, and in the lower back, are perhaps the commonest. There often seems to be a combination of physical and mental factors, as when people with spondylitic changes in the neck get much more pain there when they are feeling tense. Poor posture also plays a part and a combination of lumbar lordosis, stooping shoulders and tension is often found in those who complain of back ache for which no convincing 'organic' cause can be found.

Chronic back ache is one of the commonest complaints to doctors in our society and leads to much time off work. In many cases standard investigations are of little help, as is standard treatment. A psychiatric history often reveals great feelings of tension, usually based on domestic conflict, and a manipulative element is also not uncommon. Many of these patients seek help from non medical practitioners, such as osteopaths and chiropractors and a well organised study of different approaches to treatment would be interesting.

Relatively few patients with tension states are referred to psychiatrists, but they are very common in general practice, where they may be diagnosed in various ways. Many present with headache and musculo-skeletal pain, some with dyspepsia or other abdominal pain, usually colicky.

They are usually hard working, conscientious and relatively successful people, insecure and striving in temperament and continually feel that the tasks they have to fulfil (at work and in the home) are only just manageable, and that they cannot relax their efforts. They have no time, or perhaps no inclination, to relax and enjoy themselves and life seems a grim struggle. They may take to alcohol to relieve the continual feelings of strain with which they live. Holidays are often very helpful, but never long enough. Their families nearly always diagnose them correctly as being unable to relax and as taking everything too seriously. They are 'worriers' in the ordinary sense of the word, rather than 'anxiety prone', with evidence of autonomic over-activity and true anxiety symptoms.

Diagnosis is not difficult, but co-existence of depression must be carefully excluded. If headache or musculo-skeletal pain is a new development, investigations to exclude significant physical disorder may be needed.

Treatment is obvious — to the onlooker — but often very difficult to implement because of the patient's temperament and his frequent belief that if he relaxes his efforts he may lose his grip on the situation, something which is disturbing to contemplate for people who have spent their lives establishing control. More pleasurable activities, shorter working hours, and regular exercise, are all helpful. A careful scrutiny of how he spends his time and consideration of why he lives as he does can be educational and psychotherapeutic. Specific relaxation exercises and other related techniques, such as yoga based exercises, can also be helpful. The sort of 'anxiety and stress management' techniques offered by some behavioural psychologists (p. 406 and see bibliography) combines most of these and other approaches, and is worth trying in severe and resistant states of tension.

Benzodiazepines should be avoided because they will produce marked and rapid relief of tension, but as the patient's life style and attitudes will not thereby change, the danger is of increasing tolerance and dependence.

The prognosis is, quite simply, of improvement, deterioration or no change. The symptoms do not change in quality and no other condition supervenes as a result of deterioration, except that depression and alcoholism become more likely. Treatment is essentially a matter of education and changing attitudes and can be very successful. Many patients continue, with minor fluctuations, until they retire or their life situation changes in some major way so that they can also change. Unfortunately, the sort of people who have found it difficult to relax and enjoy life because they are too worried about work are not well prepared for retirement.

PHOBIC STATES

These conditions have much in common with obsessional states and are often classified with them for reasons which will be made clear. However, anxiety is one of their principal symptoms, and in many ways they more closely resemble the anxiety states, and are therefore considered here in this book.

A phobia is an irrational fear, in which the irrationality is recognised, realised usually to be essentially ridiculous, and is struggled against with a sense of tension. These features are exactly parallel to those of obsessional thoughts with which these phobias overlap at times, and explain the alternative classification. Phobias do not lead to compulsive acts, although the patient may well modify his life in order to cope with them. They are of two main types: the simple and the complex, and this distinction is of great importance clinically in several ways. It is the simple monosymptomatic phobias which most closely resemble obsessional thoughts; the complex phobias arise mainly in people with neurotic character disorders in interaction with their spouses, or other family members. There is a borderland between the two where they merge. Much the commonest complex phobia is agoraphobia. Social phobias deserve separate consideration.

Simple phobias (monosymptomatic phobias)

Under this heading we can put all the very common fears of spiders, mice, insects of various sorts, heights, water, lifts or other confined spaces, wide open spaces, crowded streets, feathers and almost any other object one can think of. Less often there are such activities as vomiting, as described in the section on behaviour therapy (p. 406), or of certain diseases or types of dirt. They are described as 'simple' because the principal effect is only on the person who has the phobia, whose life may be made quite uncomfortable or unpleasant by them. In that they differ from the complex phobias, in which other people's lives are markedly affected, as described later, and into which they occasionally develop, depending on personalities and circum-stances.

The simple phobias usually occur in people of rather tense and anxiety prone personality, who perhaps form conditioned reflexes rather easily. They have often been brought up by someone who has had a similiar phobia and naturally inculcated it. In others there is a clear cut and convincing history of some earlier and fearful experience associated directly or indirectly with the phobic object. When there is a phobia of entering even shallow water for example, there is often a history of being thrown into the deep end of a pool or of feeling about to drown; and someone who has fainted in a tube train and woken up on the floor may be unable to travel by tube without anxiety after that. In other people no such clear account is given but one can imagine some similar understandable chain of circumstances in many sufferers. In others the phobic object may seem to have some symbolic, particularly sexual, meaning, as with fear of snakes which may be reacted to as phallic symbols. In yet others, the underlying meaning may be related to some unacceptable and largely unconscious thought, as described in the next chapter on obsessions, when a phobic fear of knives arises from the repression of antagonistic feelings towards the children.

Another example of the importance of the unrecognised thought was of a man who suddenly developed a phobia of driving away from home in his car, unless accompanied by his wife. The fear began shortly after his wife had made a suicidal gesture by swallowing pills, complaining about the very long hours he was away from home as an insurance salesman. He did not spontaneously link the overdose and the phobia.

There are therefore various ways in which these simple phobias can arise, although the presenting symptoms are very alike. They can all be understood as over-learnt conditioned responses. Some of these phobias are very widespread, particularly that of spiders, and many otherwise stoical people are less happy about picking up a spider than a beetle, although why this should be so is not clear.

When confronted by the phobic object, for example a spider, the severely phobic individual feels rapidly mounting anxiety or fear, often to an unbearable degree, so that he has to leave the site. With pounding heart, sweating palms, tremor, dry mouth, vision blurred by pupillary dilation, gooseflesh, unsteadiness, butterflies in the stomach, perhaps an urge to micturate or defaecate, and an overwhelming desire to run away, the patient can experience a full blown panic attack, and very often feels he is about to lose consciousness, lose control and 'go beserk', or even die. This extremity of fear is of course not so common as are milder attacks, but even the less severe panics are very unpleasant, and the patient naturally goes out of his way to avoid whatever situation seemed responsible. A process of generalisation can occur, using the terminology of learning theory to describe the development of further conditioned fear responses. For example someone with a phobia of snakes might at first be unable to go into the reptile house at the zoo, later be unable to visit the zoo at all, and later feel a twinge of anxiety even at the sight of the word 'zoo'.

Patients with these monosymptomatic phobias only present to doctors when they are severe, and a host of minor phobias are tolerated. Sometimes there is a severe exacerbation of a long-standing minor phobia, either in a setting of depression or associated with some new emotionally stressful situation. A typical example was of a girl with a lifelong minor insect phobia who went on holiday with her boyfriend. He told her that he was attracted to another girl and left her on the beach; she developed a panic attack apparently focused on the flying insects nearby, which until then she had almost ignored. Over the next few months the phobia increased in intensity until her life was severely curtailed, and she was unable to go to college each day in case a flying insect brushed her face.

These phobias, of all psychiatric conditions, respond most rapidly and completely to behaviour therapy (p. 406). Antidepressants, especially clomipramine and phenelzine (q.v.) can also help, and benzodiazepines produce temporary relief. It can be taken as a general rule that any phobia which does not affect the life of another person, and from which there is no secondary gain of hysterical type, such as can come from avoiding some responsibility, will respond well to treatment if the patient is prepared to follow a properly designed course of treatment.

Complex phobias

This term is used here to describe phobias in which there are pronounced effects on other people's lives. The nature of the feelings of fear or panic is the same, although they are often more severe than are the simple phobias. They are very much more common in women. The actual phobic object need not be different, but in practice *agoraphobia,* which literally means fear of the market place, but is mainly used for a fear of being out in the open away from home, is much the commonest. If an agoraphobic woman has no notice taken of her complaints by husband and family, and is left to 'get on with it', or if she avoids involving others in her disabilities and symptoms, then it remains a simple phobia, and has a relatively better prognosis with treatment.

Much more commonly the situation develops as follows: for some reason a woman develops a fear of being out of the house on her own. It may begin with a severe panic attack while out shopping. There then develops, rapidly or slowly, a fear of going into that shop, then of approaching it, then of going to that part of town, and so on until she is unable even to go out of the house. Usually, but not always, those affected can manage to go out with the husband, or some other person. In some cases a child or a dog will do, or even an empty pram may be pushed along, and brings some security. The term 'house-bound housewife' is used for this condition, which is extremely common, and may never come to medical attention in any way. Some people are housebound for decades at a time, and it is not uncommon to be told when taking a psychiatric history that some relative has not been able to go out alone since the birth of a child who is now grown up.

As the woman's symptoms develop, and she is progressively less able to go out, the husband, or less often another relative, has to start doing the shopping. At first this is only at the distant shop where the trouble began, but gradually he has to do more and more, until he is doing it all. He also is the one who attends parent-teacher meetings at the school, visits aged relatives, and fulfills all other demands of this type.

Quite commonly as the symptoms worsen in severity she either has to have the husband with her, or has to know exactly where he is, or if his whereabouts cannot be known because of his job, some other person has to be with her. A kindly neighbour may do this, but usually a sister, mother or child has to, and if necessary the child is kept off school for that period. Gradually the woman's symptoms come to dominate the lives of her husband and other members of the family, and their every action may need to be accounted for or controlled. If these demands are not met then the housebound woman may have a very severe panic attack, the idea of which is so disturbing to her and the family that it is never allowed to happen. In fact, in some of these cases the last true panic was years before, and the whole extraordinary life style they follow has been dictated by the fear of a panic attack developing.

The husbands in these situations have certain important things in common. They tend to be rather passive, gentle, kindly and indulgent men. One does not see these complex phobic developments in the wives of aggressive and harsh men, who would refuse to do the shopping unless the wife is ill enough to be in hospital. In those cases one sees agoraphobic women who manage to struggle to the nearby shops to get the rations, because they fear the consequences, but are unable to go out on their own for social purposes or to enjoy themselves.

The rôle of the husband in these cases is crucial. It is our experience that sexual factors play a major part in about two-thirds of the fully developed complex phobias we see, in a curious manner. The husbands are usually not very active sexually, in keeping with the personalities described earlier. The wives have chosen men who are non-threatening sexually, but who are kind and 'understanding'. They appreciate these qualities, but at another level crave for a different type of sexual partner, romantic and passionate. It will often be found that the women concerned had been involved in important sexual affairs either just before the onset or actually at the time; or that fantasies about lovers from the past played an important part in their lives. Unlike the simple phobias, which can be mainly seen in terms of over-development of conditioned responses, these complex agoraphobias have the quality of 'approach-avoidance' conflicts, to use the terms of experimental psychology. In other words the woman stays at home to remain secure from her own sexual temptations — an idea put forward by Freud many years ago. (These factors do not appear in those agoraphobias which remain simple.)

Two examples make the thesis plain. The first is of a woman whose husband was exactly as described above, and who had been severely housebound for many years. At the relevant time she was attending a day hospital, to which she was taken each morning by her husband and collected afterwards. Even the idea of going out of the house on her own provoked fear and nausea. She met, at the day hospital, a rather psychopathic man, and travelled alone to one of the main London railways stations where she met her intended lover by arrangement, and where both were fortuitously met also by the present author! She remained non-agoraphobic until her lover left her, when her symptoms returned. Shortly afterwards her long-suffering husband finally turned, took a girl friend and stopped cherishing and tolerating his wife, whereupon she again lost her agoraphobic symptoms, and became quite seriously depressed.

The second example is of a woman whose husband was again as described above, whom she had married about 15 years before, for security, after the breakup of a passionate love affair with an Italian. She was completely housebound except for a long, weekly rail trip into London to see a behaviour therapist, whom it turned out she had come to regard as a kind of fantasy substitute for her old lover. When this was realised and pointed out, she immediately left her husband, travelled to Italy, and sought out and found the other man, all without any serious anxiety. However, more years had passed than she had clearly thought about, and she found a middle-aged, married man, happily domesticated. She returned to England and her husband, reverted to severe agoraphobia and gave up treatment.

The complexity and the presence of manipulative and controlling elements, with secondary emotional gains of hysterical type, make these agoraphobic syndromes very difficult to treat. Behaviour therapy using desensitisation methods and 'implosion' (q.v.) can be helpful, as can group and other psychotherapy. Drug treatment, with clomipramine, other tricyclics, or MAOI drugs such as phenelzine, can be helpful although it has to be continued for a long time and many relapse when it is stopped. It is our practice, in severe cases, to use phenelzine, and then to admit, if necessary and practicable, to a day hospital where both behaviour therapy and group psychotherapy can be offered. As with drug treatment alone there is a high relapse rate. This failure rate is understandable if the mechanisms and motives set out above are in fact operating, because there is no satisfactory resolution to the conflict. Quite a number of the women who do lose their symptoms go on to leave their husbands, although some return and again become phobic. In others the marriage breaks up permanently, and the new relationship rarely proves satisfactory. The patients then sometimes return later to the psychiatrist, no longer agoraphobic, but depressed and lonely, and sometimes dependent or even addicted to alcohol or other drugs.

It should again be emphasised that although a large proportion of severe complex agoraphobics have underlying conflicts of this type, it is not true of all. In some the syndrome dates from a puerperal depression, incompletely treated, and this group seems to do best with phenelzine or with other antidepressants. In yet other cases the original trigger to the phobia can be found in some physical illness. We have seen a patient in whom a virus infection of the inner ear (vestibular neuronitis) caused severe vertigo and some unpleasant falls in the street. The patient had always been of anxious and obsessional temperament, and a severe complex agoraphobia developed, aided by the oversolicitude of her husband, who was soon doing all the shopping. This disorder responded rapidly to simple explanation and advice about going out for a progressively longer distance each day, and it really belongs with the simple phobias as an overlearnt conditioned response, despite the effect on the husband's daily life.

Social phobia is a term used to describe a fear of confronting people in a public place such as a restaurant, and merges into ordinary shyness. It tends to improve with age and the normal social practice of life although, unfortunately, not in everyone. It is commonest in young men of reserved and inhibited temperament, who suffer from marked feelings of inferiority and of diffidence with the opposite sex, and they usually have mild ideas of reference — that is, the feeling that people are taking some special and critical note of them. Occasionally such a phobia is prodromal to schizophrenia, in which case the ideas of reference develop into truly delusional beliefs. If such phobic people become depressed the ideas of reference can also become much more severe, and they can pose diagnostic difficulties, perhaps being considered as schizophrenic. However, they have none of the other characteristic symptoms of schizophrenia, the picture is otherwise depressive, and responds to antidepressants, although a pheno-thiazine can usefully be added. This is one of the borderlands of psychiatric diagnosis, where syndromes overlap, and the correct diagnosis may not be clear for a long time.

Common sense advice about mixing more with other people, making suggestions to join tennis clubs, or whatever is appropriate to the patient's interests, is usually worth while. The more severely affected are just incapable of following such advice, and may need more positive help, by a behaviour therapy approach such as social skills training, or by group psychotherapy where appropriate. With severe social phobias, phenelzine and tricyclic antidepressants can be useful, as described in Chapter 16.

HYSTERICAL AND OTHER PSYCHOGENIC STATES

The terms 'hysteria' and 'hysterical' are amongst the most unsatis-factory in medicine, owing to the differing meanings they are given.

They tend to be used as synonymous with 'psychogenic' or 'functional' or even with 'emotionally determined', when applied to clinical states in which there are physical symptoms which do not fit readily into known clinical syndromes.

They are also used to describe uncontrolled-seeming outbursts of emotion, particularly if the observer, usually unsympathetic, feels that the degree of emotional distress is being exaggerated, or that there is an element of 'making a fuss'. There are important cultural differences in the way in which fear, grief and other emotions are expressed, and Italian or Greek manifestations of grief might well seem exaggerated and hysterical to a middle aged Englishman. (The term 'hysterical personality' is linked to the concept of exaggerated displays of emotion see p. 215).

Most dangerous is the use of the term 'hysterical' to describe some as yet undiagnosed condition, because the examination and investigations have not produced the answer, rather than because there is good psychiatric evidence of hysteria. This is more likely to happen if the doctor feels that the patient is exaggerating the degree of pain, disability and so on, or is emotionally disturbed or, particularly, if the doctor feels some degree of antagonism towards the patient. In one famous series of patients diagnosed in a neurological department as 'Hysterical', long-term follow-up showed that about half the patients had had serious progressive physical illnesses such as multiple sclerosis. A combination of the lack of physical signs (common in the early stages of many illnesses) and of the interactions of the personalities of patients and doctors, as outlined here, were presumably the main factors which led to the mis-diagnoses.

Another use of the term has been relatively recently developed in the United States. 'Hysteria' is used to describe a syndrome of multiple physical symptoms, extending over very many years, with associated anxiety and other psychiatric symptoms. It is also called Briquet's syndrome, and Somatisation Disorder in the United States and is considered in more detail on page 280.

Definition of hysterical states

We recommend that the term 'hysterical' is used in a narrow and specific sense; that is, for cases in which emotional factors initiate, maintain or worsen symptoms or disabilities, and in so doing bring the patient some benefit or *secondary gain* of which the patient is not fully aware. The motivation is *unconscious*.

In *hysterical conversion states*, the patient is unable to cope with some emotionally painful situation, and by a process or mental mechanism, not understood but which we call *'dissociation'*, the emotional distress lessens or vanishes, and is 'converted' (hence hysterical conversion) into some physical disability such as paralysis or blindness, or into some psychological impediment such as loss of memory. The loss of emotional pain is often referred to as *primary gain;* some other benefit in life, such as avoidance of responsibility, financial gain, resolution of conflict or other changes in important relationships, constitutes the *secondary gain.*

By *hysterical elaboration* and *exaggeration* we mean that similar mechanisms are at work in someone who has some organic illness, which is thereby prolonged or made more disabling.

Hyterical conversion states in this narrow sense are not common in our society, although hysterical elaboration and exaggeration are. Hysterical conversion is much more common in less developed cultures and in less intelligent and less sophisticated people in our own. There is often a very primitive and naive symbolism in acute hysterical conversion states such as was seen under battle conditions when an exhausted and terrified soldier, unable to run away and leave his comrades, but unable to take any more, would suddenly go blind, or even develop paralysis of the right hand so that he could no longer pull the trigger. The extreme conditions of war time and similar situations of prolonged fear and exhaustion, can lead to a greater incidence of hysterical states in people of more normally robust temperament, than does ordinary civil life. As with anxiety states (p. 240) there is a continuum of interaction of stress and of the ability of the individual to cope.

A profound difficulty in the confident diagnosis of hysterical conversion states should be apparent to the reader. We have no objective method of telling whether someone is conscious or unconscious of his motives, but must decide whether or not we believe what he tells us. If we do not believe him we must regard his complaints as deliberately exaggerated, or even as malingering. Naturally, the clinical details, the appearance of the patient, what we can find out about his previous record and personality, and so on, all come into the judgment.

The attitudes, training and motives of the doctor make a great difference here. A regimental medical officer in wartime, faced with a man who describes some symptoms which might prevent him performing an unpleasant duty, will probably be cynical in the absence of expected physical signs. Similarly, a doctor employed by an insurance company to assess disability after an industrial accident might be sceptical of some person's claims that the accident has caused an anxiety state. The doctor who has been treating that same individual and has developed a good rapport with him, is more likely to feel some identification with his patient, and to try and help him when he is asked to give a report on the consequences of the same accident. These differences of attitude and response among medical witnesses can be very important in medico-legal disputes, and all doctors should be aware of them. Other people important in the patient's life will also be reacting in their own particular ways determined by their own attitudes and experience of the patient, in his immediate environment. The emotional state of the patient with a hysterical conversion state is often remarkably untroubled, and is classically described as 'bland', or the patient is said to show 'belle indifference'. Instead of being deeply troubled by, say, paralysis of the legs, the patient is smiling and the affect is 'incongruous', although the use of that term is traditionally restricted to schizophrenia. This untroubled state of mind fits, of course, with the 'primary gain', that is the manner in which intolerable emotional conflicts or pressures have been 'switched off' and 'converted' into a disability. In patients with some organic disability, for example, a stroke, in which hysterical exaggeration or elaboration has occurred, there may be the same belle indifference, or there may be normal-seeming concern over lack of progress.

Psychogenic states (non-hysterical)

This term implies that emotional factors initiate, maintain or worsen physical symptoms or disabilities, or affect memory or concentration, but that these disturbances bring no secondary gain. The term *functional* means much the same thing, although it is rather illogical to use 'functional' as the polar opposite of 'organic', as is common in medicine, when most organic disorders disturb function.

Psychogenic states or disorders without hysterical secondary gains are extremely common, and have no exact diagnostic boundary. For example, an anxious patient with distressing palpitations who presents to his doctor with fears of heart disease, has a psychogenic state. The same is true of a patient with headache secondary to tension and depression or someone with an irritable bowel syndrome worsened by marital conflict. In each of these three examples, a different diagnosis would probably be used: anxiety state, depressive state and irritable bowel syndrome.

Other doctors might put each of these three examples under the heading of 'psychosomatic disorder', another useful but poorly-defined term (see p. 351). The terms psychogenic disorder and psychogenic state are not often used as diagnostic categories. The important thing is to realise that there are very many people presenting to doctors with emotionally determined physical symptoms, in whom there is no element of secondary gain.

Another very important difference between these patients and those with hysterical states, is that in the non-hysterical psychogenic states, the patient remains aware of his distressing emotions and does not display belle indifférence. He might not realise that his palpitations or abdominal colic are due to emotional factors, but he remains aware of his emotional distress. He can say 'Yes, I was feeling very worried about getting married again when the palpitations began'. The classical hysterical picture is that of someone who denies emotional stresses or problems, and the hysterical patient is more likely to say something like: 'I was feeling absolutely fine until this paralysis, and was really looking forward to getting married again next week, but it wouldn't be fair to her to marry me if I can't walk'.

Suppose that we have a patient whose arm has been immobilised for some time in a plaster cast and who finds that he cannot use that arm when the plaster is removed, although there is no organic cause for such disability. His condition is functional, but it may or may not be hysterical. If his inability arises merely from a fear of permanent paralysis that he has gradually come to accept as a fact, the condition is functional but not hysterical. Such a state may become hysterical if its existence serves a particular purpose for the person, such as enabling him to avoid something that he does not wish to do, or gains him something that he desires whether material in the form of financial compensation, or more spiritual in the form of sympathy and consideration. Again, if a person reacts by fainting to some psychological shock, such as witnessing an unpleasant accident, we should regard that as psychogenic, but not as hysterical unless there were also some clear evidence of its serving some gainful purpose. Similarly, vomiting may be psychogenic, but becomes hysterical only if it is purposive, as, for example, if used to lead to termination of an unwanted pregnancy.

Case I

A man of 50, conscientious and tense by temperament, was knocked down by a car and was briefly unconscious after a head injury. After this for a few weeks he was forgetful, had poor concentration and was prone to headaches, especially when he returned to work in his tobacconists shop, where he worked with his wife. These symptoms cleared completely, but a few months later a nearby factory closed, and the work force which had provided most of his customers no longer appeared. He began to get into debt. His wife then became seriously ill and each evening he had to visit her in hospital, keeping all his business worries to himself. He began to get increasing headaches and poor concentration, was anxious and rather depressed and became sure that his head injury was the cause of his problems, and that some serious brain damage must have occurred.

At interview, anxious, depressed and concerned as described above, he presented with a *psychogenic* disorder, which could also be described as 'functional' or 'emotionally determined' and could easily be understood as a reaction to external stress.

As he brooded angrily on the injustice of it all, a friend pointed out that he was entitled to compensation for all these problems if his symptoms were due to the head injury and a lawyer agreed that he had a good case. For the first time he saw some possibility of relief from debt and worry, and he also had a powerful motive for not getting better too quickly, although he did not see it like that. He began to visit various medical specialists for assessment of disability, and without consciously realising it, he began to distort the account he gave. He no longer made it clear that his post-traumatic symptoms had completely resolved at one stage, and that for some months his concentration had been normal; nor did he indicate that his symptoms had begun after his wife's illness. Increasingly his symptoms and resentments, and the outcome of the case, came to dominate his life. *Hysterical elaboration* and *exaggeration* had developed, prolonging his symptoms and increasing his disability in a manner of which he was not fully aware, and presumably not *wanting* to be aware.

The case dragged on, but then his solicitors told him that there was an excellent chance of settlement soon, with the chance of a sizeable award. He began to feel more relaxed and confident. One day he suddenly realised that he had just watched a long television programme with interest, and without headache or blurred vision. At this point, as he confessed some years later, he decided not to tell anyone, but to keep quiet about it until the case was over. He felt in any case that he had been very badly treated, that he deserved some recompense for all that had happened to him. He was now *malingering*.

Case 2

A middle-aged business man had done badly in his business for some time and had a poor relationship with his wife, of whom he was frightened. In order to build up his own image with her and her family he had spent money quite lavishly, although he knew he was seriously in debt. The day before he knew he was to be summonsed he disappeared from home, and was found wandering in the Scottish highlands a few days later. The weather was cold and wet and he was wearing only ordinary city clothes. He had slept out on the moors, without food or proper shelter, and was suffering from exposure and admitted to hospital when finally found.

He could not remember who he was, nor anything about his past life. His first memory was of waking in a stone hut on the moors that morning and knowing that he must get food and warmth. He was carrying a wallet with the usual details in it, but had not looked in it, saying that he 'did not know what it was for'.

This is an example of an *hysterical fugue* (fugue meaning flight), with hysterical *amnesia*. If he had been running away from his difficulties as a conscious effort, he might have planned it rather better than to risk his life and suffer severe discomfort in the mountains. There is an understandable secondary gain, but it is a very mal-adaptive response. He recovered his memory in a few days, but after being made bankrupt, separated from his wife.

Case 3

A 20-year-old woman, 'A', whose parents had always found her wayward, unpredictable and emotionally demanding, went to France with a friend after a serious family quarrel. She bought an old car and they enjoyed their trip until the other girl, driving the car on her own, crashed it and broke her neck, sustaining a tetraplegia, which persisted until death some years later. After the injured girl had been flown home to England, 'A' was left to face criminal charges because of her uninsured and unroadworthy car, and during the interview with her lawyer collapsed in a dramatic fashion on the floor. On 'waking' she had complete paralysis of the legs, without any abnormal neurological signs. Her mother was informed, flew out, they were reconciled, charges were dropped, and she returned to England and was admitted to hospital.

The condition was clearly 'psychogenic'. The way in which the illness resolved her difficulties in France reunited her with her mother, and brought her home, amounted to a massive secondary gain.

Once back in England she remained 'paralysed' below the waist, with no neurological signs. She seemed cheerful, and showed the classical 'belle indifférence'. It was expected that with some face-saving physiotherapy and supportive psychotherapy, she would soon recover, but many months passed without change. Finally, by means of an intravenous methohexitone interview it was discovered that she was receiving almost daily, letters from the mother of her severely injured friend, which were full of hate and blame, repeatedly saying that it was A who should be lying in hospital with bed sores, waiting to die, and so on. When this was brought to light, she suddenly became very deeply depressed, remorseful, and — briefly — suicidal. Her paralysis resolved over a few days, but she remained seriously depressed, slowly recovering with medication and psychotherapy.

This case illustrates some of the complexities and uncertainties found in hysterical conversion. Not only was there an obvious secondary gain which seemed to overshadow everything else, but there was a less apparent extremely important primary gain, in that severe distress, guilt and depression were seemingly kept out of the patient's consciousness by this process we call *dissociation*.

Aetiology

Hysterical symptoms may occur in anyone. They are usually shown par excellence by those with the hysterical type of personality (see p. 215), but they may occur even in normal people under sufficient stress, as was mentioned earlier in the context of soldiers in battle. In general however, they occur in people who throughout have shown low tolerance of stress, and may have had earlier episodes of conversion symptoms; in other words, those who are constitutionally predisposed.

Constitutional factors

Such constitutional predisposition may be genetically determined to some extent in that, although specific genes do not appear to be involved, it is common to find a history of marked personality disorders and minor forms of nervous instability in the sibs and antecedents of hysterical patients.

Hysterical personalities tend to be characterised by a labile emotionalism of a shallow kind leading to rapid enthusiasms that are rapidly dropped, instability of mood reflected in a vocabulary that makes special use of exaggeration, an egocentricity that makes for possessiveness and selfish attitudes with self-display and exaggeration of such personal attainments as there may be, the whole being coloured by emotional dependence on others and a fondness for the dramatic. Hysterical personalities are not solid people but mirror others and so, while themselves trying to appear more than they are, are really easily influenced and abnormally suggestible. This suggestibility is itself an aid to self-deception. Such people are inclined to act emotionally rather than reasonably, and so to take flight into feeling rather than into effective action when confronted by difficulty. In this they resemble children, whose emotional immaturity they share. Hysterical women often have great difficulty in dealing with sexuality and sexual relationships at any level other than the mild flirtation, and it is very common for them to be intensely attached to their fathers, well into adult life, with transference problems of the type considered at the beginning of this chapter. Sexual frigidity is also common, but not invariable or essential to the diagnosis. Adolescence is a common time for the first development of hysterical reactions.

Physical factors

The development of hysterical behaviour is likely to be facilitated by physical damage to the brain, and especially to the frontal lobes which appear to play some part in emotional control. Thus, severe concussion or injuries resulting in more gross damage may often be followed by hysterical symptoms, even in those who have shown little or no such trends before. It is an excellent rule to suspect organic cerebral disease in patients who first develop hysterical conversion states in middle life, even if there is a clear emotional background and 'secondary gain' is apparent.

Again, hysterical symptoms are especially common in dullards and in the mentally handicapped; this partly because duller people can accept grossness of self-deception more easily than can educated and cultivated people, but also because the integration of their emotional control is less highly organised than in the normal, just as is their intellectual function.

Finally, the development of organic disease may precipitate hysterical symptoms when long, debilitating illnesses lead to physical and mental exhaustion. The patient becomes more fearful, more suggestible, and regresses into a kind of childish manipulation, demanding increasing attention by exaggerating what might be already a serious incapacity. Hysterical elaboration of organic disease is also considered below.

Psychological factors

The more that a person is pre-disposed the less is the stress required to provoke hysterical reactions. It would be impossible to provide a list of stresses which might provoke hysterical symptoms through their emotional effects, but common among them are engagements, matrimonial difficulties, unwanted pregnancies, bereavements and conflicts between duty and desire. As regards marriage, it is often found that the hysteric enjoys the romance and attention that usually precedes it, but shrinks from the responsibility and finality of marriage; hysterical symptoms may well provide opportunity for prolonging the engagement on the plausible ground that it would not be right to contract a marriage that might be jeopardised by ill-health. As regards matrimonial difficulties, hysterical patients often use their symptoms to get their own way, to keep the partner in subjection and their children in ministering attendance. Bereavements, by removing some source of protection or object of emotional dependence, may provoke hysterical manifestations designed to secure some substitute for what has been lost. Conflicts between duty and desire may often be solved by the development of hysterical symptoms whose continued presence provides grounds for excusing the patient from his obligations.

In summary, we may say that hysterical reactions may occur in anyone under sufficient stress, but tend especially to occur in the predisposed. To such predisposition both heredity and upbringing may contribute. Hysterical personalities, who show hysterical reactions par excellence, are emotionally immature. Puberty and adolescence are favourite times for hysterical developments. These are also facilitated by such physical factors as head-injuries and organic illnesses, especially of a debilitating kind; and by such psychological factors as psychiatric illness, by difficulties, conflicts, and any situations that heighten emotional tension. Crude hysterical reactions are commoner in the immature and in people of dull intelligence.

Hysterical elaboration

This term refers simply to those rather common situations in which some physical or psychological illness or disability is exaggerated or prolonged in a manner which brings some benefit or 'secondary gain' to the patient. The motivation may be entirely unconscious, as was discussed earlier, but as with other hysterical reactions it shades imperceptibly into deliberate simulations or malingering.

The situation in which hysterical elaboration occurs may be of any clinical type. One often seen is when some elderly widow with a grown up family has a stroke which leads to hospital admission; when discharged she is left with a greater or lesser disability. Often enough before the stroke the family will have largely drifted apart, and visits to mother may have become increasingly rare. When she is taken ill every one begins to visit, daughters rally round to do the shopping, grandchildren arrive to do the garden, and the old parental home is fuller, busier and for the patient happier than for many years. It is natural then that there are powerful forces preventing complete recovery, as that might only mean a return to isolation.

Similar elaboration can occur with industrial accidents when compensation is in the offing, or in many other situations, in which complete recovery from the original illness has disadvantages. An example of this was a 60-year-old man who had had a minor stroke, from which he had made a good recovery so far as could be judged neurologically. However, he remained unable to walk without falling down. He was a caretaker of a block of council flats, in which he had kept order among the near delinquent adolescents by his rough tongue and fists; and he believed he was correspondingly unpopular. He expected to be beaten up if he returned as a semi-invalid to his own home in the block, but recovered well when he was promised a transfer to a similar place elsewhere. Hysterical elaboration differs from hysterical conversion only in that the basis of the symptoms and signs is determined by some already existing pathology.

Hysterical conversion states

These, and their distinction from 'psychogenic' states, have already been considered on pages 265-271.

It must be remembered that the absence of physical signs and a series of negative laboratory investigations do not justify a diagnosis of hysterical conversion. There must be a positive psychiatric diagnosis. To make a diagnosis positively, the state should be psychologically comprehensible in its setting, motivation and the form of the symptoms, and the secondary gain should be apparent. If the label 'hysterical' is once applied to a patient then doctors tend to stop thinking about other possibilities and it is better for all concerned to say 'not yet diagnosed' if there is doubt. Again, do not be misled by a florid display of emotion or an over emphatic or histrionic manner of speech, which is often a culturally-determined matter and may become intensified as the patient realises that his doctor does not understand the problem.

Symptoms and signs

These may be literally of any sort. In general it may be said that the hysterical patient will complain of whatever pays him to complain of. There are fashions in hysteria as in other forms of human behaviour, and at the present time the trend is for hysterical symptoms to be more subtle and vague and less obvious than they were 70 years ago. That is why the symptoms and signs described in the older textbooks seem surprising to the present-day reader. The hysterical manifestations described by Charcot in the 19th century are now seldom, if ever, seen; the gross hysterical phenomena seen in the 1914–18 war were seldom repeated in the war of 1939–45.

At the present time the commonest hysterical development is the elaboration of some already existing physical illness, or of some mental disturbance such as forgetfulness, anxiety or mood disturbance. As other forms do still occur, however, though much less often than in the past, it is necessary to describe them, but the student should note that the more gross hysterical manifestations, such as paralysis, blindness, or deafness, are comparatively uncommon. Hysterical fits are now very rare, except perhaps in the small number of institutionalised epileptics who exist.

Hysterical manifestations can be conveniently grouped under the three headings of psychological, motor, and sensory.

Psychological

Of the more gross hysterical symptoms, the commonest psychological one is perhaps loss of memory. Such loss of memory is usually of a convenient kind, which enables the patient to avoid some difficulty or to escape from some unpleasant situation; or it may occur after some imprudent behaviour which the patient prefers to forget. Such amnesias may lead to the development of *fugues*. In these the patient takes flight in a literal sense. He wanders off, and may be found later many miles from home, often alleging uncertainty as to his identity, and professing no knowledge of how he arrived where he did. These also are usually naive escapes from difficulty. In the war, such fugues were common in the Army and tended to happen at the end of periods of leave; in the Navy they were rare, presumably because it was known that they were treated by disciplinary rather than medical methods. The genuineness of the amnesia varies from case to case. Often the memory is fully accessible and is regained completely. But where the patient has been under real psychological stress, wrestling with some insoluble conflict or grossly preoccupied with some real difficulty to which he is reacting emotionally but with poor control, such pre-occupations may have so much absorbed his attention as to have rendered him unaware of his surroundings, at any rate for much of the time, and to that extent he may be only vaguely aware of what he has been doing. These amnesias and fugues are distinctly more common in those who have had head injuries with disturbances of memory in the past, perhaps years ago. It is as if that remembered experience provides a model for the hysterical reaction.

Trances and twilight states. Allied to fugues are the so-called trances and twilight-states. Trances are dream-like states into which the patient withdraws so that he is temporarily insulated from the world about him. They resemble the hypnotic state not only clinically but also in that they are producible by suggestion and their development is facilitated by practice. Many mediums have developed very markedly the capacity to enter a trance. Hysterical twilight states, often called Ganser states after the Berlin prison doctor who first described them, are extremely rare even in prison practice. They consist of a mild disturbance of consciousness akin to the trance state, but with the addition of such symptoms as a lay person imagines a lunatic to show. The patient gives incorrect answers to questions, but his replies are of a kind to suggest that the correct answer exists somewhere in his mind. Thus, if asked to multiply three by three, the patient will say 10 or 8, but never 9. The traditional example of how his answers are approximate but just wrong is the response to the question, 'How many legs has a cow?' Again, the patient answers three or five, but never four. Somewhat similar to the Ganser state, but differing from it in that there is no disturbance of consciousness, is *hysterical pseudo-dementia*. This is particularly prone to occur in the mentally handicapped when under stress. The condition may closely resemble an organic dementia, so that the differential diagnosis may not be easy, but depends on that accurate observation which will show that the performance of the hysteric is more patchy and less well sustained than that of the organic dement, and improves when his co-operation is gained.

Multiple personality. A rare phenomenon that has much in common with amnesias, fugues, trances and twilight states, in that they all depend essentially on dissociation, is the occasional occurrence of so-called dual or multiple personality. The patient is usually a woman with a number of contrasting traits of character which she has not managed to combine harmoniously within herself, and so has a poorly integrated personality. Thus, there may be inferiority feelings leading to outward diffidence, but contrasting with an inner conceit and aggressiveness; likewise an external primness and conformity to convention may conceal passionate thoughts and longings of an unorthodox and unconventional sort. This is a not uncommon state of affairs which often causes people to feel dissatisfaction. Given the tendency to disssociate, such a patient may express her inner self by allowing the appearance of the concealed personality traits while suppressing those that she is more accustomed to show. In this way, a mincing and prudish maiden may transform herself into a seductive enchantress. Extreme cases have been recorded in which such patients would reserve different names and styles of dress for their different roles, and when playing them would deny their real identities or that they had undergone any change. On return to the normal personality there would commonly be an amnesia for the interlude. It will be seen that the self-deception required is great, and such rare cases seem to have resulted from suggestions made, whether wittingly or not, in course of treating persons with a marked capacity for dissociation and a strongly hysterical predisposition.

We have had a case in which a hysterically predisposed man, about to be ordained as a priest, was the subject of religious conflicts. He was a diffident, hesitant, insecure, inadequate man, given to histrionic but shallow emotionalism. After a trivial head injury he developed an amnesia for the previous four years of his life, which included his marriage and the period of his theological studies. He failed to regain his memory. After some weeks in hospital he was having a conversation about the hesitations with which he had approached marriage, when suddenly (within 30 seconds) he changed into a gay, swashbuckling, hearty type of undergraduate who slapped his doctor on the back, and was without a care in the world. This was presumably the role of jolly muscular Christian that he had always wanted to fulfil. The change was accompanied by a complete and instantaneous reversal of his amnesia. Before the change the only part of his *recent* life that he could remember, or would remember, was the month that he had spent with us in hospital. After the change he remembered the whole of his previous life (but denied that he had ever felt the least hesitation over marriage) but could recall nothing of the month that he had just been spending in hospital. He carried this so far as to insist that the doctor, who had seen him almost daily and with whom he had been talking for half an hour before the transformation took place, was a total stranger who had entered his life for the first time at that moment. All this was something more than an act, although it was certainly melodramatic and stagey; it indicated a capacity for dissociation that is fortunately denied to more normal people.

The subject of dual or multiple personality, on account of its interest and fascination, bulks more largely in psychiatric literature than is warranted by its importance or the frequency with which it is encountered. Some of the more famous cases have probably been elaborated by the patient in response to the credulous enthusiasm of the doctors and journalists involved. It is mentioned at some length here because it is difficult to explain briefly, but it is emphasised that the condition is a very rare one.

Hysterical pseudo-psychoses. The Ganser state has already been mentioned as a form of hysterical twilight state (p. 276). Rarely fantastic imagery and ideas may develop without the apparent clouding of consciousness of the twilight state, and schizophrenia or a toxic state may be suspected. There may be visual or auditory hallucinations which do not however, have the qualities of true sensory perceptions, but are more vivid imagery. The patient is often curiously relaxed and describes the disturbances with some relish: for example visions of ghosts flitting around the room or of the image of a long dead grandfather appearing as a comforter. The more active the interest and credulity of the audience, family or medical, the more elaborate the description tends to become.

Motor symptoms

These may take the form either of paralysis or of abnormal movements. The paralysis may involve the limbs, trunk, or speech mechanism. The abnormal movements may take the form of jerks, spasms, tremors or fits.

Where paralyses are involved, the secondary gain is usually obvious even if basically mal-adaptive, as in the dissatisfied machine-operator whose hysterical paralysis of the right leg prevented him from operating his treadle, or the girl who was 'struck dumb' with emotion when her fiancé found her less reliable than he had supposed. Disordered gaits, often of a fantastic kind, may be seen usually associated with hysterical ataxia, (so-called astasia-abasia).

Where jerks, spasms and tremor occur, the differential diagnosis from organic conditions may be difficult, e.g. choreiform movements. But observation will show that such manifestations change considerably according to the circumstances and setting in which the patient is placed and according to the suggestive effect of these upon the patient. The diaphragmatic spasm on which pseudo-cyesis (hysterical imitation of pregnancy) depends may, for instance, be abolished if the patient can be successfully induced to relax. Hysterical fits can usually be distinguished from epileptic ones without too great difficulty. The clouding of consciousness is usually much less; the patients generally do not hurt themselves, bite their tongues or pass water; they do not pass through the typical tonic and clonic phases, but tend instead to show purposive movements; and they seldom, if ever, have attacks when they are alone. The pupils are often widely dilated and respond poorly to light; the tendon reflexes are normal and equal, and a Babinski response is never seen. Finally, such fits are precipitated by emotional causes and tend to vary in intensity according to the presence and absence of spectators.

Sensory symptoms

The more gross sensory symptoms in hysteria take the form of blindness, deafness or the production of areas of anaesthesia. Again, the immediate gain is obvious, at least symbolically, and often their onset is dramatic. For example, a hysterical medical student who found dissection of the cadaver aesthetically offensive and failed in his anatomy examination, developed hysterical blindness on hearing the news, and was thus absolved from continuing with his studies. Deafness may similarly occur in an emotional setting, but has been known to develop gradually as a protection against a nagging partner, and to disappear when freedom has been gained. Areas of anaethesia may occur in suggestible people after injuries, and often after medical examinations. These occur more commonly in neurological practice than elsewhere, for obvious reasons. They are becoming increasingly rare with the increasing recognition of how they are produced.

All these hysterical imitations of illness are generally very rough, since they represent only the patient's guess as to what the illness is like. Thus, the hysterical anaesthesiae are usually of a glove and stocking type, i.e. limited to what the patient regards as a functional unit and without regard for the anatomical distribution of nerves. Hysterical paralysis is usually a rough and ready affair also, and some finer points in its differential diagnosis will be mentioned later. The more informed the patient, the better the imitation; greater difficulties may therefore arise when dealing with hysterical doctors and nurses, and especially with hysterical neurologists, who are luckily rare.

More subtle symptoms

With the increasing spread of medical knowledge, these cruder hysterical manifestations have tended to be confined to less intelligent and less educated patients. Those with higher intellectual and cultural endowments are more likely to have vaguer and more subtle complaints, such as headaches, giddiness and faintness. In these physiological mechanisms are often involved, particularly over-breathing, leading to dizziness and clouding of consciousness.

Mass hysteria This is also known as epidemic hysteria, and refers to outbreaks of 'illness' which sweep through such communities as schools, at first appearing to be epidemic infections or perhaps due to some obscure poison but which are in fact, psychologically produced.

Many children learn to over-breathe, and then perform a Valsalva manoeuvre (that is, the attempt to breathe out forcibly while mouth and nose are firmly closed, thus raising intrathoracic pressure), which often leads to a faint, with genuine loss of consciousness. It has been known for a few individuals in a school to do this deliberately, and then for a wave of anxiety to run through the school among children who were not in the plot. Some of them promptly develop anxiety symptoms, feel faint, in some cases overbreathe with predictable results, including actual fainting. That is a simple form of mass hysteria, usually self-limiting in a few days, after parental anxiety has been raised to fever pitch, and the school has been closed for a few days. Such epidemics are particularly likely to happen if some ususual illness has affected nearby communities.

There have been some famous epidemics in institutions, for example among the nurses of a large hospital, in which even after full investigation it has not been quite clear whether or not the illness was due to mass hysteria or to, for example, a virus encephalitis, or to secondary anxiety and hysteria after some cases of encephalitis.

'Briquets Syndrome' (also called Somatisation Disorder) This is a diagnosis increasingly used in the United States, where unfortunately it is also known simply as 'hysteria' at times. The term 'Somatisation Disorder' has been adopted officially in the new diagnostic system in the USA.

The term is used for a group of people, almost all women, who in this country would be categorised in various ways — none of them very satisfactory — as for example, chronic hypochondria, chronic anxiety states with somatic symptoms and so on. They would all have extremely thick medical folders, perhaps in more than one hospital.

The criteria for inclusion in the syndrome are detailed, and include the following principal points: a dramatic or complicated medical history starting before the age of 35; with at least 25 symptoms distributed among 9 out of 10 groups of symptoms, only a few of which are given here. They include the following:

(1) feeling sickly for most of one's life
(2) The commoner gross hysterical conversion symptoms such as blindness or paralysis
(3) Dysmenorrhoea and frigidity
(4) The common somatic anxiety symptoms such as palpitations and dyspnoea, general nervousness, depression and fears and many others.

In other words, a life time of multiple complaints of symptoms from every bodily system, with anxiety and other psychological disturbances, and including classical hysterical conversion states. The diagnostic formulation does not include secondary gain as a necessary part.

There are many such patients in existence, haunting their general practioners and hospital outpatients, continually being re-investigated by new doctors who are afraid, very naturally, of missing something organic. Like everyone else, such people do develop ordinary physical illnesses, which are likely to be missed because of all that has gone before.

In the American studies on this group, a massive family history of psychiatric illness, alcoholism and personality disorder has been shown, and the patients are generally personally and socially incompetent.

In our view this group of patients includes many with grossly hysterical personalities, and secondary gain will indeed be prominent in many of them. We regard it as misleading to call it 'hysteria' because that introduces yet another different use of a name which has too many meanings already and is, in our opinion, best used only in a qualifying form such as 'hysterical conversion' or 'hysterical elaboration', as suggested earlier in this book. We also consider that the definition of the syndrome produces an artificial cut-off from related conditions, and does not properly allow for the manner in which abnormal personality and various abnormal reactions form a continuous distribution. Nevertheless, the concept has value, and draws our attention to an important problem in medicine.

Attitudes in hysterical patients

The whole clinical picture may be additionally coloured by the patient's attitudes; blandness and 'belle indifférence' have already been described. This seems to be a product of the primary gain, that is, the loss of the distressing emotions which have been 'converted' into some other disorder; and of the secondary gain — the benefit which the new symptoms themselves bring. The more the symptoms are obviously being used, the more that other people are being manipulated, the more likely it is that the apparent indifference will be replaced by some form of more ostentatious display of symptoms in which there is an obvious demand for attention or sympathy. The longer a hysterical condition lasts, the more likely it is that this will develop, and the more likely onlookers will feel that the patient is consciously and deliberately simulating the symptoms. In the acute phases of a hysterical paralysis, the primary gain (loss of awareness of emotional distress) often seems the most prominent feature; as time passes the secondary gain increasingly predominates and the patient increasingly loses the sympathy of others. This loss of sympathy and interest can lead to an increasing display or a change of symptoms.

Hysterical patients also adopt a characteristic attitude towards the doctor, which after a little experience is often easy to recognise. The basis of it seems to be that they want to make a special impression and to strike up a specially personal and emotional rapport. They often start by politely belittling the help that they have previously received with an implication that they realise they are now in better hands; they seek to establish themselves as special favourites by the occasional introduction of coy flattery or by striking some more markedly personal note than is usual in the consulting room. In this way they are likely to show a mixture of something near obsequiousness that is coupled with affectionate over-familiarity. The student should be on his guard. Meantime, the history is unfolded usually with a wealth of detail and the introduction of small dramatic touches. 'She said I had turned ashen, positively ashen, not a drop of blood left in me, and she thought it a miracle that I survived ... ' The observations attributed to doctors in such situations are often of an extraordinary sort. The long-windedness of the history, unlike that of obsessional patients who are anxious to be careful and to avoid misleading the doctor, is determined by egocentricity and enjoyment of being the centre of affairs.

It will be realised that the extent to which these attitudes are shown will vary much from case to case. The normal personality who has suffered a hysterical breakdown under severe stress will probably show none of them. The moderately habitual hysteric will show some of them. They will be shown par excellence only by those in whom the hysterical personality is fully developed, and in whom there has been a long series of successive hysterical states.

Underlying depression

The possibility of severe depression underlying the hysterical state should be borne in mind before trying dramatic 'cures' using hypnosis or drug induced suggestions, unless there is adequate supervision and control. Occasionally the removal of an hysterical disability in such a way, without doing anything for the underlying problem to which the disability is a response, leads to suicidal attempts. As was pointed out earlier, there is a wide range of susceptibility to hysterical reactions, and some develop them with little apparent provocation, others only when the stress is severe. It is obviously in the latter that serious underlying problems or depression may be present. (See p. 270)

Differential diagnosis

It has already been emphasised (p. 265) that neither the absence of physical signs nor the presence of histrionic complaints is enough to justify the diagnosis of a hysterical disorder. The hysterical reaction should be psychologically comprehensible in terms of (1) the form that the symptoms take, (2) the value of the symptoms to the patient (secondary gain), and (3) the setting in which they occur.

The form taken by the symptoms is unlikely to resemble that of any recognised organic condition unless the patient has had personal experience of that condition before. The more that the symptoms do resemble those of organic disease the less likely does the diagnosis of hysteria become. An account of the symptoms that is clear cut as regards their nature, localisation, onset, duration and relief, and that is given in substantially the same terms at different times, is on the whole unlikely to be an account of hysterical symptoms. The less that the symptoms resemble those of organic disease, and the more vague, widespread and variable that they are, the more likely does the diagnosis of hysteria become. The patient's choice of symptoms should be comprehensible in terms of his past experience and their suitability for whatever purpose they may be serving.

The value of the symptoms to the patient and the setting in which they occur can only be understood by taking a careful chronological history, supplemented by information from the relatives. This should show whether the symptoms can be reasonably construed as a reaction to circumstances, and whether such reaction can be reasonably construed as being purposive. A point of diagnostic value is that some cases show hysterical behaviour only in a particular environment. The occurrence of similar reactions in the past is of importance, although sometimes the history may reveal only a very sheltered and self-indulgent previous life, so that no gross hysterical manifestations appeared because there was no occasion for their display. A useful guide in the differential diagnosis is to ask oneself: does this breakdown come as a surprise? Most hysterical reactions do not come as a surprise, either to the patient's relatives or to the doctor who knows the case. In general, the reaction shown should be compatible with the personality that the history has revealed, and this judgment must be made on common-sense grounds.

The following case may illustrate the points involved. We were asked to see a man aged 43, who had been diagnosed as suffering from hysteria. His two children were ill, and one of them had cried incessantly for 48 hours, worrying both the patient and his wife, and causing them to feel worn out. In this setting the patient had suddenly, at ten minutes past eight in the morning and while trying to calm the child, felt faint and dazed, and had been obliged to sit down. He appeared confused and out of touch. He was brought to hospital where he was found to be lucid at some moments, but inaccessible at others, and at others again accessible but confused. In fact, there was fluctuation in his level of consciousness. Even if the sudden onset of the symptoms did not suggest a vascular accident, and even if it were not realised that such fluctuations of consciousness indicated some intracranial pathology (see p. 46, 102), the history would have made the diagnosis of hysteria excessively improbable. From the wife's account the patient was a conscientious, hardworking man of responsible kind with an excellent work record, who had never shown hysterical trends before. To suppose that he was escaping by the sudden development of symptoms of this kind from the worry and fatigue caused by his child's illness was a naïve oversimplification of the clinical picture. In fact, he had a haemorrhage from an intracranial angioma.

Differential diagnosis of specific hysterical symptoms

Complaints of anxiety and depression are common symptoms in hysterical states, and may be the principal ones. A careful comparison of the subjective complaints and of the degree of objective disturbance, including pulse rate, sweating, fine tremor, pupil dilation and weight loss may be helpful. If the depressive symptoms are of the endogenous pattern they should not be regarded as hysterical.

With regard to more specific hysterical symptoms, those of a psychological kind can usually be diagnosed without great difficulty if a satisfactory history has been obtained. This should enable hysterical amnesia to be distinguished from those caused by head injury, alcohol or epilepsy. Fugues may have to be distinguished from post-epileptic automatism, and trances and twilight states from disturbances of consciousness due to other causes. The significant difference is that in post-epileptic automatism the behaviour is simple and purposeless compared with the complicated and purposive actions in the fugue, which show that the patient is still capable of using the higher levels of function in a coordinated way. Similarly, in trances and twilight states such disturbance of consciousness as there may be is of a partial kind that enables the patient to use the higher levels of function in a selective way that suits his needs. The hysteric is thus able to adapt himself rapidly to altering circumstances, which the patient in epileptic confusion is not. Ganser's syndrome (see p. 276) may simulate schizophrenia; prolonged observation may be necessary to establish the diagnosis, which may be clinched in the end by the variability of the condition, particularly in relation to different circumstances and the effects of suggestion.

Hysterical pseudodementia may be hard to distinguish from true organic dementia, and observation may be required before the diagnosis becomes assured. In all these cases, should doubt persist, the position *may* be clarified by (1) investigation of the mental state under hypnosis or drugs (e.g. methohexitone given intravenously), and (2) the electro-encephalograph. The former method tends to lower the patient's resistance and enables relevant facts to be more easily ascertained; the latter may give indications of epileptic disturbance or brain disease. Neither method however, is entirely reliable, but long term observation will be in the end.

With regard to the motor symptoms, hysterical paralyses can usually be distinguished from organic ones by the normality of the reflexes (the rare condition 'familial periodic paralysis' is sometimes mistaken for hysteria but is distinguishable, apart from on other grounds, by the disappearance of the reflexes in the paralytic phase), and by the fact that if asked to make a particular movement the patient will often actively prevent it by visible contraction of the antagonistic muscles that are also supposed to be paralysed. Hysterical paralysis of the forearm can usually be detected by flexing the supported elbow in supination and allowing the forearm to fall; in organic paralysis the forearm automatically undergoes pronation to fall with the palmar surface of the hand downwards, but the hysterical patient, unless forewarned, will allow the arm to fall in the same supine position in which it started.

In paralysis of the leg, the diagnosis can be established by 'Babinski's second sign'. The recumbent patient is asked to sit up by using his trunk muscles and without using his hands. In the normal person both legs will rise off the ground equally. In the patient with organic paralysis the affected leg will rise higher than the normal one. The hysterical patient, unless forewarned, will keep his paralysed leg on the floor. Jerks, spasms and tremors may be very difficult to distinguish from choreic or extrapyramidal symptoms of organic type, but observation over a period will probably show that the hysterical forms vary very greatly in pattern and intensity, according to circumstances and the effects of suggestion. Disordered gait due to hysterical ataxia can usually be recognised through the patient's tendency to overdo it; such cases commonly show fantastic gaits, repeatedly nearly falling over (though seldom if ever hurting themselves) but saving themselves at the last moment by what the observer can recognise as skilled coordination and balance. Even then it is possible to make errors, and we have known a patient with a mid-line cerebellar tumour, and a grossly abnormal gait, who was diagnosed as 'hysterical', because of his histrionic manner and long history of social incompetence. The differential diagnosis of hysterical from epileptic fits has already been considered.

With regard to the sensory symptoms, hysterical blindness and deafness must be diagnosed on general grounds coupled with the absence of appropriate physical signs. Areas of hysterical anaesthesia can be detected, unless the patient is unusually well-informed, by the fact that they do not correspond with the anatomical distribution of the nerves that supply the area. It is possible to confuse a glove and stocking anaesthesia with peripheral neuritis but in the latter loss of tendon reflexes is almost invariable, and it is usually also possible to diminish or extend quite markedly the area of hysterical anaesthesia by suggestion so that the findings become quite inconstant. The EEG can be helpful by showing normal evoked potentials on sensory stimulation of the affected area.

The most subtle hysterical symptoms and the organ neuroses must be judged on their merits and differentiated from other conditions by their onset, development ano course in the light of the patient's personality and circumstances, coupled with the physical findings.

In patients in whom there is hysterical elaboration of some already present condition, it can be most difficult to assess the patient's capacity accurately.

Finally, it must also be remembered that hysterical reactions can be facilitated by organic disease, and this factor should always be suspected when the past history is free from hysterical episodes and the personality is stable. In particular, organic mental changes provide a fertile soil for physical conversion symptoms of all kinds.

Course and prognosis

The immediate prognosis of the individual hysterical reaction is good and becomes all the better if the special difficulties that gave rise to it have passed or are capable of resolution. A bad prognosis is more likely in those whose personality has always been lacking in resilience and who have found life difficult to cope with, and also where there are unresolvable conflicts. The more robust the personality, and the more severe the precipitating stress (so long as it has passed), the better the outlook. In those with recurrent hysterical episodes the level of recovery after previous breakdowns is the best guide to what is likely to happen.

Treatment

One of the main difficulties in the treatment of hysteria derives from the fact that hysterical personalities are apt to arouse a strong emotion of irritation and dislike in the hearts of many doctors; they seem such selfish hypocrites and take up so much time. The tragedy of the persistent hysteric is that the immediate and short-term gains that are unconsciously sought are usually quite outweighed by the long-term losses. Hysterical behaviour in the end tends to alienate sympathy and affection. The more that is demanded, the less is received. Those who are unable to conquer their revulsion towards hysterical personalities may be helped by bearing in mind that physical conversion symptoms can and often do develop in patients of quite a different type, who do not exhibit hysterical characteristics any more than they may do themselves. We are all capable of and have all practised some hysteria.

General management

In treatment the first question is: how seriously must the symptoms be regarded? This involves considerations of whether the patient should remain at work, should have a change of environment, should be further investigated, or should be admitted to hospital. The answer depends not only on the severity of the symptoms themselves but on how far they are likely to be benefited by such changes. It is not possible to supply a formula that will apply to all cases. Each patient must be thoroughly examined and appropriately investigated at the outset, but if the diagnosis is well established, not only by the absence of physical signs but also in positive psychiatric terms, further investigations for each new variation in the complaints should be avoided. To admit a wavering hysteric into hospital for full but unnecessary investigations is to provide a focal point for the development of further symptoms both immediately and in the future, and to provide a landmark in his medical history that will be exploited and will obscure the issue in his future medical consultations. The error, if there must be one, should be on the side of encouraging the patient to keep at work. 'People are seldom better employed,' said Benjamin Jowett, 'than in earning their own living'. And this (though Jowett refused to recognise science or to believe in the existence of the knee-jerk) may be taken as the golden rule in the treatment of hysteria.

It may well be otherwise, however, as regards the advisability of changing the home environment, if the stresses or conflicts precipitating the hysterical episode are centred in the home, as they often are.

Treatment of specific symptoms

The removal of single symptoms can sometimes be easy, but at other times the underlying distress is too great or the secondary gain too powerful. When symptoms can be relieved by the simple measures described here, that is not necessarily the end of treatment. It may be the beginning of an attempt to help someone cope more effectively and happily.

Those in trances or twilight states can often be brought to full awareness by the application of some powerful stimulus that causes them fully to mobilise themselves; a suitable one is the application to the nostrils of cotton wool treated with strong ammonia. When full awareness is regained its continuance must be insisted on by obliging the patient to undertake some activity, such as conversing, washing, drinking a cup of tea or eating, after which it is much harder for him to sink into his former state.

The hysterically deaf can often be persuaded to hear by persuading them to listen to questions through a stethoscope; with any initial success the loudness of the stimuli is then gradually decreased until it is plain to the patient that he can hear better than he supposed. Again, he must not be given opportunity to lose his newly rediscovered auditory acuity.

Hysterical aphonia can often be overcome by squeezing the patient's chest very suddenly, which usually produces the distinct sound 'Oh' and 'Ah'. It is then pointed out that he can produce this sound and he is made to do it again. The syllables are then elaborated until words are formed. He must then be made to continue in conversation and also to talk to other people, which similarly makes relapse more difficult to achieve with plausibility.

Patients with amnesia, who are also inaccessible in so far as they are unable to furnish that account of themselves which is essential for understanding the case, may often be led to recover their memory by firm persuasion and encouragement. If the amnesia is for the whole past life it can soon be demonstrated that they have not forgotten everything and from small beginnings (such as what season of the year does it appear to be, roughly what year it is, is it A.D., or B.C., and what do those terms mean?) it may be possible to extend their memories indefinitely. Intravenous methohexitone can be helpful in resistant hysterical amnesia; and faradism can help to demonstrate that apparently paralysed muscles can move.

When a patient has had some symptom or disability for some time he cannot be expected just to lose it, for no reason other than persuasion. Apart from anything else, the expectations and attitude of the family are important, and the patient must not be humiliated. Some face-saving treatment and alternative explanation may be useful in that way, both to the patient and family.

Rehabilitation

Removal of particular symptoms in this way is only scratching at the surface of the problem. They will recur in one form or another unless an attack is made on the underlying psychological difficulty by discussion and psychotherapy, involving the family where appropriate. The chances of success depend largely upon the personality of the patient and on his possession of what may perhaps be called mental honesty. Markedly hysterical personalities are usually incapable of more than verbal insight, and this incapacity is a bar to successful psychotherapy. The most fruitful approach is usually then indirect and environmental.

Relatives will often ask for advice in handling the patient. There can be no set formula. But in general, over-solicitude is to be strongly discouraged; the symptoms should be disregarded as far as is compatible with reasonable humaneness and courtesy; and judicious firmness should be shown. Even so, it is a mistake to suppose that there is always a solution to every problem. The husband of a woman of chronically and intractably hysterical disposition said to us, 'All through our married life friends have told me to be firm. But in the end I've found that it just doesn't pay.' In fact, resort must be had to bargaining.

SEXUAL DIFFICULTIES

The sexual deviations are separately considered on page 223. We are concerned here with problems that are more incidental, but which may occur as part of a personality problem that is not necessarily specifically sexual in itself.

SEX PROBLEMS

Personal sexual problems leading to distress frequently occur in adolescents and young men and women. The commonest complaint to doctors currently seems to be of feelings of sexual inadequacy, coupled with general feelings of inferiority, shyness of the opposite sex, and doubts about homosexual leanings. All aspects of sex are much more freely discussed nowadays, and sexual intercourse is common in young people and generally accepted by society. There is great pressure on young people from all sides to be sexually active, and modern advertising and films seem to intensify feelings of inadequacy in the shy and slow to develop. At least in London we less commonly see young people in whom the problems arise from suppression or a refusal to recognise sexual drives and feelings, who have received no instruction, and have been brought up in an atmosphere of rigid sexual morality. However, these sexual repressive problems are still not infrequent especially in older people, and some are prone to keep the whole topic of sex in some special separate compartment of their minds, a compartment that they feel is better left unopened. They thus tend to split off from the rest of their conscious considerations such sexual stirrings as they may feel, and may do so to the extent of refusing to recognise them for what they are.

In general, the more frankly that sex is regarded, the more readily and unembarrassedly that the questions of children are answered as they are asked, and the more matter-of-factly that the subject is dealt with as a whole, the better adjusted will the child be to stirrings of puberty and the onset of menstruation, and the less difficulty will there be in regulation of the sex life in adolescence.

Where other attitudes have been adopted, leading to furtiveness of thought and approach, and even to refusal of recognition, problems may arise according to the conscientiousness and moral scruples of the individual. It can be helpful to discuss the problems with a sympathetic listener, and to have them put in a different perspective. For those people greatly troubled by sexual tension, who are against any pre-marital sexual experience or masturbation, the only sensible advice is to avoid sexual stimulation as much as possible, and to try and fill life with interesting and rewarding activities. It is not the place of psychiatry to undermine people's religious or moral beliefs on grounds of 'mental hygiene', although many people believe that it is.

An extremely common complaint in older people is that one sexual partner is much more interested in sex than the other. The increased freedom of discussion and journalistic publicity has led people to be less satisfied with an imperfect situation than they previously were, but unfortunately less can be done to alter libido and sexual activity than many have been led to expect, as these are so much a matter of basic constitution and many are therefore disappointed. A similar problem of sexual dissatisfaction and frustration arises quite frequently in marriages in which the sexual drives of one partner decline with age more rapidly than those of the other. This decline seems to be more frequent in men, and can lead to great unhappiness if it intensifies feelings of inferiority, or becomes one of the battlegrounds in the marriage in which one is repeatedly criticising the other. The desire to test an apparently failing virility with another woman, having wondered how much his declining libido is the result of boredom or lack of attractiveness in the wife, is a very common cause of the breakup of apparently stable marriages. It is remarkable how often couples have not discussed the problem at all, and sometimes it helps them to do so jointly with a doctor or other suitable person. No change in sexual drive takes place, but the situation is often eased.

In recent years there has been much greater emphasis on the need for the education of sexually incompatible couples, for instance using the intensive techniques of Masters and Johnson, details of which should be sought in their books. Those authors made very detailed studies of male and female sexual physiology, and applied their findings to sexual technique; using counselling, detailed explanation and practical advice; and for some people even providing experienced sexual partners for instruction. This last, although perhaps only a formalisation of what many people have done secretly throughout history, has naturally led to much criticism, and has been largely dropped. Many clinics have been set up to offer treatment and help based on these lines. When the clinics are run by psychiatrists and psychologists many other problems between the couple other than the purely sexual ones come to light, and the work becomes closely integrated with marital psychotherapy.

Extremely good results for these techniques were claimed at first, especially by Masters and Johnson themselves, but more recently it has become apparent that the results were in a specially selected population, and are not being reproduced now. However, the techniques are valuable.

Masturbation

For some part this is a source of distress, guilt and self-reproach. Such feelings are not necessarily an anomaly but in some they may be quite excessive. Since masturbation has been practised by practically everyone at one time or another, the patient may be reassured that the practice is normal rather than otherwise. If he has been taught that it will drive him mad, send him blind, cause his eyes to drop out or totally undermine his health (and we have known patients to have been taught and to believe all of these), he may be reassured to the contrary. Over emphasis on the benefits of masturbation should be avoided, as it can become too permanent a substitute, and lessen the chances of establishing a happy and more mature sexual life.

Shyness and anxiety in feminine company

These are often a source of worry to adolescents, and may sometimes be coupled with a fear of homosexuality. They are by no means necessarily an indication of the latter. Their occurrence depends much upon the personality, upbringing and attitudes of the patient. In general, discussion, explanation and reassurance will be indicated, together with encouragement to mix and, where possible, the provision of means of doing so. Specific help can be provided at times in psychotherapeutic groups, and by behaviour therapy methods (q.v.) aimed at easing social anxieties.

Homosexual arousals

These are a cause of concern to many adolescents who fear them to indicate established homosexuality. In fact, they are common in normal adolescents, are influenced largely by the environment (e.g. by some pleasurable seduction, restriction to the company of the same sex, adolescent hero-worship), and are not necessarily indications of a homosexual constitution at all. If heterosexual arousals are also experienced there need be no undue pessimism. What is more significant, is where the patient has never experienced any hetero-sexual feelings, but is able to feel completely friendly and at ease in feminine company while sexually quite uninterested. Discussion and explanation can be very helpful in relieving ill-based fears, and simple, practical advice about how to seek feminine company more effectively may also help. In severely worried individuals, behavioural psycho-therapy is indicated.

It is common for young men who have marked feelings of inferiority and are too shy of girls to approach them, to wonder if their lack of success is due to being homosexual. They may even decide to test this by seeking homosexual experiences, which are often easier to find because they do not have to overcome the barrier of shyness actively, but merely wait to be approached. They usually find the experience disappointing sexually, which is helpful.

Psychosexual immaturity

Though patients seldom come for treatment on account of sexual immaturity alone, this often forms the foundation of a maladjustment that leads to other difficulties for which advice is sought.

It may show itself in various ways. Masturbation, though a normal transitional stage of sexual development, is usually a sign of immaturity if it persists. Other signs are undue prudishness: reluctance to participate in sexual activity through ignorance, apprehensiveness, or refusal to recognise it as a normal biological expression; frigidity and inability to find a sexual partner.

The ease with which such attitudes may lead to conflicts, dissatis-factions, inferiority feelings and matrimonial quarrels, will be readily appreciated. All these will have their effect in impairing the general social adjustment.

The causes of psycho-sexual immaturity are obscure, and it is usually accompanied by evidence of some personality disorder (see p. 209) with pronounced vulnerability or hysterical traits. In some, there is delayed development of secondary sexual characteristics, suggesting important constitutional elements.

Any treatment must depend, of course, not only on the cause but on the nature of the problem for which advice is sought. Where the predominant aetiological factors appear to be physical, endocrinological advice should be sought. It is worth trying the effect of testosterone analogues such as mesterelone 50 mg b.d. for 4–6 weeks, as in some men this does seem helpful.

On the other hand, where the predominant factors are psychological something may be achieved. Friendly discussion of the patient's attitudes and of the factors that have led to them may lead to some readjustment with beneficial effect. Where there have been previous traumatic experiences which have helped to 'condition' the patient unfavourably towards sexual expression, elicitation of the facts and ventilation of the associated emotions may provide relief and an easier frame of mind. Where the sexual difficulty is related to justified fear of pregnancy, or further pregnancy, contraceptive advice may be helpful. Where it seems due more to faulty technique, suitable advice to the patient or partner, as to considerateness, gentleness, the adequacy of preliminary wooing, forbearance in not making each attempt at intercourse a test situation, and so forth, may promote a more satisfactory state of affairs. In some cases of frigidity, where such advice is not likely to lead to undesirable complication, benzodiazepines or even alcohol may be prescribed as a temporary measure in order to help in overcoming an initial resistance. Other cases will require help in readjustment in a more general and less specifically sexual way; this, again, can only be achieved if at all — by mutual discussion of the difficulties, such re-education of the attitudes as may be practicable, and the planning of life along lines such as may yield more satisfaction than had previously been gained.

Impotence and premature ejaculation

These are very common problems. Impotence means an inability to achieve penetration during sexual intercourse. Premature ejaculation means, as it says, that an erection cannot be maintained as long as desired before ejaculation, and includes cases where ejaculation occurs both before and soon after penetration. In other words only some people with premature ejaculation are truly impotent; successful impregnation can easily occur with premature ejaculation if it takes place after penetration. Most importantly, the degree of prematurity is very variable, and the reaction of both man and woman to it depends on their expectations and needs. An easily aroused and satisfied woman may have no complaints about her sexual experiences with a man who may be unable to satisfy someone else. From the man's point of view both impotence and seriously premature ejaculation are very serious problems, in which there is a profound blow to self esteem. Very many men in this situation regard themselves as 'less than men', and their wives often take the same attitude.

The most important feature of all cases of persistent psychogenic impotence is the fear of failure, which in turn leads almost inevitably to the failure they dread. Few men can manage well sexually if they are haunted by the thought 'will I be able to do it this time?'. If the partner is abrupt, obviously disappointed, critical, or worst of all mocking, then matters are made much worse. A tolerant, loving, and encouraging sexual partner is much more likely to get the best out of the situation. The men affected are nearly always somewhat anxious sexually anyway, with doubts about their potency. One or two bad experiences of failure, felt as humiliating by the man, and perhaps triggered off by overfatigue or unsuitable circumstances, can have disastrous effects in the long run. Over-anxiety and inexperience on the wedding night or the first sexual adventure; over excitement and anxiety after a long separation; some worrying thoughts about, for instance, homosexuality; attempts at intercourse in order to please a wife for whom at the time he has little feeling or with whom he has been quarrelling; or the inability to shed from the mind the cares of daily life, may all lead to failure. In most people, such a setback has little long-term effect; but in those sexually and otherwise unsure of themselves, with anxious and ruminative temperaments, a vicious circle is easily established in which the fear of failure is ever present, and the thought of love making is like an approaching serious examination which he expects to fail. If the man has rather low sexual drives in any case, the condition may well become intractable. Sometimes the man is suffering from an unrecognised depressive illness, from which the problem stems, and effective antidepressant treatment is all that is required.

From the foregoing it is clear that the key to successful treatment is the abolition of anxiety and restoration of confidence. Simple counselling of both husband and wife, with explanation and advice to her about the importance of her responses, is often helpful in cases which are not too serious; and alcohol or a tranquilliser before attempting intercourse may help, as may the use of a condom to lessen sensitivity.

A fair number of patients can be helped by the use of MAOI drugs, particularly phenelzine 15 mg q.d.s. and isocarboxazide 10 mg t.d.s. or q.d.s. These drugs have as a side effect the prolongation of erection and prevention of ejaculation, from a direct peripheral autonomic effect. In addition, these drugs, particularly phenelzine, lessen anxiety of phobic type, and in a way there is an element of phobic avoidance in the fear of sex and of failure which develops. Tricyclic drugs can also be helpful, and are also worth trying. In those who seem generally low in sexual drives mesterolone 25 mg q.d.s. can be added. If this drug treatment is going to work it does so within six weeks, and should not be prolonged beyond that time if unsuccessful. If it does help it should be continued for many months in long-standing cases, and then the dose gradually reduced.

In at least two thirds of cases this drug treatment will have little or no effect. There are various behavioural approaches to these sexual problems, but all are based on desensitisation to the anxiety-provoking situation, by attempting to teach the patient to relax and enjoy the sensuous aspects of erotic contact without arousing the fear of failure in a 'test situation', so that the vicious circle of anxiety is interrupted. The full understanding and cooperation of the partner is almost essential to the success of these behavioural approaches, which include the techniques of Masters and Johnson mentioned before. Formal psychotherapy, with detailed exploration of early life experiences usually does more harm than good in these patients.

It is essential to remember that organic factors may play an important role in these conditions. More rapid decline of libido with age in the man than in the woman has already been mentioned; and diabetic neuropathy is an occasional cause. A useful indicator is the total absence of dreaming or waking erections for months at a time. This strongly suggests that the problem is partly, if not mainly, organic. Any morning or other erection indicates that the mechanism is functioning and excludes diabetic neuropathy. Patients who have suffered head injuries or strokes often become partially or totally impotent, usually but not always with diminished libido, and no treatment seems helpful.

It is worth emphasising again that depressive states often lead to lack of sexual drive and may present as impotence. The decline in libido may be the first symptom to appear and the last to go.

12

Obsessional states

These are described apart from 'personality reactions' and the other neurotic states in the previous chapter, because they cannot usually be seen as straightforward reactions of personality.

Obsessions may be defined as thoughts and feelings that cannot be got rid of by voluntary effort, but which recur to the mind persistently and against the will, and into the abnormality of which the patient has insight. Since their repeated intrusion occurs not only involuntarily but against the will, the patient feels himself to be under compulsion. The involuntary and compulsive nature of the process is shown by the facts that the patient (a) recognises such intrusions to be illogical, and (b) finds that efforts to resist them lead to their more forcible return, as well as to uneasiness and anxiety.

The thoughts are recognised as belonging to the individual affected, and do not have the quality of a thought inserted into the mind from outside, as happens in schizophrenia.

The element of compulsion is the essence of the obsessional state, and distinguishes an obsession from a mere pre-occupation. The layman may consider that Romeo was 'obsessed' by Juliet, or that a person is 'obsessed' with a grievance if he airs it persistently, but such pre-occupations are not obsessional in the technical sense unless an attempt is made to resist them, which fails but which generates a sense of tension, and unless their recurrence is recognised as unreasonable by the sufferer.

Obsessionalism may be confined to the realm of thought, but usually gives rise to obsessional impulses and acts, since thought so often prompts activity. Thus, an obsessional thought that the gas has not been turned off, with its accompanying feeling of uneasiness, may give rise to an impulse to go and see, and even to the act of inspection, although the person may know perfectly well that the gas has been turned off in fact. Such acts are known as compulsions, and when obsessions and compulsions co-exist (as is usual) the condition is often referred to as an obsessive-compulsive neurosis.

It thus happens that obsessional patients not only 'have to' think certain thoughts, but usually 'have to' perform certain acts prompted by those thoughts. At any rate, they experience uneasiness and anxiety until they have done so. There thus tends to be some correlation between obsessionalism on the one hand, and repetitive behaviour with the taking of precautions, on the other. These last are characteristic of the *obsessional personality* (see p. 216) with its tendency to weigh each pro and con, and to be meticulous and overconscientious. The correlation is, however, by no means exact. Obsessional symptoms often develop in people who do not have obsessional personalities. And, while the obsessional personality is more liable to become disabled by obsessional symptoms than is any other one personality type, the majority of its possessors escape the need for psychiatric care, while among those that do break down, it is usually the development of anxiety, depression and exhaustion (see p. 248) that calls for treatment rather than frank obsessionalism itself.

There is no sharp line of demarcation between obsessional symptoms and normal experiences. Everyone knows of the difficulty there may be in banishing a tune that runs persistently in the mind. All children experience certain compulsions; they 'have to' walk on or avoid the cracks in the pavement, and they 'have to' put their toys in certain places. Most adults order certain of their activities so that disturbance of the routine is disturbing to the mind. This varies in intensity, and when such disturbance occurs all transitions may be observed from momentary irritation, through the more obsessional state of being a slave to habit and forced to obey certain rules, up to full-blown obsessionalism.

It may be difficult, but usually is not, to decide when obsessionalism is within normal limits and when it becomes pathological. Most patients who seek advice for obsessional symptoms will be found to be dominated by them to an extent that constitutes a real handicap, although they have insight into its unreasonable nature.

Aetiology

This is complex and calls for the usual consideration of constitutional, physical and psychological factors. Among the *constitutional* factors, heredity is important; in any large group of obsessional patients, obsessional traits will be prominent in about one third of the parents and one fifth of the siblings. The personality has already been referred to, and it often appears that the upbringing has contributed to its obsessional elements. Thus, the inculcation of excessively regular habits, exposure to undue strictness and fussiness, emphasis on high moral standards and lofty ideals, and the expectation of especially good conduct, may often be found as part of the early history of obsessional patients; and where the person has been taught to feel anxious or insecure should he deviate from such standards, the likelihood of obsessional developments is increased.

That *physical* factors play their part is suggested by the fact that obsessional and compulsive symptoms may appear for the first time following organic disease, such as injury to the brain or encephalitis lethargica. The latter may lead not only to obsessive-compulsive phenomena in the ordinary sense, but to parallel developments in the motor field, such as coordinated tics and oculo-gyric crisis. It is uncertain, however, whether such symptoms arise de novo after the disease or injury, or arise on a hitherto unsuspected constitutional basis that the disease or injury has brought to light. For instance, it is occasionally found that organic cerebral changes in old age are accompanied by florid obsessional developments not previously in evidence; but careful investigation will then usually show that such trends were previously discernible in milder form, but appear more nakedly owing to diminished self-control.

Psychological factors have an obvious importance, but again it is difficult to know how far they are causal or how far they merely activate a constitutional predisposition. Whatever the basis, obsessional symptoms can often be traced to conflict, usually between the moral standards of the personality and more primitive urges, often of a sexual or aggressive sort. As one patient actually said, 'It's due to my wishes colliding with my conscience'. Such conflicts commonly produce anxiety; that they should lead to obsessional developments as well suggests that the constitutional background is an essential factor.

Psychoanalysts put the origin of obsessional symptoms at about the time of bowel control. It is not possible for those who have not descended so deeply into the evolution and workings at the unconscious mind to affirm or deny such a statement, but follow-up studies of children brought up in different ways of potty training do not show any clear association between any method and the development of obsessionalism.

Symptoms and signs

In the mental sphere obsessions are generally divided into ideas, impulses and phobias. *Obsessional ideas* are commonly connected with religious or philosophical problems. The patient may be unable to escape from brooding over the meaning of the Universe, of the existence of God or meaningless questions may recur repeatedly to his mind on negligible provocation, such as 'Why is that so?' 'Why is God?' 'Why is not nothing?' Inconclusive and repetitive brooding of this kind is often referred to as *obsessional rumination*. Other patients are unable to escape from ruminating on whether they should or should not have pursued some course of action, the idea repeatedly recurring to their minds without a decision being reached. This has something in common with the repetitive 'revolving in neutral without getting into gear' of the depressive, and it is noteworthy that obsessional symptoms are particularly apt to flourish in depressive states. An extreme form of this indecisiveness is seen in *obsessional doubt*, in which a patient may feel so far compelled to examine every aspect of a course of action and to scrutinise its every disadvantage or advantage that he is not only unable to arrive at any decision, but is beset by increasing doubt as to whether the premises from which he started can be correct. In this way he may follow endless trains of thought, each raising further doubts until he even becomes uncertain of the existence of anything, and may become lost in a maze of thought involving questions as to the nature of reality. He may then seek re-assurance as to whether he has done things which he knows quite well that he has done, and corroboration of which he can quite well see for himself, e.g. whether he has or has not dropped food on the tablecloth or is or is not wearing his watch. Obsessional ideas, leading in this way to rumination and doubt, may in rare instances become completely paralysing.

In most of those paralysed by obsessional rumination and indecision, the personality has always lacked drive, and there is a feebleness of will and general incapacity which showed even before the formal symptoms began. In these patients, the sense of struggle *against* the obsession is at its weakest.

Obsessional impulses are often sexual or aggressive. The patient may feel impulses, quite at variance with his ordinary feelings, to harm people, to assault them sexually or otherwise, to behave irreverently on solemn occasions, or to say or shout lewd or obscene things. Such patients rarely, if ever, give way to such impulses, but the experiences cause them anxiety and self-criticism, and lead often to fears of impending insanity. Perhaps the commonest and most distressing of this type of impulse is the urge to damage an infant, often a newborn baby in a setting of puerperal depression. Very rarely do such obsessional impulses lead to baby battering, which mainly occurs in psychopathic and poorly controlled women especially those taking long-term benzodiazepines or alcohol, but it is natural that such thoughts lead to great distress.

Obsessional phobias are irrational fears, which repeatedly recur and are commonly of open or closed spaces, heights, knives or sharp instruments, disease or contamination. Where they are severe, they may interfere considerably with life, restricting travel and even causing confinement to the home, or limiting the amount of social intercourse owing to the difficulty of taking the necessary precautions or avoiding-action when in public places or in other people's houses. They are considered in more detail in the previous chapter, because anxiety is the principal symptom. The categories we use for convenience are not always mutually exclusive, and these phobias have elements of both anxiety states and obsessional disorders.

Apart from the mental sphere, obsessionalism may lead, as has been said, to *compulsive* acts. The obsessional patient is usually anxious, and compulsive acts are usually designed to reduce the anxiety. It is quite normal for a householder to check that the house is locked, windows bolted, gas turned off, and the television set unplugged. The obsessional will check these, usually in some exactly repeated sequence. But then, having gone upstairs to bed, may again experience the anxiety of doubt, and feel compelled to go through the ritual again, perhaps many times before an exhausted spouse forces him to go to bed. This kind of repetitious checking is one of the commonest obsessional symptoms.

Similarly, those with fears of contamination or disease may feel the need to wash repeatedly, and this may spread until it involves anything with which they have come in contact. They may thus feel obliged to wash and re-wash clothes, towels, bed-linen, shoes, money, cushion-covers, and even to scrub the upholstery of chairs and sofas.

The most common washing compulsion is that associated with the obsessional thought there is some dirt or contamination by germs on the hands. Although recognised as ridiculous and struggled against, the individual washes his hands again and again, perhaps scrubs them, uses disinfectants, box after box of clean paper towels (as more likely to be sterile), and then, in many cases, wears freshly cleaned gloves or more paper towels to open doors, pull lavatory chains or touch anything else which might be contaminated. The anguish and suffering experienced can be extreme, as was painfully clear in one patient who was observed to scrub at bleeding hands, exposing raw granulation tissue. He explained that the pain of scrubbing was less than the mental pain of leaving his hands 'contaminated'.

Compulsive acts of this sort, however exaggerated, are aimed at allaying some more or less specific anxiety. Often, however, the obsessional patient's anxiety may not be specific but vague and generalised. The feeling, so common in states of anxiety, that some nebulous catastrophe is about to happen may then impel the patient to take steps to avoid it. But as his anxiety is not specific, there is no specific antidote. The usual course of action is then to put things straight, apparently on the basis that the more that things are in order, the less likely are things to go wrong. The fact that the things that may go wrong have no sort of relation to the things that he puts straight is recognised by the patient, but the sense of compulsion overrides the illogicality. Thus, the patient may take to straightening the curtains, eiderdown or tablecloth, ensuring that ornaments are in place, folding and re-folding clothes, towels and anything else that may be to hand. Such acts are superstitious, and superstition may be directly involved, so that the patient has to perform such acts three times, or in multiples of three, or in other ways, according to what his knowledge, experience and preference in superstitions may dictate. In severe cases these activities may also be completely disabling.

Deeper significance of obsessive-compulsive symptoms

These obsessional ideas, doubts, impulses and phobias, together with compulsive acts which may be ritualistic, are the main symptoms and signs found in obsessional states. In the occasional case they seem to occur as a phenomenon in themselves, without ulterior meaning. But as a rule they are only the outward manifestation of deeper disturbances, and have meaning in relation to the basic attitudes and emotional difficulties, even though the patient may be unaware, or only partially aware, of the relationship. In fact, obsessional behaviour is usually symbolic and a substitute in consciousness for something else, rather as such swear-words as 'dashed' and 'blooming' are substitutes for others whose real significance is readily forgotten.

The substitution may be partial and incomplete. In cases where respectable women of irreproachable behaviour experience impulses, which they cannot understand, to perform irreverent acts, to say lewd things, or to look suggestively at men in the street, it is likely to be found that underlying their scrupulous propriety there are contrary and rebellious trends which admit at most of only partial recognition. Likewise, where there are obsessional impulses to violence, to the surprise of a gentle personality, it is probable that there is underlying aggression whose recognition has been forbidden by a sense of duty. Again, where a patient ruminates obsessionally on religious or philosophical themes, it is likely that there is some underlying conflict of a religious or ethical kind, which there is such difficulty in solving that it is shelved, and its more remote and less personal implications become the subject of rumination instead. Shelving the problem has not altered its accompanying emotional currents, and the persistence of these, though their origin may be unrecognised, serves as a reminder of its existence, and stimulates the return into consciousness of the substituted activity.

In other cases the substitution may be more thorough. Fears of dirt and contamination are commonly related to the sex life, especially where there has been marked insistence on 'purity' and 'clean-living' with emotional effect on a conscientious personality. The emotional concern that may be engendered by conflict between moral standards and desire may be expressed more palatably in terms of fear of dirt and bacterial contamination. (Indeed, members of the so-called 'Oxford Group' have been known to speak of 'antiseptic relationships'.) Some patients with such conflicts have an obsessional preference for the right; they must use the right hand, enter by the right-hand door, walk on the right, turn to the right and so forth; the real antithesis in such states is not 'left' but 'wrong'. Other patients whose conflicts, however unrecognised, spur them to action find it preferable to touch palings, chair legs, pillars, and so forth, rather than yield to some baser desire.

Often there is a whole series of substitutions. The woman who, harassed by the children, dutifully repressed feelings of antagonism towards them, developed a fear of knives by which she might do them harm; she developed a ritual of putting away the cutlery and locking it so that the knives were out of sight, and then transferred her phobia to the key, and thence to keys in general. The substitutions are often, however, much more complicated than that, and may be simultaneously symbolic of many associated things. Thus, one patient felt obliged repeatedly to think 'The moon is turned to gold', a phrase which had no meaning to her, but whose significance was gradually, in part at least unravelled. It was a substitution for a phrase she had learned in a Bible class, 'The moon shall be turned to blood'. Blood was for her symbolic of menstruation, confinement, the sexual life, violence, her hatred of a relative and everything 'bloody' (a word which she would have liked to use, but did not permit herself), and her sex life and the relative concerned had been sources of perturbation. When she had violent and 'wicked' thoughts she was wont to distract herself from them by quotations from the Bible. One day, after an argument with her hated relative, the phrase that unfortunately occurred to her was 'The moon shall be turned to blood'. The emotional associations that it had for her increased her perturbation. She substituted for it 'The moon is turned to gold'. This was because 'gold' was to her symbolic of goodness, security and general worth, as opposed to violence and evil, and because the accomplished fact of the present tense was more re-assuring than the threat implied by the future one. She came to use this phrase as a talisman against evil. Over the years its origin and meaning had become quite lost to her, but in times of emotional stress it would recur automatically and involuntarily to her mind. In so far as its recurrence was meaningless it became a nuisance, and the more so since it was beyond her control and against her will. When, after patient search, its meaning and origin were regained it ceased to trouble her, though it would still recur from time to time.

Course and prognosis

In our view the obsessional states have been regarded with undue prognostic pessimism in psychiatric textbooks. These states are undeniably resistive to treatment, and it may be that the discouragement thus engendered has helped to promote an atmosphere of hopelessness. But in fact, and regardless of treatment, many cases seem to recover spontaneously.

It is generally agreed that where obsessional symptoms develop in association with recurrent depressive illnesses, as they often do, they may be expected to clear as the depression occurs. But apart from that, obsessional symptoms of pure kind and without such association will, in our opinion, clear spontaneously more often than seems generally to be supposed. Obsessional episodes occurring in childhood, at puberty, in adolescence and in the early twenties, quite often do so within a year and obsessional phobias of disease are often likewise episodic.

There seems to be some relationship between obsessionalism and age, in that the majority of patients referred to psychiatrists for obsessional disorders are young people, and the frequency of such referral diminishes with the decades. Similarly, studies of life histories show that although obsessional episodes are common in childhood, in the 'teens, twenties and thirties, they occur less commonly thereafter, and even obsessional illnesses of considerable severity in the earlier years tend to fade with the passing of time. To meet a severe obsessional episode in a patient in the early twenties need not, therefore, lead to undue pessimism since the majority get better, while even established conditions may wane in severity over the years.

A certain number of cases, however, do tend to be chronic. The difference between the episodic and chronic cases seems to depend largely on the extent to which the patient shows the obsessional personality. About 50% of obsessional cases show this type of personality in more or less marked form, but about 50% of cases do not. The more that the symptoms seem to arise from and to be bound up with the personality, the greater is the likelihood of chronicity. Conversely, the less that the symptoms seem related to the personality structure and the more that they seem related to some particular stress, the better is the prognosis. In brief, the possibility of a good prognosis is particularly true of those cases whose obsessional symptoms cannot reasonably be regarded as the cumulative result of the previous personality characteristics.

An ominous prognostic feature is the possession of a personality always lacking in drive, indecisive, and without serious interests in anything. Such people tend to be ineffective even without the burden of obsessional doubts, ruminations, or compulsive rituals, and with that burden they may be rendered incapable.

It is a bad sign when the patient does not really regard the obsession or compulsion as inappropriate or ridiculous, even though he knows that others do. For example, a woman who was continually washing and scrubbing her hands for fear of germs felt that others should really be doing the same; that her standards were the more desirable even if inconvenient. In this case there was no development of schizophrenia, which can occur in those who lack insight in this way.

Recurrences and fluctuations in the severity of obsessional symptoms may occur in relation to recurrent stresses such as lead to conflict or otherwise engender anxiety. Even so, such tendency seems to be reduced, as has been said, with increasing age.

Exceptions to the foregoing principles occur when (1) the symptoms appear for the first time after organic disease or cerebral injury or as part of a senile or pre-senile state. Though they may fluctuate, they then tend to be more chronic. (2) When the patient uses the symptoms in a hysterical way for the sake of some secondary gain that they may bring, and so encourages his invalidism. (3) When the pre-occupations, usually in a young patient, are specially bizarre or remote from reality and are held with less insight than would be expected. They may then be the heralds of a developing schizophrenia, in which the obsessional state gradually becomes a delusional one.

Differential diagnosis

Obsessional states have a characteristic quality that renders the diagnosis easy as a general rule. But, as with other conditions, mistakes are possible and these can be considered under the headings of (1) failing to recognise obsessionalism even though it may really be the foundation of the patient's complaints, (2) failing to recognise that the obsessionalism, though present, is incidental rather than fundamental.

The only cases in which the first of these mistakes is likely to be made with any frequency are those that present with hypochondriacal complaints. These last quite often arise on an obsessional basis, so that it is as well to be alive to this possibility. Persistent hypochondriasis, in the absence of depression and without marked previous concern over health, quite often occurs either in the form of a phobic state usually related to some more or less specific disease, or as an intensification and prolongation of symptoms that have had a genuine organic basis. Such cases will usually be found to have an underlying obsessional personality. Recognition of the basically obsessional nature of the complaints may not be of direct help as regards actual removal of the symptoms, but will help in the understanding and general management of the case.

The second mistake referred to, that of failing to recognise when the obsessionalism is incidental to some other condition rather than fundamental in itself, is liable to be made in two types of case quite different from the foregoing and from each other. The first and commoner type is where a depressive illness is accompanied by an efflorescence or exacerbation of obsessional symptoms to an extent that the latter dominate the clinical picture so that the depression goes unrecognised. It must be borne in mind that this association of depression with obsessionalism is a common one. Indeed, certain cases that show circumscribed recurrences of obsessional behaviour associated with mild mood disturbance are really recurrent depressions. The other type of case in which the obsessionalism is not basic but is incidental has been referred to in considering the course and prognosis. It is characterised by (1) the patient showing little affective response to the symptoms but tending to accept their presence apathetically, (2) the pre-occupations being of a kind that is either bizarre or remote from reality, (3) there being doubt as to the extent of the patient's insight into the abnormality of his symptoms. All these features may be suggestive of a developing schizophrenia.

Apart from these sources of possible difficulty, the diagnosis of obsessional states will depend on the presence of rumination from which the patient cannot escape, usually associated with compulsive acts which may be elaborated into rituals with a sense of struggle against the thoughts, associated with tension, and the whole accompanied by some anxiety but with insight into the irrational nature of the condition so that there is social preservation and usually every outward appearance of normality.

Treatment

Obsessional-compulsive symptoms are notoriously difficult to treat, unless they occur as part of a basically depressive illness (see later). The whole life of the patient should be considered in the treatment plan, as for example in the need to have work which suits the individual in terms of avoiding demands for rapid decision taking, often very difficult for people of obsessional temperament, and in encouraging reasonable entertainment and diversion in someone who finds it difficult to stop worrying about work.

If the obsessional symptoms have recently been precipitated by some stressful situation, especially one in which there is conflict between duty and inclination, it can be helpful to discuss this, to make the symptom more understandable. Occasionally, marked improvement can occur with this in acute cases. In the more commonly found chronic cases, this is unlikely to have much effect, and insight-directed psychotherapy and psychoanalysis are rarely useful in well-established obsessional states. They are difficult to implement practically in obsessional people, with their tendency to brood endlessly about details, as the problems uncovered by the psychotherapy can become the focus of new obsessional ruminations.

Antidepressants

If the obsessional compulsive symptoms have developed or worsened as part of a depressive state, or if secondary depression is prominent, antidepressant treatment, especially with clomipramine, will usually help a great deal. Clomipramine is sometimes helpful even if no significant depression is present and is always worth a trial. The dosage needed varies from person to person more than with any other antidepressant, from 30 mg to 300 mg daily. It is wise to start on a small dose, such as 10 mg b.d., and advise the patient to build steadily up to 150 mg daily, or as much as can be comfortably tolerated. If there is no improvement after 4 weeks on a full dose, a larger dose can be cautiously tried, even up to 300 mg daily. If it does help, then treatment may need to be prolonged for years if the symptoms are of long standing, and some people stay on the drug more or less indefinitely. Other antidepressants can also be used. Benzodiazepine drugs should be used sparingly, as in all conditions likely to be chronic, because of the danger of dependency.

Behaviour therapy

This is for many people the most helpful treatment, especially in those in whom there is little depression. Clomipramine and behaviour therapy together are in many patients more effective than either alone. Details of some behavioural techniques used are given on page 406, and see also the bibliography.

Psychosurgery

Occasionally very severe and crippling obsessive-compulsive illnesses fail to respond to all forms of treatment normally used, and a leucotomy or other appropriate psychosurgical procedure may be justified — and may indeed be strikingly successful. (see p. 436).

Psychosurgery comes under the provisions of the new Mental Health Act (1983), concerning consent to treatment, and the reader is referred to page 461 for the details.

SUMMARY

Definition

An *obsession* is a thought, or feeling, recognised as the product of the individual's own mind, which repeatedly recurs, which is regarded as inappropriate, ridiculous, disgusting or otherwise undesirable, which the sufferer tries, unsuccessfully, to push out of his thoughts, an effort which is associated with tension.

A *compulsion* is an act, physical or mental (such as hand washing or ritualised counting) prompted by an obsession.

Aetiology

Not simple reactions to stress. Common in depression. If bizarre may herald schizophrenia. Occur in some organic states.

Prognosis and treatment

Many improve spontaneously with time. Clomipramine helps especially if depression is marked. Behaviour therapy very useful. Very occasionally psychosurgery advisable.

13

Mental handicap

Mental handicap is a state in which there is both impairment of intelligence and of social functioning, and is not solely a matter of low intelligence. This must be kept in mind. Most people of low intelligence, as measured with IQ tests, can function quite well and happily in society, and do not seek help from doctors or anyone else, although they may have needed special educational help. Of course, the lower the intelligence the more likely social incapacity becomes.

In recent years there have been changes of terminology, most recently in the new Mental Health Act of 1983, concerning those few mentally handicapped people in whom compulsory hospital admission might be necessary. (See Ch. 17 for the legal aspects).

Arrested or incomplete development of mind refers to both intellectual and social functioning, and is therefore a clumsy synomyn for mental handicap, *Mental impairment* and *severe mental impairment* imply that in addition to handicap there is also 'abnormally aggressive or seriously irresponsible conduct', and only with a diagnosis of one of these forms of mental impairment can compulsory admission be used. In other words, low intelligence alone can never justify compulsory hospital admission.

The *psychiatry of mental handicap* is a term increasingly used. It emphasises the trend of the last few decades to limit the role of medicine and nursing in the mentally handicapped to those who are mentally ill or otherwise disturbed, while the vast majority of mentally handicapped people need social or educational help, if indeed they need any help at all. In the past large numbers of mentally handicapped people were kept in 'sub-normality hospitals', for reasons which would now be regarded only as an indication to offer help to an individual or family in the community. Even with someone who is severely handicapped intellectually, the present trend is to provide accommodation of a more home-like type, with supervision by social workers rather than by doctors or nurses, unless there is some psychiatric or physical reason.

The mentally handicapped do find life more difficult than others and many of them suffer from anxiety, depression, various neurotic symptoms, transient severe emotional reactions, schizophrenia, and the whole range of psychiatric disturbances. There is, therefore, still plenty of scope for psychiatry, and most research in the field has been within the general framework of medicine.

The care of the mentally handicapped has three main aspects:

1. The vast majority can live in the community, where special educational and social help can be offered if necessary both to themselves as individuals and to the family in which they are living.

2. Those who suffer from psychiatric disorders may need outpatient or inpatient treatment again, of course, considering the social situation, as in all psychiatry.

3. A very small number show 'abnormally aggressive or seriously irresponsible conduct' and may need compulsory admission to hospital under the Mental Health Act.

One should also remember that many of the most mentally handicapped may also have severe physical handicap, and may need to stay in hospital for that reason.

As will be seen later, in the large majority of cases of mental handicap the subnormal development can be regarded as a variation of the normal, comparable with very short people; these cases may be distinguished from the much smaller group whose abnormalities are so gross that they cannot be considered variations of the normal, and for which there tend to be more or less specific and clear-cut causes such as perinatal brain damage or one of the genetic abnormalities. To continue the analogy of height, these last cases are not comparable to very short people, so much as to pathological dwarfs.

Intelligence level and social incapacity

It is important to be quite clear on this point: while intellectual ability as measured by intelligence tests is an important factor that must be given consideration, the social incapacity that constitutes mental handicap does not depend on that alone. Recent work has drawn attention to the wide range of factors which should be taken into account such as those proffered by one author: 'genetic and developmental history, *present* intellectual ability, emotionality, economic status, family composition, status in family group, moral standards, vocational skill, community tolerance and potential or latent capacity for the development of social competence under favourable conditions.'

It may be emphasised that in order to classify in such a way as to lead to appropriate action being taken in both the individual's and the community's interests, far more is involved than a simple judgment based on the result of intelligence tests, although such tests do remain important and useful.

The intelligence level can be estimated with reasonable accuracy by tests and is then referred to as the Intelligence Quotient, or IQ (see p. 319). The IQ expresses the intelligence as a percentage of the normal, which is taken as 100%. Persons of average intelligence are grouped around the mean of 100, and an IQ of 75 is usually taken as the borderline of subnormality. This is arbitrary, and it has been pointed out that many patients in hospitals for the mentally handicapped have IQs above 70. The hospitals contain most of the very severely handicapped, and many who are much less handicapped, who could probably manage in residential homes and hostels with relatively little supervision, if the accommodation were available.

As the IQ rises above 60, a diminishing proportion show such a degree of social incapacity as to warrant detention under the Mental Health Act, and the indications for compulsory detention then increasingly depend on the existence of factors other than mere intellectual backwardness, such as anti-social behaviour or marked instability. Very special reasons of this kind must be present before persons with IQs of above 75 are recommended for compulsory detention on the ground of mental impairment, to use the new legal terminology. If such reservations are not made a wide variety of people could be compulsorily detained under the Mental Health Act on the grounds of social incompetence irrespective of their actual intelligence quotient. Apart from the legal dangers of such procedures, the establishment of rehabilitation schemes for such a heterogeneous group as might thus be lumped together would be a hopeless and impossible task.

Incidence and prevalence

Very many of the most severely handicapped who are born die in early life, and there is therefore a diminishing prevalence in this group as time passes. In the last few decades abortion has been offered freely to mothers in whom foetal defects have been detected before birth, using amniocentesis and other types of screening, which has led to a diminished incidence. Over the same period there has been a marked increase in the longevity of those with Down's syndrome, thus relatively increasing later prevalence. These points are made only to indicate that there are complex epidemiological problems, as a background to the figures set out here. It must be understood also that there are no British statistics using the new terminology of the 1983 Mental Health Act, and most large scale surveys rely on IQ almost exclusively for the categories used.

The table below is derived from a World Health Organisation publication of 1968.

	IQ	No. per 1000 general population (Prevalence)
Profound handicap	0–20	0.5
Severe	20–35	3.0
Mild	50–75	20–30

It is worth remembering that approximately 160 per 1000 (16%) of the general population falls between IQ 70–85, so that roughly one-fifth of the population has an IQ of 85 or below. An approximately equal number have IQs of 115 and above. (The curve of normal distribution of intelligence in the population is distorted by those with major pathological causes of handicap).

For practical purposes, the IQ level of 50 is an important one, separating mild from moderate and severe handicap. Of children with an IQ <50 only about 15% become independent in adult life, whereas many of those with higher IQ ratings who are registered as mentally handicapped and have special schooling and so on, become independent and need no further special help. This improvement does not necessarily mean that they show a rise in IQ, but that they mature personally and make a good-enough social adjustment — intelligence as measured by tests is not the only problem. If, in addition to having low intelligence, there is a behaviour disorder, such a person remains handicapped.

Aetiology: moderate and severe handicap

In the moderately and severely handicapped, with an IQ <50, the causes are clear-cut pathological conditions, which can be divided into extrinsic and intrinsic. Only a few of the major causes will be mentioned, and the reader is referred to the bibliography for more information.

Extrinsic. These can be divided as follows:

(1) *Ante-natal* — including infections such as rubella and cyto-

megalo virus, rhesus incompatibility, toxins including alcohol, and many others.

(2) *Peri-natal* — trauma and anoxia are the principal factors.

(3) *Post-natal* — in the early post-natal period, haemorrhage, infections (such as meningitis) and trauma, can lead to permanent handicap, as can unrecognised thyroid deficiency (cretinism). Premature and low birth weight infants are particularly at risk, being more vulnerable to all harmful influences.

Intrinsic. The major pathological causes are genetic and chromosomal. Approximately one third of those with IQ <50 have Down's syndrome (the term Mongolism has largely been dropped, as it is felt to have unpleasant connotations). Recessive genetic disorders such as galactosuria, unrecognised and therefore untreated phenylketonuria, microcephaly and many others form the rest. Many of these recessive genetic disorders have enzyme deficiencies, and the example of phenylketonuria in which heterozygous carriers can be identified and in which treatment is available, holds out hope that similar progress will follow in others of these 'inborn errors of metabolism', such as Adreno-genital syndrome, Tay-Sachs disease, Hartnup disease and cystinuria.

Many severe abnormalities are sex-linked (X-linked) disorders, without identifiable enzyme deficiencies. Examples are muscular dystrophy Duchenne type and diffuse cerebral sclerosis, and many more, all uncommon.

Clinical pictures

Moderate and severe handicap. The essential criterion is the degree of independence of which the child (or adult) is capable. The IQ will be mainly below 50. The most severely affected will be almost inaccessible, capable of little more than grunts and moans, incapable of walking unsupported, incontinent of urine and faeces, and needing total care to preserve life. In the upper reaches of this grade the individual will be able to converse simply and will be quite active physically, but will still need guarding from dangers, especially fire and traffic. Some will be capable of concentrating on assembly tasks in occupational therapy, and enjoy social interchange, games, and so on depending of course, on the presence or absence of the physical handicaps which often exist. Epilepsy is also common.

In those of a calm and sunny disposition the burden of care is very different from those who are aggressive, prone to tantrums, or otherwise turbulent.

Mild handicap. Most in this group will have an IQ between 50 and 70, and of course in the upper reaches are likely to be living in society without any special problems. They do need special schooling to help them learn to read and write, and many fail to cope with these skills. At work they are capable of enjoyable and productive jobs, and may live quite normally, including bringing up children. Their work is best simple and repetitive. There are many such jobs which are too boring for people of higher intelligence, although progressively fewer with technological change.

The medical profession has little need to be involved with these people unless they become ill or emotionally disturbed, and their care and supervision is largely the task of the educational and social services. In the lower grades there are often associated physical and mental anomalies which require nursing and medical care.

Psychiatric illness is common in the mentally handicapped, who are prone to psychotic episodes, often difficult to diagnose in the conventional categories; they are also rather more likely to develop schizophrenic illnesses than the intellectually better endowed. When schizophrenia does develop the prognosis is poor. Illnesses resembling bipolar manic-depressive psychoses are also quite common, and, depending on the level of verbal communication present, these may mainly present as episodes of over-activity or of retardation. In those of a higher grade of intelligence, depression often presents with bizarre hypochondriacal complaints. A careful comparative account by someone who knows the patient well is often most useful here.

The mentally handicapped do tend to find life difficult. Even the more intelligent are slow to learn and easily bewildered, and in many there is a lack of foresight, poor tolerance of frustration, and a tendency to be easily led astray. As a result they are often repeatedly involved in petty crime, sometimes by more intelligent people who exploit them for this purpose.

Low intelligence plays a large part in the self-perpetuating cycle of unplanned children who cannot be coped with, who thus themselves grow up dull and deprived, and who, for both genetic and environmental reasons, continue the cycle. Repeated production of illegitimate children and repeated petty crimes are often indications of mental handicap.

SPECIAL FORMS OF MENTAL HANDICAP

These are numerous. It is proposed here to mention only a few of special interest.

Cerebral palsy

This condition varies in severity from very mild to gross physical and mental handicap. It can be due to trauma, severe jaundice, anoxia and other factors. Most are of low birth weight, and the incidence is lower with expert ante-natal care. The degree of handicap varies both as regards spasticity and intelligence, between which there is no real correlation. In many children the physical difficulties impede their mental development so that they seem duller than they really are, and of these quite a number will later display a high degree of intelligence. Microcephaly (the result rather than the cause of cerebral hypoplasia) occurs in about 35% of cases and is characterised by a small skull (circumference usually about 17 inches or less) with flattened occiput and receding forehead. These, coupled with receding chin, provide an unfortunate profile often called 'birdlike'. Most of those with microcephaly are severely handicapped.

Tay-Sachs disease

This is rare, but is mentioned because of its genetic interest (single recessive gene). It was originally thought to occur only in Jewish children. It is now realised, however, that it occurs in other races, and also in adults in a form that is pathologically indistinguishable. Special signs are muscular weakness and wasting, particularly involving the head and neck, blindness due to macular degeneration (seen as grey patch with a cherry red spot at its centre) and progressive apathy with subnormality. Microscopically, cortical changes are the most marked and are characterised by ballooning of the cells by lipoid substances which replace the Nissl substances, while there is also an increase of neuroglia. There is an enzyme deficiency, so far untreatable, of hexosaminidase A.

Tuberose sclerosis (Syn. Epiloia)

This is a heredito-familial disease transmitted by a single dominant gene. It is characterised by three groups of symptoms: nervous symptoms (mental handicap and epilepsy); cutaneous symptoms (adenoma sebaceum, plaques of 'peau de chagrin', café-au-lait spots); and fibromata (tumours of the retina, the heart and the kidneys).

Mental subnormality is not present in all cases; where it exists its onset is always in the first two years of life, the first manifestation being development delay in speech, gait and habits. In a large proportion mental subnormality is very profound; in some cases superimposed psychotic (catatonic) features make it appear even worse than it may be. All types of epileptic manifestations, general convulsions, Jacksonian fits, and petit mal, may be observed. Adenoma sebaceum consists of a nodular rash of yellow-red or brownish colour which covers, if fully developed, a butterfly-shaped area over the nose, the naso-labial folds (where it often begins) and part of the cheeks.

Cretinism

Endemic as well as sporadic, is often combined with mental handicap, the degree of which varies from mere dullness to the most severe. The first definite symptoms, mainly physical, appear as a rule, within the first two years of life. The mental development is retarded. The main features of the cretin's psychological state are lack of initiative, slowness, and clumsiness. Cretins are claimed to be good natured and easily manageable. The physical appearance is very characteristic. The results of thyroid treatment on the mental state may be considerable if treatment is started early in life. Cretins are now rarely seen in hospitals for the mentally handicapped.

Down's syndrome (Chromosome 21 Trisomy)

The term 'Mongolism' has been generally abandoned for this condition. It is much the most common of the special forms of handicap, comprising about one third of the moderately and severely mentally handicapped, that is with an IQ of <50 on the whole. One in every 660 live births is affected, but it is much more likely to happen with older mothers, and the risk is 1:50 for mothers aged 45 or over.

There are various forms of chromosomal abnormality involved in Down's syndrome, although all have trisomy of chromosome 21. The trisomy may be complete or mosaic, that is, with only a proportion of cells affected. A third type is due to translocation, which means that material from another chromosome fuses with chromosome 21; these individuals may have few or many of the stigmata of Down's syndrome, and are much more likely to be of normal intelligence. There is a marked familial element in Down's syndrome.

Affected individuals have a characteristic appearance. They are all dwarfed. The face is flat with oblique palpebral fissures which suggest the old name of the condition. The nose is short, the tongue large, fissured and often protruded. The skin is flabby, the muscles hypotonic, the joints abnormally flexible. There is often an umbilical hernia. Congenital heart disease and severe myopia are common. The resistance to common infections is low but an increasing number survive to adult life with antibiotics, correction of heart defects and so on, and an increasing number are surviving to about sixty. They age quickly, and seem often to develop Alzheimer's disease.

In appearance those with Down's syndrome are often astonishingly alike, but there is a wide range of ability. A few are quite intelligent and a few are very severely subnormal. The majority, though severely handicapped mentally, are docile, cheerful and trainable, so that they can look after their daily needs and live in a family. A minority are dull, introverted and untrainable. They are often said to show a special fondness for music. In fact, most of them like to join in music and dancing as part of play, but they have no special musical or rhythmical sense. They can continue to improve and respond to education and training for a very long period, even if slowly.

Phenylketonuria

Most sufferers from this condition are severely subnormal. Aetiologically, it appears to be due to the effect of a single recessive gene which results in biochemical abnormality, the essence of which is an enzyme failure to break down phenylalanine which accumulates in the blood with excretion of phenylpyruvic and other acids in the urine. Nearly all sufferers have fair hair and blue eyes and show muscular hypertonus with exaggerated reflexes. The diagnosis should be made immediately after birth by examination of the urine and estimation of phenylalanine in the blood, (The Guthrie test). This is of some consequence as it is possible to prevent mental handicap from developing by a phenylalanine-free diet.

DIAGNOSIS OF MENTAL HANDICAP

The ease or difficulty of diagnosis will depend on the age of the patient and the type of handicap shown. Where the latter is one of the special types described above, with characteristic signs, the diagnosis can be made within the first year of life. Apart from these types, mental handicap may be suspected (but cannot be diagnosed with certainty) if the child remains abnormally inert, uninterested and unresponsive, despite apparently sound physical health.

If, subsequently, there is a failure of the normal development in the second and third years, particularly as regards talking, walking and toilet training, the diagnosis of handicap becomes very probable. During the ensuing years, the educational standard attained, the adjustment to school, and the results of intelligence tests (see p. 319) may clinch the diagnosis.

During adolescent and adult years the question of educability becomes of secondary importance compared with that of general social adaptation, as has been emphasised. This is especially so where compulsory detention under the Mental Health Act is involved. Intelligence tests may give a reasonably accurate indication of the degree of intellectual handicap, and therefore of the diagnostic category, but there would be no point in considering compulsory detention if the social adjustment of the patient were satisfactory.

In general, diagnostic difficulties will be encountered only among the higher grades.

To those who specialise in the psychiatry of the mentally handicap, the problems of diagnosis and assessment are presented early, by family doctors, social workers, and from the schools. The more severe forms of mental handicap do not present to the general psychiatrist, but some degree of low intelligence is quite a common feature in patients in a general psychiatric clinic, and is clinically important. The intellectually handicapped, as mentioned earlier, find life more difficult than do most people; and it is necessary to modify appropriately explanations, discussion, type of occupational therapy, and job expectations.

A careful psychiatric history and examination, which goes into schooling and job record, and follows up any clues by checking on literacy, general knowledge, and degree of understanding, is usually sufficient. Psychometric testing is advisable to check on clinical impressions.

The diagnosis of underlying mental handicap should also be suggested by certain types of breakdown, characterised by a mood which is shallow and inconsistent as well as by the fact that the history frequently discloses that the breakdown has been precipitated by very simple stress. In brief, these breakdowns are often very childish and naive and readily affected by changes in the environment. Frank hysterical conversion symptoms are frequently seen, the psychogenesis of which is often patently clear. These patients, as mentioned before, are also liable to short-lived psychotic episodes of an anomalous type which occurring in a more intelligent individual would be strongly suggestive of schizophrenia. Thus confusion and hallucinosis may be shown and paranoid ideas are very common.

Formal intelligence tests

Many of these have been devised. The first one of all was that devised by the Frenchmen, Binet and Simon. The most widely used in Britain are probably the Wechsler Adult Intelligence Scale (W.A.I.S.), and the Wechsler Intelligence Scale for Children (W.I.S.C.), but there are several other reputable ones. They consist of two main sections. A verbal scale measures vocabulary, which gives us the 'verbal IQ', and a scale based on various sub-tests, including mathematical, visuo-spatial, memory, logical problems and others, gives us the 'performance IQ'.

These tests consist of a series of questions. The questions are based on what intensive trial and experiment have shown that average children of each age level are capable of answering. Most tests take 16 as the age at which adult intelligence is achieved, which is an approximation only. If the 8 year-old child is unable to pass the tests geared to the 8 year level, then his mental age is considered to be less than his chronological age; on the other hand, if he can pass the tests at the 9 year level, his mental age is considered to be greater than his chronological age. The performances of different patients are rendered comparable by introducing a common denominator. This is done by dividing the mental age (MA) by the chronological age (CA) and multiplying by 100. This expresses the intelligence as a percentage of the normal, and is called the IQ or Intelligence Quotient. Thus, if a 10-year-old child achieves a mental age of thirteen years, the IQ = MA 13/CA 10 × 100 = 130. Similarly, if a child of 12 years and 4 months achieves a mental age of 9 years and 6 months, the IQ = MA 114 months/CA 148 months × 100 = 77.

IQs between 90 and 110 can be considered within normal limits. IQs above or below these limits indicate superior or inferior intelligence. Medical students may be gratified to learn that they probably rank in the top 10% of the population. IQs of 70 or below indicate that the patient is unlikely to be able to benefit from education in ordinary schools.

Many objections to the foregoing procedures have been raised. For example, the concept of MAs is obviously an artificial one if applied to adults. A grown-up person with a mental age of, say, 10 years will be quite different from a normal child of 10. To say that he has the mentality of a child of 10 is incorrect. All that a mental age of 10 years means is that the patient is able to score on certain tests only what an average child of 10 would score which is quite a different thing. The W.A.I.S. and the W.I.S.C. use appropriate questions for adults and children respectively.

The number of available tests of all these kinds is very large indeed. The students must bear in mind, however, that such tests do not provide absolute answers to clinical problems, and there is no test that is free from involvement with a cultural background.

Finally, the student should be aware that the dissatisfaction of academic psychologists with the method of recording results in terms of MAs and IQs has led to the revival of the method of percentiles, which was invented by Galton in the last century. But percentiles are inconvenient to handle statistically, and they are not for many people a natural or easy way of thinking about the relationship of measurements. A percentile rank of say 30 means that 30% of a representative population are below and 70% above in regard to their performance in the particular test employed. The ranks between 25 and 75 may be accepted as normal, if it is supposed that half of the population can be so regarded. But it is important to know against what objective criterion a test has been checked ('validated') in order to know what it means in terms of what is wanted — for example, the probabilities or possibilities of efficiency in some particular job.

Intelligence testing is also useful in the investigation of organic deterioration (p. 86); and in tracking down reasons for repeated job failure, as when we find someone who has a markedly higher verbal than performance IQ, and thus at interview tends to appear more intelligent than he is in practical matters.

TREATMENT IN MENTAL HANDICAP

Moderate and severe handicap

There have been advances in the last few decades in both understanding and treatment of some of the more specific forms, especially phenylketonuria. Improved physical care, including orthopaedic, cardiac and neurological surgery, has improved the well-being of some physically extremely disabled children and adults. Improved anticonvulsant treatment of the epilepsy which is so common, and developments in phenothiazines, thioxanthenes, antidepressants and lithium therapy have helped those who are also psychotic or otherwise disturbed.

The fact that a 'purely' genetic condition like phenylketonuria has been shown to be preventable by a change of environment (in the broad sense) has stimulated research and the hope that other apparently inevitable disorders will also be preventable or treatable. (More could be done in the fields of antenatal and perinatal care, as a sizeable amount of irreversible damage occurs at these times, and mortality and morbidity rates in the United Kingdom are poor by comparison with many European countries).

There is, however, no way in which major improvements in intelligence can occur, unless some treatable condition such as cretinism or phenylketonuria is present, and then only if treatment is begun early.

Mild handicap

The main change in this field has been parallel to developments in psychiatry as a whole, in emphasising the benefit of community care, and trying to lessen the number and size of hospitals for the mentally handicapped. The present trend is to offer social support to the families keeping the child, or backward adult, at home; to provide more day centres and hostels; and to build small residential units where inpatient treatment can be offered.

Treatment for most of the affected individuals is not medical or psychiatric, but more educational and social. The traditional role of the medical profession in supervising and controlling the environment in which so many patients lived, that is in the large hospitals, has been strongly challenged by educationalists and social workers, who have highlighted the disadvantages of big hospitals for these patients.

For the very severely handicapped, especially those with associated physical disabilities or who need much nursing care, and for the mentally more disturbed who need psychiatric treatment, only the medical and nursing professions are really able to cope. For the less severely handicapped social training, appropriate special education, occupational therapy and training for work where possible, are the main aims.

As with the big mental hospitals, the dangers and difficulties of big, understaffed subnormality hospitals are easy to see. Institutionalisation, neglect of physical and psychological needs by overworked staff, and the inevitable morale and other problems of the staff themselves. However, it is naive to imagine that these problems cannot develop in small units run by social workers as the years pass and enthusiasm wanes. The burden on the family can also be considerable, as with chronic schizophrenics discharged from hospital under similar policies.

Governments tend to favour cheap alternatives in health care, and unless money is found to provide good facilities in the local communities, the big old hospitals will be run down and nothing suitable will take their place.

Many mentally handicapped individuals, especially if they have no associated psychiatric disturbance, can be trained to useful and stimulating work, although they are usually better placed in some form of sheltered workshop.

Information about the social and educational services available can be had from the National Association for Mental Health, 39 Queen Anne Street, London, W.1., from another voluntary organisation MENCAP, 123 Golden Lane, E.C.1 or from local branches.

14

Alcoholism and drug addiction

ALCOHOLISM

Moderate drinking is a normal habit in these Isles. This habit becomes a medical problem only (1) if it leads to symptoms calling for medical aid, (2) if the individual develops symptoms when the supply of alcohol is interrupted, (3) when signs of organic deterioration appear, or (4) when the family is adversely affected.

Alcoholism is steadily increasing in almost all Western countries, and is a very serious health problem. It leads to cirrhosis of the liver and other physical diseases, as well as to the syndromes described in this chapter. Alcohol is a factor in road accidents, crime, baby battering, poverty, industrial inefficiency and, overwhelmingly, in unhappy family life. There is much unrecognised heavy drinking in all social classes, and heavy drinking occurs among much younger people than was the case a few years ago. Many people attending hospital, especially those with abdominal symptoms, are in fact alcoholics, and several studies in the past decade have shown that about one-quarter of all patients in acute general hospital beds are excessive drinkers.

There are many social and psychological factors associated with heavy drinking as described later, but availability and cost are probably more important than any of them overall. Alcohol is much cheaper, in real terms, in the United Kingdom than it was before the Second World War, and is growing progressively cheaper. The best way to combat alcoholism would be to increase the tax on it, rather than rely on treatment methods of unproven efficacy.

Acute alcoholic intoxication

People vary much both in their tolerance to alcohol and in the sequence in which signs of intoxication appear. In some, physical signs such as slurred speech and other evidence of motor incoordination appear very early; in others mental changes alone may be observed until intoxication is severe. Usually, the first signs are those of disinhibition, i.e. increased talkativeness and mild euphoria. These are succeeded by impaired concentration with forgetfulness owing to defective registration of what is happening. Later, there is superficial thinking, lack of judgment and insight, with frank impairment of memory and often irritability. Patients with cerebral disease or injury, especially epilepsy, are liable to show severe intoxication (drowsiness, irritability, excitement) after quite small doses of alcohol, and this is a point to remember where there is some legal involvement.

Intoxication may lead to various legal and other difficulties. Psychotropic drugs, which are very commonly taken now, often increase the effects of alcohol. Both the benzodiazepines and tricyclic drugs can lead to unexpected drunkenness and even to confusional states with paranoid ideas, if taken with alcohol. No one on these, or other psychotropic drugs, should ever drink before driving.

The formerly frequent medico-legal problem of fitness or unfitness to drive a car after alcohol has become infrequent since the introduction of the Road Safety Act, 1967. This requires a suspected person to submit to breath tests and, if these are positive, to blood or urine testing, and it is an offence to refuse. Under this procedure the role of the medical man is confined to taking a blood sample. No examination is called for. Whatever his clinical state the driver will have committed an offence if the concentration of alcohol is more than 80 mg per 100 ml of blood or urine. If, however, the police choose to proceed under the Road Traffic Act, 1960, (e.g. if they think the 'breathalyser' has failed in its purpose) the subject *may* refuse medical examination. If he does not, special attention should be paid to the smell of the breath, the presence of flushed face, full and rapid pulse, dilated and sluggish pupils, and evidence of motor incoordination e.g. the ability to walk straight, to write adequately, and whether there is any disorder of articulation, traditionally tested by repeating phrases such as "the Leith police dismisseth us". As regards the mental state, note should be taken of the mood, type of language used, memory for recent events and the ability to do simple arithmetic.

Treatment

This is seldom called for in simple intoxication, except for the occasional case who shows violence and excitement. Such have sometimes been referred to as *mania a potu*, an unfortunate term since it has nothing to do with mania. These are usually explosive reactions occurring in people liable to be explosive whether drunk or sober, and who are specially susceptible to alcohol. The prime necessity is to get enough help to restrain the patient and to remove anything potentially dangerous to himself or others. The excitement can then be reduced by intramuscular injection of chlorpromazine, 250–500 mg depending on the size of the patient.

Alcoholic coma

All comatose cases require careful examination. It is most unwise to attribute a comatose state to alcohol unless it seems certain from the history that the condition can be explained on that ground alone. The development of symptoms after an overdose of insulin may be very similar to that of alcoholic intoxication. Nor is the smell of the patient's breath a reliable guide; a drunk person may be diabetic, or may have sustained a head injury through falling; and people are often given brandy or whisky on feeling faint, though they may have had no other drinks.

Treatment

The only immediate practical measure is to aspirate the stomach and examine the contents. So long as there is doubt as to the cause of coma, the patient should be kept under observation, with repeated attention to temperature, pulse, respiration, blood pressure and the development of eye signs and other neurological signs.

Acute alcoholic hallucinosis

This is a rare condition which generally starts after a heavy drinking bout. The patient hears hallucinatory voices, usually reproachful or threatening, without much clouding of consciousness. The mood is usually one of fear (as in delirium tremens which, indeed, may subsequently develop) though there may be traces of alcoholic jocularity. Some cases turn out to be schizophrenics who have taken alcohol to drug themselves in the first stage of an acute schizophrenic episode.

CHRONIC ALCOHOLISM

This condition develops in recognisable stages. It is possible to be a heavy drinker without being an addict to alcohol; indeed, it is estimated that only about one heavy drinker in twenty becomes addicted. The difference is that the heavy drinker can do without alcohol if he chooses; the addict can not, because he has become habituated to and physiologically dependent on it. It is difficult to know why this happens, although genetic factors are responsible in part.

The definition of alcoholism is uncertain, and there are two main approaches: first, we can define it narrowly by the existence of physiological addiction with tremor or withdrawal ('morning shakes'); or by the development of some clear cut alcoholic syndrome such as delirium tremens, cirrhosis of the liver, Korsakoff's psychosis, dementia, hallucinosis, and so on. This leads to fairly low incidence figures, but has the benefit of being more easy to identify accurately. It is also reasonable to consider alcoholism as a 'disease' using this limited definition.

Second, we can use a looser definition and say that a person is an alcoholic if the drinking damages his or her health, or adversely affects the lives of others. This is the view taken by the World Health Organization. It has obvious advantages in recognising the effects of alcoholism on others, but means that reliable statistics are almost impossible to collect, particularly for any international or historical comparisons; and makes the 'disease' concept of alcoholism less appropriate. It is wise to keep these two different attitudes to diagnosis clear in one's mind, as many people confuse them.

Aetiology

Alcohol is an inherent part of our culture, and almost everyone has taken alcohol by late adolescence or early adulthood. Only a few go on to become heavy drinkers, and even fewer to develop physiological addiction or one of the recognised complicating syndromes. Price and availability, as mentioned earlier, are extremely important in determining the general level of alcohol consumption in any community, and other environmental factors affect the individual.

In Britain, the Royal College of Psychiatrists have suggested that the following should be regarded as the daily upper level of safe drinking: four pints of beer, four doubles of spirits; or one bottle of wine. Although there is very great individual variation, above these levels alcoholism becomes increasingly frequent.

There are some simple environmental factors. Thus, publicans, bar-keepers and business representatives ("reps") often drink as a normal part of their occupations. Businessmen and women with frequent expense account lunches are very much at risk. Drinking is also a normal function of certain social sets, especially among those who live in outposts which are often in difficult climates with few distractions, and among colleagues whom they would not ordinarily have chosen as associates. Such may have quite normal personalities. Social factors of a more general kind, such as poverty and slum life, that used to encourage periodic trips to Nirvana, are less important than they used to be.

More commonly, the reasons for excessive drinking must be sought in the personality of the patient rather than in his environment. Thus, many alcoholics are psychopathic personalities, especially inadequate psychopaths, whose impulsiveness, poor control, inability to take a long-term view, tendency to feel a few drinks below par and to be troubled by an awareness of their inadequacy, may combine to encourage the habit. In other people, not necessarily psychopathic, excessive drinking may arise from personal problems. Some may be constitutionally anxious, yet determined to overcome fear. Others experience dissatisfaction and frustration through, for example, marital difficulties, homosexuality, failure to achieve ambition and to adjust to that failure. These may use alcohol because it is a powerful solvent of reality — for the time being. As a once talented actor, less successful than his wife, expressed it: 'Once I'd had that failure it was difficult to meet my equals as I had before, and frankly I preferred to be cock of my own dunghill in the local.' Such drinking comes under the heading of *neurotic reaction*.

Some excessive drinking is symptomatic of more specific psychiatric illness. The lack of restraint in early deterioration may facilitate alcoholism, as may hypomania. Certain people with recurrent depression turn to alcohol for relief of symptoms. Some manic-depressive patients thus show that recurrent and periodic form of drinking known as *dipsomania*; others, having started the habit, may drink between attacks. In all symptomatic cases a history of symptoms preceding the alcoholism may be of diagnostic importance, particularly for forensic purposes.

There are also very important cultural factors in alcoholism. For example, the Irish closely followed by the Scots, are much more prone to heavy drinking and alcoholism than are most other inhabitants of the British Isles, a fact which is related to cultural attitudes to alcohol and its place in life. Traditionally Irish men associate heavy drinking with manliness, despise the non-drinker and centre all their social life around alcohol. These attitudes of mind persist for several generations after emigration, so that in the United States second and third generation Irish Americans still have higher alcoholism rates than, for instance, Italian Americans. The Italians can also be compared interestingly to the French. Both Italy and France produce large quantities of wine, and there are no significant racial differences, yet alcoholism is commoner in France than Italy.

Women traditionally have had a lower alcohol intake than men, and have had much lower alcoholism rates. The woman alcoholic usually has a more disordered personality, which has led to the abnormal drinking, and they do correspondingly worse with treatment. They also have a lower physiological tolerance of alcohol and develop serious complications more easily. With women increasingly competitive with men in life outside the home, more and more alcoholism in women is seen, but in people of relatively more normal personality.

The development of heavy drinking is thus dependent on many factors, both personal and social. The development of alcoholic addiction, but not that of heavy drinking alone, is known to be largely influenced by genetic factors; an old idea recently confirmed by Scandinavian studies of twins and of adopted children similar to those used to unravel the genetic component in schizophrenia. There are probably inherited differences in the way in which alcohol is handled by the body, as there are known to be for several other drugs. It has also been claimed that peoples of Mongolian extraction, including Red Indians and Eskimos, metabolise alcohol differently, and are more prone to ill-effects from alcohol; which if true partly explains the ease of conquest of the West, and the high alcoholism rates of the North American Indian now, although there are also many unfavourable social factors acting in their case.

Symptoms and signs

The first or *premonitory* phase is usually marked by alcohol forming a keynote in the patient's life. An agreeable event calls for celebration by, and a difficulty calls for consolation from, a drink. A bar is regarded as the only conceivable place for a rendezvous. A drink is essential in the transaction of business. Drinks are a necessary preliminary to meals even if the latter have to be delayed. Social occasions are preceded by a drink or two before setting out, and anxiety is felt as to whether the supply of alcohol will be adequate, so that a few quick drinks are taken as soon as possible after arrival. When travelling, thought is given to reserve supplies. More time tends to be spent away from home. There is a reduction, at first hardly noticeable, in initiative, efficiency and amount of trouble taken, with a tendency to be behindhand and uncommunicative in the mornings. At this stage the patient may worry about his alcoholic intake, and may express this in the form of jocose references to the subject.

The *established* stage is marked by the patient finding himself unable to feel comfortable in the absence of alcohol. Patients have difficulty in describing this, but they seem to suffer from a restless, irritable malaise, with a sense of discontentment and difficulty in settling to things. This is temporarily dissolved by alcohol so that a need for it is felt. One drink now leads to the need for another, and the patient does not control the quantity even when he has reached a 'comfortable concentration'. He therefore subsequently experiences a different malaise of the hang-over type. If this is severe, it may cause him to stop drinking for a day or so, but he will almost immediately start again. He needs to drink more, and more quickly than his former associates; while with them, he may excuse himself and sneak extra drinks elsewhere. His application and initiative are now more definitely affected; he does less work and does it less effectively and attentively. Any originality in thinking or conversational adroitness disappears; he relies on his former stock-in-trade and speaks in clichés. He drops his outside interests and forms no new ones. Financial difficulties now often arise; he becomes less scrupulous and may indulge in gambling with poor judgment. In the home he is self-centred, inconsiderate, and evasive of his responsibilities, often with more or less plausible excuses. If taken to task he may show an aggressive irritability, often expressing a morbid jealousy that may be related to increasing impotence; this may alternate with a maudlin self-pity and remorse if he is feeling physically prostrated. Violence to wife and children becomes increasingly common, particularly in those already prone to aggressive behaviour, but also in people who have never been like that before. The life of the family often becomes desperately unhappy.

The *advanced* stage of chronic alcoholism is marked by anorexia, with failure to take enough food, morning nausea often with vomiting, tremor, a constant preoccupation over supplies, and the necessity for drinks in the morning before activity is undertaken and the tremor can be controlled. A morning tremor ('shakes') controlled by alcohol, is a definite sign of addiction. Alcohol is also necessary to achieve sleep, although alcohol is itself a cause of early morning wakefulness. Abstinence leads at once to anxiety, which may be severe.

The stage of *alcoholic breakdown* is then reached, with almost chronic intoxication, weakness from lack of food, vomiting, and the toxic direct effects of alcohol. Lack of initiative is total, except for getting more drink about which there may be every unscrupulousness. The mood is one of anxiety, depression and remorse. The patient thinks only of himself, how he feels, and the next drink, shows a reduced tolerance so that he is drunk on little, with impaired time-sense and only a vague appreciation of recent events. There is now commonly a considerable aversion to alcohol and a full recognition that he wishes to dispense with it but cannot.

Accompanying these developments there will have been various degrees of upset both at work and at home. Complaints will have been made, and relations will have become strained. Paranoid developments may have occurred, with suspiciousness and actual delusions (p 332), with possible attempts at testing the fidelity of the spouse by traps and detective work almost always based on the patient's alcohol-induced impotence. These may have encouraged increased consumption of alcohol as a solace, with the creation of a vicious circle.

Specially ominous indications in the foregoing sequence are: (1) a falling off in the patient's capacity to hold his liquor, (2) the occurrence of patches of amnesia after only small amounts of alcohol; these are evidence of cerebral damage, (3) enlargement and tenderness of the liver (which may later give place to shrinkage and induration), (4) tenderness of the muscles and nerve trunks with defects of sensation, referable to peripheral neuritis from lack of thiamin (Vitamin B_1).

Alcoholics tend to be singularly deficient in insight, cannot be convinced that their troubles arise from their habits, refuse to admit defeat ('Give it up? Why, that would be giving in'), and insist that they can manage the situation in the teeth of overwhelming evidence to the contrary. In many, the lack of insight and perhaps the inability to exert their will power sufficiently, may be because significant brain damage has already occurred (p. 331). They are plausible and almost always untruthful as to the extent of their consumption. Women have a greater tendency to drink secretly than do men, and many have more opportunity of doing so.

Many alcoholics are men and women of the world with remnants of a personality that was once engaging. This may lead them to show an apparent frankness, with a spurious charm that is really allied to shamelessness, and connected with a vain refusal to face the humiliation of confessing the facts. Phrases like 'To be perfectly frank ... ', 'To be quite candid ... ', 'If I'm really honest ... ', may help to put the doctor on his guard and to recognise that when an alcoholic claims to have put all his cards on the table, a number are probably face down.

OTHER ALCOHOLIC SYNDROMES

Korsakoff's psychosis

This is described on page 105.

Alcoholic dementia

In addition to Korsakoff's psychosis, which is secondary to thiamin deficiency, alcohol can cause direct brain damage, a fact that has been increasingly recognised recently. Very many alcoholics show slight permanent intellectual impairment, even after prolonged abstinence; and a few show quite severe decline, with demonstrable cerebral atrophy. The lack of insight and will to cooperate which many advanced alcoholics show may well be due in part to some degree of dementia.

Computer assisted tomography (CAT scanning) has demonstrated dilatation of cerebral ventricles in quite young adult alcoholics, which apparently recovers in many if they abstain for months. In the past dilatation of cerebral ventricles has been assumed to be permanent, but in these cases the changes are presumably due to shrinkage of brain substance without permanent cell death. In any case, the existence of anatomical brain changes in quite young alcoholics is linked with impaired memory and intellectual functions. In more advanced cases ventricular dilatation is permanent.

Chronic alcoholic hallucinosis

This is also rare. It may develop from an acute hallucinosis or it may be insidious in onset. In either event the patient hears hallucinatory voices in clear consciousness and without much disturbance of behaviour. Characteristically, these are repetitive and rhythmical — 'idiot, idiot, idiot', or 'beggar, beggar, beggar'. The condition tends to be very persistent. Some patients get used to the voices and carry on in spite of them, but most develop paranoid misinterpretations as a result of the voices and come to need institutional care. Such patients may, however, be appreciably helped by phenothiazines (p. 412).

Alcoholic paranoid states

Alcohol can play a part in the production of states that may closely resemble paranoid schizophrenia, or, when a grandiose colouring is added, general paralysis of the insane, but with a much better prognosis. Jealousy is usually a prominent feature, and the delusions are usually related to it; the paranoid alcoholic accuses his spouse of infidelity, especially when impotence has occurred as part of the alcoholism. Important points to look for are (a) the alcoholism, and development of symptoms in relation to it, (b) a greater variability in the clinical picture than occurs in paranoid schizophrenia or general paralysis, (c) organic mental features (p. 78).

Delirium tremens

This is most often precipitated by sudden alcohol withdrawal, and is more common in spirit drinkers. It begins 6–8 hours after the last drink, and is at its peak a further 40 hours later. It occurs especially in those whose diet has led to deficiency of vitamins. The onset is often acute, precipitated by a drinking bout with insufficient food intake, by a physical illness or injury, or admission to hospital with consequent alcohol withdrawal. Delirium tremens is seen as often in orthopaedic wards as in psychiatric units. On the other hand, the onset may be subacute and preceded by nocturnal anxiety, nightmares, hypnagogic hallucinations, sometimes with confusion at night, though in the waking state. This may happen for a few nights before the delirium begins; such an occurrence should at once bring to mind the possibility of an incipient delirium, however normal the patient may seem during the daylight hours. A few cases start with an epileptic fit. If a known heavy drinker is admitted to a general hospital for surgery or other treatment it may be advisable to give alcohol, in diminishing amounts, to prevent acute withdrawal symptoms developing.

The clinical picture does not differ materially from that of other delirious states (p. 100). Special features characteristic, though not diagnostic, of the alcoholic delirium are: *physically*, tremor of the tongue, lips, fingers and hands, often coupled with signs of polyneuritis, cramps, sweating, tachycardia, nausea and retching, and restless insomnia. In many cases these physical disturbances, and accompanying mental distress occur, but the more florid mental disturbances of true delirium do not develop. In more severe states, with delirium proper, there is a mixture of anxiety or even terror, alternating with jocularity, the occurrence of rapidly moving hallucinations of small animals (mice, rats, insects), and the imaginary pursuit of his own occupation by the delirious patient. References to alcohol, intentional or inadvertent, in the patient's remarks, and requests for gin, whisky or brandy, are diagnostic pointers.

It is not always realised that this is a serious condition. The mortality used to be about 10%, though this has been reduced by modern methods of treatment. The commonest cause of death is circulatory failure. The length of the attack can now be reduced to about three days or less; formerly, it was three to seven days, and usually five. Of the survivors, about one-third may be left with Korsakoff's psychosis (p. 105) unless thiamin is given in large doses for a prolonged period.

Treatment of delirium tremens includes a careful search for any precipitating infection or other illness; intravenous fluids with a potassium supplement if there is marked dehydration with hypokalaemia, which is common, and thiamin. Chlormethiazole 500–1500 g six-hourly on a reducing schedule, keeping pace with improvement. Chlormethiazole is an addictive drug and should not be given to outpatients. Chlordiazepoxide in large doses (30–60 mg six-hourly) may also be tried.

More details of the clinical features and treatment of the delirium are given on page 102). When that has recovered the problem of alcoholism has to be dealt with if possible, as described below.

Epileptiform fits

Grand mal convulsions can occur in alcoholics in more than one setting. Principally they occur on sudden withdrawal in chronic alcoholics, during a period of delirium tremens for example. In this way they are like the withdrawal fits of barbiturate abusers. They can also occur in acute severe alcohol intoxication — 'rum fits'. During withdrawal from alcohol in hospital, the use of chlormethiazole or chlordiazepoxide will probably prevent fits, and the latter can be used as an anticonvulsant in other situations, as can diazepam.

Treatment

It is a sad fact that we cannot yet be confident that any particular type of treatment regime is of any overall value, although special units for alcoholics are frequently established. Their main function should really be in research into treatment methods. That is not to say that no alcoholic can be helped, but the results depend mostly on the personality of the patient, and particularly on genuine motivation and determination, on the personalities of those offering help, and on the family and work setting in which he lives, rather than on a particular method of treatment.

The alcoholics who do best with treatment are those whose drinking is secondary to some treatable psychiatric syndrome, especially depression; and those in whom some relevant clear cut environmental problem can be overcome. The more abnormal the underlying personality, the worse the outlook.

It is important to give clear and accurate information about the risks of his drinking to every alcoholic, with details of liver and other damage, as this can be the necessary motivational spur.

Before the established stage is reached, attempts should be made at encouraging moderation. Difficulties, anxieties and situations that encourage drinking should be discussed, and clarification of the whole problem and possible means of dealing with it should be attempted, in the hope of altering the habit-pattern and devising alternative satisfactions.

It is also necessary to be quite clear that, once the patient has entered the established stage of chronic alcoholism, total abstinence should be the aim. Every alcoholic patient who comes for treatment hopes to be turned into a controlled drinker, but this is only possible for a few, and people entering treatment should not be aiming at it. Though treatment does not often succeed unless the patient comes actually asking for help, usually as the result of some crisis, there are some patients who after admission to hospital has enabled them to 'dry out' and regain perspective, will see the light although they may have come reluctantly in the first place. Such cases may be deterred from accepting treatment if the need for total abstinence is stressed too soon. But a patient seen in the premonitory phase, before his addiction is actually established, may be sobered into changing his habits if the ultimate need for total abstinence is put to him with sufficient cogency.

It is so difficult to control alcoholism outside hospital that admission is almost always essential if addiction or some other complicating syndrome is present. Even then, many patients show a facile optimism about their future and discharge themselves too soon. In hospital, care should be taken to ensure that the patient does not have a secret supply of alcohol. Sudden withdrawal may precipitate delirium tremens and/or epileptic fits, as already described. (The treatment of delirium tremens is described earlier in this section on p. 332.)

The withdrawal symptoms are relatively mild as long as delirium does not supervene. Restlessness, irritability, emotional lability and anxiety may be shown, with anorexia, tremulousness, sweating and diarrhoea. These should be reduced by sedation with phenothiazines, chlormethiazole or benzodiazepines, and large doses of vitamins such as are given in delirium tremens, which may also help to prevent delirium from developing. Benzodiazepines and chlormethiazole should not be continued for long in alcoholics after the withdrawal symptoms have died down, because of the risk of dependency and even addiction.

When the patient's general condition has been improved, specific *physical* treatments may be considered as an adjunct to the general psychological management.

Detoxication units. For some years many North American hospitals have had special wards for drying out alcoholics, many of whom are severely deteriorated and have been taken there by the police who might otherwise have arrested them as 'drunk and disorderly', or under some equivalent charge. Suitable patients are then offered more prolonged treatment. There are some similar units in the United Kingdom. They will lessen the burden on the prison service, but most of those admitted are likely to be untreatable by current methods, so it is to be hoped that they will be developed for research purposes at first.

Aversion treatments. These are no longer used very much, not because they were proven to be less effective than other methods, but because they became unfashionable, not fitting into the philosophy of modern practice. Apomorphine and emetine hydrochloride were most widely used, setting up a conditioned response by associating vomiting and alcohol intake. In the hands of enthusiastic and skilled doctors and nurses, good results were certainly obtained in some patients.

Controlled drinking. A different attitude to that expressed here has been that many alcoholics can learn to control their drinking behaviour, using behavioural psychological techniques. These methods were developed mainly in the United States and early results were very encouraging, although recently more gloomy reports have been published. The present writer remains unconvinced that the approach has a wide application.

Disulfiram treatment. Antabuse, disulfiram, interferes with the metabolic breakdown of alcohol with the effect of causing acetaldehyde to accumulate in the blood-stream. This can be fatal. Disulfiram should, therefore, never be given to an intoxicated person. The treatment is best begun in hospital. The patient, detoxicated, is given 400 mg daily for about one week, reducing to 200 mg daily. More will be needed if the reaction with alcohol is not severe enough. On the fifth day alcohol is given as a test, in the form which the patient prefers. A suitable quantity is 50 ml of gin or whisky. Some degree of acetaldehyde poisoning develops. Its extent depends on the amount of antabuse given, on the amount of alcohol given and the rate at which it is absorbed. It may be unwise to let the patient pour drinks for himself and drink at his normal rate. A suitable régime is to give repeated doses of 50 ml of spirits every 15 minutes, with the patient resting, and having his blood pressure and pulse recorded every 10 minutes. Most patients experience some effect after about 15 minutes; those who do not should be given more alcohol.

The initial effect is that the patient feels hot in the face with flushing that extends to the conjunctivae, giving rise to the 'bull-eyed' appearance which makes him look more uncomfortable than he really is. This is followed by palpitation, a sense of constriction in the chest and neck, with pounding of the vessels in the neck and head leading to headache. The patient now feels ill, uncomfortable and apprehensive, even in fear of death. There is a rise in pulse rate and a fall in blood pressure that is usually gradual, but occasionally rapid. In course of this, the flushing gives place to pallor with general malaise, nausea and sometimes vomiting, while the patient may say he is experiencing the worst 'hang-over' he has ever known.

If the patient shows a satisfactory reaction and drinks are given every 10 minutes, the stage of pallor will usually be reached in 45–60 minutes. We do not give alcohol beyond this point and most patients will already have refused to continue.

The patient should be kept under supervision in bed for the rest of the day as delayed reactions of fainting or vomiting may occur. Many patients will go to sleep an hour or so after the start of treatment, and they tend to wake up feeling particularly well.

If the effects have not been sufficiently unpleasant to make an impression on the patient, the procedure may be repeated with increased dosage or antabuse and/or alcohol, or with more rapid alcoholic intake.

The patient then has to be persuaded to take maintenance doses of antabuse (200–400 mg daily), if necessary under supervision, in the hope that knowledge of what will happen if he drinks will deter him from doing so. Disulfiram is of most help when the patient takes it himself daily as a kind of commitment 'to be sober today'.

The commonest complications are (a) cardio-vascular collapse, and (b) coronary thrombosis. The former may be alarming and blood pressure elevating drugs (e.g. mephentermine sulphate 15 mg) should be at hand during treatment. It should be avoidable by controlling the rate of intake of alcohol. That coronary thrombosis can occur owing to the antabuse-alcohol reaction dictates caution where there is a suspicion of coronary arterial disease. Other indications for caution are other cardiac disorders, cirrhosis of the liver, nephritis, diabetes and thyrotoxicosis. Patients on maintenance doses may sometimes complain that they feel rather less alert. A rare but startling complication is the occasional development of psychotic states in patients who have had antabuse in large doses or over a long period of time; these take the form of organic confusional states but they may also have markedly schizophrenic features. They may last for some days after withdrawal of the drug, but show spontaneous recovery. Citrated calcium carbimide (Abstem), is a less severe and more rapidly acting drug of similar type. The dose is 50–100 mg daily by mouth.

Rehabilitation. This is essential. Without it nothing will be achieved save improving the patient's physical condition sufficiently to encourage further drinking. In many parts of Britain the initial withdrawal from alcohol and treatment of physical and mental complications, is undertaken in general psychiatric units, and the patients then are referred on to specialist alcoholic units after a few weeks. The stay in the alcoholic unit is usually a few months. At present these specialised units emphasise education about the dangers of alcohol, with group therapy aimed at greater understanding of underlying problems, of the effect on the family and so on, and also foster a sense of belonging to the group. Most work closely with Alcoholics Anonymous when possible.

In many alcoholics the family not only suffers from the drinking, but contributes to it, and some alcoholics find it easier to remain abstinent if they separate from their spouses. This is particularly so when the male drinker feels humiliated by his wife, either sexually because of low potency which precedes or follows the alcoholism, or for some other personal feeling of inadequacy. Very commonly it is the drinker's initial heavy drinking, that leads to the wife's very attitudes that later the drinker blames as the cause of his troubles — in an endless circle of recrimination.

Families can also be involved by discussing joint problems and airing conflicts in a professional situation, instead of attempting only to blot them out with alcohol; and many wives of alcoholics find support and help from Alanon, a kind of parallel organisation to Alcoholics Anonymous itself. Alcoholics Anonymous (A.A.) can be of great help to some drinkers, and every alcoholic should be informed about them, and told how to contact the local branch. The members have considerable knowledge of alcoholism through previous personal experience and have acquired a certain expertise in helping to prevent recurrences of the habit. They hold meetings, discussions and social occasions, and individual members can be called on by the drinker who feels he is relapsing. Patients who are introduced will find themselves welcome as new members and may also find a niche in which they may be useful to others, which is always helpful in restoring self-esteem.

There are various branches, and particulars may be obtained from the London Office, at present at 11 Redcliffe Gardens, S.W.10.

Other voluntary organisations have sprung up to help the alcoholic, for example Accept, which offers support, counselling, education, and a day centre for the unemployed alcoholic. Several other organisations (e.g. the Cyrenians) provide hostel accommodation for the down-and-out drinker. It is worthwhile for any doctor to find out whatever is available in the local area in which he or she practises.

Follow up after discharge, offering personal support, encouragement and advice, is also very important. If possible, the outpatient should see the same individual doctors, nurses, psychologists, or social workers (all of whom have active treatment roles in most alcoholic units) as during his inpatient stay.

During this after-treatment, care may be required to tide the patient over special events, and the better one knows the patient the more will one be prepared. Festive occasions such as Christmas may call for special precautions, as may such other events as anniversaries, births, marriages and wakes.

DRUG ADDICTION

Drug addictions can be divided into two main groups. The first comprises addiction to those drugs which involve only an *emotional* dependence, such as marihuana, cocaine, analeptics such as the amphetamines and phenmetrazine (Preludin), and bromides. True physiological addiction does not develop, so that they can be given up without physical symptoms.

The other group comprises addiction to those drugs which involve a *physical* dependence, and this is a very real thing in that the patients develop abstinence symptoms of a physical kind if supply of the drug is discontinued. The nature of the withdrawal symptoms varies according to the drugs to which the patient is addicted, but these fall easily into two sub-groups, namely (1) the opiate group, and (2) the alcohol-barbiturate-benzodiazepine group. The withdrawal symptoms of the opiate group are characterised by nervous instability — and this is no fancy on the part of the patient or the observers — with autonomic dysfunction but *without* the development of convulsions or delirium. The withdrawal symptoms of the alcohol-barbiturate group are characterised, if the addiction is sufficiently severe, by the development of convulsions and delirium. Benzodiazepines have been increasingly recognised as occasionally causing true addiction of this type, although rarely in proportion to the vast numbers of people who take these drugs regularly.

The growth of opiate addiction in Great Britain has been parallel to that in the rest of the western world, although not so great as in some countries. Between 1936 and 1960 the average number of opiate addicts annually was 336; with a high of 620 in 1937 and a low of 199 in 1947. The figures were reliable because there were no illegal sources of morphine and heroin. Most of those on these drugs were patients who had been given the drugs for some severe pain and became addicted; and many were doctors, nurses, pharmacists and so on who had easy access to the drugs. There was no 'drug culture' and young people were rarely involved.

The new wave of drug takers developed here from 1960 onwards, much increased by North American heroin addicts who came to this country because here the drugs could be legally prescribed for addicts, whereas in their own countries it was a crime to take and to prescribe them. By 1965 there were 259 new cases of heroin addiction known, of whom 145 were under 20 years. There was no significant change in morphine and pethidine addiction, all the increase was with heroin, though later Methadone became important.

The rate continued to climb, and in 1968 there were 2624 new notifications in Great Britain of narcotic addicts. Of this total 2096 were on heroin, 214 on Methadone, and 314 were on other drugs. As a response to the extremely rapid growth of heroin addiction new legislation was brought in. Heroin prescribing became restricted to a very few doctors, centred almost exclusively in special drug clinics in hospital outpatients departments, and with special inpatient units to back them up, which stopped over-prescribing by 'rogue' doctors, many of whom were just too credulous and unable to say 'No'. The effect of the new (1968) legislation and organisation of drug clinics was striking: by 1970 there were 762 new notifications, of whom only 353 were on heroin; but there has been a marked increase since then. In 1981 there were 3,800 narcotic addicts in the United Kingdom known to the Home Office, of which 2,300 were newly notified. Huge drug smuggling operations are carried out by international organisations such as the Mafia, and the situation is almost out of control again.

An unknown number of addicts remain outside the system, variously estimated as between 20 and 100% of the known totals, and it is possible that some addicts manage to register themselves at more than one clinic. Narcotic addiction was largely centred in London, but in the past few years has spread to nearly all large towns in the United Kingdom.

Many other drugs are turned to by opiate addicts, especially if heroin is in short supply, and by drug abusers who have never been on heroin. A growing practice has been to crush up barbiturates and inject the incomplete solution intravenously — with frequent local abscesses, septicaemia, and a fairly high mortality as consequences. Intravenous methedrine has been withdrawn from the market by the manufacturers, and oral amphetamines are at present being voluntarily outlawed in many areas and hospitals. Mandrax, a mixture of methaqualone and diphenhydramine, has many devotees and should in our opinion not be prescribed either. We have no exact knowledge of the numbers of addicts, even of heroin, because we do not know how many others each known addict may be supplying. There is no machinery to ascertain the frequency of barbiturate addiction, but surveys of various populations some years ago indicated it to be very common, especially in middle aged housewives who had little, other than their addiction, in common with the younger addicts. Barbiturates are prescribed much less now, but benzodiazepines are still far too freely handed out. Amphetamine prescribing has also declined. In recent years large and small scale thefts of drugs from chemists' shops and hospital pharmacies have increased the amounts in circulation, but careless over-prescribing remains the chief source.

Aetiology

Here, many factors are involved, and it is not a simple matter at all. There are social, personal, physical and pharmacological factors.

Under *social* factors, the first is availability; addiction starts where the drugs are to be found, and the best way to become an addict is to know one. Addiction is almost a contagious disease.

So the basic social factors are availability and the sort of person who takes to addiction. In the United States the great majority of addicts belong to minority groups from the same areas of the same cities, slum areas with a high incidence of other social problems, delinquency, crime, venereal disease, and unstable family structures. It looks as though addiction, like delinquency when that occurs on any large scale, is a social function of a problem population, stemming from contact with each other and so handed on by local tradition. However, the drug culture also attracts large numbers of young people from quite privileged backgrounds, but of unstable and inadequate personality. Addiction in Great Britain, by comparison on a small scale, has not yet assumed the fixity of the American social pattern. Many of our young currently view drug-taking with complacency, even approval, and there is evidence of a Rakes' Progress from marijuana and amphetamines to 'hard' (opiate) drugs.

So much for the basic social factors of availability, and the social problem group which spreads the contagion. But since enormous numbers of people subjected to the same social circumstances do not become addicts there must be *personal* factors also. As regards these, it would appear that anyone *can* become addicted. But just as alcohol is a 'detector of psychic weakness' the same is true of drugs, and the more the 'psychic weaknesses', the more is the person at risk. Fundamentally, it seems to us that addicts are people who just like taking things in accordance with a narcissistic, childlike preoccupation with their own needs. Safeguards against addiction are to be obsessionally careful and emotionally cold. Dangers are to be incautious, impulsive, unduly emotional and of a dependent type. Some young addicts are impulsive hedonists out for a thrill who get into bad company, part of the 'teenage explosion'. Others may be serious students with adolescent needs, hoping to achieve creativeness and greater self-knowledge, questing for new sensations and experience in an attempt at greater self-fulfilment. Among those of more complex psychopathology, some may take drugs as an aggressive protest against reactionary society. The more tormented may take them to reduce the moodiness arising from their awareness of the difference between their ideal and actual selves, or from their sexual and interpersonal problems, finding themselves more bearable and life less threatening, however transiently, under the effect of drugs.

Most adult addicts seem to be immature and dependent people who look for and expect props, who take flight into feeling rather than effective action in face of difficulty, and the self-centred dependence of many encourages a selfish possessiveness of others that renders relationships complicated and unsatisfactory. There may then be a tendency to retreat into pseudo-illness with demand for drugs and increasing use of those as solvents of the reality they do not wish to face. These are the anxious-hysterical group. Addiction becomes even commoner where there is an admixture of psychopathy. Then, having got into the company of addicts the patient finds, in Isbell's words, he has entered a 'distinct social group with its own language, customs and code'; he feels himself to belong, he is at less disadvantage than in ordinary company, and if he tries to extract himself, he is lonely, bored, has lost his friends and feels he has nothing in common with non-drugtakers, to whom he easily feels inferior because of their greater success in coping with life. Too commonly, addicts deliberately encourage acquaintances and friends to take drugs, playing down the disadvantages, gaining satisfaction from pulling others down to their own level and expressing their own resentment at a world with which they cannot cope.

Narcotic drug users have a high crime rate, even before they start on drugs, and nearly all of them are convicted of an offence at some time. The female addicts have relatively higher delinquency rates, before the addiction starts, than do the males; an expression of disordered personality in another field.

Next, we come to *physical* factors. Some patients have genuinely developed an addiction through attempts to relieve genuine pain, but this is also often put forward as an excuse, with the alleged condition having been elusive and obscure, defying diagnosis in a way that creates scepticism as to how founded in reality it was.

Last, we come to *pharmacological* factors. It is usually thought that the choice of the drug has been more rather than less accidental, depending on chance and availability, but this may not be altogether so, in that opiate addicts like the reduction of general (including erotic) appetite, while experiencing from intravenous injection a transient thrill akin to orgasm though centred in the abdomen, after which they feel a tranquil freedom to get on with what they want to do; whereas barbiturate addicts are more often aggressive people (even though also immature and inadequate) who like a high degree of sexual stimulation and to live in an emotional vortex, for which the disinhibiting effect of barbiturates may be useful. Benzodiazepine dependency occurs in people of varying temperaments, most commonly in anxious and tense people, in whom it produces a welcome relaxation and screen from reality, very like that of alcohol.

It is now known that opiates, because of their molecular structure, in some way 'fit into' brain receptors for endogenous endorphins, almost as a key fits into a lock, which goes some way to explaining the pain relief they provide. Electrical self-stimulation of the brain (e.g. in animal experiments on the 'pleasure areas' of Olds) is known to release endorphins or analogous substances, and it is therefore possible that opiates also produce their euphoriant effect by acting on this system. Benzodiazepines similarly seem to 'fit into' receptor sites of other endogenous neuro-transmitters involved in emotional responses.

Symptoms and signs

Emotional dependence group

Marijuana (Cannabis indica), also known as pot, hash, grass and by other names, is mainly smoked but can be eaten. Various types are produced from different countries, but the main active ingredient of each is delta tetra hydrocannabinol. It leads to a wide variety of effects, partly depending on what the drug taker is expecting, his stage of mind, and the social setting. Often there is a sense of calm elation, with distortions of space and time, and perceptual distortions with illusions or even hallucinations can occur. Outwardly the subject looks distant and dreamy, 'stoned', and may be giggling over little things. As with many drugs there may be a sense of deep creative thinking or of cosmic awareness, but the ideas are usually flat and obvious to the unintoxicated, and even to the subject afterwards.

Occasionally, cannabis is followed by an intense feeling of anxiety, amounting to terror, which usually settles down with time, aided by chlorpromazine. This seems to happen if the subject takes a much stronger preparation than usual, or one prepared in a different way, as for example when an American smokes Algerian hash for the first time. Currently we are now seeing in large British cities acute florid psychoses associated with heavy cannabis intake, especially in the form of 'Ganja', favoured by West Indian Rastafarians. These psychotic states are brief, but can be most difficult to differentiate from acute functional psychoses such as schizophrenia.

Cannabis is now taken very frequently in the western world, and probably has no more serious ill effects than alcohol, which has plenty. There is a strong movement to make it legal. One serious disadvantage, not widely recognised, is that there is a cannabis 'hangover', a not unpleasant apathy, unlike the subjective distress caused by alcohol. Students in particular can be affected badly, because a weekend heavy session may be followed by 2 or 3 days in which no work gets done. When the apathy wears off the student starts to worry about not having done enough work, and too often smokes more pot to assuage his anxiety. The drug is implicated in many student failures.

Cocaine can confer a sense of extreme well-being with increase of psychomotor activity and abolition of fatigue and hunger. This is very short-lived. When the dose is repeated toxic symptoms may appear with central nervous stimulation and autonomic sensitisation: elevation of blood pressure, pulse and respiration, with sweating, exophthalmos and mydriasis, increased reflexes with tremors, twitches and even spasms of muscle groups. Finally, a toxic psychosis may appear with disorientation and failure of grasp, visual, auditory and tactile hallucinations, a persecuted suspiciousness — a sub-delirium that may become a full delirium.

There has been a huge increase in cocaine taking in the past few years, especially among the prosperous and fashionable. In this country, psychiatrists are not seeing many harmful effects from this habit although there are harmful local effects, such as damage to the nasal septum in cocaine sniffers. In the USA, more ill-effects are being recorded, including panic attacks, paranoia, convulsions and violence.

The picture with *amphetamine* is similar: abuse is commoner in the poorer and less fashionable and 'speed' as it is often called is widely used as an excitant, and may be indiscriminately mixed with alcohol, diazepam or other drugs by those seeking an exciting night out. Regular large amounts of amphetamines can lead to an 'amphetamine psychosis', in which a florid paranoid psychosis develops without clouding of consciousness but with delusions of persecution, great fear, excitement and auditory hallucinations. However, first-rank symptoms of schizophrenia are lacking (p. 148). This psychosis enters into the differential diagnosis of schizophrenia. It settles with chlorpromazine and avoidance of amphetamines.

With *bromide* there is an increasing calm with inter, ils of somnolence and, as the dose climbs, a gradually increasing sub-delirious state, starting at night, which may progress to full delirium; there may or may not be acneiform eruptions. With none of these drugs is there any abstinence syndrome.

With the *alcohol-barbiturate-benzodiazepine* group (other main members: paraldehyde, chloral, meprobamate (Equanil) glutethimide (doriden)) true addiction can occur. The clinical picture is one of more or less chronic intoxication. At high levels of intoxication there will be a muddled, fuddled confusion, with impaired intellectual function and diminished emotional control, and neurological manifestations such as dysarthria, nystagmus, ataxia and other evidence of incoordination, perhaps with the physical accompaniment of unexplained bruises, grazes or burns sustained through falls. At lower levels of intoxication, diagnostic pointers include the following:

Reluctance to tolerate reduction of the dose with or without devices aimed at preventing it, e.g. statements that the prescription or the pills have been lost, or short measure given. A general falling off in efficiency and effort; the housework does not get done, letters are unanswered, bills are unpaid or paid twice through memory impairment, meals are delayed. Oscillation of mood from an anxious, irritable, depressed disgruntlement and then back to equable cheerfulness, without obvious external cause. Oscillations of behaviour from a disinhibited over-talkativeness with restlessness to a slow, forgetful fuddledness with somnolence at the wrong times, but sometimes with night being turned into day by the added introduction of stimulants, for many barbiturate addicts like to offset the sedative barbiturate effect. There may be also the development of an aggrieved antagonism with grumbling accusations, sometimes with a germ of twisted truth achieved by altering the emphasis of something that has been said or the motive of something that has been done. In general, such changed behaviour may reveal something of the underlying discontent that may have led to taking drugs in the first place, its expression being released by their disinhibiting effect. Particularly, in the more purely intellectual sphere, there may be rambling conversation that does not reach a point, telling the same story twice, asking the same thing again and again, repeatedly seeking confirmation, muddles over dates, missing appointments, forgetting to relay messages or making telephone calls at extraordinary hours through impairment of time sense or judgement, finding entries in diaries with inability to remember when they were made and to what they refer, or a story of seeing a client on a Thursday without recollection of having seen him on Tuesday, even though notes had been made.

With the *opiate* group, (main members: morphine, diacetyl-morphine (heroin), methadone (physeptone), hydromorphone (dilau-did), levorphanol (dromoran), pethidine and phenadoxone (heptalgin)), morphine may be taken as the paradigm. The intoxication that occurs with alcohol and barbiturates is not seen. The initial effects of depression of blood pressure, pulse rate, temperature and respiration are not maintained as tolerance is acquired, but the pupils remain constricted, constipation is always present, sexual function remains depressed, and there is continued irritability of the longer reflex arcs. In the early stages the candidate for addiction may show increased activity followed by drifting into a light sleep, from which he may wake suddenly and then drift back again. It is in this stage of drift from sleep to wakefulness that the opium dreams occur. But as tolerance increases, this tendency to light sleep decreases. To outward observation the opiate addict is not abnormal as long as he can continue to take a satisfactory dose, and he will be quite able to carry on a skilled technical job. The only outward evidence may be constricted pupils, injection marks, and loss of weight secondary to reduced food intake though in general the productivity, is likely to be less and more time may be spent in daydreaming. The moral decay emphasised by the older text-books need not occur except in so far as the addict may be unscrupulous over trying to maintain supplies.

Solvent Sniffing. A recent worrying development has been a large increase in sniffing of solvents, such as those found in many modern glues, or of dry cleaning fluid, petrol and similar fat solvents. Fatal liver damage has occurred and brain damage is a possibility. Those involved are mainly rather unintelligent and inadequate young people, often from seriously deprived backgrounds, and with hopeless and apathetic responses to family and society. The effects are rather like those of alcohol although addiction does not occur. There is no specific treatment for the solvent sniffing as such, but anything which will help the individual to feel better and to cope better may be helpful.

Withdrawal symptoms

As regards the first group — those drugs involving emotional dependence only — the only withdrawal symptoms of note are moodiness and malaise and withdrawal may be abrupt without danger. With the alcohol-barbiturate-benzodiazepine group, the withdrawal symptoms may be serious. Their severity varies with the dose taken, the degree of intoxication and its length. Withdrawal symptoms are to be expected if the patient has been taking more than 800 mg of barbiturate per day for any significant length of time, but as regards alcohol and benzodiazepines, there are more individual variations so that it is less easy to be precise. With barbiturates, the usual course of events is that after a latent interval of about eight hours, anxiety, restlessness, headache, tremor, twitching of various muscle groups, weakness, vomiting and postural dizziness make their appearance. These increase, accompanied by electro-encephalographic changes in the form of slow waves with spike and wave formation. Between about the thirtieth and forty-eighth hour of withdrawal epileptiform fits may be expected in about three cases out of four. Thereafter, the patient may begin to recover, but, on the other hand, about two out of every three are liable to increasing insomnia with the development of delirium, usually starting at night. Barbiturate delirium does not differ significantly from delirium tremens, and the attitude of the patient towards it may vary between, occasionally, amusement at the queer things that he is observing and, more often, fear that may become desperate with frantic efforts to escape from imaginary enemies. Agitation may lead to exhaustion and exhaustion to death. While the onset of delirium may be prevented by judicious use of barbiturate or alcohol, its course cannot be so influenced after it has begun.

Benzodiazepine withdrawal similarly may produce epileptic convulsions (like the barbiturates, benzodiazepines are themselves effective anti-convulsants) or a picture like that of 'delirium tremens in slow motion', coming on about 48 hours after withdrawal, and preceded by unpleasant withdrawal symptoms as with alcohol.

On withdrawal of morphine and other opiates the symptoms are less dangerous but are distressing both to experience and to observe. Their intensity depends to some extent on the dose that the patient has been accustomed to take. For the first 14 hours the patient feels reasonably well, but there then develop yawning, lacrimation, rhinorrhoea and perspiration with a restless, uneasy sleepiness. After about twenty-four hours the patient awakens to a persistent insomnia, with intensification of the foregoing symptoms now coupled with severe cramp-like pains in the back and legs and 'cold flashes' which lead to curling up with demand for more blankets whatever the atmospheric temperature. Objectively, there are recurring waves of gooseflesh with twitching of various muscle groups. After about 36 hours there is an intense increase of restlessness, with retching, vomiting, diarrhoea, total anorexia and increase of temperature, respiration and blood pressure, with loss of body weight. This state reaches its height at about 48 hours after withdrawal, continues much the same until about the seventy second hour of abstinence, and then starts to abate. After a week or so objective signs have disappeared, but the patients may yet complain of weakness, aches and difficulty in sleeping.

Treatment

In this, whatever the addiction, there are several stages. The first is to get the patient to see the need for treatment. This may be difficult. The second is to wean the patient from the drug. This can only be done satisfactorily in a controlled environment, i.e. an institution, away from sources of supply. Even so many patients will cheat, or try to, by bringing in supplies more or less cunningly concealed or by claiming to need more than was stated at the preliminary consultation. The third, and much the most difficult, is to try to help the addict to feel better, to live in and to cope with the world, and to enjoy it without drugs. Unfortunately psychotherapy, of conventional kinds at least, seems to be of little benefit to addicts.

With the cocaine, marijuana, amphetamine and bromide group abrupt withdrawal will not much matter since immediate withdrawal carries on ill-effects, and there is of course no true addiction. With the alcohol-barbiturate-benzodiazepine group to withdraw abruptly may be to endanger life. A few diminishing doses of alcohol should suffice to avoid delirium tremens. The patient should be out of hazard if he survives without discomfort an alcohol-free period of about 24 hours. With *barbiturates*, the best practice seems to be to substitute pentobarbitone (nembutal) since its length of action is such that four oral doses daily should suffice to prevent withdrawal symptoms without producing more than mild intoxication. The 'stabilising dose' can be established by observing the patient over a period of about 48 hours. Tremulousness and postural hypotension are the main indicators of underdosage. When the patient appears comfortable on the stabilising dose, this should be gradually reduced by 100–200 mg each day. If tremulousness, twitching, hypotension and weakness occur, the reduction should be suspended for 24 hours, and it may be advisable to nurse the patient on a mattress on the floor. Severely addicted patients may require gradual withdrawal over a month or more, specially if there are cardiovascular or other organic complications. Since the barbiturate delirium cannot be reversed once it occurs, it is best to err on the side of caution and even to increase the dose if the warning signs are marked. Phenothiazines are best avoided owing to risk of their potentiating the liability to epileptic developments. Benzodiazepines can relieve some of the symptoms, and have an anticonvulsant effect.

With the *opiate group*, immediate withdrawal (the so-called 'cold turkey' treatment, having reference to the cold flashes and the goose-flesh) rarely involves risk to life but may be considered cruel, as it has no deterrent effect against relapse. The substitution method is again to be preferred. Methadone is the drug of choice because it is a sufficient substitute for the others of the opiate group, its effects are of quite long duration, and its own abstinence symptoms are milder. It is best given orally to wean the patient away from his liking for syringes and whatever symbolic significance they may have. The patient should be observed on what seems to be the suitable minimum dose. If the guess is a good one, two doses a day should keep the patient comfortable and enable 'stabilisation' to be achieved within 48 hours. It is usual to substitute 1 mg of methadone for every 3 mg of morphine, and 1 mg of methadone for every 2 mg of heroin that the patient claims to have been taking. The stabilising dose may then be halved and gradual reduction carried out, arriving at complete withdrawal within seven to ten days. This can be achieved with only slight discomfort. Most heroin addicts do not really want to come off all drugs, and the standard British practice is to provide oral methadone as a substitute at a Drug Dependency Clinic, although some people may continue to be prescribed heroin. The individuals concerned, who rarely see themselves as 'patients', usually try to get large amounts of the drug by giving an exaggerated account of how much they need, so that they can sell the surplus on the drug black market.

Prognosis

This is apparently better than is generally thought, though accurate figures are hard to obtain since addicts are notoriously shiftless, changeable and unreliable so it is difficult to follow them up. Many die prematurely, occasionally of an acute, massive pulmonary oedema, the cause of which is hard to explain, more often through failure of antiseptic precautions in self-injection leading to liver failure, bacterial endocarditis, septicaemia, etc. Many seem abnormally susceptible to intercurrent infections. Of the survivors, the prognosis seems to depend on two main factors. One is the length of the treatment. Early relapse is associated with its brevity. The second main factor is concerned with the social circumstances to which the patient has to return. Those with satisfactory personal relationships and some qualification to undertake interesting work have a better chance than the thrill-seeking, restless, personality-disordered addicts who neither work nor have social attachments except to other addicts. It is probably because of this that of those who started addiction for medical reasons 60–70% were able to make some more or less satisfactory drug-free adjustment. The results with doctors and nurses in the United States who had satisfactory and interesting work to which to return and who by law had to be followed up for 5 years, were even better and reached the surprisingly high figure of about 90%. So, prognostically, there is great variation from case to case. It has been estimated that over a longer period of 10–12 years, about half the 'teen-age addicts will be off all drugs for no obvious reason except perhaps that the process of maturation enables them to dispense with thrills, props and artificial aids to a better adjustment.

LSD (lysergic acid diethylamide)

This, though not properly a drug of addictive type, may be mentioned here because its indiscriminate use — mainly by personality-disordered adolescents — has created much anxiety. Although chemically unrelated to mescal (see p. 131) its effects are similar. Visual illusions and hallucinations occur, but visual experience of the actual scene is also enriched and enhanced, while movement and changing relationship of the surroundings may appear to be happening. Time sense is disturbed. Memories may be recaptured with a special vividness and intensity of feeling. These, and the visual experiences and the emotions felt, may become invested with a special significance and importance, so that a new world may be felt to have been revealed.

LSD has been used therapeutically in attempts to 'explore the personality in depth' and as treatment for alcoholism and various neurotic disturbances. Its value is not established, and acute psychotic episodes and chronic schizophrenia-like psychoses have followed its use. Therapeutic use has almost stopped. Both LSD and marijuana are sometimes followed by anxiety states with depersonalisation and fears of permanent mental damage which can be very distressing. They usually respond to chlorpromazine. 'Flashbacks', with the sudden onset of severe anxiety and perceptual disturbances even months after taking the drug, are a distressing complication, the mechanisms of which are not understood. In some people schizophrenic illnesses of classic type follow the use of LSD. Whether they occur in people who were on the point of breakdown, or whether LSD truly causes schizophrenia is unknown.

The 'opening of a new world' idea has led the intellectually curious as well as the personality-disordered into experimentation with LSD. Certainly this may be fascinating; certainly it is also dangerous. The altered judgements under its influence may lead to difficult situations, e.g. accidents involving innocent people, unwanted pregnancies, things said and acts done that are later regretted. There have also been reports of serious self-damage through lack of judgement, as by walking out of a window in the belief that he can fly. 'Trip-takers' and devotees of 'psychedelic experience' should be discouraged from taking LSD.

15

Psychomatic medicine

This is a very large subject, and one in which because of the several distinct meanings of the word 'psychosomatic', it is easy to generate more heat than light. In this chapter we briefly consider those different meanings, some of the conditions most widely regarded as psychosomatic, and various related subjects. The interested reader is referred to the bibliography, and particularly to 'The Foundations of Psychosomatics' edited by Christie and Mellett.

(1) The commonest use of the term psychosomatic illness refers to illnesses of proven structural or biochemical pathology, regarded as caused — to some important degree — by psychological factors. Many physicians believe that emotional factors play an important role in the development of duodenal ulcer, coronary artery disease and myocardial infarction, hypertension, asthma, ulcerative colitis, eczema and some other skin diseases, and possibly other illnesses too. Others think that there is no sound reason for believing that emotional factors play a more than secondary role, although everyone recognises that emotional disturbances will worsen the symptoms, and often the prognosis, of all of the above named illnesses, and many more.

(2) Another common use of the term 'psychosomatic' refers to the physical symptoms of anxiety or of some other powerful emotion, which are due to overactivity or dysfunction of the autonomic nervous system. Palpitations, dyspnoea, sweating, butterflies in the stomach or other unpleasant sensations, nausea and vomiting, colicky lower abdominal pain, frequency of micturition or of bowel function — the latter often amounting to diarrhoea — dry mouth and choking sensations are the commonest. These complaints make up a large number of those for which people consult their general practitioners, and they are of course the same as those found in anxiety states (see p. 245). They are the reason that so many anxious people are convinced they have some physical illness — especially of the heart.

(3) A related aspect is the study and intercorrelation of various somatic and psychological measures, not necessarily studying patients

or illness, but in a psycho-physiological way. One example is the study of the effects of different mood states on endocrine function and, conversely, the effect of hormone changes on mood states, such as those in women throughout the menstrual cycle. This type of study, into what is often called 'The psychophysiology of emotion', is increasingly frequent, and should help to provide a firmer basis for clinical psychosomatic medicine.

(4) An important field, not usually considered under the heading of psychosomatic medicine, but reasonably mentioned here, is the patient's emotional reaction to any illness. This is especially important in those with long illnesses which affect earning prospects, and lead to prolonged hospitalisation. Likewise, the reactions to mutilation, to the threat to life of a heart attack or stroke with the inevitable fear of recurrence, or to a diagnosis of cancer, must all be taken into account by those caring for such patients in any way. The reactions depend of course on the personality and life situation of the patient as well as on the nature of his illness, and include denial of the truth, depression, anxiety, despair, anger, frustration, hopeless 'giving up' and hysterical manipulation. Most people of course react with constructive coping and realistic acceptance, even if they have difficulties in doing so.

(5) In recent years there has been increasing interest in the idea that emotional factors influence the resistance of the individual to disease, through hormonal or immunological mechanisms. For example bereavement has been shown to affect the immunological system, with depression of T-lymphocyte function. At present there is much research into the possibility that such factors affect resistance to neoplasia, testing the notion put forward long ago by a famous surgeon 'cancer doesn't happen to happy people'.

(6) The broadest application of the term psychosomatic is concerned with the relationship between emotional and personality factors and a wide range of accidents and physical illnesses. For example: the emotional aspects of heavy cigarette smoking mean that cancer of the lung has a psychosomatic background in many cases; motor cycle accidents and injuries are commoner in rather psychopathic and aggressive young men; alcoholics and heavy drinkers have many more road accidents than others; physical fitness, including control of body weight, is related to coronary heart disease, and obviously depends largely on personality and attitudes. Many more examples could be adduced to illustrate the point, that personality factors largely determine someone's life style which in turn partly determines the type of illness he will develop.

Having outlined various ways in which emotional factors can be involved in the development of physical illness, it must be made clear that even in cases where the importance of these factors seems obvious, psychiatric and psychological treatment will not necessarily be helpful. It can be taken as a good working rule that if someone has psychiatric symptoms which justify treatment in their own right, and also has some physical illness, successful treatment of the former often helps the latter. If the patient is not aware of any emotional disturbance or is someone obviously 'disturbed' to others, but who refuses to discuss or face it, psychiatric treatment is likely to have no effect or may even be harmful. The benefits of psychiatric treatment are seen quite frequently in those cases of eczema and hypertension who come to psychiatric attention for coexisting depression or anxiety, and improve a great deal physically after psychiatric treatment. Even malignant hypertension, with papilloedema, has been known to be reversed by pre-frontal leucotomy carried out for a coexisting psychiatric illness.

Reactions to illness

The reactions of patients and their families to illness are usually as expected — appropriate concern and action, and most people can display great fortitude when it is really necessary. Problems may arise unexpectedly when a patient's reactions seem inappropriate to the situation. A common cause of this is the fear of cancer or some grave illness, even if to the doctor there is nothing serious. In other cases the opposite happens, and the patient seems unable to face the reality of a serious situation, failing to consult the doctor about obviously sinister developments such as a lump in the breast or haematuria. People can deny to themselves the reality of intolerable worries not only about physical illness, but about situations such as the impending death of a child, or the probability that the spouse is having an affair. There is in fact a wide spectrum of possible responses, from excessive hypochondriacal worry, through realistic concern, to total denial.

Nearly all serious illnesses need not only physical resistance and effective treatment, but cooperation by the patient and some spirit and will to live. When someone loses this the prognosis worsens, and people can give up and die unexpectedly. A man to whom this applied was a 50-year-old who had been caring for his hemiplegic wife after a stroke, when he had a myocardial infarct, and consequent renal damage. He coped well with renal dialysis, awaiting a renal transplant, until each of his brothers refused to donate a kidney. He became depressed and apathetic, ceased to cooperate actively, and died a few months later.

It is common for people suffering from chronic painful conditions to become depressed. Chronic rheumatoid and osteo-arthritis, with the limitations they impose on life, and the feeling of hopelessness they engender, are good examples. Depression lowers the individual's capacity to cope, and often leads to an increased awareness of the pain and stiffness, lessens the ability to take an interest in other things, and generally intensifies the patient's suffering. Many of these patients can be helped by antidepressants and by lessening social isolation, and the doctor should always be alert to the possibility of depression, and not regard it as inevitable and untreatable in this type of illness.

Physical symptoms and emotional disturbances

Emotional disturbances and psychiatric illnesses can present with physical symptoms which suggest, or even mimic, physical disease, and can be very misleading. Some of these presentations are briefly mentioned in later sections, as are constipation, anorexia, and weight loss in depression. Usually these are obviously secondary to depression, but sometimes one or more may become the major presenting problem. For example, constipation in an elderly man, in whom the depression is not recognised, may lead to detailed investigation for a bowel neoplasm, and the patient's increasing agitation is then regarded as due to natural worry about cancer. A patient with anorexia and weight loss, again secondary to depression, may be similarly investigated for carcinoma of the stomach. These are natural mistakes, and in fact the clinical picture may demand such investigation. What is a clinical error is to fail to think of depression as a cause after negative investigations, and turn the patient away with reassurances which do nothing for the underlying depression. It is as important for the physician, or surgeon, to be able to examine the mental state briefly, as for a psychiatrist to be able to do a basic neurological examination.

There are several other very common misleading presentations, and a host of uncommon ones. Palpitations and tachycardia due to anxiety, often associated with chest pain and dyspnoea, are perhaps the most common, and rarely go unrecognised by the doctor after screening investigations, especially for thyrotoxicosis. Unfortunately, many patients experience cardiac symptoms in panic attacks, with a fear of passing out or impending death, and they can be very difficult to reassure. If they fail to improve after reassurance it is not enough to prescribe a benzodiazepine and discharge them. They should be examined psychiatrically and treated appropriately.

A closely related and equally common problem presents when a patient reacts to some organic illness with an abnormal degree of anxiety. This is perhaps most common with cardiovascular disease, when anxiety raises blood pressure, causes tachycardia, dyspnoea, easy fatigue, and other symptoms which could be due either to the illness or to the patient's reaction. The heart has profound connotations as the very mainspring of life and seat of the emotions, and heart disease is a frightening idea to almost everyone.

Many patients after myocardial infarction need psychological rehabilitation as well as appropriate physical treatment. It has been demonstrated that psychological counselling, with discussion of the fears about activity, especially of sexual intercourse and its risks, and similar anxieties, improves functional recovery after myocardial infarcts, and greatly lessens the hypochondriacal invalidism which is a common sequel.

There are some very common conditions in which it is almost impossible to sort out organic or physical factors from the patients emotional reactions and problems. As an example we can take a major cause of disability, chronic backache; especially in those cases in young or middle aged people who have lumbar pain, absent or slight radiological evidence of disease, and no neurological signs.

Back pain often has a 'dragging' and wearing down quality, and if severe and long lasting often leads to some depressive feelings. Difficulties in the home or at work, especially if there is much unexpressed resentment, commonly cause emotional tension, which in turn leads to muscular tension. If there is already some spasm of the lumbar muscles the emotional tension increases this, and a vicious circle of increasing pain, irritability, domestic tension and inability to work in comfort, is soon established. This situation is a common one, and responds badly to treatment, especially if the pain began after an industrial accident for which there is a possibility of compensation (see p. 94 for compensation neurosis). The patients involved tend to be tense and resentful people, with a complaining quality, but how much this is basic to the personality, and how much secondary to chronic pain and a lack of relief from treatment by doctors, is uncertain in many cases.

A related problem is chronic neck ache in depressed and tense people, more in older women than in others, in whom there is pain and spasm in the shoulder girdle and posterior neck muscles. The slightly stooping, head bowed posture of the depressive; the presence of strong resentments and tensions in the home — often unexpressed because of fear of the consequences — and some degree of cervical osteo-arthritis, combine to form a very characteristic picture, in which treatment by physical means alone is rarely successful. Several old sayings sum up the role of resentment and other emotions in causing pain, discomfort, and so on. 'He gives me a pain in the neck' and 'you make me sick' are common, and often relevant. How much such emotions can lead to structural pathology is a different matter, but they can certainly intensify symptoms if pathology is already present.

These few examples are given only to illustrate the kind of inter-relationships of physical and emotional problems which are so common in general practice. In any patient who fails to improve as expected from some straightforward seeming condition, it is worth reviewing not only the diagnosis and the treatment used, but also to consider whether some conflict, important life problem, hidden alcoholism, or depression is delaying recovery.

Reactions to death and dying

It is a common observation that over the past 60 years there has been a reversal of attitudes about death and sex. The public expression of grief and mourning has declined, and people have become embarrassed to show their sadness to the world and to their friends, while the opposite has happened with the overt discussion and almost morbid exploitation of sex.

This is relevant to the care of dying patients, whom it is too easy to avoid as soon as there seems to be no more active treatment to offer, because even doctors and nurses can be uncertain how to approach the patient, and to talk about impending death. Even clergymen are less able to do this now, and rarely attempt to help people 'prepare their souls to meet their Maker', as few have this type of religious belief now, and seem to be more involved in a form of social work.

The dying can become sadly isolated, and in addition to the careful relief of pain and other distressing symptoms it can help to give them the time and encouragement to talk about their situation, feelings, regrets and hopes. Most people dying realise it, even though they may not discuss it with their family, each side sometimes thinking that the other could not cope with it if it were brought out into the open.

Psychosomatic theories and research

As has been mentioned, the commonest use of 'psychosomatic' refers to illnesses of known organic pathology, in which emotional factors are thought to play a truly causal role, at least in some patients. Peptic ulcer, ulcerative colitis, bronchial asthma, hypertension, neuro-dermatitis, thyrotoxicosis and rheumatoid arthritis were those classically described, and others have been added to the list by various authors. The two main concerns of earlier psychosomatic theories and studies were first, the *stresses* which lead to some people to break down into physical illness, and second, the *personalities* or *particular conflicts* which render those people vulnerable to stress in this way. More recent psychosomatic studies and theories have been less concerned with the classical psychosomatic illnesses and more with the 'psychophysiology' of emotion as mentioned earlier.

Stress. This is a vague but extremely important concept, which lies at the heart of most people's views of psychosomatic medicine. It overlaps and in some ways includes such concepts as long standing anxiety, being 'hard driven', and the response to a sequence of life events, as described later in this section. To say that someone is 'over stressed' implies that he feels that he cannot continue to cope in the long term with the demands made upon him, without feeling unwell in some way. (It might perhaps have been better to distinguish stress from 'strain' as engineers do, where strain is what stress causes. The terminology however is too well established.) If the stress is sudden and intense, there may be rapid collapse and inability to function, but in the psychosomatic context we are usually considering long-term stress which the individual can more or less cope with, perhaps for months or many years, but only at the expense of increasing feelings of fatigue, tension and inability to relax. Thus, in many cases as the stressful circumstances continue, both mental and physical symptoms appear: tension is often the first complaint then anxiety, feelings of depression and irritability are common as are headache, muscular aches and pains, dyspepsia and the full range of somatic symptoms found with anxiety (p. 245). Alcohol is often taken to relieve the tension and other symptoms and this is one of the ways in which alcoholism may develop.

It is this kind of long continued stress that all doctors recognise as harmful to health in some way, even if they remain unconvinced that physical illness, with organic pathology, is likely to occur as a result. The general public in its folk wisdom has probably always believed in the causal connection, and in the past 20 or 30 years the idea of 'stress-induced illness' has been very widely accepted as proven, is written about in the newspapers and so on, and yet has left unconvinced many physicians and surgeons.

Selye's theory of stress and adaptation

The work of Selye had a great influence in those interested in psychosomatic medicine, although he mainly studied the effects of prolonged physical stress on experimental animals such as rats. He found that rats exposed to prolonged heat, cold, starvation or fatigue leading to death all showed very similar pathology, independent of the type of stress used. They showed adrenal swelling and cellular pathology ('exhaustion'), shrunken thymus glands and very often had bleeding gastric ulcers.

He defined stress as something which called forth a response from the organism in order to cope with it, and saw 'general adaptation' as largely dependent on the capacity to respond of the adrenal glands. First came the *alarm reaction*, with outpouring of ACTH and of steroid hormones. Then came an adaptation or resistance phase, in which the organism coped with whatever demands were made on it. If stress were too prolonged or severe, the stage of *exhaustion* developed, with adrenal failure and death.

This model was flexible and realistic, accepting all types of mental and physical stress as relevant; and, much modified by increased knowledge over the past 30 years, is still useful.

In fact, the evidence for the association between long continued stress of the type described and illnesses such as duodenal ulcer, myocardial infarction and hypertension, is extremely difficult to pin down, and is overall only convincing for myocardial infarction. There is ample and daily evidence that dyspepsia, pain in the chest and headaches are stress induced, but that does not mean that peptic ulcer and coronary artery disease are also. The acute gastric ulcers of the experimental animal are not really identical with the chronic duodenal ulcers of humans.

Very many illnesses are clearly multifactorial, and we can expect that many more will later be shown to be the same. There has been a steady decline in the incidence of duodenal ulcer in the Western world for about 30 years, after it built up to a peak in the 40s and 50s of this century. Myocardial infarction has been less and less frequent in the USA in the past decade, and is perhaps starting to decline now in England and Wales, where the incidence is already lower than in Scotland. Nevertheless, it is striking that in 2320 survivors of acute myocardial infarction rated for levels of life stress and social isolation, those who scored highest on these scales had a subsequent mortality *four* times higher than the least stressed and isolated group. Although diet, exercise, smoking, and heredity may be more important, psychosocial factors must be allowed for *after* the infarct if not before. It is the original causative link that is most difficult to establish.

It has long been known, of course, that emotional upsets, particularly anger or anxiety, will, by increasing the heart rate, bring on an attack of chest pain in someone subject to angina pectoris. Major emotional turmoil will precipitate a fatal myocardial infarction or a cerebral haemorrhage, in someone who at post mortem can be shown to have extensive arterial disease. What is uncertain is whether emotional or personality factors play a *direct* part (as opposed to acting through dietary or exercise factors) in the development of the atherosclerosis itself.

One major research difficulty is that of quantifying stress convincingly. If a man has a demanding job, with an awkward boss and a long journey to work, then has to take in his elderly mother to live with him, which in turn antagonizes his wife who, after a few months, leaves him to cope alone, no one would be surprised if he became unwell in some way, physically or mentally, and if his general practitioner gave him a certificate to be off work for a while. How would that rate on a 'stress scale' compared to that experienced by a woman whose husband dies leaving her with three young children, one of whom is autistic, and who has to move out of their comfortable home into makeshift accommodation because he did not insure his life?

Life events schedules (see later) do provide a measuring instrument, but they are crude instruments and concentrate on discrete events over a short period of time, rather than with long continued stress of the type illustrated in the previous paragraph, or with the even more difficult to quantify stress which arises from internal conflict.

One convincing study has, however, shown a relationship between hypertension and stress at work. It was of air traffic controllers, whose work demands continual vigilance and great responsibility, and which at busy airports is extremely taxing. It was shown that staff who were posted to busier air stations, although starting with similar blood pressures, developed hypertension significantly more often than those at quieter bases.

Human and animal experiments have produced plenty of evidence of disturbed physiology in all types of emotionally stressful laboratory situations, and in animals death can easily be produced. For example, the famous 'executive monkey' experiments showed that if monkeys had to remain vigilant, pressing levers in order to avoid electric shocks, many of them broke down physically, and death from intestinal lesions was common, as in the exhaustion phase of Selye's theory (p. 358).

Monkeys in a similar situation, except that they were powerless to avoid the shocks (not in themselves damaging), survived unharmed. Naturally it is tempting to extrapolate from monkeys to men, and many have done so. Interestingly, even in this type of study, personality differences in monkeys show through, and animals of stable and unexcitable temperament coped better and showed less pathology.

Another type of study, increasingly popular recently, is that in which the experimental subjects, mainly human, are equipped with ECG and other telemetry equipment, so that the ECG, blood sugar and other variables can be studied while the subject lives an active life. The ECG changes in rock climbers and of those driving in heavy traffic or having a disagreement at work are open to inspection, and can be correlated with, for example, changes in noradrenaline output as measured by urinary metabolites afterwards, or by simultaneous blood sampling.

Personality types and other factors

In the same way that 'stress' as a general factor has been seen as a cause of psychosomatic disorder, so tense, restless, hard-driven people were the first to be described as especially prone to certain illnesses, particularly to myocardial infarction. It proved difficult to demonstrate this type of relationship objectively, but in the last few years there has been a lot of evidence collected to show that 'Type A personality', which is an almost identical concept to the older one, is related to myocardial infarction (see later).

Another widely held idea was that sufferers from these psychosomatic disorders tended to be more *obsessional* than others. Again, this has not been supported by objective study. It is probable that the earlier psychiatrists and psycho-analysts who had an interest in psychosomatics, and saw these patients with physical illnesses, were seeing people who were indeed more 'hard driven' and obsessional than the general population, having been specially selected in some way.

Anxiety has been thought to play an important part in psychosomatic illness for many years, largely because people seen in outpatients for hypertension, duodenal ulcer and other illnesses were found to be more anxious than normal, both at interview and when tested by standard questionnaires. When cases were identified by population surveys, however, they were not more anxious. The explanation for this difference, between patients seeking help and those identified by survey, is that people who attend their doctor are on average more anxious than those who do not. Many consult the doctor for headache, dyspepsia and chest pain essentially due to anxiety and they are therefore more likely to have (for example) their blood pressures recorded than those who do not see the doctor, and so some cases of hypertension are identified. This type of selection factor has invalidated my studies.

Nevertheless, despite the lack of epidemiological evidence that anxiety and hypertension in particular are related, it is a plausible association. We know that anxiety raises the blood pressure transiently, as does any mental activity in fact, and that beta-blockers are effective hypotensive agents. Relaxation exercises with and without bio-feedback have also been shown to lower blood pressure in established hypertension of mild and moderate degree while leucotomy performed for intractable depression and tension has been known to reverse even malignant hypertension, with papilloedema.

Repressed hostility. This concept has also been widely proposed, especially in hypertension. It is based on the idea that if someone is unable to express the anger and resentment which he feels, perhaps to his parents or spouse, because of the way in which his personality has developed, and has no way of expressing such feelings — so that he may not even be fully aware of them — he has to 'bottle up' his rage. This in turn has been thought to lead to a build up of noradrenaline or metabolites, or to some distorted pattern of autonomic activity, which in turn leads to hypertension. Again, as with anxiety, this seems a possible, even plausible mechanism, but it has proved impossible to substantiate it by large scale surveys, and no one has yet been able to demonstrate that repressed hostility is more common in hypertension than in others.

It should be realised that in order to demonstrate such an association objectively and convincingly a measuring instrument, almost certainly a questionnaire filled in by the patient or a check list filled in by a skilled interviewer, would have to be developed. The technique used would have to detect accurately and reliably changes in feelings of which the subject is only partially aware, and of which he may be truly unconscious! The task is beyond our present capabilities but the questionnaires which measure conscious hostility, a much easier thing to do, show no relationship with hypertension.

'Giving up — Given up'. Another very influential hypothesis in psychosomatic medicine has been that of the 'giving up — given up' complex, developed in the USA, like so many of the important ideas in psychosomatics. This emphasises the way in which physical illness

tends to occur at a time in someone's life when he feels unable to struggle any more against adverse circumstances, when it 'all seems too much' and when the individual feels helpless and powerless to change things. Many studies in this field have been published and the idea is attractive and plausible. It is compatible with, for example, the way in which physical and mental illnesses tend to occur in clusters and tend to follow 'life events' as described later in this section. Unfortunately, in many of the studies published, it is impossible to distinguish accurately the patient's 'giving up' feelings from the effects of the illness itself. For example, take the case of a severely hypertensive man who has a stroke, after a period of a few months in which he feels unable to cope and struggle effectively: his impaired coping is just as likely to be due to hypertensive cerebral arterial disease as to be the cause of the stroke which follows.

Nevertheless, many experienced clinicians believe that people who put up a fight are more likely to survive serious illness, and that to 'turn one's face to the wall' is to usher in death. The body's defensive mechanisms, immunological and otherwise, are presumably those through which such psychological effects could show themselves.

Life Events. 'Life events' schedules are also mentioned in considering the precipitation of schizophrenia and affective disorders (p. 165), in each of which there is a marked tendency for illness to follow about 3 weeks after a number of significant life events. The schedules contain a list of events of many types, ranging from loss of employment to bereavement, getting married or moving home, to the death of a pet or the engagement of a sibling. A careful attempt is made to distinguish truly independent events from those, such as breaking off one's own engagement, which might be an early sign of disturbance, rather than a precipitant. The use of these schedules has shown statistically significant associations in diverse illnesses, including sub-arachnoid haemorrhage (in patients without aneurysms or angiomas), and myocardial infarction. The more rigorous the scientific methodology, the less striking the associations are, as is so often the case.

Perhaps the most striking of this type of association, demonstrated without a life events schedule, is the way in which the death rate increases very markedly in the surviving spouse after bereavement, at least in widowers aged 55 and over, in whom these developments are most marked. The commonest cause of death in these circumstances is from heart disease and there have now been several studies which have shown objectively that people do indeed die from 'a broken heart'. The death rate in the survivors rises sharply in the first 6 months, but then falls *below* that of the matched control population. After a few years it can be seen that overall the death rate has been the same in the spouses and the non-bereaved control group. In other words, the deaths of a very significant number, who have been in some way especially vulnerable, have been brought forward, and those who survive that danger period of 6 months or so are presumably the more robust or were less emotionally disturbed.

Type A Personality. So far criticisms have been made of the lack of objective evidence produced in many psychosomatic studies, but that certainly does not apply to the concept of Type A personality. The concept was developed by Friedman and Rosenman in the USA that coronary artery disease was much commoner in people of what they called 'Type A' personality: characterised by being competitive, restless, striving for success in work, very aware of time pressures, with a feeling of urgency and being rather aggressive and hostile in attitude to others. 'Type B' was used to describe people who did not share these attributes, which are ranged along a continuum of course, but which can be scored on a questionnaire, so that groups can be defined by scores and cut-off points.

Many prospective studies in the USA have demonstrated that those who can be classed as Type A are much more prone to develop coronary artery disease when followed-up for several years. They also tend to have such risk factors as raised plasma triglyceride and cholesterol, and increased diurnal noradrenaline output. Interestingly, Type A personality does not appear to be related markedly to hypertension, although that is itself a major risk for coronary artery disease. In the last few years there has been an increasing number of negative studies, especially from outside the USA. The epidemiology of myocardial infarction also does not fit the Type A concept; not only is the illness now declining in the Western world, but it is commoner in the unskilled and semi-skilled working classes, whereas Type A is commoner in managerial and professional groups. In one huge survey of 270 000 employees of Bell Telephone, poor education was more strongly associated with coronary disease than executive stress. The interaction of physical and emotional factors is obviously immensely complex and may well be different in different individuals and societies.

Alexithymia. More recently, another theoretical approach to the psychosomatic problem has become quite popular but unfortunately it is one of those without any real objective evidence to support it. The concept of 'alexithymia' is that people with psychosomatic illnesses have an inability to express their feelings in words, and that conflicts and emotional disturbances thus express themselves in bodily disorders and physical disease. It is certainly true that unsophisticated and 'non-verbal' people will complain more of physical symptoms when depressed or anxious than will those who are more used to putting their feelings into words. Where a depressed university lecturer may talk of his difficulties in communication with his wife, a depressed farm labourer might complain of a pain in the abdomen and of feeling 'choked', although he has rather similar difficulties with his wife also. These differences are well-known and widespread. It is, however, quite a different matter to relate causally an inability to put feelings into words with physical pathology. In fact, no studies have been published which produce any hard evidence on the subject and so far, no convincing measurement of degrees of alexithymia has been developed.

Specific conflicts. Psycho-analytic theorising about psychosomatic illness was for many years very influential although now mainly of historical interest. It concentrated on the existence of specific unconscious conflicts in specific personality types, leading on to particular physical illnesses. A good example is that of duodenal ulcer, in which one of the influential hypotheses put forward can be expressed as follows: the individual has a deep need for dependency, of an infantile and 'oral' type, but has learnt never to show it and feels shame and guilt about what he is barely conscious of. He keeps up a front of independence, but inability to reach emotional security activates his underlying needs and he develops increased gastric secretion, which leads on to ulceration. The increased gastric secretion is a manifestation of his 'oral' needs, that is for milk from his mother's breast, and the gastric hypersecretion is appropriate in that way.

SOME SPECIFIC DISORDERS

This book cannot provide a detailed account of the field of psychosomatic medicine, and the preceding section should be seen as an introduction to the subject, and in particular to the idea that emotional and more generally psycho-social factors are always relevant and sometimes of prime importance throughout medicine. It should also have demonstrated some of the difficulties there are in studying the subject scientifically.

There remain a number of conditions and subjects which justify separate consideration.

EATING DISORDERS

The commonest eating disorder in the western world is overeating, which leads to obesity and its many complications. Only rarely is this associated with obvious psychopathology although many psychological studies of the obese have been made. Some very obese people seem to use their obesity as a screen which protects them from, for example, sexual relationships with which they feel unable to cope. For most of the obese, the psychiatrist has little practical to offer. There are, however, the important syndromes, anorexia nervosa and bulimia nervosa which must be described.

Anorexia nervosa

This illness is serious in many cases and is one of those in which emotional and physical factors are continuously, and obviously interacting. The patient, nearly always an adolescent girl or single young woman, becomes emaciated through persistent refusal of food, the condition often beginning with a normal-seeming slimming diet which they gets out of control. She may well make no complaint herself about her emaciation, which she in fact desires, but is brought for treatment by her parents. The appetite may be in abeyance, even with revulsion at the thought or sight of food; but more often the patient feels ready to eat, but complains of feeling distended after only a mouthful, and resists all efforts to make her eat more. When pressed to eat, such patients usually resort to vomiting, while others purge themselves with laxatives, and almost always show both determination and ingenuity in hiding or otherwise disposing of food that they pretend to have eaten. The degree of emaciation may be quite alarming, and is the more striking in view of the remarkable energy and activity that such patients usually contrive to sustain. Amenorrhoea is part of the syndrome. A certain number of patients vary between overeating with obesity, overeating with vomiting, and food avoidance. In many of the sufferers there is a distorted image of their own body size and shape, and they seem to see themselves as larger than they really are.

Anorexia nervosa seems to be increasing in frequency in the Western world, a fact perhaps related to the increase in overeating and obesity in our societies, and the parallel fashionable interest in being thin; and perhaps related also to the increasing cultural pressure on young people to be sexually active even if they are not ready for it. In many families of anorexic girls food and eating seem to play a very large part; and in nearly all the patients affected there is a fear of sexuality, and a feeling of inability to cope with sex or even with sexually-toned relationships. The sexually unappealing skinniness and the amenorrhoea can be seen as a way of removing oneself from the fray, and prolonging childhood; and many patients worry a great deal, as they begin to gain weight with treatment, that they will attract sexual attention. As well as specifically sexual anxieties, other aspects of maturation are problems to these girls such as the independence/dependence conflicts with parents which occur in adolescence. It is much commoner in the more prosperous upper classes than in working-class families.

In some cases the illness seems to have the function of keeping the parents together as a married couple, if the patient believes that they are likely to split up 'when the children have grown up'. This kind of manipulative hysterical element is common in anorexia nervosa, and makes treatment more difficult.

Another common background factor is depression, perhaps precipitated by an unhappy love affair, which at first seems much like any other depression with anorexia and weight loss, but in which a kind of 'gear change' occurs. the depressive feelings fade into the background as the anorexic syndrome develops, and attention is more and more centred on food and weight. This sub-type of the illness is commoner in those with a relatively normal personality and family background and is the most responsive to treatment, often being helped by antidepressants.

Another common feature is marked obsessionalism, affecting various aspects of life, and associated with a tendency to brooding rumination on all the details of calories, grams gained and lost, and on various unhappy experiences of the past. Patients in whom there is marked obsessionalism do rather badly, and those who are markedly hysterical and manipulative do worst of all.

Course and prognosis are very variable, but overall this is a serious illness, with a mortality of up to 10% in the long run, in those who come to specialist attention. There are many milder cases who do not reach specialist units because they recover spontaneously or respond rapidly to treatment. Death occurs from malnutrition with electrolyte imbalances (especially common in those who vomit or use laxatives to induce diarrhoea), intercurrent infections, the complications of alcoholism which often develops in long standing anorexia, and from suicide. In some cases the starvation has a suicidal quality in itself.

These girls and, rarely, boys avoid all food, especially carbohydrates, and are sometimes described as having a 'phobia' of weight or of fatness. It is important to realise that the starvation itself affects the mental state profoundly, so that one is not only having to deal with the underlying emotional problems, but with mental abnormalities which arise secondarily from the starvation and consequent metabolic changes. These secondary changes are often difficult to understand and to empathise with, and, combined with the dishonesty about refusal and hiding of food, make these patients difficult to like, so that nursing staff and doctors tend to get irritated by them.

Treatment must be aimed at restoring weight to normal levels, and then trying to prevent relapse. In any but a mild case it is best to admit to hospital, as these patients need skilled nursing, and the situation in the family may be extremely disturbed and disturbing; the patient is often playing one parent off against another, as well as causing concern by her illness. In a mild case it may be worth agreeing a 'contract' with the patient, that if she manages to attain a certain weight by a certain date admission may not be necessary. The same type of treatment contract is useful in hospital, in that the patient is kept in bed until a certain agreed weight is reached; and a programme is drawn up in which various privileges and rewards are gained as weight is gained. Drug treatment is usually necessary especially at first and chlorpromazine or other sedative phenothiazine may be used and has the benefits of lessening tension and agitation, and also lessening the tendency to vomit which many of the patients have. Antidepressants are indicated if depression is marked; and psychotherapeutic discussions, involving the family where appropriate, are very important. Psychotherapy may be impossible in the early stages, but as the mental state improves with better feeding and restoration of normal metabolism, it becomes easier.

In a few patients, in whom all other treatments have failed, some psychosurgical procedure (see p. 436) may be necessary as a last resort.

Prevention of relapse in those who have responded to treatment is another problem. Essentially, these girls must be helped to develop and mature emotionally, a process which takes time, but can be aided. Emotional support over a long period is helpful with discussions aimed at developing a different view about life problems, especially about sexual relationships and family tensions, and interviews with the family where appropriate. Even in those who do fairly well there are often prolonged difficulties in the ensuing years, including depression and phobic states, and many abuse alcohol.

Bulimia nervosa

This is a syndrome in which the sufferer, almost always a girl or young woman, has bouts of eating excessively — in brief binges on high carbohydrate foods — and prevents weight gain by self-induced vomiting and, less often, purgation. It merges into anorexia nervosa, and some individuals show both clinical pictures at different times. There is rarely much weight loss and the sufferers may function apparently normally in most aspects of life; the binge eating and vomiting both being secret. They tend to be better adjusted personally and socially including sexually, than anorexics but are usually sensitive and feel unable to cope with the tensions of day-to-day life. In a mild form the syndrome is very common, and remains unrecognised unless some specific survey is being made.

In severe cases the frequent vomiting and purging can lead to severe electrolyte imbalances, with epileptiform convulsions, profound muscle weakness and tetany among the symptoms. Alcoholism develops later in many, as with anorexia nervosa. The binge eating often disgusts the girl herself, and depression and guilt are very common. Sometimes the amounts eaten in a short time are enormous, and severe abdominal pain is common, and even rupture of the stomach has occurred.

As in anorexia nervosa there is a morbid fear of fatness, but the threshold of fatness is set higher, as it were. The underlying psychosocial family problems in the severe cases are often as found with anorexics, but in mild cases no unusual family or personal problems may be obvious, only those so common in all families, and the underlying causes include social pressures to be slim combined with poor impulse control.

Treatment has not been noticeably successful but recent studies suggest that a behavioural approach with strict monitoring by a sympathetic but firm therapist, introducing 'discipline' into eating habits, with counselling for personal problems is helpful. The associated depression may need antidepressant medication.

Pre-menstrual syndrome

This is perhaps more widely known as 'Pre-Menstrual Tension', but tension is only one of many symptoms experienced. Almost all women are aware of some alteration of feeling or behaviour in the pre-menstrual phase, and in a sizeable proportion these can be troublesome or even disabling symptoms, and in some quite marked behavioural disturbances. The 'premenstrual phase' varies from woman to woman, but is usually up to 7 days before the period begins. Although contraceptive pills are widely used to treat the premenstrual syndrome, the symptoms can occur while taking them.

The symptoms can be either emotional or physical in nature. For example: a depressive and unstable mood, tension, anxiety, irritability, 'confusion' and feeling muddled and poor concentration are all common on the psychological side. Physically, there are often tender breasts, generalised aches and pains especially in the head, back, and stomach, feelings of nausea, dizziness, faintness and feeling bloated. In a large number of women there is also a feeling of physical clumsiness, and impaired efficiency both mental and physical and the irritability can lead to problems with the husband and other people, perhaps at work.

There is also evidence that women are more likely to commit suicide, fail examinations, have car crashes and commit criminal acts more frequently during the premenstrual phase and this has been used as a defence in court in recent years. It is possible, however, that this increased frequency of crimes is more related to the underlying personality and associated psychiatric disturbance than to purely premenstrual factors.

There is a greater incidence and greater severity of pre-menstrual psychological symptoms in those who are psychiatrically disturbed than in the mentally healthy, who are more likely to have physical symptoms if any.

The cause of the pre-menstrual syndrome is uncertain. One popular theory is that there is a relative lack of progesterone, and another attributes it to excessive prolactin; neither is well substantiated. It is worth noting here that many women feel especially well around the time of ovulation, which fits in with the idea that hormonal changes are important. It is also the present author's view that treatment with progesterone (which can be given as 200 or 400 mg suppositories for about one week before menstruation) can be very helpful. Diuretics are commonly prescribed and many find them helpful. Pyridoxin has also been recommended.

Nocturnal enuresis

This term is generally taken to apply to bed-wetting that persists after the age of 5 years. Recent large scale surveys show that the condition is very common, most cases show no psychological disturbance, and the problem is largely one of maturation of bladder control. Doctors, and psychiatrists especially, see a selected series in which psychological factors are prominent.

Perhaps the simplest possible cause is lack of adequate training, owing to the symptom having been passively accepted as inevitable so that it has persisted as a habit. This must be a rare state of affairs except in young children, but it seems occasionally to happen. We treated successfully a man of 27, who had never had one dry night in his life. His parents and all their siblings, and all his own siblings suffered from the same complaint. For them, enuresis was not only a family weakness but a family tradition. Explanation, persuasion and re-education relieved the patient of the symptom. Overall enuresis is commoner in boys than girls and a positive family history is common.

From the physical point of view, enuresis is sometimes associated in children with other conditions causing local irritation. If only for this reason, a proper examination must always be made, including testing of the urine.

The symptom certainly improves with age, and seems more likely to do so the less the patient is troubled by it or by other things. It usually ceases by the time puberty is reached, but is commoner in adults than might be supposed. Where it does persist, we are struck by the apparent absence of adequate psychogenesis, and by the frequent, though not invariable, association with other symptoms. Thus, the patients very commonly have 'irritable' bladders, in the sense that they are liable both to frequency and urgency of micturition, while they usually sleep abnormally heavily. It is usual to find that they were accustomed to leave the schoolroom for the lavatory more often than their schoolmates, that they prefer aisle seats in cinemas, theatres and churches, and are unable to sit through lengthy performances of any sort. They are peculiarly difficult to arouse at night, and often have to be dragged from their beds when due to get up in the morning. This is suggestive of physiological abnormality. It is said that enuresis in children usually occurs within 2 hours of going to sleep and that the volume of urine passed is remarkable in view of the short lapse of time since the bladder was emptied. We agree that the volume of fluid passed is often remarkable, but, on the other hand, we are much struck by the extreme inconstancy of the time at which it occurs. We also agree that the volume of fluid passed, and the part played by the hypothalamus, both in the regulation of sleep and in the liberation of anti-diuretic hormone from the posterior part of the pituitary, which is ineffective in deep sleep, are relevant considerations in the aetiology of enuresis as a whole.

Regular arousal at night in order to ensure emptying of the bladder is usually ineffectual. If the patient has not passed water before being aroused, he seems just as likely to do so after it. The most generally useful treatment, effective in about 75% of sufferers, is the electric alarm apparatus set off by the first few drops of urine allowing current to flow through a circuit. The apparatus is now widely available commercially and through child welfare clinics.

Drugs are useful in some cases, especially in those who sleep very deeply. Amphetamines (e.g. 15–30 mg Amphetamine sulphate at night) are well proven; but their use is generally discouraged now. Imipramine 25 mg at night is sometimes helpful, also on the basis of lessening the depth of sleep.

We regard most cases of adult enuresis as having some physiological disturbance rather than a primarily psychological one.

Stammering

This, again, is commonly considered a psychogenic disability, but is far more probably a condition to which psychological factors make only a partial contribution. Those who have studied it most fully ascribe it to an instability of integrated cortico-vocal function, probably related to a failure of either of the cerebral hemispheres to become the clearly dominant one. This is, however, another unsolved problem. The instability of function becomes more obvious when the patient is under stress. Such stress is commonly afforded by the feelings of diffidence and inferiority that the stammering itself arouses in the sufferer. Recent intensive study by psychologists (as opposed to psychiatrists) has rendered this a highly specialised field with the development of new and widely differing techniques which have changed the prognosis much for the better.

The most effective treatment is speech therapy, but psychotherapy and psychological management may be of help where there is an associated personality disorder, whether arising from the difficulties engendered by the stammer or from other causes.

We have occasionally treated stammerers with more or less success by hypnosis, since they may speak well under conditions of relaxation and may be so far encouraged by their success as then to feel more confident, but the effects have not been lasting.

Sleepwalking

This, though fairly common in children, is rare in adults. In children it may be associated with so-called 'night terrors', in which the child starts up from sleep, apparently terrified, but in a stage of consciousness intermediate between sleeping and waking in which he remains inaccessible. If there is such association, the condition will usually yield to glucose drinks taken at bedtime, since it apparently arises in relation to glycopenia. In other instances, it may represent the acting out, in a semi-sleeping state, of some conflict with which the child is preoccupied. In that event, the behaviour is more or less purposive, though not executed in full consciousness, and is likely to indicate the nature of the conflict. Treatment should be directed towards resolving this. The sleepwalking is unlikely to lead to danger, but for reassurance purposes it may be wise to prescribe small doses of sedatives, gradually to be discontinued as the psychological adjustments are effected.

In adults, we have encountered sleepwalking of two kinds, quite different from each other. One form has occurred in hysterical and exhibitionistic patients, whose hysterical symptoms verged on malingering. In their nocturnal disturbances they did appear to be asleep, but their behaviour was purposive, and had a stagey quality that encouraged one to suppose that they could have arrived at full wakefulness with very little effort. It appeared to be a dissociated state, comparable with that of the fugue (p. 275), but coloured by some degree of sleepiness. No fears were felt that such behaviour would involve any danger.

The other form occurred in stable men, who were known to have been quite sober, and whose sleepwalking seemed quite without motive or conscious direction. In these, danger was certainly involved. One patient fell 40 feet out of a window; another was rescued when found by a nurse hanging over the edge of a balcony. Both had a complete amnesia up to the moment when they were found, and each gave a history of having walked in his sleep on more than one occasion before. There was no evidence of epilepsy in either. The nature of the disturbance was not understood, but was not believed to be psychogenic. Beyond giving advice to sleep on the ground floor whenever possible, and otherwise to play for safety by taking hypnotics when sleeping above that level, it is difficult to know what treatment to prescribe for cases of this sort.

Tics and spasmodic torticollis

Tics are commoner in children but may persist into adult life. They occur most commonly in states of fatigue and debility or in situations in which the patient feels self-conscious or is under other stress. They are thus influenced by both physical and emotional factors. Sometimes a case may be considered essentially psychogenic, in that the tic may represent symbolically some aspect of a conflict with which the patient is preoccupied; for instance, a patient not previously subject to tics, developed a sudden jerking of the right forearm in a setting of conflict over whether or not to get engaged. He had long been in the habit of urging himself to action by saying to himself 'Get a jerk on'. He saw the connection for himself, and the tic stopped as soon as he had done so, although he remained in conflict for some time. In some patients tics and facial grimaces seem to represent suppressed anger directed at some close family member, and in many there seems to be some instability of cortical motor activity enhanced by emotional stress. Many cases of tic, especially in children, respond to haloperiodol. The dose should be built up steadily from 0.5 mg b.d. until benefit is achieved or Parkinsonian side effects appear. As emotional tension and anxiety make tics worse, other psychological help may be useful.

Spasmodic torticollis, which is also often considered essentially psychogenic, appears to us to arise from an instability of motor function manifesting itself in periodic disturbances of tone. It occurs only in adults and is commonest in middle age. It may or may not be associated with emotional stress; where it is, such stress appears contributory rather than causal. The condition is peculiarly resistant to treatment of any sort. Psychological treatment seems to exert no influence on the basic condition, though it may sometimes improve the patient's adjustment to it. Recently, promising surgical techniques have been devised in the form of a stereotactic attack on the ventromedial region of the thalamus in which small, distinctive lesions can be made by thermocoagulation, electrolysis, or chemical means.

Acute intermittent porphyria

This rare, dominantly inherited abnormality of pyrrole metabolism, commoner in women than in men, may come to psychiatric notice either because of mental symptoms or because 'attacks' otherwise hard to explain have encouraged an erroneous diagnosis of hysteria. The 'attacks' may involve abdominal, neurological or mental symptoms, but these may occur separately or together. Most noteworthy are bouts of unlocalised abdominal pain with severe vomiting and constipation (occasionally diarrhoea), which may previously have led to laparotomy; they usually subside after about 48 hours. Apart from or together with those, there may be focal lesions of the central nervous system, e.g. peripheral neuritis, facial palsy, optic atrophy, wasting. Possible mental symptoms, occurring in association with the foregoing or independently, range from those of organic neurasthenia (p. 88), through histrionic display and aggressive contrariness, to confusional states and delirium. The 'attacks' are often precipitated by the patient having taken barbiturates — sometimes sulphonamides. The best hope in diagnosis lies in finding porphyrins in the urine, though a history of having taken barbiturates and/or a family history may be suggestive. There is no specific treatment, though phenothiazines (e.g. chlorpromazine 25–100 mg q.d.s) may allay excitement and confusion. Barbiturates are to be avoided. The condition is rare, but should come to mind when otherwise inexplicable periodic abdominal and/or mental symptoms are encountered.

16

Treatment

We have repeatedly emphasised that in every patient there are constitutional, physical and psychological factors in aetiology. Our treatment should bear this in mind. Although there are as yet no treatments which will change the constitution, constitutional factors will often determine response.

All treatments in psychiatry can be considered under three main headings: (a) environmental change, (b) psychological treatment, and (c) physical treatments, and these should not be considered as in any way mutually exclusive. In nearly every patient each of them is relevant to some extent, although in many one will be more important than the others, and we hope to make clear in this chapter what is included under each heading.

As an example we can take the case of a middle-aged woman with a serious depressive illness of mixed endogenous and reactive pattern, as so many are. She has been increasingly failing to cope with her husband, a chronic invalid since a fall while drinking. Their relationship has always been turbulent, and just before his accident she had told him to 'go away or die' and leave her in peace. Her guilt about her ill wishes to him, which were immediately almost fulfilled, have led her to refuse a home help from the local authority. In this case an important *environmental change* is brought about by admitting him to a medical and her to a psychiatric ward, where she is given *physical treatment* by antidepressants and ECT successfully. She is then helped *psychotherapeutically* by discussions of the problems with her husband. Her guilt, already lessened by the improvement in depression, is further helped, and she is persuaded to have a home help on discharge. If her husband still has a drink problem, or needs further treatment for his disabilities, to do something about these is again part of the therapeutic environmental change. This kind of combined approach is the essence of psychiatric treatment, and the three main headings should always be in the back of the doctor's mind in planning treatment.

It is important not to view physical and psychological treatments as mutually exclusive, as too often happens when people have dogmatic theoretical views: our theories are not good enough to justify dogmatism.

We should not take the naive view that a disorder precipitated by psychological stresses must of necessity be treated by psychological means. We know, for example, that many depressions precipitated by grief respond to physical treatments. The view is naive because by ignoring constitutional and physical factors it regards 'precipitation' and 'cause' as interchangeable concepts. Nor should we fall into the opposite error, and think that physically determined illnesses can only be treated by physical means. If someone has a pre-senile dementia, environmental change by hospital admission and support for the family are among the most useful things we have to offer.

There are two more very important points to appreciate in considering psychiatric treatment, which are much less obvious in the field of general medicine. The first is the aspect of 'social trouble', the sheer nuisance value to relatives, neighbours, friends and society at large, caused by the behaviour of some patients including those with organic dementia and confusional states, and also many psychotic and psychopathic people. This is not often a problem in, for example, the surgical wards. If it is, and someone's behaviour is too troublesome to be borne, the psychiatrist will often be asked to cope, and the diagnosis will indeed usually be of dementia, confusional state, schizophrenia, mania or personality disorder. All this means that the way we have to treat many of our more disturbed patients is determined by society's dislike of them or of their behaviour, as well as by what is actually best for them.

The second of these general difficulties is the problem of psychopathic disorders of personality (p. 219). These are rarely amenable to treatment, being so much a part of the constitution. When severe they can cause unhappiness for the individual and others, and can lead to behaviour which seems to the ordinary person so strange and 'crazy', so infuriating and disturbing, that people feel that they must be 'ill' and therefore a psychiatric case. The personality of the patient and of those treating him always interact, and the relationships which develop, and the nature of the people concerned, have a marked influence on the type of treatment offered, and on many aspects of it. If the patient has a severe personality disorder, accompanying a psychiatric illness, then the usual treatments may be impossible to carry out, because, for example, of unreliability with appointments or medication, or because the patient is just unable to sustain interest in anything long enough.

The personality, whether seriously disordered or not, also sets limits to the results of treatment. The habitually gloomy and anxious remain so even after the successful treatment of a serious depression. This is a limitation which is not always recognised, and often it is only by talking with someone who knows the patient well that we realise that we have made as much progress as we are likely to. The same applies in the opposite sense. We may not realise how much potential for improvement the patient has until we speak to someone else, who may make it plain that the patient has not at all returned to normal, that further efforts must be made, and that it is our treatment which is at fault, rather than the patient's personality. This is an important message.

The therapeutic plan

When a diagnosis has been made, and the patient's personality and life situation assessed, a therapeutic plan must be made and environmental change, psychological treatment, physical treatment, or the desired combination of the three, decided upon.

In some cases rather different treatment is needed for the immediate relief of distressing symptoms, from that aimed at the underlying illness. For example, in a patient with a depressive illness there might be marked anxiety symptoms. *Symptomatic* treatment for the latter with a benzodiazepine could start before the more *specific* electrical treatment (ECT) for the former. Similarly, we may have to treat intercurrent infections, or make up for a prolonged period of poor appetite by adding vitamins. All this should be part of the therapeutic plan.

ENVIRONMENTAL CHANGE

The ideal therapeutic plan is that which combines the best chance of benefiting the patient with the least dislocation of his normal life. The first consideration is likely to be whether or not the patient needs to be off work. Most psychiatric patients do not; the great majority are better at work, and they should be encouraged to continue.

Indications for hospital treatment

The main indications for inpatient treatment are:

(1) *To remove the patient from a stressful or harmful environment*, such as a very tense home situation.

(2) *For the patient's own protection*, e.g. to prevent suicide, to prevent social embarrassments which the patient and family might have difficulty in living down, to prevent undue expenditure and extravagance arising from mental illness.

(3) *For the protection of others*, usually to avoid violence or the threat of it, or where the patient is socially a public nuisance, e.g. if delusional beliefs lead him repeatedly to make complaints or to threaten legal action, or if he repeatedly shows deteriorated behaviour in public, e.g. exposing himself or appearing unclad.

(4) *For providing treatment* which offers reasonable chance of benefit, without which the patient would get worse or would recover more slowly and with greater suffering.

In practice, the majority of cases that come under these headings are those with the major illnesses, i.e. the psychotic cases. Under this heading we include those with the so-called functional psychoses (schizophrenia and affective psychoses), and those with organic psychoses, e.g. toxic deliria, organic confusional states, and those cases of senile and pre-senile deterioration who are unable to manage their own affairs and have no one who can satisfactorily look after them.

With regard to *schizophrenic* cases, those who are young and have not undergone appropriate treatment should usually be sent to hospital, in view of the seriousness of the illness. Chronic schizophrenics who have been treated but with limited success, may do better outside hospital than in, according to the amount they can do, the amount of satisfaction they can get from life, the adequacy of their social adjustment, and their living conditions. But the more they live in isolation and have to fend for themselves without supervision, the more they are likely to deteriorate. For people with schizophrenia with late onset, in early middle age, usually of the paranoid or paraphrenic variety, admission to hospital is less essential; if their circumstances are suitable, it may be best for them to live in the community, especially if they are socially well-preserved and able to remain acceptable to their associates.

As to *manic-depressive* cases, it may be said that the manic patient should always be in hospital since he will be unmanageable in the outside world; the hypomanic should be placed in hospital, if possible, when he is wearing out himself, his relatives and his bank-balance, as well as when he is drinking to excess. The depressive should be admitted to hospital when there are (*a*) serious risks of *suicide*, (*b*) *delusions, ideas of reference*, or *guilt feelings*, and (*c*) if the patient is too unwell to cope at home or is deteriorating with outpatient treatment. these mean that the case is beyond ordinary conversational approach and requires special handling.

With regard to cases with *organic psychoses*, the necessity for admission to hospital may be very variable. Admission to hospital is often necessary for detailed diagnostic observation and investigation. After that, it depends on the state of the patient and the home situation. (More details are given in Chapter 7, on the problems of the demented old.) The disposal of those with toxic deliria or organic confusional states depends on the underlying cause and the physical condition of the patient.

While the foregoing psychotic cases constitute the bulk of those who will require admission, there are of course many others, perhaps with relatively minor conditions, who may benefit from hospital care. Such are cases of *reactive depression* who have become suicidal risks, or who require removal to a sheltered environment before improvement can be expected. *Severe hysterics* may require hospital care, and something of the control that goes with it, especially where their relatives are unable to manage them satisfactorily, or encourage them into invalidism through mistaken beliefs or undue solicitude. Cases of *anxiety with exhaustion* who have become debilitated and demoralised may benefit from rehabilitation carried on in the supportive atmosphere of hospital. *Severe obsessionals*, and other neurotic cases (including alcoholics) whose symptoms have become conditioned by, and habitually related to, their daily routine, may be helped by the de-conditioning effect of removal to hospital, and an inpatient programme of behaviour therapy (p. 406). Finally, a certain number of cases in whom the diagnosis remains doubtful may need to be admitted for investigation and further observation before any satisfactory treatment can be begun.

Environmental adjustment in hospital

Admission to hospital involves, apart from anything else, a sudden and complete change of environment; such a simple measure may bring about a striking change in the clinical picture. To effect this to best advantage care should be devoted to such questions as which ward would be the most suitable, whether the patient would be better in a single room, whether he is favourably or unfavourably influenced by certain other patients or nurses. His reactions should be observed carefully and suitable alterations made accordingly, as far as may be possible. The extent to which they are possible is often surprising.

The desirability of some occupation has already been stressed. In hospital this is met by '*Occupational Therapy*'. The name is perhaps unfortunate as tending to emphasise the aspect of filling in time, whereas stress should be laid on the far more important aspects of relieving unhappiness or discomfort by distraction, affording an opportunity for the recovery of real pleasure in activity, increasing self-confidence by tangible evidence of a capacity that had been doubted or unrealised, and often enough frank training in better habits of concentration and work. For patients in hospital, and for chronic patients of whatever sort whether in hospital or not, this form of treatment is invaluable. It is not achieved by suggesting a little knitting as an alternative to brooding or the depressing exchange of rival symptoms with other patients. It should be definitely organised and recognised as a form of treatment which the patient is expected to undergo, just as he is expected to take his medicines and whatever else may be prescribed. In this way a corporate spirit is developed, and handicraft classes come to develop a sociable atmosphere that has a value of its own. Apart from arts and crafts, occupational therapy includes industrial units (manufacturing and assembly work), games and recreations, which do much to reduce the patient's isolation, all an integral part of the occupational programme.

Resocialisation of the shy and isolated is another important aspect in occupational therapy; in work-like situations, domestic activities such as cooking and baby-care where appropriate, and in more purely recreational pursuits, the occupational therapists try to foster social contact, interest, and self-respect.

Apart from its value in treatment, occupational therapy can have some diagnostic value in doubtful cases, and it can throw considerable light on the extent to which the individual patient has progressed. The patient's behaviour in the work or occupational situation can be very revealing.

The more chronic the condition of the patient the more should his occupation serve some useful function to the community in which he lives. Thus, in mental hospitals the employment of suitable patients on the farm, in the gardens, about the house, and in maintenance work, is of mutual benefit in that the patient's own self-esteem is maintained through service to the community. The more such work resembles that which the patient will resume on discharge from hospital, the more valuable it is in his rehabilitation. Unfortunately in many hospitals in the United Kingdom union opposition to the employment of patients has hampered rehabilitation. The transition to a fully independent life can also be aided if facilities can be arranged for the patient to work outside the hospital for a time before discharge, whilst spending his leisure time under its medical supervision and within its sheltered atmosphere.

Day hospitals, hostels, and rehabilitation centres

Day hospitals are increasingly recognised as very useful treatment centres, not only for chronic patients, but for a wide range of acute disorders. A well run and well staffed day hospital can cope with all but the most severely disturbed, and the list of indications for admission as an in-patient also applies to day patients. In some cases the patient is too severely ill, the home environment too unsuitable, or daily travel impractical in which situations inpatient care is better. The benefits of a day hospital over inpatient treatment are several: most importantly there is less emotional regression and institutionalisation, and family and social life are much less disrupted when the patient is only in hospital during normal work or school hours; nursing and medical staff work shorter hours without the need to provide 24 hour care; and there are economies in all other areas too. The current policy of the Department of Health and Social Security is to provide 40 day hospital and 30 inpatient places for each 60 000 of catchment area population, excluding provision for psychogeriatric patients, which indicates well the recognition now given to day care.

Hostels and Halfway Houses. These are provided for those who are able to live outside hospital and work, but are liable to relapse if left to fend for themselves, or if they return to an emotionally intense home with which they cannot cope — and which cannot cope with them. They are therefore principally for chronic schizophrenic patients. Unfortunately, although many promises have been made by the government and by local authorities, far too few of these hostels have been provided, and charitable organisations such as the Cheshire Homes and Richmond Fellowship have done much of what has been achieved.

Group homes. These are mainly for patients who have spent many years in mental hospitals, usually with chronic schizophrenia, and who are markedly institutionalised. They are provided with a house in the community, shared between four or five ex-patients, and look after themselves, but are visited by social workers, community nurses or voluntary helpers, or by all three. A good deal of preparatory rehabilitation, especially in domestic training, shopping, and so on, is needed before they move into the group home.

Rehabilitation Centres likewise offer a haven to psychiatric patients who are not too disturbed for an active regime, in which treatment, whether psycho-therapeutic or physical, is combined with an elaborate occupational and recreational programme, the former involving the use of workshops where new skills or trades may be learned and the latter providing educational facilities in the form of films, lectures and discussion groups which, to a varying extent, may be organised and run by the patients themselves. Some areas have *Training Centres* for the mentally handicapped; and other types of *Day Centres* are provided by Local Authorities.

Mention may also be made of *Industrial Rehabilitation Units*, which may or may not be residential, and which are designed to cater for those who, having been obliged to change their employment for physical or other reasons or having been industrial misfits for whatever cause (including mental handicap), need help in their readjustment. Their aptitudes can be tested, decisions can be made as to the best use to which these can be put, and instruction given accordingly in the establishment's workshops.

Day hospitals, hostels, rehabilitation centres and industrial rehabilitation units are attempts to answer social problems that cannot be dealt with individually but need to be dealt with en masse. As such, they are or should be functions of the community, and it is to be hoped that such facilities will be extended in the way successive governments have advised and promised.

Care of the patient at home

The following professionals may be involved in the care of the patient in the community, either at home or in a hostel, group home, or other accommodation: the general practitioner, psychiatrist, community psychiatric nurse, social worker, district nurse, health visitor, and home help. It is the demented elderly person who is likely to have the greatest number of services offered, and the chronic schizophrenic also often needs a lot. If the patient is at home, dependent on relatives, the relatives themselves may need much help and support, as the burdens borne by them are often great. With so many different helpers, from several agencies, confusion and inefficiency are common, and a close watch should be kept on this.

Community Psychiatric Nurses have proved to be one of the most successful developments in psychiatric care of recent years. They are psychiatric nurses with additional training, and work either as part of a hospital based or general practice based team. One of their principal tasks has been the assessment and supervision of chronic schizophrenic patients in the community, where they can give depot injections as necessary, help the family in their reactions to and relationships with the patient, and keep in touch with medical and social work staff also involved.

They also play a part in the treatment of other types of patient, for instance, in supervising behaviour therapy programmes for agoraphobics, and in visiting a depressed patient, encouraging them to activity and self care, and so on. As in all aspects of psychiatric treatment, personal relationships are all-important, and to have a skilled and interested nurse visiting the home regularly can make a very big difference and have much more impact than an occasional visit to psychiatric outpatients. Thus the long-term care of many of the psychiatrically disabled needs a well organised community psychiatric service.

Links with community services

For patients with chronic or relapsing illnesses, especially schizophrenia, and for those members of vulnerable and problem families who are so often psychiatric casualties, inpatient and outpatient treatment are only part of the network of services which must be used. Increasingly social workers may be called on to help. They can visit the home regularly, provide emotional support, try and reduce emotional tensions in the family, encourage the patient to take his medication and to attend outpatients, and keep in touch with both G.P. and hospital doctor. They are able to note the development of emotional disturbance in other members of the family and give appropriate advice or refer for treatment; and they are also able to guide patients through the intricacies of the state industrial and sickness benefit schemes etc. In providing a psychiatric service to an area it is essential to have effective links with the local authority and its social workers. A few years ago the recommendations of the Seebohm Committee for the reorganisation of the social services were implemented. The divisions between mental welfare, child care, and other specialised skills were largely abolished; and 'social work skills' of a generic type are supposed to be offered by one social worker only to a family or person. The effects, from the viewpoint of psychiatry, were almost entirely harmful; and the administrative disruption and growth of bureaucracy in social service departments generally led to less efficiency. Recently however, there has been a return in practice to the more specialised social worker, after a basic training in common with other members of the profession.

Agreement and refusal to enter hospital

If admission to hospital is advised, the majority of patients will accept the idea readily enough. A certain number, however, will refuse. Of these, a few will be quite sensible people with reasons of their own. These need not be pressed. A few will have hysterical personalities and take pleasure in making themselves the centre of other people's difficulties. These need not be pressed unless they are proving an intolerable burden to others. Other patients will be rigid and obstinate people who refuse 'on principle' because they feel such a step would be 'giving in'. More or less trouble should be taken to persuade them according to the benefits that are likely to be gained. Others again will be vacillatingly indecisive depressives whose illness prevents them from making up their minds to any course of action. With these much trouble should be taken and they will usually respond to firm pressure, especially if the support of the relatives is enlisted. Alcoholics will often agree to enter hospital, but will change their minds at the last moment with various plausible excuses; the relatives should be warned of this contingency so that they are prepared for it. The remainder of those patients who refuse will be psychotic cases, hypomanic, manic, schizophrenic or with organic brain damage, who lack insight into the seriousness or abnormality of their condition. They may sometimes be persuaded to enter hospital on the score of treatment or investigation of some physical symptoms from which they may incidentally complain; but where this is not feasible compulsory detention in hospital must be considered. (This is considered in Ch. 17.)

The psychiatric emergency

These sometimes arise, such as the sudden development of catatonic excitement or threats of and attempts at suicide. The assessment of suicidal risk is described on page 201. An immediate decision may be required as to the patient's fitness to remain at large. If unfit, admission to hospital should be arranged forthwith, if necessary, under compulsion.

In the meantime, until the necessary arrangements have been made, the patient should be put to bed, where he can best be controlled, and his clothes removed. In dealing with excited patients, drugs will be needed in most cases in which hospital admission is necessary, although very often excitement dies down in a calm atmosphere after the opportunity to talk. The most widely used drug is intramuscular chlorpromazine, of which up to 600 mg may be used for a very excited strong man. Intramuscular haloperidol, in large doses of up to 60 mg, has the benefit of causing less hypotension and somnolence, and is extremely effective against psychotic delusions and hallucinations. It should be remembered that violent excitement and agitation most often follows fear and paranoid misinterpretation, and all concerned should be as calm and non-threatening to the patient as possible. Other helpers should be recruited, if necessary from neighbours or police, but should keep out of sight unless finally needed. The patient must be carefully watched (e.g. accompanied to the lavatory), with help remaining at hand, especially as some time may elapse before arrival of suitable transport or the local authority employed social worker whose help may be called upon (see p. 443). Suicidally inclined patients need equally careful watching, but milder sedation should suffice.

General Problems of Adjustment

Before considering more formally the main methods of treatment in psychiatry, we must remember the importance of all sorts of factors, many of which could come under the heading of 'Environmental Change' used at the beginning of this chapter. They are often quite obvious to all concerned, are the most important, and yet it may be possible to do little about them. Examples include loneliness, bad housing, aggressive and noisy neighbours, chronic physical illness, uncongenial work, the care of elderly and demanding relatives, and so on. A knowledge of what services are available through the local Department of Social Services, and voluntary organisations, and which particular office or person is likely to be most helpful, can be most valuable.

PSYCHOLOGICAL TREATMENT

This heading covers a wide range of activities and approaches, including various types of formal psychotherapy, several of which are described in more or less detail in this section, including psycho-analysis, group psychotherapy, behaviour therapy and so on. In its broadest sense, psychological treatment also includes all those interactions between people which go on day by day in the doctors' surgery, outpatient clinics and in hospital wards, and which are often difficult to identify and describe, but which play so important a part in creating the right atmosphere, and in helping people to feel better and to respond to treatment.

The beginning of the first interview with the patient is perhaps the most important time of all. It determines whether the patient will feel able to talk freely, will be able to trust the doctor, and will later follow the recommended treatment. Even the contact between patient and reception staff or nurses has an influence in this way, and to a lesser extent so do the physical characteristics of waiting rooms, consulting rooms, hospital wards, and the whole general setting. These continue to exert an influence throughout the patient's visit or hospital stay. The importance of them, and of many other factors, should not be underestimated.

Interview technique is briefly described in Chapter 5, the essentials being adequate time, good listening by the doctor, and the avoidance of leading questions and moralising. Privacy and quiet are also needed. It is almost impossible to make a detailed assessment of a patient's problems and mental state in a busy medical ward, separated from the next patient by only a curtain and a few feet of space.

Simple psychotherapy

Psychotherapy aims at relieving symptoms of psychic origin by adjusting the attitudes that have led to their development. It is an art rather than a science, and cannot be learned from books any more than can surgical technique. It is, however, possible to state some underlying principles of general applicability.

There are two essential preliminaries. The first is to gain the patient's confidence. Successful psychotherapy must depend basically on obtaining a good grasp of the case, and the facts cannot be gained without the patient's confidence being gained also. The sort of approach that is necessary for gaining a good history has been outlined on page 66. Some course must be steered between a booming heartiness under which the patient remains submerged but unsatisfied, and a nervous diffidence which he will come quickly to reflect. The second essential preliminary is the careful collection of the facts. The sort of facts that are required are listed on pages 69–74, and the sort of conclusion that should be reached is outlined in general terms on pages 74–76. A detailed study of this kind may render the symptoms immediately intelligible in the light of what has been going on in the patient's mind, whether the connection is recognised by him or not. But this is, of course, by no means always so, and in complex cases several interviews may be necessary before the case becomes reasonably intelligible in psychological terms. It is unwise to jump to conclusions; careful ascertainment of the facts must always precede any attempts at interpretation of the symptoms.

Even these essential preliminaries are not without therapeutic value in themselves. The opportunity of discussion may have come to the patient as a relief, and the formulation of the trouble into words will have helped towards a more objective view. The combined effect is to reduce the size of the difficulties in that the patient sees both them and the symptoms in better proportion, with the effect that he can face them more easily and constructively. In a sense, therefore, the treatment has already begun, with *ventilation* of feelings and *clarification* of problems.

When these essential preliminaries have been completed the treatment proceeds by stages which are often referred to as *explanation, suggestion, persuasion* and *re-education*.

Explanation consists in interpreting the symptoms to the patient in the light of the psychological processes that have led to their development. Many patients, although they should not be told that there is 'nothing wrong with them' or that 'it is only nerves', are able and even pleased to accept the reassurance that their symptoms are due only to psychological causes and will not seriously affect their physical fitness or mental faculties. Many sufferers from states of anxiety have no difficulty in grasping the principle that the mind affects the body, that their symptoms are the *normal* accompaniments of emotional disturbance, and find that the symptoms cease or are tolerable once their origin has been understood. Where technical matters are involved, such as that muscular tension leads to tremor, the explanation will have to be direct. The art of this depends on the ability to adapt explanation not only to the patient's intellectual level but also to his emotional needs. Hence the importance of the manner that is adopted. But aside from such technical matters as the relation between anxiety and autonomic function, it is wise to proceed by a Socratic method so that the patient, stimulated and encouraged by the therapist, looks for and finds the explanations for himself. It is only thus that he will fully realise the connection between his symptoms and his situation. If such explanations are imposed upon the patient he may reject them. If he finds them for himself, they are the more convincing to him, and his understanding of them will be both more complete and lasting. In explanation, therefore, the patient should play an active role; the role of the therapist should be confined to helping the patient where to look to find the causes.

Explanation, as has been indicated, may provide relief in simple cases, but there will usually remain decisions as to future action. These are likely to be necessary for such reasons as mitigating the stress to which the patient has been subject, or preventing its recurrence. In general, it is best not to give direct advice, but to help the patient to form his own course of action by discussion of the advantages and disadvantages of the possible alternatives. It may be necessary also to encourage the patient towards the development of firmer, or more yielding, or different attitudes, as the case may be. In making these adjustments, both internal and external, *persuasion* will play its part. This is usually considered to mean influencing the patient by reasoning. But in persuasion, there is always also a large element of *suggestion*. This may be indirect, arising from the doctor's personality, and from the atmosphere of the hospital or consulting room; it may be more or less indirect, as when matters are put subtly to the patient so that he brings forward as his own idea something constructive that has been hinted at by the therapist; or it may be altogether direct, in the form of plain advice, where other methods have failed, or when implanted in the patient's mind under hypnosis (p. 427).

When adjustments have been made in these ways, continued supervision in the form of periodic interviews may be necessary in order to ensure that such gains as may have been made are maintained. It is this process of helping the patient to apply his newly acquired attitudes and understanding of himself to the life-situation, and so to maintain his improvement, that is referred to as *re-education*.

Supportive psychotherapy is the term used to describe the 'propping up' of patients who can be helped to cope with the difficulties of life by regular, if infrequent, interviews with their doctor, psychiatrist or any other suitable person. An example is found with those elderly ladies, recovered from depression after the death of husbands on whom they were emotionally dependent, but who gain a surprising confidence from the knowledge that in a few weeks' time they will be able to see their doctor, tell him some of their problems, and thus share some of their burdens.

Supportive psychotherapy should concentrate on the positive aspects of the patient's character whenever possible. It should encourage independence of thought and action by the rewards of discreet flattery and approval, and generally aim at supporting self-esteem. It should not, if at all possible, be purely an occasion for repetitive complaints which are answered by non-constructive sympathy. The importance of some of these relationships is shown by the very marked deterioration which can follow the death or unexpected departure of the doctor, and the danger of creating unnecessary dependence should be remembered when arranging supportive interviews.

Psychoanalysis

This is sometimes equated with psychiatry as a whole by those who are ill-informed, and it has been variously described as 'the greatest discovery of modern times' and as 'the biggest hoax in history'. Its origins have been mentioned on page 10. It requires a special training for the understanding of its concepts and technique. On this account it has become somewhat divorced from medicine and from the rest of psychiatry, and the mystery surrounding it has been enhanced by the use of a special jargon which is difficult to understand. This last, together with the meagreness of published data, makes its results difficult to assess. Increasingly it has been supplanted, for treatment, by more brief psychotherapies often based on psychoanalytic theory.

Theory

Mental illness is regarded by most psychoanalyists as arising from abnormality of emotional development thought to be largely determined by early childhood experiences. The underlying theory was developed by Freud from the study of cases believed to have been hysterical, but now thought by some possibly to have been chronic schizophrenics. Although Freud included physical and constitutional factors in his original concepts, these have come to be increasingly ignored by his disciples and the emphasis is heavily on the psychological.

As psychoanalysis has been extremely influential, and is still a very prominent feature of psychiatry as practised in the United States, the student may welcome a brief presentation of the Freudian theory. Freud believed the mainspring of human behaviour to be an urge, which he called the *libido*, and which he considered to be an urge to gain satisfaction in accordance with the 'pleasure-pain principle'. And Freud believed this urge to have a fundamentally sexual basis. The underlying idea, derived from the fantasies and infantile experiences of his patients, is that the libido is the basic factor underlying the pleasure-pain principle of life. Freud believed that other methods of gaining satisfaction, of a not specifically sexual kind, were substitutes for the fundamental and universal one, but arising from the same driving force. In this sense, all satisfactions came to be sexual, and

Freud included under this heading much that would ordinarily be called 'sensual', and that is *far* removed from sexual as the latter word would ordinarily be used.

Freud believed this libido to be present in all people from birth onwards, but that the form in which it found expression varied at different ages. He shocked public opinion by drawing attention to the fact that even infants experience enjoyment that may legitimately be considered to be of a sexual kind. He described the development of the sex life through a series of phases. The newly born child was called *auto-erotic*, receiving sexual (or sensual) pleasure through stimulation of the skin, as when caressed. Later in the auto-erotic phase came satisfactions derived from the stimulation of particular areas or 'erogenous zones', first the mouth and later the anus. Oral satisfaction was gained first through sucking, later through biting. Anal satis-faction was gained first through retention of the faeces, later through their expulsion. Subsequently, the genital area became the main erogenous zone. Having passed through these oral, anal and genital phases of the auto-erotic phase, the child became, after about the first eighteen months of life, able to distinguish between himself and his environment, so that his desires became attached to things outside himself. This was the *allo-erotic* phase. His interest, however, was still mainly directed towards himself, with derivation of pleasure from exhibiting his own body, calling for approval from those around him, and sensual (or frankly sexual) self-stimulation. This, the narcissistic phase, was characterised by such overtly sexual pleasure as mastur-bation and love-play, but also by attraction towards the parent of the opposite sex. From about the age of 5 or 6, there followed the so-called 'latency period', during which the more frankly sexual feelings remained for the most part in abeyance under the influence of repression until revived by pubescence. The child was believed then to pass, in the natural course of events, through a homosexual phase in adolescence, followed by the final establishment of heterosexuality.

As to the less specifically sexual development, Freud conceived of the personality as coming to consist of three parts, which he called the *id*, the *ego* and the *superego*. The *id* was basic, and consisted of the individual's general energy, instinctively and unconsciously directed towards gaining satisfaction in accord with the pleasure-pain principle. He regarded the *ego* as responsible for the individual's adaptation to life in so far as it provided, through knowledge and reasoning, a conscious regulation and control over the rest of the personality; and also responsible for coping with the reality of the outer world. He believed the *superego* also to be a controlling force, but in an unconscious way, as being derived from those standards and injunctions inculcated into child by parents or other authorities and accepted so that they became an automatic regulating force exerting control without the intermediary of conscious reasoning.

Freud conceived that tension between these three aspects of the personality could result in mental symptoms in certain circumstances: for example, if conflicts of the ego, under the influence of id impulses and superego limitations, could not be satisfactorily resolved.

The smooth progress of the individual from one phase of development to the next depended on sublimation, i.e. the libido is redirected into channels permitted by the superego that are acceptable substitutes. When such normal development was unsuccessful, *fixation* occurred, and the individual remained fixated at a more primitive level of development than normal. Thus, according to the Freudian theory, the sexual perversions arise from fixations that have occurred in the oral or anal phases of development, so that the individual is left with a lingering inclination to oral or anal satisfactions, as opposed to genital ones. It will be realised further that such fixations are believed to take place at a very early age, so that according to psychoanalytic views the development of the person may be determined to a very considerable extent by the age of, say, 18 months. By then the seeds of personality traits may have been sown, particularly with regard to attitudes towards authority and the subsequent development of *complexes*, i.e. systems of reaction to conflicting feelings, tending to lead to the development of symptoms and arising from repressed sentiments.

Two of these at least may be mentioned, since their names are so well known, even if their meaning is seldom understood; these are the *Oedipus* and *Electra complexes*. (There seems nowadays to be some trend towards using the former to cover both sexes.) Freud believed, as already stated, that in the allo-erotic phase the child experienced attraction towards the parent of the opposite sex, with the effect that he wishes the other parent out of the way and experiences jealousy and resentment. The sexual attraction is frustrated because adequate satisfaction is impossible, the jealousy and resentment may give rise to conflict and, if sublimation fails, the sentiments may then be repressed into the unconscious in an attempt to resolve that conflict. When, after the latency period, the sex life begins again at puberty, the old conflicts are revived although at an unconscious level, with renewal of attraction towards the same parent, and revival of mixed feelings that include resentment towards the other parent. The individual has difficulty in managing these feelings through unawareness of their origin, and their persistence causes him difficulty both in social adaptation and in arriving at emotional independence. It will be remembered that Oedipus, though unaware of the parental relationships, paved the way for marrying his mother by killing his father, while Electra gained revenge for the murder of her father by her mother, by assisting in the subsequent murder of the latter.*

Treatment

The above are some of the main points of psychoanalytic theory. The analysis consists of interviews, lasting about an hour at a time, repeated up to six times a week, and continuing — it may be — for years. Traditionally, but subject to modern modification, the patient lies on a couch and is asked to say whatever comes into his mind, however apparently irrelevant and objectionable. The analyst is meantime behind the patient and out of sight. He encourages the patient to continue, taking special note when the stream of talk fails as this is thought to indicate resistance and therefore the proximity of repressed material. Apart from such stoppages, the patient's talk is supposed to depend on 'free association', one idea suggesting the next without conscious direction or control, so that dominant topics ordinarily kept under the patient's 'mental censor' are allowed to rise to the surface.

The data thus provided are interpreted by the analyst to the patient in the light of psychoanalytic theory, leading to further trains of thought and further exploration. In course of this, old situations are re-lived, the emotions associated with them are ventilated and the reasons for symptoms are exhibited. Meanwhile, the patient develops a special attitude towards the analyst who, as the person encouraging the revival of these experiences, comes to be associated in the patient's mind with the various persons, parents, siblings, bosses, etc., involved in them. This attitude of patient to analyst is known as *transference*, and the nature of the transference changes from time to time

---

*It has been a source of surprise to us that no place seems to have been found in the warp and woof of psycho-analytic theory for Dymphna, a Princess of Ireland, who escaped from her father in the seventh century, and eluded his pursuit as far as Gheel in Belgium, where he overtook and murdered her because she refused to yield to his incestuous desires. The apparent omission is the more striking since she was later canonised and became the tutelar saint of the mentally afflicted, so that her shrine became a psychiatric Lourdes and formed the nucleus of the now famous Gheel colony, where psychotic patients live at large under the care and in the private houses of the residents of that town.

according to the emotions that are activated. In fact, it is the transference situation that reveals the patient's basic attitudes, and the belief has now come about that it is on the analysis of this transference between patient and analyst that the success of analytic treatment depends. At the present time there seems much more emphasis than formerly on dealing with current as well as past experiences in course of the analysis, while current stresses and situations as well as the analytical relationship itself are regarded as factors in the recovery of repressed material. It is supposed that through the treatment the patient is enabled to understand his own emotional development, and through understanding to make appropriate adjustments. Apart from this, and in the absence of a formal course of treatment, analytic techniques may be of use in providing explanations for unexpected behaviour or attitudes that have developed in particular situations.

It will be seen that the theory, even as judged by this presentation of its bare outline, is elaborate and at some points far-fetched. Unfortunately, many of its later adherents have come to regard it not as a theory but as a creed or dogma, with consequent failure to review its shortcomings. This adds to the danger that any given case may be moulded to fit the preconceptions of the therapist. Its application has also come to be extended far beyond Freud's original intentions. Such attitudes and excursions have done nothing to enhance its reputation. Its aims are laudable, and especially in this respect, that the intention is to equip the patient to deal with life in whatever form and without stooping to those manipulations and adjustments of the environment that must sometimes be advocated by those, including ourselves, who practise other methods. In this respect its aims are basic and radical, but whether or not they are achieved is quite another matter.

Offshoots. The psychoanalytic schools of Adler and Jung are offspring of the Freudian school, whose legitimacy is not accepted by the parent. They differ in being far less specifically directed towards the sexual aspects of life. That of Jung makes a wider use of symbolism, and involves the conception of the 'collective unconscious', an 'unconscious' mind that is inherited and common to all mankind, that gives rise to common urges, not specifically sexual, that are not conscious nor related to rational thinking but are symbolically expressed in dreams, myths and legends; it is the collective unconscious, according to Jung, that is responsible for all the alleged essential similarity in the myths and legends of all races.

The Adlerian school is based mainly on the two concepts of 'organ-inferiority' and the 'will-to-power'. Here the prime desire for mastery of the environment, failure to satisfy which leads to conflict. Conflict results in the formation of symptoms which, by a sort of 'escape into illness', are an attempt at its solution. Both the pattern of the symptoms, and the fears of failure that give rise to them, are believed to be determined by 'organ inferiority', arising in gross form from some actual physical disability, or less obviously from some more subtle defect that has led to over-sensitiveness.

Whether the theories of the various psychoanalytic schools find general acceptance or not, whether their claims are justified or not, and whatever their limitations in practice, they have made contributions to a further understanding of the mind and its more subtle mechanisms. There has however been a most striking decline in the position of psycho-analysis in the United States in the past few years.

Formal psychotherapy (major psychotherapy)

By the term 'formal psychotherapy' we mean that the patient is taken on for a course of treatment, consisting of a series of interviews or meetings, which are devoted to helping him by purely psychological means. There is no clear cut distinction from simple psychotherapy (p. 386), but the latter usually takes place during the course of interviews devoted also to other matters, such as the result of drug treatment, and is essentially brief and limited. Formal psychotherapy is usually carried out by someone with special training, or by someone gaining that special training and being supervised in so doing. In practice, the general psychiatrist usually refers a patient for psychotherapy, or for an opinion on its desirability, rather in the way that a physician will refer a patient to a surgeon — seeking specialist knowledge and skills. If he is suitably trained he can do it himself.

There have been many changes in the field of psychotherapy in the last twenty years. A large number of therapies, mainly originating in the United States, have sprung up, and in some cases have spread to this country, but remain quite outside the range of psychiatry as it is usually practised. We will mainly describe the well-established.

Formal psychotherapy really began with *psychoanalysis*, as developed by Freud (see p. 389), and as modified by many other psychoanalysts. Psychoanalysis includes several different schools of thought and dogma, which often differ sharply, and is a very long drawn out procedure nowadays, taking an hour at a time, 3, 4 or 5 days weekly, for several years. In our opinion it should not be regarded as a therapeutic procedure, but more as part of the training of those interested in practising as psychoanalysts or psychotherapists of that school. It can be seen as a voyage of exploration of the human psyche which can lead to shipwreck, as well as to a sense of knowledge and satisfaction at journey's end.

Psychoanalytic (dynamic) psychotherapy implies that the therapy is based on psychoanalytic concepts and practice, usually by people who have been analysed, who may or may not be medically qualified. It is the original form of what can be called '*insight-directed*' psychotherapy, as opposed to supportive psychotherapy and behaviour therapy (q.v.). 'Insight-directed' means that the therapist tries to give the patient's symptoms and problems in adult life a deeper psychological meaning, very often relating them to problems in early life experiences with the parents or other important childhood figures. These are so-called 'transference' problems (see p. 392), and the therapist uses *interpretations* in dealing with them, and with other types of conflict or problem.

Interpretations are used to lead the patient to realise the unconscious forces which are at work, affecting and often distorting his emotional responses to other people. They are better illustrated than defined: for example, if a man loves and marries an older, rather motherly woman, is sexually impotent with her but is potent with other women, for whom he cannot feel strong affection, his therapist might comment that he has married someone like his mother — answering some deep need — and that this has inhibited his sexuality because of an unconscious feeling that this would be incestuous. The therapist's remarks, however phrased, are the interpretation, and the ability to profit from such interpretations is regarded as a precondition for successful insight directed therapy.

In psychoanalytic psychotherapy, as in psychoanalysis itself, the relationship which grows between patient and therapist is regarded as extremely important, because of the development of transference (p. 392). The patient is seen as responding to the therapist in a way which is more appropriate to his parents, or to someone else important in his childhood, and the interpretation of these transference feelings is another of the main features of this type of therapy.

Some schools of psychotherapy avoid interpretations of the psychoanalytic type, as in the American '*client-centred*' *psychotherapy* of Carl Rogers and his school. This concentrates on helping the patient (or 'client' to these non-medical therapists) to express and recognise his feelings by putting them into words. The therapist tries to help in this process of clarification, to share the distressing feelings, and to aid the client in coming to terms with his past and present.

This group has done some of the most important research in psychotherapy of recent years by identifying three of the personal characteristics of the therapist which are related to improvement. These personal characteristics they identified as 'accurate empathy' 'non-possessive warmth' and 'genuineness'. It has long been evident to those outside the main schools of psychotherapy that the personality of the therapist is more important than any theory used, but the Rogerian school were the first to go into this seriously. They do not claim that these are the only factors which count, just that they are the only ones they have so far identified. (Studies elsewhere have shown that the enthusiasm of relatively untrained therapists can at times outweigh the experience of their seniors, who are, perhaps, more world weary.)

'Accurate empathy' is the ability to express in words to the patient what he is feeling at that time — a clarification and a demonstration that the therapist *understands*. 'Non-possessive warmth' means that the patient does not have to earn the therapist's regard and personal interest by being pleasant or worthwhile, and that he feels a sense of warmth and interest without any sense of possessiveness or attempt at control. 'Genuineness' means that the therapist seems to mean what he says, is not putting on an act of, for example, simulated interest and compassion. These characteristics presumably apply to all forms of psychotherapy, and are stressed here for that reason, although the Rogerian school is not very active in Britain. These findings contrast fascinatingly with the classical manner of the psychoanalyst, which was supposed to be essentially blank and impersonal, so that the patient could more freely react as though to his parents, or with some expression of transferred emotions in keeping with the central role of transference and its interpretations in psychoanalysis.

Brief psychotherapy is a term used for a form of dynamic (psychoanalytic) therapy, increasingly popular recently in this country, in which only a limited number of sessions are used — perhaps twenty or thirty — and only certain specified personal problems tackled. Other forms of insight directed therapy have tended to have more diffuse and often unrealistic aims of causing major change in the personality, and have usually been unlimited in time. As such, they tend to stretch out for years, with the risk of harmful effects from excessive dependence and continual brooding introspection. Full scale psychoanalysis, lasting for years and years, is the most prone to produce these side effects.

Marital and family therapy. A family approach to the problems of children has been in use for very many years, as the effect of family problems and conflict on children has long been obvious, and to extend the idea to the treatment of adults is a natural step. One of the main emphases of family therapy is to see the patient who actually presents with symptoms as a kind of scapegoat, who carries the burdens and problems of the family, and who, in some way, helps to keep the rest of the family functioning smoothly by being 'sick'. Therapists of this persuasion use the phrase 'the sick rôle' a good deal, and put less emphasis on the personal characteristics which have led that particular family member to break down and develop symptoms, although he might have behaved differently if he had been different in his constitutional make-up. A family approach can be very illuminating and helpful, even though it is not suitable in every case, because it is certainly in the family that passions and problems tend to be most intensely felt.

In family therapy both husband and wife and any suitable children are usually present, but other relatives and even neighbours and friends are brought in by some enthusiastic therapists.

In marital therapy only husband and wife are involved, and it merges into the kind of counselling offered by the Marriage Guidance Council and similar organisations. A recent development is the use of behaviour therapy techniques, which sound comically simple but can be helpful, as when one spouse gives the other tokens (which may be pieces of wood or printed paper) to 'reward' the other for something which has been pleasant — such as not nagging for 12 hours or helping with the washing up. People often do not realise the harm they do by continuing in habitual ways, and an approach of this type, undertaken in a light-hearted manner though with serious intent, can help people to adjust to each other.

Parallel to these family and marital therapy developments, and closely associated in theory and practice, has been the growth of the sexual therapies, especially that based on the techniques of Masters and Johnson (see Bibliography). All of these methods and approaches are used flexibly, and have remained free from the kind of isolated dogmatism which developed in the various schools of psychoanalysis, especially between the two world wars. There is, however, the disadvantage that their protagonists tend to see all psychiatric disturbances in terms of family pathology, and inter-relationships, ignoring much else of personal meaning, and ignoring also the physical and constitutional aspects.

In the western world marriages and family life have been breaking up with increasing frequency, as divorce gets easier and easier, and the increasing interest in these marital and family therapies is perhaps a natural consequence. It seems to this writer however, paradoxically, that the therapies are themselves part of that same philosophy, or attitude to life, which is leading to the breakdown. The point is that too much emphasis is put on marriage as an institution designed to make people happy, with the assumption that if it does not do so then it should be mended or 'treated', and that if the treatment is of no avail, then the marriage might as well be scrapped.

Marriage as a social contract and institution has developed in some form in all societies, as a way of providing a stable environment for the vulnerable human young. When it also led to happiness that was good fortune. Now that its principal function has been diverted into the manufacture of happiness, and it can so easily be scrapped if not successful in that, the young are not getting the stable environment they need. Nor do the divorced and remarried necessarily find their second and third marriages any more successful. In marriages the commonest form of unhappiness lies in the unrealistic demands the partners so often make of each other. We see this for example when immature couples, marrying very young, seek qualities of security and stability in each other — like some ideal parent, always loving, tolerant and reliable — which they are quite incapable of providing. At the same time, each may be wanting an exciting companion and a perfect lover, such as they have been led to expect by our culture and its media of communication, and, of course, by serious minded marriage guidance counsellors, marital therapists and psychiatrists!

Group therapy. Group therapy became popular in the armed services in the Second World War, although sporadically used before that. It was at first mainly seen as a way of educating groups of neurotically-disabled servicemen into the nature and cause of their symptoms, but soon lost this didactic quality. It became more a way of sharing experiences and emotions, of thus gaining relief from distress and more knowledge about others and oneself; and, as a group forms a kind of microcosm of life in which the relationship problems of the world outside are repeated relatively harmlessly, the therapy offered a way in which people could learn to react differently to others.

Group therapy has been extremely popular with the organisers of psychiatric treatment because of its economy and flexibility. Therapeutic groups can be held for outpatients and inpatients, can be supportive and relatively superficial, or can deal with the most intimate and distressing personal matters as in individual therapy. There are several theoretical schools, which differ sharply from each other. Some more or less conduct individual psychotherapy in public, as it were; others have an almost mystical view of the existence of a group spirit or matrix, which is seen as the most important therapeutic agent. Some have a closed membership once they start, others are 'open', and new members come in as others leave. Some have one therapist, others have two, preferably one of each sex; some are officially leaderless, with no therapist in charge, although one can be consulted if necessary. Many have sprung up quite independently of psychiatric services or psychological schools, and have developed into the encounter groups so common in the USA, in which people come together, sometimes for a day or more at a time, in some of which physical and even sexual exploration is encouraged and expected. *Sensitivity groups* are also common, in which groups of interested people, perhaps would-be counsellors, personal advisers, psychotherapists and so on, discuss their own and the others feelings, trying to enhance their sensitivity and openness to others.

Most commonly in this country, free discussion and straightforward self-disclosure are encouraged among not more than eight patients at a time — the ideal number, as Lord Houghton declared, for 'a polite dinner party', though, especially as the interactions develop, the groups are not always 'polite'. They usually meet weekly, for about 90 minutes at a time, and after overcoming initial diffidence those attending may be eased by finding that they are not alone in their difficulties, and the belonging and participating helps those who feel isolated and unneeded. In a cohesive group in which people are working well together, the group influence may be remarkably powerful, but suitable selection of patients is essential for this.

Group therapy has the advantages over individual therapy that the patient is not in such a subservient rôle; he may accept insight and criticism better from his peers than from an authoritarian-seeming therapist; unhealthy dependence on the therapist is much less likely; and he can contribute to the welfare of the others by his own contributions, which enhances self-esteem. For many more sensitive individuals, groups provide too rough and tumble an experience, as people battle for dominance or express their anger, and many drop out for this reason.

Indications and contra-indications for formal insight directed psychotherapy

Unfortunately there is no general agreement about what type of patient is most suitable for psychotherapy, nor which particular type of psychotherapy is most suitable in various conditions. We do know, however, that the personality of the therapist is of great importance.

Many psychotherapists, especially in the USA, have taken the view that almost all patients should be treated by psychotherapy, even those with florid psychoses such as schizophrenia or mania, believing that by so doing they were treating the fundamental problems, while drug therapy could only treat symptoms. This misconception arises from viewing all mental illness as a purely psychological reaction to stress and conflict, and ignoring the physical and constitutional aspects, including genetic and biochemical factors; and also from ignoring the accumulated published evidence. On the whole, those who have taken that view, which has been less popular in recent years, have not had many dealings with psychotic patients in fact.

In our opinion, the role of psychotherapy in the psychoses is a limited one, and only useful after the acute illness has settled down. It can then undoubtedly be helpful in the resolution of conflicts, both internal and in the family, which may be adding to difficulties of life and raising the patient's level of anxiety or arousal. If such problems can be more clearly understood and thus ameliorated, not necessarily by prolonged or elaborate psychotherapy, the chance of relapse can be lessened. A common example of this is in the young schizophrenic, in conflict with one or both of his parents, and continually 'stirred up' emotionally. Sometimes family attitudes and reactions can be usefully modified; more often it is best for the young patient to leave home for some more neutral emotional atmosphere. Psychotherapeutic help can ease this move for both patient and parents.

The following case report provides another example of the useful, but limited, role of psychotherapy in the psychoses:

A 30-year-old woman had had recurrent schizophrenic illnesses, remained well on depôt injections of fluphenazine decanoate, but relapsed each time the drugs were stopped. She was in continual conflict with her mother with whom she and her husband continued to live. The latter was rather like her dead father, and was an unassertive man who suffered from premature ejaculation, and she was continually angry at him for this, and for his inability to stand up to her mother and to herself. After a series of individual and joint therapy sessions and successful sexual therapy, the couple were much better adjusted and found their own place to live. They were both happier and calmer, and her medication was reduced successfully, but when the drugs were stopped completely as a trial a year later, she again relapsed, exactly as before, and with no apparent precipitant. There is no doubt the psychotherapy was worthwhile in its own right, but it did not affect the basic course of the schizophrenia. In other rather similar cases longer drug-free remissions can be produced by psychotherapy and environmental change, but the patient remains vulnerable to any upheaval or 'life event', as described in Chapter 8, and not just to specific conflicts or problems.

The psychotherapy used in these schizophrenic patients should usually avoid the more challenging interpretations, for example, about infantile sexual drives and the Oedipus complex, which may be appropriate in neurotic patients who have stronger defences, and are better able to make use of such interpretations. To the schizophrenic, with his disturbance of abstract thought and fragmented psyche, 'deep' interpretations can be distressing and harmful. Support, explanation, and guidance of a somewhat prosaic kind, are usually more appropriate.

In bipolar manic-depressive psychoses, psychotherapy can again be helpful in dealing with conflicts and problems if any can be identified which deserve treatment in their own right, or which have a role in precipitating the major mood swings. If no relevant neurotic problems or conflicts can be identified, as is more often the case, there is no point in offering formal psychotherapy for manic depressive illnesses as such. The important stresses in this group of illnesses are, in practice, more commonly environmental, as described in Chapter 9, but the environment does include other family members, and psychotherapy can be useful here at times.

Formal insight directed psychotherapy is very rarely helpful in people with obsessional disorders, because of the ruminative style of thinking of these patients, as described later. For obsessional and compulsive symptoms behaviour therapy is usually more appropriate.

In individuals with marked psychopathic disorders outpatient psychotherapy is more or less useless, and only some kind of group in a special inpatient unit is likely to be helpful. Special units for psychopaths have been developed throughout the world, some firmly disciplined, as in prison psychotherapy units, some more or less run by the patients on group therapy lines. Unfortunately, because of the lack of well-controlled studies, it is impossible to know what, if anything, such attempts at treatment achieve. Similar scientific assessment problems afflict the whole of psychotherapy, as is outlined later, but most would agree that a good response to treatment in psychopathic personality disorder is hard to find.

Another important contraindication is found when the patient is too seriously depressed to begin the psychotherapeutic exploration of any underlying problems which may exist. If someone is having serious suicidal ideas or is unable to cope with the business of daily life, he or she is almost certainly too depressed to cope with psychotherapy, which may indeed lead to deterioration, and treatment is best aimed first at symptoms by antidepressant drugs, and psychotherapy can appropriately be started after discharge. Most psychiatric hospital admission wards are not well suited to formal insight directed psychotherapy, as they are more geared to coping with seriously disturbed people who need symptomatic treatment and support. A prolonged stay in such a ward while having psychotherapy can lead to rapid institutionalisation, sapping energy and initiative. Some special inpatient psychotherapy units do exist, but they are run on different lines. Inpatient behaviour therapy (p. 406) is, however, sometimes advisable because of the controlled environment which may be needed.

The principal uses of insight directed psychotherapy are in people with neurotic personality reactions and neurotic character disorders, as described in Chapter 11. Some of those described in Chapter 10 under the heading Disorders of personality and sexual devlopment can be helped to come to terms with their own nature, and gain other benefits, and the vulnerable can gain from support although they run the danger of excessive dependence.

The first essential is that the patient should regard himself as someone who has personal problems or conflicts, and not just symptoms, and he must be eager to change. If motivation to change is lacking, and the patient is more interested in talking about himself because he is such a fascinating subject, no useful result is likely. He must be reasonably capable of introspection. The first realisation that the problems exist quite commonly follows discussion with the psychiatrist, and one of the main functions of the diagnostic interview is indeed to seek for such problems.

In psychotherapy the personality of the therapist is one of the important factors, as described earlier, and the relationship which develops between therapist and patient, or between members of a group, is crucial. Another essential is an adequate grasp of the language. The patient need not be of superior intelligence as is often thought, but must be bright enough to cope with the situation verbally. It is interesting to know that most studies of those to whom psychotherapy is offered, at least in the United States, show that young, attractive, well-educated females of the upper social classes are the most favoured, even when fees are not involved. The poor, and poorly educated, the less personally attractive, less intelligent and the generally deprived, are less likely to get psychotherapy. It is presumably the same in this country.

It is also advisable that there should be a limited number of identifiable neurotic conflicts or problems, and that the patient should otherwise function fairly well in society. The more areas of life which are disturbed — work, social, sexual, family relationships — the worse the outlook. The impulsive and lacking in forethought, that is, the somewhat psychopathic, do badly, as already mentioned. The patient should be able to accept and benefit from interpretations, assuming they are appropriately made, being able to see something in a new light, with a new emotional response. It is not bad for the patient to put up some reasoned resistance to interpretations, and argue about them, so long as the discussion is constructive, and not purely obstructive. (Unconsciously determined resistance to psychotherapy is something the therapist must be alert to.)

The patient's style of thought should not be too ruminative and indecisive, as happens so often with obsessional personalities. Psychotherapy can become bogged down in endless, pointless theorising, or painful brooding on some sad episode or inadequacy; and unsuccessful psychotherapy, if prolonged, seems to intensify this type of problem.

Indications for group psychotherapy. These are similar to those for individual psychotherapy on the whole, but a group is a socialising influence, especially for the shy and those who are socially inept. Benefit can come simply from the regular social interactions, independent of more specific insights and so on, and this forms, therefore, a supporting indication. The realisation that many other people have similar problems can also be a great relief. As groups lead to less individual dependence on the therapist, they may be preferred in passive and dependent-seeming people for this reason.

Results of psychotherapy

In the past 20 years in all branches of medicine and surgery there has been an increasing sophistication in the assessment of results, and many well-established treatments have been scrutinised and discarded. The use of random allocation trials helps to overcome problems of comparability of patients and of diagnosis, and double-blind methods in drug trials help with observer bias; but in assessing the results of psychotherapy double-blind methods are not appropriate, and random allocation trials have proved very difficult to organise on a big scale although some informative small ones have been done.

There have been several large scale studies of patients referred for psychotherapy who never received it, but who, when followed up, showed the same degree of improvement (roughly two thirds improved, one-third not) that has appeared in many small scale studies as a result of treatment. From this many writers have concluded that psychotherapy has no sizeable effects and that this improvement rate represents the natural history of neurotic disorders. This has provoked supporters of the various therapies into passionate defence, but sadly not into the organisation of random allocation studies on a large scale.

Every doctor who has practised any form of psychotherapy has seen patients who have clearly been helped, sometimes with dramatic rapidity, and therefore most practising psychiatrists, as well as non-medical psychotherapists, have found the large scale 'no benefit' studies mentioned difficult to accept, as they seem to contradict daily clinical experiences. It is always difficult for anyone to be cold-bloodedly objective about something like this, and almost impossible to ask them to contemplate as useless something to which they have devoted themselves personally and professionally. A surgeon informed that radical mastectomy is a useless and unnecessarily traumatic procedure, as is now said by some, must experience the same difficulty; and similarly that surgeon must have seen patients in whom it was 'obvious' that the operation had been marvellously successful, even though a random allocation study might suggest otherwise.

There is much more evidence to support the usefulness of psychotherapy than clinical impression alone. Many studies show that identifiable, and measurable change, can come about through inter-pretations for example; and small scale studies have shown greater symptomatic relief from therapy in patients than occurs in controls, but in most of the studies there have unfortunately been flaws in the methods of assessment.

One very important factor in all psychotherapy which makes a medical type of assessment more difficult, is that many patients who enter psychotherapy do not in fact have symptoms as such, and even if they do the therapist might well consider these of little importance. A simple example is provided by someone referred after recovery from a depressive illness because the referring psychiatrist thinks that neurotic conflicts within the marriage have been among the factors leading to the depression. A symptom-free patient therefore begins therapy with the aim of discussing and sorting out various marital and personal conflicts, during the course of which therapy much distressing discussion may take place, leading to anxiety and even depression in the patient. Nevertheless, the therapy may be experienced as helpful, although a standard symptom rating scale might suggest the opposite.

Many people go into psychotherapy who have never been overtly disturbed at all psychiatrically, and have certainly not been 'ill'. They may feel unhappily inhibited in personal relationships or unable to form an enduring sexual relationship, be lonely and fearful, feel that they are achieving less in life than they should do, wish to experience things more deeply, or just want to find out more about themselves. In this country the National Health Service does not cater much for these people, but in private practice they form a large part of those in psychotherapy and psychoanalysis, and in the USA an enormous number of people have had psychotherapy of one kind or another for problems like these, and have invested much time and money in it. There is some evidence that the public's enthusiasm for orthodox psychotherapy for the mentally not-too-bad is waning now in the USA, but other methods of 'life enhancing' therapy keep springing up, most of which appeal principally to the young.

Psychotherapy, which began as part of medicine, offering treatment to the ill, has slowly become seen as a way of helping people to happiness and fulfillment. In a society in which most people do not have to worry about satisfying the need for food, warmth and shelter, there is progressively less to be concerned with apart from problems which probably would have seemed incomprehensible to our early ancestors; and people seem increasingly dissatisfied with the quality of their lives as their standard of living improves. In this setting of personal and social dissatisfaction it can be imagined that an objective assessment of the effect of psychotherapy is extremely difficult. It is also of little importance to us here. What we do need is to clarify its contribution in the more limited field of psychiatric disturbance.

There remains another important aspect to consider when trying to make sense of the negative findings of some large scale studies, and the way these contradict smaller studies and personal experience. In the research work by the Rogerian school already referred to, in which accurate empathy, genuineness and non-possessive warmth were confirmed as valuable, it was found in the early studies that many patients offered psychotherapy actually became worse during treatment. Deterioration was associated with an absence of the three desirable characteristics mentioned; but we should consider this in a broader way. Most treatment studies in all branches of medicine use categories such as: No change; improved; much improved, and cured. The idea that some people might be made worse is too often not seriously contemplated, and that has certainly been true of many psychotherapy, and other, outcome studies, although with increasing sophistication has gone an increasing honesty about this. In some groups of patients as many may be harmed as helped. In any follow-up study there are many patients who cannot be contacted for various reasons, and also many drop outs; we can assume that these will include many of those who feel that the treatment is irrelevant or positively harmful, but their absence is easily ignored in the final statistics.

It is probable that the personal and clinical impressions of individual improvement are correct but that those who do badly are not recognised as so doing, or if they are, we naturally tend to forget them. This is at least a partial explanation of the contradictory results. Our response should be further research into the refinements of psychotherapy. Patients should not be referred for 'psychotherapy', any more than they are for 'surgery', but we should consider the details of which type of treatment, when, under what conditions, for how long, and by whom. The last is perhaps the most important consideration, and indicates the importance of the training of the psychotherapist, as well as of the need for further research.

Behaviour therapy

This term covers several disparate methods of treatment. The early methods were all based on psychological theories of learning derived essentially from Pavlov's work on conditioning. (More recently cognitive therapies and other methods, not based on conditioning and so on, still come under the general heading of 'Behaviour Therapy'.) They aim to abolish old, or to set up new, conditioned reflexes, and are aimed entirely at symptoms, deliberately avoiding attempts to treat 'the cause'. Behaviour therapists see neurotic symptoms simply as learned patterns of behaviour; a very different approach from that of psychoanalysts and psychotherapists, who tend to see symptoms as superficial manifestations of deep seated conflict and personality disturbances. There has been much unnecessary and unwise argument between behaviour therapists and psychotherapists, both claiming to be members of the only true church, and both making excessive claims for the efficacy of their treatments, but recently there have been some joint studies by behaviour therapists and psychotherapists trying to establish which method is most suitable for particular patients in particular situations.

Aversion therapies

These were the earliest behavioural treatments to become popular and were used extensively in alcoholism in the form of apomorphine and emetine regimes. Their importance now is mainly historical. The aim of the treatment is to produce a conditioned avoidance response to alcohol so powerful that it outweighs the patient's craving to drink.

This is done by giving intramuscular apomorphine 5–30 mg and offering the patient his favourite drink shortly afterwards, seconds before the apomorphine causes violent nausea and vomiting. This is continued day and night, in an atmosphere of increasing exhaustion and disgust, the patient sitting surrounded by unemptied vomit bowls, being exhorted and preached at (sometimes by tape recorded messages), until the very idea of alcohol is sufficient to provoke nausea and vomiting. The technique has physical dangers, is distressing both for patients and staff, is no more effective than less traumatic methods, and has been largely abandoned.

Faradic stimulation then became the most popular method of aversion therapy, and was used mainly in sexual disorders — transvestism, fetishism and homosexuality particularly. As an example of the technique, a homosexual would be shown photographs which he had previously selected as being erotically exciting, and would be given a painful shock to his forearm by the therapist at appropriate times. It is usually more effective not to give a shock every time a picture is shown, but to give it intermittently, so that the patient never quite knows what is going to happen. A refinement is to use the penis plethysmograph, which indicates even minimal penile enlargement on a mercury gauge like a sphygmomanometer, so that the therapist has some guide to the patient's feelings other than his statements. As the treatment proceeds, usually with daily one hour sessions, the patient's sexual interest in the photographs wanes, and in successful cases, his general homosexual interest wanes.

One of the greatest problems with this technique in treating any sexual deviation, is that it is purely negative, and heterosexual feelings do not necessarily fill the emotional void created by the loss of homosexual or other urges. The patient's life is to that extent emptier, and he may be more lonely and unhappy with no sexual life at all than as a homosexual, fetishist or transvestist. Positive conditioning techniques cannot yet help much, and so the most successful treatment is in those in whom normal sexual feelings and behaviour have also been clearly present.

During the course of treatment, depression and anger directed at the therapist quite often develop, and unstable and aggressive or psychopathic people do badly with these techniques, as with all others. These methods have also largely been abandoned, not least because homosexuals hardly ever present asking for a change in their sexual orientation, as social attitudes have changed so much. They can however still be used where appropriate, for example in men with urges to touch girls or women on the genitals or buttocks. If possible the aversive treatment for that behaviour should be accompanied by help in relationships with women generally.

Desensitisation therapies

These are more generally used than aversion techniques, mainly in the treatment of phobic or other anxiety. The aim is to lessen the anxiety which is associated with some particular situation by getting the patient to relax while in a situation which would usually provoke anxiety. As Wolpe, who largely developed these methods, said 'if a response inhibitory to anxiety can be made to occur in the presence of anxiety evoking stimuli, it will weaken the bond between these stimuli and the anxiety'. The provocation of anxiety can be either by putting the patient directly in contact with the real life object or situation, or by the patient using his imagination to conjure it up. *Real life desensitisation.* If the patient has a single monosymptomatic phobia of, say, spiders, he can, in many cases, be rapidly desensitised to them. He is taught to relax on a couch or in a chair, and is presented with a graded series of small pictures of spiders, working up through small dead spiders in glass boxes, through a series of progressively larger and nearer spiders. At each stage he deliberately relaxes, and does not pass on to the next until he is quite comfortable and free from anxiety. It is with these simple phobias, which rarely come to psychiatric attention, that the most successful results from behaviour therapy are obtained.

Real life desensitisation is much less successful in agoraphobic syndromes, which are difficult to treat effectively by any means. They are usually complex neurotic syndromes, with major disturbances in the relationships between family members, and the syndromes are usually only the tip of an iceberg. One method of treatment consists of taking the patient, usually a 'housebound housewife' for progressively longer trips out of the house. This may be effective, but often does not last beyond the period of treatment. The patient frequently becomes over-dependent on and emotionally over-involved with the therapist, who may become a kind of substitute for the husband in the mind of the patient. There is often an hysterical element in the agoraphobias, and the patients tend to manipulate the treatment situation — including the therapist — for more attention or some other secondary gain. However, as part of a wider treatment regime, as for instance when a patient is being treated with phenelzine (p. 423) or with psychotherapy, the patient should always be encouraged to go out for gradually increasing distances, either on her own, with a nurse, or with a group of other patients.

Another approach is to use a 'flooding' technique. Instead of a gradual desensitisation the patient is exposed immediately to the situation he dreads, although usually accompanied by a therapist for support and encouragement. A man with a travel phobia, for example, would be taken straight onto a bus, and encouraged to remain on it despite intense anxiety amounting to panic. This having been successfully completed progress can then be very rapid in some patients.   *Desensitisation in imagination.* This technique can be used in patients who can, while lying on a couch, produce a fantasy vivid enough to make them anxious, of their own particular phobic object or situation. They first work out, with the aid of the therapist, a finely graded hierarchy of anxiety provoking situations. Having been taught to relax on the couch, which may take several sessions using, if necessary, a semihypnotic technique, they then imagine the fear inspiring situations. Starting at the bottom of the hierarchy with the mildest situation, and only moving up to the next when completely relaxed and comfortable with each lower stage, they work up to the top.

A simple example is that of a young girl student, with a fear of vomitus and of people vomiting. Her grandmother apparently had had the same fear to a milder extent, but in the patient it limited her life quite markedly. She was unable to travel on a bus, sit in a lecture hall or cinema, etc., or sit in someone else's house, except in the seat nearest the door. Thus, if by chance someone began to vomit she could escape without having to go past the vomitus. She felt unable to marry and have children in case she had to cope with husband or child vomiting. This last situation was at the very top of the hierarchy, and even talking about it during an interview made her feel faint and dizzy with anxiety. She was taught to relax, using a mental image of a pleasant hillside scene where she had been very happy as a child, and she could bring this into her mind at will, with an immediate sense of calm and happiness. In eight weekly one-hour sessions, she lost all her fears of travel and cinemas, etc., and could contemplate child care with only slight anxiety; she remained well.

Desensitisation in imagination can be used both in simple monosymptomatic phobias like that just described, and in the more complex agoraphobic states, but the latter respond less effectively. As a general rule, treatment in neurotic states is less successful the more other people's lives are affected by the patient's symptoms: as for example, when a husband has to stay at home a great deal in order to lessen his wife's feelings of anxiety, and there is therefore the possibility of hysterical secondary gain arising from the symptoms.

Positive conditioning therapies

These differ from aversion techniques in that the desired behaviour is rewarded rather than undesired behaviour, e.g. drinking, being punished (positive as opposed to negative reinforcement). The electric alarm bell and pad widely used for enuresis fits into this category in a way, in that the alarm produces the reward of a dry bed, and there is no 'punishment' for wetting. A *Token economy* is a method of running a psychiatric hospital ward in which the patients are rewarded for good behaviour by being given tokens with which they can buy sweets, cigarettes or certain privileges. The technique is used mainly for chronic and regressed schizophrenics who are withdrawn and possibly mute. Each time they speak or make any personal contact they are rewarded with a token, but undesired behaviour is ignored as far as possible. There is no evidence that the method produces better results than skilled nursing and occupational therapy of conventional type, but these are often in short supply in mental hospitals, and the token method is still experimental. Similar 'operant conditioning' techniques have been used in disturbed children, and have also been applied to other neurotic conditions. It is too early to assess their value.

Another recent development in behaviour therapy is the teaching of *social skills*. The shy and socially inept person who feels unable to chat to others, especially if attractive and of the opposite sex, can often be helped by quite simple instruction. How long to look someone in the eyes before turning away, how to shake hands, how to develop and practise a few introductory phrases, how to be a bit more assertive and stand up for one's rights in a shop (or with one's spouse) and many other applications. They can be done individually or in small groups. The need for this training is clearly related to deficiencies in early training in many cases, especially when the patient has socially withdrawn parents, who never learnt the skills and so could not pass them on. For the prosperous classes in Britain the public schools have long seen this type of training as one of their proper functions.

Modelling techniques are increasingly used in behaviour therapy. They essentially rely on imitation and practice, so that, for example, the patient who has an obsessional fear of dirt watches the therapist picking up objects from the floor and is encouraged to copy him, while being given approval and support. Modelling of this type can lead to marked changes in behaviour, and there are complex psychological mechanisms at work, including desensitisation and social rewards. It forms part of many other behavioural techniques, as for example when the patient observes, and can 'model', the therapist's own calmness in a crowded store.

Side effects and contra-indications of behaviour therapy

If the psychoanalytic approach is correct, then purely behavioural treatment of neurotic symptoms, without attempting to treat the underlying conflicts, could lead to some other symptom developing as a substitute. In fact, this does not seem to happen in the simple monosymptomatic phobias at all, probably because they are rarely the expression of deep seated underlying conflicts, and are mainly examples of 'over learning' in anxiety prone individuals. In more complex neurotic states, particularly agoraphobia, behaviour therapy is not very successful on its own anyway, and is mainly used in conjunction with other methods of treatment. In our experience, the main side effects in agoraphobia follow improvement in the patient, and arise from changes in the family — as, for example, when a woman loses her symptoms and then leaves her husband. We have known such patients later return to the husband and settle down again with agoraphobic symptoms as housebound housewives. In others, quite severe depression has followed otherwise successful treatment, but agoraphobia often runs a fluctuating course and depressive episodes are common without treatment. Altogether, true symptom substitutes seem to be rare.

In the aversive treatments for alcoholism and sexual deviations, aggressive outbursts and depressive spells are common. The therapist must always be able to deal with these himself, or have suitable help if he is a psychologist trained only in behavioural techniques. Aggressive and psychopathic people do badly, as do those with severely obsessional or hysterical personalities.

PHYSICAL METHODS OF TREATMENT

These are most important in the psychotic illnesses, but have applications throughout psychiatry. They can be considered under three main headings: treatment by drugs; electrical treatment: and cerebral surgery, in order of importance.

Treatment by drugs

Before 1953 the drugs most used in psychiatry were (1) sedatives, for allaying agitation, restlessness or excitement, (2) hypnotics, for promoting sleep, and less often (3) analeptics, for stimulating those who suffered from lassitude and variable depression.

Chlorpromazine, a phenothiazine, was introduced in 1953, and found to be of great value in schizophrenia especially; and later the monoamine oxidase inhibiting (MAOI) and tricyclic compounds were developed as antidepressants. By 1960 the treatment of both schizophrenic and affective illnesses had been revolutionised, and many advances have been made since then.

Phenothiazines and other antipsychotic drugs

These now form the mainstay of drug treatment in schizophrenic illnesses, in which they calm agitation and fear, allay restlessness and excitement, lead to detachment from and then often to actual loss of delusions, hallucinations and ideas of reference, and control thought disorder and passivity experiences. They are therefore much more than 'tranquillisers', a term now used mainly for the 'minor' tranquillisers named in a later section. On the negative symptoms —loss of drive and of affect — they have much less effect. It is currently thought that their antipsychotic effects stem from their anti-dopaminergic actions on the meso-limbic system.

All schizophrenic patients should have an adequate trial of these drugs, and most of them will be helped. Some are suited more by one than the other, and as a general rule the more sedative members of the group (chlorpromazine and thioridazine) are indicated in markedly disturbed patients in whom the sedative controlling action calms them subjectively and objectively. In less florid illnesses, and particularly in patients during rehabilitation and after discharge from hospital, the less sedative trifluoperazine or fluphenazine, or one of the non-phenothiazine drugs such as flupenthixol, may be preferred.

The phenothiazines act quickly. The sedative and controlling effect of intramuscular chlorpromazine in adequate dosage occurs within a few minutes in even the most disturbed patients; and oral doses on an empty stomach take effect within 10 or 15 minutes. After weeks or months of normal dosage a patient may stop the drugs only to suffer a relapse, sometimes after a delay of several months. The failure to take continued phenothiazines after discharge from hospital is a common cause of relapse leading to readmission, a fact which all doctors should know, as it is not uncommon for the drugs to be stopped on advice from a doctor who does not realise the importance of continued medication. Most often however, the patient stops them because he feels so well, or because he very understandably resents the idea of being dependent on drugs. It is well worth while spending time with patients and relatives in explaining the need to take the drugs. If this is still unsuccessful long acting depôt injections may be useful (see p. 416).

We do not yet know how long it may be necessary to continue these drugs, but it is our practice to advise long term phenothiazines to those who have twice needed readmission after stopping them. In patients admitted for a first illness, who remain well on discharge, it seems reasonable to withdraw the drugs under supervision after 12 months. If they relapse on drug withdrawal after a full year of good symptomatic recovery, a longer period — 2 or 3 years on medication — should be tried before stopping it again. Even in those on long-term medication, as many chronic schizophrenics are, it is always proper to try reducing the dose and stopping it, perhaps every 1 or 2 years, under proper supervision, especially if the patient is keen to do so. So long as the drug is started again quickly if symptoms recur, nothing will be lost.

In some schizophrenic patients the 'activity' of the illness seems so great that continuous drug treatment is necessary, whatever the living conditions of the patient. In most, however, the drug treatment protects against relapse brought about by the patients' abnormally intense reaction to environmental stresses, often quite trivial seeming to the onlooker, but none the less sufficient to disturb the patients' equilibrium. Most often relapse in the non-medicated occurs about three weeks after the stressful event, which may be something like a move of house or change of job. The rôle of these 'life events' in the course of schizophrenia is considered in Chapter 8.

In practice drug therapy may be found continuously necessary in some patients until they change their environment in some important way: perhaps by leaving an unhappy home, making a happy marriage, being admitted to hospital or in some other way.

The phenothiazines are also valuable in other psychiatric patients. Chlorpromazine in particular is useful in calming and controlling the manic or hypomanic patient; it helps to relieve the agitation of the melancholic; and the restlessness and paranoid ideas of the demented, confused and delirious. Phenothiazines also potentiate the use of barbiturates and other hypnotics, help reduce the distress of intractable pain, partially control withdrawal symptoms in drug addiction, and are useful antiemetics.

On the whole the phenothiazines are of little value in the minor neurotic and depressive states mainly treated by general practitioners, despite some of the claims of their manufacturers. In the major mental illnesses they are invaluable, and they have replaced deep insulin treatment for schizophrenia, almost abolished the use of pre-frontal leucotomy for conduct disturbance in chronic schizophrenia, and greatly reduced the need for electrical treatment in mania and hypomania.

There are so many phenothiazines available that any clinician can develop experience of only a few of them. Those mentioned in more detail are therefore those which we have mainly used.

Undesirable side effects are common but rarely serious. They include postural hypotension with occasional syncope; and drowsiness, dullness, and apathy. These are most common with high dosage of chlorpromazine and thioridazine, as is excessive weight gain. All these foregoing side effects suggest that the dosage needs to be reduced.

Extrapyramidal disturbances ranging from a curious pottering restlessness to muscular rigidity and frank Parkinsonism are common with all phenothiazines, but especially with the less sedative members of the group, such as trifluoperazine (Stelazine) and fluphenazine (Moditen), and others which contain a piperazine ring and a fluorine atom. In some patients more severe and dramatic extrapyramidal disturbances occur, with continued restless movements of the legs (akathisia); or writhing, forced athetoid like movements particularly of the neck, and also of limbs, trunk, facial, tongue and pharyngeal muscles; and sometimes oculogyric crises occur. These disturbances are accompanied by feelings of great anxiety and tension. These extrapyramidal disturbances respond to antiparkinsonian agents such as orphenadrine (Disipal) 50–150 mg daily; benzhexol (Artane) 4–20 mg daily; or benztropine (Cogentin) 2–4 mg daily. Benztropine 2 mg and procyclidine (Kemadrin) 10 mg can be given intravenously for the more severe disturbances with immediate relief. Some patients, especially older or brain damaged, develop permanent abnormal muscular movements, affecting mainly the tongue, pharynx and face, known as *tardive dyskinesia*. This is an increasingly serious problem, much commoner with long term treatment, and very difficult to treat.

The extrapyramidal side effects are thought to be due to the dopamine-blocking effect of the drugs on the striato-nigral system. An uncommon side effect is galactorrhoea (milk secretion from the breast), secondary to a rise in circulating prolactin, which in turn results from dopamine blockade in the hypothalamus, where a prolactin-inhibiting factor is usually produced.

The anti-parkinsonian drugs sometimes produce a feeling of euphoria, and some patients became dependent on them, and may take excessive amounts leading to confusional states.

Phenothiazines may facilitate epileptic disturbances; and fluid retention with dependent oedema can occur. Patients on chlorpromazine may develop marked photosensitivity leading to unexpected and severe sunburn; and all phenothiazines may lead to pyrexia, and occasionally to urinary retention. On prolonged treatment opacities may appear in the lens and cornea, due to melanin also accumulated in the skin. Thioridazine can cause retinal degeneration. Cholestatic jaundice occurs particularly with chlorpromazine, and may lead on to hepatocellular damage; and rarely blood dyscrasias of various types develop due to marrow suppression. Liver damage and blood dyscrasias have been responsible for most of the deaths reported. Phenothiazines should be avoided in those with liver and renal damage, leucopenia, persistent tachycardia, and marked hypotension. Their tendency to potentiate the action of other central nervous system depressants (barbiturates, alcohol, general anaesthetics), and their epileptogenic properties should be remembered.

The side effects and complications may sound formidable, but should be seen against the enormous extent to which these drugs are prescribed without incident throughout the world. In particular jaundice and blood dyscrasias now seem very rare. Extra-pyramidal disturbances, and especially tardive dyskinesia, are the most serious problem without doubt, and tardive dyskinesia is appearing in more of those now very chronic and elderly patients who have been on phenothiazines for many years. It is essential to keep dosage to the minimum needed, and to try every now and then to manage without the drug, as described above.

Chlorpromazine. (Largactil. Thorazine.) This is the oldest and most thoroughly tried. It can be given by mouth or by intramuscular injection, but intravenous injection can be fatal. The useful dosage range varies from 25–50 mg at night for restless and disturbed senile cases to the relatively enormous doses sometimes necessary in young and very disturbed psychotic patients in whom up to 1000 mg daily or more may be given. Normally dosage should be increased gradually from 50 mg b.d. or t.d.s., and most schizophrenic patients will need not more than 150–500 mg daily in divided doses. In schizophrenia dosage must be prolonged, as mentioned before, but in other conditions the dose can be gradually withdrawn as symptoms abate.

Thioridazine (Melleril). This drug is similar to chlorpromazine in its sedative effect, and in dosage. Prolonged use may lead to retinal degeneration, but otherwise it is relatively free from side effects.

Promazine (Sparine) is less potent than chlorpromazine, and the dosage is approximately double, but it is claimed to have no toxic effect on the liver and has less hypotensive effect. It is therefore useful in the management of alcoholic patients as well as for the elderly. It can be injected painlessly.

Perphenazine (Fentazin) is about five times as potent as chlorpromazine, seems very free from toxic effects and causes little drowsiness, but extrapyramidal disturbances are common. Dosage ranges from 2 mg t.d.s. to 60 mg daily, and antiparkinsonian agents are often needed with the bigger doses.

Trifluoperazine (Stelazine) is of very high potency, leads to little drowsiness, and of all phenothiazines seems to us the most effective against the hallucinatory, delusional, thought disturbance and passivity experiences of schizophrenia. Liver damage and other toxic effects are rare but extrapyramidal disturbances common and sometimes severe. Doses ranging from 5–30 mg per day are usual, and antiparkinsonian agents are again often needed. A very useful proprietary preparation is the delayed release capsule of Stelazine 'spansule' 10 or 15 mg which need only be given once in 24 hours, preferably at night.

Thioxanthenes

This group of drugs has been developed in Scandinavia as a parallel range to the phenothiazines, with less sedative and more sedative members. They are, like the phenothiazines and all drugs useful against schizophrenic symptoms, dopamine blocking agents. Only two, flupenthixol and clopenthixol, are in use in Britain.

Flupenthixol (Fluanxol). By mouth, this drug is not much used in schizophrenia, although as flupenthixol decanoate it is a widely used depôt injection described later. It has useful antidepressant and tranquillising properties when given by mouth in a dose of 1–3 mg daily (in 0.5 mg tablets).

Depôt injections

Although phenothiazines are so valuable in the treatment and maintenance of schizophrenic patients, many stop their drugs, often because they feel well and are convinced that drugs are not necessary, or because of an objection to being dependent on medication. Others simply forget them. Depôt injections of fluphenazine, of two thioxanthenes, and of haloperidol are available, which slowly release the active drug into the circulation for several weeks after deep intramuscular injection.

These depôt drugs are most useful in patients who are unreliable about their medication. Slowly developing over-dosage can be a problem, leading to apathy and dullness, as well as to extrapyramidal side effects. A careful watch must be kept, and dosage can usually be reduced as time passes. An upheaval in life might need a temporary increase in dose to protect the patient from the over-reaction, leading to relapse a few weeks later, which is so characteristic of the schizophrenic.

When first used these depôt drugs were said to precipitate severe depression and suicide, but in fact this is not so, and the incidence of depression is no greater than in those on oral medication, and less than that in the untreated.

Fluphenazine enanthate (Moditen). Fluphenazine is a well established phenothiazine by mouth. As a depôt injection, the enanthate was the first to be introduced; it needs to be repeated every two to three weeks. After a test dose of 12.5 mg to exclude over-sensitivity, the usual starting dose in a Seriously disturbed young person might be 50–100 mg, and an average maintenance dose 25 mg fortnightly.

Fluphenazine decanoate (Modecate). This preparation lasts longer than the enanthate, and is preferable for maintenance, with monthly injections. Again, a 12.5 mg test dose is advisable and dosage usually settles down at 25–37.5 mg monthly.

Flupenthixol decanoate (Depixol). This is a thioxanthene. The injections need to be repeated every two to four weeks; a test dose of 10 mg is advisable, and the average maintenance dose is 20–40 mg every 2, 3, or 4 weeks.

Some patients are suited better by this preparation, which seems rather less sedative, but it is probably not quite so effective in controlling severe schizophrenia as is fluphenazine.

Clopenthixol decanoate (Clopixol). This is a more sedative and longer acting thioxanthene, recently introduced in Britain but well established in Scandinavia. A 50 mg test dose is needed, and the average maintenance dose is 200–400 mg every 3 or 4 weeks.

Haloperidol (Serenace; Haldol). This is not a phenothiazine but a substituted butyrophenone. It is potent and rapid acting, and most useful in the control of very excited and disturbed schizophrenics and in hypomania and mania. Intravenous injection of 5–30 mg will rapidly reduce major excitement, but most patients will respond to divided oral doses of 4.5–15 mg daily. Some need very much larger doses, of 100 mg daily or more. Extrapyramidal disturbances are common and severe, but otherwise it seems a safe drug. It has a distinctly depressant effect and as hypomanic patients improve the dose should be gradually reduced. It is sometimes used as a minor tranquilliser for which it seems ill-suited to us. It is available as a depôt preparation, with a 50 mg test dose, and average dosage of about 200 mg monthly.

Pimozide (Orap). This drug is a diphenylbutylpiperidene. It helps maintain some patients symptom free, without sedation, although of little use in treating disturbed patients. The dosage varies from 4 to 10 mgm daily by mouth. It is relatively free of side effects.

Very high dosage therapy. The usual range of doses of antipsychotic drugs has been outlined above, but very much greater doses of some phenothiazines and of haloperidol can be given, and at times prove extremely useful. Schizophrenic patients, resistant to more usual doses, can be given steadily increasing doses either until adequate improvement occurs, or until unacceptable side effects develop. Several hundred milligrams every two weeks of fluphenazine enanthate, or even up to 140 mg daily of haloperidol can be given. It is very remarkable that extrapyramidal side effects are not marked with these huge doses. It is thought that the anticholinergic effect of these drugs makes them act as their own antiparkinsonian agent when given in such large amounts.

Rauwolfia serpentina. Alkaloids of rauwolfia (e.g. reserpine) are also included under the major tranquillisers, but have largely been abandoned owing to the marked tendency to cause severe depression, and because of the superior effectiveness of the phenothiazines.

Anxiolytics (Minor tranquillisers)

This category includes drugs of widely different composition, but in recent years the benzodiazepines have almost supplanted the others, and are the only ones considered here. They are prescribed in vast quantities for the relief of anxiety and tension, and should be used much less. Their disadvantages have become more and more obvious over the past decade.

Benzodiazepines. These are powerfully anxiolytic, and there are many of them, with similar effect, differing mainly in the duration of action. Some are marketed principally as hypnotics, when they are used in larger doses. Dependence quite rapidly develops and tolerance more slowly. A genuine withdrawal syndrome can develop, including a picture-like delirium tremens, although in 'slow motion' compared to that of alcohol.

They are safe even in large overdose, but they do impair reaction time and judgment and should not be taken before driving. It is not widely enough known that they also interfere with learning. Students who combat examination nerves with benzodiazepines or use them to get to sleep regularly before examinations are likely to perform worse than expected, and the anxiety-relieving properties and impairment of judgment can make someone live in a fool's paradise. They also interfere with other learning, as for example in psychotherapy and behaviour therapy, and should be kept to a minimum then.

The problem of learning and of reaction mentioned above are mainly found with those drugs which have a long half-life, and thus last well into the next day if used as hypnotics, and may be truly cumulative. Flurazepam (Dalmane) is perhaps the worst in this respect, and in the opinion of the writer should never be prescribed. Nitrazepam also, for long an extremely popular hypnotic, can be cumulative. Especially in the elderly, regular use can lead to increasing confusion.

Another problem with benzodiazepines is that as the effect of the drug wears off there is often a sharp 'rebound' of anxiety. With some of the very short acting ones this can be a serious disadvantage, especially if used as a hypnotic, because the patient can wake early feeling even more anxious.

On the whole those of medium duration, such as temazepam and lor-metazepam are suitable for use as hypnotics unless there is marked depressive early waking when the longer acting diazepam may be better. For daytime use, lorazepam is non-cumulative, diazepam is longer acting and is slightly cumulative, and these two are as good as any others.

Because of the immediate relief of distress they provide, they lead to emotional dependence; and as tolerance develops the dose often creeps up, and the side effects become more serious as the dose increases. There is mental slowing, and physical unsteadiness, and dysarthria is common. As with alcohol, there is often release of normally inhibited aggression, as well as impairment of judgment; and many cases of baby battering are associated with benzodiazepines. Recent evidence incriminates them in road accidents too. They have a summative effect with alcohol, of a rather unpredictable type.

Tricyclic antidepressants have a useful anxiolytic effect, especially the more sedative ones like amitriptyline and trimipramine, and these two are also effective hypnotics. They are dangerous in overdose however, and have side effects such as dry mouth, and other anti-cholinergic effects.

Benzodiazepines are often prescribed by doctors in the mistaken belief that they have an antidepressant effect. In fact, they often worsen depression, and if taken by a patient in whom anxiety symptoms are part of a depressive illness they can be positively harmful. Worst of all they are handed out much too freely to the chronically worrying and vulnerable members of our society, to lessen the impact of day to day stresses. As such, they induce drug dependence, lessen the ability to cope and encourage the belief — much too widely held — that any discomfort or distress is an affront and must be relieved by someone or something.

Benzodiazepines are powerful anticonvulsants, and intravenous diazepam 10–20 mg is useful in status epilepticus. Sudden withdrawal after prolonged use can precipitate convulsions.

The use of these drugs should be restricted to brief courses in moderate dosage, for example, diazepam 2–5 mg up to three times daily for some self limited condition. Thus, they can usefully be given in depressed patients who are already on an antidepressant if anxiety symptoms are prominent; or can be used to allay a phobia of flying so that someone can go abroad. They should not be given for a long standing problem, nor to lower the general level of anxiety in someone who is chronically tense and anxious.

Beta-blockers

Beta-blocking drugs have been in use for several years in the treatment of anxiety symptoms. They block the activity of the β-adrenergic fibres, thus lessening the intensity — in theory — of all those anxiety symptoms which are mediated through this system. These are particularly palpitations, tremor, and gastrointestinal symptoms such as 'butterflies in the stomach'. The most commonly used is propanolol, 80–160 mg daily. They seem to help some patients, but our experience of them is disappointing. They were also proposed as a treatment for schizophrenia, used in large doses, but are probably ineffective in that condition.

Indications for drug therapy in depressive states

It is not always clear which patients will benefit from antidepressants. There are many chronically unhappy and low spirited people, vulnerable to the pressures of life, in whom these drugs are useless; and there are people with neurotic personality problems who become depressed in a purely reactive manner in certain situations who similarly cannot be helped with drugs. Antidepressants are most clearly indicated in those in whom the depression has a clear cut onset, arising in a person whose spirits are usually good. The more the depression resembles the classical endogenous pattern, with 'biological' symptoms, the more likely it is to respond to physical treatments, and the relevant symptoms should be carefully enquired into (see Ch. 9.)

In patients with severe depressive illnesses, with delusions, marked psychomotor retardation or agitation, impaired fluid intake and marked weight loss, it is better to use electrical treatment (described later) without delay. In many actively suicidal patients it is better to use ECT early, before trying antidepressants.

When antidepressants are given a trial they should not be persevered with unchanged for more than four weeks if there is no response to full dosage. After successful treatment the drugs should not be stopped too soon, as relapses may occur, and they should be continued for at least four months before tapering them off. The longer the illness has lasted before successful treatment, the longer should be the period on the medication. Twelve months of an antidepressant is not uncommonly needed.

Amphetamines

The use of amphetamines (Benzedrine) and dextroamphetamine (Dexedrine) or mixtures of these drugs with barbiturates (e.g. Drinamyl) is not recommended. They often lead to addiction, and their action is brief and frequently followed by tension and worsening in the depression. Amphetamines are necessary in narcolepsy and at times in hyperkinetic children in whom they are paradoxically sedative, but should otherwise not be prescribed.

Anti-depressants (thymoleptics)

The principal antidepressants used now belong to three main groups: Tricyclic drugs, Monoamine oxidase inhibitors (MAOI) and tetracyclic compounds.

The modes of action of these drugs are not really understood, but they have been linked with the so-called 'Catecholamine' hypothesis of depression. This postulates that depressive illnesses are caused by a fall in the level of available monoamines (noradrenalin, 5-hydroxytryptamine), as illustrated for example by the depression which often follows the use of reserpine, a known cause of monoamine depletion of platelets. It is thought that tricyclic drugs work by inhibiting the re-uptake of nor-adrenaline and 5-hydroxytryptamine from the synaptic cleft; while MAOI drugs inhibit breakdown by monoamine oxidase centrally. The two main tetracyclic antidepressants, maprotiline and mianserin, differ from each other. Maprotiline is more like a tricyclic in structure and actions; mianserin seems to act by blockade of pre-synaptic α-adrenoceptors. All of these explanations of how antidepressants work should be regarded as hypothetical.

Tricyclic drugs

These are closely related chemically to chlorpromazine. Imipramine (Tofranil) and amitriptyline (Tryptizol) are the best known, and in double blind trials have been effective in from 60–80% of outpatient depressives, compared to 40–55% of patients given placebo. The effective dose is about 150 mg daily, although less should be given to the elderly. The antidepressant effect is delayed for 10–21 days usually. Other well tried tricyclic drugs are doxepin (Sinequan), desipramine (Pertofran), nortriptyline (Aventyl) and trimipramine (Surmontil). The last is the most sedative, amitriptyline slightly less so. These more sedative drugs can be very useful as hypnotics. Protriptyline (Concordin) is given in the smaller dosage of up to 60 mg daily, and is non-sedative. Clomipramine (Anafranil) is worth special mention because of its striking effectiveness in obsessional disorders, and in phobic states to a lesser extent.

The side effects of the tricyclic drugs are largely due to their central anti-cholinergic actions: with dry mouth, constipation, retention of urine, impaired visual accommodation, sweating, and occasional impotence. Postural hypotension is common and may be serious, especially in the old, in whom they also cause ataxia at times, and in whom the atropine-like effect may precipitate glaucoma. Rarely a toxic confusional state develops, especially with amitriptyline; and alcohol may lead to unexpected and prolonged drunkenness. Epileptic fits are another rare complication. Major toxic effects on liver or other body systems are very uncommon, and these drugs are relatively safe, except in overdosage, when they can cause cardiac dysrhythmias and death. Doxepin is the only tricyclic which should be given to people with any history which suggests cardiac dysrhythmia; including therefore patients who have had a myocardial infarct within the previous 4 months or so. Although minor side effects of the tricyclics are common they are usually transient and need not be feared, except in the elderly.

Tetracyclic drugs

Until recently there has been general agreement that the tricyclics were the antidepressants of first choice, but in our opinion mianserin, a tetracyclic drug, is probably preferable. It is as effective an antidepressant as amitriptyline and has almost no anticholinergic effects. Consequently, it does not lead to the unpleasant, and in the elderly, dangerous atropine-like side effects of the tricyclics. It is also non-toxic to the heart, and therefore much safer in accidental or suicidal overdose. As it has been in use only a few years some caution is reasonable before assuming that the tricyclics have been genuinely supplanted.

Mianserin causes drowsiness and some postural hypertension, particularly in the first few days. It is advisable to build the dose up from 10 to 20 mg to 60 mg, though up to 120 mg can be used, increasing as the drowsiness allows. It is as effective taken all at night as in divided doses. It does in some people lead to marrow suppression, and agranulocytosis may also occur. A blood count after 5 weeks on the drug seems an adequate safeguard.

The tetracyclic drug maprotiline is more like a tricyclic drug in structure and actions, and is also an effective antidepressant. It has some atropine-like side effects, and occasionally causes convulsions, like the tricyclics. It seems safe in those with cardiac dysrhythmias. The usual dose is 150 mg daily for an adult.

Monoamine oxidase inhibitors (MAOI)

The first of this group to be used was iproniazid (Marsilid), but although effective it is also toxic, especially to the liver, and is now rarely prescribed. The most generally effective seems to us isocarboxazid (Marplan), of which the dose is 20–40 mg daily in divided doses. Phenelzine (Nardil) (30–60 mg daily) is also valuable, and is rather more sedative. Tranylcypromine (Parnate) is also very effective, and somewhat stimulating, almost in an amphetamine like way for some patients. Phenelzine is widely recommended for phobic anxiety states and agoraphobia, and for the latter it is the drug of choice. In both of these drugs the benefits appear only after about 7–21 days.

The most serious side effect of the MAOI group is the *hypertensive crisis*, in which a rise in blood pressure occurs which is so rapid and severe that subarachnoid or intracerebral haemorrhage may occur. This happens when the MAOI drug has inactivated those enzymes which destroy pressor amines, and the usually innocuous amines thus accumulate in large amounts. These pressor amines include tyramine (found in cheese, and to a lesser extent in Marmite, Bovril, broad beans, Chianti, pickled herring and joghurt); others are ephedrine, amphetamines, and various substances used as nasal decongestants or 'cold cures'. Other drugs are potentiated by MAOI compounds, in particular morphine, pethidine, and related drugs, and some hypotensives. These may all lead to sudden *vasomotor collapse* with *respiratory failure and coma*. Anaesthetists, surgeons, and dentists should be told when patients are having MAOI treatment. It is extremely important that patients should be warned of these foods and drugs, and deaths still occur, although less frequently. Tranylcypromine (Parnate) was most often incriminated in the hypertensive crises. Tricyclic drugs have been included on the list of drugs to avoid, but in our experience and that of many others, a combination of amitriptyline and isocarboxazid at least is safe and often effective, as is trimipramine and tranylcypromine.

Apart from these serious drawbacks the MAOI drugs are relatively free from side effects, although they have been suspected of causing jaundice; and fluid retention may occur.

Lithium carbonate

In the last few years lithium carbonate has been shown to lessen the frequency and severity of recurrent hypomanic and manic illnesses, and, although less markedly, the depressive episodes in people with bipolar manic depressive illnesses. In some patients it is also useful in the immediate control of hypomania. It is less useful in the prevention of recurrent depressive illnesses alone, although worth trying in many cases.

Lithium salts are toxic; and regular serum lithium estimations are necessary. The optimal levels are between 0.8 and 1.2 millimols for most patients, but many can be maintained adequately around 0.7 millimols. Above 1.6 mmols toxic effects become more common, and 2.0 mmols is dangerously high as cardiac arrhythmias or renal damage may develop. Signs of toxicity include anorexia, coarse tremor, vomiting, diarrhoea, and marked thirst. Lithium salts may also cause direct gastric irritation. Longer term side effects include hypothyroidism and nephrogenic diabetes insipidus. Both are reversible when the drug is stopped, except that two cases of permanent renal damage have been described. A suitable preparation is Priadel, a delayed release form. Initial dosage is 800–1600 mg daily for up to a week, to reach a suitable blood level, followed by 400–800 mg daily as a maintenance dose, depending on the serum estimations.

Lithium and haloperidol used together have often proved very effective in states of mania and acute schizophrenic excitement. Unfortunately it seems that together they are particularly likely to cause side effects, and they have been incriminated in the *malignant neuroleptic syndrome*. In this condition progressive collapse with confusion and hyperpyrexia occurs, and may be fatal.

Sedatives

The use of daytime sedatives in the old fashioned sense has been replaced by anxiolytic drugs. These have relatively less effect on the level of consciousness than, say, barbiturates, which calm the acutely distressed at the cost of sedation. In our opinion barbiturates should not be prescribed except as anticonvulsants or anaesthetics, except in patients who have taken them in a stable dosage for a long time, and in whom it is not worth trying to wean them off. They are too often addictive to be used freely.

Paraldehyde should also not be used. By injection it is painful and can cause sterile abscesses; by mouth it smells and tastes disgusting.

Chlorpromazine, if necessary by intramuscular injection, up to 500 mg or more, will calm the most excited psychotic patient. A benzodiazepine, such as diazepam, by mouth or injection, of up to 20 mg will adequately tranquillise, and sedate to some extent as well.

Chlormethiazole (Heminevrin) is a very useful drug for controlling withdrawal symptoms in alcoholics, and is powerfully sedative. It is unfortunately also addictive, and can cause nocturnal confusion, especially in the elderly. It is best kept for use in alcoholics, in short courses only.

Treatment of insomnia

Sleep disturbance is an important symptom of depressive illnesses, where the complaint of early waking is classic (Chapter 9). Strangely, when observed by others or if sleep is recorded automatically in some way, depressives often do not seem to waken especially early and it may be more because they feel so desperate as they lie awake that they complain. The treatment of such insomnia is the treatment of the depression and often a sedative antidepressant is helpful. It is important to avoid inducing dependency to benzodiazepines, so if they are used the patient should be told in advance of the need to tail them off later.

Much more common are the complaints of insomnia made by non-depressed patients, many of whom demand relief from doctors and too many of whom are given benzodiazepines. All types of people can complain of longstanding sleep difficulties. Very unhappy people, especially the unoccupied elderly, are dissatisfied with the 6–8 hours of sleep they get because their lives are so empty and dull when they are awake. Women complain more than men, and especially thin older women, with long standing neurotic difficulties, who smoke heavily and take more alcohol than most — people seeking relief from miserable lives. However, one should note that people who sleep less than 6 hours per night have generally higher mortality rates from all sorts of illnesses and there do seem to be various metabolic differences between good and poor sleepers, shown by variations in body temperature, for example.

Sometimes there are very obvious factors such as taking caffeine in coffee or tea in the evening; (nicotine disturbs sleep in many). Alcohol, although helpful in small amounts as a nightcap, is a common cause of broken sleep in the heavier drinker, perhaps because of a kind of withdrawal symptom.

Poor sleep in the chronically anxious or tense can be helped by relaxation techniques, including the use of tape recorded instructions and specific exercises, or by yoga-type techniques. Psychologists have much to offer in anxiety management for the more difficult patients. Regular exercise can be most helpful in aiding sleep. Regular hours, avoiding disturbing late night films on television, a soothing book and a hot milk drink are all worth recommending. It is also important to educate the patient to realise that sleep should not be regarded as something to induce automatically with drugs, and also to recognise the dangers of habituation, dependence and even true addiction which can occur to benzodiazepines.

If drugs are necessary, then even in those who are not suffering from depression, tricyclic antidepressants have the advantage of being non-addictive. Trimipramine, 25–100 nocte is especially useful. These drugs, however, can be fatal in overdose, so a proper history is important, as indeed it is before a benzodiazepine is prescribed.

A related problem is that of weaning people off sleeping pills, which now means benzodiazepines almost exclusively. The aspects mentioned above are all relevant, but there are some details which depend on which drug is currently taken. As described earlier, benzodiazepines differ principally in their duration of effect, depending on breakdown and elimination. If they have a very short half-life (such as triazolam), the patient may experience a kind of withdrawal 'rebound' of anxiety after a few hours. If the drug has a very prolonged action, such as flurazepam which is markedly cumulative, there is no rebound but there may be prolonged intoxication, with errors in driving and other types of judgment. Flurazepam can thus be more easily stopped abruptly than some others. The very short acting ones are the most difficult to withdraw, and it may be advisable to transfer the patient to say diazepam with a medium duration of effect to make withdrawal less painful.

Continuous narcosis

This, sometimes called sleep treatment, is of use in some patients with severe chronic tension and anxiety, not responding to simpler régimes. the aim is to keep the patient asleep for from 16–20 hours a day, for 7–12 days, and a combination of chlorpromazine 200–400 mg and dichloralphenazone (Welldorm) 2 G can be given every 6 hours or so to produce this. The method is of least value in those who clamour for it most on the basis of 'if I could only get away from it all'.

Narco-analysis and hypnosis

Situations sometimes arise in which the persistence, despite treatment, of symptoms believed to be psychogenic leads to the suspicion that there are operative factors that the patient has not disclosed. The patient can often be helped to talk more freely under the influence of drugs, as is known to every reader of spy stories. In reality, however, there is no such thing as the 'truth drug', and the patient may not only continue to conceal facts, but may tell eye-opening lies when drugged. Some care is therefore called for in interpretation of what is said, and it is advised that reliance should not be placed on the statements of drugged patients where legal issues are involved. There are, however, a number of cases in which the increased communicativeness of patients, achieved by this means, may be useful in treatment, though it will be realised that sympathetic doctors who secure good rapport will need to use this method less often than other therapists.

Methohexitone or thiopentone are useful for narco-analysis, and are given intravenously. The amount required will vary from case to case, and the most satisfactory method is probably to encourage the patient to count while the injection is made slowly, and to stop at the point at which speech becomes markedly slurred. This can be of particular value for the recovery of episodes for which the patient is amnesic, and the elicitation of other factors that have been repressed, or which the patient has been unable to bring himself to disclose. While the patient is under the influence of the drug it is often possible to undertake treatment by suggestion.

The principle of narco-analysis is the same as that underlying hypnosis. There are various hypnotic techniques, most of which depend on getting the patient to fix his attention on some particular object while disregarding the rest of the environment. Suggestions are then made to him, in a confident but soothing fashion, that he is relaxed and comfortable. The idea is then gradually instilled, by repetition of suitable phrases, that this relaxation is giving place to sleep. The patient may then be told that his eyelids are becoming increasingly heavy, are gradually closing, and that when they do close he will be asleep. If the patient is cooperative and suggestion skilfully made, the desired result will be achieved. The depth of the hypnosis can then be further increased by suggestion that the sleep is 'deeper and deeper'. In this state the patient's suggestibility is much increased and, with suitable encouragement, information may be obtained from him in much the same way as under the influence of drugs. While this is done the 'depth of sleep' must be maintained by repeating the suggestion. The heightened suggestibility of this state may also be useful in removing symptoms, e.g. by implanting the idea that the patient will waken free from anxiety, buoyant, and confident. In cases of hysterical paralysis and aphonia the patient can often be brought rapidly to full use of the affected parts while in the hypnotic state, during which it can also be suggested that this recovered function will continue on wakening. Although the results can be dramatic, the value of hypnosis is very limited, except when used by someone particularly skilled or gifted, and with suitable patients.

Abreaction

The release of pent-up emotion is called abreaction, for which the above methods can be used. Patients carrying a heavy emotional load and unable to discharge it may be helped thus in much the same way as some people 'get it off their chest' by having a drinking bout. Some prefer ether inhalations for this, in that these seem specially to facilitate emotional release. The main indication for abreaction is the suspected repression of painful traumatic memories or experiences. It must be realised that hypnosis, narco-analysis, and abreaction constitute only a part of treatment which will require to be carried further. Abreaction was more valuable for the dramatic traumata of war time than it is for the stresses of peace.

Deep insulin treatment

This, also called Insulin Coma Treatment, was introduced by Sakel of Vienna in 1935. It had for some time been known that insulin was effective in improving both the physical and mental state in cases of severe anorexia, and it was with this in view that Sakel tried its effect in combating withdrawal symptoms in cases of morphine addiction. The results were encouraging, especially when the doses used were sufficient to produce clinical evidence of hypoglycaemia, which was found to be controllable without difficulty if adequate precautions were taken. Sakel was encouraged to try the method empirically on schizophrenics. Its modus operandi was considered to be through biochemical changes occurring as a result of the hypoglycaemia. For many years this method was the accepted way of treating schizophrenia, and generated much therapeutic enthusiasm, which was of great value to psychiatry generally at the time. The method fell rapidly into disuse after a controlled trial in which patients treated with insulin coma therapy were found to fare no better than those given intravenous barbiturate coma.

Electrical treatment

This is often known as ECT, standing for 'Electrical Convulsant Treatment' or 'Electroconvulsive Therapy'. It is also commonly known as 'Electric Shock Treatment'. We feel this last term is unfortunate owing to the alarming emphasis. For the same reason, the alternative term 'electroplexy' has been coined. We prefer the still simpler 'electrical treatment', which stresses the therapeutic aspect without alarming the patient, since electricity is familiar enough not to be frightening, while still mysterious enough to most people to convey an encouraging suggestion of science allied to magic. However, ECT is firmly entrenched in British use.

The treatment consists in passing an electric current through the skull between electrodes placed on the temples. It is generally held that the current should be of such strength as to produce a convulsion, since weaker currents tend to be inadequate in their effects. Despite the strength of the current, the convulsion itself can be prevented from occurring by special means which will later be described.

If reasonable precautions are taken, there need be nothing alarming about the treatment, either to those who give or receive it. It is very safe, and carries little more risk than that of being run over in the street. Nor need there be any complications of note.

Development

In 1933 von Meduna of Budapest, when studying a large number of case records, was struck by the low incidence of epilepsy in schizophrenics and by the rarity of schizophrenia in epileptics. He found this sufficiently striking to formulate the hypothesis that the two conditions were 'biologically antagonistic' to each other. The corollary was that to induce fits in a schizophrenic might lead to improvement of the schizophrenia. Such fits were induced chemically, usually by the intravenous administration of camphor compounds. Despite the unsoundness of the underlying theory, considerable improvement was often found to occur. With increasing experience it came to be realised that such improvement depended, in the main, on controlling disturbed behaviour and in clearing those disorders of the mood, whether of excitement or depression, with which schizophrenia is so often associated. That is, the improvement was for the most part symptomatic rather than affecting the essential underlying illness. This led to the use of the treatment, on a symptomatic basis, in the treatment of mood disorders, whether related to schizophrenia or not. In these, it proved considerably effective. Indeed, this treatment revolutionised the treatment of severe depressive illness, and it is in this field that its chief use lies. But it has also been found of unexpected benefit in certain rarer conditions which will be described.

In 1937, as the value of the treatment was becoming established, Cerletti and Bini devised a machine for giving fits electrically. These are more easily induced, are less severe, and produce fewer complications, so that this has become the method of choice. Electrophysiological research is still being conducted with a view to finding improved forms of current and technique, but the existing machines, though capable of refinement, are therapeutically effective.

Even with electrically induced fits, there remained a certain group of patients with co-existing physical disabilities that were a contraindication to convulsive treatment. Efforts were therefore made to devise means of abolishing or attenuating the actual fit. This was achieved by the use of curare and its derivatives, and later by polarising agents, each of which prevents the peripheral spread to the muscles of the electrical impulses initiated by the current. In this way the treatment has come to be virtually without physical hazards.

Modus operandi

This is an empirical treatment. As its success became established, various theories to account for its action were sought in psychological terms, such as that it satisfied a desire for punishment, was an expiation of guilt-feelings, was a symbolic re-birth after death, and so forth. These have been discarded, and no doubt is felt that the treatment works through its physiological effects, presumably on hypothalamic and brain stem functions. There is some evidence that it affects brain mono-amines, and some that it enhances post-synaptic receptor responses to the amines, so that the effects are similar to those of the antidepressant drugs.

Indications

Although it has been used in a wide variety of conditions, often more in despair than in hope, the treatment is mainly of value in (1) states of depression, and (2) states of excitement. As to (1), electrical treatment is of remarkable value in those depressive illnesses of endogenous pattern, leading to recovery in about 70% and marked improvement in about 90% of cases. The sort of syndromes that benefit par excellence are described on pages 172–178, but the treatment can also be effective in some schizophrenics with depressive colouring, particularly if there is any suggestion of clouding of consciousness, or much anergia. As to (2), electrical treatment is of value in controlling acute schizophrenic excitement, hypomanic and manic excitement, and the periodically disturbed and violent behaviour of chronic schizophrenics but is rarely needed now because of the more effective use of anti-psychotic drugs. States of catatonic stupor, mutism and marked perplexity and bewilderment in schizophrenia can all be helped dramatically by ECT. Rarely, when a confusional state persists after the organic causes have cleared up, ECT may be valuable in ending the confusion.

Contraindications

Wisdom must naturally dictate caution in the treatment of cases who are feeble, frail or suffering from organic disease, especially where the psychiatric state justifies expectant treatment. Age is no barrier, and good results have been obtained in patients over eighty. Patients advanced in pregnancy have also been successfully treated. Almost the only physical contraindications are recent strokes, coronary thrombosis, heart failure, and active chest infection. Apart from physical contraindications, the treatment is best withheld from patients in whom the pattern of symptoms is more reactive, especially if important neurotic conflicts are present. It is a mistake to use it in doubtfully depressed people of hysterical or markedly obsessional temperament.

Complications

Serious complications are rare, with about three deaths yearly in England and Wales, at a time when 80 000–90 000 treatments were probably given annually. This is no greater than the death rate associated with anaesthetics in minor medical or surgical procedures, but should not be accepted as inevitable. The commonest cause of death is vagal inhibition leading to cardiac arrest. (It must be remembered that there is a sizeable death rate from suicide in depression.)

In the last few years, beginning in the USA but spreading to Europe, there has been a strangely passionate movement against the use of ECT, mainly outside the medical profession. The treatment has been criticised for causing severe mental impairment, especially of memory; regarded as an assault on the patient by an authoritarian psychiatric profession which is interested more in controlling and subduing innocent victims than in helping distressed patients, and said to be useless as a treatment in any case.

The campaign against ECT has had some harmful effects, in that psychiatrists in the USA have become afraid to use it even when it is obviously needed, for fear of litigation. Unfortunately, the campaigners have tended to be equally passionate in their belief that psychotherapy or some social change is always the treatment of choice, whatever the nature of the depression, and in the USA many deeply depressed patients who really need a physical treatment have had to continue with non-productive psychotherapy because of the power of this particular lobby. Unfortunately ECT has been included in the new Mental Health Act (1983) and that of Scotland (1984) as one of those treatments considered as 'hazardous', and for which the special consent procedures have been introduced. (See p. 462.) In fact medication has as many hazards as ECT.

There is, however, no doubt that ECT, like any treatment, can be abused. There is no justification for giving large numbers of treatments close together as memory disturbances do then become increasingly likely. Between 6 and 10 ECT, given at a rate of one treatment twice or thrice weekly is enough for almost any patient, and 12 treatments should be regarded as the maximum unless there are very good reasons, such as a previous genuinely good response to a larger number than that. Memory disturbance is common after a course of ECT, but is nearly always transient, and it is often forgotten that depression is associated with impaired concentration and memory in many cases. In older patients, and with bilateral rather than unilateral treatment, more persistent complaints of forgetfulness are commoner. Psychometric testing often fails to demonstrate the deficit, but this may be a reflection on the tests used.

Complaints of memory disorder are overwhelmingly more common in patients who did not have the classical indications for ECT — that is, the presence of an endogenous pattern of symptoms, as described on page 174. People prone to obsessional ruminations, continually examining themselves by minute introspection, are also likely to focus on quite minor and transient memory loss, and worry about this so much that it becomes another symptom.

Another major group of patients who may complain bitterly are people who, even in good health, find it difficult to live up to the intellectual demands made on them by their jobs, or who have intellectual ambitions and interests which outrun their capacities. A course of ECT is then seen as the cause of their failure to achieve the success which eludes them, even if to the onlooker it seems more likely that the failure to achieve was a factor in causing the depression. There are many men and women of high intellectual calibre who return to productive and creative life after ECT, but they rarely talk or write about it.

The campaign against ECT also casts doubt on its efficacy, and as a result a number of controlled experiments have been done, and more are under way. This is never a bad thing in medicine, and one must remember that insulin coma therapy (q.v.) was also considered very effective until it was found to be no more so than an intravenous barbiturate anaesthetic. (Perhaps it would have been logical to have used barbiturate coma as a treatment, but this was not done. The experiment was done in the early years of phenothiazine treatment, the efficiency of which has been proven in sophisticated trials.) Most controlled trials have shown clear evidence in favour of ECT, and the weight of evidence is still firmly on the side of the treatment.

Despite all that has been devoted to this problem here, in daily clinical practice ECT is given usefully, and without disagreement, to many patients every year, although it has been progressively less used as antidepressants have improved.

Use with out-patients

Patients not sufficiently ill to need admission to hospital may be satisfactorily treated as out-patients. All patients should be escorted home after electrical treatment, but, apart from questions of memory disturbance, many may feel unable to fend for themselves in an empty house, especially if at all inclined to the development of hysterical or anxiety reactions. Patients with any suggestion of schizophrenia should be given phenothiazines or other anti-psychotic drugs at the same time, as occasionally schizophrenic symptoms may be released by the electrical treatment.

Technique

The patient should wear loose clothing and should have had no food for four hours, and no fluids for two and a half hours. His bowels and bladder should be evacuated before treatment. Metal hair clips and dentures should be removed. The presence of loose teeth should be noted for fear of their being dislodged. The anaesthetic and relaxant are given intravenously. The electrodes, soaked in saline, are placed on the temples to which a little 'contact paste' may previously have been applied. A gag may be placed in the mouth before the current is applied, or at the moment when the patient opens his mouth as the tonic phase of the attenuated 'fit' begins.

The current must be sufficient to induce a generalised epileptic convulsion, although the convulsive movements themselves are almost totally abolished by the use of a muscle relaxant. Increasing the duration of the current increases memory disturbance, without improving the antidepressant effect. Many contemporary ECT machines are not correctly designed with this in mind. A minimum of 10 Joules of electrical energy is advisable, as lower quantities may fail to produce a fit. A brief pulse is desirable.

The best anaesthetic is probably intravenous methohexitone, with suxamethonium chloride or bromide (30–60 mg) from a different syringe, through the same needle, as a muscle relaxant. Intravenous atropine can be given with the methohexitone, to lessen the brady-cardia and the likelihood of vagal inhibition leading to cardiac arrest.

Artificial inflation of the lungs with oxygen is necessary on account of the respiratory paralysis; various types of machine are available for this. Very occasionally, *laryngeal spasm* may occur, so that it is advisable for those giving the relaxant to have experience of passing a laryngeal tube.

After the treatment the patient must be kept under supervision and lying down until consciousness is fully restored.

Unilateral application is advisable for routine use, although it seems to us to work rather more slowly and in some patients bilateral application is still necessary. Older women in particular seem to do better with bilateral ECT. In the unilateral method both electrodes are applied to the skull on the non-dominant side, in the frontal and temporal regions. The benefit is that there is much less immediate memory loss and confusion.

Frequency and duration of treatment

A series of such treatments is given, the number being determined by the clinical improvement. It is usual to give two or three in the first 7 days, and two in each subsequent week as far as may be necessary. The number required may be reduced if thymoleptic drugs are also given, but without them it varies as a rule between three and ten; with an average of six, if bilateral and eight if unilateral. It is fairly often the case that the markedly depressed patient experiences no subjective improvement from the first three or four treatments, even though it may be apparent to those around that improvement has actually occurred. Where the diagnosis is certain, therefore, it is a mistake to abandon the treatment too soon. Improvement in sleep and in spontaneous activity are usually the first signs of response, and these are later followed by subjective awareness of improvement. Even where recovery is apparent, the patient should be kept under observation for a period as relapses may occur. If the improvement is held over a period of 2 weeks from the last treatment, it will be maintained for at least a year in over 90% of cases.

The estimated recovery rate with electrical treatment in uncomplicated cases varies from about 70% to about 90% according to the cririaadopted. About 90% of cases can expect considerable improvement at least. A curious feature is that the treatment sometimes succeeds later in the attack when it has failed to confer benefit before. This is usually so only when the previous attacks have been lengthy, and is a contraindication to undue therapeutic pessimism.

The only substantial disadvantage is that the treatment does not prevent recurrence of subsequent attacks, and antidepressants should usually be continued for several months after the electrical treatment has been given. Attempts to prevent relapse by giving, say, monthly treatments over long periods regardless of whether the patient is ill or well (such a measure being reserved, of course, only for the rapidly recurrent cases) have sometimes been reported to be successful, but are often disappointing. A possibility to beware of is that a depressive phase may sometimes be converted to a hypomanic one in course of this treatment.

Psychosurgery (cerebral surgery)

This section on psychosurgery is far longer and more detailed than might be expected in view of the rarity of these operations currently. It is however, a very interesting subject, and a contentious one, and the section was largely written by the late Dr M. Partridge, who had an unrivalled experience of the results of leucotomy.

Cerebral surgery was previously limited to pre-frontal leucotomy, but several different operations are now available. They are rarely performed, but still have a place in psychiatric treatment for those patients disabled by severe tension or depression, from whom no other treatment offers relief. These operations also come under the special consent procedures of the new Mental Health Acts. (See p. 461.) In earlier years chronic schizophrenia was treated by leucotomy, but this is no longer advisable, unless the patient has severe tension as well as schizophrenic symptoms.

Although the surgical treatment of mental illness had been attempted in the 1880s, this operation was conceived by Moniz, the professor of neurology at Lisbon and father of angiography. He developed the idea that where a patient had fixed delusions, it might be possible to disorganise them by disorganising the neural substrate that he supposed to be responsible for their formation. The frontal lobes seemed the logical point of attack, both because they were then believed to be the seat of the intellectual life and because they had no other clearly assignable function. Moniz was further encouraged by experimental work reported at a neurological congress held in London in 1935, in which extensive ablation of the frontal areas in apes was shown to have improved their emotional stability at small cost to their intellectual function. He initiated the work in the same year. It was found that the delusions and hallucinations were virtually unaltered, but that, as in apes, the emotional stability was improved in that the patients were much less disturbed by their symptoms and acquired a greater ease of mind.

Techniques

Several different techniques were developed over the decades. For years the standard operation was a free hand and essentially blind procedure aimed at severing the white matter of the centrum ovale just in front of the anterior horns of the lateral ventricles; and various other less extensive freehand operations followed this. They have been replaced by stereotactic procedures in which small lesions are placed accurately, or by open operations such as removal of parts of the temporal lobe for temporal lobe epilepsy. (Stereotactic procedures in neurosurgery are those in which X-rays outline the skull and cerebral ventricles, so that a guided probe can be exactly placed in relation to certain 'landmarks'. They are very safe.) These small accurately placed lesions are much less likely to cause harmful personality change, such as apathy or excessive disinhibition, than the older blind operations.

The most favoured operations in this country are: (a) stereotactic tractotomy, in which fibres from the orbital cortex are interrupted by radioactive yttrium seeds; and (b) stereotactic limbic leucotomy, in which lesions are made in the fronto-limbic pathways, and in the cingulum. Both of these operations are aimed at the relief of symptoms, namely depression, anxiety and tension, especially that associated with obsessional-compulsive states. Operations such as amygdalotomy and hypothalamotomy have been used, mainly in other countries, to lessen aggressive and violent behaviour. There are major ethical problems with these latter operations, particularly as they tend to be offered mainly to prisoners rather than to patients.

The tractotomy and limbic leucotomy interrupt fronto-limbic connections, which are involved in emotional and autonomic functions centred in the limbic system.

General effects

Clinically, the usual physical effects are improvement of appetite and sleep, restoration of lost weight and of regularity of previously irregular menstruation. The mental effects may be summarised under the headings of: (1) Reduction of the patient's emotional charge, so that he feels and reacts less intensely, with a reduced tendency to worry; in line with this there is liable to be some reduction in spontaneous activity and initiative. (2) Release of inhibition, so that the patient feels less restrained, imposes less check upon himself than before and may say and do things more impulsively and with less deliberation than he would have shown before operation. (3) Intellectual changes, which are often of a subtle kind. The patient tends to think more in concrete than in abstract terms, to attend to the immediate rather than the remote, to have some difficulty in the adroit distribution of his attention when attending to the various aspects of any complex matter, so that his judgments tend to be simpler and made with less deliberation and thoroughness. These are not absolute changes but are broad, general trends. The extent to which they occur depends on the amount of damage done by the operation, and on the pre-morbid personality, of which the post-operative one is a modification. the better the pre-morbid personality the better the postoperative results are likely to be. The difficulty is to devise an operation which gives adequate relief of symptoms without causing untoward personality and intellectual changes. The more extensive operations tended to do both, but the more accurate and limited modern operations cause less damage. Many patients who would otherwise have been hopeless chronic invalids have been enabled to lead useful lives after operation at a cost that is small by comparison, and may be apparent only to those who knew the patient well before. In brief, there are always changes, but it should not be supposed that the operation reduces the patients to robots or renders them necessarily difficult to live with. On the contrary, many are pleasanter to live with than they were before, and we have known clergymen, university professors, business executives etc., resume their work satisfactorily even after the standard operation.

Indications

This is a symptomatic treatment and must be used on a symptomatic basis. The main indications are, therefore, afforded by cases incapacitated by tension, agitation and distress. It is rare to offer these operations to patients who have been intractably ill for less than 5 years, and have had every other appropriate form of treatment.

Among the *affective disorders*, states of severe anxiety with tension, and of depression with agitation, are those that do best. Manic-depressive illnesses of classical kind with regularly recurrent manic and depressive phases show disappointing results in that, though there is less post-operative tendency for recurrence of depression, the recurrence of manic phases is little influenced, though it is true that the severity of the recurrences is usually reduced. Nor is the operation as effective as might be hoped in cases of chronic or recurrent mania without depression. In cases of recurrent depression without manic attacks the results are much better.

In the *schizophrenic illnesses*, only those with severe depressive or tension symptoms are likely to be helped, and the operation is rarely performed.

Incapacitating *obsessional states*, notoriously resistant to other forms of treatment, are among the cases that do best of all, and the chances are better the more the symptoms are confined to rumination and the less they involve repetitive rituals.

In some patients with severe intractable pain cerebral surgery may be necessary to make life bearable; and in cases of severe anorexia nervosa it may be necessary to preserve life. The operations are uncommonly performed for both conditions.

Contraindications

Operation is an irreversible procedure, and should be regarded as a treatment of last resort. There are, therefore, two absolute contraindications: (1) If there still remains untried some form of treatment from which benefit may reasonably be expected. (2) If there remains any serious chance of spontaneous recovery occurring before permanent deterioration has set in.

The other contraindications are only of a relative sort. Physically, hypertension increases the risk of haemorrhage at or after operation. But many patients with severe hypertension have been operated on successfully; it is wise, however, to keep them at rest and in bed for a few weeks as a preliminary. (It is interesting that malignant hypertension has been known to recover after leucotomy.) Psychiatric-ally, cerebral surgery should be avoided in patients who have been aggressive or lacking in drive and in the capacity to struggle against adversity. Lessened restraint can lead to troublesome aggression; the apathetic will become more so.

The lessened restraint may also be of importance in cases with homosexual trends, since operation may lead to their frank release; whether it does so or not will depend on the patient's recognition of and pre-operative attitude towards them, as well as on the extent of his social conscience and powers of self-control. People who are well controlled before operation are likely to remain reasonably well controlled after it. People who are naturally self-indulgent are likely post-operatively to be more so.

The patients who are likely to be difficult after operation are those who have always shown poor social adjustment, who do not adapt themselves, are egocentric with lack of regard for others, have poor powers of effort, hold grudges, and show little depth of feeling. The possession of such a personality cannot in itself be considered a contraindication to operation, if the symptoms experienced are totally disabling and of a kind from which operation might confer relief. But where the symptoms are not totally disabling and the patient is able to lead some sort of a life, even though under handicap, it may be better for him to continue as he is rather than become an even less satisfactory personality though with fewer symptoms. Such decisions may be very difficult indeed.

Complications

The overall mortality using modern techniques is very small. Any intracranial operation carries some risk of post-operative epilepsy, and the more extensive the approach the greater is the risk. Thus, post-operative epilepsy occurs in about 16% of cases after gyrectomy or topectomy, but in only about 10% of cases after simpler operations. Even so, many of these have but one single attack, and we have never known post-operative epilepsy to constitute any serious problem. Urinary incontinence is an occasional complication but is nearly always transient. Urgency and frequency of micturition may persist but seldom to any degree that causes embarrassment. Such formidable complications as rectal incontinence, hemiparesis, etc., that were reported after some of the early cases, are so rare as to be negligible.

After-care

The post-operative rehabilitation is very important. The patients are usually in an accessible, tractable and accepting frame of mind after operation, and every advantage should be taken of this to encourage them into more satisfactory attitudes and habits, both as regards occupying themselves, attending to their duties, and learning to live with and to manage their residual symptoms. Behaviour therapy may be more effective, as may drug treatment, after operation. A considerable amount of re-education may be necessary, especially in those who have long been psychotic. Occupational therapy is indispensable.

Most neuro-surgeons advise that the patient should take small doses of anti-convulsants; many patients, however, will not bother about this if it is left to themselves.

It is always advisable to follow up the patients after discharge until one is satisfied that the maximum improvement has been gained and the patients' stability established. In this connection, it must be borne in mind that the immediate post-operative result is no guide to what the future holds; many patients continue to improve slowly and to make further adjustments over periods of many months and even years after operation.

17

The legal aspects of mental illness

The Mental Health Act (1983) applies to England and Wales, and came into force on 30th September 1983, when the 1959 Act and its minor modifications of 1982 were largely repealed. As this goes to press many difficulties are occurring in making the new Act work, and many psychiatrists are unhappy about some of its provisions, especially those covered by the heading 'Consent to Treatment' (p. 461). That part of the Act interferes with the independence of clinical judgment which has characterised British medical practice until now and which is so much valued by doctors. There are, naturally, fears that this interference may be extended and not restricted only to psychiatric treatment.

The aim of the Act, however, is clearly to extend the rights and protect the civil liberties of mentally ill people who are so often at a disadvantage in their dealings with others. It makes it more difficult for them to be detained in hospital against their will and more difficult for doctors to give treatments which are irrevocable (such as psychosurgery) or which are seen by some as potentially harmful. The Act also contains numerous minor modifications of the older Act.

In this account few references will be made comparing the new Act to that of 1959. The earlier one was itself a great step forward. It brought about an enormous change in practice and attitudes by making admission to mental hospitals, for the great majority of patients, the same as going into any other hospital — something without legal implications. Until then almost everyone was 'certified' in one way or another, and a magistrate was needed in most cases, along with medical recommendations and an application by the nearest relative. Even voluntary patients had to sign an application form to be admitted and could only leave if they gave 72 hours notice of their desire to do so. Society must have legislation to protect itself and to protect the rights of its members, both healthy and sick. The older emphasis was more on the protection of society but since 1959 the emphasis has been shifting.

441

Anyone who wishes to compare the 1959 and 1983 Acts could consult an older edition of this book and those who need more detail than is given here should consult the Act itself (available from Her Majesty's Stationery Office) and its explanatory guide, the *Memorandum to the Mental Health Act 1983*, published by the Department of Health and Social Security.

SOME DEFINITIONS

The Act concerns 'the reception, care and treatment of mentally disordered patients, the management of their property, and other related matters'.

Mental disorder

This includes four specific categories: 'mental illness, arrested or incomplete development of mind, psychopathic disorder or any other disorder or disability of mind'.

Mental illness is undefined, and its usage is left to clinical judgment.

Mental impairment and *severe mental impairment* differ in degree, and are used in cases where 'arrested development of mind' is combined with abnormally aggressive or seriously irresponsible conduct. '*Arrested development of mind*' includes both significant impairment of intelligence and of social functioning and is another term for mental handicap. Although the distinction between *mental impairment* and *severe mental impairment* is a matter only for clinical judgment, it has important practical and legal implications because there are differences in the grounds on which those suffering can be detained. It must be clearly understood that limited intelligence alone is never a justification for detention in hospital or for being received into guardianship (described later), but that there must also be serious impairment of social functioning in some way.

Psychopathic disorder

This means 'a persistent disorder or disability of mind (whether or not including significant impairment of intellect) which results in abnormally aggressive or seriously irresponsible conduct on the part of the person concerned'. The use of the word 'persistent' distinguishes psychopathic personality disorder from any mental illness which might lead to 'abnormally aggressive or seriously irresponsible conduct', such as damage to the frontal lobes or mania. An individual with psychopathic disorder cannot be detained in hospital compulsorily unless it is stated that 'medical treatment is likely to alleviate or prevent a deterioration of his condition'.

This is perhaps an appropriate place to record that people are not regarded as suffering from mental disorder, in the meaning of the Act, solely because of promiscuity, other immoral conduct, sexual deviance or dependence on alcohol or drugs. Alcohol and drug dependence can of course lead to mental disorders which might come under the Act.

ADMISSION TO HOSPITAL

Before reading the following sections, which are mainly concerned with methods of imposing control or treatment, it should be remembered that the overwhelming majority of patients go into hospital voluntarily, without legal formality, and that most of those who go in under some form of compulsion stay in hospital informally after the expiry of the compulsory powers. Compulsory powers are used if the patient refuses treatment, which is considered necessary for his 'own health or safety or for the protection of others'.

Compulsory admission

There are three sections of Part II of the Act (Sections 2, 3 and 4) which details three different procedures whereby patients can be admitted compulsorily from the community, and one (Section 5) which covers compulsory detention of someone already in hospital informally.

Section 136 deals with the admission of mentally disturbed people found in public places by the police while several other sections concern the various ways in which the courts can order people to be detained in hospital, only some of which will be described in this book.

Application for Admission

In the three main methods of compulsory admission, Sections 2, 3 and 4, an application must be made on the appropriate form by the nearest relative* or by an approved social worker. The application is made to

---

*Consideration of who is the nearest relative is long and quite complex in the Act, and a hierarchy is set out which is headed by husband or wife, then son or daughter, father or mother, brother or sister and so on. The oldest in a category takes precedence, but if the patient lives with a relative, 'or persons acting as such', that person will take precedence. Common-law spouses are acceptable.

the managers of the hospital, and must be supported by one or two medical recommendations, according to which section is used, and must be made out on the correct forms.

For admissions under Section 4, only one medical recommendation is needed, and the doctor concerned must have seen the patient in the previous 24 hours, as must the applicant. For admissions under Sections 2 and 3, two medical recommendations are needed, one of which should come from a practitioner approved as having 'special experience in the diagnosis or treatment of mental disorder', and the other should, if possible, be from a doctor previously acquainted with the patient, and will usually be the general practitioner. No more than 5 days should pass between the two medical examinations. Only one recommendation may be from a doctor on the staff of the hospital admitting the patient; in the case of private patients both recommendations must be from doctors who are not on the staff of the hospital.

Section 2 Admission for Assessment (Forms 1, 2, 3 and 4)

This lasts for 28 days, and allows treatment as well as assessment. Two medical recommendations are needed. The patient must be regarded as suffering from mental disorder of a nature or degree which warrants his detention in hospital, and it must be considered necessary in the interests of his own health or safety, or for the protection of others. He may appeal to the Mental Health Review Tribunal in the first 14 days. Treatment may be given during this period of assessment.

Section 3 Admission for Treatment (Forms 8, 9, 10, 11)

This lasts for 6 months in the first instance. Two medical recommendations are needed, the patient must be suffering from one of the four specified forms of mental disorder and detention must be regarded as necessary, as for Section 2. If he suffers from psychopathic disorder, it must be stated that it is likely that treatment will alleviate the condition or prevent deterioration. The patient may appeal to a Mental Health Review Tribunal within the first 6 months and *must* be reviewed after 6 months in any case and also after every 3 years if detained for longer periods, whether he appeals or not.

Section 4 Admission for Assessment in cases of Emergency (Forms 5, 6, 7)

This lasts for up to 72 hours, and only one medical recommendation is needed. It should only be used if there is urgent necessity and the normal procedure (which is under Section 2) would involve undesirable delay. The patient should be placed under Section 2 before the 72 hours expires, by having a second medical recommendation, unless of course the urgent assessment indicates that in fact longer detention is not necessary.

Section 5 Detention of Patients already in Hospital

Sections 2 and 3 may be applied to patients who are already in hospital, but in an emergency Section 5 may be used, in one of two ways.

Section 5(2)(Form 12). An informal patient may be detained for up to 72 hours by a single doctor, using Form 12. The completed application, given to the hospital managers, states the reasons why informal treatment is no longer appropriate, and that 'an application ought to be made under Part II of the Act', in other words, that Section 2 or Section 3 should now be used. The doctor entitled to implement Section 5 (2) is described as 'the registered medical practitioner ... in charge of the treatment' of the patient and this means the consultant. He is allowed one nominated deputy on the hospital staff and according to guide-lines issued in the first few weeks of the use of the Act, it is hoped that this deputy will be a consultant or a senior registrar. This might well prove impractical in many hospitals, in which case other arrangements will have to be made.

In the case of a patient in a general hospital, if he is already having psychiatric treatment his consultant psychiatrist (or nominated deputy) would have to be called for Section 5 (2); if he has no psychiatrist, the consultant responsible for his care in that hospital must provide the report.

Doctors must be familiar with this part of the Act, even if they are working in general hospitals and have no intention of being involved in psychiatry. Psychiatric emergencies are not rare in general hospitals and the junior doctors, and of course the nurses, are in the front line.

Section 5 (4) Nurses six-hour holding power (Form 13). It has always been the case that a nurse would be expected to keep a patient on a ward against his will, if it seems likely that by leaving he might harm himself or others, but there has not previously been any recognised statutory authority by which he might be held. This Act now gives that formal authority, with some stringent controls.

A 'first level nurse' — that is one with the Registered Mental Nurse qualification (RMN) or one trained in mental handicap — may detain an informal patient *who is already being treated for mental disorder*, for up to 6 hours, if it appears to the nurse that it is necessary for his health and safety or for the protection of others and it is not possible to get a doctor, qualified to detain him under Section 5 (2), quickly enough. The nurse must complete Form 13 and send it to the hospital managers. The power lapses when the doctor arrives, or after 6 hours. If the patient is then held under Section 5 (2) the 6 hours counts as part of the 72 hour total.

The Act, and the published guidelines already mentioned, make it clear that only the responsible consultant or his nominated deputy are able to implement Section 5 (2), and although junior doctors must be called for advice and help, they apparently cannot extend the nurse's holding power. As mentioned above, it seems that these subsections 5 (2) and 5 (4) will prove very difficult to implement at times: if, for example, either the consultant or his nominated deputy cannot reach the hospital within 6 hours of a telephone call because they are both in cars driving away from the hospital to Outpatient Clinics, through heavy traffic in distant parts of large cities, or if one is unexpectedly ill or injured.

None of this means that a nurse should not use his or her own judgment in an emergency, and detain someone while a doctor or more senior nurse is called. So long as the nurse acts in good faith, and takes immediate steps to contact someone more senior, the correct thing has been done. This is true also in a general hospital ward. A nurse should prevent a patient leaving the ward, in for example, a state of severe confusion or if apparently suicidal, although such situations are not apparently covered by the Mental Health Act. Suicide is quite common in general medical wards and nurses should not feel paralysed by this legislation and prevented from acting in the best interests of the patient.

Sections 135 and 136

These sections are also concerned with emergencies in that Section 135 empowers a police officer to enter and search premises, armed with a warrant from a magistrate, if a social worker suspects that some mentally disordered person there is being neglected or ill-treated or is incapable of reasonable self-care. The patient may then be taken to hospital and detained for 72 hours, while assessed. It is unlikely to be used very often.

Section 136 is, however, frequently used in some places and is the same as Section 136 of the 1959 Act. It empowers the police to take to a place of safety any person apparently 'suffering from mental disorder' in a public place and who seems to be in need of immediate 'care or control'. The place of safety is almost always a hospital but can be a residential old people's home, a police station or other suitable place where a medical examination can be carried out. The period of detention lasts 72 hours.

In big cities particularly, the police pick up many people in the streets who are obviously mentally disordered in the meaning of the Act, but the Act specifically excludes from the definition of mental disorder 'alcohol or drug abuse alone'. Many of those brought to hospital are drunk or under the influence of drugs, of course, but the police naturally prefer to play safe.

Powers of the Courts and Home Secretary

The sections of the Mental Health Act 1983 so far considered have had some possible relevance to the daily clinical practice of nearly all doctors. Only psychiatrists, however, are likely to be involved in those described next, so the accounts are brief. It should be noted that courts cannot force hospitals to accept patients under these sections, but the hospitals must agree to admit.

Section 35 Remand to hospital for a report on the accused's mental condition

This section empowers the court to remand someone *before trial* if he is suspected to be suffering from mental disorder (that is mental illness, psychopathic disorder, mental impairment or severe mental impairment) to a hospital for a psychiatric report, instead of keeping him on remand in a prison where psychiatrists have to visit him. A single medical recommendation is needed and the order lasts 28 days, extendable to 12 weeks. (This section is due to come into effect at some unspecified time after the rest of the Act). Like Section 36, it cannot be used when the charge is of murder.

Section 36 Remand to hospital for Treatment

This enables a Crown Court (not a Magistrates' Court), with two medical recommendations, to detain in hospital someone *not yet tried*, for treatment of mental illness or severe mental impairment, for 28 days extendable to 12 weeks. Note that psychopathic disorder and mental impairment (not severe) are excluded. This section comes into force with Section 35.

Section 37 Hospital (and Guardianship) Orders

A Court can use this when someone has been *tried and convicted* of an offence (other than murder) which is punishable by imprisonment and will use it if psychiatric treatment in hospital seems the most helpful thing to do. Two medical recommendations are needed, both giving the same diagnosis, stating that the prisoner suffers from either mental illness, psychopathic disorder, mental impairment or severe mental impairment and that detention in hospital is appropriate. If the diagnosis is psychopathic disorder, it must be stated that treatment is likely to alleviate the condition or prevent deterioration. Finally, a hospital must agree to take him within 28 days.

The patient may be discharged by the consultant in charge and may apply to the Mental Health Review Tribunal after 6 months, which must in any case review the case at 6 months and every 3 years, whether appealed to or not, as for Section 3. Nearest relatives may also apply after 6 months.

Section 38 Interim Hospital Order

This section provides for a 'trial of hospital' for the same categories of convicted offender as Section 37, so that the effect of treatment can be assessed before final sentencing. Two medical recommendations are needed. The order lasts for 12 weeks, extendable to a maximum of 6 months. Extensions and also a conversion to a Section 37 Hospital Order may be made without further appearance at court, so long as the patient is represented there by a lawyer. (Again, this section is to be brought into use on some, so far, unspecified date).

Section 41 Restriction Order

This empowers a Crown Court (not Magistrates' Court) to ensure that the patient is detained either for some minimum period or indefinitely, removing the power of discharge from the doctor in charge and making it dependent on the Secretary of State (Home Secretary) to whom the doctor must report. The patient may however, apply to, and be discharged by, a Mental Health Review Tribunal after 6 months.

A Magistrates' Court may refer a prisoner to a Crown Court for consideration of Section 41, and have him detained in hospital while he waits for the case to be heard (Sections 43 and 44).

Section 47 (and 48) Transfer to hospital of prisoners

This enables a sentenced prisoner to be transferred to hospital for treatment, if two doctors report as for Section 37. The hospital order expires at the end of his sentence.

Restrictions can be placed on patients transferred from prison (Section 49), as under Section 41.

Non-sentenced prisoners (i.e. those in prison on remand, or people detained by the immigration authorities for example) can be transferred to hospital similarly under *Section 48*

Criminal Procedure (Insanity) Act 1964

Under this Act, which still applies, a defendant before a Crown Court may be found either 'not guilty by reason of insanity' or 'unfit to plead' (also called 'under disability') in which latter situation no trial takes place. In either of these cases the defendant will be admitted to hospital under Section 5 (1) of that 1964 Act, and will be detained without limit of time. If the defendant who was found 'unfit to plead' later recovers, he should then be tried for the offence, so that he has the opportunity of having his guilt or innocence decided by a court.

Guardianship

An individual suffering from mental disorder (that is, one of the four specific categories listed above) can be placed under guardianship, under Section 8 of the Act, 'in the interests of the welfare of the patient or for the protection of other persons', as a way of ensuring reasonable care and protection by exerting some control and guidance whilst living outside hospital. The guardian can determine where the patient should live, in order to stop him sleeping rough or perhaps being exploited by others. He can be made to attend for medical treatment (but not to accept it), occupational therapy, education or training and so on, and also be obliged to provide access to doctors or social workers at his place of residence. If the patient does not conform to these rules, he can be admitted to hospital.

Guardianship can only be applied to those over 16 years of age, and applications and two medical recommendations must be made on designated forms, as for compulsory hospital admissions. The guardian can be a private individual, such as a relative, or the local social services authority. As this subject has little relevance to most students and doctors, no further details are given here. As there are no real powers or sanctions given to the guardian it does not look like being a very useful measure.

Mental Health Review Tribunals (MHRT)

Each of the Regional Health Authorities of England and Wales has its own MHRT, composed of lawyers, other lay people and doctors. In certain defined circumstances, patients, relatives and others may apply to them for a review of the case of a compulsorily-detained patient. The tribunal visits the hospital, interviews the patient and doctors concerned, and the patient's legal representative, if there is one and has access to all notes. It has the right to discharge the patient or to recommend transfer or a period of leave. Tribunals can also consider the cases of patients detained under hospital orders by the courts and even order the discharge of someone who has been placed under a restriction order by a Crown Court, if they are satisfied he no longer fulfills criteria which justify detention.

Patients detained under Section 2 (28 days) may apply only within the first 14 days of detention. Those under Section 3 may apply within 6 months, and must be reviewed at 6 months anyway, whether or not they apply. If the authority for detention under Section 3 is renewed, the tribunal must review the case again after 3 years or after 1 year if the patient is under 16 years of age. (It is the responsibility of the managers of the hospital to refer the cases to the tribunal at the proper times.)

Mental Health Act Commission (MHAC)

This is a new special authority, with about 80 members drawn from medicine, nursing, law, psychology, social work and other walks of life. Its task is to oversee the care and welfare of compulsorily-detained patients, and specifically to examine the validity of their consent to treatment. The medical members must also give opinions on the appropriateness of certain treatments, as described in the next section. (In the Scottish Mental Health Act 1984, their Mental Welfare Commission serves the functions of both MHRT and MHAC with other and broader interests too.)

CONSENT TO TREATMENT

Part IV (Sections 56–64) of the 1983 Act is concerned with consent to treatment, and introduces radically different concepts and practices as 'safeguards'. The aim is to make it more difficult to give patients certain forms of treatment without prolonged consideration and full consent.

Treatment requiring consent and a second opinion. (Section 57). (This applies to both compulsorily detained and informal patients).

Psychosurgery is the only treatment named in the Act itself, but the wording leaves it open for others to be included, and in the Regulations (a kind of addendum to the Act) the implantation of hormones to reduce male sex drive is included. When these 'most serious treatments' are considered, the patient's informed consent must first be given, after a full explanation of what is involved, and if he is not capable of such consent or does not give it, the treatment cannot be given. If he does consent, the next step is to approach the Mental Health Act Commission, who will send a doctor and two non-medical members to consider the matter. They will first assess the validity of the patient's consent, and if that is upheld, the doctor member of the visiting team will consider the appropriateness of the treatment proposed. He must have access to the notes and should interview not only the patient but also a nurse and a psychologist or social worker, each of whom must have been involved in the patient's care. Form 37 must be completed before treatment is carried out.

Treatment requiring consent or a second opinion. (Section 58) (This applies only to compulsorily detained patients).

In the Act this applies only to drug treatment given for more than 3 months in the period of detention, but electroconvulsive therapy (ECT) is named in the Regulations, and other treatments could be included by the Secretary of State.

If a detained patient agrees to continued medication or to ECT, and is capable of giving fully valid consent, this must be recorded on Form 38 by the doctor and the treatment can go ahead. If he does not consent, and the consultant (or equivalent acting as 'responsible medical officer') feels that the treatment is necessary, he should contact the Mental Health Act Commission (MHAC) which will send a doctor to consider the case, who must interview a nurse and another professional involved as for Section 57. The visiting doctor must complete Form 39 if he agrees the treatment should be performed without the patient's consent.

The Act specifically includes consideration of complete plans of treatment of which medication or ECT might be a part.

Urgent Treatment. (Section 62).

Any treatment may be given which is immediately necessary to save a patient's life — something uncommonly needed in psychiatry, except for the prevention of suicide. Examples would be of someone with a severe depressive illness or catatonic stupor who is refusing all food and drink and resists attempts at parenteral feeding, and who might die without ECT. Physical illnesses are not covered by this Act, and doctors treating them should follow their usual treatment policies.

Treatment can also be given urgently without consent, in order to prevent serious deterioration, so long as the treatment is not 'irreversible', which in practice must mean psychosurgery.

Treatment which is not 'irreversible' or 'hazardous' (the latter term defined as 'significant physical hazard') can be given in order to alleviate serious suffering by the patient.

Similarly, a treatment neither irreversible nor hazardous can be given urgently to prevent a patient behaving violently or being a danger to himself or others — this covers urgently needed medication for very disturbed patients.

These urgent treatment clauses enable the doctor responsible to act without waiting for the Mental Health Commission to visit and report, but there are many uncertainties in the wording of the Act. For example, are we to consider ECT as having a significant physical hazard? The risk is much the same as for having a general anaesthetic for any minor operation, and in certain circumstances would be much less than the risk of death by suicide or refusal of food and drink.

Although there are difficulties of interpretation and definition, and the intrusion of committees into decisions on treatment profoundly alters the traditional role of doctors, the aims of the Act are praiseworthy. By the time this edition is published we should be able to form an opinion of its practicality.

Table 17.1a Mental Health Act (England & Wales) 1983: Principal compulsory admission procedures

Section	Title	Detention	Comments	Forms
2	Admission for Assessment	28 days	Two doctors. Treatment also allowed. MHRT appeal within 14 days	21, 2, 3, 4
3	Admission for Treatment	6 months	Two doctors. MHRT appeal within the first 6 months. Automatic review at 6 months	8, 9, 10, 11
4	Admission for Assessment in cases of Emergency	72 hours	One doctor. Should be followed by Section 2	5–7
5(2)	Application in respect of a patient already in hospital	72 hours	One of two specified doctors. Followed by Section 2	12
5(4)	Nurses 6 hour holding power	6 hours	Qualified psychiatric (or mental handicap) nurse. Usually followed by Section 5(2)	13
136	Mentally Disordered Persons found in Public Places	72 hours	Police take those apparently mentally disordered to a 'place of safety'	

Table 17.1b   Mental Health Act (England & Wales) 1983: Powers of the Courts

Section	Power	Duration	Comment
35	Remand to hospital for report on mental condition	28 days	One doctor. Order extendable to 12 weeks. Used before trial or before sentence. Not used if convicted of murder
36	Remand to hospital for treatment	28 days	Two doctors. Extendable to 12 weeks. Before trial or before sentence. Not used if convicted of murder
37	Hospital and Guardianship orders	6 months (and as for Section 3)	Two doctors. After conviction (not if for murder). Appeal to MHRT only after 6 months. Discharge by doctor or by MHRT.
38	Interim Hospital Order	12 weeks extendable to 6 months	A 'trial of hospital' to help decide sentence. Two doctors
41	Restriction Order	Unlimited or limit specified	Crown Court adds restriction on discharge to Section 37. Discharge by Home Secretary, or by MHRT (may apply after 6 months)
	Criminal Procedure (insanity) Act 1964	Unlimited	For defendants found 'not guilty by reason of insanity' or 'unfit to plead'; can be detained indefinitely

Table 17.1c Mental Health Act (England & Wales) 1983: Consent to treatment

Section	Treatments	Applies to	Requires	Forms
57	Psychosurgery Hoemone implants	Detained *and* informal	Consent *and* MHAC approval	37
57	ECT	Detained only	Consent or Approval of MHAC doctor (second opinion)	38
	Medication for >3/12	Detained only		39
		Urgent Treatment —	*Detained patients only*	
			Consultant's decision only	
62	Any treatment		— to save life	
	Any non-irreversible treatment		— to prevent serious deterioration	
	Any non-irreversible and non-hazardous tratment		— to alleviate serious suffering	
	Any non-irreversible and non-hazardous treatment		— to prevent violence or danger to self or others	

The Mental Health Act (England and Wales) 1983 – some important features

It is for the reception, care and treatment of mentally disordered patients, the management of their property and other related matters.

Mental disorder means 'mental illness, arrested or incomplete development of mind, psychopathic disorder or any other disorder or disability of mind'.

The Act is mainly concerned with four specific categories:

Mental illness   — undefined.

Mental impairment ⎫
                   ⎬ — mental handicap combined with
Severe mental   ⎭   abnormally aggressive or seriously
impairment   irresponsible conduct

Psychopathic disorder — a persistant disorder, with or without
                         impairment of intelligence, resulting
                         in abnormally aggressive or seriously
                         irresponsible conduct. (Note the overlap
                         possible with 'mental impairment')

Individuals with mental impairment or psychopathic disorder can only be admitted compulsorily to hospital if treatment is likely to 'alleviate or prevent a deterioration'.

In the following tables only sections which doctors are more likely to encounter are included.

Note that the powers of the courts to commit people to hospital only apply if the offence was punishable by imprisonment.

THE MENTAL HEALTH (SCOTLAND) ACT 1984

Scotland, being a different country, has a different legal system (much more influenced by Roman law than that of England and Wales) and consequently has its own Mental Health Act. This resembles very closely that for England and Wales issued in the previous year, but there are significant differences. The outline provided here will, it is hoped, be of value to Scottish medical students, doctors and others interested. The general comments made about the Act for England and Wales, and the doubts expressed about the consent to treatment sections, apply also, in the writers' view, to the Scottish Act.

The sub-headings of Parts, Sections and sub-sections are those used in the Act itself.

Part I

The Act is concerned with the reception, care, treatment and related matters of persons suffering from mental disorder, which means mental illness and mental handicap, however caused. The definitions of 'mental impairment' and 'severe mental impairment' which recur in the Act are as for the England and Wales Act (see p. 442). The Act does not apply to people by reasons only of promiscuity or other immoral conduct, sexual deviancy or dependence on alcohol or drugs.

Part II Mental Welfare Commission (MWC)

The Mental Welfare Commission (MWC) will exercise a protective function for the mentally disordered and have powers of enquiry into possible ill treatment, improper detention, misuse of property and so on. They will also have a large number of statutory duties associated with compulsory admission and detention of patients in hospital and their release, and will be expected to advise the Secretary of State, Health Boards and so on on matters to do with mental health. They will have considerable powers in holding enquiries, functioning very much as a court at times.

PART V Admission to and detention in hospital, and Guardianship

This refers only to compulsory admission of course, and not to the vast majority of informal admissions.

SECTION 17 Grounds for Admission

The patient must suffer from mental disorder (that is, mental illness or handicap) of sufficient severity; and the Act allows what is usually described as 'psychopathic personality' as grounds for admission, if treatment 'is likely to alleviate or prevent a deterioration in his condition'. In the Act it is described as 'persistent . . . manifested only by abnormally aggressive or seriously irresponsible conduct'.

Mental handicap by itself does not justify compulsory admission. Unless there is 'mental impairment' or 'severe mental impairment', that is handicap with marked behaviour disturbance, admission is not justified under the Act.

Compulsory admission for any of these conditions must be necessary for 'the health or safety of that person or for the protection of other persons.'

SECTION 18 (and following sections) Admission and Detention of Patients

This leads to detention in hospital for 6 months. It needs an application by the nearest relative or by a Mental Health Officer (MHO: a social worker approved by the local authority) and recommendations by two doctors. One should be approved as having special experience in mental disorder and the other should preferably be the general practitioner. They must examine the patient within 5 days of each other and use the same general diagnosis; they should not work in the same hospital and should have no financial interest in the hospital or treatment. (The relative or MHO must have seen the patient within 14 days of the application).

The application is then submitted by the MHO to the Sheriff, who may make any enquiries he thinks fit, including discussions with relatives. If he approves, the patient must be admitted within 7 days. The hospital then informs the local authority, which must arrange a social report by an MHO within 21 days of admission, and the Mental Welfare Commission (MWC) must also be informed.

Between 21 and 28 days after admission the Responsible Medical Officer (RMO) must submit a report, having consulted others involved in the patient's care, and if he considers admission still necessary, must inform the MWC, the nearest relative, the local authority, and the managers of the hospital.

This section may be extended for a further 6 months, and thereafter at yearly intervals, by appropriate reports from the RMO, made after consultation with nurses and others involved in treatment, if the basic grounds (Section 17) still apply. The MWC must be informed each time, as must the patient and the nearest relative.

The RMO can of course, discharge the patient, as can the MWC, and the patient can appeal to the Sheriff who has wide powers of inquiry and discharge. The nearest relative can apply for discharge, but this can be blocked by a report from the RMO.

Section 24 Emergency Admission

In cases of urgent necessity a single doctor may make 'an emergency recommendation' leading to admission for up to 72 hours. He must if possible obtain the consent of the nearest relative or an MHO, or state why neither was possible, and he must examine the patient the day he signs the recommendation. The hospital managers must then inform the nearest relative, the MWC, and some responsible person who resides with the patient.

A Section 24 cannot be repeated when it expires, but must be followed by another section, e.g. 26, if compulsory detention is considered still necessary.

Section 25 Detention of Patients already in hospital

25(1). Someone already in any hospital can be detained for 72 hours by a single doctor using Section 24. It may then be converted to Section 26.

25(2) A patient already receiving psychiatric treatment can be detained by a 'nurse of the prescribed class' for up to 2 hours — for the patient's health or safety, or for the protection of others — while awaiting a doctor who has the power to use Section 24/25(1). The nurse must keep a record, and deliver it to the hospital managers as soon as possible, who must inform the MWC.

Section 26 Short term detention

This lasts 28 days. Both sections 24 and 25 can be converted into Section 26 by the recommendation of a second, approved, doctor on the usual grounds of the patient's health or safety or for the protection of others. If possible the consent of the nearest relative or MHO should be obtained. Similar safeguards to those of Section 18 apply. At present, in the early months of the Act, Section 26 is mainly implemented by converting Sections 24 and 25.

The hospital managers must inform the MWC, nearest relative and local authority, which must arrange for a social report. The patient may appeal to the Sheriff. Section 26 cannot be extended, and must be followed by Section 18 if necessary.

Sections 27, 28 and 29

These deal with leave of absence from hospital, powers of recall, those who go absent without leave and transfer of patients to other hospitals and into guardianship. Details will not be given here, but there are extensive powers, with specified safeguards, allowing the control of patients movement in and outside of hospital. If a patient goes absent without leave and remains out more than 28 days, he becomes no longer liable to detention.

Sections 117 and 118 are actually from part XI of the Act, but they seem more appropriately mentioned at this point.

Section 117 Entry to Premises

This empowers a MHO or a medical commissioner to enter premises with a warrant and inspect, if there is reasonable cause to believe that a mentally disordered person is being ill-treated there in some way, or is alone and uncared for. If such is the case, a Justice of the Peace (or a sheriff or stipendiary magistrate) may be informed and a police officer, accompanied by a doctor, can be given a warrant to enter and remove the patient, by force if necessary, and take him to a place of safety (usually a hospital). The admission order lasts 72 hours and can be converted to Section 18 or 26 if necessary. Under the same section, a patient already under some section of the Act, who has absconded from hospital, may be apprehended and returned to hospital.

Section 118 Mentally disordered persons found in public places

This empowers a police officer to take to a place of safety, where he may be detained for 72 hours, anyone found in a public place who seems to the constable to be suffering from mental disorder and to be in immediate need of care and control, either in that person's interest or for the protection of others.

In practice the police have the difficult task of distinguishing the effects of alcohol and illicit drug abuse (which are not grounds for detention under the Act) from mental illness.

Sections 37–52 Guardianship

These sections are very like those in the Act for England and Wales, except for methods of appeal and so on, there being no Sheriffs in England and Wales. The reader is referred to page 449, where the general aim of Guardianship is made clear.

PART VI Detention of Patients concerned in Criminal Proceedings etc.

These sections in Part VI are generally of little interest to medical students and doctors not in psychiatric practice, so few details will be given.

Section 60 Hospital Orders

These apply to convicted prisoners, who can be transferred to a hospital and treated, very much as though they were non-prisoners under part V.

Section 62, 65 (Restriction Orders, Restriction Directions)

These deal with the way in which the Courts, or the Secretary of State, can alter the normal regulations about leave, appeal, expiry of section and so on. Various restrictions can be imposed and, for example, patients may be returned to prison under certain circumstances when treatment has finished.

Section 70. Transfer Orders

This deals with the way people in custody who have not been tried or sentenced can be transferred to hospital as under Part V (Section 18). Two medical recommendations and the agreement of the hospital are needed.

Section 71

This considers similar transfers for people who are serving terms of imprisonment already, and have become mentally ill while in prison. Again, various special restrictions can be imposed by the Court or Secretary of State.

Part X Consent to Treatment

The most novel feature of the new Act is the introduction of formal checks on the right of Consultants to prescribe what form of treatment each considers proper. The wording of these sections is almost identical with that of the Act for England and Wales, and the intentions of the two Acts are the same, except that in England and Wales the equivalent section to Section 97 applies to informal patients also.

Other differences reflect, for example the fact that in Scotland the doctor appointed to confirm or negate the treatment proposed comes from the Mental Welfare Commission, in England and Wales from the Mental Health Act Commission.

Section 97 Treatment requiring consent and a second opinion

This section applies to 'any surgical operation for destroying brain tissue or for destroying the functioning of brain tissue; and to any other treatment which may be specified by the Secretary of State.' (So far only surgical implantation of hormones in order to reduce male sexual drive has been specified). *It applies only to those compulsorily detained.*

The treatment cannot be given unless the patient consents (which has always been the case) and a doctor and two non-medical persons, all appointed by the MWC, certify that the patient is capable of understanding the nature, purpose and likely effects of the operation, and has consented to it; and the appointed doctor has certified that the treatment should be given. Before doing this he must consult 'such person or persons who appear to him to be principally concerned with the patients medical treatment.'

Section 98 Treatment requiring consent *or* a second opinion

This applies to drug therapy, given to a compulsorily detained patient, if 3 months have elapsed since he first began it, and to any other treatment which the Secretary of State might specify. (Electroconvulsive therapy has been specified.)

In these circumstances, *either* the RMO must certify that the patient is capable of understanding its nature, purpose and likely effects and has consented; or a doctor appointed by the MWC must, after consulting others involved, certify that the patient is not capable of understanding, but that the treatment is appropriate and should be given.

Section 102 Urgent Treatment

The two sections 97 and 98 can be set aside in certain urgent circumstances, although the wording of the Act is unfortunately not entirely clear. Treatment can be given:

(1)   which is immediately necessary to save a patient's life *or*

(2)   which (not being irreversible) is immediately necessary to prevent a serious deterioration in his condition *or*

(3)   which (not being irreversible or hazardous) is immediately necessary to alleviate serious suffering by the patient *or*

(4)   which (not being irreversible or hazardous) is immediately necessary and represents the minimum interference necessary to prevent the patient from behaving violently or being a danger to himself or others.

The Act then says that 'treatment is irreversible if it has unfavourable irreversible physical or psychological consequences and hazardous if it entails significant physical hazard.'

Obviously, psychosurgery is never an emergency procedure, and although it is not specifically stated here ECT and medication are presumably the treatments considered. Presumably ECT is regarded as entailing significant physical hazard, although that may be much less than keeping someone sedated for a period, on doses of medication liable, for example, to cause hypotension. The uncertainty in the wording is most unfortunate and the Act seems badly drafted but again, time will show what problems do arise in practice.

CRIMINAL RESPONSIBILITY

A person who is found to be obviously insane at the time of trial is found 'unfit to plead' and is not tried. Main issues here are whether the person is capable of giving instructions for his defence and of following the evidence. When during the trial of an accused person he is found to have been insane at the time of the commission of the act, the jury shall, if satisfied that he committed the offence, return a verdict of 'Guilty but insane'. In either case the person may be detained in custody during Her Majesty's pleasure.

In dealing with insanity, the Courts follow the rules laid down by the judges in connection with the case of McNaghten, a paranoid patient, who had been tried for the wilful murder of Sir Robert Peel's private secretary. The important points in these rules are:

1. 'In order to establish a defence on the ground of insanity it must be clearly proved that at the time of committing the act the party accused was labouring under such defect of reason from disease of the mind as not to know the nature and quality of the act he was doing, or if he did know it, that he did not know he was doing what was wrong.'

2. 'If the accused labours under "partial delusions" only, and is in all other respects sane, he should be considered in the same situation as to responsibility as if the facts with respect to which the delusion exists were real.'

These rules have been subjected to much criticism. The words 'nature and quality' refer essentially to the physical aspects of the act, i.e. if a man has a gun, does he know that it is a gun? Does he know that, if he discharges it, the effect may be damaging to other people? The word 'wrong' does not refer to any question of abstract values, but as used here is synonymous with 'punishable by law'. Thus, the question

'Does he know that it is wrong?' must be taken legalistically to mean 'Does he know that it is wrong in law and punishable accordingly?'

From these considerations it is clear that the first of the rules quoted has the possible advantage of rendering it almost impossible for any guilty person to escape the rigours of the law on the ground of insanity. The rule may be considered liable, however, to fall rather hardly on some people who, though guilty of the act, were nevertheless significantly mentally disturbed by ordinary psychiatric standards at the time. As a learned judge put it 'Hardly anyone is mad enough to come under the McNaghten Rules'.

The second of the rules quoted is unrealistic, since the idea of partial insanity takes no cognisance of the necessity for assessing people in terms of the total personality, nor of the fact that instinctual and emotional factors are far more important in controlling a person's actions than are intellectual processes.

Diminished Responsibility

The McNaghten rules were being increasingly ignored or cleverly evaded for some time before a new act, the Homicide Act of 1957, introduced the concept of diminished responsibility into English law, although it had been available in Scottish law since the 19th century. In practice the laws and rules are applied variously depending on whether or not the accused is viewed sympathetically by the court or not.

The concept of diminished responsibility allows the court to find the defendant guilty of manslaughter with diminished responsibility, rather than murder and this has been wide enough in some cases to include severe premenstrual tension and 'disorders of impulse control' — in other words, psychopathic personality disorder. People suffering from mania, depression and schizophrenia are of course also covered.

Medico-legal reports

It is traditional that a doctor should help his patient. Indeed, most doctors feel some obligation to try to do so. The fact that a person has sought medical advice is thus liable to create a special personal relationship. But where the doctor, patient and the law are all concerned together, the relationship is not bilateral but triangular. Students and doctors who are inexperienced but show enthusiasm for the normal professional role are not always at ease in the triangular situation. In making reports or recommendations they are sometimes liable to assume something of the role of advocate instead of that of impartial observer, owing to a certain sense of obligation to the patient. But it should not be supposed that a man is better treated by medical than legal measures merely because he has sought medical advice. Conversely, even though punishment may sometimes be valuable, it should never be prescribed by a doctor.

CIVIL LAW

The question of mental disorder may arise in all provinces of Civil Law, but only three aspects will be mentioned here:

(1) Management of property and the court of protection

The function of the Court of Protection is to manage the property and affairs of persons who, by reason of mental disorder, are unable to do so themselves. The Court is only directly concerned with patient's property, not with their persons; but through control of their property, it is able to exercise considerable control over such questions as to where the patient shall live or whether the patient shall enter or leave hospital or nursing home.

The need for protection of this kind is obvious in many old people who, owing to confusion or forgetfulness, may make a hash of their finances, e.g. by leaving bills unpaid or cheques or dividends uncashed; or who may neglect themselves or be imposed upon or sponged upon by others. But the need for protection is not confined to the senile. It is also, for example, evident in many of the mentally handicapped and in that ever-enlarging group of the brain-damaged as the result of head injuries. Patients with manic-illnesses often need financial control, and so do some with schizophrenia.

Except for temporary relief in emergencies, the Court must have medical evidence to establish its jurisdiction. The relevant part (VII) of the Mental Health Act 1983 is in effect so all-embracing that any form of mental disorder suffices to give the Court jurisdiction if by reason thereof a person is incapable of managing his property and affairs. In Scotland the equivalent powers are described in part IX, and the MWC may petition for the appointment of curator bonis.

It should be clearly understood that, in providing a medical certificate or affidavit to this effect (1) the responsibility of taking action, or not taking action, falls entirely on the shoulders of the Court, the doctor merely being the reporting agent; and (2) the issue in question, namely whether the patient is capable of managing his property and affairs, is quite a separate issue from the desirability of compulsory detention in hospital. The majority of the patients under the jurisdiction of the Court of Protection are not in hospital, nor could they or should they be compulsorily detained in hospital. Conversely, the fact that a patient is in hospital, whether voluntarily or compulsorily, is not in itself sufficient to establish that he is incapable of managing his affairs.

It is most important that both doctors and relatives should realise that incapacity to manage affairs and the need for compulsory admission to hospital are quite unrelated.

The normal procedure of the Court — and except in most exceptional circumstances it can only act on medical evidence — is to appoint a Receiver who may be a relative or friend, a Solicitor or Bank Trustee, or in many cases the Official Solicitor of the Supreme Court. The Receiver is invested by the Court of Protection with various powers of acting on behalf of the patient, and must render an account of his stewardship.

It is quite often supposed that the need for the jurisdiction of the Court of Protection and the appointment of a Receiver in a patient who is manifestly incapable of managing his affairs, can be avoided by getting the patient to give a Power of Attorney. But if a patient is incapable of managing his affairs he cannot in law give a valid power of attorney. Further, a Power of Attorney, which may be valid when given, is revoked by the patient becoming incapable.

It is the duty of the family or hospital doctor to inform the relatives when the time has come for the appointment of a Receiver. The relatives should be told to consult a solicitor or write direct to the Chief Clerk of the Court of Protection, Store Street, London, W.C.1.

A patient placed under the care of the Court of Protection does not have to remain so permanently. If his mental state improves the order can be rescinded by an Order Determining Proceedings.

A word may be added about the Lord Chancellor's Visitors, who are not officers of the Court of Protection but are appointed by the Lord Chancellor, and who have been described as the 'eyes and ears' of the Court of Protection. Their function is to visit patients who are, or who are thought to be, incapable of managing their affairs and to report to the Court either generally on their mental capacity and welfare, or more specifically on any matter on which the Court may require information, such as the testamentary capacity of the patient. The medical visitors have certain statutory rights, such as requiring the production of medical records; and any interference in the carrying out of their duties is an offence punishable by imprisonment.

(2) Testamentary capacity

This is not an uncommon question in examinations, and is quite often an important practical problem. The medical man should satisfy himself on the following essential points: Does the patient (*a*) understand the nature of a Will; (*b*) the effect of a Will; (*c*) appear to have a reasonable knowledge of his estate and has he any delusions thereon; (*d*) has he the capacity to appreciate which dependants, relatives or friends might reasonably be entitled to his bounty; (*e*) has he any delusions which would per se cause him to omit any person or persons as beneficiaries, who otherwise might reasonably have been included; (*f*) has he any delusion which would cause him to make a gift which he might not have made in the absence of such delusion; (*g*) does he appear to understand the importance attached to his act; (*h*) if the medical practitioner sees the draft of the Will, do the bequests appear to him to be reasonable?

A patient who is compulsorily detained may possess testamentary capacity and one who is not may not. In summary, to have testamentary capacity a man must understand the nature of a Will, he must be able to understand the extent of his property, and he must be able to form a proper judgment as to the nature of the claims on his bounty.

A medical practitioner asked to advise as to testamentary capacity should show by his report that he has considered each of these three essentials, and if he is not given the necessary particulars, he should refuse to advise until he is properly instructed.

Recent legislation gives the Court of Protection power to make a will, or make a codicil to an old will, on behalf of a patient under its jurisdiction. The court would of course need medical evidence to show that the patient himself lacks testamentary capacity, and the doctor must be prepared to give his reasons as well as an opinion.

(3) Divorce

Insanity can be a reason for divorce and for nullification of a marriage. A petition for divorce may be presented on the ground that the respondent is 'incurably of unsound mind and has been continuously under care and treatment for a period of at least 5 years immediately preceding the presentation of the petition'. 'Under care and treatment' means either compulsory detention or informal stay provided the latter follows directly on a period of compulsory detention. An important amplification of what is meant by being incurably of unsound mind was given in a recent judicial decision (Whysall v Whysall):' ... if in the light of medical knowledge at the time of the inquiry it is said that the patient's mental state is such that the best that can be hoped for is discharge to conditions where he will not be required to manage himself or his affairs but will live an artificial existence protected from the normal incidents and problems of life he will properly be termed incurable.'

Nullification of a marriage may take place if either party was at the time of the marriage of unsound mind, or mentally handicapped, or subject to recurrent fits of insanity or epilepsy. The condition of such a decree is that the petitioner was at the time of the marriage ignorant of the facts alleged. The petition has to be filed within a year from the date of marriage. With regard to nullification no details about the type or degree of insanity have as yet been laid down; at any rate, to have been compulsorily detained is not the only necessary condition.

TERMINATION OF PREGNANCY

By the Abortion Act of 1967 a pregnancy may be terminated by a registered medical practitioner if two registered medical practitioners are of the opinion, formed in good faith:

1. (a) that the continuance of the pregnancy would involve risk to the life of the pregnant woman, or of injury to the physical or mental health of the pregnant woman or any existing children of her family, greater than if the pregnancy were terminated; or (b) that there is a substantial risk that if the child were born it would suffer from such physical or mental abnormalities as to be seriously handicapped.

2. In determining whether the continuance of a pregnancy would involve such risk of injury to health as is mentioned in paragraph (a) of subsection (1) of this section, account may be taken of the pregnant woman's actual or reasonably foreseeable environment.

The practitioners concerned must fill in a 'green form' (Certificate A) which is sent to the Department of Health and Social Services. The operation must be carried out only in National Health Service hospitals, or in private hospitals or nursing homes approved after inspection as being suitable.

This act has raised many problems. The phrasing, 'injury to the physical ... health of the pregnant woman' is open to the interpretation that any pregnancy may be terminated, as the risks of early abortion in skilled hands are less than the risks of pregnancy, labour, and the puerperium. The psychiatric aspects 'injury to the ... mental health' taking into account 'the pregnant woman's actual or reasonably foreseeable environment', is a problem because it is so difficult to define mental health. In patients who have had serious depressive illnesses associated with childbirth in the past, or who are schizophrenic, there is general agreement that termination of pregnancy is helpful if the woman does not want the child. There is also general agreement to terminate in those women with low incomes and large families, often of dull intelligence and socially incapable, in whom each extra child depresses the general level of the family's well being and the mother's health. In these cases sterilisation should also be considered.

In the early years after the Act was passed, psychiatrists were often involved in the recommendations. The problematical cases were those who presented and still present in the largest numbers: women who did not want the baby, were not mentally ill, may or may not have had some disorder of personality and who were unhappy. They were not always single, but usually felt lonely and insecure, distressed at the idea of having a young child at home to look after so that they would lose a job and so on. They were unlikely to become mentally ill, but felt that they would be generally unhappier and live more stressful lives.

Currently, at least in London, psychiatrists are almost never involved. Abortion is available on demand for practical purposes and the medical recommendations are a matter between the general practitioner and gynaecologist. Easy abortion is undoubtedly one of the ways in which the population of the United Kingdom has been stabilised and it has become accepted widely and rapidly, in a surprising manner to many older people, who recall the fierce arguments of a few years ago.

The *published* evidence on the effects of termination of pregnancy suggests that it has few undesirable after effects, in that marked guilt and depression do not develop as often as used to be thought, and most of the women are pleased and happier. A sizeable proportion become pregnant again soon, and go to term; while a few again ask for termination. Follow up studies abroad do not show any increase in serious mental illness, and most cope adequately. It is generally recognised that suicide in pregnancy is rare, although often it used to be threatened.

Bibliography

A small selection of books useful to the student

PSYCHOLOGY

Introduction to psychology, 6th ed. Hilgard E R, Atkinson R C, Atkinson R L 1975. Harcourt Brace Jovanovich Inc., New York
A very readable and informative book

PSYCHOPATHOLOGY

Psychopathology. Kraupl-Taylor F 1966. Butterworth, London
Clinical psychopathology. Schneider K 1959. Grune & Stratton, New York
New introductory lectures on psycho-analysis. Freud S 1948 (Trans. Sprott). Hogarth Press, London

CLINICAL PSYCHIATRY

American handbook of psychiatry, 2nd ed. Arieti (ed) 1974, 1981. Basic Books, New York
A very large seven-volume compendium, useful for reference and browsing

Clinical psychiatry, 3rd ed. Mayer–Gross W, Slater E T O, Roth M 1969. Bailliere, Tindall and Cassell, London
Although outdated, contains much valuable clinical description

Companion to psychiatric studies, 3rd ed. Kendell R E, Zealley A K (eds) 1983. Churchill Livingstone, Edinburgh
A well written detailed textbook, very suitable for psychiatrists in training and others

Organic psychiatry (the psychological consequences of cerebral disorder). Lishman A 1978. Blackwell Scientific Publications,

470

Oxford
A modern classic

Fears and phobias. Marks I M 1969. Heinemann, London

Psychiatric disorders in old age. Whitehead T 1979. HM and M Publishers, Aylesbury
A short but useful guide to doctors and others concerned

Recent advances in clinical psychiatry, Nos. 2, 3, and 4, Granville-Grossman K L 1976, 1979 and 1982. Churchill Livingstone, Edinburgh
Review articles, with detailed lists of references

Contemporary psychiatry. Silverstone T, Barraclough B (eds) 1975. Royal College of Psychiatrists and Headley Bros Ltd, London
A collection of review articles from the British Journal of Hospital Medicine, a journal which has regular useful reviews of psychiatric topics

Alcoholism Kessel N, Walton H 1965. Penguin, London

TREATMENT
PHYSICAL METHODS

An introduction to physical methods of treatment in psychiatry, 5th ed. Sargant W W, Slater E T O 1972. Livingstone, Edinburgh

Drug treatment in psychiatry, 3rd ed. Silverstone T, Turner P 1982. Routledge & Kegan Paul, London

PSYCHOTHERAPY

An introduction to the psychotherapies. Bloch S (ed) 1979. Oxford University Press

Introduction to psychotherapy. Brown D, Pedder J 1979. Tavistock, London
These books do not, despite their titles, cover the same ground

Cognitive Therapy and the Emotional Disorders. Beck A T 1976. International University Press, New York

Handbook of psychotherapy and behaviour change. Bergin A E, Garfield S L (eds) 1971. Wiley, New York

Handbook of psychotherapy and behaviour and behaviour change. Bergin A E, Garfield S L (eds) 1971. Wiley, New York
(Especially the chapter on 'The Evaluation of Therapeutic Outcomes', Bergin, A E)

Behavioural Techniques. Stern R 1978. Academic Press, London

Persuasion and healing. Frank J D 1961. Johns Hopkins Press, Baltimore

Archives of General Psychiatry Vol. 24 p. 107–118 Theoretical Hierarchy of adaptive ego mechanisms. Vaillant G E 1971

CHILD PSYCHIATRY

Basic child psychiatry, 4th ed. Barker P 1983. Crosby Lockwood Staples, London

MENTAL HANDICAP

Mental handicap. Kirman B, Bicknell J (eds) 1975. Churchill Livingstone, Edinburgh

Tredgolds Mental Retardation, 12th ed. Craft M (ed.) Baillere Tindall, London

PSYCHOSOMATICS

Foundations of Psychosomatics Christie M, Mellett P G 1981 John Wiley and Son Ltd, London

Modern trends in psychosomatic medicine No 3. Hill O (ed) 1979. Butterworth, London
Volumes 1 and 2 are also worth reading

SEXUAL PHYSIOLOGY AND THERAPY

Human sexual response. Masters W H, Johnson V E 1966. Little Brown, Boston

Human sexual inadequacy. Masters W H, Johnson V E 1970. Churchill, London
These books have been extremely influential

HISTORY OF PSYCHIATRY

History of psychiatry. Ackerknecht E H (Trans. Wolf S) 1969. Hafner, New York

Three hundred years of psychiatry. Hunter R A, MacAlpine I 1963. Oxford University Press, London
    The former gives an overall view; the latter a more detailed and vivid account from British historical documents

Index

Abortion Act of 1967, 468
Abreaction, 428
Abstein, 337
Acute brain syndromes, 99
Addiction
  to alcohol, *et seq.* 323
  to other drugs, 338
Adler, 393
Admission to hospital
  assessment (Sect. 2), 444
  by a police officer (section 136), 446
  emergency (Section 4), 444, 445
  from courts, 447 *et seq.*
  in Scotland, 457 *et seq.*
  treatment (Section 3), 444
Aetiology of mental illness, 17 *et seq.*
Affect
  disturbances of, 51, 136 *et seq.*
  incongruity of affect, 52, 136
  loss of, 52, 137
Affective disorders, 160
Aggressive psychopath, 221
Agoraphobia, 261
Alanon, 337
Alcoholics Anonymous, 337
Alcoholism, 323 *et seq.*
  aetiology, 326
  delirium tremens and, 332
  dementia in, 331
  dipsomania and, 327
  epileptiform fits in, 333
  hallucinosis in, 331
  Korsakoff's psychosis and, 105, 331
  paranoid states in, 331
  symptomatic, 327
  treatment of, 333 *et seq*
Alexithymia, 363
Alzheimer's disease, 107
Ambivalence, 52
Amentia, 55
Amine hypothesis of depression, 171
Amitriptyline, *see* Tricyclic drugs

Amnesia, 54
  alcoholic, 330
  hysterical, 275
  post-traumatic, 89
Amphetamine psychosis, 344
Amphetamines, 344, 421
Anaesthesia, hysterical, 279
Anal phase, 390
Anafranil, *see* Clomipramine
Anancastic personality, *see* Obsessional
  personality
Anorexia nervosa, 365
Antabuse, 335
Anterograde amnesia, 44, 54
Antidepressant drugs, 420 *et seq.*
Antiparkinsonian drugs, 414
Anti-psychotic drugs, 412 *et seq.*
Anxiety, 52
  catastrophic, 78, 80
  in depression, 182, 250
  in organic states, 78, 242
  in schizophrenia, 137
Anxiety neurosis, *see* Anxiety state
Anxiety proneness, 213
Anxiety state, 240 *et seq.*
Anxiolytics, 418
Apomorphine, 406
Arteriopathic dementia, 120 *et seq.*
Assessment of intellectual impairment,
  86
Astasia-Abasia, 278
Asthenic physique, 26
Ataractics, *see* Minor tranquillisers
Athletic physique, 27
Attention, disturbance of, 45
Autochthonous ideas, *see* Delusions,
  primary
Auto-erotic phase, 390
Automatic obedience, 47
Autonomic symptoms, 52
  with anxiety, 240 *et seq.* 351
Aventyl, *see* Tricyclic drugs

475

Aversion therapies, *see* Behaviour
      therapy
Avitaminosis, 105

Babinski's second, sign, 286
Baby battering, 419
Backache, 257
Barbiturate abuse, 344
Behaviour therapy, 406 *et seq.*
   aversion therapy, 406
   cognitive therapy, 189
   desensitisation techniques, 408
   flooding, 409
   positive conditioning techniques, 410
Belle indifference, 282
Benperidol, 228
Benzedrine, *see* Amphetamines
Benzhexol, 414
Benzodiazepines, 418
   dependence, 344
Bereavement and depression, 166
Beta-blockers, 420
Binet-Simon test, 319
Biochemistry and depression, 171
Biochemistry and schizophrenia, 131
Bipolar manic-depressive psychosis, 189
      et seq.
   course, 195
   depressive phase, 190
   flight of ideas, 193
   hypomania, 191
   manic phase, 190
   symptoms and signs, 191 *et seq.*
   treatment, 196 *et seq.*
Birth injury, 312
Blindness, hysterical, 279
Blocking of thought, 48
Brain biopsy, 113
Brain damage, 91 (*see also* Organic
      Mental States)
Brietal sodium, *see* Methohexitone
Briquets' syndrome, 280
British Epilepsy Association, 105
Bromide
   delirium, 344
Bulimia Nervosa, 368

Cannabis, 342 *et seq.*
Cardiac neurosis, 248
Case taking, 66 *et seq.*
CAT Scanning, 113, 131, 331
Catalepsy, 46, 140
Catastrophic anxiety, 78

Catatonic excitement, 47, 139
Catatonic schizophrenia, 139
Catecholamine hypothesis of depression,
      171
Cattell 16 P.F. Questionnaire, 210
Cerebral angiography, 113
Cerebral injury–long term effects, 88
      (*see also* Organic Mental States)
Cerebral palsy, 315
Cerebral surgery, *see* Psycho-surgery
Cerletti and Bini, 430
Chloral abuse, 344
Chlordiazepoxide, *see* Minor
      tranquillisers
Chlormethiazole, 333
Chlorpromazine, *see* Phenothiazines
Chromosome 21 Tri-somy, 316
Chronic brain syndromes, 99
Circumstantiality, 48
Citrated calcium carbimide, 337
Classification of mental disorders, 59
Claustrophobia, 259
Clomipramine, in obsessional states, 307
Clopenthixol, 417
Clouding of consciousness, 45, 100 *et seq.*
Cocaine addicts, 343
Cognitive Therapy in Depression, 189
Collective unconscious, 393
Community psychiatric nurse, 382
Community services, 381, 383
Compensation problems, 92, 94, 355
Complexes, 391
Comprehension, disturbed, 82
Compulsive acts, 301
Compulsive thoughts, 301
Compulsory detention, 443 *et seq.*
Computer assisted X-ray tomography,
      see CAT scanning, 111, 113, 131
Concentration
   impairment of, 44, 81
   tests of, 73
Concrete thinking, 81
Concussion, 89 *et seq.*
Confabulation, 54, 105
Confusion, 45,
   in elderly, 117
Confusional states, 99
   in the elderly, 117
   post-traumatic, 90 *et seq.*
Consciousness, clouding of, *see* Clouding
      of consciousness
Consent to treatment (*see* Mental Health
      Acts)
Constitution, 17, 19 *et seq.*
Continuous narcosis, 427

de Costa's syndrome
Court of Protection, 465
Cretinism, 316
Crentzfeldt-Jakob disease, 109
Criminal responsibility, 463
Curatov bonis, 465
Cyclothymic personality, 164, 215
Cyclothymic personality, 164, 215
Cyproterone Acetate, 228

Dartalan, *see* Thiopropazate
Day centres, 360
Day hospital, 381
Deafness
    hysterical, 279
    and paranoid developments, 117
Death and dying, reactions to, 356
Deep insulin treatment, 428
Defence mechanisms, *see* Ego
        defence mechanisms
Déjà vu, 55
Delirium, 51, 100 *et seq.*
    post-traumatic, 90
    tremens, 332
Delusional mood, 49
Delusional perception, 49
Delusions, 49 *et seq.*
    in affective illnesses, 177, 194
    primary, 49, 140, 148
    secondary, 49
Dementia, 107, 118 *et seq.*
    arteriopathic (arteriosclerotic), 120
    differential diagnosis of, 110
    investigation of, 111
    multi-infarct, 120
    praecox, 124
    presenile, 107 *et seq.*
    senile, 118 *et seq.*
    'treatable', 110
Denial, 40
Depersonalisation, 58
Depôt injections, in schizophrenia, 416
Depression, 160 *et seq.*
    aetiology, 163 *et seq.*
    biochemical aspects, 170
    biological symptoms, 173
    delusions in, 177
    differential diagnosis, 185
    elderly, in the, 116
    endogenous pattern, 160, 172
    genetic aspects, 163
    hormones and, 171
    hypothyroidism and, 172
    life events and, 165

manic-depressive, 189
menopause, 168
neurotic, 161
physical factors, 168
physical symptoms, 173, 177, 181
post-natal, 169
premorbid personality, 164
prognosis, 183
psychotic, 161
puerperal, 169
reactive pattern of, 180
schizophrenia and, 157
shoplifting and, 178
strokes and, 78, 116
symptoms and signs, 172 *et seq.*, 180 *et
        seq.*
transient depressive reactions, 236
treatment, 186 *et seq.* 196
vitamin B_{12} deficiency and, 172, 185
Derealisation, 58
Desensitisation therapies, *see* Behaviour
        therapy
Despiramine, *see* Tricyclic drugs
Deterioration, intellectual, 80, 91 *et seq.*
        (and *see* Dementia)
    assessment of, 86 *et seq.*
    epileptic, 96
    schizophrenic, 139, 152
Diazepam, 418
Dichloralphenazone, 427
Dipsomania, 327
Disabled Resettlement Officer
        (D.R.O.), 157
Disorientation, 45, 90, 100 *et seq.*
Displacement, 40
Dissociation, 54, 266
Distortions of content, 61, 72
Distractibility, 46
Disulfiram, 335
Divorce, 467
Diurnal variation of mood, 173
Doctor-patient relationship, 12
Dopaminergic receptors, 131
Doxepin, *see* Tricyclic drugs
Down's syndrome, 316
Drinamyl, 399 (*see* Amphetamines)
Drug addiction, 338 *et seq.*
    aetiology, 340
    frequency of, 339
    opiates and, 345
    personality in, 341
    treatment, 347
    withdrawal symptoms, 346
Drug dependence, 338 *et seq.*
Drugs in treatment, 411

Dual personality, *see* Multiple personality
Dysmnesic syndrome, *see* Korsakoff's psychosis

Echoing thoughts, 57
Echolalia, 47
Echopraxia, 47
Ecstasy, 52
E.C.T., *see* Electrical treatment
Ectomorphy, 27
Ego, 390
Ego defence mechanisms, 40
Elation, 51
Electra relationship, 391
Electrical treatment, 429 *et seq.*
 in deliria, 105
 in depression, 188, 431 *et seq.*
 in manic phase, 199
 in schizophrenia, 158
 unilateral, 434
Electro-encephalography, 111
Electroplexy, *see* Electrical treatment
Emergency admission to hospital, 445
Emotional
 disturbance in schizophrenia, 142 *et seq.*
 incontinence, 51, 83
 lability, 51
Endomorphy, 27
Endorphins (and opiates), 342
Enuresis, 369
Environmental change (as treatment), 377 *et seq.*
Epilepsy, 95 *et. seq.*
 alcohol withdrawal and, 333
 post-leucotomy, 440
 schizophrenia-like psychoses of, 98
 temporal lobe, 96
Epileptic
 deterioration, 95
 personality, 95
 psychoses, 96
 twilight states, 96
Epiloia, *see* Tuberose sclerosis
Examination of patient, 67 *et seq.*
Excitement
 in mania, 193
 in schizophrenia, 144
 normal, 162
Exhibitionism, 229
 in mania, 193
Extroversion, 210
Eysenck Personality Inventory, 210

Fentazin, *see* Perphenazine
Fetishism, 230
First rank symptoms (of schizophrenia), 148
Fits, *see* Epilepsy
 hysterical, 275
 withdrawal, 333, 346
Fixation, *see* Psychoanalysis
Flashbacks, 350
Flexibilitas cerea, 46, 140
Flight of ideas, 48, 193
Flooding (behaviour therapy), 409
Flupenthixol decanoate (Depixol), 417
Fluphenazine enanthate, 417
Fluphenazine decanoate, 417
Flurazepam, 419
Folic acid deficiency
 and depression, 185
 and dementia, 110
Folie à deux, 145
Free association, (*see* Psychoanalysis)
Freud, 10, 389 *et seq.*
Frigidity, 293
Frontal lobe syndrome, 83
Fugues, 54, 275
Functional psychoses, 60

Ganser states, 276
Guardianship, 449
General paralysis of the insane (GPI), 109
Genetic influences, 26, 29, 126, 163, 313, 328
George III, 7
Giddiness in anxiety, 245
Gluthêmide, abuse, 344
Grasp
 impairment of, 44
Group homes, 381
Group therapy, 398, 403
Guilt feelings, 25, 175
Guthrie test, 317

Hallucinations, 56–58
 auditory, 57
 hypnagogic, 56
 in alcoholism, 325, 331
 in deliria, 103
 in affective illnesses, 176
 in schizophrenia, 141 *et seq.*
 olfactory, 57
 tactile, 57
 visual, 56

Haloperidol, 417
Headache
  in anxiety, 245
  post-traumatic, 92
  with tension, 256
Head injury, 88 *et seq.*
Hebephrenia, 144
Heminevrin, *see* Chlormethiazole
Heredity, *see* Genetic influences
Heroin, 339, 345
High Expressed Emotion, 128
History of psychiatry, 7
Homicide Act (1957), 464
Homosexual phase, 390
Homosexuality, 224 *et seq.*
Hostels, 381
Housebound housewives, *see*
  Agoraphobia
Huntington's chorea, 108
Hydrocephalus–normal pressure, 110
Hydromorphone, 345
Hyperparathyroidism and dementia, 110
Hypertensive crisis (and M.A.O.I.
  drugs), 423
Hyperventilation, 245
Hypnagogic hallucinations, 56
Hypnosis, 427
Hypnotics, 425
Hypochondriasis, 205, 281
  in depression, 177, 181
  in schizophrenia, 141
Hypomania, 189 *et seq.*
Hypothyroidism
  and depression, 185
  and dementia, 110
Hysterical states, 264 *et seq.*
  conversion states, 265, 274 *et seq.*
  depression and, 283
  differential diagnosis, 283 *et seq.*
  dissociation, 266
  elaboration, 273
  fugues, 275
  mass hysteria, 280
  personality, 215
  pseudo-dementia, 276
  symptoms and signs, 275 *et seq.*
  treatment, 287
  twilight states, 276

Id, *see* Psychoanalysis
Ideas of reference, 49
  in depression, 175
  in mania, 194
Illusions, 56

pareidolic, 142
Imipramine, *see* Tricyclic drugs
Impotence, 294
  in alcoholism, 329
  in depression, 173
Incoherence, 48
Incongruity of affect, 52
Incontinence,
  emotional, 51
Industrial Rehabilitation Units, 382
Initiative, lack of, 46
Insight, 74
Insomnia, treatment of, 425
Insulin coma treatment, 428
Intellectual impairment after brain
  damage, 86
Intellectualisation, 40
Intelligence, 74
  development of, 29
Intelligence quotient, 311, 319 *et seq.*
Intelligence tests, 311, 319
Interview technique, 66 *et seq.*
Introversion, 210
Involutional melancholia, 177
Iproniazid, 423
Irritability, 51
Isocarboxazide, 423
Isotope scan, 113

Jakob-Creuzfeldt disease, *see*
  Creuzfeldt-Jakob disease
Jung, 393

Kelly's Repertory Grid, 211
Kinsey, 224
Kleptomania, 47
Korsakoff's psychosis, 105, 333
  post traumatic, 106
Kraepelin, 8, 9
Kretschmer, 27

Lability, emotional, 51
Largactil, *see* Chlorpromazine
Lead poisoning, 110
Learning tests, 88
Legal aspects of mental illness, 441
  seq.
  compulsory detention, 443 *et seq.*
  criminal responsibility, 463
  informal admission, 443
  management of property, 465
  testamentary capacity, 467

Leptosomatic physique, 26
Leucotomy, see Psychosurgery
Libido, 389
Librium, see Chlordiazepoxide
'Life events,' 127, 165, 362
Lithium carbonate, 424
Local authorities, see Community
    services and Social worker
Lorazepam, 419
Lord Chancellor's Visitors, 466
Lysergic acid diethylamide (L.S.D.),
    349

McNaghten Rules, 464
Management of property, 466
Mandrax, 340
Mania, 189 et seq.
Mania a potu, 324
Manic-depressive psychosis, see Bipolar
    manic-depressive psychosis
Mannerisms, 140
M.A.O.I. drugs, see Monoamine oxidase
    inhibitor drugs
Marijuana, 342 et seq.
Marplan, see Isocarboxazide
Marriage Guidance Council, 397
Marsilid, see Iproniazid
Masochism, 230
Mass hysteria, 280
Masturbation, 292
Medico-legal reports, 464
Melancholia, see Depression and
    involutional
Memory, disturbance of, 53 et seq.
    organic impairment, 81, 86 et seq.
    hysterical, 275
Mental age, 319
Mental deficiency, see Mental Handicap
Mental handicap, 309
Mental Health Act (1983), 441 et seq.
    (1984) Scotland, 453 et seq.
Mental Health Act Commission
    (MHAC), 450
Mental Health Review Tribunals, 450
Mental illness
    aetiology, 17 et seq.
    frequency, 4 et seq.
Mental impairment, 309, 442
Mental mechanisms, 38 et seq.
Mental Welfare commissions (Scotland),
    457
Mental Welfare Officer (M.W.O.), see
    Social worker
Meprobamate abuse, 344

Mescal, 349
Mesomorphy, 29
Methadone, 339, 345
Meyer, Adolf, 10
Mianserin, 422
Microcephaly, 315
Middlesex Hospital Questionnaire, 211
Minnesota Multiphasic Personality
    Inventory, 211
Minor tranquillisers, 418 et seq.
Misinterpretation, 141
Modecate, see Fluphenazine decanoate
Modelling, 410
Moditen, see Fluphenazine enanthate
Mogadon, see Nitrazepam
Mongolism, 316
Moniz, 436
Monoamine oxidase inhibitor drugs, 423
Monro, Thomas, 9
Morphine addiction, 345
Motility, disturbances of, 139
Multi-dimensional diagnosis, 65
Multi-infarct dementia, see
    Arteriopathic demetia
Multiple personality, 276
Myxoedema, see Hypothyroidism

Narcissistic phase, 390
Narco-analysis, 427
Narcosis, continuous, 427
Nardil, see Phenelzine
National Association for Mental Health,
    158
National Schizophrenia Fellowship, 158
Negativism, 46
Neologisms, 48
Neurasthenia,
    organic, 88
Neuritis, peripheral, 105
Neuroses, 59 et seq. 236 et seq.
Neurosis, post traumatic, 93 et seq.
Neurotic character disorder, 238
Neurotic depression, 161
Neuroticism, 237
Neurotic personality, 237 et seq.
Neurotic states, 236 et seq.
Nitrazepam, 419
Nocturnal enuresis, 369
Nortriptyline, see Tricyclic drugs

Obsessional doubt, 300
Obsessional ideas, 50
Obsessional impulses, 300

Obsessional neurosis, 297 *et seq.*
Obsessional personality, 216
Obsessional phobias, 301
Obsessional rituals, 301
Obsessional ruminations, 300
Obsessional symptoms
    and sex, 303
    in depression, 176, 306
Obsessive-compulsive neurosis, *see*
    Obsessional neurosis
Occupational therapy, 380
Oculogyric crises, 414
Oedipus complex, *see* Psychoanalysis
Oral phase, *see* Psychoanalysis
Organ inferiority, 393
Organ neurosis, 248
Organic deterioration and dementia, 77
    et seq. 118 *et seq.*
Organic mental states, 77 *et seq.*
Organic mental symptoms, 44 *et seq.*
    55, 79 *et seq.*
Organic neurasthenia, *see* Neurasthenia,
    organic
Organic psychoses, 88 *et seq.* 99 *et seq.*
    118 *et seq.*
Orientation, 72
Overactivity, psychomotor, 46, 191 *et
seq.*

Paedophiliacs, 226
Paraldehyde, 425
    abuse of, 344
Paralysis, hysterical, 278
Paranoia, 145
Paranoiac, 145
Paranoid, 50
    personality, 217
    psychosis in the elderly, 117
    trends in alcoholics, 330, 331
        in delirium, 103
        in mania, 194
Paranoid schizophrenia, 144
Paraphrenia, 144
Pareidolic illusions, 142
Parentrovite, 104
Parkinsonism
    drug induced, 414
    post-encephalitic, 99
Parnate, *see* Tranylcypromine
Passivity feelings, 50, 143, 148
Pavlov, 406
Percentiles, 320
Perceptual impairment, with brain
    damage, 79

Peripheral neuritis, *see* Neuritis,
    peripheral
Perphenazine, 416
Perseveration, 47
Personality
    anancastic (*see* obsessional)
    disorders of, 214
    assessment of, 209 *et seq.*
    cyclothymic, 215
    hysterical, 215
    inadequate, 221
    multiple, 276
    neurotic, 237 *et seq.*
    obsessional, 216
    paranoid, 217
    psychopathic, 219
    reactions, 236 *et seq.*
    schizoid, 219
    sociopathic, 219
    Type 'A', 363
    vulnerable, 218
Personality change
    after brain damage, 83 *et seq.*
    after encephalitis lethargica, 99
    after psychosurgery, 437 *et seq.*
Personality tests, 210
Personality traits, 212 *et seq.*
Pertofran, *see* Desipramine
Pethidine, 345
Phenelzine, 423
Phenothiazine drugs, 412 *et seq.*
Phenylketonuria, 317
Phenylpyruvic amentia, *see*
    Phenylketonuria
Phobias, 52, 258
    agoraphobia, 261
    complex, 261
    monosymptomatic, 259
    obsessional, 301
    simple, 259
    social, 264
Physical symptoms and emotional
    disturbance, 237, 240, 354 *et seq.*
Pick's disease, 108
Pimozide, 418
Pinel, 7
Porphyria, 373
Positive conditioning, 410
Post-concussional syndrome, 92 *et seq.*
Post-encephalitic states
Post-traumatic amnesia, 89
Post-traumatic neurosis, 92
Postural hypotension, drug induced, 414
Predominant ideas, 48
Prefrontal leucotomy, *see* Psychosurgery

Pregnancy, termination of, 468
Preludin, see Phenmetrazine
Premature ejaculation, 294
Premenstrual Tension, 368
Presenile dementia, 107 et seq.
Priadel, see Lithium carbonate
Procyclidine, 414
Projection, 41
Promazine, 415
Protriptyline, see Tricyclic
      antidepressants
Proverbs test, 87
Pseudo-cyesis, 279
Pseudo-dementia, 276
Pseudo-hallucinations, 142
Pseudo-neurotic schizophrenia, 145
Pseudo-psychosis, 278
Psychiatric teaching, aims of, 15
Psychiatry
   definition, 1
   development of, 7
Psycho-analysis, 10, 389 et seq.
Psychobiology, 11
Psychogenic states, 267
Psychological treatment, 385 et seq.
Psychology, 1
Psychometric testing, see Assessment of
      intellectual impairment
Psychomotor agitation, 176, 177
Psychomotor overactivity, 46, 191 et seq.
Psychomotor retardation, 46, 176
Psychoneurosis, see Neurosis
Psychopathic personality, 219 et seq.
   in addictions, 340 et seq.
   legal definition, 442
Psychoses
   classification, 59 et seq.
   functional, 60
   organic, 60, 99 et seq.
Psychosexual immaturity, 293
Psychosomatic medicine, 351 et seq.
Psychosurgery, 436 et seq.
Psychotherapy,
   brief, 396
   client-centred, 395
   contra-indications, 399 et seq.
   family therapy, 396
   formal (major), 394
   group, 398
   indications, 399
   major (formal) 394
   marital, 396
   psycho-analytic, 395
   results, 403
   Rogerian, 395

simple, 386
   supportive, 388
Psychotic depression, 161
Puerperal psychoses, 133, 169
Pyknic physique, 27
Pyromania, 47

Radioactive isotope scan, 113
Rapport, loss of, 137
Rauwolfia, 418
Reactive depression, 160, 178 et seq.
Recall, 53
Reference, ideas of, 49
   delusions of, 141
Registration, 53
Rehabilitation, 155, 289
Rehabilitation centres, 381
Repression, 40
Reserpine, 418
Retardation, see Psychomotor
      retardation
Retention, 53
Retrograde amnesia, 54
Rhesus incompatibility, 313
Rigidity, 80
Rituals, 301
Rorschach test, 211
Rostral leucotomy, see Psychosurgery
Rubella, 312

Sadism, 230
Sakel, 428
Scans, see Computer assisted
      tomography (CAT scan), 113
   radioactive isotope, 113
Schizo-affective psychosis, 151
Schizoid personality, 219
Schizophrenia, 124 et seq.
   aetiology, 126 et seq.
   affect-laden, 151
   biochemical aspects, 131
   catatonic, 139, 144
   computed tomography in, 131
   course, 150 et seq.
   delusions in, 140
   differential diagnosis, 147
   disturbances of affect (emotion), 136
   disturbances of motility, 139
   disturbances of thought, 134
   disturbances of will, 138
   dopaminergic pathways and, 131
   epidemiology, 125
   family interactions and, 129

Schizophrenia (*contd.*)
  first rank symptoms in, 148
  genetic aspects, 126
  hallucinations in, 141
  hebephrenic, 144
  'high expressed emotion' in, 128
  life events and, 127
  neuropathological studies, 131
  paranoia and, 145
  paranoid, 144
  paraphrenic, 144
  premorbid personality, 132
  pseudoneurotic, 145
  psychophysiology, 130
  simple, 144
  'spectrum', 127
  thought disorder, 134
  treatment, 152 *et seq.*
  withdrawal, 140
Schizophrenia-like psychoses of
  epilepsy, 98
Schizophreniform psychoses, 147
Schneider, Kurt, 148
Scotland, Mental Health Act (1960), 453
  et seq.
Secondary gain, 265
Sedatives, 425
Self-poisoning, 204
Self-reproach, 175
Selye's theory of stress and adaptation, 358
Serenace, *see* Haloperidol
Severe mental impairment, 309, 442
Sex problems, 290 *et seq.*
Sexual anomalies, 223 *et seq.*
Sex therapy, 291, 397
Shallowness of affect, 51, 136
Shoplifting, 178
Sleepwalking, 372
Social skills, 410
Social worker, rôle of, 382, 383, 443 *et seq.*
Sociopath, *see* Psychopath
Solvent sniffing, 345
Somatisation Disorder, 280
Sparine, *see* Promazine
Spasmodic torticollis, 372
Special investigations in organic brain
  disease, 111
Stammering, 371
Stelazine, *see* Trifluperazine
Stereotactic cerebral surgery, 437
Stereotyped movements, 47, 140
'Stress', 357 *et seq.*
Strokes, psychological effects of, 78
Stupor, 46, 139, 176
Subdelirious states, 100 *et seq.*

Sublimation, 41 (*see also* Psychoanalysis)
Subnormality, *see* Mental Handicap
Suggestibility, 47
Suggestion, 47
Suicidal gesture, 200 *et seq.*
Suicide, 201 *et seq.*
Superego, *see* Psychoanalysis
Surmontil, *see* Trimipramine
Syphilis, cerebro-vascular, *see* General
  paralysis of the insane

Tardive dyskinesia, 414
Tay-Sacks' disease, 315
Temporal lobe epilepsy, 96
Tension, 52, 256
Termination of pregnancy, 468
Testamentary capacity, 467
Tests, *see* Intelligence tests, Personality
  tests
Tetracyclic antidepressants, 422
Thematic Apperception Test, 211
Thiamine (in alcoholics), 106
Thiopropazate, 108
Thioridazine, 415
Thioxanthenes, 416
Thought block, 48, 134
Thought broadcasting, 51, 148
Thought disorder, 48, 134
Thought echo, 148
Thought insertion, 51, 148
Thought withdrawal, 51, 148
Thymoleptics, 421
Tics, 372
Tofranil, *see* Imipramine
Token economy, 410
Torticollis, 372
Tractotomy, stereotactic, 437
Trances, 276
Tranquillisers, *see* Benzodiazepines
Transference, 13, 392
Transexualists, 232
Transvestism 230
Tranylcypromine, 423
Treatment of mental illness, 375 *et seq.*
Tribunals, Mental Health Review, 450
Tricyclic antidepressants, 421
Trifluperazine, 416
Trimipramine, *see* Tricyclic
  antidepressants
Tryptizol, *see* Amitryptiline
Tuberose sclerosis, 315
Tuke, 8
Twilight states, 45
  epileptic, 96

Twilight states (*contd.*)
  hysterical, 276
  post-traumatic, 91
Type A personality, 363
Tyramine, 423

Unconscious, the, *see* Psychoanalysis

Valium, *see* Diazepam
Visual hallucinations, 56, 103, 142
Visuo-spatial impairment, 79
Vitamin B$_{12}$
  deficiency and depression, 185
  deficiency and dementia, 110
Vitamins, use of, 101, 105, 332

Volition, disturbances of, 46, 138
Vulnerable personality, 218

Wechsler Adult Intelligence Scale, 319
Wechsler Intelligence Scale for
    Children, 319
Welldorm, *see* Dichloralphenazone
Will, disturbances of, 138
Withdrawal fits, 333
Withdrawal symptoms, 346
Wolfenden report, 224
Word salad, 136

XYY Chromosome abnormality, 222